EXAM✓PREP

D0789343

CCNA
Second Edition

Jeremy Cioara, David Minutella, Heather Stevenson

CCNA Exam Prep, Second Edition

Copyright © 2008 by Pearson Education, Inc.

ISBN-13: 978-0-7897-3713-7
ISBN-10: 0-7897-3713-2

Library of Congress Cataloging-in-Publication Data

Cioara, Jeremy.

  CCNA exam prep : (exam 640-802) / Jeremy Cioara, David Minutella, Heather Stevenson. -- 2nd ed.

     p. cm.

  ISBN 978-0-7897-3713-7 (pbk. w/cd)

  1. Electronic data processing personnel--Certification. 2. Computer networks--Examinations--Study guides. I. Minutella, David. II. Stevenson, Heather. III. Title.

  QA76.3.C4779 2007

  004.6076--dc22

                        2007044227

Printed in the United States on America

First Printing: December 2007

Trademarks

Warning and Disclaimer

Bulk Sales

Que Publishing offers excellent discounts on this book when ordered in quantity for bulk purchases or special sales. For more information, please contact

  U.S. Corporate and Government Sales

  1-800-382-3419

  corpsales@pearsontechgroup.com

For sales outside of the U.S., please contact

  International Sales

  international@pearsoned.com

Associate Publisher	David Dusthimer
Executive Editor	Brett Bartow
Senior Development Editor	Christopher Cleveland
Technical Editors	David Camardella
	Steve Kalman
Managing Editor	Patrick Kanouse
Project Editor	Mandie Frank
Copy Editor	Gayle Johnson
Indexer	Ken Johnson
Proofreader	Williams Woods Publishing Services, LLC
Publishing Coordinator	Vanessa Evans
Designer	Gary Adair
Page Layout	TnT Design, Inc.

Contents at a Glance

Table of Contents

About the Authors

Jeremy Cioara (CCIE, CCVP, CCSP) works in many facets of the Cisco networking realm. As an author, he has written multiple books for Cisco Press and Exam Cram. As an instructor, he teaches at Interface Technical Training (www.interfacett.com) in Phoenix, Arizona. Likewise, Jeremy has recorded many E-Learning titles at CBTNuggets (www.cbtnuggets.com). Finally, Jeremy is the CIO of AdTEC Networks and works as a network consultant focusing on Cisco network and Voice over IP (VoIP) implementations. What's more? Jeremy also runs the Cisco Blog (www.ciscoblog.com) in his "free time." Thankfully, he is married to the Certified Best Wife in the World (CBWW) who helps him manage his time and priorities and prevents him from getting an enormous Cisco-logo tattooed across his chest.

Dave Minutella (CCNP, CCDP, INFOSEC, CISSP, CTP, MCSA, MCDST, Security+, Network+, A+) has been working in the IT and telecom industry for over 14 years. He currently serves as Vice President of Educational Services for Training Camp. Before that, he was the lead Cisco instructor, primarily teaching CCNA, CCDA, and CCNP courses. Dave is also the technical author of *CSVPN Exam Cram 2* from Que Publishing and is the present Cisco certifications expert for SearchNetworking.com's Ask the Networking Expert panel.

Heather Stevenson (CCNP) has over 7 years of experience in the IT industry and is currently a senior network engineer at a global manufacturing company. She has written a number of technical training guides and mentored fellow IT professionals throughout her career. When she is not working, Heather still loves spending time with her network of friends and family.

Dedications

From Jeremy: *I'd like to dedicate this book to my newest daughter, Isabella. She's currently six months old and is staring at me right now from a soft blanket on the floor. By the time she's old enough to read this, this book will probably be outdated as we will all have Ethernet ports implanted in our skull (I'm opting for a wireless connection, myself). Hopefully, if we remember to pull this book off the shelf and read this dedication I can tell her what amazing joy she has brought me. This tiny, arm flailing, cooing, cheesy-grinning, soft, delicate, playful, yet scandalously sly, giggling little girl has become my addiction. I hope I can always help her know how incredibly special she is to me.*

From Dave: *This book is dedicated to my soon-to-be daughter, Chloe. By the time this book is printed, you will be born and your exquisite mother and I can have longwinded debates about which event was more distressing. I very well may have written books about Cisco technology and whatnot, but as for incredible blessings, it's you who wrote the book.*

From Heather: *I would like to dedicate this book to anyone and everyone who has ever helped me in my pursuit to learn. I have been fortunate enough to have many wonderful teachers in my life. Not just school teachers, but family and friends who have given me their hand along the way.*

Acknowledgments

From Jeremy: My number one acknowledgment always goes to God who has blessed me in more ways than I even realize. Thank you for granting me the talent to be successful in the realm of Cisco networking. Please allow me to use these talents to accomplish more for Your kingdom than an Ethernet cable ever could. Thanks to my darling wife, Susan. You are my eyes and ears that help me to see what is REALLY going on around me. I love you! And last, but not least: Thank you fish swimming in the big fish tank next to me. You bring me much peace and serenity as I sit here typing these acknowledgments. Especially the big yellow Butterfly fish that swims this way and that. Swish, swish, swish. Swish, swish.

From Dave: As always, I would like to put to paper yet again my undying gratitude and love to my wife, Marsha. Your beautiful spirit outshines the sun even on the brightest of days. I also would like to thank my family and family-in-laws for your unwavering support. I especially want to honor my mother-in-law, Pattie, who touched so many throughout her life. Words cannot fill the sorrow in our hearts, but your memories and spirit give us strength. We will miss you.

From Heather: I would like to send out a huge hug and thank you to my parents and my Dustin. Dustin has been by my side for as long as I have been working in this industry. He even took me to my junior prom many, many years ago. His support is immeasurable. I am so lucky to have amazing people around me to keep me sane. Finally, DYB Bear and Grumpy Nigel also deserve a special hello. Hello!

We Want to Hear from You!

As the reader of this book, *you* are our most important critic and commentator. We value your opinion and want to know what we're doing right, what we could do better, what areas you'd like to see us publish in, and any other words of wisdom you're willing to pass our way.

As an associate publisher for Que Publishing, I welcome your comments. You can email or write me directly to let me know what you did or didn't like about this book—as well as what we can do to make our books better.

Please note that I cannot help you with technical problems related to the topic of this book. We do have a User Services group, however, where I will forward specific technical questions related to the book.

When you write, please be sure to include this book's title and author as well as your name, email address, and phone number. I will carefully review your comments and share them with the author and editors who worked on the book.

Email: scorehigher@pearsoned.com

Mail: Dave Dusthimer
         Associate Publisher
         Que Publishing
         800 East 96th Street
         Indianapolis, IN 46240 USA

Reader Services

Visit our website and register this book at www.examcram.com/title/9780789737137 for convenient access to any updates, downloads, or errata that might be available for this book.

Cisco ICND1/ICND2/CCNA Exam Objectives

Cisco ICND1 Exam Objectives

Interconnecting Cisco Networking Devices Part 1 (ICND1)

Exam Number: 640-822 ICND1

Associated Certifications: CCENT and CCNA

Duration: 90 Minutes (50-60 questions)

Exam Description

The 640-822 Interconnecting Cisco Networking Devices Part 1 (ICND1) is the exam associated with the Cisco Certified Entry Network Technician (CCENT) certification and a tangible first step in achieving the Cisco Certified Network Associate certification. Candidates can prepare for this exam by taking the Interconnecting Cisco Networking Devices Part 1 (ICND1) v1.0 course. This exam tests a candidate's knowledge and skills required to successfully install, operate, and troubleshoot a small branch office network. The exam includes topics on networking fundamentals; connecting to a WAN; basic security and wireless concepts; routing and switching fundamentals; the TCP/IP and OSI models; IP addressing; WAN technologies; operating and configuring IOS devices; configuring RIPv2, static and default routing; implementing NAT and DHCP; and configuring simple networks.

Exam Topics

The following topics are general guidelines for the content likely to be included on the Interconnecting Cisco Networking Devices Part 1 exam. However, other related topics may also appear on any specific delivery of the exam. In order to better reflect the contents of the exam and for clarity purposes, the guidelines below may change at any time without notice.

Describe the operation of data networks

- ▶ Describe the purpose and functions of various network devices
- ▶ Select the components required to meet a given network specification
- ▶ Use the OSI and TCP/IP models and their associated protocols to explain how data flows in a network
- ▶ Describe common networking applications including web applications
- ▶ Describe the purpose and basic operation of the protocols in the OSI and TCP models
- ▶ Describe the impact of applications (Voice Over IP and Video Over IP) on a network
- ▶ Interpret network diagrams
- ▶ Determine the path between two hosts across a network
- ▶ Describe the components required for network and Internet communications
- ▶ Identify and correct common network problems at layers 1, 2, 3 and 7 using a layered model approach
- ▶ Differentiate between LAN/WAN operation and features

Implement a small switched network

- ▶ Select the appropriate media, cables, ports, and connectors to connect switches to other network devices and hosts
- ▶ Explain the technology and media access control method for Ethernet technologies
- ▶ Explain network segmentation and basic traffic management concepts
- ▶ Explain the operation of Cisco switches and basic switching concepts
- ▶ Perform, save, and verify initial switch configuration tasks including remote access management
- ▶ Verify network status and switch operation using basic utilities (including: ping, traceroute, telnet, SSH, arp, ipconfig), SHOW & DEBUG commands
- ▶ Implement and verify basic security for a switch (port security, deactivate ports)
- ▶ Identify, prescribe, and resolve common switched network media issues, configuration issues, autonegotiation, and switch hardware failures

Continues on Following Page

Implement an IP addressing scheme and IP services to meet network requirements for a small branch office

▶ Describe the need and role of addressing in a network

▶ Create and apply an addressing scheme to a network

▶ Assign and verify valid IP addresses to hosts, servers, and networking devices in a LAN environment

▶ Explain the basic uses and operation of NAT in a small network connecting to one ISP

▶ Describe and verify DNS operation

▶ Describe the operation and benefits of using private and public IP addressing

▶ Enable NAT for a small network with a single ISP and connection using SDM and verify operation using CLI and ping

▶ Configure, verify, and troubleshoot DHCP and DNS operation on a router.(including: CLI/SDM)

▶ Implement static and dynamic addressing services for hosts in a LAN environment

▶ Identify and correct IP addressing issues

Implement a small routed network

▶ Describe basic routing concepts (including: packet forwarding, router lookup process)

▶ Describe the operation of Cisco routers (including: router bootup process, POST, router components)

▶ Select the appropriate media, cables, ports, and connectors to connect routers to other network devices and hosts

▶ Configure, verify, and troubleshoot RIPv2

▶ Access and utilize the router CLI to set basic parameters

▶ Connect, configure, and verify operation status of a device interface

▶ Verify device configuration and network connectivity using ping, traceroute, telnet, SSH, or other utilities

▶ Perform and verify routing configuration tasks for a static or default route given specific routing requirements

▶ Manage IOS configuration files (including: save, edit, upgrade, restore)

▶ Manage Cisco IOS

▶ Implement password and physical security

▶ Verify network status and router operation using basic utilities (including: ping, traceroute, telnet, SSH, arp, ipconfig), SHOW & DEBUG commands

Explain and select the appropriate administrative tasks required for a WLAN

▶ Describe standards associated with wireless media (including: IEEE WI-FI Alliance, ITU/FCC)

▶ Identify and describe the purpose of the components in a small wireless network. (including: SSID, BSS, ESS)

▶ Identify the basic parameters to configure on a wireless network to ensure that devices connect to the correct access point

▶ Compare and contrast wireless security features and capabilities of WPA security (including: open, WEP, WPA-1/2)

▶ Identify common issues with implementing wireless networks

Identify security threats to a network and describe general methods to mitigate those threats

▶ Explain today's increasing network security threats and the need to implement a comprehensive security policy to mitigate the threats

▶ Explain general methods to mitigate common security threats to network devices, hosts, and applications

▶ Describe the functions of common security appliances and applications

▶ Describe security recommended practices including initial steps to secure network devices

Implement and verify WAN links

▶ Describe different methods for connecting to a WAN

▶ Configure and verify a basic WAN serial connection

Cisco ICND2 Exam Objectives

Interconnecting Cisco Networking Devices Part 2 (ICND2)

Exam Number: 640-816 ICND2

Associated Certifications: CCNA

Duration: 75 minutes (45-55 questions)

Exam Description

The 640-816 Interconnecting Cisco Networking Devices Part 2 (ICND2) is the exam associated with the Cisco Certified Network Associate certification. Candidates can prepare for this exam by taking the Interconnecting Cisco Networking Devices Part 2 (ICND2) v1.0 course. This exam tests a candidate's knowledge and skills required to successfully install, operate, and troubleshoot a small to medium size enterprise branch network. The exam covers topics on VLSM and IPv6 addressing; extending switched networks with VLANs; configuring, verifying and troubleshooting VLANs; the VTP, RSTP, OSPF and EIGRP protocols; determining IP routes; managing IP traffic with access lists; NAT and DHCP; establishing point-to-point connections; and establishing Frame Relay connections.

Exam Topics

The following topics are general guidelines for the content likely to be included on the Interconnecting Cisco Networking Devices Part 2 exam. However, other related topics may also appear on any specific delivery of the exam. In order to better reflect the contents of the exam and for clarity purposes, the guidelines below may change at any time without notice.

Configure, verify and troubleshoot a switch with VLANs and interswitch communications

▶ Describe enhanced switching technologies (including: VTP, RSTP, VLAN, PVSTP, 802.1q)

▶ Describe how VLANs create logically separate networks and the need for routing between them

▶ Configure, verify, and troubleshoot VLANs

▶ Configure, verify, and troubleshoot trunking on Cisco switches

▶ Configure, verify, and troubleshoot interVLAN routing

▶ Configure, verify, and troubleshoot VTP

▶ Configure, verify, and troubleshoot RSTP operation

▶ Interpret the output of various show and debug commands to verify the operational status of a Cisco switched network

▶ Implement basic switch security (including: port security, unassigned ports, trunk access, etc.)

Implement an IP addressing scheme and IP Services to meet network requirements in a medium-size Enterprise branch office network

▶ Calculate and apply a VLSM IP addressing design to a network

▶ Determine the appropriate classless addressing scheme using VLSM and summarization to satisfy addressing requirements in a LAN/WAN environment

▶ Describe the technological requirements for running IPv6 (including: protocols, dual stack, tunneling, etc)

▶ Describe IPv6 addresses

▶ Identify and correct common problems associated with IP addressing and host configurations

Configure and troubleshoot basic operation and routing on Cisco devices

▶ Compare and contrast methods of routing and routing protocols

▶ Configure, verify and troubleshoot OSPF

▶ Configure, verify and troubleshoot EIGRP

▶ Verify configuration and connectivity using ping, traceroute, and telnet or SSH

▶ Troubleshoot routing implementation issues

▶ Verify router hardware and software operation using SHOW & DEBUG commands

▶ Implement basic router security

Implement, verify, and troubleshoot NAT and ACLs in a medium-size Enterprise branch office network

▶ Describe the purpose and types of access control lists

▶ Configure and apply access control lists based on network filtering requirements

Continues on Following Page

- ▶ Configure and apply an access control list to limit telnet and SSH access to the router
- ▶ Verify and monitor ACL's in a network environment
- ▶ Troubleshoot ACL implementation issues
- ▶ Explain the basic operation of NAT
- ▶ Configure Network Address Translation for given network requirements using CLI
- ▶ Troubleshoot NAT implementation issues

Implement and verify WAN links

- ▶ Configure and verify Frame Relay on Cisco routers
- ▶ Troubleshoot WAN implementation issues
- ▶ Describe VPN technology (including: importance, benefits, role, impact, components)
- ▶ Configure and very PPP connection between Cisco routers

Cisco CCNA Exam Objectives

Cisco Certified Network Associate (CCNA)

Exam Number: 640-802 CCNA

Associated Certifications: CCNA

Duration: 90 Minutes (50-60 questions)

Exam Description

The 640-802 Cisco Certified Network Associate (CCNA) is the composite exam associated with the Cisco Certified Network Associate certification. Candidates can prepare for this exam by taking the Interconnecting Cisco Networking Devices Part 1 (ICND1) v1.0 and the Interconnecting Cisco Networking Devices Part 2 (ICND2) v1.0 courses. This exam tests a candidate's knowledge and skills required to install, operate, and troubleshoot a small to medium size enterprise branch network. The topics include connecting to a WAN; implementing network security; network types; network media; routing and switching fundamentals; the TCP/IP and OSI models; IP addressing; WAN technologies; operating and configuring IOS devices; extending switched networks with VLANs; determining IP routes; managing IP traffic with access lists; establishing point-to-point connections; and establishing Frame Relay connections.

Exam Topics

The following topics are general guidelines for the content likely to be included on the Cisco Certified Network Associate exam. However, other related topics may also appear on any specific delivery of the exam. In order to better reflect the contents of the exam and for clarity purposes, the guidelines below may change at any time without notice.

Describe how a network works

- ▶ Describe the purpose and functions of various network devices
- ▶ Select the components required to meet a network specification
- ▶ Use the OSI and TCP/IP models and their associated protocols to explain how data flows in a network
- ▶ Describe common networked applications including web applications
- ▶ Describe the purpose and basic operation of the protocols in the OSI and TCP models
- ▶ Describe the impact of applications (Voice Over IP and Video Over IP) on a network
- ▶ Interpret network diagrams

- ▶ Determine the path between two hosts across a network
- ▶ Describe the components required for network and Internet communications
- ▶ Identify and correct common network problems at layers 1, 2, 3 and 7 using a layered model approach
- ▶ Differentiate between LAN/WAN operation and features

Configure, verify and troubleshoot a switch with VLANs and interswitch communications

- ▶ Select the appropriate media, cables, ports, and connectors to connect switches to other network devices and hosts

- Explain the technology and media access control method for Ethernet networks
- Explain network segmentation and basic traffic management concepts
- Explain basic switching concepts and the operation of Cisco switches
- Perform and verify initial switch configuration tasks including remote access management
- Verify network status and switch operation using basic utilities (including: ping, traceroute, telnet, SSH, arp, ipconfig), SHOW & DEBUG commands
- Identify, prescribe, and resolve common switched network media issues, configuration issues, auto negotiation, and switch hardware failures
- Describe enhanced switching technologies (including: VTP, RSTP, VLAN, PVSTP, 802.1q)
- Describe how VLANs create logically separate networks and the need for routing between them
- Configure, verify, and troubleshoot VLANs
- Configure, verify, and troubleshoot trunking on Cisco switches
- Configure, verify, and troubleshoot interVLAN routing
- Configure, verify, and troubleshoot VTP
- Configure, verify, and troubleshoot RSTP operation
- Interpret the output of various show and debug commands to verify the operational status of a Cisco switched network.
- Implement basic switch security (including: port security, trunk access, management vlan other than vlan1, etc.)

Implement an IP addressing scheme and IP Services to meet network requirements in a medium-size Enterprise branch office network

- Describe the operation and benefits of using private and public IP addressing
- Explain the operation and benefits of using DHCP and DNS
- Configure, verify and troubleshoot DHCP and DNS operation on a router.(including: CLI/SDM)
- Implement static and dynamic addressing services for hosts in a LAN environment
- Calculate and apply an addressing scheme including VLSM IP addressing design to a network

- Determine the appropriate classless addressing scheme using VLSM and summarization to satisfy addressing requirements in a LAN/WAN environment
- Describe the technological requirements for running IPv6 in conjunction with IPv4 (including: protocols, dual stack, tunneling, etc).
- Describe IPv6 addresses
- Identify and correct common problems associated with IP addressing and host configurations

Configure, verify, and troubleshoot basic router operation and routing on Cisco devices

- Describe basic routing concepts (including: packet forwarding, router lookup process)
- Describe the operation of Cisco routers (including: router bootup process, POST, router components)
- Select the appropriate media, cables, ports, and connectors to connect routers to other network devices and hosts
- Configure, verify, and troubleshoot RIPv2
- Access and utilize the router to set basic parameters.(including: CLI/SDM)
- Connect, configure, and verify operation status of a device interface
- Verify device configuration and network connectivity using ping, traceroute, telnet, SSH or other utilities
- Perform and verify routing configuration tasks for a static or default route given specific routing requirements
- Manage IOS configuration files. (including: save, edit, upgrade, restore)
- Manage Cisco IOS
- Compare and contrast methods of routing and routing protocols
- Configure, verify, and troubleshoot OSPF
- Configure, verify, and troubleshoot EIGRP
- Verify network connectivity (including: using ping, traceroute, and telnet or SSH)
- Troubleshoot routing issues
- Verify router hardware and software operation using SHOW & DEBUG commands.
- Implement basic router security

Explain and select the appropriate administrative tasks required for a WLAN

- Describe standards associated with wireless media (including: IEEE WI-FI Alliance, ITU/FCC)

Continues on Following Page

▶ Identify and describe the purpose of the components in a small wireless network. (Including: SSID, BSS, ESS)

▶ Identify the basic parameters to configure on a wireless network to ensure that devices connect to the correct access point

▶ Compare and contrast wireless security features and capabilities of WPA security (including: open, WEP, WPA-1/2)

▶ Identify common issues with implementing wireless networks. (Including: Interface, miss-configuration)

Identify security threats to a network and describe general methods to mitigate those threats

▶ Describe today's increasing network security threats and explain the need to implement a comprehensive security policy to mitigate the threats

▶ Explain general methods to mitigate common security threats to network devices, hosts, and applications

▶ Describe the functions of common security appliances and applications

▶ Describe security recommended practices including initial steps to secure network devices

Implement, verify, and troubleshoot NAT and ACLs in a medium-size Enterprise branch office network

▶ Describe the purpose and types of ACLs

▶ Configure and apply ACLs based on network filtering requirements.(including: CLI/SDM)

▶ Configure and apply an ACLs to limit telnet and SSH access to the router using (including: SDM/CLI)

▶ Verify and monitor ACLs in a network environment

▶Troubleshoot ACL issues

▶Explain the basic operation of NAT

▶Configure NAT for given network requirements using (including: CLI/SDM)

▶Troubleshoot NAT issues

Implement and verify WAN links

▶ Describe different methods for connecting to a WAN

▶ Configure and verify a basic WAN serial connection

▶ Configure and verify Frame Relay on Cisco routers

▶ Troubleshoot WAN implementation issues

▶ Describe VPN technology (including: importance, benefits, role, impact, components)

▶ Configure and verify a PPP connection between Cisco routers

Introduction

The Cisco Certified Network Associate (CCNA) accreditation has become the leading introductory-level network certification available today. The CCNA certification is recognized by employers as providing candidates with a solid foundation of Cisco networking concepts, terminology, and skills. The CCNA exam covers a broad range of networking concepts to prepare candidates for the technologies they are likely to work with in today's network environments.

This book is your one-stop shop. Everything you need to know to pass the exam is in here. You do not have to take a class in addition to buying this book to pass the exam. However, depending on your personal study habits or learning style, you might benefit from buying this book *and* taking a class. Taking a CCNA certification class gives you dedicated study time and precious hands-on experience with live Cisco equipment.

Exam Preps are meticulously crafted to give you the best possible learning experience for the particular characteristics of the technology covered and the actual certification exam. The instructional design implemented in the *Exam Preps* reflects the task- and experience-based nature of Cisco certification exams. The *Exam Preps* provide the factual knowledge base you need for the exams and then take it to the next level, with exercises and exam questions that are required in the CCNA certification.

Cisco has split the single CCNA test into two separate exams, ICND1 and ICND2. Although the single CCNA exam still remains, Cisco recommends that only those who are recertifying an existing CCNA certification take this exam. This *CCNA Exam Prep* title prepares you for both the ICND1 exam, which covers the foundational Cisco network concepts and configurations, and the ICND2 exam, which covers the more advanced network concepts and configurations. Personally, we recommend that you follow Cisco's advice on taking the two-exam path rather than the single CCNA exam. Although it may be tempting to go after the one-test "fast-track," this single exam is extremely difficult and has discouraged many potential CCNA candidates from continuing on their Cisco certification journey.

How This Book Helps You

This book takes you on a self-guided tour of all the areas covered by the CCNA exam and teaches you the specific skills you need to achieve your certification. This book also contains helpful hints, tips, real-world examples, and exercises, as well as references to additional study materials. Specifically, this book is set up to help you in the following ways:

▶ **Organization:** This book is organized by individual exam objectives. Every objective you need to know for the CCNA exam is covered in this book. It presents the objectives in an order as close as possible to that listed by Cisco. However, we did not hesitate to reorganize them where needed to make the material as easy as possible for you to learn. We also make the information accessible in the following ways:

  ▶ The full list of exam units and objectives is included.

  ▶ Each chapter begins with an outline that provides an overview of the material and the pages on which particular topics can be found.

  ▶ The objectives are repeated where the material most directly relevant to them is covered.

▶ **Instructional features:** This book provides multiple ways to learn and reinforce the exam material. Following are some of the helpful methods:

  ▶ **Exam Alerts:** These provide specific exam-related advice. Such tips might address what material is covered (or not covered) on the exam, how it is covered, mnemonic devices, or particular quirks of that exam.

  ▶ **Review breaks and summaries:** Crucial information is summarized at various points in the book in lists or tables. Each chapter ends with a summary as well.

  ▶ **Key terms:** A list of key terms appears at the end of each chapter.

  ▶ **Notes:** Notes contain various kinds of useful or practical information, such as tips on technology or administrative practices, historical background on terms and technologies, or side commentary on industry issues.

  ▶ **Warnings:** When using sophisticated information technology, there is always the potential for mistakes or even catastrophes because of improper application of the technology. Warnings alert you to such potential problems.

  ▶ **In the Field sidebars:** These relatively extensive discussions cover material that might not be directly relevant to the exam but that is useful as reference material or in everyday practice. In the Field sidebars also provide useful background or contextual information necessary for understanding the larger topic under consideration.

  ▶ **Exercises:** Found at the end of the chapters in the "Apply Your Knowledge" section and in the Challenges found throughout chapters, exercises are performance-based opportunities for you to learn and assess your knowledge.

▶ **Extensive practice test options:** This book provides numerous opportunities for you to assess your knowledge and practice for the exam. The practice options include the following:

> ▶ **Exam questions:** These questions appear in the "Apply Your Knowledge" section. You can use them to help determine what you know and what you need to review or study further. Answers and explanations for these questions are provided in a separate section, titled "Answers to Exam Questions."

> ▶ **Practice Exam:** A practice exam is included in the "Final Review" section of the book.

▶ **Final Review:** This part of the book provides two valuable tools for preparing for the exam:

> ▶ **Fast Facts:** This condensed version of the information contained in the book is useful for last-minute review.

> ▶ **Practice Exam:** A practice test is included. Questions on this practice exam are written in styles similar to those used on the actual exam. Use the practice exam to assess your readiness for the real thing. Use the extensive answer explanations to improve your retention and understanding of the material.

This book includes several other features, such as a "Suggested Readings and Resources" section at the end of each chapter. It directs you to additional information that can aid you in your exam preparation and your real-life work. Also included are a glossary and an appendix describing what is on the CD-ROM.

For more information about the exam or the certification process, refer to the Cisco website at www.cisco.com/certification.

Network Hardware and Software Requirements

As a self-paced study guide, *CCNA Exam Prep* is meant to help you understand concepts that must be refined through hands-on experience. To make the most of your studying, you need to have as much background in and experience with both common operating systems and network environments as possible. The best way to do this is to combine studying with work on actual networks. These networks need not be complex. The concepts involved in configuring a network with only a couple of routers and a switch follow the same principles as those involved in configuring a network that has hundreds of connected systems. This section describes the recommended equipment for a solid practice environment.

To fully practice some of the exam objectives, you need to create a network with two (or more) routers networked together with one (or more) Cisco switches. We recognize that your finances may be limited, so we suggest purchasing routers from the Cisco 800 or 3600 series (primarily the 851W, 3620, and 3640 routers). These can commonly be found for between $100 and $500 through a used-equipment vendor or online auction. A Catalyst 1912 or 1924 switch can typically be found for less than $50. Some of the syntax on the 1900 series switches may be slightly different from Cisco's mainline switches, but most of the commands are similar. Remember that Cisco has strict restrictions about using used or remanufactured equipment in production networks. Although Cisco hardware can be resold, the software that runs it (Cisco IOS software) cannot. Before used or remanufactured equipment can be used in a production environment, Cisco IOS software must be relicensed through Cisco or an authorized reseller. Be sure to verify these regulations before using your lab equipment in a production network.

If you are looking to build a lab environment, the following is a more detailed list of the minimum equipment you need. Keep in mind that this is the minimum equipment that we suggest for the CCNA. If you plan on moving into the CCNP, CCVP, or CCSP programs, you may want to look into the more advanced (and expensive) Cisco equipment such as the 2800 routers.

- ▶ At least one Cisco 851W router, which has four 10/100Mbps Ethernet ports to test configurations such as NAT, one fixed port to simulate WAN connectivity, wireless LAN with a detachable antenna, up to five VPN tunnels, and SDM capabilities.

- ▶ One additional Cisco router, such as the 2501, with one Ethernet port and two serial ports to create and test WAN connectivity.

- ▶ A DB-60 DTE to DB-60 DCE cross-over serial cable.

- ▶ At least one Cisco switch, ideally a 2900XL or 2950; however, a 1900 series switch will also suffice. If you decide to use a 1900 series switch, be sure it is equipped with the Enterprise IOS version, which includes the command-line interface. The Standard IOS for the 1900 allows only a menu-driven configuration.

- ▶ At least one rollover console cable.

- ▶ Multiple straight-through and cross-over network cables.

- ▶ Optionally, adding one or more PCs to the network can add realism and troubleshooting advantages. These PCs can be connected to the switch and act as network clients in your scenarios.

It's easy to get access to the necessary computer hardware and software in a corporate business environment. It can be difficult, however, to allocate enough time within the busy workday to complete a self-study program. Most of your study time will occur after normal working hours, away from the everyday interruptions and pressures of your regular job.

Advice on Taking the Exam

Keep this advice in mind as you study:

> ▶ **Read all the material:** Cisco has been known to include material that is not expressly specified in the objectives. This book includes additional information that is not reflected in the objectives in an effort to give you the best possible preparation for the examination—and for your real-world experiences to come.

> ▶ **Complete the exercises in each chapter:** They will help you gain experience in using the specified methodology or approach. Cisco exams require task- and experienced-based knowledge and require you to understand how certain network procedures are accomplished.

> ▶ **Use the exam questions to assess your knowledge:** Don't just read the chapter content; use the exam questions to find out what you know and what you don't know. If you are struggling, study some more, review, and then reassess your knowledge.

> ▶ **Review the objectives:** Develop your own questions and examples for each objective listed. If you can develop and answer several questions for each objective, you should not find it difficult to pass the exam.

NOTE

Exam-Taking Advice   Although this book is designed to prepare you to take and pass the Cisco certification exam, there are no guarantees. Read this book, work through the questions and exercises, and when you feel confident, take the practice exam. Your results should tell you whether you are ready for the real thing. Keep in mind that lots of capable, intelligent people fail these exams one or more times. Cisco exams are some of the most difficult in the industry; if you do fail the exam, use it as a tool to help you focus your studies in the areas where you felt weak. As overused as this guidance is, we still need to say it: Don't give up. Every author writing this book has hit his or her own low points in the certification journey. Trust us—after you pass the CCNA exam, the benefits far outweigh the cost.

When taking the actual certification exam, be sure that you answer all the questions before the time limit expires. Do not spend too much time on any one question. If you are unsure about a question, answer it as best you can and move on. This especially applies to simulation-based questions. Partial credit is given on these questions if you have completed the majority of the steps, so don't get hung up on any one simulation objective for an extended time.

Remember that the primary objective is not to pass the exam but to understand the material. When you understand the material, passing the exam should be simple. Knowledge is a pyramid; to build upward, you need a solid foundation. This book and the CCNA certification are designed to ensure that you have that solid foundation.

Good luck!

CHAPTER ONE

Standard Internetworking Models

Objectives

This chapter covers the following Cisco-specific objectives for the "Describe how a network works" section 640-802 CCNA exam:

▶ **Use the OSI and TCP/IP models and their associated protocols to explain how data flows in a network**

▶ **Describe common networked applications including web applications**

▶ **Describe the purpose and basic operation of the protocols in the OSI and TCP models**

▶ **Determine the path between two hosts across a network**

Outline

Study Strategies

▶ Read through the exam objectives at the beginning of the chapter.

▶ Review the characteristics of each internetwork and keep in mind which network would be appropriate based on a given company and its individual requirements.

▶ Identify the names and primary functions of each OSI model layer. Create a mnemonic device to help you remember the seven layers.

▶ Identify the protocols and standards that are used at each layer of the OSI model. Pay close attention to the application protocols used at the Application layer.

▶ Review and memorize associated UDP and TCP port assignments for several well-known protocols.

Introduction

Whether you already work in the computer technology industry, or you are trying to enter the field as a newcomer, it is important in this day and age to back up your resume with a vendor-specific certification. If you search job postings on the Internet, it is commonplace for hiring companies today to require or recommend that an applicant have at least one vendor certification. Other companies ask that their current employees obtain certifications as a way to meet goals for advancement. Regardless of the underlying reason, studying for the CCNA is a smart move.

The CCNA certification was developed by Cisco to test your knowledge of networking at a beginner's level. Cisco wants to identify individuals capable of installing, configuring, and maintaining small-scale networks, which include Local Area Networks (LANs) and Wide Area Networks (WANs).

The purpose of this first chapter is to provide a general overview of the concepts that will ultimately be the foundation for the rest of this book. To start this chapter, the first step is to define the term *internetwork*. It then reviews the general concepts that pertain to LAN and WAN internetworks, as well as the Metropolitan Area Network (MAN), Storage Area Network (SAN), and Virtual Private Network (VPN). Later chapters go into more detail regarding the technologies that are related to both LAN and WAN.

This chapter also gives an in-depth look at the three networking reference models that are likely to be tested on the CCNA exam. These are the Open Systems Interconnection (OSI), Transmission Control Protocol/Internet Protocol (TCP/IP), and Cisco 3-Layer Hierarchical models. Being familiar with these models is fundamental to understanding how networks operate, as well as how various devices and protocols fit into their structure. By using these models, you can design an infrastructure based on a given organization's specific requirements.

What Is an Internetwork?

Simply put, an internetwork is the connection of more than one network. These networks are linked together by an internetworking device to provide communication between the networks. Internetworks may also be referred to as an *internet*. Notice the lower case *i* at the beginning of the word *internet*—this differentiates it from the Internet. The Internet is considered to be the largest internet in the world. I know the phrase sounds odd, but it is a great example of how thousands of smaller networks are joined together to form one large global internetwork. Another example of an internet would be the connection of individual LANs to form a WAN.

The term *internetworking* signifies the industry, products, and processes that are required to handle the challenges of network interoperability. Such issues can be quite complex because of the existence of multiple vendors and protocols.

Types of Internetworks

There are various types of internetworks discussed in greater detail. I already mentioned LAN and WANs, which are the most common types of internetworks. Other important internetworks include MANs, SANs, and VPNs, which are also reviewed in this section.

Local Area Network (LAN)

Like the name suggests, LANs are limited to a local or small geographical area. An example of a LAN would be a network of individual computers or workstations that are connected in a single department. These users have shared access to resources such as data and network devices. Users on a LAN segment can share a network printer and communicate with one another via email. Also, they are governed by one authoritative administrator.

> **NOTE**
>
> LAN is the smallest network in geographical size.

Given the size constraints, downsides of a LAN network are limited distance that data can travel and a limited number of computers that can be connected. An upside of a LAN is fast data transfer with data speed that can reach up to 10Gbps.

Xerox Corporation worked in collaboration with DEC and Intel to create ethernet, which is the most pervasive LAN architecture used today. Ethernet has evolved and has seen significant improvements in regard to speed and efficiency.

Other significant LAN technologies are Fiber Distributed Data Interface (FDDI) and token ring.

> **EXAM ALERT**
>
> An understanding of LAN technology is required for the CCNA exam. Each ethernet version is discussed in detail in Chapter 3, "Data Link Networking Concepts."

Local area networking uses switches, bridges and/or repeaters, and hubs to interconnect LANs and increase overall size. Routers are used to connect a LAN to a WAN or MAN. Both of these scenarios form an internetwork.

Figure 1.1 provides an example of a LAN. A single switch connects to all the peripheral network devices in this example.

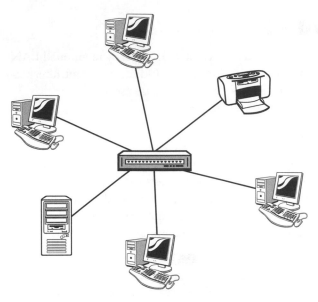

FIGURE 1.1 Example of a LAN.

Metropolitan Area Network (MAN)

A MAN is larger than a LAN but smaller than or equal in size to a WAN. Think of it as the size of a city or college campus network, which can range anywhere from 5 to 50km in diameter. MANs are typically owned and managed by a single entity. This could be an ISP or telecommunications company that sells its services to end-users in that metropolitan area. For all intents and purposes, a MAN has the same characteristics as a WAN with distance constraints.

Wide Area Network (WAN)

WANs cover more than one geographical area. This is ideal for a company that has offices in different cities around the country or even the world. Each office can connect to the other sites in the WAN via a router. Connectivity from router to router is a circuit leased from a telephone or communications company, such as AT&T to name one. The larger the circuit a company needs to transmit data, the more it costs to lease. The company also needs to pay close attention to the performance of its WAN connection because that cost can directly impact its ability to do business. It is important to keep an eye on the amount of traffic that is going over each circuit to ensure that you have sufficient throughput. *Throughput* refers to the amount of data transferred in a specified timeframe.

NOTE

Earlier I mentioned that the Internet is the perfect example of an internetwork. It is also an excellent example of a WAN network where thousands of small networks are joined together to form one large global network.

The following are WAN encapsulations that are reviewed in Chapter 22, "Wide Area Network Connections":

▶ Frame Relay

▶ PPP

▶ HDLC—Cisco standard

EXAM ALERT

WAN characteristics, protocols, services, and troubleshooting techniques are all possible exam topics. Therefore, WAN technologies are discussed in length in Chapter 22.

Figure 1.2 provides an example of a WAN. In this example, a central router connects two LANs to create the WAN. Each LAN has a switch connected to its local end-user devices.

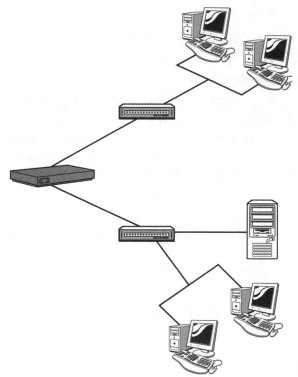

FIGURE 1.2 Example of a WAN.

Storage Area Network (SAN)

SAN may be referred to as a subnetwork or special purpose network. Its special purpose is to allow users on a larger network to connect various data storage devices with clusters of data servers. Cisco offers this service with its Cisco MDS 9000 Series Multilayer SAN Switches. These switches provide scalable storage solutions for the end user.

Virtual Private Network (VPN)

VPN is a private network that can access public networks remotely. VPN uses encryption and security protocols to retain privacy while it accesses outside resources. When employed on a network, VPN enables an end user to create a virtual tunnel to a remote location. Typically, telecommuters use VPN to log in to their company networks from home.

Open Systems Interconnection (OSI) Model

Objectives:

▶ Use the OSI and TCP/IP models and their associated protocols to explain how data flows in a network

▶ Describe common networked applications including web applications

▶ Describe the purpose and basic operation of the protocols in the OSI and TCP models

By now you understand the concept of an internetwork. Now the OSI model will help you see just how an internetwork operates by using a *layered architecture*.

The International Organization for Standardization (ISO) created the OSI model as the first major attempt to internetwork various vendor-specific networks, the ultimate goal being that these different vendor networks could work together in harmony. This model consists of seven layers. Although it is not widely used today, the terminology is prevalent in the networking community. The OSI model may also be helpful when troubleshooting a network issue.

First of all, it is important to know the name of each layer and its corresponding layer number. This will help you remember where the layers reside in the OSI model. You may also hear the layers referred to by number, so knowing them will also help in that respect. Table 1.1 provides a list of all seven layers.

TABLE 1.1   The Seven Layers of the OSI Model

Layer Number	Layer Name
7	Application
6	Presentation
5	Session
4	Transport
3	Network
2	Data Link
1	Physical

In general, each layer communicates with the adjacent layers on the OSI model and the corresponding layer on another system. For example, the Presentation layer communicates with the Application layer, the Session layer, and also with the Presentation layer of another connected system.

EXAM ALERT

It is crucial that you learn the layers of the OSI model and their respective functions. Also know that the OSI model helps with multi-vendor integration. The functions are reviewed in this chapter. For now, to help you remember the names of the layers and their order, it may be helpful to come up with a mnemonic device. The most commonly used phrase is "All People Seem To Need Data Processing." There are many other phrases out there, some of which are quite crass, but it is ultimately up to you to decide whether this will help.

Upper Layers

Now that you know the layers in order, it is also important to know that the layers may also be referred to as the *upper* and *lower* layers. Primarily, the upper layers of the OSI model define communications between applications that reside on end-user stations. This is generally related to software communication. Table 1.2 provides a list of the layers considered as the upper layers.

TABLE 1.2   The Upper Layers of the OSI Model = Applications

Layer Number	Layer Name
7	Application
6	Presentation
5	Session

Application Layer

Layer 7 provides an interface between a host's communication software and any necessary external applications (such as email, file transfers, and terminal emulation). This layer can also evaluate what resources are necessary to communicate between two devices and determine their availability.

Layer 7 also provides the following functionality:

▸ Synchronization of client/server applications

▸ Error control and data integrity between applications

▸ System-independent processes to a host

Table 1.3 provides a list of the protocols supported by the Application layer.

TABLE 1.3   Application Protocols Supported by the Application Layer

Application Protocols	Function
Telnet	A TCP/IP protocol that provides terminal emulation to a remote host by creating a virtual terminal. Secure CRT is one program that can be installed on a user computer to create telnet sessions. This protocol requires authentication via a username and password.
Hypertext Transfer Protocol (HTTP)	Enables web browsing with the transmission of Hypertext Markup Language (HTML) documents on the Internet.
Secure Hypertext Transfer Protocol (HTTPS)	Enables secure web browsing. A secure connection is indicated when the URL begins with https:// or when there is a lock symbol at the lower-right corner of the web page that is being viewed.
File Transfer Protocol (FTP)	Enables a user to transfer files. Provides access to files and directories. Securely implemented with telnet, which allows remote authentication to an FTP server.
Trivial File Transfer Protocol (TFTP)	A bare-bones version of FTP that does not provide access to directories. With TFTP you can just send and receive files. Unlike FTP, TFTP is not secure and sends smaller blocks of data.
Domain Name System (DNS)	Resolves hostnames such as www.cisco.com into IP addresses.
Simple Mail Transfer Protocol (SMTP)	Sends electronic mail across the network.
Post Office Protocol 3 (POP3)	Receives electronic mail by accessing an Internet server.
Network File System (NFS)	Enables users with different operating systems (for example, NT and Unix workstations) to share files.
Network News Transfer Protocol (NNTP)	Offers access to Usenet newsgroup postings.
Simple Network Management Protocol (SNMP)	Monitors the network and manages configurations. Collects statistics to analyze network performance and ensure network security.

TABLE 1.3 *Continued*

Application Protocols	Function
Network Time Protocol (NTP)	Synchronizes clocks on the Internet to provide accurate local time on the user system.
Dynamic Host Configuration Protocol (DHCP)	Works dynamically to provide an IP address, subnet mask, domain name, and a default gateway for routers. Works with DNS and WINS (used for NetBIOS addressing).

EXAM ALERT

Know the Protocols. Be prepared to identify which protocols are used at the Application layer of the OSI model. Also familiarize yourself with the general functions of these protocols.

Presentation Layer

Layer 6 presents data to the Application layer and acts as a data format translator. Format translation is necessary to ensure that the data can be read by applications. Layer 6 also handles the structuring of data and negotiating data transfer syntax to Layer 7. Processes involved include data encryption, decryption, compression, and decompression.

NOTE

The Presentation layer is the only layer that can actually change data.

Layer 6 protocols include the following:

- ▶ Joint Photographic Experts Group (JPEG)
- ▶ American Standard Code for Information Interchange (ASCII)
- ▶ Extended Binary Coded Decimal Interchange Code (EBCDIC)
- ▶ Tagged Image File Format (TIFF)
- ▶ Graphic Image File (GIF)
- ▶ Picture (PICT)
- ▶ Moving Picture Experts Group (MPEG)
- ▶ Musical Instrument Digital Interface (MIDI)
- ▶ QuickTime
- ▶ Rich Text Format (RTF)

> **NOTE**
>
> Graphic and visual images use PICT, TIFF, and JPEG. Audio and video formatting uses MIDI, MPEG, QuickTime, and RTF.

Session Layer

Layer 5 is primarily concerned with dialog control among devices. This layer determines the beginning, middle, and end of a session or conversation that occurs between applications. In this way, the Session layer acts as an intermediary for those applications. Table 1.4 lists the Session layer protocols and their functionality.

TABLE 1.4   Session Layer Protocols and Their General Functionality

Session Layer Protocol	Function
Network File System (NFS)	Accesses remote resources transparently and represents files and directories as if local to the user system. Developed by SUN and used on Unix workstations.
Structured Query Language (SQL)	Functions as a query language that requests, updates, and manages databases. Developed by IBM and compatible with XML and HTML.
Remote Procedure Call (RPC)	Basis for client/server communications. Calls are created on the client and then carried out on the server.
AppleTalk Session Protocol (ASP)	Also client/server–based communications, but specific to AppleTalk client and server devices.
X Window	Communicates with remote Unix machines and enables the user to operate the device as if attached locally.
Digital Network Architecture Session Control Protocol (DNA SCP)	A proprietary Digital Equipment Corporation Networking (DECnet) protocol, also referred to as a DECnet session.

Lower Layers

The lower layers of the OSI model focus on data transport, which can be achieved via a router, switch, or a physical wire. They are listed in Table 1.5.

TABLE 1.5   The Lower Layers of the OSI Model—Responsible for Data Transport

Layer Number	Layer Name
4	Transport
3	Network
2	Data Link
1	Physical

Transport Layer

Layer 4 is responsible for end-to-end connections and data delivery between two hosts. The ability to segment and reassemble data is a key functionality of this layer. For example, when one system is sending data to another system, that data can be segmented into smaller data blocks and transmitted across the network. The receiving system can then reassemble the segmented data blocks at the Transport layer. Transmissions occur via logical connectivity between the sender and destination. Layer 4 provides transparent data transfer by hiding details of the transmission from the upper layers.

> **EXAM ALERT**
>
> Segmenting and reliable end-to-end data delivery occurs at the Transport layer.

Layer 4 also provides the following functionality:

▶ Fault detection

▶ Error recovery

▶ Establishing, maintaining, and tearing down virtual circuits

The Transport layer can provide reliable networking via acknowledgments, sequencing, and flow control.

▶ **Acknowledgments**—Delivered segments are acknowledged to the sender. If they are not acknowledged, the sender will retransmit.

▶ **Sequencing**—Data segments are sequenced into their original order when they arrive at the destination.

▶ **Flow Control**—Provides buffer controls that prevent packet flooding to the destination host. Buffers store bursts of data for processing when the transmission is complete.

Layer 4 protocols include the following:

▶ Transmission Control Protocol (TCP)

▶ User Datagram Protocol (UDP)

▶ Sequenced Packet Exchange (SPX)—A reliable communications protocol created by Novell NetWare

> **NOTE**
>
> TCP and UDP protocols are important to know for the exam. These are discussed later in this chapter, under the "Transport Layer" section of the TCP/IP model.

Network Layer

Layer 3 is where the best path determination is made for packet delivery across the network. Routed protocols such as IP are used to determine logical addressing, which can identify the destination of a packet or datagram. The most common network device found at the Network layer is a router; however, Layer 3 switches may also be implemented.

A router at the Network layer follows these general steps to ensure proper data transport:

1. The router checks the destination IP address of the incoming packet on the router interface.

2. Packets destined for that router are processed, whereas packets destined for another router must be looked up in the routing table.

3. The router determines an exit interface based on the routing table and sends the packet to the interface for framing and forwarding. If there is no route in the routing table, the packet is dropped by the router.

A routing table on a router contains the following information:

▶ Network Address

▶ Interface—Exit interface used to forward packets

▶ Metric—Distance to reach a remote network

There are two packet types utilized at Layer 3:

▶ **Data Packets**—Transport data across the internetwork and are supported by IP and IPX protocols.

▶ **Route Update Packets**—Send updates to neighbor routers about all networks connected to that internetwork and are supported by routing protocols such as RIP, EIGRP, and OSPF.

Layer 3 routed protocols include the following:

▶ Internet Protocol (IP)

▶ Internet Packet Exchange (IPX)—Part of the IPX/SPX protocol suite created by Novell NetWare

▶ AppleTalk DDP—Datagram delivery protocol used by Apple

EXAM ALERT

For the exam, this book focuses on IP, which is reviewed in Chapter 5, "Implementing IP Addressing."

NOTE

Routers and logical addressing (that is, IP addresses) are used at Layer 3. Data at Layer 3 is in the form of packets or a datagram.

Data Link Layer

Layer 2 ensures reliable data transfer from the Network layer to the Physical layer for transmission across the network.

Two domains determine data transport reliability:

▶ **Broadcast Domain**—A group of nodes that can receive each other's broadcast messages and are segmented by routers.

▶ **Collision Domain**—A group of nodes that share the same media and are segmented by switches. A collision occurs if two nodes attempt a simultaneous transmission. *Carrier Sense Multiple Access Collision Detection (CSMA/CD)* is an access method that sends a jam signal to notify the devices that there has been a collision. The devices then halt transmission for a random back-off time.

EXAM ALERT

Routers segment broadcast domains, whereas switches segment collision domains.

Data received from the Network layer is formatted into frames to be transmitted to the Physical layer. Physical addressing or hardware addressing (rather than logical addressing) ensures that data is delivered to the appropriate node on the LAN. This layer is also responsible for error notification (not correction), network topology, and flow control.

This is the only layer of the OSI model that has sublayers. The two sublayers in question define the IEEE Ethernet 802.3 frame, which in turn provides physical addressing and flow control. Also, routed protocol information (IP, IPX, AppleTalk, and so on) is provided to the upper layers.

The IEEE Ethernet 802.3 sublayers are Media Access Control (MAC) and Logical Link Control (LLC), and are described in the following sections.

Media Access Control (MAC)

The MAC address is the hard-coded address on the network interface controller (NIC) of the Physical layer node attached to the network. Although the source address will always be a unicast or single destination address, the destination address can be a unicast, multicast (a determined subset of nodes), or broadcast (all nodes in a broadcast domain) address.

Each MAC address must be unique and follow this format:

▸ It must consist of 48 bits.

▸ It must be displayed by 12 hexadecimal digits (0-9, A-F).

▸ The first 6 hexadecimal digits in the address are a vendor code or organizationally unique identifier (OUI) assigned by the NIC manufacturer.

This is an example of a MAC address: 00:00:07:A9:B2:EB

EXAM ALERT

Know the structure of a MAC address and that the broadcast address value is FFFF FFFF FFFF.

Logical Link Control (LLC)

The LLC sublayer complements the MAC sublayer in the ethernet model; the LLC is responsible for framing, error, and flow control. LLC provides a service access point (SAP) identifier in the frame. The SAP field of the frame consists of one byte that identifies an upper layer protocol (for example, 06 = IP, whereas E0 = IPX). The LLC inserts a destination SAP (DSAP) and a Source SAP (SSAP) in the frame. Figure 1.3 provides an example of an ethernet frame.

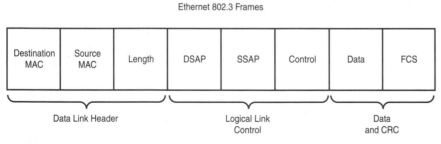

FIGURE 1.3 Example of an ethernet frame.

Two devices are used at the Data Link layer:

▸ **Bridges**—Bridges connect two segments in a single network or two networks together. They simply forward data between those segments/networks without performing an analysis or redirection of the data.

▶ **Switches**—At Layer 2, switches are multi-port bridges that utilize Application Specific Integrated Circuit (ASIC) to forward frames. Each port of the switch has a dedicated bandwidth.

> **EXAM ALERT**
>
> Dedicated bandwidth enables the switch port to guarantee the speed assigned to that port. For example, 100Mbps port connections get 100Mbps transmission rates.

Although both devices create a separate collision domain for each connected device, all the devices connected to either are a part of the same broadcast domain. Remember that broadcast domains are segmented at the Network layer by routers.

Switches and bridges identify MAC addresses by scanning for the source MAC address of each frame received.

> **NOTE**
>
> Bridging and switching are discussed in more detail in Chapter 3.

Physical Layer

Layer 1 moves bits between nodes. Electrical, mechanical, procedural, and functional requirements are defined at the Physical layer to assist with the activation, maintenance, and deactivation of physical connectivity between devices.

Other attributes of Layer 1 include the following:

▶ Specification of voltage, wire speed, and pin-out cables

▶ Capability to receive and transmit a data signal

▶ Identification of the interface that is set up between the data terminal equipment (DTE) and the data communication equipment (DCE)

> **NOTE**
>
> Although DTE is the locally attached device, DCE is typically found at the service provider. DTE services can be accessed with either a model or a channel service unit/data service unit (CSU/DSU). For additional information on associated Layer 1 technologies, continue on to Chapter 2, "Physical Layer Networking Concepts."

Devices at the Physical layer include hubs and repeaters. Hubs and repeaters *extend* a network, whereas Layer 2 and Layer 3 devices *segment* a network.

OSI Layered Communications

Now that you have reviewed all seven layers of the OSI model, it is a good time to see how those layers communicate with each other. Each layer passes information to adjacent layers by using Protocol Data Units (PDUs). The PDU includes both the message and the protocol/control information from the forwarding layer. That control information can be in the form of a header or trailer. The process of adding a header or trailer to the PDU at each layer of the OSI is called *encapsulation*.

Each layer has an associated control information name, which is listed in Table 1.6.

TABLE 1.6   OSI Model Layers and Their Control Information Names

OSI Layer	Control Information Name
Application Presentation Session	Data
Transport	Segment
Network	Packet
Data Link	Frame
Physical	Bit

Based on this chart, you can see how information is encapsulated as it travels down through the various layers. The correct order for data encapsulation is data, segment, packet, frame, and bit.

EXAM ALERT

It is important to know the control information name for the OSI layers and the correct order for data encapsulation.

REVIEW BREAK

Let's take a few minutes to go over the OSI model. Table 1.7 lists the seven layers and significant aspects of each layer.

TABLE 1.7   OSI Model Layers and Their Respective Functionalities

OSI Layer	Important Functions
Application	Provides an interface between a host's communication software and any necessary external applications. Evaluates what resources are necessary and the available resources for communication between two devices. Synchronizes client/server applications. Provides error control and data integrity between applications. Provides system-independent processes to a host.
Presentation	Presents data to the Application layer. Acts as a data format translator. Handles the structuring of data and negotiating data transfer syntax to Layer 7. Processes involved include data encryption, decryption, compression, and decompression.
Session	Handles dialog control among devices. Determines the beginning, middle, and end of a session or conversation that occurs between applications (intermediary).
Transport	Manages end-to-end connections and data delivery between two hosts. Segments and reassembles data. Provides transparent data transfer by hiding details of the transmission from the upper layers.
Network	Determines best path for packet delivery across the network. Determines logical addressing, which can identify the destination of a packet or datagram. Uses data packets (IP, IPX) and route update packets (RIP, EIGRP, and so on). Uses routed protocols IP, IPX, and AppleTalk DDP. Devices include routers and Layer 3 switches.
Data Link	Ensures reliable data transfer from the Network layer to the Physical layer. Oversees physical or hardware addressing. Formats packets into a frame. Provides error notification. Devices include bridges and Layer 2 switches.
Physical	Moves bits between nodes. Assists with the activation, maintenance, and deactivation of physical connectivity between devices. Devices include hubs and repeaters.

TCP/IP Model

Objectives:

▶ Use the OSI and TCP/IP models and their associated protocols to explain how data flows in a network

▶ Describe common networked applications including web applications

▶ Describe the purpose and basic operation of the protocols in the OSI and TCP models

▶ Determine the path between two hosts across a network

The TCP/IP model, also known as the Department of Defense (DoD) model, was created by the DoD when they developed the TCP/IP protocol suite. Their goal was to provide reliable networking and data integrity in the event of a disaster. This model is prevalent in the current networking community. Although the OSI model is rarely used (except for the terminology), TCP/IP communications are ingrained in today's networking fabric and are a focal point on the CCNA exam.

> **NOTE**
>
> So far, the Internet has been a great example of an internetwork and a WAN. It's also a great example of the TCP/IP protocol suite at work.

Essentially the TCP/IP model has many similarities to the OSI model. Table 1.8 lists the layers of the OSI model in the left column and the related layers of the TCP/IP model in the right.

TABLE 1.8   Layers of the OSI and TCP/IP Models

OSI Layer	TCP/IP Layer
Application Presentation Session	Application
Transport	Transport
Network	Internet
Data Link Physical	Network Access

Application Layer

This layer combines functionalities of the three top layers of the OSI model and may also be called the Process/Application layer. Also, some of the most popular applications (email, file transport, and so on) interface with this layer to communicate with other applications on the network.

If you'll remember, the description of the Application layer of the OSI model included a list of application protocols and their primary functions. (Refer to Table 1.3.) These applications are also relevant to the Application layer of the TCP/IP model.

Table 1.9 provides a quick list of the protocols at their respective layers of the TCP/IP model.

TABLE 1.9   Protocols for Each Layer of the TCP/IP Model

TCP/IP Layer	Protocols			
Application	Telnet	HTTP/HTTPS	FTP	TFTP
	DNS	SMTP	POP3	NFS
	NNTP	SNMP	NTP	DHCP
Transport	TCP		UDP	
Internet	ICMP	ARP	RARP	IP
Network Interface	Ethernet	Fast Ethernet	Token Ring	FDDI

Transport Layer

The Transport layer corresponds with the Transport layer of the OSI model and is also known as the Host-to-Host layer. Not only is this layer responsible for reliable data delivery, but it can also make certain that data arrives in the proper order. You will see two transport layer protocols on the CCNA exam. These protocols are TCP and UDP. The following sections cover each protocol and its related applications.

TCP

TCP is a reliable connection-oriented protocol. TCP uses acknowledgments, sequencing, and flow control to ensure reliability (please refer back to the "Transport Layer" section of the OSI model for definitions of these terms). A TCP segment contains fields for the Sequence, Acknowledgment, and Windowing numbers. These fields help make sure that datagrams arrive undamaged. This is considered to be reliable delivery.

TCP uses Positive Acknowledgment and Retransmission (PAR):

▶ The source device begins a timer when a segment is sent and retransmits if the timer runs out before an acknowledgment is received.

▶ The source device keeps track of segments that are sent and requires an acknowledgment for each segment.

▶ The destination device acknowledges when a segment is received by sending a packet to the source that iterates the next sequence number it is looking for from the source.

Figure 1.4 shows the TCP segment header format.

Source Port	Destination Port
Sequence Number	
Acknowledgement Number	
Miscellaneous Flags	Window (Flow Control)
Checksum	Urgent
Options	

FIGURE 1.4 TCP segment header format.

EXAM ALERT

Memorize the TCP header format for the exam.

Flow control via TCP includes *windowing*. Windowing is a method for traffic congestion control where a window is determined by the receiving system to limit the number of data segments (bytes) that can be sent by the source device without an acknowledgment from the recipient. The size of a window determines the number of unacknowledged data segments allowed by the receiving system. Window sizes vary and can change throughout the duration of a connection. Increasing a window size enables more data segments to be transmitted to the recipient before acknowledgment, whereas decreasing the window size allows for fewer data segments to be transmitted before an acknowledgment is sent.

As mentioned at the beginning of this section, TCP is a connection-oriented protocol. When a source device is ready to transmit data, it sets up a Connection-Oriented Communication session with the intended recipient. This is a *call setup* or a *three-way handshake*. When the data is successfully transmitted, a call termination occurs to disconnect the virtual circuit.

The three-way handshake includes the following steps:

1. A "connection agreement" segment is sent to the recipient asking to synchronize systems. This step is associated with the term *SYN packet*.

2. The second and third segments acknowledge the request to connect and determine the rules of engagement. Sequencing synchronization is requested of the receiving device. A two-way connection is established. This step is associated with the term *SYN-ACK packet*.

3. A final segment is sent as an acknowledgement that the rules have been accepted and a connection has been formed. This step is associated with the term *ACK packet*.

For the exam you may also be asked to identify the applications that use TCP and their respective port numbers. Both TCP and UDP use port numbers. Public applications are assigned port numbers below 256. Numbers 256-1023 are allocated to companies. Numbers above 1023 are dynamically assigned by an application. Access lists can use port numbers to filter traffic. Table 1.10 lists applications that use TCP.

TABLE 1.10 Applications Using TCP

Application	Port Number(s)
FTP	20, 21
Telnet	23
SMTP	25
DNS (zone transfers)	53
HTTP	80
POP3	110
NNTP	119
HTTPS	443

EXAM ALERT

The application and port identifiers used by TCP and UDP should be memorized for the exam.

UDP is the other protocol that is used at the Transport layer of the TCP/IP model.

UDP

UDP is much simpler than TCP because it is a connectionless protocol. UDP headers contain only the source and destination ports, a length field, and a checksum. Because of the lack of a sequence, acknowledgment, and windowing field, UDP cannot guarantee delivery. Because there are no delivery guarantees, UDP is considered unreliable. With this protocol, it is up to the application to provide reliability. Figure 1.5 shows a UDP segment header.

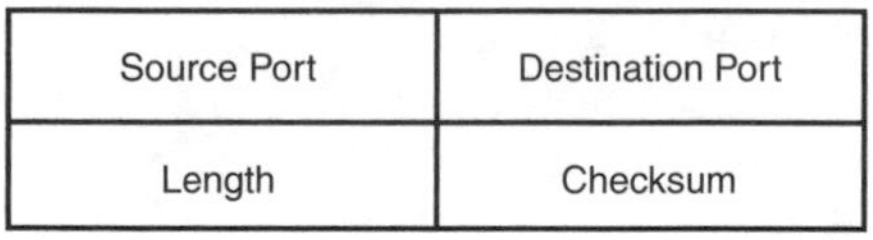

Source Port	Destination Port
Length	Checksum

FIGURE 1.5 The UDP header.

On the plus side, UDP is considerably cheaper to implement and has faster transfer rates. Table 1.11 lists the applications that use UDP.

TABLE 1.11 Applications Using UDP

Application	Port Number(s)
DHCP	67, 68
DNS (name resolution)	53
TFTP	69
NTP	123
SNMP	161

NOTE

DHCP uses UDP as its transport layer protocol. UDP port number 67 identifies the DHCP server port, while UDP port number 68 identifies the DHCP client port.

EXAM ALERT

Note that DNS is listed for both TCP and UDP because it can be used with both protocols. With TCP, DNS is used for zone transfers and with UDP, it is used for name resolution.

Challenge

As mentioned in the TCP section of this chapter, knowing the applications that use TCP and UDP is important for the CCNA exam. It is also important that you know which port number is assigned to each application. Fill in the blanks that are given in each of the following tables. You may reference Tables 1.10 and 1.11, but I strongly suggest that you keep using these charts until you have this information memorized.

Applications Using TCP

Application	Port Number(s)

Applications Using UDP

Application	Port Number(s)

Internet Layer

The Internet layer corresponds with the Network layer of the OSI model.

The following protocols relate to the logical transmission of packets:

▶ IP

▶ ICMP

▶ ARP, RARP, and Proxy ARP

IP

IP uses logical or virtual addressing to get a packet from a source to its destination. IP addresses are used by routers to make forwarding decisions.

Some key characteristics of IP addresses include the following:

▶ Addresses are allocated by the Internet Assigned Numbers Authority (IANA).

▶ IPv4 IP addresses are 32 bits, divided into four octets (8 bits each). An example of an IP address in dotted decimal format would be 172.16.122.204.

▶ The minimum value (per octet) is 0 and the maximum value is 255.

▶ IPv6, which is the future of IP addresses, is 128 bits.

Figure 1.6 shows the data fields that make up an IP datagram.

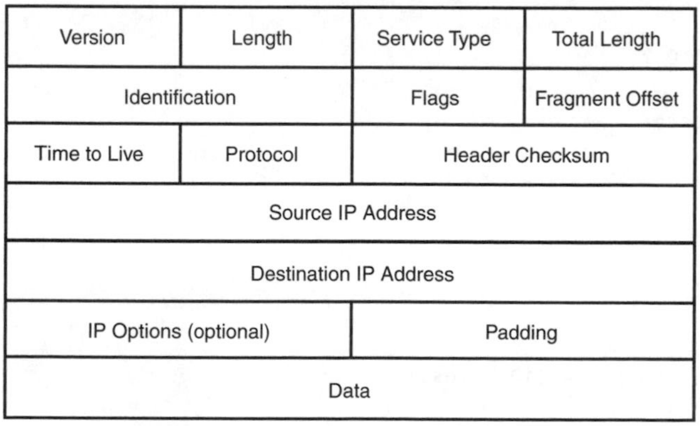

Version	Length	Service Type	Total Length
Identification		Flags	Fragment Offset
Time to Live	Protocol	Header Checksum	
Source IP Address			
Destination IP Address			
IP Options (optional)		Padding	
Data			

FIGURE 1.6   IP datagram.

NOTE

IP addressing is a topic discussed with additional detail in Chapter 5.

ICMP

Internet Control Messaging Protocol is used by ping and traceroute utilities.

Ping (Packet Internet Groper) enables you to validate that an IP address exists and can accept requests. The following transmissions are used by the Ping utility:

▶ Ping sends an echo request packet to receive the echo response.

▶ Routers send Destination Unreachable messages when they can't reach the destination network and they are forced to drop the packet. The router that drops the packet sends the ICMP DU message.

The following is an example of a successful ping test run from a computer command prompt:

```
C:\Documents and Settings>ping 10.0.0.1

Pinging 10.0.0.1 with 32 bytes of data:

Reply from 10.1.1.1: bytes=32 time<1ms TTL=255
Reply from 10.1.1.1: bytes=32 time<1ms TTL=255
Reply from 10.1.1.1: bytes=32 time<1ms TTL=255
Reply from 10.1.1.1: bytes=32 time<1ms TTL=255

Ping statistics for 10.0.0.1:
    Packets: Sent = 4, Received = 4, Lost = 0 (0% loss),
Approximate round trip times in milli-seconds:
    Minimum = 0ms, Maximum = 0ms, Average = 0ms
```

The following is an example of an unsuccessful ping test run from a computer command prompt:

```
C:\Documents and Settings>ping 10.0.0.2

Pinging 10.0.0.2 with 32 bytes of data:

Request timed out.
Request timed out.
Request timed out.
Request timed out.

Ping statistics for 10.0.0.2:
    Packets: Sent = 4, Received = 0, Lost = 4 (100% loss)
```

> **EXAM ALERT**
>
> Ping is used at the Internet layer of the TCP/IP model and network layer of the OSI model.

Traceroute traces the route or path taken from a client to a remote host. Traceroute also reports the IP addresses of the routers at each next hop on the way to the destination. This is especially useful when you suspect that a router on the route to an unreachable network is responsible for dropping the packet.

> **NOTE**
>
> Extended ping enables you to select a datagram size and a timeout.

ARP, RARP, and Proxy ARP

The Address Resolution Protocol (ARP), Reverse Address Resolution Protocol (RARP), and Proxy Address Resolution Protocol (Proxy ARP) are all protocols used at the TCP/IP model's Internet layer.

ARP maps a known IP address to a MAC address by sending a broadcast ARP. When the destination IP address is on another subnet, the sender broadcasts ARP for the router's ethernet port or default gateway, so the MAC address sent back is that of the router's ethernet port.

RARP maps a known MAC address to an IP address.

Proxy ARP enables a router to respond to an ARP request that has been sent to a remote host. Some Unix machines (especially Solaris) rely on Proxy ARP versus default gateways.

Network Interface Layer

This layer corresponds with the Data Link and Physical layers of the OSI model. As mentioned earlier in the chapter, this layer manages hardware addressing and physical data transfer.

Cisco 3-Layer Hierarchical Model

When I think of the word *hierarchy* outside the realm of networking, I think of the military. Each branch of the military has a list of ranks that is assigned to each soldier. In the Army for example, the ranks range from an enlisted private all the way up to the General of the Army. Each soldier reports to a higher-ranking soldier, and each rank has its own group of functions and responsibilities, much like the layers of the Cisco hierarchical model.

The term *hierarchy* as it pertains to this model is the classification of a group of functions or responsibilities into a logical layer where each layer is subordinate to the layer above it in the hierarchy. This model is most effective when you plan to implement a small- to moderate-sized network.

The following sections start from the bottom and work up through the ranks to the top of the hierarchy. First though, take a look Figure 1.7 for an example of the Cisco hierarchical model in its entirety.

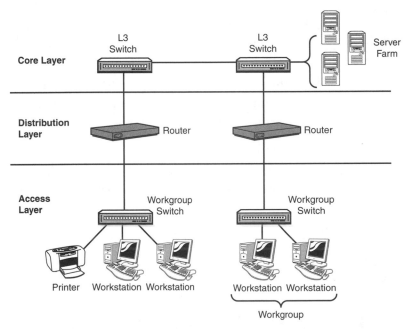

FIGURE 1.7 Cisco hierarchical model.

Access Layer

End users are connected at the Access layer; therefore, this layer may also be referred to as the *desktop* layer. These end users may also be combined to form a workgroup. Virtual LAN (VLAN) workgroups are defined by virtual access lists or filter lists at the Access layer to allow for a continuation of the policies implemented at the Distribution layer. This functionality further controls internetwork resource access granted to each end user or workgroup. Users may access locally available resources at this level or they may be directed to the Distribution layer to access remotely available resources.

Distribution Layer

In the hierarchy, the Distribution layer is the middle man between the access and core layers. You may also hear this layer called the *workgroup* layer. Although the Distribution layer acts as a gathering point for the Access layer devices, it also uses a router or Layer 3 switch whenever necessary to determine how to traverse packets to the core layer.

You achieve traffic control at this layer by using various policies that ultimately provide network management and security.

Primary functions of the Distribution layer include the following:

- Routing (best path determination)
- Routing between VLANs
- Filtering—Access lists provide packet filtering, Quality of Service (QoS), network address translation (NAT), and route filtering
- Accessing WAN
- Defining broadcast and multicast domains
- Translating between different types of media (for example, ethernet and token ring)

Core Layer

The Core layer is the foundation or backbone of the network. Much like a building would falter without its foundation, a network would fall apart without the structure provided by the core layer. As mentioned before, the Distribution layer manages access to the core. This enables the core to focus on speed and reliability. The goal is to provide high-speed switching as quickly and efficiently as possible. Any latency or delay can affect everyone on that network. Because speed is of the essence, the policies implemented at the Distribution layer (for example, filtering, access lists, and so on) should not occur at the Core layer.

Redundancy and fault tolerance are also important to the successful design of a core. If a network is set up with full redundancy, any failures should be transparent to the end user, which is the definition of a fault tolerant network.

> **NOTE**
>
> You might see Enterprise servers (server farms) connected to the core. Devices used at the Core layer may include the Catalyst 6500 series switch or the 7000 series routers. These devices also are reviewed in Chapter 6.

If you were tasked with the design of a new network, would you select a Layer 2 core or a Layer 3 core? Although the Layer 2 core consists of a switched hierarchical setup, a Layer 3 core consists of a routed hierarchical setup.

The answer depends upon the individual requirements of the company in question. If the primary requirement is speed, perhaps a Layer 2 core is appropriate. If a stated desire is the additional network control that is available with a routed solution, then a Layer 3 core would fit the bill.

> **EXAM ALERT**
>
> Remember that routers segment broadcast domains (Layer 3 core) while switches segment collision domains (Layer 2 core).

Challenge

This chapter discusses three different layered models, including the Cisco 3-Layer Hierarchical model. To enhance your understanding of network communications with a layered architecture, please list each layer of the hierarchical model in the correct order and also list its primary responsibilities.

Layer Name	Layer Responsibilities

Although the hierarchical model is typically mentioned in published reviews for the CCNA examination, Cisco also created the Enterprise Composite Network Model (ECNM) for larger-scale network implementations.

The hierarchical model can assist in the implementation of a small- to moderate-sized network. The composite model goes a step further and provides a guide for creating a larger network. Because Cisco has a group of topics listed as "Planning and Designing," it is important to have a general knowledge of their models for network design.

Chapter Summary

The term *internetworking* signifies the industry, products, and processes that are required to handle the challenges of interconnecting networks. Various internetworks can be used, depending on the user's specific needs. For example, a LAN is a small network that is confined to a local geographical area. A LAN can connect to another LAN via a switch, bridge, or repeater. If a LAN attempts to connect to a MAN or WAN, it needs to interconnect via a router. WANs are much larger in scope. WANs are good for a company that has offices in multiple cities around the country. LAN and WAN technology are discussed in greater detail in later chapters of this book.

This chapter also discusses the importance of layered reference models such as the OSI model, TCP/IP model, and the Cisco 3-Layer Hierarchical model. The OSI model is important to discussions of internetworking because the terminology related to each layer has endured the test of time. Seven layers essentially map out the transmission of data from one end-user system to another. Multiple protocols relate to the interoperation of each layer. Special focus is placed on the Application layer protocols and their primary functions.

The TCP/IP model is implemented in a large portion of the networks that are set up today. The model is a condensed version of the OSI model with four related layers. The two most important protocols discussed in the TCP/IP suite for this first chapter are TCP and UDP. TCP is a connection-oriented protocol that provides for reliable data transport. UDP is a connectionless protocol that is considered unreliable. There are advantages and disadvantages to each protocol. Although TCP is reliable, it also costs more to implement on a network.

Overall, this chapter was designed to provide a general overview of standard internetworks and the layered architecture that was designed to represent network interactions. Now that you have gone over all of the internetworking models that are relevant to the exam, you are ready to move on to Chapter 2 and review the concepts related to networking at the Physical layer.

Key Terms

- internetwork
- LAN
- MAN
- WAN
- SAN
- VPN
- OSI model
- Application layer
- Telnet
- HTTP
- HTTPS
- FTP
- TFTP
- DNS
- SMTP
- POP3
- NFS
- NNTP
- SNMP
- NTP
- DHCP
- Presentation layer
- Session layer
- NFS
- SQL
- RPC
- ASP

- X Window
- DNA SCP
- Transport layer
- segment
- acknowledgment
- sequencing
- flow control
- buffers
- Network layer
- packet
- datagram
- data packets
- route update packets
- Data Link layer
- broadcast domain
- collision domain
- CSMA/CD
- grame
- MAC
- MAC address
- LLC
- ridge
- switch
- Physical layer
- hub
- repeater
- bit

- DCE
- DTE
- CSU/DSU
- encapsulation
- PDU
- TCP/IP model
- TCP/IP
- TCP
- PAR
- windowing
- UDP
- IP
- ICMP
- ARP
- RARP
- proxy ARP
- Cisco 3-Layer Hierarchical model
- VLAN
- routing
- filtering
- packet filtering
- route filtering
- QoS
- NAT

Apply Your Knowledge

Exercise

1.1 OSI Layered Model Identification

This has been mentioned throughout the chapter, but it is extremely important for the CCNA exam to know the seven layers of the OSI model and their general functions. If you have not decided on a mnemonic device that you like, you may want to take another look because most people find them to be very helpful with this type of exercise.

Estimated Time: 10 minutes

List the name of the appropriate layer next to the number listed and then identify two primary functions of that layer. Refer to Table 1.7 to check your responses.

1. _____Layer

   Functions: _____

2. _____Layer

   Functions: _____

3. _____Layer

   Functions: _____

4. _____Layer

   Functions: _____

5. _____Layer

   Functions: _____

6. _____Layer

   Functions: _____

7. _____Layer

   Functions: _____

Review Questions

1. Briefly list the communication application protocols that are used at the Application layer of the OSI model and what service they provide.

2. Describe how information is passed through the layers of the OSI model.

3. Define Positive Acknowledgments and Retransmission (PAR).

4. Describe the steps involved in a three-way handshake.

5. List the differences between TCP and UDP.

6. List the key functionalities of the Access layer of the Cisco hierarchical model.

7. List the key functionalities of the Distribution layer of the Cisco hierarchical model.

8. List the key functionalities of the Core layer of the Cisco hierarchical model.

Exam Questions

1. What information can DHCP provide to clients? (Choose the 3 best answers.)

   ○ **A.** Clock information

   ○ **B.** IP information

   ○ **C.** DNS information

   ○ **D.** Gateway information

2. Which of the protocols are used by email? (Choose the 2 best answers.)

   ○ **A.** POP3

   ○ **B.** SMTP

   ○ **C.** SNMP

   ○ **D.** DHCP

3. What takes place when a collision occurs on an ethernet network? (Choose the 3 best answers.)

   ○ **A.** Every device stops transmitting for a short time.

   ○ **B.** A jam signal is sent to notify devices of a collision.

   ○ **C.** A collision signal is sent to notify devices of a collision.

   ○ **D.** A random back-off algorithm starts.

4. What is the OUI of the MAC address 01:AB:4D:F2:89:10?

   ❍ **A.** 01

   ❍ **B.** F2:89:10

   ❍ **C.** 01:AB

   ❍ **D.** 01:AB:4D

5. A MAC address is… (Choose the 2 best answers.)

   ❍ **A.** A unique hardware address in a broadcast domain

   ❍ **B.** A unique IP address in a broadcast domain

   ❍ **C.** Provided by the manufacturer of the NIC

   ❍ **D.** Configured manually by the network administrator

6. At what layer of the OSI model do you find MAC addresses?

   ❍ **A.** Transport

   ❍ **B.** Network

   ❍ **C.** Data Link

   ❍ **D.** Physical

7. At what layer of the OSI model do you find sequence numbers?

   ❍ **A.** Application

   ❍ **B.** Presentation

   ❍ **C.** Session

   ❍ **D.** Transport

8. At what layer of the OSI model do you find IP addresses?

   ❍ **A.** Transport

   ❍ **B.** Network

   ❍ **C.** Data Link

   ❍ **D.** Physical

9. What kind of PDU is used at the Data Link layer of the OSI model?

   ○ **A.** Bit

   ○ **B.** Segment

   ○ **C.** Packet/Datagram

   ○ **D.** Frame

10. What kind of PDU is used at the Network layer of the OSI model?

   ○ **A.** Segment

   ○ **B.** Packet/Datagram

   ○ **C.** Bit

   ○ **D.** Frame

11. What kind of PDU is used at the Transport layer of the OSI model?

   ○ **A.** Segment

   ○ **B.** Data

   ○ **C.** Frame

   ○ **D.** Bit

12. What is the correct order for data encapsulation?

   ○ **A.** Segment, packet, frame, data, bit

   ○ **B.** Data, segment, packet, frame, bit

   ○ **C.** Bit, frame, packet, segment, data

   ○ **D.** Data, packet, segment, frame, bit

13. Routers look at the _____ when making a routing decision.

   ○ **A.** Destination IP address

   ○ **B.** Source IP address

   ○ **C.** Destination MAC address

   ○ **D.** Source MAC address

14. What protocol is assigned to port numbers 20 and 21?

    ○   **A.**   DNS

    ○   **B.**   Telnet

    ○   **C.**   FTP

    ○   **D.**   SMTP

15. What protocol is assigned to port number 80?

    ○   **A.**   SNMP

    ○   **B.**   HTTP

    ○   **C.**   POP3

    ○   **D.**   DHCP

16. Which of the following are TCP? (Choose the 2 best answers.)

    ○   **A.**   Telnet

    ○   **B.**   HTTP

    ○   **C.**   TFTP

    ○   **D.**   NTP

17. Which of the following are UDP? (Choose the 2 best answers.)

    ○   **A.**   DHCP

    ○   **B.**   SMTP

    ○   **C.**   SNMP

    ○   **D.**   POP3

18. What commands use ICMP? (Choose the 2 best answers.)

    ○   **A.**   Show cdp neighbor

    ○   **B.**   traceroute

    ○   **C.**   Telnet

    ○   **D.**   ping

19. What protocol maps a known MAC address to an IP address?

   ○ **A.** RARP

   ○ **B.** ARP

   ○ **C.** ICMP

   ○ **D.** Proxy ARP

20. What TCP/IP protocol provides terminal emulation to a remote host?

   ○ **A.** HTTP

   ○ **B.** VPN

   ○ **C.** Telnet

   ○ **D.** SNMP

Answers to Review Questions

1. The following is a list of the protocols utilized at the Application layer of the OSI model and the functionality of each protocol.

   Telnet—Terminal emulation to a remote host

   HTTP—Web-browsing service

   HTTPS—Secure web browsing

   FTP—File transfer

   TFTP—Bare-bones file transfer

   DNS—Name management

   SMTP—Send emails

   POP3—Receive emails

   NFS—File sharing

   NNTP—Usenet newsgroups

   SNMP—Network management

   NTP—Time management

   DHCP—Dynamic host configuration

2. The upper layers (Application, Presentation, and Session) pass data to the Transport layer. The Transport layer encapsulates the data into a segment that is handed down to the Network layer. The Network layer encapsulates the segment into a packet (or datagram) to be handed down to the Data Link layer. The Data Link layer encapsulates the packet (or datagram) into a frame and sends it to the Physical layer. The Physical layer then encapsulates the frame into a bit to be sent over the network.

3. Used by TCP, PAR is the process by which the source device begins a timer when a segment is sent and retransmits if the timer runs out before an acknowledgment is received. The source device keeps track of segments that are sent and requires an acknowledgment for each segment. The destination device acknowledges when a segment is received by sending a packet to the source that iterates the next sequence number for which it is looking from the source.

4. First, a connection agreement segment is sent to the recipient asking to synchronize systems. Second, a second and third segment acknowledge the request to connect and determine the rules of engagement. Sequencing synchronization is requested of the receiving device. A two-way connection is established. Third, a final segment is sent as an acknowledgment that the rules have been accepted and a connection has been formed.

5. The following table lists comparisons of the key characteristics of the TCP and UDP protocols.

TCP	UDP
Uses sequenced data transmissions	Does not use sequenced data transmissions
Reliable protocol	Unreliable protocol
Connection-oriented	Connectionless
Expensive to implement	Inexpensive to implement
Sends acknowledgments	Does not send acknowledgments
Uses windowing flow control	Does not use windowing or flow control

6. The following list includes the key functionalities of the Access layer of the Cisco hierarchical model:

Desktop layer

End-user connectivity

Virtual LAN (VLAN) workgroup definition

Continuation of the policies implemented at the distribution layer by using virtual access lists or filter lists

User access to locally available resources

7. The following list includes the key functionalities of the Distribution layer of the Cisco hierarchical model:

   Control layer

   Middleman between the access and core layers

   Acts as an aggregation point for access layer devices

   Determines how and when to traverse packets to the core layer

   Policy implementation

   Network security

   Routing (best path determination)

   Routing between VLANs

   Filtering

   Access lists

   Packet filtering

   Quality of Service (QoS)

   Network address translation (NAT)

   Route filtering

   WAN access

   Defines broadcast and multicast domains

   Translates between different types of media (i.e. ethernet and token ring)

8. The following list includes the key functionalities of the Core layer of the Cisco hierarchical model:

   Backbone layer

   The Distribution layer manages access to the core.

   High-speed switching

   Reliability

   Redundancy

   Fault tolerance

   Low latency

   Enterprise servers (server farms)

Answers to Exam Questions

1. **B, C, D.** DHCP works dynamically to provide IP address, DNS, and default gateway information. Answer A is incorrect because the Network Time Protocol (NTP) provides clock information.

2. **A, B.** POP3 receives email on an Internet server and SMTP sends email across a network. Answer C is incorrect because SNMP is a network management protocol and answer D is incorrect because DHCP is the dynamic host configuration protocol.

3. **A, B, D.** When a collision occurs on an ethernet network a jam signal is sent to notify devices of a collision and a random back-off algorithm starts while every device stops transmitting for a short time. Answer C is incorrect because a jam signal is sent rather than a collision signal.

4. **D.** The OUI of a MAC address is the organizationally unique identifier that is assigned by the manufacturer of the network interface card (NIC). The OUI consists of the first 6 hexadecimal digits. Answer A is incorrect because it only consists of 2 hexadecimal digits. Answer B is incorrect because it is not the first 6 hexadecimal digits of the MAC address 01:AB:4D:F2:89:10. Answer C is incorrect because it only consists of 4 hexadecimal digits.

5. **A, C.** The MAC address is a unique hardware address in the broadcast domain and the manufacturer of the NIC provides MAC addresses. Answer B is incorrect because IP addresses are logical addresses used by the Network layer. Answer D is incorrect because a MAC address is not configured manually by a network administrator.

6. **C.** MAC addresses are found at the Data Link layer of the OSI model. Answers A, B, and D are incorrect because MAC addresses are not found at the Transport, Network, or Physical layer of the OSI model.

7. **D.** The Transport layer uses sequence numbers. Data segments are sequenced into their original order when they arrive at the destination. Answers A, B, and C are incorrect because sequence numbers are not found at the Application, Presentation, or Session layer of the OSI model.

8. **B.** Answer B is correct because IP addresses are found at the Network layer of the OSI model. IP addresses are logical or virtual addresses that are assigned at Layer 3 to identify the destination of a packet or datagram. Answers A, C, and D are incorrect because IP addresses are not found at the Transport, Data Link, or Physical layer of the OSI model.

9. **D.** The Data Link layer uses frame PDUs to encapsulate data. Answers A, B, and C are incorrect because segments are used at the Transport layer, whereas packet/datagrams are used at the Network layer and bits are used by the Physical layer of the OSI model.

10. **B.** The Network layer of the OSI model uses packets/datagrams. Answers A, C, and D are incorrect because the Application, Presentation, and Session layers of the OSI model transmit data.

11. **A.** Segments are used at the Transport layer of the OSI model. Answer B is incorrect because the three upper layers of the OSI model transmit data. Answer C is incorrect because the Data Link layer transmits frames, and answer D is incorrect because the Physical layer transmits bits.

12. **B.** Encapsulation occurs from the Application layer and then is passed down through the lower layers of the OSI model. The PDUs are sent by the Application layer as data and then they are encapsulated with a segment at the Transport layer. At the Network layer the segment is encapsulated into a packet/datagram that is passed down to the Data Link layer, which encapsulates a frame and hands it off to the Physical layer, which uses bits.

13. **A.** Routers look at the destination IP address to determine where to forward the packet. Answers B, C, and D are incorrect because a router does not examine the source IP address, destination MAC address, or source MAC address to make forwarding decisions.

14. **C.** FTP is assigned to port numbers 20 and 21. Answers A, B, and D are incorrect because Telnet is assigned port number 23, DNS is assigned port number 53, and SMTP is assigned port number 25.

15. **B.** HTTP is assigned port number 80. Answers A, C, and D are incorrect because SNMP is assigned port number 161, POP3 is port number 110, and DHCP is assigned ports 67 and 68.

16. **A, B.** Telnet and HTTP are both protocols that use TCP. Answers C and D are incorrect because TFTP and NTP use UDP.

17. **A, C.** DHCP and SNMP use UDP, whereas answers B and D are incorrect because SMTP and POP3 use TCP.

18. **B, D.** Traceroute and ping are both commands that use ICMP. Traceroute traces the route or path taken from a client to a remote host. Ping enables you to validate that an IP address exists and can accept requests. Answers A and C are incorrect because neither `show cdp neighbor` nor Telnet use ICMP.

19. **A.** RARP maps MAC addresses to an IP address, whereas answer B is incorrect because ARP maps an IP address to a MAC address. Answer C is incorrect because ICMP sends messages across the network via ping, and traceroute enables a router to respond to an ARP request that has been sent to a remote host. Answer D is also incorrect because some Unix machines (especially Solaris) rely on Proxy ARP rather than default gateways.

20. **C.** Telnet provides for terminal emulation to a remote host. Answers A, B, and D are incorrect because HTTP is a web-browsing application, VPN is a private network that can access public networks remotely, and SNMP is a network management application.

Suggested Readings and Resources

The following are some recommended readings on the subject of standard internetworking models:

1. "Open Systems Interconnection Protocols," http://www.cisco.com/univercd/cc/td/doc/cisintwk/ito_doc/osi_prot.htm.

2. "OSI Model," http://en.wikipedia.org/wiki/OSI_model.

3. "TCP/IP Overview," http://www.cisco.com/univercd/cc/td/doc/cisintwk/ito_doc/osi_prot.htm.

4. "TechEncyclopedia," www.techweb.com/encyclopedia.

CHAPTER TWO

Physical Layer Networking Concepts

Objectives

This chapter covers the following Cisco-specified objectives from the "Describe how a network works" and "Configure, verify and troubleshoot a switch with VLANs and interswitch communications" sections of the 640-802 CCNA exam:

▶ **Interpret network diagrams**

▶ **Select the appropriate media, cables, ports, and connectors to connect switches to other network devices and hosts**

▶ **Describe the purpose and functions of various network devices**

Outline

Study Strategies

▶ Identify the four physical network topologies discussed in this chapter.

▶ Know the different types of network cables and the characteristics that differentiate them from one another.

▶ Review the wireless technology standards.

▶ Be able to identify devices that are used at the Physical layer.

Introduction

Chapter 1, "Standard Internetworking Models," went over the layers of the OSI and TCP/IP models. This chapter goes into more detail regarding the Physical layer. Remember that electrical, mechanical, procedural, and functional requirements are defined at this layer. Such requirements provide assistance with the activation, maintenance, and deactivation of physical connectivity between devices.

Concepts covered include the topologies, cabling, and devices that are relevant at the physical level and important to understand when studying for the CCNA exam. Also, because wireless communications are constantly evolving and are flourishing in today's marketplace, several significant wireless technologies are covered as well.

Network Topologies

Objective:

▶ Interpret network diagrams

Topology can be defined as either the physical or logical layout of a network. Typically, a physical topology is documented with a network diagram, such as a Visio diagram. Diagrams can prove to be extremely helpful when troubleshooting a network issue. Most companies keep a database with copies of their entire network as well as individual site connections. If you work in a sales capacity, diagrams are drawn up to plan out the network setup and to ensure that all bases are covered to meet customer expectations.

Just as you might imagine, a physical topology consists of the cables, workstations, and other peripheral devices that comprise the network. A logical topology refers to how the network actually communicates. This may differ from the physical topology; therefore, this section covers the four most common physical network topologies and what the associated logical network topology is for the physical star network.

The Bus Topology

A *bus network* topology may also be referred to as a *linear bus* topology. This topology is set up so that the network nodes are connected via a single cable (also referred to as a *trunk* or a *backbone*). Electrical signals are sent from one end of the cable to the other. When this occurs, all connected devices receive that electrical signal transmission. Network devices are connected directly to the trunk with a T connector. Both ends of the trunk use a terminator to stop the electrical signal from echoing back down the cable. Figure 2.1 represents a physical bus topology.

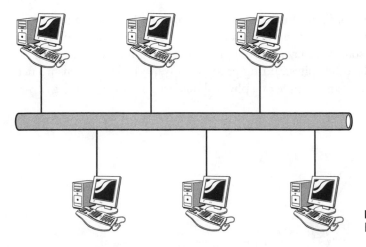

FIGURE 2.1 Example of a physical bus topology.

Because the bus topology uses a single cable, it is a low-cost option that is easily implemented. The downside to this setup is the lack of redundancy. If the cable breaks, the entire network goes down.

The Ring Topology

A *ring network* topology is set up so that one device is directly connected to two other devices on the same network. When a device emits a data signal transmission, the transmission is sent in a single direction to the next connected device. The transmission continues to pass along each device successively until it arrives back at the original transmitting device. This method creates a ring or a loop. Figure 2.2 shows an example of a physical ring topology.

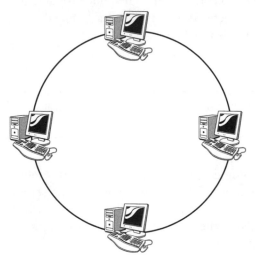

FIGURE 2.2 Example of a physical ring topology.

With this topology, a single ring configuration lacks a failover solution. If there is a break any-where on the ring, it brings down the entire network. This was the same situation with the bus network topology. For this reason, you may also configure a dual ring topology. If there is a failure on one physical ring, the other physical ring passes data transmissions to ensure net-work operability. Figure 2.3 shows an example of a physical dual ring network topology.

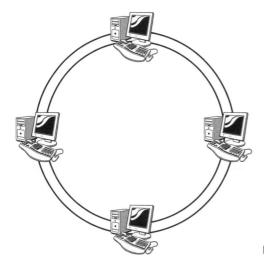

FIGURE 2.3   Example of a physical dual ring topology.

The Star Topology

The *star network* topology is the most commonly implemented network design. With this topology, there is a central device with separate connections to each end node. Each connec-tion uses a separate cable, which adds to the cost of implementation. When hubs are used in a star topology, a logical bus is created. This type of network star is called a hub-and-spoke topology. Figure 2.4 shows an example of a physical star topology.

> **NOTE**
>
> Although the star topology is a physical star, it also can be referred to as a logical bus topology because hubs are used to control communication.

Because there are separate connections between end nodes and the central device, this topol-ogy enables the network administrator to add or remove end nodes without affecting service to all other nodes on that network. This is also possible with the token ring topology, which enables you to add multistation access units (MAUs) to the network without disrupting serv-ice. The same cannot be said for the physical bus network topologies.

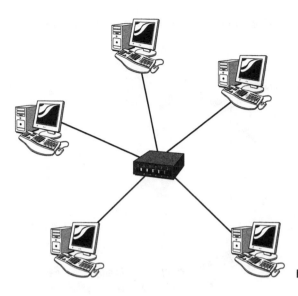

FIGURE 2.4   Example of a physical star topology.

The Mesh Topology

The full mesh network topology is set up so that each device is directly connected to every other device on the network. This connection method has built-in redundancy. If one link goes down, the device transmits via another link. Figure 2.5 shows an example of a physical full mesh topology.

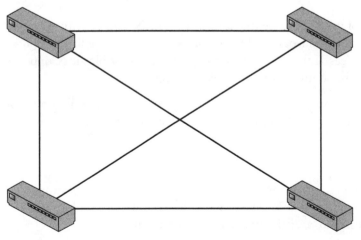

FIGURE 2.5   Example of a mesh topology.

A partial mesh network topology has direct connectivity between some of the network devices, but not all of them, as the full mesh topology does. Figure 2.6 shows an example of a physical partial mesh topology.

Overall, mesh topologies are much more expensive to implement. However, the cost may be acceptable given the reliability of this design.

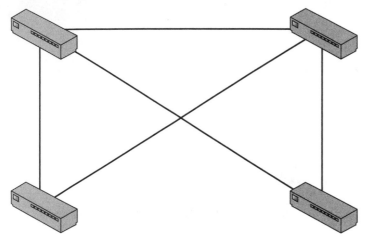

FIGURE 2.6   Example of a partial mesh topology.

Cabling

Objective:

▶ Select the appropriate media, cables, ports, and connectors to connect switches to other network devices and hosts

This section reviews the types of media or cable that are used for LAN connectivity. The primary media types include coaxial, twisted-pair, and fiber-optic cables. Cable media offer physical connectivity to network devices. Cables may consist of metal, glass, or plastic. Copper is the most popular metal cable. Fiber-optic uses glass or plastic cabling.

Before you look at each medium in greater detail, it's a good idea to discuss several important terms related to data transmission that are directly affected by what type of cable media is used on a network.

Review the following terminology:

▶ **Bandwidth**—The total amount of information that can traverse a communications medium, measured in bits per second. Measurement of bandwidth is helpful for network performance analysis. Also, availability is increasing but limited.

> **EXAM ALERT**
>
> For the exam, remember that bandwidth is used to analyze network performance and that although availability is increasing, it is also limited.

▶ **Attenuation**—Occurs over long distances as a signal loses strength.

▶ **Electromagnetic Interference (EMI)**—Interference or noise caused by electromagnetic signals, which can decrease data integrity.

▶ **Crosstalk**—An electrical or magnetic field originating from one communications signal that can affect the signal in a nearby circuit.

  ▶ **Near-end Crosstalk (NEXT)**—Crosstalk measured at the transmitting end of a cable.

  ▶ **Far-end Crosstalk (FEXT)**—Crosstalk measured at the far end of the cable from where the transmission was sent.

> **EXAM ALERT**
>
> Know the terms NEXT and FEXT and what they represent for the CCNA exam.

Coaxial Cable

Coaxial cables for data consist of a single copper wire surrounded by a plastic insulation cover and a braided copper shield. Primarily, two types of coaxial cables are used in conjunction with Ethernet LAN networks. They are called *thin* and *thick coax*.

Thin coax has the following characteristics:

▶ Also called thinnet

▶ .25 inches in diameter

▶ Maximum cable length = 185 meters

▶ Uses Bayonet Neill Concelman connectors (BNCs)

▶ 10BASE-2 ethernet standard

> **NOTE**
>
> The Institute for Electrical and Electronics Engineers (IEEE) ethernet standards are reviewed in Chapter 3, "Data Link Networking Concepts."

Thick coax has the following characteristics:

- Also called thicknet

- Maximum cable length = 500 meters

- Uses vampire taps (where the tap goes through the shield to touch the copper wire)

- Uses attachment unit interface (AUI) adapters

- 10BASE-5 ethernet standard

The coaxial cable media is not nearly as popular as twisted pair or fiber optic. It is not as flexible or cost effective as other options. You may see this cable implemented on an older network.

Twisted-Pair Cable

Just as the name indicates, twisted-pair cables twist two wires together to form a pair. This solution helps to reduce interference and attenuation. There are two types of twisted-pair cabling defined by the Telecommunications Information Association (TIA). Those types are unshielded twisted pair (UTP) and shielded twisted pair (STP). UTP is the more common and cost-effective solution. STP has an additional shield, which provides additional reduction of interference and attenuation, but also makes it the more expensive solution. For the exam, UTP is reviewed in greater detail.

UTP key characteristics include the following:

- Eight color-coded wires

- Four pairs

- Uses an RJ-45 connector

- Vulnerable to EMI

- Maximum, practical length is 100 meters

- 10BASE-T, 100BaseT, and 1000BaseT ethernet standards

TIP

When reviewing for the exam, note that UTP is vulnerable to EMI and uses an RJ-45 connector.

EXAM ALERT

Because attenuation causes a signal to lose strength as the length of a cable increases, the maximum, practical length of a UTP cable is 100 meters.

UTP can be broken down into six more categories. You may have heard someone talk about a Cat5 cable. They are referring to a Category 5 UTP cable. Each category has different characteristics:

▶ **Category 1**—Telephone cable that is not used for data transmission.

▶ **Category 2**—Data cable that can handle speeds up to 4Mbps. This is no longer fast enough for networks today.

▶ **Category 3**—Data cable that can handle speeds up to 10Mbps. It is faster than the Cat2 cable, and this was quite popular until network speeds surpassed the 10Mbps threshold.

▶ **Category 4**—Data cable that can handle speeds up to 16Mbps. Meant to be used with token ring.

▶ **Category 5**—Data cable that can handle speeds up to 100Mbps. This is currently the most popular cable selection.

▶ **Category 5e**—Data cable that can handle speeds up to 1Gbps. This is a popular choice for Gigabit Ethernet networks.

▶ **Category 6**—This cable was created to exceed speeds of 1Gbps.

It is also important to know the pinouts for twisted-pair cables. The term *pinout* is used in the electronic industry to describe the purpose of each pin in a connector. When choosing your cable, you need to know which pinout is appropriate to connect the devices on your network. The following sections cover the straight-through and cross-over cables.

Straight-Through Cable

Straight-through cables use four wires and pins 1, 2, 3, and 6. Given those pins, pin 1 is connected on one end of the cable to pin 1 on the opposite end of the cable. Pin 2 at one end is connected to pin 2 on the far end, and so on. Figure 2.7 shows an example of a straight-through cable pinout.

These cables are meant only for interface to interface connections on ethernet networks, so you cannot use them with token ring, ISDN, and so on.

Use a straight-through cable for the following connection types:

▶ From a PC to a switch or a hub

▶ From a router to a switch or a hub

TIP

> For the CCNA exam, you need to know which devices can be connected with a straight-through cable. Remember that straight-through cables are used to connect unlike device interfaces. Different devices = straight-through cable.

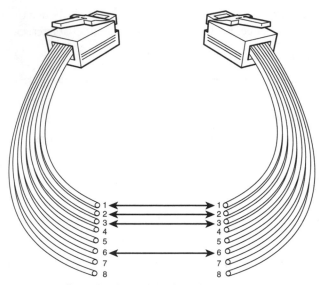

FIGURE 2.7 Example of a straight-through cable pinout.

Cross-Over Cable

Cross-over cables also use four wires and pins 1, 2, 3, and 6. The difference is in how the pins are connected at each end. With cross-over cables, pin 1 connects to pin 3 and pin 2 connects to pin 6. Figure 2.8 shows an example of a cross-over cable pinout.

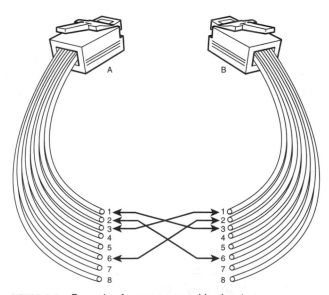

FIGURE 2.8 Example of a cross-over cable pinout.

Use a cross-over cable for the following connection types:

▶ From a switch to another switch

▶ From a router to another router

▶ From a PC to another PC

▶ From a PC to a router

▶ From a hub to another hub

▶ From a hub to a switch

TIP

For the CCNA exam, you need to know which devices can be connected with a cross-over cable. Remember that for the most part cross-over cables are used to connect similar device interfaces.

Rolled Cable

Rolled or rollover cables use eight wires and connect from a host to a console serial communications (com) port on a router. You may also hear this cable referred to as a *console cable*. Make sure not to confuse a rollover cable with a cross-over cable for the CCNA exam.

Challenge

Knowing the type of twisted-pair cable that is used to connect one device to another is an important networking concept. If you use the wrong cable, you will not have a working connection. So in this challenge I give you various connectivity scenarios and you must decide whether you should use a straight-through or cross-over cable between the devices.

Connecting a...	Type of Cable
Switch to a switch	
Hub to a switch	
PC to a switch or hub	
PC to a PC	
Hub to a hub	
Router to a router	
PC to a router	
Router to a switch or hub	

Fiber-Optic Cable

Fiber-optic cables use light rather than electric signals to send data transmissions. These optical light signals travel a fiberglass core and you may hear this technology referred to as *fiber optics* or *optical cabling*.

Two categories of fiber-optic cabling are

▶ *Multimode (MM)*—This is generally used for shorter distances and is ideal for a campus-sized network. MM also has a larger diameter of optical fiber than SM fiber.

▶ *Single-mode (SM)*—This mode is used to span longer distances. SM also allows for a higher data rate than MM and faster data transmission speeds.

Fiber-optic cables may use a subscriber connector (SC), straight tip (ST), or MegaTransfer-Registered Jack (MT-RJ) connector. There are several Layer 2 ethernet protocols that can pass data over fiber-optic cables. Those Layer 2 ethernet standards are 10BASE-FL, 100Base FX, 1000BaseSX, 1000BaseLX, and 1000BaseZX.

All in all, fiber is the best choice for a secure connection over longer distances. Because fiber uses optical light signals for data transmission, it is not as easy to "eavesdrop" on communications as it is with copper cabling using electrical signals. Fiber is not susceptible to EMI and crosstalk, as coaxial and twisted-pair cables are. It also offers the highest maximum speed of the different cable types. You may have already guessed, but fiber is also the most expensive option.

> **TIP**
>
> Fiber-optic cables are not susceptible to EMI.
>
> On the CCNA exam, you may see the terms *Main Distribution Frame (MDF)* and an *Intermediate Distribution Frame (IDF)*. A distribution frame is a physical rack that allows for the termination and interconnection of cables. This process creates network cross-connects. With that in mind, the MDF provides a point of interconnection between external telecommunications cabling and internal cabling in a facility. The IDF is the point of interconnection for cabling between the MDF and end-user devices.

Wireless

Wireless technology uses radio transmissions rather than data transmissions over copper wire or fiber-optic media. With wireless LANs (WLANs), a physical connection is no longer necessary. Electromagnetic energy, whose existence was proven way back in 1867, passes through the atmosphere in varied wavelengths. Different wavelengths are differentiated by their different names. Spread Spectrum WLANs determine how data traverses the Radio Frequency (RF) media. The most common applications for wireless technology are Wireless Fidelity, Infrared, and Bluetooth technologies. Because of the widespread popularity of wireless technology in business today, an entire section of this book is now devoted to wireless networking.

> **TIP**
>
> Keep in mind that Spread Spectrum WLANs allow for high-speed transmissions over short distances. There are two types of spread spectrum radio: Direct Sequencing Spread Spectrum (DSSS) and Frequency-Hopping Spread Spectrum (FHSS).

Wireless Fidelity (Wi-Fi)

IEEE created the 802.11 designation as the standard for wireless networking. IEEE 802.11 may be further defined by three more specific standards: 802.11a, 802.11b, and 802.11g. The speed, distance, and features of 802.11 specifications are variable. The most common of these specifications is the 802.11b standard, which may also be referred to as Wireless Fidelity (Wi-Fi) or High Rate 802.11. IEEE 802.11b can allow for transmission speeds of up to 1–2Mbps. It also uses a Radio Frequency (RF) of 2.4GHz.

> **TIP**
>
> For the CCNA exam, remember that the 802.11b standard is also known as Wi-Fi or High Rate 802.11.

802.11 can also be broken down again into the following wireless standards:

- 802.11a
  - RF is 5GHz.
  - Speed up to 54Mbps.
  - Range of transmission is generally lower than that of 802.11g.
- 802.11b
  - RF is 2.4GHz.
  - Uses different channels to cover subfrequencies in the 2.4Ghz band.
  - Speed up to 11Mbps.
  - Range of transmission is generally greater than that of 802.11a and 802.11g.
- 802.11g
  - RF is 2.4GHz.
  - Speed up to 54Mbps.
  - Range of transmission is generally lower than that of 802.11b.

Based on these summarizations, you can see the similarities and differences of each standard. Please note that only 802.11a uses a different RF. This means that 802.11a is not compatible with either 802.11b or 802.11g.

Infrared

Infrared resides in a region of the electromagnetic spectrum just beyond the red end of our visible spectrum. Infrared wireless technology uses infrared beams to pass data across a network. Your television remote uses infrared technology to send requests to the television set. Speeds can reach a maximum of 16Mbps and signals are used for short-distance communications.

Infrared can eliminate the need for those pesky cables that connect your keyboard or mouse to your PC and cause clutter in your workspace. On the other hand, infrared may be easily refracted or reflected so it should not be used near windows or glass objects.

Bluetooth

Bluetooth technology utilizes a short-range wireless radio connection to enable various devices to interconnect. Such devices include cell phones, PCs, and Personal Digital Assistants (PDAs). The only requirement to establish connectivity is a 10-meter range (approximately 33 feet) between communicating devices. When in range, Bluetooth uses an RF link in the 2.4GHz range that has a 720Kbps per channel capacity to transfer voice or data. The Bluetooth specification also has two power levels defined; a lower power level that covers the shorter personal area within a room, and a higher power level that can cover a medium range like the range within a home.

Physical Layer Devices

Objective:

▶ Describe the purpose and functions of various network devices

The discussion so far of physical layer networking concepts has gone over the physical network topologies, cables, and wireless technology standards. Several network devices also are utilized at the Physical layer. Those include repeaters, hubs, and network interfaces.

Repeaters

Chapter 1, with its discussion of the Physical layer, mentioned that repeaters and hubs extend a network rather than segment a network. In fact, repeaters were introduced to increase or extend the distance between end nodes. A repeater consists of a transmitter and a receiver.

When a signal is received by the repeater, it amplifies the signal and then retransmits. This effectively enables the signal to travel over a greater distance.

Please note that repeaters are an outdated technology. A separate device is no longer needed to perform this functionality. Both active hubs and switches can be used in place of a repeater.

Hubs

A *hub* can be defined as a multiple port repeater. A hub consists of 2 to 24 ports and may be called a *workgroup hub*. When data is received, the hub then retransmits that data out on all the other ports. Physical connectivity is achieved via a twisted-pair cable.

There are active and passive hubs. Active hubs have a separate power supply to assist with the gain of a signal before it is forwarded out all connected ports. *Gain* is an electrical term used to identify the ratio of signal output to signal input of a system. A power signal increased by a factor of 10 would indicate a gain of 10. Passive hubs do not regenerate the incoming signal.

Although they are very inexpensive, hubs may not be the best solution if you require a more efficient use of bandwidth and its distribution among ports. Traffic may become congested because of collisions on the network. Traffic is being forwarded out on all ports of a single collision domain. To decrease congestion, the network administrator might consider replacing the hub with a switch.

> **TIP**
>
> Know that a viable solution to decrease network congestion is replacing a hub with a switch. A switch creates a separate collision domain for each network segment, therefore increasing the number of collision domains.

> **EXAM ALERT**
>
> Hubs and repeaters are Layer 1 devices that can be used to increase the size of a single LAN segment.

Network Interfaces

A network interface provides connectivity from an end-user PC or laptop to the public network. Depending on the interface, you might see up to three light-emitting diodes (LEDs) that help to determine the connection's status. The link light LED should light up if you have connectivity. The activity light LED should flicker if there is activity on the line. There may also be a speed light LED that is used to verify the connection speed in a 10/100/1000Mbps network. Blinking lights and colors other than green can indicate error conditions that can be investigated by a technician.

Chapter Summary

Chapter 2 has taken the Physical layer and expanded the discussion to include physical network topologies and various network components. All these concepts are relevant when mapping out the design of a new network. Many of the topics in this chapter also touch upon ethernet technologies, which Chapter 3 continues to discuss, along with devices that are used at the Data Link layer.

Key Terms

- physical topology
- logical topology
- bus topology
- ring topology
- dual ring topology
- star topology
- full mesh topology
- partial mesh topology
- bandwidth
- attenuation
- EMI
- crosstalk

- NEXT
- FEXT
- coaxial cable
- twisted-pair cable
- unshielded twisted-pair cable
- shielded twisted-pair cable
- straight-through cable
- cross-over cable
- fiber-optic cable
- multimode

- single-mode
- wireless fidelity
- 802.11
- 802.11a
- 802.11b
- 802.11g
- infrared
- Bluetooth
- repeaters
- hubs
- network interface

Apply Your Knowledge

Exercise

2.1 UTP Cable Categories

Each category of UTP cabling has different characteristics. In this exercise, please list the characteristics of each category of UTP cable.

Estimated Time: 10 minutes

UTP Category	Characteristics
Category 1	
Category 2	
Category 3	
Category 4	
Category 5	
Category 6	

Review Questions

1. Draw out a simple physical bus topology.

2. Draw out a simple physical single ring and dual ring topology.

3. Draw out a simple physical star topology.

4. Draw out a simple physical partial mesh and full mesh topology.

5. Describe the pinout of a straight-through cable.

6. Describe the pinout of a cross-over cable.

Exam Questions

1. Which physical network topology is shown in the following diagram?

    ○ **A.** Ring

    ○ **B.** Bus

    ○ **C.** Star

    ○ **D.** Mesh

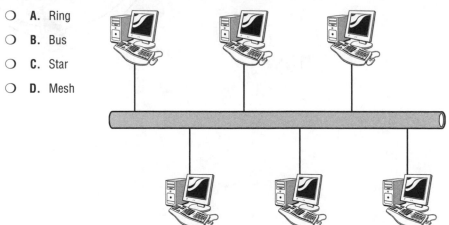

2. Which physical network topology is shown in the following diagram?

   ○ **A.** Ring

   ○ **B.** Bus

   ○ **C.** Star

   ○ **D.** Mesh

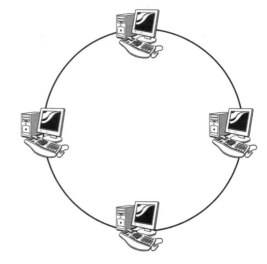

3. Which physical network topology is shown in the following diagram?

   ○ **A.** Single ring

   ○ **B.** Partial mesh

   ○ **C.** Full mesh

   ○ **D.** Dual ring

4. Which physical network topology
   is shown in the following diagram?

   - ○ **A.** Ring
   - ○ **B.** Bus
   - ○ **C.** Star
   - ○ **D.** Mesh

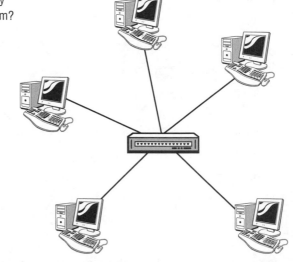

5. Which physical network
   topology is shown in the
   following diagram?

   - ○ **A.** Single ring
   - ○ **B.** Partial mesh
   - ○ **C.** Dual ring
   - ○ **D.** Full mesh

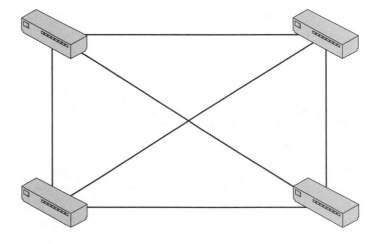

6. Which physical network
   topology is shown in the
   following diagram?

   - ○ **A.** Single ring
   - ○ **B.** Partial mesh
   - ○ **C.** Dual ring
   - ○ **D.** Full mesh

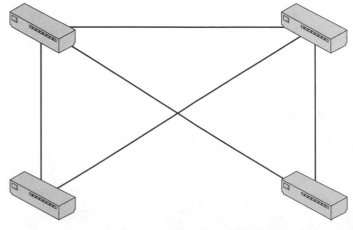

7. Which of the following is not susceptible to EMI?

   ○ **A.** Fiber

   ○ **B.** Thin coaxial cable

   ○ **C.** Category 3 UTP cable

   ○ **D.** Category 5 UTP cable

8. Which connector does a UTP cable use?

   ○ **A.** MT-RJ

   ○ **B.** SC

   ○ **C.** ST

   ○ **D.** RJ-45

9. Because of attenuation, the maximum, practical length of a UTP cable is _____.

   ○ **A.** 10 meters

   ○ **B.** 100 meters

   ○ **C.** 200 meters

   ○ **D.** 500 meters

10. The total flow of information over a certain time period on a communications medium measured in bits per second is called _____.

    ○ **A.** Bandwidth

    ○ **B.** Crosstalk

    ○ **C.** Attenuation

    ○ **D.** Electromagnetic interference

11. Which cable consists of a single copper wire surrounded by a plastic insulation cover and a braided copper shield?

    ○ **A.** Coaxial cable

    ○ **B.** UTP

    ○ **C.** STP

    ○ **D.** Category 5 cable

12. What type of UTP cable would you use to connect a switch to a router?

    ◯ **A.** Coaxial cable

    ◯ **B.** Straight-through cable

    ◯ **C.** Cross-over cable

    ◯ **D.** Thin coax

13. What type of UTP cable would you use to connect a PC directly to another PC?

    ◯ **A.** Coaxial cable

    ◯ **B.** Straight-through cable

    ◯ **C.** Cross-over cable

    ◯ **D.** Thick coax

14. If you have a network that is connected through a hub and experiencing congestion, which of the following is the best solution to decrease congestion on your network?

    ◯ **A.** Install a second hub.

    ◯ **B.** Replace the hub with a repeater.

    ◯ **C.** Replace the hub with a switch.

    ◯ **D.** Replace the hub with a network interface.

15. What is the IEEE standard for wi-fi?

    ◯ **A.** 802.1q

    ◯ **B.** 802.11b

    ◯ **C.** 802.3u

    ◯ **D.** 802.3ab

16. Which IEEE wireless standard uses a 5GHz radio frequency and is not compatible with other wireless standards?

    ◯ **A.** 802.11

    ◯ **B.** 802.11a

    ◯ **C.** 802.11b

    ◯ **D.** 802.11g

17. Which cable pinout is shown in the following diagram?

   ○ **A.** Thin coax cable

   ○ **B.** Thick coax cable

   ○ **C.** Straight-through cable

   ○ **D.** Cross-over cable

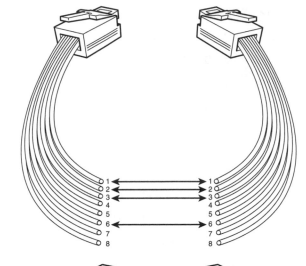

18. Which cable pinout is shown in the following diagram?

   ○ **A.** Thin coax cable

   ○ **B.** Thick coax cable

   ○ **C.** Straight-through cable

   ○ **D.** Cross-over cable

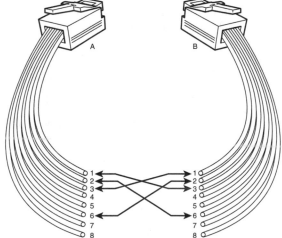

19. Which of the following connectors are used by fiber? (Choose the 3 best answers.)

   ○ **A.** MT-RJ

   ○ **B.** SC

   ○ **C.** ST

   ○ **D.** RJ-45

20. Which of the following are wireless technologies? (Choose the 3 best answers.)

   ○ **A.** Fast Ethernet

   ○ **B.** Bluetooth

   ○ **C.** Infrared

   ○ **D.** Wi-fi

Answers to Review Questions

1. Refer to Figure 2.1 to check your design of a physical bus topology.

2. Refer to Figure 2.2 to check your design of a physical single ring topology and Figure 2.3 to check your design of a physical dual ring topology.

3. Refer to Figure 2.4 to check your design of a physical star topology.

4. Refer to Figure 2.6 to check your design of a physical partial mesh topology and Figure 2.5 to check your design of a physical full mesh topology.

5. Straight-through cables use four wires and pins 1, 2, 3, and 6. Given those pins, pin 1 is connected on one end of the cable to pin 1 on the opposite end of the cable. Pin 2 at one end is connected to pin 2 on the far end. Pin 3 is connected to pin 3 and pin 6 is connected to pin 6.

6. Cross-over cables also use four wires and pins 1, 2, 3, and 6. The difference is in how the pins are connected at each end. With cross-over cables, pin 1 connects to pin 3 and pin 2 connects to pin 6.

Answers to Exam Questions

1. **B.** This diagram represents the physical bus topology or the linear bus topology. This topology uses one cable as the trunk or backbone.

2. **A.** This diagram represents the physical ring topology. Each device is connected to two other devices on the network. Data traverses the network and creates a ring or loop.

3. **D.** This diagram represents the physical dual ring topology. Unlike a single ring topology, this design offers redundancy if either ring breaks.

4. **C.** This diagram represents the physical star topology. It may also be referred to as a hub-and-spoke topology.

5. **D.** This diagram represents the full mesh topology. All the devices on the network are directly connected to every other device on that same network.

6. **B.** This diagram represents the partial mesh topology. Some but not all of the devices are connected to all of the other devices on the network.

7. **A.** Fiber is not susceptible to EMI. Answers B, C, and D are all incorrect because thin coaxial cable, category 3 UTP, and category 5 UTP are all susceptible to EMI.

8. **D.** UTP cables use RJ-45 connectors. Answers A, B, and C are incorrect because fiber uses ST, SC, or MT-RJ connectors.

9. **B.** Because of attenuation, the maximum, practical length of a UTP cable is 100 meters.

10. **A.** The total flow of information over a certain time period on a communications medium measured in bits per second is called bandwidth. Answer B is incorrect because crosstalk is an electrical or magnetic field that is a result of one communications signal affecting the signal in a nearby circuit. Answer C is incorrect because attenuation occurs over long distances as a signal loses strength. Answer D is incorrect because EMI is the interference caused by electromagnetic signals.

11. **A.** A coaxial cable consists of a single copper wire surrounded by a plastic insulation cover and a braided copper shield. Answer B is incorrect because UTP cables use eight colored wires in four pairs. Answer C is incorrect because STP has an additional layer of shielding. Answer D is incorrect because Category 5 is a UTP cable.

12. **B.** When connecting a switch to a router you must use a straight-through UTP cable.

13. **C.** When directly connecting two PCs you can use a cross-over UTP cable.

14. **C.** The best answer here is to replace a hub with a switch. Switches can segment the network. Answers A and B are incorrect because a repeater or an additional hub simply extends the network further. Answer D is incorrect because the network interface connects a PC or laptop to the public network.

15. **B.** The IEEE standard for Wireless Fidelity is 802.11b. Answer A is incorrect because IEEE standard 802.1q defines VLAN. Answer C is incorrect because IEEE standard 802.3u defines Fast Ethernet. Answer D is incorrect because IEEE standard 802.3ab defines Gigabit Ethernet on a Category 5 cable.

16. **B.** 802.11a uses a 5GHz RF. Answer A is incorrect because IEEE standard 802.11 is the basis for the 802.11a, 802.11b, and 802.11g wireless standards. Answers C and D are incorrect because 802.11b and 802.11g use 2.4GHz RF. 802.11a is not compatible with 802.11b and 802.11g.

17. **C.** A straight-through cable uses pins 1, 2, 3, and 6. Given those pins, pin 1 is connected on one end of the cable to pin 1 on the opposite end of the cable. Pin 2 at one end is connected to pin 2 on the far end, and so on. Answers A and B are incorrect because pinouts do not apply to coaxial cable because it is a single copper wire. Answer D is incorrect because cross-over cables also use four wires and pins 1, 2, 3, and 6. The difference is in how the pins are connected at each end. With cross-over cables, pin 1 connects to pin 3 and pin 2 connects to pin 6.

18. **D.** Cross-over cables also use four wires and pins 1, 2, 3, and 6. The difference is in how the pins are connected at each end. With cross-over cables, pin 1 connects to pin 3 and pin 2 connects to pin 6. Answers A and B are incorrect because pinouts do not apply to coaxial cable because it is a single copper wire. Answer C is incorrect because straight-through cable uses pins 1, 2, 3, and 6. Given those pins, pin 1 is connected on one end of the cable to pin 1 on the opposite end of the cable. Pin 2 at one end is connected to pin 2 on the far end, and so on.

19. **A, B, and C.** Fiber uses an MT-RJ, SC, or ST connector. Answer D is incorrect because RJ-45 is used by a UTP cable.

20. **B, C, and D.** Bluetooth, infrared, and wi-fi are all wireless technologies. Answer A is incorrect because Fast Ethernet is an ethernet LAN technology.

Suggested Readings and Resources

The following are some recommended readings on network components and related terminology:

1. Habraken, Joe. *Absolute Beginner's Guide to Networking, fourth edition.* Que Publishing, 2003.

2. "Fiber Optic Connector Guide," http://www.commspecial.com/connectorguide.htm.

3. "Network Cabling Help," www.datacottage.com.

CHAPTER THREE

Data Link Networking Concepts

Objectives

This chapter covers the following Cisco-specified objectives for the "Describe how a network works" and "Configure, verify and troubleshoot a switch with VLANs and interswitch communications" sections of the 640-802 CCNA exam:

▶ **Describe the purpose and functions of various network devices**

▶ **Select the components required to meet a network specification**

▶ **Use the OSI and TCP/IP models and their associated protocols to explain how data flows in a network**

▶ **Interpret network diagrams**

▶ **Explain the technology and media access control method for Ethernet networks**

Outline

Study Strategies

▶ Read the objectives at the beginning of the chapter.

▶ Familiarize yourself with token ring and FDDI protocols.

▶ Define the IEEE MAC unicast, broadcast, and multicast addresses.

▶ Review the ethernet family of protocols and be able to identify the characteristics of each protocol.

▶ Name the devices that are used at the Data Link layer and important traits of each device.

▶ Define duplex.

▶ Describe microsegmentation.

Introduction

Several data link networking concepts were first introduced in the discussion of the Data Link layer or Layer 2 of the OSI model in Chapter 1, "Standard Internetworking Models." Again, it is important to understand the layered architecture of the OSI model to grasp the fundamentals of how a network operates. Although Chapter 2, "Physical Layer Networking Concepts," went over concepts that define the Physical layer of the OSI model, this chapter goes over concepts that define how a network operates at the Data Link layer specifically.

Important Data Link LAN topics to understand for the CCNA exam include the protocols, addressing, and devices that are used at Layer 2. Cisco specified several objectives related to LAN technologies, which are prevalent at Layer 1 and Layer 2. Let's begin with three Data Link layer protocols: token ring, FDDI, and ethernet.

> **NOTE**
>
> Remember that the Physical and Data Link layers are combined in the TCP/IP model to form the Network Interface layer.

Data Link Protocols

Objectives:

- ▶ Explain the technology and media access control method for Ethernet networks
- ▶ Interpret network diagrams
- ▶ Use the OSI and TCP/IP models and their associated protocols to explain how data flows in a network

In this section, you will learn about network protocols that can be utilized at the Data Link layer of the OSI model. These protocols include token ring, FDDI, and ethernet. Ethernet Data Link protocols are broken out into addressing and framing standards.

Token Ring

Token ring is a LAN protocol that utilizes a token-passing media access technology in a physical ring or physical star topology, which creates a logical ring topology. This protocol was first developed by IBM but then standardized by IEEE with the 802.5 specification. With token-passing, a three-byte token (or special bit pattern) is inserted in a frame and passed in a single direction from one node to another until it forms a complete loop. The node that has possession of the token is the only one that can send data at any given time on that LAN. Because only one node can send data at a time, collisions are avoided.

Rather than using a hub or switch, Token ring uses a multistation access unit (MAU) to send a token across the network. The MAU has Ring In (RI) and Ring Out (RO) ports. The RO of the first MAU is connected to the RI of the next MAU. This continues until the final MAU, which connects back to the first MAU RI port via its own RO port. As mentioned, a logical ring is created with this setup. Figure 3.1 shows how a token ring network operates with MAUs.

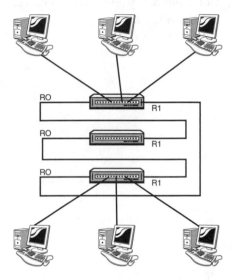

FIGURE 3.1   Token ring network.

A token ring LAN can run at either 4Mbps or 16Mbps. Each device must be configured for the same speed; otherwise the token-passing does not work at all. Overall, although this protocol provides a collision-free network, it is also more expensive to implement than ethernet. This is a major reason why ethernet is the most popular Data Link layer protocol, making token ring a rather distant second.

Let's recap what you've learned about token ring:

▶ Standardized by the IEEE 802.5 specification

▶ A token-passing media access technology

▶ Set up as a physical ring or physical star topology

▶ Creates a logical ring topology

▶ Speeds are assigned as either 4Mbps or 16Mbps

▶ Utilizes an MSAU rather than a switch or hub

▶ Provides collision-free data transfer

▶ High overhead

FDDI

FDDI is a LAN protocol that utilizes a token-passing media access method on a dual ring topology. This protocol was created by the American National Standards Institute (ANSI) with the ANSI X3T9.5 specification. Data transmission occurs on fiber-optic cables at a rate of 100Mbps. Primarily, FDDI was developed to run data across the network backbone of a larger company. Dual ring is configured for FDDI to provide redundancy and fault-tolerance. Also, because it runs over fiber it is not susceptible to EMI like other media options. Figure 3.2 shows the dual ring topology of an FDDI network.

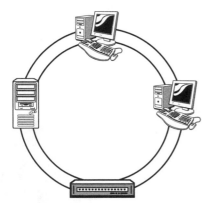

FIGURE 3.2   FDDI network.

> **NOTE**
>
> Copper Distributed Data Interface (CDDI) is a 100Mbps token-passing protocol that runs over copper wire rather than fiber-optic cable.

FDDI uses a method called *beaconing* to signal when a failure is detected on the network. Beaconing enables a device to send a signal informing the other devices on that LAN that token passing has stopped. The beacon travels around the loop from one device to the next until it reaches the last device in that ring. To troubleshoot, the network administrator can find the beacon at that last device and then check the connection between that device and the next connected device on the FDDI network.

Like token ring, FDDI is costly to implement, which is a disadvantage when designing a small network.

Let's recap what you've learned about FDDI:

▶ Developed by ANSI with the ANSI X3T9.5 specification

▶ A token-passing media access technology

▶ Set up as a dual ring topology

▶ Redundant, fault-tolerant network

▶ Speed is 100Mbps

▶ Runs over fiber-optic cable

▶ Not susceptible to EMI

▶ Provides collision-free data transfer

▶ Fault-detection provided by beaconing

▶ High overhead

Ethernet at the Data Link Layer

Ethernet, ethernet, ethernet...

The most popular LAN by a mile, ethernet is a group of protocols and standards that work at either the Physical or Data Link layer of the OSI model. This section covers ethernet technology that is relevant to Layer 2. Ethernet is defined by the IEEE 802.3 specification. As technology advancements occur, IEEE has defined additional classifications of 802.3, which include Fast Ethernet, Gigabit Ethernet, 10-Gigabit Ethernet, and Long Reach Ethernet. The physical implementations of each Ethernet standard are covered in greater detail in a moment, but first I would like to review ethernet addressing and ethernet framing. Ethernet addressing can be achieved with unicast, multicast, or broadcast addresses at the Data Link layer.

Ethernet Addressing

The Data Link layer uses physical or hardware addressing to make sure data is delivered to the appropriate end device in a LAN. Physical addresses or what are commonly referred to as *MAC addresses* are used at Layer 2. Before you go any further, it's a good idea to take a minute to review what you learned in Chapter 1.

The Data Link layer of the OSI model is the only one that has sublayers. Table 3.1 shows the breakout of Layer 2.

TABLE 3.1   Data Link Layer and Sublayers

OSI Model Layer	Sublayer
Data Link Layer	Media Access Control (MAC) IEEE 802.3
	Logical Link Control (LLC) IEEE 802.2

A MAC address is hard-coded (burnt in) on the network interface controller (NIC) of the Physical Layer device attached to the network. Each MAC address must be unique and use the following format:

► The address must consist of 48 bits (or 6 bytes).

► It must be displayed by 12 hexadecimal digits (0–9, A–F).

► The first 6 hexadecimal digits in the address are a vendor code or organizationally unique identifier (OUI) assigned to that NIC manufacturer.

► The last 6 hexadecimal digits are assigned by the NIC manufacturer and must be different from any other number assigned by that manufacturer.

An example of a MAC address would be 00:00:07:A9:B2:EB. The OUI in this example is 00:00:07.

EXAM ALERT

MAC Address Structure   Know that a MAC address consists of 48 bits and is expressed as 12 hexadecimal digits from either 0–9 or A–F. Also, know that the vendor code or OUI is the first 6 hexadecimal digits of the MAC address.

NOTE

Check out an actual example of a physical address on your own PC. From the Start menu, select Run. Then type in **cmd** to enter the command prompt for your PC. You should see a new window open on the screen where you can type in **ipconfig /all** at the prompt. Among other things, the output includes the physical or MAC address of your PC.

Ethernet LAN addresses can be broken down into two subcategories: individual and group addresses. An individual address is referred to as a *unicast address*. A unicast address identifies the MAC address of an individual LAN or NIC card. The source address on an ethernet frame will always be a unicast address. When a packet from the Network layer is framed for transport and is being forwarded to a single destination, a unicast address is also the destination address on an ethernet frame. Figure 3.3 represents an example of frame forwarding between a unicast source and a unicast destination device. Cisco devices typically use three groups of four hexadecimal digits separated by periods, such as 0000.0C12.3456. Cisco's OUI is 0000.0C.

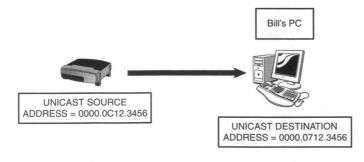

Bill's PC

UNICAST SOURCE
ADDRESS = 0000.0C12.3456

UNICAST DESTINATION
ADDRESS = 0000.0712.3456

FIGURE 3.3 Unicast frame transmission.

In the example in Figure 3.3, Bill's computer checks the destination address on the ethernet frame. If the destination address is the MAC on his computer, the frame is processed. If the destination address does not match up, the frame is dropped.

Group Ethernet LAN addresses classify more than one LAN or NIC card. Multicast and broadcast addresses are both classified as group addresses and can be described as follows:

▶ **Multicast addresses**—Addresses where a frame can be sent to a group of devices in the same LAN. IEEE ethernet multicast addresses always begin with 0100.5E in hexadecimal format. The last three bytes can be any combination of hexadecimal digits. The IP routed protocol supports multicast addressing with three groups of four hexadecimal digits separated by periods (like Cisco devices), so it appears as 0100.5Exx.xxxx, where the x's can represent any hex digit from 0–9 or A–F. Figure 3.4 shows a frame that is being forwarded from a unicast source to an IP multicast destination address.

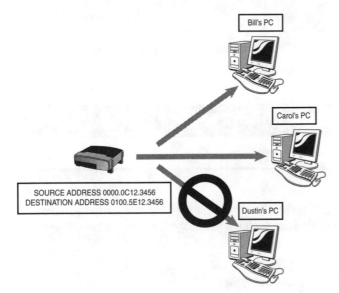

SOURCE ADDRESS 0000.0C12.3456
DESTINATION ADDRESS 0100.5E12.3456

FIGURE 3.4 Multicast frame transmission.

In this example, the switch sends a frame from its own unicast address to the multicast address of 0100.5E12.3456. Each device in that LAN segment checks the destination address to see whether it should be processed. Although Bill and Carol's computer will review and process the frame, Dustin's does not care about it and therefore drops the frame.

▶ **Broadcast addresses**—Addresses where a frame is sent to all devices in the same LAN segment. Multicast and broadcast addresses are limited to a LAN or network segment. Broadcast addresses are always the same value, which is FFFF.FFFF.FFFF. Figure 3.5 shows a switch sending a frame to the destination address FFFF.FFFF.FFFF. Because this is the broadcast address value, all the devices in that LAN should process the frame.

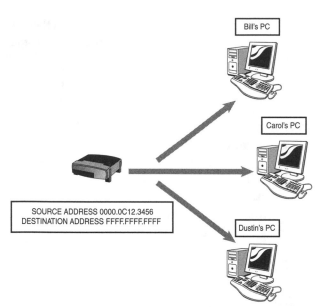

SOURCE ADDRESS 0000.0C12.3456
DESTINATION ADDRESS FFFF.FFFF.FFFF

FIGURE 3.5 Broadcast frame transmission.

EXAM ALERT

The broadcast address value is FFFF.FFFF.FFFF.

Challenge

You should be able to recognize the difference between a unicast, multicast, and broadcast address for the exam. In this challenge, I give you an address and ask that you identify whether it is a unicast, multicast, or broadcast address.

TABLE 3.2   Unicast, Multicast, and Broadcast Addresses

This Address Is...	Unicast, Multicast, or Broadcast
0100.5C12.3456	
0100.5E11.2345	
FFFF.FFFF.FFFF	
0100.5E12.3456	
0000.0C12.3456	

Ethernet Framing

As you will recall from Chapter 1, data traverses the layers of the OSI model and is encapsulated from layer to layer.

Table 3.3 shows the process of using the OSI model to encapsulate data.

TABLE 3.3 OSI Model Layer and Related Control Information

OSI Layer	Control Information Name
Application	Data
Presentation	
Session	
Transport	Segment
Network	Packet
Data Link	Frame
Physical	Bit

EXAM ALERT

The correct order for data encapsulation is data, segment, packet, frame, and bit.

The Data Link layer uses frames to transport data between layers. Framing is the process of interpreting data that is either received or sent out across the network. The 802.2 LLC Data Link sublayer is an extension of 802.3 and is responsible for framing, error-detection, and flow control. Figure 3.6 represents an 802.3 frame.

802.3 Ethernet Frame

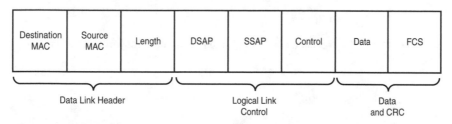

FIGURE 3.6 802.3 frame.

EXAM ALERT

For the CCNA exam, review the structure of the 802.3 frame, specifically, the Destination/Source MAC address fields of the data-link header, the DSAP/SSAP fields of the LLC portion of the frame, and the FCS field of the Data and CRC data-link trailer.

The three main parts of an 802.3 frame can be broken down and described as follows:

▶ The Data Link header portion of the frame contains the destination MAC address (6 bytes), source MAC address (6 bytes), and length (2 bytes).

▶ The Logical Link Control portion of the frame contains Destination Service Access Point (DSAP), Source Service Access Point (SSAP), and control information. All three are 1 byte long. The Service Access Point (SAP) identifies an upper-layer protocol such as IP (06) or IPX (E0).

▶ The data and cyclical redundancy check (CRC) portion of the frame is also called the *data-link trailer*. The data field can be anywhere from 43 to 1497 bytes long. The frame check sequence (FCS) field is 4 bytes long. FCS or CRC provides error detection.

Error detection is used to determine whether bit errors happened during frame transmission. The sender and receiver of a frame use the same mathematical formula to analyze the information in the FCS field of the data-link trailer. If the calculations match up, there were no errors on that frame transmission.

EXAM ALERT

The FCS field of a frame is used for error detection.

Challenge

Given the necessity that you know the layout of the 802.3 frame, I will provide you with an outline. Fill out the fields that belong to each portion of the frame.

Data Link Header	Logical Link Control	Data and CRC

Now that you have filled out the fields, provide the full names of the following acronyms that are used in conjunction with the 802.3 frame.

MAC =

LLC =

DSAP =

SSAP =

CRC =

FCS =

I mentioned how the SAP in the 802.3 frame identifies an upper-layer protocol with 1 byte or 2 hexadecimal digits. The IP SAP is 06. Well, it turns out that 1 byte was insufficient for the number of protocols that need to be recognized by an 802.3 frame. To accommodate the influx of protocols, IEEE permitted for an additional header in the 802.3 frame called a *Subnetwork Access Protocol (SNAP)* header.

The SNAP header serves the same purpose as the DSAP field; however, it consists of 2 bytes. For example, 0800 is the hexadecimal format assigned to IP with SNAP. RFC 1700 identifies all the values that are associated with SAP and SNAP.

Physical Ethernet Standards

Objective:

▶ Select the components required to meet a network specification

Have I said that ethernet is the most popular LAN protocol? Ethernet started in the 1970s when Xerox needed a networking system to connect personal computers. Xerox joined forces with Digital Equipment Corp. (DEC) and Intel to develop the protocol, which is why the very first ethernet standards were referred to as DIX Ethernet. This section covers the progression of ethernet standards from the earlier 10Mbps connections to the more recent 10 gigabit ethernet connections.

Each standard has a maximum connection length and speed. Individual ethernet standards also specify which cables and connectors can be used for network connectivity. You will be introduced to each group of standards starting with the 10Mbps ethernet connections, then the 100Mbps Fast Ethernet connections, 1Gbps ethernet, and 10Gbps ethernet connections.

Ethernet

The IEEE 802.3 ethernet standards are covered in the following sections. The following list contains all the ethernet standards that are covered in this chapter, in order.

▶ 10BASE2

▶ 10BASE5

▶ 10BASE-T

▶ 10BASE-FL

▶ 100BASE-T4

▶ 100BASE-TX

- ▸ 100BASE-FX

- ▸ 1000BASE-T

- ▸ 1000BASE-TX

- ▸ 1000BASE-CX

- ▸ 1000BASE-SX

- ▸ 1000BASE-LX

- ▸ 10GbE

10BASE2

10BASE2 networks are connected with RG-58 coaxial cables that use Bayonet Neill Concelman (BNC) connectors. There are no other hardware devices such as hubs or switches to connect devices, just the coaxial cables. This creates a physical bus topology. An electrical signal is sent by each device that wants to transmit data on that network. If more than one device sends a signal at the same time, this causes a collision and the signal is lost. To prevent loss of data transmissions, an algorithm called *Carrier Sense Multiple Access Collision Detection (CSMA/CD)* was defined. This algorithm sends a jam signal to notify the devices that there has been a collision. The devices then halt transmission for a random back-off time. CSMA/CD must be activated for 10Base ethernet LANs that are connected with a hub.

> **EXAM ALERT**
>
> For the exam, know the definition of CSMA/CD and its capability to act as an arbitrator for devices in an ethernet LAN.

The name 10BASE2 breaks down as follows:

10—10Mbps data transmission speed

BASE—Represents baseband, the signaling mode where the media can only send one signal per wire at a time

2—Actually refers to 185m or the maximum segment length (where 185 is rounded up to 200 and 2 is a multiple of 100m)

> **NOTE**
>
> So what you can see from the naming scheme is that the first number represents the speed, the word *base* means the baseband signaling mode, and the last helps you determine the type of cable used.

10BASE5

10BASE5 has the same characteristics as 10BASE2, but with a maximum segment length of 500m. The 5 is also a multiple of 100m.

10BASE-T

10BASE-T has a maximum segment length of 100m and has a 10Mbps data transmission speed. 10BASE-T can use Category 3, 4, or 5 unshielded twisted-pair (UTP) or shielded twisted-pair (STP) cables for connectivity. If you recall, UTP is the more common and cost-effective solution. STP has an additional shield that provides additional reduction of interference and attenuation, but it is also the more expensive solution. The following cables can be used with a 10BASE-T connection:

- ▶ **Category 3**—Data cable that can handle speeds up to 10Mbps.

    Although it is faster than the Cat2 cable, this was quite popular until network speeds surpassed the 10Mbps threshold.

- ▶ **Category 4**—Data cable that can handle speeds up to 16Mbps and is meant to be used with token ring LANs.

- ▶ **Category 5**—Data cable that can handle speeds up to 100Mbps and is currently the most popular cable selection.

> **EXAM ALERT**
>
> UTP is vulnerable to electromagnetic interference (EMI) and uses an RJ-45 connector.

10BASE-FL

10BASE-FL also has a 10Mbps data transmission speed, but it runs over fiber-optic cables. This option allows for a maximum segment length up to 2km.

Table 3.4 compares the 802.3 ethernet characteristics, listing the key characteristics of each specification.

TABLE 3.4   Summary of Ethernet 802.3 Characteristics

Standard	Speed	Maximum Distance	Media Type	Connector Used
10BASE2	10Mbps	185m	RG-58 coaxial	BNC
10BASE5	10Mbps	500m	RG-58 coaxial	BNC
10BASE-T	10Mbps	100m	Category 3, 4, or 5 UTP or STP	RJ-45
10BASE-FL	10Mbps	Up to 2km	Fiber-optic	SC or ST

As you can see, the early standards are all limited to 10Mbps. More recent ethernet specifications allow for faster data transmission speeds and are more popular for today's networks.

Fast Ethernet

Fast Ethernet was derived for networks that needed speeds in excess of 10Mbps. The IEEE 802.3u defines standards for 100BASE-T4, 100BASE-TX, and 100BASE-FX. You may also hear them collectively referred to as 100BASE-X. Based on what you learned from the 10Base naming scheme, you would be correct to infer that the 100 represents 100Mbps. Also, all three standards are baseband like the 10Mbps family of protocols.

> **NOTE**
>
> Fast Ethernet is defined in the IEEE 802.3u standard.

100BASE-T4

100BASE-T4 has the same characteristics as 100BASE-TX except that it can use Category 3, 4, or 5 UTP or STP cables.

100BASE-TX

100BASE-TX, like 10BASE-T, uses either UTP or STP. Category 5 UTP cable is used with this implementation. 10BASE-T has a maximum segment length of 100m.

100BASE-FX

100BASE-FX uses either single-mode or multimode fiber-optic cables to connect. Multimode (MM) fiber set for half-duplex can reach a distance of 412m. Single-mode (SM) fiber set for full-duplex can reach a distance of 10,000m. SC or ST connectors can be used. The drawback, as mentioned before with fiber implementations, is the high overhead.

▶ **Multimode (MM) fiber**—This is generally used for shorter distances and is ideal for a campus-sized network. MM also has a larger diameter of optical fiber than SM fiber.

▶ **Single-mode (SM) fiber**—This mode is used to span longer distances. SM also allows for a higher data rate than MM and faster data transmission speeds.

> **EXAM ALERT**
>
> Fiber-optic cable is not susceptible to EMI, Near-end Crosstalk (NEXT), or Far-end Crosstalk (FEXT).

REVIEW BREAK

Table 3.5 compares Fast Ethernet 802.3u standards.

TABLE 3.5 Comparison of Fast Ethernet 802.3u Characteristics

Standard	Speed	Maximum Distance	Media Type	Connector Used
100BASE-T4	100Mbps	100m	Category 3, 4, or 5 UTP or STP	RJ-45
100BASE-TX	100Mbps	100m	Category 5 UTP or STP	RJ-45
100BASE-FX	100Mbps	412m with half-duplex MM fiber 10,000m with full-duplex SM fiber	Fiber-optic	SC or ST

Gigabit Ethernet

Gigabit Ethernet standards all have a data transmission speed of 1000Mbps (1Gbps) and use a baseband signaling mode. Gigabit Ethernet can be broken down into two IEEE standards, 802.3ab or 1000BASE-T and 802.3z or 1000BASE-X.

1000BASE-T 802.3ab

1000BASE-T or 1000BASE-TX is defined by the 802.3ab standard and can reach a maximum total distance per segment of 75m. This standard uses a minimum of Category 5 UTP cable with an RJ-45 connector.

▶ **Category 5e**—Data cable that can handle speeds up to 1Gbps; a popular choice for Gigabit Ethernet networks.

▶ **Category 6**—Cable that was created to exceed speeds of 1Gbps.

Table 3.6 summarizes the primary points of interest that are relevant for the 1000BASE-T standard.

TABLE 3.6   Summary of Gigabit Ethernet 802.3ab Characteristics

Standard	Speed	Maximum Distance	Media Type	Connector Used
1000BASE-T or 1000BASE-TX	1000Mbps or 1Gbps	75m	Category 5 UTP or higher	RJ-45

1000BASE-X 802.3z

1000BASE-X is the collective name for 802.3z standards 1000BASE-CX, 1000BASE-SX, and 1000BASE-LX that have the following characteristics respectively:

► **1000BASE-CX**—1000BASE-CX is the unique standard in this family because it uses shielded copper wire cable with a 9-pin shielded connector instead of fiber-optic cable for connectivity. The maximum total distance per segment is a mere 25m.

► **1000BASE-SX**—1000BASE-SX transmits short-wavelength laser over fiber-optic cable. Either 50-micron or 62.5-micron (diameter) MM fiber can be used with this option. Lengths may vary depending on the type of MM fiber and duplex chosen for each connection as follows:

  ► Half-duplex 62.5-micron MM fiber connections can reach a maximum segment length of 275m.

  ► Half-duplex 50-micron MM fiber connections can reach a maximum segment length of 316m.

  ► Full-duplex 62.5-micron MM fiber connections can reach a maximum segment length of 275m.

  ► Full-duplex 50-micron MM fiber connections can reach a maximum segment length of 550m.

  As you can see, the 50-micron MM fiber can offer longer segment distances. The 62.5-micron MM fiber reaches the same maximum segment length of 275m regardless of the duplex.

► **1000BASE-LX**—1000BASE-LX transmits long-wavelength laser over fiber-optic cable. Either 50-micron or 62.5-micron (diameter) MM fiber can be used with this option. SM fiber can also be used with 1000BASE-LX, which differentiates this standard from 1000BASE-SX. The same MM fiber length restrictions apply based on the implementation of half- or full-duplex. The following lengths apply when SM fiber is used:

  ► Half-duplex SM fiber connections can reach a maximum segment length of 316m.

  ► Full-duplex SM fiber connections can reach a maximum segment length of 5000m.

  Using full-duplex SM fiber allows for a huge increase in distance. As you can imagine, this is also the more expensive option.

Table 3.7 compares Fast Ethernet 802.3z standards.

TABLE 3.7   Comparison of Gigabit Ethernet 802.3z Characteristics

Standard	Speed	Maximum Distance	Media Type	Connector Used
1000BASE-CX	1000Mbps or 1Gbps	25m	Shielded copper wire	9-pin shielded connector
1000BASE-SX	1000Mbps or 1Gbps	275m with half or full-duplex 62.5-micron MM fiber 316m with half-duplex 50-micron MM fiber 550m with full-duplex 50-micron MM fiber	MM fiber-optic	SC or ST
1000BASE-LX	1000Mbps or 1Gbps	275m with half- or full-duplex 62.5-micron MM fiber 316m with half-duplex 50-micron MM fiber or SM fiber 550m with full-duplex 50-micron MM fiber 5000m with full-duplex SM fiber	MM or SM fiber-optic	SC or ST

EXAM ALERT

Gigabit Ethernet comprises the 802.3ab and the 802.3z standards.

10-Gigabit Ethernet (10GbE)

You guessed it: 1Gbps just wasn't a fast enough option. Actually, it is just the nature of technology to constantly strive for faster speeds. Yet another new standard was defined by IEEE and labeled 802.3ae. Earlier in this chapter you saw 10BASE-2, which has data transmission speeds of 10Mbps. 10-Gigabit Ethernet transmits data at 10,000Mbps. That is quite an upgrade! IEEE 802.3ae uses 62.5-micron MM, 50-micron MM, or SM fiber-optic cabling for connectivity and a baseband signaling mode.

NOTE

All of the ethernet standards, regardless of their speed, use the same 802.3 MAC and 802.2 LLC headers and trailers.

Long Reach Ethernet

Cisco Long Reach Ethernet (LRE) was developed to provide broadband service over existing telephone-grade or Category 1, 2, or 3 wiring. Speeds vary between 5–15Mbps and can reach a maximum segment length of up to 5000m. Cisco LRE may be a viable networking solution for a LAN or MAN that already has Category 1/2/3 cabling installed. A hotel could benefit from Cisco LRE to provide high-speed Internet or video conferencing solutions to their clientele.

> **NOTE**
>
> Broadband is a signaling method that supports various frequencies such as audio and video.

Data Link Layer Devices

Objective:

▶ Describe the purpose and functions of various network devices

At the Data Link layer, either a bridge or a Layer 2 switch can be installed to segment a LAN. Hubs and repeaters at the Physical layer only serve to extend a network. With segmentation, switches and bridges create a separate collision domain for each connected node, which effectively reduces the number of collisions that occur on that network.

Remember from Chapter 1 that a collision domain is a group of nodes that shares the same media and are segmented by switches or bridges. A collision occurs if two nodes attempt a simultaneous transmission within the same collision domain. This reinforces the need for an increased number of collision domains. Figure 3.7 demonstrates how a bridge creates two collision domains.

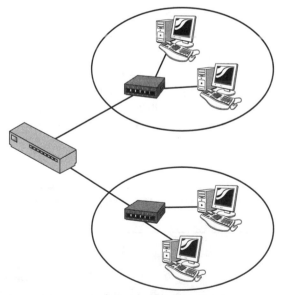

FIGURE 3.7   Example of a bridged network.

Figure 3.8 provides an example of a situation in which a switch creates separate collision domains.

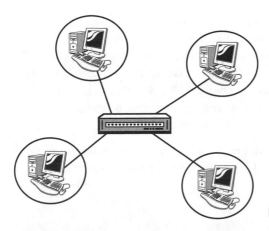

FIGURE 3.8 Example of a switched network.

Bridges

Bridges were created to alleviate several expansion-related network issues. As networks were growing and becoming more complex, hubs and repeaters no longer provided sufficient network resources. Because they do not segment the network, all the devices connected to a hub or repeater had to share the same bandwidth. Also, if one device sent a frame it could collide with a frame from another device on that LAN. This meant that all devices on that LAN had to take turns sending frames. Again, this is not very efficient as additional devices are added to a network.

Transparent bridges were introduced and helped solve these growing pains. The word *transparent* is used to indicate that the other devices on a network are not aware of its existence. Bridges use a software application to forward frames.

The following are the primary tasks performed by both bridges and switches:

▶ The source MAC address of every inbound frame is examined to learn its MAC address.

▶ Frames may either be forwarded or filtered depending on the destination MAC address (they can also be flooded if the destination is unknown).

▶ Eliminates loops that are caused by redundant connections by configuring Spanning Tree Protocol (STP).

Learned MAC addresses and their interfaces are stored in a *bridge table* on the bridge or switch. When a new frame arrives on that bridge or switch, the device refers to the bridge table to decide how to forward or filter the frame. If the frame's destination MAC address is on a different segment of that LAN, the device forwards the frame to that segment. If the frame's destination MAC address is on the same segment as the source MAC address, the device filters the frame. That frame reaches its destination without the assistance of a bridge or switch. Figure 3.9 shows a segmented LAN with the MAC addresses of each end user.

As frames are received by the bridge or switch from each end user, it updates its bridge table with their MAC addresses and the interface on which the frame came into the device. Table 3.8 shows the bridge table of this bridge.

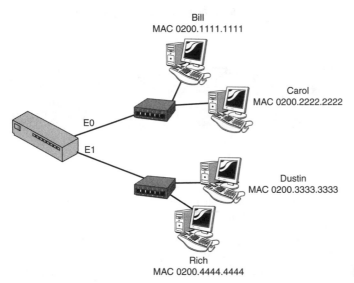

FIGURE 3.9 Bridge LAN.

TABLE 3.8   Example Bridge Table for Figure 3.9

MAC Address	Interface
0200.1111.1111	E0
0200.2222.2222	E0
0200.3333.3333	E1
0200.4444.4444	E1

If the incoming frame destination address is...

▶ **Unicast**—The bridge checks the bridge table first. If the destination unicast address is not in the bridge table, it forwards the frame to all interfaces except for the interface that originally sent the frame. If the destination unicast address is in the bridge table and on a different interface than the interface that originally sent the frame, it forwards the frame. If the destination unicast address is in the bridge table and on the same interface as the sender, the frame is filtered.

▶ **Multicast**—The bridge forwards the frame to all interfaces except for the interface that originally sent the frame.

▶ **Broadcast**—The bridge forwards the frame to all interfaces except for the interface that originally sent the frame.

Challenge

Based on what you just learned about bridge and switch frame filtering or forwarding, take a look at Figure 3.10 and fill out the bridge table for this network that is using a switch for connectivity.

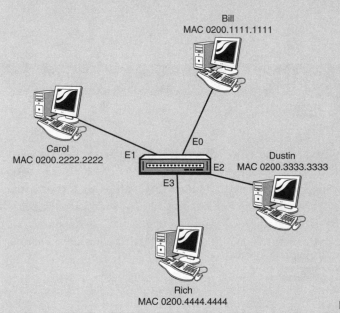

FIGURE 3.10 Switch LAN.

Bridge Table

Address	Interface

Using the same diagram and your new bridge table, I will give you a source and destination address. Please fill out whether the frame will be filtered or forwarded. If it is forwarded, also fill out the outbound interface to which the frame will be sent.

TABLE 3.9   MAC Filtering or Forwarding

Source Address	Destination Address	Filter or Forward	Outbound Interface(s)
0200.1111.1111	0200.2222.2222		
0200.2222.2222	0200.3333.3333		
0200.3333.3333	0200.4444.4444		
0200.2222.2222	FFFF.FFFF.FFFF		
0200.4444.4444	0200.1111.1111		
0200.1111.1111	0100.5E12.3456		

EXAM ALERT

Bridges and switches examine the source MAC address of each inbound frame to learn MAC addresses.

Switches

Layer 2 switches are multi-port bridges; therefore, they have all the same functionality of bridges. There are differences that differentiate a switch from a bridge. For example, switches utilize hardware or Application-Specific Integrated Circuit (ASIC) chips to forward frames rather than software. Also, each port of the switch has a dedicated bandwidth. If the dedicated port on a switch is 10Mbps, the connected LAN segment has a dedicated bandwidth of 10Mbps. This works in the same manner for 100Mbps and 1000Mbps dedicated switch ports. This feature also sets a switch apart from a bridge that has a low port density.

EXAM ALERT

For the test, know that switches are multi-port bridges that use ASIC hardware chips for frame forwarding. Dedicated bandwidth enables the switch port to guarantee the speed assigned to that port. For example, 100Mbps port connections get 100Mbps transmission rates.

A popular ethernet switch port is the 10/100 ethernet port, where you can set the port to pass traffic at 10Mbps or 100Mbps. Chapter 6, "Introduction to Cisco Routers and Switches," goes into more detail regarding specific Cisco devices, including the 2950 series switches.

Challenge

Do you recall the difference between straight-through and cross-over cables? Both cables are used with ethernet networks. In Chapter 2, Figure 2.7 and Figure 2.8 demonstrate the differences between straight-through and cross-over. Selecting the right cable for your network connections is vital. The following connections are all related specifically to switch connectivity. Please determine whether you should use a straight-through or cross-over cable between the devices.

Connecting a...	Type of Cable
Switch to a switch	
Switch to a hub	
Switch to a PC	
Plugged into a dedicated switch port	
Switch to a router	

Duplex

It is important that you understand duplex logic and how it affects traffic on a network. The communication mode of a device may either be half-duplex or full-duplex, depending on the connection type.

Half-duplex allows for one-way communication, which means that a device can only send or receive a data transmission at any given time. This option does not allow for simultaneously sending and receiving data. As part of a shared collision domain, hubs are inherently set up for half-duplex. Bandwidth suffers because a collision detection technology such as the CSMA/CD algorithm must be implemented. Collision detection can chew up 50–60% of the bandwidth on that ethernet LAN.

Full-duplex allows for two-way communication, which means that a device can simultaneously send and receive data transmissions. Full-duplex is available with dedicated switch port connections to a single device. If a switch port connection is configured for full-duplex, the CSMA/CD algorithm must be disabled. An ethernet connection set for full-duplex allows for 100% transmission speeds in both directions. For example, a 100Mbps connection can transmit data simultaneously at 100Mbps in each direction.

With ethernet, if a switch port and NIC offer multiple speed options as well as half- and full-duplex settings, autonegotiation can be configured on both devices. The switch and NIC automatically negotiate the connection speed and duplex so that the settings on both ends match. You may have heard of a 10/half or 100/full connection before. The term 10/half refers to a 10Mbps half-duplex connection. It is more likely that you will see 100/full, which indicates a 100Mbps full-duplex connection.

NOTE

Autonegotiation may not always be a reliable option. There have been some instances where the switch port goes into error disable mode because of massive errors. Configuring or "hard coding" the port and NIC to the appropriate speed and duplex settings may resolve the issue when the port is reactivated.

EXAM ALERT

Hubs use half-duplex technology. Switches can be set up for full-duplex.

Microsegmentation

Microsegmentation occurs when a switch creates a dedicated path for sending and receiving transmissions with each connected host. Each host then has a separate collision domain and a dedicated bandwidth.

Chapter Summary

Many important functions occur at the Data Link layer of the OSI model. Different technologies can be implemented at Layer 2 to transmit data across the network. Token ring and FDDI networks use token-passing to send frames, whereas ethernet uses the 802.3 frame standard with 802.2 LLC specifications. Ethernet framing and ethernet addressing are both significant topics for the CCNA exam. Other key ethernet functions include error detection and arbitration. Although the FCS field of the 802.3 frame detects errors on a LAN, the CSMA/CD algorithm arbitrates how data is transmitted on a LAN.

Data Link layer devices include bridges and switches. Switches are really multi-port bridges, so they share the same general functionalities. New networks are most likely to use a Layer 2 switch in place of a bridge. Switches have been improved upon over the years and offer more options for the consumer, such as dedicated bandwidth and full-duplex communications.

Although the Data Link layer uses frames to transmit data, the Network layer uses Internet Protocol or IP addresses to route traffic. Chapter 5 discusses IP addressing and subnetting at length. Both topics are imperative for the CCNA exam.

Key Terms

- token-passing
- token ring
- 802.5
- MSAU
- RI
- RO
- FDDI
- ANSI X3T9.5
- unicast
- multicast
- broadcast
- frame
- 802.2
- MAC
- LLC
- SAP
- DSAP

- SSAP
- SNAP
- 802.3
- 10BASE-2
- 10BASE-5
- 10BASE-T
- 10BASE-FL
- 802.3u
- 100BASE-T4
- 100BASE-TX
- 100BASE-FX
- 802.3ab
- 1000BASE-T
- 802.3z
- 1000BASE-CX
- 1000BASE-SX
- 1000BASE-LX

- ▶ 802.3ae
- ▶ 10GbE
- ▶ baseband
- ▶ broadband
- ▶ LRE
- ▶ EMI
- ▶ coaxial cable
- ▶ unshielded twisted-pair cable
- ▶ shielded twisted-pair cable
- ▶ fiber-optic cable

- ▶ multimode
- ▶ single-mode
- ▶ switch
- ▶ ASIC
- ▶ bridge
- ▶ transparent bridges
- ▶ Spanning Tree Protocol
- ▶ duplex
- ▶ microsegmentation

Apply Your Knowledge

Exercise

3.1 IEEE 802.3 Ethernet Standards

You may be asked to identify the standards associated with IEEE Ethernet on the CCNA exam. In this exercise, I am listing the ethernet specification and want you to complete the table to include the IEEE-defined standard, the associated speed, and the cable or media type used for each specification. You may refer back to Tables 3.4, 3.5, 3.6, and 3.7 to check your answers.

Estimated Time: 10 minutes

IEEE Standard	IEEE Standard #	Maximum Speed	Cable or Media
10BASE-2			
10BASE-5			
10BASE-T			
10BASE-FL			
100BASE-T4			
100BASE-TX			
100BASE-FX			
1000BASE-T or 1000BASE-TX			
1000BASE-CX			
1000BASE-SX			
1000BASE-LX			
10GbE			

Review Questions

1. Define token-passing.

2. List the characteristics of a token ring network.

3. List the characteristics of an FDDI network.

4. Define unicast, multicast, and broadcast.

5. Describe CSMA/CD.

6. What are the primary tasks performed by both bridges and switches?

7. Describe half- and full-duplex.

8. Define microsegmentation.

Exam Questions

1. Which of the following is the IEEE standard for token ring?

   ○ **A.** 802.2

   ○ **B.** 802.3a

   ○ **C.** 802.3u

   ○ **D.** 802.5

2. ANSI X3T9.5 is the specification for which LAN technology?

   ○ **A.** Token ring

   ○ **B.** Fast Ethernet

   ○ **C.** FDDI

   ○ **D.** LLC

3. What Data Link layer technology inserts a three-byte token (or special bit pattern) into a frame and passes it in a single direction from one node to another until it forms a complete loop?

   ○ **A.** Token-passing

   ○ **B.** Unicast

   ○ **C.** Multicast

   ○ **D.** Broadcast

4. Which of the following LAN protocols use token-passing for frame transmission? (Choose the 2 best answers.)

   ○ **A.** Fast Ethernet

   ○ **B.** Token ring

   ○ **C.** Gigabit Ethernet

   ○ **D.** FDDI

5. This MAC sublayer address type identifies the MAC address of an individual LAN or NIC card.

   ○ **A.** Unicast

   ○ **B.** Multicast

   ○ **C.** Broadcast

   ○ **D.** Token

6. Which of the following addresses is an example of a unicast address? (Choose all that apply.)

   ○ **A.** 0000.0C12.3456

   ○ **B.** 0100.5E12.3456

   ○ **C.** FFFF.FFFF.FFFF

   ○ **D.** 0200.1111.1111

7. This MAC sublayer address type sends a frame to a subset of devices on the LAN.

   ○ **A.** Unicast

   ○ **B.** Multicast

   ○ **C.** Broadcast

   ○ **D.** Token

8. Which of the following addresses is an example of a multicast address?

   ○ **A.** 0000.0C12.3456

   ○ **B.** 0100.5E12.3456

   ○ **C.** FFFF.FFFF.FFFF

   ○ **D.** 0200.1111.1111

9. This MAC sublayer address type sends a frame to all the devices on the LAN.

   ○ **A.** Unicast

   ○ **B.** Multicast

   ○ **C.** Broadcast

   ○ **D.** Token

10. Which of the following addresses is an example of a broadcast address?

    ○ **A.** 0000.0C12.3456

    ○ **B.** 0100.5E12.3456

    ○ **C.** FFFF.FFFF.FFFF

    ○ **D.** 0200.1111.1111

11. The OSI model Data Link layer uses _____ to transport data between layers.

    ○ **A.** Bits

    ○ **B.** Frames

    ○ **C.** Packets

    ○ **D.** Segments

12. Which field of a frame is used for error detection?

    ○ **A.** SAP

    ○ **B.** DSAP

    ○ **C.** SSAP

    ○ **D.** FCS

13. Which IEEE Ethernet standards define Gigabit Ethernet? (Choose all that apply.)

    ○ **A.** 802.3u

    ○ **B.** 802.3ab

    ○ **C.** 802.3z

    ○ **D.** 802.3ae

14. Bridges and switches segment a network and create an additional _____ domain for each segment.

    ○ **A.** Collision

    ○ **B.** Broadcast

    ○ **C.** Unicast

    ○ **D.** Multicast

15. Bridges and switches examine the _____ of each inbound frame to learn MAC addresses.

    ○ **A.** Multicast MAC address

    ○ **B.** Broadcast MAC address

    ○ **C.** Source MAC address

    ○ **D.** Destination MAC address

16. Which device uses ASIC hardware chips for frame forwarding?

    ○ **A.** Hub

    ○ **B.** Repeater

    ○ **C.** Bridge

    ○ **D.** Switch

17. With a 10Mbps ethernet LAN, dedicated bandwidth enables a switch port to guarantee what data transmission speed?

    ○ **A.** 10Mbps

    ○ **B.** 100Mbps

    ○ **C.** 1000Mbps

    ○ **D.** 10,000Mbps

18. This Data Link protocol eliminates loops that are caused by redundant connections.

    ○ **A.** CRC

    ○ **B.** FCS

    ○ **C.** CSMA/CD

    ○ **D.** STP

19. This communication mode allows for only one-way data transmissions at any time.

❍ **A.** 10Mbps

❍ **B.** 100Mbps

❍ **C.** Half-duplex

❍ **D.** Full-duplex

20. This communication mode allows for simultaneous two-way data transmissions.

❍ **A.** 10Mbps

❍ **B.** 100Mbps

❍ **C.** Half-duplex

❍ **D.** Full-duplex

Answers to Review Questions

1. Token-passing is a Data Link protocol that inserts a three-byte token (or special bit pattern) into a frame and passes it around the network in a single direction from one node to another until it forms a complete loop. The node that has possession of the token is the only one that can send data at any given time on that LAN. Because only one node can send data at a time, collisions are avoided.

2. Standardized by the IEEE 802.5 specification

A token-passing media access technology

Set up as a physical ring or physical star topology

Creates a logical ring topology

Speeds are assigned as either 4Mbps or 16Mbps

Utilizes an MSAU rather than a switch or hub

Provides collision-free data transfer

High overhead

3. Developed by ANSI with the ANSI X3T9.5 specification

A token-passing media access technology

Set up as a dual ring topology

Redundant, fault-tolerant network

Speed is 100Mbps

Runs over fiber-optic cable

Not susceptible to EMI

Provides collision-free data transfer

Fault-detection provided by beaconing

High overhead

4. A unicast address identifies the MAC address of an individual LAN or NIC card.

A multicast address forwards a frame to a subset of devices in the same LAN. IEEE ethernet multicast addresses always begin with 0100.5E in hexadecimal format. The last three bytes can be any combination.

A broadcast address sends a frame to all devices in the same LAN. Broadcast addresses are always the same value, which is FFFF.FFFF.FFFF.

5. CSMA/CD or Carrier Sense Multiple Access Collision Detection is an algorithm that sends a jam signal to notify the devices that there has been a collision. The devices then halt transmission for a random back-off time.

6. The primary tasks performed by both bridges and switches are as follows:

The source MAC address of every inbound frame is examined to learn its MAC address.

You can decide whether to forward or filter a frame based on the destination MAC address.

Eliminate loops that are caused by redundant connections by configuring Spanning Tree Protocol (STP).

7. Half-duplex allows for one-way communication, which means that a device can only send or receive a data transmission at any given time. As a part of a shared collision domain, hubs must use half-duplex.

Full-duplex allows for two-way communication, which means that a device can simultaneously send and receive data transmissions. Full-duplex is available with dedicated switch port connections to a single device. If a switch port connection is configured for full-duplex, the CSMA/CD algorithm must be disabled. Also, an ethernet connection set for full-duplex allows for 100% transmission speeds in both directions.

8. Microsegmentation occurs when a switch creates a dedicated path for sending and receiving transmissions with each connected host. Each host then has a separate collision domain and a dedicated bandwidth.

Answers to Exam Questions

1. **D**. IEEE 802.5 defines token ring. Answers A, B, and C are incorrect because IEEE 802.2 defines LLC, 802.3a defines ethernet, and 802.3u defines Fast Ethernet.

2. **C**. ANSI X3T9.5 defines FDDI. Answers A, B, and D are incorrect because they are all IEEE standards. IEEE 802.5 defines token ring, 802.3u defines Fast Ethernet, and 802.2 defines LLC.

3. **A.** Token-passing inserts a three-byte token (or special bit pattern) into a frame and passes it in a single direction from one node to another until it forms a complete loop. Answers B, C, and D are all incorrect because unicast, multicast, and broadcast are all types of ethernet addresses.

4. **B, D.** Token ring and FDDI use token-passing to send frames. Answers A and C are incorrect because Fast Ethernet and Gigabit Ethernet both use 802.3 MAC and 802.2 LLC headers and trailers for framing.

5. **A.** Unicast addresses identify the MAC address of an individual LAN or NIC card. Answer B is incorrect because multicast addresses send a frame to a group of devices in the same LAN. Answer C is incorrect because broadcast addresses send a frame to all the devices in the same LAN. Answer D is incorrect because a token is a special bit pattern used with token-passing networks.

6. **A, D.** Both 0000.0C12.3456 and 0200.1111.1111 are unicast addresses. 0000.0C is Cisco's OUI. Answers B and C are incorrect because 0100.5E12.3456 is a multicast address and FFFF.FFFF.FFFF is a broadcast address.

7. **B.** Multicast addresses send a frame to a subset of devices in the same LAN. Answer A is incorrect because unicast addresses identify the MAC address of an individual LAN or NIC card. Answer C is incorrect because broadcast addresses send a frame to all the devices in the same LAN. Answer D is incorrect because a token is a special bit pattern used with token-passing networks.

8. **B.** 0100.5E12.3456 is a multicast address. Multicast addresses always start with 0100.5E. Answers A and D are incorrect because both 0000.0C12.3456 and 0200.1111.1111 are unicast addresses. Answer C is incorrect because FFFF.FFFF.FFFF is a broadcast address.

9. **C.** Broadcast addresses send a frame to all the devices in the same LAN. Answer A is incorrect because unicast addresses identify the MAC address of an individual LAN or NIC card. Answer B is incorrect because multicast addresses send a frame to a subset of devices in the same LAN. Answer D is incorrect because a token is a special bit pattern used with token-passing networks.

10. **C.** Broadcast addresses are always represented as FFFF.FFFF.FFFF. Answers A and D are incorrect because both 0000.0C12.3456 and 0200.1111.1111 are unicast addresses. Answer B is incorrect because 0100.5E12.3456 is a multicast address.

11. **B.** Frames are used by the Data Link layer to transport data between the Network and Physical layer. Framing is the process of interpreting data that is either received or sent out across the network. Answers A, C, and D are incorrect because bits are used at the Physical layer, packets are used at the Network layer, and segments are used at the Transport layer of the OSI model.

12. **D.** The frame check sequence (FCS) field of a frame uses a mathematical formula to determine whether any bit errors occurred during data transmission. Answer A is incorrect because Service Access Point (SAP) identifies the upper-layer protocol such as IP. Answer B is incorrect because DSAP is the destination SAP or destination upper-layer protocol. Answer C is incorrect because SSAP is the source SAP or the source upper-layer protocol.

13. **B, C.** IEEE 802.3ab and 802.3z define Gigabit Ethernet standards. Answers A and D are incorrect because 802.3u defines the Fast Ethernet standard, and 802.3ae defines the 10 Gigabit Ethernet standard.

14. **A.** Collision domains are increased with the addition of bridges or switches on a network. Answer B is incorrect because routers create additional broadcast domains. Answers C and D are incorrect because unicast and multicast are both addresses used by ethernet.

15. **C.** The source MAC address of an incoming frame is examined by a bridge or switch to learn the MAC address for the bridge table. Answers A and B are incorrect because multicast and broadcast addresses can never be the source MAC address. Answer D is incorrect because the destination MAC address is not used by a bridge or switch to create the bridge table.

16. **D.** Switches use ASIC hardware chips for frame forwarding. Answers A and B are incorrect because hubs and repeaters do not forward frames because they are Physical layer or Layer 1 devices. Answer C is incorrect because bridges use software for frame forwarding.

17. **A.** 10Mbps is guaranteed with dedicated bandwidth on a 10Mbps ethernet LAN. Answers B, C, and D are incorrect because other speeds of 100, 1000, and 10,000Mbps are all faster speeds that require a different ethernet LAN standard.

18. **D.** Spanning Tree Protocol (STP) is a Data Link protocol that eliminates loops caused by redundant connections on a LAN. Answers A and B are incorrect because cyclical redundancy check (CRC) and frame check sequence (FCS) both provide error detection. Answer C is incorrect because CSMA/CD is an algorithm that is used for arbitration on an ethernet network.

19. **C.** Half-duplex allows for only one-way data transmissions at any time. Answers A and B are incorrect because 10Mbps and 100Mbps are speed classifications primarily associated with ethernet LANs. Answer D is incorrect because full-duplex allows for two-way data transmissions.

20. **D.** Full-duplex allows for simultaneous two-way data transmissions. Answers A and B are incorrect because 10Mbps and 100Mbps are speed classifications primarily associated with ethernet LANs. Answer C is incorrect because half-duplex allows for only one-way data transmissions at any time.

Suggested Readings and Resources

The following are some recommended readings for LAN networking and related terminology:

1. "TechEncyclopedia," www.techweb.com/encyclopedia.

2. "RFC 1700," www.isi.edu/in-notes/rfc1700.txt.

3. "Layer 1 & 2," www.hojmark.net/layer1-2.html#lan.

4. "Cisco Long-Reach Ethernet," www.cisco.com/warp/public/779/servpro/solutions/long_ethernet/.

5. Barnes, David and Sakandar, Basir. *Cisco LAN Switching Fundamentals.* Cisco Press, 2004.

CHAPTER FOUR

General Network Security

Objectives

This chapter covers the following Cisco-specific objectives for the "Identify security threats to a network and describe general methods to mitigate those threats" section of both the 640-802 CCNA and 640-822 ICND1 exams:

▶ **Describe today's increasing network security threats and explain the need to implement a comprehensive security policy to mitigate the threats**

▶ **Explain general methods to mitigate common security threats to network devices, hosts, and applications**

▶ **Describe the functions of common security appliances and applications**

▶ **Describe security recommended practices including initial steps to secure network devices**

Outline

Study Strategies

▶ Read the information presented in this chapter, paying special attention to tables, Notes, and Exam Alerts.

▶ Read the objectives at the beginning of the chapter.

▶ Review each class of attack.

▶ Name the specific attacks that comprise each class.

▶ Describe security threat mitigation techniques.

▶ Familiarize yourself with the Cisco devices that assist with general network security.

▶ Complete the Challenges and the Exercises at the end of the chapter.

Introduction

Information technology has evolved and provides countless resources for everyday people to create, maintain, and utilize data. If you have ever seen or read *Spiderman*, you have likely heard the quote "With great power comes great responsibility." Information is power, so it is vitally important to implement safeguards on your LAN and WAN to protect data from hackers. Everyone with a computer is susceptible and should be cautious with important private details such as credit card information. I have worked in the networking department at several types of companies, including a health-care company. Imagine if a hacker were to obtain patient medical records or a list of social security numbers from the human resources database. A company must follow special guidelines to ensure data privacy, which ties directly to network security. To make sure that companies adhere to security guidelines, annual audits are performed on their networks to identify potential weaknesses.

Even though network security has been a hot topic since the advent of computer networking, it is a new set of objectives on the CCENT and CCNA exams. To prepare yourself for the exams, you must know what classes of attack are common today, how to mitigate those attacks, and what features or hardware Cisco offers to assist in protecting your network. This chapter begins with a discussion of prevalent classes of attack.

Classes of Attack

Objective:

▶ Describe today's increasing network security threats and explain the need to implement a comprehensive security policy to mitigate the threats

Any number of motives could inspire an attacker; two motives that we touched on already are financial gain and gathering intelligence. A hacker may also simply enjoy the thrill of successfully breaking into someone's network. There are documented cases of hackers who intentionally attacked government systems simply to prove that it could be done and therefore gain notoriety.

This section discusses three classes of attack that are commonly found in today's network environment:

▶ Access attacks

▶ Reconnaissance attacks

▶ Denial of service (DoS) attacks

Each class has various more-specific subcategories of attack methods that will be covered in greater detail.

TIP

The three common classes of attack are access, reconnaissance, and DoS.

Access Attacks

An access attack is just what it sounds like: an attempt to access another user account or network device through improper means. If proper security measures are not in place, the network may be left vulnerable to intrusion. A network administrator is responsible for ensuring that only authorized users access the network. Unauthorized attacks are attempted via four means, all of which try to bypass some facet of the authentication process: password attacks, trust exploitation, port redirection, and man-in-the-middle attacks.

TIP

The four types of access attacks are password attacks, trust exploitation, port redirection, and man-in-the-middle attacks.

Password Attacks

Nowadays, it seems as if you need a password for everything. I have so many passwords that I find it hard to keep track. Although it might sound like a good idea to keep your passwords simple or to write them down, both practices are highly discouraged. The goal is to make it harder for someone to find or guess your password; therefore, password integrity is necessary. That being said, an attacker might attempt a login with false credentials. It is also important to note that not all attackers are external users. Many recorded instances of attempted and/or successful attacks have come from internal company employees.

There are alternatives to passwords, such as Terminal Access Controller Access Control System (TACACS) or Remote Authentication Dial-In User Service (RADIUS), both of which manage access to network hardware. Passwords are fast becoming as obsolete as rabbit-ear antennas or dialup Internet connections.

Cisco equipment is shipped from the factory with a standard configuration. When the device is turned on, the setup program prompts for a password and leaves all but the enable secret password in plain text. It is the responsibility of the recipient to update the password information before deploying the device on a network. Changing passwords every time an employee leaves the company or in a given time period (every 90 days) would also help protect login credentials.

Trust Exploitation

Trust exploitation can occur in one of two ways:

- ▶ Reliance on the trust a client has in a server
- ▶ Reliance on the trust the server has in the client

For example, most companies have a part of their network that lies between the wide-open Internet and the corporate internal network. This in-between part of the network is called the demilitarized zone (DMZ). Servers that communicate from the DMZ and the internal network may have a trust relationship established. The internal devices may be set up to trust information that is received from a DMZ server. An attacker can then compromise the DMZ server and initiate a connection to the internal network. This is an example of phishing. When the trust that the server has in a client is exploited, this is an example of session hijacking.

Port Redirection

Port redirection is a form of trust exploitation in which the untrustworthy source uses a machine with access to the internal network to pass traffic through a port on the firewall or access control list (ACL). The port in question normally denies traffic, but with redirection the attacker can bypass security measures and open a tunnel for communication.

Man-in-the-Middle Attacks

A man-in-the-middle attack happens when a hacker eavesdrops or listens for network traffic and intercepts a data transmission. After the transmission is intercepted, the untrustworthy host can position itself between the two communicating hosts, interpret the data, and steal information from the packets sent. The hacker can also take over the session and reformat the packets to send information to either or both communicating parties. In this situation it is possible for the hacker to capture credentials, hijack a session, or instigate a DoS attack.

Data sessions are more vulnerable when the packets are left in clear-text format and can be read without additional decryption by the human eye. Proper data encryption, with the use of an encryption protocol, makes the captured data useless.

Challenge

In this challenge, write down the four types of access attacks.

1.

2.

3.

4.

Reconnaissance Attacks

When I hear the word reconnaissance, I think of a military reconnaissance mission. The soldier is sent out to gather important information about an area of interest. The same holds true for a reconnaissance attack on a computer network. The hacker surveys a network and collects data for a future attack. Important information that can be compiled during a reconnaissance attack includes the following:

- Ports open on a server

- Ports open on a firewall

- IP addresses on the host network

- Hostnames associated with the IP addresses

As with access attacks, there are four main subcategories or methods for gathering network data:

- Packet sniffers (also known as network monitors)

- Ping sweeps

- Port scans

- Information queries

> **TIP**
>
> The four common tools used for reconnaissance attacks are packet sniffers, ping sweeps, port scans, and information queries.

Packet Sniffers

A packet sniffer may also be called a network analyzer, packet analyzer, or Ethernet sniffer. The packet sniffer may be either a software program or a piece of hardware with software installed in it that captures traffic sent over the network, which is then decoded and analyzed by the sniffer. Network administrators install monitors on dedicated machines or on their workstations when needed. A common software program available today is Wireshark, formerly known as Ethereal.

Ping Sweeps

As you may recall, ping enables you to validate that an IP address exists and can accept requests by sending an echo request and then waiting for an echo reply. A ping sweep tool can send an echo request to numerous host IP addresses at the same time to see which host(s) respond(s) with an echo reply.

> **NOTE**
>
> Refer to Chapter 1, "Standard Internetworking Models," for a review of ping, which uses ICMP.

Port Scans

A port scanner is a software program that surveys a host network for open ports. Because ports are associated with applications, the hacker can use the port and application information to determine a way to attack the network. As mentioned, these programs can be used by a third party to audit a network as well as being used by a hacker for malicious intent.

As mentioned in Chapter 1, it is extremely important that you know the prevalent applications and their matching port numbers. Table 4.1 reviews the applications that use TCP, and Table 4.2 reviews UDP-based applications.

TABLE 4.1   Applications Using TCP

Application	Port Number(s)
FTP	20, 21
Telnet	23
SMTP	25
DNS (zone transfers)	53
HTTP	80
POP3	110
NNTP	119
HTTPS	443

TABLE 4.2   Applications Using UDP

Application	Port Number(s)
DHCP	67, 68
DNS (name resolution)	53
TFTP	69
NTP	123
SNMP	161

Information Queries

Information queries can be sent via the Internet to resolve hostnames from IP addresses or vice versa. One of the most commonly used queries is nslookup. You can use nslookup by opening a Windows or Linux command prompt (CMD) window on your computer and entering nslookup followed by the IP address or hostname that you are attempting to resolve.

Here are a couple sample CMD commands:

```
C: nslookup www.cisco.com
C: nslookup 198.133.219.25
```

A multitude of websites offer an nslookup tool.

Challenge

In this challenge, write down the four common tools we discussed for gathering information for a reconnaissance attack.

1.

2.

3.

4.

Denial of Service (DoS) Attacks

DoS attacks are often implemented by a hacker as a means of denying a service that is normally available to a user or organization. For example, users might be denied access to email as the result of a successful DoS attack. IP spoofing can be used as part of a DoS attack or man-in-the-middle attack and occurs when a valid host IP address is assumed by an attacking system. This provides a way to bypass the trust a machine has in another machine.

Although it has long since been patched, a DoS attack called the ping of death occurred when an ICMP echo request packet larger than 65,535 bytes was sent to a target destination, causing it to overflow, crash, and/or reboot. A current example of a DoS attack is a teardrop, which can cause a system to crash by running the CPU up to 100%. Teardrop sends in thousands of tiny fragments with overlapping offsets.

DoS can also be in the form of a distributed DoS (DDoS) attack, TCP SYN attack, or smurf attack.

Distributed DoS (DDoS)

With distributed DoS, multiple systems are compromised to send a DoS attack to a specific target. The compromised systems are commonly called zombies or slaves. As a result of the attack, the targeted system denies service to valid users. Figure 4.1 illustrates a DDoS attack.

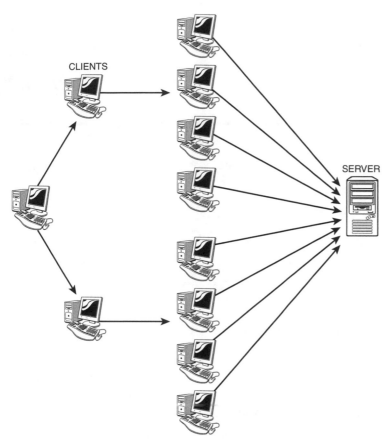

FIGURE 4.1 DDoS attack.

TCP SYN

You may recall from Chapter 1 that a TCP session is established with the use of a three-way handshake, which involves the following steps:

1. A "connection agreement" segment is sent to the recipient, asking to synchronize systems. This step is associated with the bit name SYN.

2. The second and third segments acknowledge the request to connect and determine the rules of engagement. Sequencing synchronization is requested of the receiving device. A two-way connection is established. This step is associated with the bit name SYN-ACK.

3. A final segment is sent as an acknowledgment that the rules have been accepted and a connection has been formed. This step is associated with the bit name ACK.

Figure 4.2 illustrates a proper TCP session.

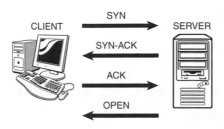

FIGURE 4.2 TCP session establishment.

In a TCP SYN attack, a SYN request is sent to a device with a spoofed source IP address. The attacking system does not acknowledge the resulting SYN-ACK, which causes the session connection queues to fill up and stop taking new connection requests. TCP intercept can be configured on a router to block a TCP SYN attack. This enables the router to terminate any sessions that have not been established within an allotted time frame.

Smurf Attack

With a smurf attack, multiple broadcast ping requests are sent to a single target from a spoofed IP address. Figure 4.3 illustrates a smurf attack. Adding the `no ip directed-broadcast` command to a router might help mitigate a potential smurf attack.

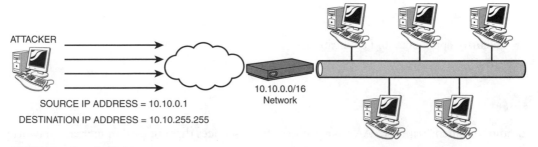

FIGURE 4.3 Smurf attack.

Challenge

In this challenge, write down the six DoS attacks that we reviewed in this chapter.

1.

2.

3.

Mitigating Network Threats

Objectives:

▶ Explain general methods to mitigate common security threats to network devices, hosts, and applications

▶ Describe the functions of common security appliances and applications

▶ Describe security recommended practices including initial steps to secure network devices

By definition, to mitigate is to lessen in force or intensity. Now that you are familiar with the various classes of attack, let's discuss what actions you can take to lessen the impact of an attack on a network. Keep in mind that we already went over some common mitigation techniques, such as password integrity, password encryption, TCP intercept, and `no ip directed-broadcast`. We will continue this chapter with a general overview of additional recommended practices and security measures. Our discussion includes the following mitigation techniques:

▶ Authentication, Authorization, and Accounting (AAA)

▶ Cisco access control lists (ACLs)

▶ Cisco Internetwork Operating System (IOS) secure management features

▶ Encryption protocols

▶ Security appliances and applications

AAA

Commonly called "triple A," AAA is a group of three services that are used to increase network security:

▶ **Authentication:** Identifies a user by login and password.

▶ **Authorization:** Determines what a user is allowed to do.

▶ **Accounting:** Assembles and sends usage information (such as logging).

AAA works in conjunction with TACACS or RADIUS to provide a secure network connection with a record of user activities.

Cisco ACLs

An access list is an ordered list of `permit` and `deny` statements that can be applied on a Cisco device to effectively determine whether a packet will be permitted or denied access to the network. A properly configured access list can help block most of the attack methods described in this chapter:

▶ IP spoofing

▶ TCP SYN attacks

▶ Smurf attacks

▶ ICMP and traceroute

> **NOTE**
>
> Chapter 19, "Using Cisco Access Lists," provides a detailed explanation of ACLs and their functionality.

Cisco IOS Secure Management Features

I mentioned earlier that it is the responsibility of the network administrator to configure Cisco equipment with a new password before deployment. You can take this a step further by performing some initial steps to secure Cisco equipment within the IOS. Configuring the following features on your Cisco device helps create a secure network environment:

▶ Secure Shell (SSH)

▶ Simple Network Management Protocol (SNMP)

▶ Syslog

▶ Network Time Protocol (NTP)

SSH

SSH is a data transmission protocol that uses strong authentication and an encrypted tunnel to ensure secure communications between an SSH client and the SSH server. SSH uses TCP port number 22 for connectivity.

SNMP

SNMP is a management protocol that monitors the network and manages configurations by collecting statistics to analyze network performance and ensure network security. It is best to use SNMP version 3, which provides cryptographic authentication and management traffic encryption. SNMP uses UDP port number 161 for connectivity.

Syslog

With syslog, log messages are collected from the Cisco device and are sent to a syslog server to keep record of any network occurrences. For syslog to work properly, NTP must be configured. Each logged message has an associated severity level. Syslog uses UDP port number 514 for connectivity. Table 4.3 lists the severity levels in order, with 0 representing the most critical message.

TABLE 4.3 Syslog Severity Levels

Security Level	Description
0	Emergency
1	Alert
2	Critical
3	Error
4	Warning
5	Notification
6	Informational
7	Debugging

NTP

NTP is a protocol that synchronizes clocks on the local network to provide accurate local time on the user system. As with SNMP version 3, NTP version 3 is preferred because of the ability to provide cryptographic authentication and management traffic encryption. NTP uses UDP port number 123 for connectivity.

Encryption Protocols

Unencrypted data can be easily read by internal or external threats to a network. This is the case when data is left in clear-text format. To help prevent an attack, it is important to encrypt or encode data. Here are three key encryption protocols:

▶ **SSH:** A data transmission protocol that uses strong authentication and an encrypted tunnel to ensure secure communications between an SSH client and the SSH server.

▶ **Internet Protocol Security (IPsec):** Consists of a set of protocols that were developed to secure the transfer of packets above the Network layer (Layer 3) of the OSI model.

▶ **Secure Socket Layer (SSL):** A protocol that provides a secure channel between two devices at the Application layer (Layer 7) of the OSI model. Asymmetric encryption and certificates are used to exchange a session key. Data is encrypted using that key and a block cipher. HTTPS is an example of an SSL secure transaction.

Security Appliances and Applications

The following are security devices used to mitigate security vulnerabilities:

▶ **Firewall:** A firewall can be either software or hardware that is installed to separate a trusted network from a less-trusted network, such as the Internet.

▶ **Intrusion Prevention System (IPS):** IPS is an active device that is inline with the traffic path on a network. An IPS listens promiscuously to all incoming traffic to identify attacks. It works with the firewall to modify rule templates to block traffic from the attacker address(es) while the attack is still in progress.

▶ **Intrusion Detection System (IDS):** IDS is a passive device that may not be inline with the traffic path on a network. An IDS also listens promiscuously to all incoming traffic to record and generate alerts and issue TCP resets if necessary.

REVIEW BREAK

Because so many possible mitigation techniques exist, let's go over them all in a quick review. Table 4.4 lists and describes each method.

TABLE 4.4   Security Mitigation Techniques

Mitigation Method	Description
AAA	A group of three services (authentication, authorization, and accounting) that are used in conjunction with TACACS or RADIUS to provide a secure network connection with a record of user activities.
Cisco ACL	An ordered list of `permit` and `deny` statements that can be applied on a Cisco device to effectively determine whether a packet will be permitted or denied access to the network.
SSH	A data transmission protocol that uses strong authentication and an encrypted tunnel to ensure secure communications between an SSH client and the SSH server. SSH protects otherwise-vulnerable services such as Telnet, news, and mail.
SNMP	A management protocol that monitors the network and manages configurations by collecting statistics to analyze network performance and ensure network security.
Syslog	Log messages are collected from the Cisco device and are sent to a syslog server to keep records of any network occurrences.
NTP	A protocol that synchronizes clocks on the local network to provide accurate local time on the user system.
IPsec	A set of protocols that were developed to secure the transfer of packets at the Network layer (Layer 3) of the OSI model.

(continues)

TABLE 4.4 *Continued*

Mitigation Method	Description
SSL	A protocol that provides a secure channel between two devices at the Application layer (Layer 7) of the OSI model.
Firewall	Either software or hardware that is installed to protect a network from outside networks, such as the Internet.
IPS	An active device that is inline with the traffic path on a network. An IPS listens promiscuously to all incoming traffic to identify attacks, which the system can then block.
IDS	A passive device that may not be inline with the traffic path on a network. An IDS also listens promiscuously to all incoming traffic to generate alerts and issue TCP resets if necessary.

Chapter Summary

After reading through this chapter, you should have a general understanding of the types of security threats that are prevalent in our high-tech, information-driven society and various ways to mitigate those threats. A responsible network administrator must be aware of these possible attacks to protect the network from any form of security breach. Cisco offers built-in security management features that can be configured before the equipment is installed on the local network. It is also possible to purchase additional hardware and software to enhance overall security. The Cisco catalog includes IOS versions of firewall, IPS, IPsec VPN, and SSL VPN. You also have a variety of network security appliances to choose from, depending on the size and needs of your particular company.

Key Terms

- Access attack
- Reconnaissance attack
- Denial of service (DoS) attack
- Password attack
- Trust exploitation
- Port redirection
- Man-in-the-middle attack
- Packet sniffer
- Port scan
- Ping sweep
- Information query
- IP spoofing
- Ping of death
- Teardrop attack
- Distributed DoS attack

- TCP SYN attack
- Smurf attack
- Authentication, Authorization, and Accounting (AAA)
- Access control list (ACL)
- Secure Shell (SSH)
- Simple Network Management Protocol (SNMP)
- SYSLOG
- Network Time Protocol (NTP)
- Internet Protocol Security (IPsec)
- Secure Socket Layer (SSL)
- Firewall
- Intrusion Prevention System (IPS)
- Intrusion Detection System (IDS)

Apply Your Knowledge

Exercise

4.1 Mitigation Methods

Based on the Cisco-provided exam objectives, you may need to "explain general methods to mitigate common security threats to network devices, hosts, and applications" on the CCNA exam. In this exercise, list the eleven mitigation methods that were covered in this chapter, and write a brief description of each one. You may refer to Table 4.4 to check your answers.

Estimated Time: 20 minutes

1. _____ _____

2. _____ _____

3. _____ _____

4. _____ _____

5. _____ _____

6. _____ _____

7. _____ _____

8. _____ _____

9. _____ _____

10. _____ _____

11. _____ _____

Review Questions

1. Define trust exploitation.

2. Describe a TCP SYN attack.

3. What are the three services that make up AAA?

4. What can a Cisco ACL help mitigate?

5. List the similarities and differences between an IPS and IDS.

Exam Questions

1. What are the three common classes of attack?

   ○ **A.** Access attack

   ○ **B.** DoS attack

   ○ **C.** Smurf attack

   ○ **D.** Reconnaissance attack

2. Which of the following are types of access attacks? (Choose three)

   ○ **A.** Trust exploitation

   ○ **B.** TCP SYN attack

   ○ **C.** Port redirection

   ○ **D.** Man-in-the-middle

3. Which of the following are tools that can be used for a reconnaissance attack? (Choose three)

   ○ **A.** Port redirection

   ○ **B.** Ping sweep

   ○ **C.** Port scan

   ○ **D.** Packet sniffer

4. Which of the following are types of DoS attacks? (Choose three)

   ○ **A.** Smurf attack

   ○ **B.** Packet sniffer

   ○ **C.** DDoS

   ○ **D.** TCP SYN attack

5. What command can be configured on a Cisco device to mitigate smurf attacks?

   ○ **A.** `ip tcp intercept`

   ○ **B.** `ip directed-broadcast`

   ○ **C.** `no ip directed-broadcast`

   ○ **D.** `no ip tcp intercept`

6. When a valid host IP address is assumed by an attacking system, it is called _____.

   ○ **A.** Filtering

   ○ **B.** Ping of death

   ○ **C.** IP spoofing

   ○ **D.** Teardrop attack

7. What do the three A's in AAA stand for?

   ○ **A.** Authentication, authorization, advertising

   ○ **B.** Authorization, accounting, activating

   ○ **C.** Authentication, accounting, activating

   ○ **D.** Authentication, authorization, accounting

8. Which protocol uses TCP port 22?

   ○ **A.** SSL

   ○ **B.** SSH

   ○ **C.** SNMP

   ○ **D.** NTP

9. Which of the following are Cisco IOS secure management features? (Choose three)

   ○ **A.** Syslog

   ○ **B.** SSH

   ○ **C.** AAA

   ○ **D.** SNMP

10. Which protocol provides a secure channel between two devices at the Application layer (Layer 7) of the OSI model?

   ○ **A.** SSL

   ○ **B.** IPsec

   ○ **C.** SNMP

   ○ **D.** NTP

Answers to Review Questions

1. Trust exploitation occurs when a device or group of devices on a shared segment erroneously trusts information that has been provided by an untrustworthy source.

2. In a TCP SYN attack, a SYN request is sent to a device with a spoofed IP address. The attacking system does not acknowledge the resulting SYN-ACK, which causes the session connection queues to fill up and stop taking new connection requests.

3. Authentication identifies a user by login and password. Authorization determines what a user is allowed to do by putting together a list of attributes. Accounting assembles and sends usage information.

4. IP spoofing
   TCP SYN attacks
   Smurf attacks
   ICMP and traceroute

5. Both IPS and IDS listen promiscuously to all incoming traffic. IPS is an active device that is inline with the traffic path. It can identify attacks and block them in the system. IDS is a passive device that may not be inline with the path of traffic. IDS can also generate alerts and send TCP resets when necessary.

Answers to Exam Questions

1. **A, B, D.** The three common classes of attack are access attack, reconnaissance attack, and DoS attack. Answer C is not a class of attack, but rather a type of DoS attack.

2. **A, C, D.** Trust exploitation, port redirection, and man-in-the-middle are all types of access attacks. Answer B is incorrect because a TCP SYN attack is a form of DoS attack.

3. **B, C, D.** Ping sweeps, port scans, and packet sniffers are all tools that can be utilized for a reconnaissance attack. Answer A is incorrect because port redirection is a type of access attack.

4. **A, C, D.** Smurf attacks, DDoS attacks, and TCP SYN attacks are all types of DoS attacks. Answer B is incorrect because a packet sniffer is a tool used for a reconnaissance attack.

5. **C.** The `no ip directed-broadcast` command can be configured on a Cisco device to block smurf attacks. Answers A and D are incorrect because they are related to the TCP SYN attack. Answer B is incorrect because it does not contain the keyword no.

6. **C.** When a valid host IP address is assumed by an attacking system, it is called IP spoofing. Answer A is incorrect because filtering is used to filter traffic. Answer B is incorrect because the ping of death is when an ICMP echo request packet that is larger than 65,535 bytes is sent to a target destination, causing it to overflow, crash, and/or reboot. Answer D is incorrect because a teardrop attack happens when the Offset field of the TCP header is changed.

7. **D.** AAA stands for authentication, authorization, and accounting. Answer A is incorrect because advertising is not a service of AAA. Answers B and C are incorrect because activating is not a service of AAA.

8. **B.** SSH uses TCP port 22. Answer A is incorrect because SSL uses TCP port 443. Answer C is incorrect because SNMP uses UDP port 161. Answer D is incorrect because NTP uses UDP port 123.

9. **A, B, D.** Syslog, SSH, and SNMP are all Cisco IOS secure management features. Answer C is incorrect because AAA consists of a group of three services that are used in conjunction with an authentication server and a software service such as TACACS or RADIUS to provide a secure network connection with a record of user activities.

10. **A.** SSL is a protocol that provides a secure channel between two devices at the Application layer (Layer 7) of the OSI model. Answer B is incorrect because IPsec functions at Layer 3 of the OSI model. Answer C is incorrect because SNMP is a management protocol that monitors the network and manages configurations. Answer D is incorrect because NTP is a protocol that synchronizes clocks on the local network to provide accurate local time on the user system.

Suggested Readings and Resources

1. "A Beginner's Guide to Network Security,"
   http://www.cisco.com/warp/public/cc/so/neso/sqso/beggu_pl.pdf

2. List of Cisco Security products,
   http://www.cisco.com/en/US/products/hw/vpndevc/index.html

CHAPTER FIVE

IP at the Network Layer

Objectives

This chapter covers the following Cisco-specific objectives for the "Implement an IP addressing scheme and IP Services to meet network requirements in a medium-size Enterprise branch office network" section of the 640-802 CCNA exam:

▶ **Describe the operation and benefits of using private and public addressing**

▶ **Calculate and apply an addressing scheme including VLSM IP addressing design to a network**

▶ **Determine the appropriate classless addressing scheme using VLSM and summarization to satisfy addressing requirements in a LAN/WAN environment**

▶ **Describe the technological requirements for running IPv6 in conjunction with IPv4 (including: protocols, dual stack, tunneling, etc.)**

▶ **Describe IPv6 addresses**

Outline

Study Strategies

▶ List the characteristics of IPv4.

▶ Make sure you know how to convert binary to decimal.

▶ Make sure you know how to convert decimal to binary.

▶ Make sure you know how to convert decimal to hexadecimal.

▶ Identify IP address classes, including their networks and hosts, and the IP range value of the first octet of each class.

▶ Define subnet masks and the IP subnet mask format.

▶ Describe CIDR notations and how to determine the CIDR notation based on the subnet mask.

▶ Define RFC 1918, NAT, and PAT.

▶ Make sure you know how to calculate hosts and networks in a subnet.

▶ Determine the Network ID, Broadcast IP, and valid IP range of a subnet.

▶ Name the devices that are used at the Network layer and important traits of each device.

Introduction

This chapter elaborates on the fundamental concepts that you learned about the Network layer or Layer 3 of the OSI model in Chapter 1, "Standard Internetworking Models." It reviews the primary functions of the Network layer and then moves right into IP addressing and formats. After you are familiar with address formats and how to convert between them, it reviews subnetting. No matter whether you decide to take the one- or two-test approach to the CCNA certification, you have to know IP address formats and subnetting. They are integral concepts to any Cisco certification. Finally, this chapter discusses network devices that are used at the Network layer, which are routers and Layer 3 switches.

Network Layer Functions

The Network layer of the OSI model serves two primary functions:

▶ Determines the best path selection for a packet based on a logical or virtual address on the network (routing)

▶ Handles ICMP, ARP, and Proxy ARP requests

First, best path determination is made at the Network layer for packet delivery across the network. Routed protocols such as IP are used to define logical addressing, which can identify the destination of a packet or datagram. Logical addresses used for routing consist of network and host bits. Routers also must determine the path through the internetwork for packet transmission. This is similar to how switches use a MAC address and interface for frame delivery. Routers also use an interface along with the logical or IP address.

Second, the Network layer also handles ICMP, ARP, and Proxy ARP requests on the internetwork. Remember the function of each protocol for the CCNA exam.

Internet Control Messaging Protocol (ICMP) is used by ping and traceroute utilities. Packet Internet Groper (ping) enables you to validate that an IP address exists and can accept requests.

▶ Ping is an echo and the response is an echo response.

▶ Routers send Destination Unreachable messages when they can't reach the destination network and they are forced to drop the packet. The router that drops the packet sends the ICMP DU message.

A traceroute traces the route or path taken from a client to a remote host. Traceroute also reports the IP addresses of the routers at each next hop on the way to the destination. This is especially useful when you suspect that a router on the route to an unreachable network is responsible for dropping the packet.

Address Resolution Protocol (ARP) maps a known IP address to a MAC address by sending a broadcast ARP. When the destination IP address is on another subnet, the sender broadcasts ARP for the router's Ethernet port or default gateway, so the MAC address sent back will be that of the router's Ethernet port.

Reverse ARP (RARP) maps a known MAC address to an IP address.

Proxy ARP enables a router to respond to an ARP request that has been sent to a remote host. Some Unix machines (especially Solaris) rely on Proxy ARP versus default gateways.

IP Addressing and Formats

Internet Protocol (IP) uses logical or virtual addressing to get a packet from a source to its destination. At the Network layer, routers use IP addresses to make best path forwarding decisions. Public IP addresses are used for packets destined for the outside world, whereas private addresses can be used if the packet needs to traverse only an internal network. The CCNA course focuses on IP version 4 (IPv4). The addresses themselves are assigned by the Internet Assigned Numbers Authority (IANA) to individual organizations based on a request for IP address space. Because the total number of IPv4 addresses is not infinite, strict guidelines are placed on IP space requests to ensure that they are justifiable.

IPv4 addresses

- ► Consist of 32 bits.

- ► Are broken into four octets (8 bits each).

- ► Use dotted-decimal format, such as 172.16.122.204.

- ► Have a minimum value (per octet) of 0 and a maximum value of 255.

- ► Have a Network ID of 0.0.0.0.

- ► Have a Broadcast IP of 255.255.255.255.

Another IP version was created in the event that the IP space from IPv4 is exhausted. That version is called IP version 6 (IPv6). IPv6 has emerged in the Cisco professional-level exams and may appear on a future CCNA exam. For this reason, IPv6 is introduced later in this chapter.

Binary

To understand IP addressing, you must first understand binary. Binary is a computer language that is represented by a bit value of 0 or 1. A 32-bit binary address would resemble 10101010101010101010101010101010. Those 32 bits can be grouped into four octets, or

10101010 10101010 10101010 10101010, for conversion to decimal format. When the bit value is 1, the bit is considered to be on and you can calculate its binary value depending on its placement within the binary octet. When the bit value is 0, the bit is off and has no corresponding binary value. Figure 5.1 displays the binary value and the calculated decimal value of each bit within an octet. Notice that the binary value increases exponentially.

Binary Value	2^7	2^6	2^5	2^4	2^3	2^2	2^1	2^0
Decimal Value	128	64	32	16	8	4	2	1

FIGURE 5.1 A list of binary and decimal conversion values.

Converting Binary to Decimal

By using the value calculated for each bit you can easily convert to decimal format. Line up the binary octet with the decimal value that was calculated in Figure 5.1. To calculate the total decimal value of each octet, you would add up the binary value of each bit that is on (1).

The example in Table 5.1 uses binary octet 00000000.

TABLE 5.1   Example #1 of a Binary-to-Decimal Conversion

Bit Value	0	0	0	0	0	0	0	0
Decimal Value	128	64	32	16	8	4	2	1

In this case, all the bit values are off (0), so there is no corresponding decimal value. The IP address octet value is also 0.

Table 5.2 uses binary octet 00010001.

TABLE 5.2   Example #2 of a Binary-to-Decimal Conversion

Bit Value	0	0	0	1	0	0	0	1
Decimal Value	128	64	32	**16**	8	4	2	**1**
				16				**1**

In this example, the fourth and last bit values are 1. Add the decimal values to get the total decimal value of that octet. That is, the total decimal value = 17 (16 + 1).

Table 5.3 uses binary octet 11111111.

Table 5.3   Example #3 of a Binary-to-Decimal Conversion

Bit Value	**1**	**1**	**1**	**1**	**1**	**1**	**1**	**1**
Decimal Value	**128**	**64**	**32**	**16**	**8**	**4**	**2**	**1**
	128	**64**	**32**	**16**	**8**	**4**	**2**	**1**

In Table 5.3, the total decimal value = 255 (128 + 64 + 32 + 16 + 8 + 4 + 2 + 1).

In this case, all the bit values are on (1), so all the decimal values are added together to calculate the IP address octet. The IP address octet value is 255.

Now, you can convert a 32-bit binary address into a dotted-decimal address. In this example the binary address is 10101010 01010101 11000011 00111100. Start with the first octet 10110000. Table 5.4 shows the conversion of 10101010 from binary to decimal value.

TABLE 5.4   Binary-to-Decimal Conversion of 10101010

Bit Value	1	0	1	1	0	0	0	0
Decimal Value	**128**	64	**32**	**16**	8	4	2	1
	128		**32**	**16**				

In Table 5.4, the total decimal value = 170 (128 + 32 + 16).

The second octet is 01010101. Table 5.5 shows the conversion of 01010101 from binary to decimal value.

TABLE 5.5   Binary-to-Decimal Conversion of 01010101

Bit Value	0	1	0	1	0	1	0	1
Decimal Value	128	**64**	32	**16**	8	**4**	2	**1**
		64		**16**		**4**		**1**

In Table 5.5, the IP octet value = 85 (64 + 16 + 4 + 1).

The third octet is 11000011. Table 5.6 shows the conversion of 11000011 from binary to decimal value.

TABLE 5.6   Binary-to-Decimal Conversion of 11000011

Bit Value	1	1	0	0	0	0	1	1
Decimal Value	**128**	**64**	32	16	8	4	**2**	**1**
	128	**64**					**2**	**1**

In Table 5.6, the total decimal value = 195 (128 + 64 + 2 + 1)

The fourth and final octet is 00111100. Table 5.7 shows the conversion of 00111100 from binary to decimal value.

TABLE 5.7 Binary-to-Decimal Conversion of 00111100

Bit Value	0	0	1	1	1	1	0	0
Decimal Value	128	64	32	16	8	4	2	1
			32	16	8	4		

In Table 5.7, the total decimal value = 60 (32 + 16 + 8 + 4).

Based on these calculations, the IP address in dotted-decimal format is 176.85.195.60.

EXAM ALERT

Whenever the last bit is 1, the decimal value is an odd number. Whenever the last bit is 0, the decimal value is an even number. The CCNA exam often uses multiple-choice questions, so you may be able to narrow down the possible correct answers quickly with this hint.

Challenge

In this challenge, you are given a bit value for four octets. You need to fill out the corresponding decimal value and then calculate the total decimal value. After you have converted all four octets, you need to fill out the IP address in dotted-decimal format.

Bit Value	1	1	1	0	1	0	1	0
Decimal Value								

Total Decimal Value = _____

Bit Value	0	1	1	0	1	1	0	1
Decimal Value								

Total Decimal Value = _____

Bit Value	0	0	1	0	1	1	0	0
Decimal Value								

Total Decimal Value = _____

Bit Value	1	0	1	0	1	1	1	1
Decimal Value								

Total Decimal Value = _____

The IP Address in dotted-decimal format is _____ . _____ . _____ . _____ .

Converting Decimal to Binary

You must also be able to convert an IP address from dotted-decimal format into binary. It helps to work from left to right when converting to binary.

Example IP address = 206.110.28.62

The first octet of 206 can be broken down as follows:

128	64	32	16	8	4	2	1
1	1	0	0	1	1	1	0

The octet value is greater than 128, so the first bit is on. Subtract 128 from 206.

206 – 128 = 78

The remainder 78 is greater than 64, so the second bit is also on.

78 – 64 = 14

The remainder 14 is less than 32 and 16, so the third and fourth bits are off. However, 14 is greater than 8, so the fifth bit is on.

14 – 8 = 6

The remainder 6 is greater than 4, so the sixth bit is on.

6 – 4 = 2

The remainder 2 is equal to the seventh bit value, so that bit is also on.

2 – 2 = 0

The last bit value is off because the remainder is 0. Remember that it is an even number, so the last bit will always be 0!

Challenge

You've already converted the first octet of 206.110.28.62 into binary. Determine the appropriate bit value for the remaining three octets.

Second octet 110:

128	64	32	16	8	4	2	1
___	___	___	___	___	___	___	___

Third octet 28:

128	64	32	16	8	4	2	1
___	___	___	___	___	___	___	___

Fourth octet 62:

128	64	32	16	8	4	2	1
___	___	___	___	___	___	___	___

Now that you all four quartets have been converted, the binary equivalent of 216.110.28.62 is 11001110 _____ _____ _____ .

Hexadecimal

Hexadecimal is a numbering system with a base of 16. Numbers 0 through 9 represent the first 10 decimal digits and the next 6 digits are the letters A through F. Each hexadecimal character is equal to four bits. Hexadecimal format was first introduced in Chapter 1, during the discussion of MAC addresses at the Data Link layer. Figure 5.2 shows the decimal values 0 through 15 and their equivalent hexadecimal values.

Decimal Value	0-9	10	11	12	13	14	15
Hexadecimal Value	0-9	A	B	C	D	E	F

FIGURE 5.2   Decimal-to-hexadecimal conversions.

Converting Decimal to Hexadecimal

There are two ways to calculate hexadecimal from decimal format. With the first method, the decimal value should first be converted to binary format.

Decimal value = 141

128	64	32	16	8	4	2	1
1	0	0	0	1	1	0	1

Binary value = 10001101

Now break the binary value into two groups of 4 bits each, which is 1000 and 1101. Then, line up the 4 bits with the last four decimal values that were calculated in Figure 5.1. Again, add up the binary value of each bit that is on (1).

1	0	0	0
8	4	2	1
8				The combined value is 8 so the hexadecimal character = 8

1	1	0	1
8	4	2	1
8	4		1	The combined value is 13 so the hexadecimal character = D

The combined hexadecimal address is 0x8D.

The second method for calculating a hexadecimal address is to divide the decimal number by 16 first. So, 141 divided by 16 equals 8 with a remainder of 13, which matches the results from the binary conversion in the first method.

> **NOTE**
>
> Recall how 8 bits for an octet equals one byte. Well, when you divide an octet into two hexadecimal fields of 4 bits each, each 4-bit field is called a nibble.

Challenge

Here are several decimal values. Calculate the hexadecimal value, using Figure 5.2 as a guideline.

Decimal Value	Hexadecimal Value
210	
193	
245	
161	

IP Address Classes

As you know, IP addresses are 32 bits long, represented by dotted-decimal notation. Each address can be divided into two parts:

▶ Network

▶ Host

The number of network octets and host octets determines the IP address class. Table 5.8 shows the three IP defined network classes.

TABLE 5.8   IPv4 Address Classes

	First Octet	Second Octet	Third Octet	Fourth Octet
Class A	Network	Host	Host	Host
Class B	Network	Network	Host	Host
Class C	Network	Network	Network	Host

TCP/IP defines two additional address classes:

▶ Class D: Used for multicast addresses

▶ Class E: Used for research purposes

Table 5.9 lists the possible values each class network can have in the first octet. With these values you can easily identify what class network is being referenced on the exam.

TABLE 5.9   Address Class Ranges

Class	First Octet Decimal Range
A	1–126
B	128–191
C	192–223
D	224–239
E	240–255

NOTE

The 127.x.x.x address range is reserved for loopback addresses.

EXAM ALERT

Memorize the decimal range for the first octet of each address class.

The network portion of an address maintains the same value for all the IP addresses that are assigned from a Class A, B, or C network. Remember that one octet is equal to 8 bits or 1 byte. The Class A network portion is 1 byte, and the host portion takes up the remaining 3 bytes. The Class B network portion is 2 bytes, with the remaining 2 bytes making up the host portion. The Class C network portion is 3 bytes, whereas the host portion is 1 byte. It stands to reason that if fewer bytes are devoted to the network portion of an address, fewer networks are possible for that class of network. With that said, the same is true for the host portion of an address. The fewer host bytes, the fewer total hosts that are available for that class of network.

When calculating the total number of Class A, B, or C networks available, you must subtract 2 from the total. This is a Cisco standard implemented for the CCNA exam. A host address must be unique for each device or interface on a network. For each Class A, B, or C network, there is always a network identifier (ID) and a broadcast IP address. For this reason, you must also subtract two to calculate the total number of valid hosts per network.

A *network ID* is the first IP address in a network. This may also be referred to as a *subnet ID*. Every host bit for the network ID address is turned off (or all 0s). An example of a Class A network ID is 16.0.0.0.

A *broadcast IP* is the last IP address in a network. Every host bit for the broadcast IP address is turned on (or all 1s). An example of a Class A broadcast IP is 16.255.255.255.

EXAM ALERT

Power of 2 When you enter the exam room, it's helpful to write down some things on the paper or white board that is supplied. I would suggest writing down the powers of 2 for quick reference when calculating networks and hosts.

Here's a calculation for the number of networks for each class:

$2^7 - 2 = 126$ total Class A networks

$2^{14} - 2 = 16,382$ total Class B networks

$2^{21} - 2 = 2,097,150$ total Class C networks

NOTE

When calculating the total number of Class A, B, or C networks, the exponent is a multiple of 7.

Now you can calculate the number of hosts per network:

For any Class A network,

Network = 1 byte (8 bits)

Host = 3 bytes (24 bits)

$2^{24} - 2 = 16,777,214$ total hosts per network

For any Class B network,

Network = 2 bytes (16 bits)

Host = 2 bytes (16 bits)

$2^{16} - 2 = 65,534$ total hosts per network

For any Class C network,

Network = 3 bytes (24 bits)

Host = 1 byte (8 bits)

$2^8 - 2 = 254$ total hosts per network

NOTE

When calculating the total number of hosts per network, the exponent is equal to the number of host bits.

Network Class	First Octet Range (Decimal)	Total Networks	Total Hosts per Network
A			
B			
C			

Subnet Masks

Sub-networks (subnets) enable you to break a large network of IP addresses down into smaller, manageable address ranges. A smaller address range means fewer hosts on a network. Each subnet becomes a separate broadcast domain. All the devices that are in the same broadcast domain receive all broadcasts. Think if it were possible to have all 16,777,214 Class A network hosts sharing a broadcast domain and receiving all broadcasts. That would be a huge amount of traffic. Subnets enable you to break this large network into smaller address ranges. In this case, smaller is better.

A subnet mask is used to identify which part of an IP address is the network portion. Like the IP address itself, a subnet mask consists of 32 bits. The network portion is represented by all 1s.

The default subnet masks for Class A, Class B, and Class C networks are as follows:

- ▸ Class A: 255.0.0.0 (11111111 00000000 000000000 000000000)
- ▸ Class B: 255.255.0.0 (111111111 1111111111 000000000 000000000)
- ▸ Class C: 255.255.255.0 (111111111 1111111111 111111111 0000000000)

Now that you know what an IP address and subnet mask are, there is a mathematical operation called Boolean AND that helps to identify some important aspects of an IP network. With Boolean AND you can determine the network ID and broadcast IP given an IP address and subnet mask.

Boolean AND works as follows:

- ▸ Determines the binary value of the IP address.
- ▸ Determines the binary value of the subnet mask.
- ▸ Lines up both binary values one on top of the other.

▶ If the lined-up bit values in both addresses equal 1, the Boolean bit is also 1.

▶ If the lined-up bit values in both addresses do not equal 1, the Boolean bit is 0.

Table 5.10 provides a Boolean example. The decimal IP address value = 124.0.0.0, and the subnet mask = 255.0.0.0.

Table 5.10   Boolean AND Example #1

IP Address Binary	01111100	00000000	00000000	00000000
Subnet Mask Binary	11111111	00000000	00000000	00000000
Boolean AND	01111100	**00000000**	**00000000**	**00000000**

The network ID in this example is 124.0.0.0. Using Boolean you can see that the host bits in the last three octets are 0 bits, which identifies the network ID. I emphasized the last host octet in Table 5.10. If you turn all of those host bits on, you will get the broadcast IP, which in this case is 124.255.255.255.

For the next example (Table 5.11), the decimal IP address value = 135.252.4.0, and the subnet mask = 255.255.0.0.

Table 5.11   Boolean AND Example #2

IP Address Binary	10000111	11111100	00000100	00000000
Subnet Mask Binary	11111111	11111111	00000000	00000000
Boolean AND	10000111	11111100	**00000000**	**00000000**

The network ID in this example is 135.252.0.0. Using Boolean you can see that the host bits in the last two octets are 0 bits, which identify the network ID. I emphasized both host octets in the example. If you were to turn all those host bits on, you would get the broadcast IP, which in this case is 135.252.255.255.

Classless Interdomain Routing (CIDR) notation may also be used to identify the subnet mask. The mask is written in slash notation as follows:

▶ Class A: /8

▶ Class B: /16

▶ Class C: /24

EXAM ALERT

The CIDR notation or prefix notation for each network class can be determined by counting the 1s in binary or the number of bits that make up the network portion of the address.

Challenge

In this challenge, please fill in the appropriate default subnet mask and CIDR notation for each network class.

Network Class	Subnet Mask (Decimal)	CIDR Notation
A		
B		
C		

Private (RFC 1918) Addressing

Objectives:

▶ Describe the operation and benefits of using private and public addressing

The previously listed Class A, B, and C addresses are all IANA assigned public IP addresses. Although it originally seemed that there was sufficient public IPv4 address space available, resources began being consumed quickly. I mentioned that IPv6 was developed in the event that IPv4 address space became exhausted. Other measures were also implemented to alleviate the shortage of IPv4 public IP address space. These measures include RFC1918, Network Address Translation (NAT), and Port Address Translation (PAT). RFC 1918 defines private IP address space. Private address space can be used for traffic that does not need to leave the internal network. Because this traffic is internal to the network, it does not matter if other organizations are using the same address space. Private IP addresses are not routable on the Internet.

IANA Private Address Space Allocations include the following IP address ranges for Class A, Class B, and Class C networks:

▶ Class A: 10.0.0.0–10.255.255.255

▶ Class B: 172.16.0.0–172.31.255.255

▶ Class C: 192.168.0.0–192.168.255.255

NAT translates one IP address to another. Typically this is done between private and public IP addresses. For example, a private IP address can be translated with NAT to a public IP address for outbound transmission to the Internet. NAT can also translate a public IP address to a private IP address for inbound transmission on the internal network. PAT can translate multiple addresses on an internal network to a single public IP address, which is called one-to-many address translation. PAT is available as NAT overloading on Cisco routers.

NOTE

Chapter 21, "Command-Line NAT Implementation," covers NAT terminology and configurations in detail.

Subnetting IP

Objectives:

▶ Calculate and apply an addressing scheme including VLSM IP addressing design to a network

▶ Determine the appropriate classless addressing scheme using VLSM and summarization to satisfy addressing requirements in a LAN/WAN environment

So far, we have focused on the network classes and key characteristics of each one. As I mentioned, each network class can also be broken down into smaller groups of IP address ranges or subnets, which may also be referred to as variable-length subnet masking (VLSM). *Subnetting* is the process of breaking down those larger IP networks into smaller sub-networks. At first, subnetting IP might seem like a daunting task, but it's not that bad after you get the hang of it. In this section you need to pull together all the knowledge that you have learned so far about binary, decimal, and subnets.

First, let's get the easy subnetting out of the way.

For an IP address that has a 255.255.0.0 or 255.255.255.0 subnet mask, you can copy the octets that have a subnet mask value of 255 from the original IP address. For the remaining octets, you will put down a 0. Here's an example:

IP address = 139.42.6.0

Subnet Mask = 255.255.0.0

The Network ID is 139.42.0.0.

To determine the Broadcast IP of this IP address and subnet mask, just replace the 0 octets from the Network ID with 255.

The Broadcast IP is 139.42.255.255.

EXAM ALERT

When a subnet mask has a value of 255.255.0.0 or 255.255.255.0, you can copy the original IP octets that match the 255 value subnet octets and then use 0 for any remaining octets to determine your Network ID. The Broadcast IP is the same original IP octets that match the 255 value subnet octets and the number 255 rather than 0 for the remaining octet(s).

To understand more difficult subnetting, you need to break down an IP address into network bits, host bits, and subnet bits. The network bits are determined by the network class. Class A has 8 network bits, Class B has 16 network bits, and Class C has 24 network bits. The network bits value is a constant. The host bits, on the other hand, must share space with the subnet bits. To determine the subnet bits for a network you need to look at the subnet mask in binary. For example,

IP address = 176.85.195.60/22

Subnet Mask = 255.255.252.0

Subnet Mask in Binary = 11111111 11111111 11111100 00000000

Network bits = 16

Host bits = 10

Subnet bits = 6

The subnet mask in binary has 22 bits with a value of 1, which means the CIDR notation is /22. Based on the first octet of the IP address you know that this is a Class B network. Class B networks have 16 network bits. That leaves 16 bits in the address. The bits that have a value of 0 determine the number of host bits. In this case there are 10 host bits. The rest of the bits are the subnet bits, so there are 6 subnet bits.

Table 5.12 is a conversion table of decimal to binary values that will help you convert addresses more quickly when taking the exam.

TABLE 5.12   Decimal-to-Binary Conversion

Decimal	Binary
0	00000000
128	10000000
192	11000000
224	11100000
240	11110000
248	11111000
252	11111100
254	11111110
255	11111111

You can use the chart to figure out more IP address values:

IP address = 100.15.209.0/23

Subnet Mask = 255.255.254.0

Subnet Mask in Binary = 11111111 11111111 11111110 00000000

Network bits = 8

Host bits = 9

Subnet bits = 15

IP address = 128.216.55.0/24

Subnet Mask = 255.255.255.0

Subnet Mask in Binary = 11111111 11111111 11111111 00000000

Network bits = 16

Host bits = 8

Subnet bits = 8

IP address = 222.110.8.61/28

Subnet Mask = 255.255.255.240

Subnet Mask in Binary = 11111111 11111111 11111111 11110000

Network bits = 24

Host bits = 4

Subnet bits = 4

Challenge

In this challenge, I supply you with the IP address and subnet mask. From there, you need to convert the subnet mask to binary and determine the number of network bits, host bits, and subnet bits for each network.

IP address = 193.216.0.0

Subnet Mask = 255.255.255.248

Subnet Mask in Binary = _____ _____ _____ _____

Network bits = _____

Host bits = _____

Subnet bits = _____

IP address = 130.101.2.0

Subnet Mask = 255.255.255.128

Subnet Mask in Binary = _____ _____ _____ _____

Network bits = _____

Host bits = _____

Subnet bits = _____

Calculating Hosts in a Subnet

To calculate the hosts in a subnet, we can use the formula $2^H - 2$. The exponent H represents the number of host bits in a network. If you use the subnetting examples, you can determine the hosts in each subnet:

IP address = 176.85.195.60/22

Subnet Mask = 255.255.252.0

Network bits = 16

Host bits = 10

Subnet bits = 6

$2^{10} - 2 = 1022$ Hosts

IP address = 100.15.209.0/23

Subnet Mask = 255.255.254.0

Network bits = 8

Host bits = 9

Subnet bits = 15

$2^9 - 2 = 510$ Hosts

IP address = 128.216.55.0/24

Subnet Mask = 255.255.255.0

Network bits = 16

Host bits = 8

Subnet bits = 8

$2^8 - 2 = 254$ Hosts

IP address = 222.110.8.61/28

Subnet Mask = 255.255.255.240

Network bits = 24

Host bits = 4

Subnet bits = 4

$2^4 - 2 = 14$ Hosts

EXAM ALERT

The formula to calculate the number of hosts created is $2^H - 2$. The *H* represents the host bits in a network.

Challenge

In the last challenge, you figured out the network bits, host bits, and subnet bits for two different IP address subnets. In this challenge, please take that information and calculate the number of hosts in each subnet.

IP address = 193.216.10.0

Subnet Mask = 255.255.255.0

Network bits = _____

Host bits = _____

Subnet bits = _____

Hosts = _____

IP address = 130.101.2.0

Subnet Mask = 255.255.255.128

Network bits = _____

Host bits = _____

Subnet bits = _____

Hosts = _____

Calculating Networks in a Subnet

To calculate the networks in a subnet, you can use the formula $2^N - 2$. The exponent N represents the number of subnet bits in a network. You can figure out the number of networks in each subnet with the formula.

IP address = 176.85.195.60/22

Subnet Mask = 255.255.252.0

Network bits = 16

Host bits = 10

Subnet bits = 6

$2^6 - 2 = 62$ Networks

IP address = 100.15.209.0/23

Subnet Mask = 255.255.254.0

Network bits = 8

Host bits = 9

Subnet bits = 15

$2^{15} - 2 = 32,766$ Networks

IP address = 128.216.55.0/24

Subnet Mask = 255.255.255.0

Network bits = 16

Host bits = 8

Subnet bits = 8

$2^8 - 2 = 254$ Networks

IP address = 222.110.8.61/28

Subnet Mask = 255.255.255.240

Network bits = 24

Host bits = 4

Subnet bits = 4

$2^4 - 2 = 14$ Networks

EXAM ALERT

The formula to calculate the number of networks or subnets created is $2^N - 2$. The N represents the subnet bits in a network.

Challenge

In this challenge, please use the subnet bit value that you calculated and determine the number of networks in each subnet.

IP address = 193.216.10.0

Subnet Mask = 255.255.255.0

Network bits = _____

Host bits = _____

Subnet bits = _____

Subnets = _____

IP address = 130.101.2.167

Subnet Mask = 255.255.255.224

Network bits = _____

Host bits = _____

Subnet bits = _____

Subnets = _____

Zero Subnet Rule

Zero subnet may also be referred to as *subnet zero*. The zero subnet is the first subnet in a network and has all binary 0s in the subnet field. For the purpose of taking the CCNA exam, you should not include the first subnet when calculating the number of networks in a larger subnet. This is one of the two reserved subnet numbers on a network and one of the reasons why you subtract from the total number of networks to get the correct answer for the test. The other network is the broadcast subnet, which has all 1s in the subnet field.

The Increment

We have been working with the IP address subnet 222.110.8.61/28. After you know how many subnets and hosts are in a subnet, you can determine the network ID for that subnet. So far, you know that 222.110.8.61/28 has 14 hosts and 14 subnets. Before subtracting 2 for the valid number of hosts/networks, your calculations were for 16 hosts and 16 networks. This means that a subnet with a 255.255.255.240 mask is part of a larger subnet with a 16-host increment. The variable part of this subnet is the last octet. So you can automatically write down the first three octets as follows:

222.110.8.x (where the x is variable and has a 16-host increment)

Octet values range from 0 to 255. So the first subnet in the larger network is 222.110.8.0. Now you want to add increments of 16 to the last octet, so you get the following networks:

222.110.8.0 (zero subnet—not valid for the CCNA exam)

222.110.8.16

222.110.8.32

222.110.8.48

222.110.8.64

222.110.8.80

222.110.8.96

222.110.8.112

222.110.8.128

222.110.8.144

222.110.8.160

222.110.8.176

222.110.8.192

222.110.8.208

222.110.8.224

222.110.8.240 (broadcast subnet—not valid for the CCNA exam)

This is a list of the Network IDs in that Class C network with a subnet of 255.255.255.240. The Network ID is always an even number. There are 16 total subnets. According to the zero subnet and broadcast subnet rule, the first and last subnet cannot be used. The IP address 222.110.8.61 is greater than 48 and less than 64, so the Network ID or subnet number for 222.110.8.61/28 is 222.110.8.48 (which is highlighted in the list of networks). To get the broadcast IP, subtract 1 from the next Network ID in your list. In this example, the broadcast IP is 222.110.8.63.

There is another math shortcut that can be used to identify the Network ID, which then helps you determine the Broadcast IP. Take another look at 222.110.8.61/28.

IP address = 222.110.8.61

Subnet Mask = 255.255.255.240

Look at the first subnet mask octet from the left that is not a value of 255 and subtract it from 256.

256 – 240 = 16

You want to find the closest multiple of 16 that is less than the last octet in the IP address, which equals 61. You are using the last octet because that is the same octet used from the subnet mask.

16×3 = 48 and 16×4 = 64

Based on the calculations, the Network ID increments are as follows:

222.110.8.48

222.110.8.64

So you use 48 because it is less than 61, and 64 is the Network ID of the next subnet. You come up with the same answer as before.

Network ID = 222.110.8.48

Broadcast IP = 222.110.8.63 (one less than the next Network ID of the next subnet)

Here's another example:

IP address = 100.15.209.0

Subnet Mask = 255.255.254.0

The first two octets in the subnet mask equal 255, so you need to use the first octet that is not equal to 255, or in this case the third octet from the left. Now you can subtract 254 from 256.

256 – 254 = 2

2×104 = 208

2×105 = 210

You can see that the valid network ID less than 209 is 208. The next network ID equals 210, so you can fill out the third octet with each value to obtain the following network ID increments:

100.15.208.0

100.15.210.0

For IP address 100.15.209.0 with a subnet mask of 255.255.254.0, you now know the Network ID is 100.15.208.0. The next network is 100.15.210.0, so you want to find the last IP address before that network ID to get the Broadcast IP. Because the value of an octet can range from 0 to 255, the last possible IP before 100.15.210.0 is 100.15.209.255.

Network ID = 100.15.208.0

Broadcast IP = 100.15.209.255

Challenge

Part I:

To help you understand incremental values, make a list of the subnet increments for address 130.101.2.167 with a subnet mask of 255.255.255.224. I will fill in the first and last network ID (neither are valid networks per the CCNA exam).

130.101.2.0

_____

_____

_____

_____

_____

_____

130.101.2.224

What is the Network ID of 130.101.2.167/27? _____

What is the Broadcast IP of 130.101.2.167/27? _____

Part II:

Given the following IP address and subnet mask, use the shortcut method to determine the Network ID and Broadcast IP.

IP address = 176.85.195.60

Subnet Mask = 255.255.252.0

Determining the Range of Valid IPs

The range of valid IP addresses in a subnet is the first IP address after the Network ID and the last IP address before the Broadcast IP address. If you are given the following IP address and subnet mask, you can determine the range of valid IP addresses:

IP Address = 210.189.16.0

Subnet Mask = 255.255.255.0

First, identify the Network ID, which in this case is 210.189.16.0. Then determine the Broadcast address, which is 210.189.16.255. In this case the valid IP range is 210.189.16.1 to 210.189.16.254.

Here are some more examples where the Network ID and Broadcast IP have already been determined:

IP address = 100.15.209.0

Subnet Mask = 255.255.254.0

CIDR = /23

Network ID = 100.15.208.0

Broadcast IP = 100.15.209.255

Valid IP range = 100.15.208.1 to 100.15.209.254

IP address = 222.110.8.61

Subnet Mask = 255.255.255.240

CIDR = /28

Network ID = 222.110.8.48

Broadcast IP = 222.110.8.63

Valid IP range = 222.110.8.49 to 222.110.8.62

EXAM ALERT

The valid range of IP addresses always starts with an odd number and ends with an even number.

Challenge

In this challenge I have supplied the IP address and subnet mask. First, calculate the binary equivalent of the subnet mask. Then determine the CIDR notation. After you have these fields completed, calculate the Network ID and Broadcast IP, using the shortcut provided for subnetting. After you identify the Network ID and Broadcast IP, you can determine the valid IP host range.

IP Address	172.17.8.122
Subnet Mask	255.255.255.224
Binary Subnet Mask	
CIDR Notation	
Network ID	
Broadcast IP	
Valid IP Range	

It is important to understand the general concepts related to IP addressing and subnetting. Figure 5.3 is a chart or quick sheet that will help you check your answers and provide you a guideline for the CCNA exam. I suggested that you memorize the powers of 2. I also suggest that you memorize this chart and write it down on your scrap paper or white board when you start the exam. I found it to be extremely helpful!

Binary Increment	128	64	32	16	8	4	2	1
Subnet Mask	128	192	224	240	248	252	254	255
CIDR	/17	/18	/19	/20	/21	/22	/23	/24
Hosts-2	32768	16384	8192	4096	2048	1024	512	256
Class B Networks-2	2	4	8	16	32	64	128	256
Class C Networks-2								

128	64	32	16	8	4	2	1
128	192	224	240	248	252	254	255
/25	/26	/27	/28	/29	/30	/31	/32
128	64	32	16	8	4	2	0
512	1024	2048	4096	8192	16384	32768	65536
2	4	8	16	32	64	128	256

FIGURE 5.3 Subnetting quick sheet.

IPv6

Objectives:

▶ Describe the technological requirements for running IPv6 in conjunction with IPv4 (including: protocols, dual stack, tunneling, etc.)

▶ Describe IPv6 addresses

IPv6 is a workable IP version that was created in anticipation of the inevitable exhaustion of IPv4 addresses. Cisco routers are capable of routing IPv4 and IPv6 traffic in the event that networks start to use IPv6 addressing on a regular basis. At this point, organizations are primarily requesting small IPv6 networks from IANA for testing purposes to make sure they are prepared for the day when IPv4 addresses are no longer available. IPv6 provides the same functionality as IPv4. Like IPv4, IPv6 also manages Network layer packet addressing and routing. The sheer size of assignable IPv6 addresses is astounding. The format of this version offers trillions of available IP addresses. For this reason, IPv6 should never experience a shortage of address space.

IPv6 Communications

There are three different types of IPv6 communications: unicast, multicast, and anycast. As you know, these terms also exist in the world of IPv4. Whereas unicast means a one-to-one communication, just as it does with IPv4, multicast and anycast take on new meaning.

With IPv6, multicast refers to one-to-many communication. Multicast can be on a local link, a local site, an organization, or even the entire Internet.

Anycast can be described as one-to-closest communication. With anycast, you assign the same IP address to multiple devices. So, when a packet is destined for this IP address, the path to the closest destination device is chosen. This can also offer redundancy. For example, if two servers have the same IP address and one of the servers goes offline, the other server is chosen as the destination.

IPv6 Address Format

This may be an understatement, but IPv6 addresses are much longer than their 32-bit IPv4 address counterparts. Each address is 128 bits long and is represented by 32 hexadecimal digits. I guess it's a good thing that we covered hexadecimal earlier in this chapter.

As you will recall, IPv4 is represented by dotted-decimal notation. Because hexadecimal digits are used, IPv6 is also written differently. First, IPv6 addresses consist of two parts:

▶ A 64-bit network prefix

▶ A 64-bit local identifier

Here is a sample IPv6 address:

2001:0BD2:0200:08F1:0000:0000:0000:16AB

As you can see, each address is broken into eight smaller groups of four hexadecimal digits that are separated by colons. In this example, the network prefix is 2001:0BD2:0200:08F1, and the local identifier is 0000:0000:0000:16AB.

IPv6 address format summary:

▶ Defined by RFC 2373 and RFC 2374.

▶ Consists of 128 bits with a 64-bit network prefix and a 64-bit local identifier.

▶ Represented by 32 hexadecimal digits broken into eight smaller groups of four.

▶ Uses CIDR notation (slash notation) to discern a subnet range. So you might see the same IP address subnetted and written out as 2001:0BD2:0200:08F1:0000:0000:0000:16AB/16.

As you can see, IPv6 addresses are quite long and complex-looking. To help make IPv6 notation a bit easier, leading zeros in a group may be removed when the address is written. Also, if there is a four-digit group of all 0s or contiguous groups of all 0s, the group or groups can be removed from the address and replaced with ::. Don't go too crazy, though. Keep in mind that the :: can be used only once in the address.

To demonstrate, the same IPv6 IP address can be written in all of the following ways:

2001:0BD2:0200:08F1:0000:0000:0000:16AB

2001:BD2:200:8F1:0:0:0:16AB

2001:BD2:200:8F1::16AB

EXAM ALERT

For the exam, know that leading 0s can be omitted from an IPv6 address and that four-digit groups of all 0s can be omitted and replaced with ::.

Types of IPv6 Addresses

IPv6 has four types of IPv6 addresses: link-local, unique/site-local, global, and multicast.

Link-Local Address

Link-local addresses have the shortest reach of the IP address types. They can go only as far as the Layer 2 domain. These addresses are autogenerated with or without the use of a DHCP server. So, when an IPv6 node goes online, this address is assigned automatically.

Link-local addresses always start with FE80. This means that the first 16 bits of this IPv6 address always begin with 1111 1110 0100 0000, followed by all 0 bits to equal the 64-bit network prefix.

The 64-bit local identifier of a link-local address is interesting, to say the least. The last 64 bits are generated using the MAC address of an interface. Remember, though, that MAC addresses consist of only 48 bits, so there is a discrepancy of 16 bits. The solution to this issue is to add FFFE to the 24th bit of the MAC address. Basically, FFFE is squeezed right into the middle of the MAC address.

Here is an example of how the last 64 bits of the IPv6 link-local address are determined:

MAC address: 0017.C101.DCF6

IPv6 local identifier: 0017:C1FF:FE01:DCF6

Unique/Site-Local Address

Two RFCs describe a unique or site-local address type. RFC 3513 originally outlined the site-local address, which was later rewritten in RFC 4193 and given the new name unique address. People are asked to use the term unique address going forward. Be sure you know this type of address by either name for the exam.

Unique/site-local addresses have a broader scope than link-local addresses. They can expand to the size of an organization and are used to describe the boundary of the organizational network. These are the private addresses for IPv6.

Figure 5.4 shows the format for a unique/site-local address.

GLOBAL ROUTING PREFIX N BITS	SUBNET ID 64 - N BITS	INTERFACE ID 64 BITS

FIGURE 5.4 IPv6 unique/site-local address format.

The first 7 bits of the address are FC00 (also written as FC00::/7). Based on the diagram, the fixed prefix written in bits is 1111 110(L). The letter L can represent the number 1 for locally assigned addresses, or the number 0 for future-use addresses. If you are assigning an address, you would use the number 1 for the eighth bit of the network prefix. As a result, site addresses actually begin with FD00 (also written as FD00::/8), which in binary form is 1111 1101.

Global Address

Global addresses have the broadest scope of all. As the name indicates, these addresses are for global use—that is, Internet communications. Figure 5.5 shows the format of a global address. The global routing prefix consists of 48 bits or less, and the first 3 bits are set to 001 (also written as 2xxx::/3). Because the number is variable, it is represented by the letter N in Figure 5.4. The subnet ID is made up of whatever bits remain after the global routing prefix. The subnet ID has 64 − N bits. As usual, the interface ID or local identifier makes up the last 64 bits of the address. If you were to go to IANA for a trial block of IPv6 address space, you would get an IP subnet from the 2001::/16 range.

1111 1111	FLAG 4 BITS	SCOPE 4 BITS	ADDRESS 112 BITS

FIGURE 5.5 IPv6 global address format.

Multicast Address

Multicast addresses for IPv6 will be extremely important because of their use in group communications and broadcast messaging. Figure 5.6 shows the multicast address format.

FIXED PREFIX 1111 110(L)	GLOBAL ID 40 BITS	SUBNET ID 16 BITS	INTERFACE ID 64 BITS

FIGURE 5.6 IPv6 multicast address format.

The first 8 bits are always 1111 1111 or FF. The next 4 bits or flag bits each have their own meaning, which can be determined using the abbreviation 0RPT:

0 indicates an unassigned bit.

R indicates whether the bit is a rendezvous point.

P indicates whether the bit is based on a unicast address.

T can be either a 0 for a permanently assigned address or 1 if not.

The scope field indicates how far the multicast address will travel. This bit is defined by one of the following seven hexadecimal digits:

1 = Interface

2 = Link

3 = Subnet

4 = Admin

5 = Site

8 = Organization

E = Global

Autoconfiguration

IPv4 uses Dynamic Host Configuration Protocol (DHCP), which allows a device to dynamically obtain the IPv4 address, default router, and DNS server if available. DHCPv6 was created to work with IPv6 addressing. DHCP and DHCPv6 are both considered stateful protocols. With a stateful protocol, a dedicated server maintains a table of the information that was gathered. Unlike IPv4, IPv6 also supports a stateless protocol for autoconfiguration. This means that a dedicated server is no longer required.

With the exception of routers, IPv6 creates a unicast global address for each device. It also allows every NIC to have multiple IPv6 addresses. These address types include link-local, site-local, and global. At a minimum, each NIC has a link-local address, but it is more likely that it will have a link-local and global address.

Example of a global address:

2001:0BD2:12C3:08F1:000C:32FF:FED2:16AB/64 scope global

Example of a local-link address:

2001:0BD2:12C3:08F1:000C:32FF:FED2:16AB/10 scope link

Integrating IPv4 and IPv6

Now that you understand both IPv4 and IPv6 better, how can we get the two versions to interact or coexist? Well, there are several ways to integrate the two versions. You can implement dual-stack, tunneling, or translation techniques to help IPv4 and IPv6 addresses to exist together on the network simultaneously. First, a dual-stack IP layer solution is in place when every node has an IPv4 and an IPv6 address. This offers comprehensive support for both protocols and can operate in one of three modes: IPv4-only when IPv6 is disabled, IPv6-only when IPv4 is disabled, or IPv4 and IPv6 concurrently.

Two tunneling techniques also can be used—manual and automatic tunneling. Manual tunneling requires that the network administrator configure a point-to-point tunnel by hand. Automatic tunneling uses a different address type such as 6to4 to set up a dynamic tunnel. In both cases, the IPv6 packet is tunneled or encapsulated into IPv4.

Finally, the translation technique translates between the two IP versions using a system such as 6to4. With this system, a 6to4 gateway or router encapsulates IPv6 packets into IPv4 packets. This is considered a temporary solution for IP integration.

ICMPv6

In addition to DHCPv6, ICMPv6 has been created to help manage IPv6 addressing. Although ICMPv6 builds on the same functionality as ICMP with ping, ARP, and RARP, there are also enhancements such as neighbor discovery (ND). ND can identify neighboring link layer devices, whether they are reachable, and if the link layer address changes. ND can also discover routers. The caveat is that ICMPv6 must be set up on all IPv6 devices.

Network Layer Devices

The most common network device found at the Network layer is a router; however, Layer 3 switches may also be implemented to create a WAN.

Both routers and Layer 3 switches can carry out these functions:

- ▶ Suppress broadcasts or multicasts
- ▶ Determine the best path for data transfer (routing)
- ▶ Strip down and add to Data Link layer frames
- ▶ Implement access lists for packet filtering (permit/deny statements)
- ▶ Set up quality of service (QoS) qualifiers to measure network performance

It is important to know that both these devices can be used at the Network layer. However, for the purpose of the CCNA exam, routers are more widely recognized and, therefore, are referred to when discussing Layer 3 functions.

Routers

Routers join a minimum of two networks together to create an internetwork or WAN. So far, we have discussed devices that are used at the Physical layer (hubs and repeaters) and the Data Link layer (Layer 2 switches and bridges). Layer 2 switches and bridges create a separate collision domain for each segment of the LAN. Routers and Layer 3 switches create a separate broadcast domain for each segment of a WAN. A broadcast domain is a group of nodes that can receive one another's broadcast messages. Figure 5.7 demonstrates how a router creates broadcast domains whereas the connected switches create collision domains.

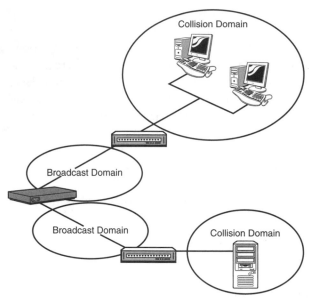

FIGURE 5.7 Broadcast and collision domains.

Figure 5.8 demonstrates a simple LAN with one router and two segments. In this network, any traffic that is generated by Matt's PC has the source MAC and source IP address of that PC. If Matt is sending a frame to the server on the other segment of that WAN, the destination IP address will be that of the server he is trying to reach. Because the server is not on the same segment as Matt, the destination MAC address is that of the router, which is the default gateway. The router takes a look at the frame and at its own routing table. It then decides what interface to use to forward the frame based on the network portion of the IP address. The router attaches its own MAC address as the source MAC address of the frame before sending the frame to the server.

A routing table on a router contains the following information:

▶ Network Address

▶ Interface: Exit interface used to forward packets

▶ Metric: Distance to reach a remote network

EXAM ALERT

For the exam, you should understand how a packet traverses the network and determine the source and destination IP and MAC address as the packet moves from device to device.

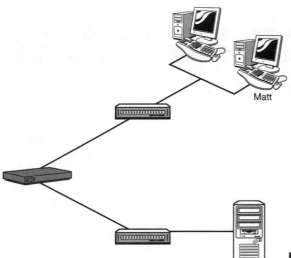

FIGURE 5.8 Frame transmission using a router.

Figure 5.9 exemplifies a WAN with two routers. Each router has a separate routing table to make best path decisions.

Routers provide packet switching between networks and can provide packet filtering based on a network address or application layer port level.

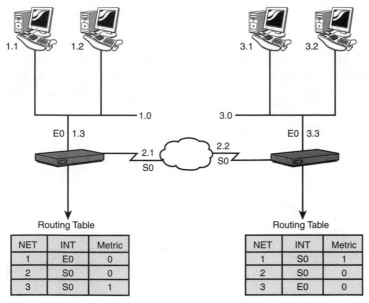

Routing Table

NET	INT	Metric
1	E0	0
2	S0	0
3	S0	1

Routing Table

NET	INT	Metric
1	S0	1
2	S0	0
3	E0	0

FIGURE 5.9 A WAN with routing tables.

EXAM ALERT

Routers provide internetwork communication, packet switching, and packet filtering.

Two packet types are used at Layer 3:

▶ Data packets: Transport data across the internetwork and are supported by routed protocols such as IP and IPX.

▶ Route update packets: Send updates to neighbor routers about all networks connected to that internetwork and are supported by routing protocols such as RIP, EIGRP, and OSPF.

NOTE

Specific Cisco router models are reviewed in Chapter 6, "Introduction to Cisco Routers and Switches."

IP configurations are covered in Chapter 8, "Foundation Cisco Configurations."

Chapter 10, "Introduction to Routing and Routing Protocols," details routing terminology.

Chapter 11, "Distance Vector Routing Protocols," reviews RIP and IGRP routing protocols.

Chapter 12, "Link-State and Hybrid Routing Protocols," discusses OSPF, RIPv2, and EIGRP routing protocols.

Layer 3 Switches

Layer 3 switches are typically called *multilayer switches*. I already listed the commonalities between routers and Layer 3 switches. There are also a couple of differences worth mentioning. The number one difference between a router and a Layer 3 switch is packet switching throughput. Whereas a router has evolved over the years to process more than one million packets per second (pps), a Layer 3 switch can process millions of pps. That said, Layer 3 switches process more traffic in a shorter time.

Whereas routers use microprocessor-based engines, Layer 3 switches use ASIC hardware to perform packet switching. Layer 2 switches use ASIC hardware to forward frames.

NOTE

The Cisco Catalyst 8500 series switch is an example of a Layer 3 switch. Layer 3 switches are recommended for Campus networks.

Chapter Summary

Take a deep breath. That was a lot to cover! IP addressing and IP subnetting are vital to studying for the CCNA exam. In fact, they are integral to understanding networking in general. This chapter touched on many of the concepts that are elaborated later in this book. A lot of device configurations are in upcoming chapters. Knowing your IP format and subnet masks is the first big hurdle when working with IP routing protocols such as OSPF and EIGRP. In addition, for the latest release of the CCNA exam, you will need to understand IPv6. The next chapter introduces Cisco routers and switches as well as other important Cisco network components. You will also be introduced to Cisco IOS Software, which you will need to understand to configure a Cisco device.

Key Terms

- ▶ IPv4 (IP version 4)
- ▶ Binary
- ▶ Network ID
- ▶ Broadcast IP
- ▶ Subnet
- ▶ Subnetting
- ▶ Subnet mask
- ▶ CIDR (Classless Interdomain Routing)
- ▶ Boolean AND
- ▶ NAT
- ▶ PAT
- ▶ Zero subnet rule
- ▶ Broadcast subnet
- ▶ IPv6
- ▶ Link-local address
- ▶ Unique/site-local address
- ▶ Global address

Apply Your Knowledge

Exercises

5.1 Converting Binary to Decimal

Practice makes perfect! Address conversion is pretty much guaranteed to be on the CCNA exam. I promise you that it is worth your while to go over these exercises until you have the system down pat. I will give you the bit values for four octets. Convert each octet to decimal and fill in the corresponding dotted-decimal IP address value.

Keep in mind that the bit values for each octet are

| 128 | 64 | 32 | 16 | 8 | 4 | 2 | 1 |

Estimated Time: 10 minutes

First Octet:

| Binary | 1 | 1 | 0 | 1 | 1 | 0 | 0 | 0 |

Decimal_____

Second Octet:

| Binary | 0 | 1 | 0 | 1 | 1 | 1 | 1 | 1 |

Decimal_____

Third Octet:

| Binary | 1 | 0 | 1 | 1 | 1 | 1 | 1 | 1 |

Decimal_____

Fourth Octet:

| Binary | 1 | 1 | 1 | 0 | 0 | 0 | 0 | 0 |

Decimal_____

IP Address = _____. _____. _____. _____

5.2 Converting Decimal to Binary

Conversions go both ways. Now, I will give you the decimal values for four octets. Convert each octet to binary and fill in the corresponding binary address value.

Estimated Time: 10 minutes

First Octet:

Decimal 224

Binary   _____

Second Octet:

Decimal 137

Binary   _____

Third Octet:

Decimal 15

Binary   _____

Fourth Octet:

Decimal 253

Binary   _____

Binary Address = _____ _____ _____ _____

5.3 Converting Decimal to Hexadecimal

You may be asked to determine a hexadecimal value given a decimal value. In this challenge I have given you the decimal value. You need to convert that to binary and then break the binary octet into two 4-bit groups.

Keep in mind that the bit values for each 4-bit group are

8   4   2   1

Also, Figure 5.2 has the decimal-to-hexadecimal values.

Estimated Time: 10 minutes

Decimal = 105

Binary = ____ ____ ____ ____ ____ ____ ____ ____

First 4 bits of the binary octet:

____ ____ ____ ____ = Decimal _____ Hexadecimal_____

Last 4 bits of the binary octet:

____ ____ ____ ____ = Decimal _____ Hexadecimal_____

The combined hexadecimal value is 0x_____.

5.4 Binary Chart

There are several useful memorization tools for the IP subnetting questions on the CCNA exam. Fill in the binary equivalent (one octet) for each of the following decimal values.

Estimated Time: 5 minutes

Decimal	Binary
0	
128	
192	
224	
240	
248	
252	
254	
255	

5.5 Identify the Network ID

In this exercise, please use Boolean AND to determine the Network ID, given the IP address 134.141.7.130 and subnet mask 255.255.255.0.

Estimated Time: 5 minutes

IP Address Binary

Subnet Mask Binary

Boolean AND

Network ID = _____. _____. _____. _____

Review Questions

1. Convert binary 00101010 00111111 11011100 11111111 to decimal format.

2. Convert decimal 150.193.6.100 to binary format.

3. What is hexadecimal 0x5F in decimal format?

4. Perform Boolean AND to define the Network ID of IP address 200.62.183.26 255.255.255.0.

5. Given the IP address 32.116.5.0 and subnet mask 255.255.255.0, what is the Network ID?

6. Given the IP address 213.50.201.0 and subnet mask 255.255.255.0, what is the Broadcast IP?

7. What is the valid IP range for 220.9.3.0/24?

8. Define the zero subnet and broadcast subnet rules.

9. Describe the process of routing.

10. List the functions performed by a router or Layer 3 switch.

Exam Questions

1. What is the decimal equivalent of 10010111 00000110 10101100 01110111?

   ○ **A.** 151.6.172.119

   ○ **B.** 151.6.172.120

   ○ **C.** 151.6.172.121

   ○ **D.** 151.6.172.122

2. What is the first octet range for Class B addresses?

- ○ **A.** 1 to 126
- ○ **B.** 128 to 191
- ○ **C.** 192 to 223
- ○ **D.** 224 to 239

3. What is the first octet range for Class C addresses?

- ○ **A.** 1 to 126
- ○ **B.** 128 to 191
- ○ **C.** 192 to 223
- ○ **D.** 224 to 239

4. How many hosts are available with a Class C network?

- ○ **A.** 253
- ○ **B.** 254
- ○ **C.** 255
- ○ **D.** 256

5. What is the network ID for a host with the IP address 124.199.7.18/28?

- ○ **A.** 124.199.7.0
- ○ **B.** 124.199.7.16
- ○ **C.** 124.199.7.32
- ○ **D.** 124.199.7.48

6. You have been assigned a Class C network address. A coworker has requested that you create 10 networks that can support 10 hosts per network. What subnet mask should you use?

- ○ **A.** 255.255.255.0
- ○ **B.** 255.255.255.224
- ○ **C.** 255.255.255.240
- ○ **D.** 255.255.255.248

7. Which of the following are valid host addresses in the 208.62.15.0 network with a 255.255.255.224 subnet mask? (Choose the two best answers.)

   ○ **A.** 208.62.15.0

   ○ **B.** 208.62.15.1

   ○ **C.** 208.62.15.30

   ○ **D.** 208.62.15.32

8. Given the network address 192.131.10.0 and subnet mask 255.255.255.0, what is the total number of networks and the total number of hosts per network?

   ○ **A.** 1 network / 255 hosts

   ○ **B.** 1 network / 254 hosts

   ○ **C.** 2 networks / 62 hosts

   ○ **D.** 6 networks / 30 hosts

9. How many valid host IP addresses are available with a network address of 218.41.99.24 and a subnet mask of 255.255.255.252?

   ○ **A.** 2

   ○ **B.** 6

   ○ **C.** 14

   ○ **D.** 30

10. If you need at least five subnetworks with a Class C network and you want to have as many hosts as possible on each network, what subnet mask would you use?

    ○ **A.** 255.255.255.252

    ○ **B.** 255.255.255.240

    ○ **C.** 255.255.255.248

    ○ **D.** 255.255.255.224

11. How many hosts are available with a Class B network?

    ○ **A.** 254

    ○ **B.** 64,000

    ○ **C.** 65,534

    ○ **D.** 16,777,214

12. What is the Broadcast IP for 196.23.250.32/27?

   ○ **A.** 196.23.250.32

   ○ **B.** 196.23.250.33

   ○ **C.** 196.23.250.63

   ○ **D.** 196.23.250.64

13. What subnet mask would you use if you had a Class B address and you would like 250 networks?

   ○ **A.** 255.255.255.0

   ○ **B.** 255.255.254.0

   ○ **C.** 255.255.252.0

   ○ **D.** 255.255.248.0

14. How many subnets can you have with subnet mask of 255.255.240 on a Class B network?

   ○ **A.** 6

   ○ **B.** 14

   ○ **C.** 16

   ○ **D.** 30

15. How many hosts are available if you have a Class B network with a subnet mask of 255.255.255.128?

   ○ **A.** 254

   ○ **B.** 256

   ○ **C.** 128

   ○ **D.** 126

16. Which of the following are considered private addresses per RFC 1918? (Choose the three best answers.)

   ○ **A.** 1.0.0.0

   ○ **B.** 10.10.10.20

   ○ **C.** 172.30.255.10

   ○ **D.** 192.168.128.128

17. What is the CIDR notation for the 128.250.62.0 network with a subnet mask of 255.255.255.0?

　　　○　**A.** /23

　　　○　**B.** /24

　　　○　**C.** /25

　　　○　**D.** /26

18. Which of the following network classes do not define public IP address space? (Choose the two best answers.)

　　　○　**A.** Class B

　　　○　**B.** Class C

　　　○　**C.** Class D

　　　○　**D.** Class E

19. What is the valid IP host range for 160.254.101.167/27?

　　　○　**A.** 160.254.101.128 to 160.254.101.254

　　　○　**B.** 160.254.101.129 to 160.254.101.254

　　　○　**C.** 160.254.101.160 to 160.254.101.191

　　　○　**D.** 160.254.101.161 to 160.254.101.190

20. Given this network diagram, if the Philadelphia router sends a packet to 172.23.0.51, what interface will the Milford router use to forward the packet?

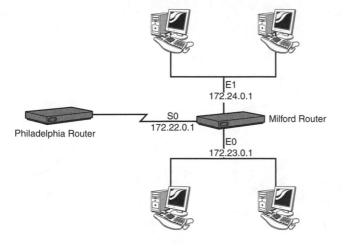

○ **A.** E0

○ **B.** E1

○ **C.** S0

○ **D.** S1

21. Given the IPv6 address of 2001:0A20:D201:0000:0000:DC3F:0000:011D, which of the following are valid ways to write the same address? (Choose two)

○ **A.** 2001:A20:D201:0:0:DC3F:0:11D

○ **B.** 2001:A20:D201::DC3F:0:11D

○ **C.** 2001:A2:D201::DC3F:0:11D

○ **D.** 2001:A20::DC3F::11D

Answers to Review Questions

1.	128	64	32	16	8	4	2	1
	0	0	1	0	1	0	1	0

32+8+2 = 42

128	64	32	16	8	4	2	1
0	0	1	1	1	1	1	1

32+16+8+4+2+1 = 63

128	64	32	16	8	4	2	1
1	1	0	1	1	1	0	0

128+64+16+8+4 = 220

128	64	32	16	8	4	2	1
1	1	1	1	1	1	1	1

128+64+32+16+8+4+2+1 = 255

The correct answer is 42.63.220.255.

2.	128	64	32	16	8	4	2	1
	1	0	0	1	0	1	1	0

128	64	32	16	8	4	2	1
1	1	0	0	0	0	0	1

128	64	32	16	8	4	2	1
0	0	0	0	0	1	1	0
128	64	32	16	8	4	2	1
0	1	1	0	0	1	0	0

The correct answer is 10010110 11000001 00000110 01100100.

3. The first hexadecimal character is 5, which is the same as the decimal value.

8 4 2 1

0 1 0 1

The second hexadecimal character is F, which is 15 in decimal.

8 4 2 1

1 1 1 1

Now you can combine the two 4-bit groups to get 01011111, which converts to 95 in decimal.

4. IP Address Binary = 11001000 00111110 10110111 00011010

Subnet Mask Binary= 11111111 11111111 11111111 00000000

Boolean AND = 11001000 00111110 10110111 **00000000**

The correct answer is 200.62.183.0.

5. This is considered an easy mask. You just write down the original octets with a subnet mask value of 255 and a 0 for each octet with a 0 value in the subnet mask.

The correct answer is 32.116.5.0.

6. Because this has an easy subnet mask, you can copy the first three octets and then replace the last octet with 255.

The correct answer is 213.50.201.255.

7. This IP address subnet mask is 255.255.255.0, so the network ID is 220.9.3.0. The broadcast IP is 220.9.3.255.

The correct answer is 220.9.3.1 to 220.9.3.254.

8. Zero subnet may also be referred to as subnet zero. The zero subnet is the first subnet in a network and has all binary 0s in the subnet field. For the purpose of taking the CCNA exam, you should not include the first subnet when calculating the number of networks in a larger subnet. This is one of the two reserved subnet numbers on a network and one of the reasons why you subtract from the total number of networks to get the correct answer for the test. The other network is the broadcast subnet, which has all 1s in the subnet field.

9. Traffic that is generated by a device has the source MAC and source IP address of that device. If a frame is sent to a server on another segment of a WAN, the destination IP address is that of the server the frame is trying to reach. Because the server is not on the same segment, the destination MAC address is that of the router, which is the default gateway. The router takes a look at the frame and at its own routing table. It then decides what interface to use to forward the frame, based on the network portion of the IP address. The router attaches its own MAC address as the source MAC address of the frame before the frame is sent to the server.

10. Suppress broadcasts or multicasts.

   Determine the best path for data transfer (routing).

   Strip down and add to Data Link layer frames.

   Implement access lists for packet filtering (permit/deny statements).

   Set up quality of service (QoS) qualifiers to measure network performance.

Answers to Exam Questions

1. **A.** The decimal equivalent of 10010111 00000110 10101100 01110111 is 151.6.172.119. Answers B and D can be eliminated right away because both IP addresses end with an even number.

2. **B.** The first octet range for Class B addresses is 128 to 191. Answers A, C, and D are incorrect because the range of 1 to 126 is Class A, 192 to 223 is Class C, and 224 to 239 is reserved for multicast.

3. **C.** Answer C is correct because the first octet range for Class C addresses is 192 to 223. Answers A, B, and D are incorrect because the first octet range for Class A addresses is 1 to 126, for Class B is 128 to 191, and 224 to 239 is reserved for multicast.

4. **B.** There are 254 hosts per Class C network. For any Class C network there are 24 network bits and 8 host bits: $2^8 - 2 = 254$.

5. **B.** The Network ID of 124.199.7.18/28 is 124.199.7.16. If you write out the subnet mask it is 255.255.255.240. Subtract 240 from 256 and you have 16; 16×1 = 16, which is the first valid increment that can be the network ID. The next network ID is 124.199.7.32.

6. **C.** Subnet mask 255.255.255.240 allows for 14 networks and 14 hosts. Answer A is incorrect because subnet mask 255.255.255.0 allows for only one network with 254 hosts. Answer B is incorrect because subnet mask 255.255.255.224 allows for 6 networks and 30 hosts, and answer D is incorrect because subnet mask 255.255.255.248 allows for 30 networks and 6 hosts.

7. **B, C.** 208.62.15.1 and 208.62.15.30 are valid host addresses in the 208.62.15.0 network with a 255.255.255.224 subnet mask. Answer A is incorrect because 208.62.15.0 is the network ID and therefore is not a valid host address. Answer D is incorrect because 208.62.15.32 is the network ID of the next network and is not valid.

8. **B.** The network address 192.131.10.0 and subnet mask 255.255.255.0 has one network with 254 hosts.

9. **A.** With a network address of 218.41.99.24 and a subnet mask of 255.255.255.252, 2 valid host addresses are available. Answer B is incorrect because subnet mask 255.255.255.248 has 6 available hosts. Answers C and D are incorrect because subnet mask 255.255.255.240 has 14 available hosts, and subnet mask 255.255.255.224 has 30 available hosts.

10. **D.** Subnet mask 255.255.255.224 would allow for 6 networks with 30 available hosts per network. Answer A is incorrect because subnet mask 255.255.255.252 allows for 62 networks but only 2 hosts per network. Answers B and C are incorrect because subnet mask 255.255.255.240 allows for 14 networks with only 14 hosts per network, and subnet mask 255.255.255.248 allows for 30 networks with only 8 hosts per network.

11. **C.** There are 65,534 hosts available for a Class B network. Answers A and D are incorrect because a Class C network has 254 possible hosts, and a Class A has 16,777,214 possible hosts.

12. **C.** The broadcast IP for 196.23.250.32/27 is 196.23.250.63. Answer A is incorrect because 196.23.250.32 is the Network ID of 196.23.250.32/27. Answers B and D are incorrect because 196.23.250.33 is the first valid IP in the /27 network and 196.23.250.64 is the Network ID of the next network.

13. **A.** The only subnet that allows for 250 networks is 255.255.255.0. Subnet mask 255.255.255.0 can create 254 subnets. Answer B is incorrect because subnet mask 255.255.254.0 can create 126 subnets. Answer C is incorrect because subnet mask 255.255.252.0 can create 62 subnets. Answer D is incorrect because subnet mask 255.255.248.0 can create 30 subnets.

14. **B.** You can have 14 subnetworks with a Class B network that has a subnet mask of 255.255.240.0.

15. **D.** Answer D is correct because there are 126 possible hosts for a Class B network with a subnet mask of 255.255.255.128. Answer A is incorrect because a Class B network with a subnet mask of 255.255.255.0 has 254 possible hosts. Answers B and C are incorrect because the Network ID and Broadcast IP addresses were not subtracted from the total number of IPs in each subnet.

16. **B, C, D.** RFC 1918 defines the following private IP address ranges: 10.0.0.0 to 10.255.255.255, 172.16.0.0–172.31.255.255, and 192.168.0.0 to 192.168.255.255. Answer A is incorrect because the address 1.0.0.0 is a Class A public address.

17. **B.** /24 is the correct CIDR notation for the 128.250.62.0 network with a subnet mask of 255.255.255.0. Answer A is incorrect because /23 is the CIDR notation for 255.255.254.0. Answer C is incorrect because /25 is the CIDR notation for 255.255.255.128, and answer D is incorrect because /26 is the CIDR notation for 255.255.255.192.

18. **C, D.** Class D defines multicast address space and Class E defines IP address space reserved for research. Answers A and B are incorrect because Classes B and C are both defined for public use.

19. **D.** The valid host range for 160.254.101.167/27 is 160.254.101.161 to 160.254.101.190. Answers A and B are incorrect because both 160.254.101.128 to 160.254.101.254 and 160.254.101.129 to 160.254.101.254 are part of a 255.255.255.128 subnet. Answer C is incorrect because with the range 160.254.101.160 to 160.254.101.191, the first IP is the Network ID and it is not a valid host IP address.

20. **A.** The Milford router forwards the packet through the E0 interface because the network matches the 172.23.0.0 network. Answer B is incorrect because interface E1 is going to the 172.24.0.0 network, and answer C is incorrect because interface S0 is going to the Philadelphia router via the 172.22.0.0 network. Answer D is incorrect because interface S1 does not exist in this scenario.

21. **A, B.** Leading zeros and contiguous groups of zeros can be taken out of the IPv6 address and replaced with "::" when written. Answer C is incorrect because a trailing zero was removed from the second group. Answer D is incorrect because there are two sets of "::", which is not a valid format.

Suggested Readings and Resources

The following are some recommended readings on IPv4, private and public IP addressing, subnetting, and routing:

1. "IPv4," http://en.wikipedia.org/wiki/IPv4

2. "RFC 1918," http://www.faqs.org/rfcs/rfc1918.html

3. "IP Addressing and Subnetting for New Users," http://www.cisco.com/warp/public/701/3.html

4. "IP Address Subnetting Tutorial," http://www.ralphb.net/IPSubnet/

5. "Network Calculators," http://www.subnetmask.info/

6. Andrew Colton. *Cisco IOS for IP Routing*. Rocket Science Press, Inc., 2002.

CHAPTER SIX

Introduction to Cisco Routers and Switches

Objectives

This chapter covers the following Cisco-specified objectives for the "Describe how a network works" section of the 640-802 CCNA exam:

▶ **Select the components required to meet a network specification**

▶ **Describe the purpose and functions of various network devices**

Outline

Study Strategies

▶ Identify the interfaces and modules used with Cisco devices.

▶ Describe the Cisco memory components ROM, Flash, RAM, and NVRAM.

▶ Familiarize yourself with Cisco Internetworking Operating System (IOS) feature sets.

▶ Review the IOS image file structure.

▶ Identify the Cisco Router models and their features.

▶ Identify the Cisco Switch models and their features.

Introduction

Up to this point, we have discussed general internetworking technologies and devices to provide a background of the material relevant to the CCNA exam. Now the scope of the discussion widens to include Cisco technology. This chapter reviews internetworking devices (routers and switches) that were developed by Cisco for network implementations. It also discusses the individual hardware components that make up a router and switch, which you must thoroughly understand before the configuration of these devices is explained. This introduction to Cisco technology leads up to Chapter 9, "Understanding the Cisco SDM," and Chapter 7, "Foundation Cisco IOS Operations," where you will delve into hands-on device operations and configurations.

Interfaces and Modules

Objectives:

▶ Select the components required to meet a network specification

▶ Describe the purpose and functions of various network devices

Networks can be connected to Cisco hardware in a variety of ways. Communication lines can be terminated to a Cisco device via hardware interfaces and modules. Interfaces provide a physical point of interaction between two networks. That hardware interface includes the cable, plug, socket, and signal that sync up together to communicate among devices.

Certain Cisco routers are built as fixed-port routers or fixed configuration routers and do not allow for additional network module installations. Cisco also offers modular-port routers. Modular-port routers allow for future system upgrades by mounting network modules in available spaces to accommodate changing network environments. A module is a self-contained component. A Cisco network module has built-in hardware interfaces to add alternate connection options on a network. Because they are modular components, Cisco routers can be upgraded easily and with minimal expense to the company. This chapter reviews the variety of physical connection types on LAN and WAN devices.

LAN Interfaces

Local area network (LAN) interfaces are used to provide a point of interconnection between Cisco switches and other network devices. Cisco provides a wide selection of switches that can be implemented on a LAN and offer end-user connectivity. In Chapter 3, "Data Link Networking Concepts," Layer 2 switches were introduced. The Cisco 2950 series switch family includes various models with different interface options, such as the Cisco 2950-12 and the Cisco 2950-24. The 2950-12 has 12 built-in ethernet ports, whereas the 2950-24 has 24 built-in ethernet ports. Certain models also have Gigabit Ethernet slots.

If Gigabit Ethernet ports are included, the front panel of a 2950 model has 10/100 ethernet ports on the left side of the switch and 2 Gigabit Ethernet slots that accommodate LAN interface modules on the right. The 10/100 ports allow for either a 10Mbps or 100Mbps connection speed. Media connects to an ethernet switch port via an RJ-45 connector. As far as the switch is concerned, each ethernet port is designated as a numbered interface for identification. The top left port is labeled 1 by the switch. Each interface begins with a 0/#, where the # sign equals the port number on the switch. The top left port is then named 0/1 on that switch. Given this formula, the bottom left port is labeled 0/2.

> **EXAM ALERT**
>
> For the CCNA exam, know how the interfaces are labeled for an ethernet port. This information is necessary for any switch configuration exercises.

The Gigabit Ethernet slots are available for Gigabit Interface Converters (GBICs). A GBIC interface module can be inserted into the Gigabit Ethernet slot to allow for different media connections to that port. The physical media can range from copper to single-mode fiber. A GBIC is also hot swappable, so you can remove and replace it without shutting off power to the switch. This helps to avoid interruption of service to that switch.

The back panel of the 2950 includes power input and the switch's console port. The console port has an RJ-45 connector and is connected to a terminal with a rollover cable for initial switch configuration.

WAN Interfaces

Wide area network (WAN) interfaces are also used to provide a point of interconnection between Cisco routers and other network devices. Types of WAN interfaces include

- ▶ Basic Rate Interface (BRI)
- ▶ Synchronous Serial
- ▶ Asynchronous Serial
- ▶ High-Speed Serial Interface (HSSI)
- ▶ T1 Controller Card

BRI

BRI is an Integrated Services Digital Network (ISDN) service that consists of two 64Kbps bearer (B) channels and one 16Kbps data channel. Voice, video, and data traffic can be carried over the B-channels. Signals between telephone company switches use the D-channel. Cisco offers an 8-port ISDN-BRI with a built-in Network Termination Type 1 (NT-1) Network Module for router installation.

> **EXAM ALERT**
>
> For the exam you should know that BRI is an ISDN line that consists of two 64Kbps bearer (B) channels and one 16Kbps data (D) channel.

The NT-1 is a telephone company requirement for an ISDN line connection. This network module has a BRI U interface, which means that the NT-1 is built in on the network module and does not require a separate NT-1 device.

Synchronous Serial

A synchronous serial interface synchronizes clocks for the bit stream of both the sending and receiving end of a serial link. This allows for the data rate to be adjusted if necessary to ensure that both ends of a serial link are functioning at the same speed.

Asynchronous Serial

An asynchronous serial interface does the opposite of a synchronous serial interface. It does not synchronize the clocks for the bit stream of the sending and receiving end of a serial link. Cisco offers a 4-port asynchronous/synchronous serial network module.

With the asynchronous/synchronous serial network module, each port can be configured individually as either asynchronous or synchronous, depending on your network setup.

HSSI

High-speed serial interfaces offer up to 52Mbps transmission rates to the WAN from a Cisco router. The higher speed capacity is relevant if the corporate backbone requires high-speed Internet access and VPN connectivity. Cisco offers a 2-port HSSI port adapter.

T1 Controller Card

Also referred to as a *digital signal level 1* (DS1) service, a T1 is a connecting line that offers a 1.544Mbps data transmission speed. A single T1 line consists of 24 digital signal level 0 (DS0) channels that are 64Kbps each and an additional 8Kbps that is reserved for management overhead. A T1 controller card can be installed in a router's T1 slot to communicate with and control the 24 DS0 channels.

Data Communications Equipment (DCE)

Data Communications Equipment (DCE) or Data Circuit-Terminating Equipment (DCE) is the term used to identify a device that connects the Data Terminal Equipment (DTE) to a service provider's communications line. The DCE side of a connection sets the clock speed for a serial connection.

DCE equipment may consist of a

- Modem
- Channel Service Unit/Data Service Unit (CSU/DSU)
- Basic Rate Interface Network Termination Type 1 (BRI NT-1)

Modems convert a digital signal into an analog signal for transmission over a telephone line. The signal is converted back into a digital format when it reaches the device on the other end of that telephone line.

A Channel Service Unit/Data Service Unit (CSU/DSU) serves as the intermediary between the service provider and the WAN router. In most cases, the CSU/DSU provides the clock speed for the router. A CSU/DSU may be a separate unit or it could be incorporated into a WAN interface card (WIC).

If it is not built in on a Cisco router via a BRI-U (Basic Rate Interface-User) interface, the service provider requires separate BRI NT-1 hardware as a termination point for the communications line. The BRI NT-1 then connects to the Cisco router.

> **EXAM ALERT**
>
> A modem, CSU/DSU, or BRI NT-1 can be used to connect a WAN router at the customer premise to a service provider.

Data Terminal Equipment (DTE)

Data Terminal Equipment is the term used to identify a device at the user end of a network and is connected to the service provider via the DCE device.

DTE equipment may consist of a

- Router
- PC
- Server

In Figure 6.1, the service provider, whom you will most likely hear called a telco, brings a communication line from its central office (CO) to the customer and terminates its line to the CSU/DSU. The CSU/DSU is then connected to the customer router. The point at which the telco terminates its line to the customer is called a demarcation point or demarc. Customer-owned equipment, such as the router and typically the CSU/DSU, is referred to as *customer premise equipment* (CPE).

FIGURE 6.1 An overview of a service provider connection to an end user.

Cabling between the CSU/DSU and router is decided by the type of CSU/DSU that is deployed on that network. If a WIC functions as a CSU/DSU, then the CPE is a telco jack and a Category 5 or Category 6 cable is used with an RJ-45 connector. If a WIC does not function as the CSU/DSU, there are several types of connections possible between a CSU/DSU and the DTE device. With routers, typically a DB-60 connector is used to connect to the router while one of the following connectors is used to connect to the CSU/DSU:

▶ EIA/TIA-232

▶ EIA/TIA-449

▶ EIA/TIA-530

▶ V.35

▶ X.21

The Electronic Industries Association/Telecommunications Industry Association (EIA/TIA) formed a standards body, which developed the 232, 449, and 530 cables. The V.35 and X.21 cables were developed by the International Telecommunication Union (ITU).

Your best bet is to position the CSU/DSU as close to the router as possible. This requires the shortest amount of cable and therefore ensures maximum speeds.

EXAM ALERT

For the exam you should know the difference between DCE and DTE equipment. Also, know that the DCE side of a connection must provide the clocking for the serial connection.

Cisco Memory Components

Objectives:

▶ Select the components required to meet a network specification

▶ Describe the purpose and functions of various network devices

Four memory components are used by Cisco devices. Those components include ROM, Flash, RAM, and NVRAM.

ROM

Read-only memory (ROM) contains the basic code for booting a device and maintaining Power on Self Test (POST), ROM Monitor (ROMmon), bootstrap, and RXBOOT. Because this type of memory is read-only, it cannot be changed by any configuration done at the networking device. ROM is nonvolatile, so data is not lost when the device is powered off.

Flash

Flash is installed on either an electrically erasable, programmable, read-only memory (EEP-ROM) or Personal Computer Memory Card International Association (PCMCIA) card. Flash memory contains the Cisco Internetworking Operating System (IOS) image. The router uses Flash by default to locate the IOS when it is booted. Configuration files may also be stored on a Flash card. Like ROM, Flash is also nonvolatile memory.

RAM

Random-access memory (RAM) is used for short-term storage of a machine's running IOS and running configuration. The IOS is copied from Flash to RAM. This is the only type of system memory that is not permanent. At times, you may hear RAM also referred to as dynamic random-access memory (DRAM). Because this type of memory is volatile, it is lost whenever the machine is shut down.

> **EXAM ALERT**
>
> RAM contains the running IOS, with the exception of Run-From-Flash (RFF) routers. RAM also contains the running configuration or the active configuration that is used after a machine is booted.

NVRAM

Nonvolatile random-access memory (NVRAM) stores the startup configuration. This is the configuration that is loaded when the machine is booted.

Cisco Internetworking Operating System

Cisco IOS software is developed and maintained by Cisco to support a full array of system functions, applications (including Internet applications), and network hardware in a single software package. IOS software is installed on each Cisco router or switch and can accommodate network growth and provide for secure data transfers. The command-line interface (CLI) for routers and switches defines the commands that are used to communicate with the IOS. Future chapters demonstrate the use of CLI commands on both network devices.

> **NOTE**
>
> A Cisco Catalyst switch may use either a Cat OS or Cisco IOS. The major difference with Cat OS is the CLI commands that are used in conjunction with the operating system software.

Cisco releases IOS software using what they call trains. Each release can be further defined by train identifiers. A train identifier determines whether a release is a Technology (T), Enterprise, or Service Provider (SP) release. When the IOS version has no train identifier, it is the mainline train. With so many features and applications being offered with each release, a train identifier can further define a specific subset of features. For example, if you have a release named 12.3(1)T, the IOS version number breaks down as follows:

▶ 12.3 refers to the mainline train that will not be added to but will be subject to IOS bug fixes.

▶ (1) represents the release number, which increments with each new release of the mainline train.

▶ T identifies the type of train release where T stands for Technology. This may also be an S (Service Provider) or E (Enterprise) train.

Feature Sets

A feature set is a package of the features that is offered in addition to the basic IOS functions of an IOS software release. You can select more than one feature set per release. Feature sets may be identified as standard, enhanced, or advanced, depending on the services that are supported. To give you an idea of the latest features available with Cisco IOS, current releases offer the following software functionality:

▶ IP Base—The base IOS image.

▶ IP Voice—Features include Voice over IP (VoIP), and Voice over Frame (VoFR).

▶ Advanced Security—Offers advanced protection via firewall, Intrusion Detection System (IDS), Secure Shell (SSH), and IP Security (IPSec).

▶ SP Services—Includes service provider services such as IPv6, Netflow SSH, ATM, Voice over ATM (VoATM), and Frame Relay.

▶ Enterprise Base—Consists of Enterprise Layer 3 routed protocols, and IBM support.

▶ Advanced IP Services—Offers a combination of the Advanced Security and Service Provider Services feature sets.

▶ Enterprise Services—Combines the Enterprise Base and Service Provider Services feature sets with full IBM support.

▶ Advanced Enterprise Services—Incorporates all the Cisco IOS feature sets.

IOS Image File Naming

The IOS image file represents the name of the system image on a Cisco router or switch. The hardware platform, feature set, compression format, IOS version, and train information are all found in the name of an IOS image file. An IOS image filename can be broken out to identify more specific information about the IOS in use by a device. This is helpful if you are troubleshooting a system issue and need to verify what version is currently in use. Cisco may be aware of an IOS bug, or the version may simply be outdated and an IOS upgrade might be the solution to your trouble. To find the IOS image filename, use the show version command from the command prompt.

Given the example filename c2600-ipbase-1.122-1.T.bin (.bin indicates binary format), from left to right, each portion of the filename represents the following:

- ▶ c2600—Hardware platform (Cisco 2600 router)

- ▶ ipbase—Feature set

- ▶ 1—File format (compressed re-locatable)

- ▶ 122—IOS version number

- ▶ 1—Maintenance release number

- ▶ T—Train identifier

EXAM ALERT

Remember the IOS image file structure. If given a filename, you should be able to break down each part of the file and what it represents.

Challenge

Understanding Cisco IOS is necessary for the maintenance and troubleshooting of Cisco routers and switches. I will provide an IOS image filename and would like you to identify the hardware platform, feature set, compression format, IOS version, and train information for that file.

IOS Image filename—c1700-entbase-1.121-1.E.bin

Maintenance Release Number _____

File Format _____

Hardware Platform _____

Train Identifier _____

Feature Set _____

IOS version number _____

Cisco Router Models and Features

Objective:

▶ Describe the purpose and functions of various network devices

Cisco offers a wide selection of router models for network implementations. The Cisco family of routers can accommodate networks that range in size and require various network interfaces for WAN connectivity. As mentioned, some router models are fixed port and fixed configuration, whereas others are modular-port routers. To help you prepare for the CCNA exam, a Cisco 2500 series router model can perform a broad range of the basic routing functions. This router can provide you with sufficient functionality to practice initial router setup and configurations.

The 2500 series hardware can support CSU/DSU, ethernet, token ring, asynchronous or synchronous serial, and ISDN connections. The 2500 series routers coupled with Cisco IOS software can support routed protocols such as IP, Novell IPX, and AppleTalk. They can also support a wide array of routing protocols. Although most of the 2500 family routers are fixed port, the 2524 and 2525 models are both modular-port routers.

In addition to the 2500 series routers, Cisco also offers the following router series:

▶ **800 Series**—Fixed-port and fixed-configuration routers that support Asymmetric Digital Subscriber Line (ADSL), ADSL over ISDN, Single-pair High-Speed DSL (G.SHDSL), Serial, and ethernet to an external cable modem or DSL connections. They can also support a small office or a home office for a telecommuter.

▶ **1600 Series**—Fixed-port routers that support ISDN, asynchronous serial, or synchronous serial connections and can support a small- to moderately-sized business.

▶ **1700 Series**—Modular-port routers that support built-in Fast Ethernet LAN ports and WAN/Voice modular slots, and can support a small- to moderately-sized business.

▶ **1800 Series**—Fixed-port and modular-port routers that build on the 1700 Series router functionality with integrated services such as IPSec VPN, firewall security, inline intrusion prevention (IPS), Network Admission Control (NAC), and URL filtering to small offices.

▶ **2600 Series**—Modular multiservice access routers that support built-in ethernet LAN ports, built-in Fast Ethernet LAN ports, and WAN/voice modular slots. They can support a small to medium office.

▶ **2800 Series**—Integrated service routers that support built-in Fast Ethernet LAN ports, built-in Gigabit Ethernet LAN ports, and WAN/voice modular slots. They can support a small to medium office, its telecommuters, and Wi-Fi connections.

▶ **3600 Series**—Modular multiservice access routers that support data, voice, video, and VPN. They can support a medium to large office or a small Internet Service Provider (ISP).

▶ **3700 Series**—Modular multiservice access routers that support built-in Fast Ethernet LAN ports and WAN/voice modular slots. They can support branch offices.

▶ **3800 Series**—Modular multiservice access routers that support built-in dual Gigabit Ethernet LAN ports and enhanced network module slots. They can support a medium to large business with integrated services.

▶ **7200 Series**—Can be used with an Enterprise Edge or Service Provider Edge environment and support links that range in size from a DS0 (64Kbps) all the way up to an OC12 (655Mbps). They can support Fast Ethernet, Gigabit Ethernet, and Packet over Sonet connections. Chassis slots are open for installation of more than 70 network interfaces.

▶ **7600 Series**—Are likely to be found in a main office of an enterprise business or at a small service provider's point-of-presence (POP) site. Each chassis can support a maximum of 4 slots. Each slot has either a 40Gbps or 720Gbps capacity with advanced optical service modules.

Cisco Switch Models and Features

Objective:

▶ Describe the purpose and functions of various network devices

The Cisco family of switches includes the Catalyst switch models, which as you learned earlier in this chapter might use the Cat OS rather than the IOS. As with Cisco routers, the switch model numbers increase as they are upgraded for enhanced overall operability. Various switches have been developed over the years to accommodate the size and functionality requirements of LANs around the world. You may have a Cisco 1900, 2800, 2900, or 2924 switch to help you study for the Cisco Certified Network Associate exam. These models should be easy to find and affordable, and they cover all the features necessary for the exam when coupled with Cisco IOS.

In addition to the 1900, 2800, 2900, and 2924 series switches, Cisco also offers the following switch series:

▶ **2950 Series**—Includes a fixed-configuration switch that can support both Fast Ethernet and Gigabit Ethernet connections.

▶ **3500 Series**—Are stackable switches that can employ Cisco Switch Clustering technology and GigaStack GBICs, and support Layer 3 functionality.

▶ **4000 Series**—Can support high-density copper, fiber-based interfaces, Fast Ethernet, Gigabit Ethernet connections, and Layer 3 functionality.

▶ **6500 Series**—Can support Power over Ethernet (PoE) devices, 10/100Mbps ethernet ports, 10/100/1000Mbps ethernet ports, 10Gbps ethernet ports, and Layer 3 functionality.

Cisco switches may also support PoE. PoE enables an end device to receive power over a copper ethernet cable. End devices that might use PoE include wireless access points, IP telephones, video cameras, and card scanners. This technology was originally developed by Cisco and called "inline power." IEEE has since standardized PoE with 802.3af.

Chapter Summary

A general knowledge of Cisco hardware and IOS is integral to your preparation for the CCNA exam. Chapter 7, "Foundation Cisco IOS Operations," shows you how to correctly navigate through the Cisco IOS. Also, Cisco router and switch configurations are presented throughout the remainder of this book.

Key Terms

- interface
- module
- GBIC
- BRI
- synchronous
- asynchronous
- HSSI
- T1 controller card
- DS0
- DS1
- T1
- BRI
- ISDN
- NT-1
- HSSI

- DTE
- modem
- CSU/DSU
- CO
- demarc
- CPE
- ROM
- Flash
- RAM
- NVRAM
- IOS
- train
- CLI
- PoE

Apply Your Knowledge

Exercise

6.1 Cisco Memory Components

You may be asked to identify the memory components that are used on Cisco devices. In this exercise, please list the four types of memory and their respective functions.

Estimated Time: 10 minutes

Memory Component	Memory Component Functionality

Review Questions

1. Describe a GBIC.

2. List the WAN interfaces and their descriptions.

3. Define DCE and DTE.

4. What is the Cisco IOS?

5. Define PoE.

Exam Questions

1. Which WAN interface is an ISDN line that consists of two 64Kbps bearer (B) channels and one 16Kbps data (D) channel?

   ○ **A.** BRI

   ○ **B.** Synchronous serial

   ○ **C.** Asynchronous serial

   ○ **D.** HSSI

2. Which WAN interface synchronizes clocks for the bit stream of both the sending and receiving end of a serial link?

- ○ **A.** BRI
- ○ **B.** Synchronous serial
- ○ **C.** Asynchronous serial
- ○ **D.** HSSI

3. Which WAN interface offers up to 52Mbps transmission rates to the WAN from a Cisco router?

- ○ **A.** BRI
- ○ **B.** Synchronous serial
- ○ **C.** Asynchronous serial
- ○ **D.** HSSI

4. Which of the following devices can be labeled Data Circuit-Terminating Equipment (DCE)? (Choose the 3 best answers.)

- ○ **A.** Router
- ○ **B.** Modem
- ○ **C.** CSU/DSU
- ○ **D.** BRI NT-1

5. Which of the following devices can be labeled Data Terminal Equipment (DTE)? (Choose the 3 best answers.)

- ○ **A.** Router
- ○ **B.** Modem
- ○ **C.** PC
- ○ **D.** Server

6. What type of memory contains the basic code for booting a device and maintaining POST, ROMmon, bootstrap, and RXBOOT?

- ○ **A.** ROM
- ○ **B.** Flash
- ○ **C.** RAM
- ○ **D.** NVRAM

7. What type of memory is nonvolatile and contains the Cisco IOS image?

   ○ **A.** ROM

   ○ **B.** Flash

   ○ **C.** RAM

   ○ **D.** NVRAM

8. This type of memory contains the running IOS and the running configuration (active configuration) that is used after a machine is booted.

   ○ **A.** ROM

   ○ **B.** Flash

   ○ **C.** RAM

   ○ **D.** NVRAM

9. This type of memory stores the startup configuration.

   ○ **A.** ROM

   ○ **B.** Flash

   ○ **C.** RAM

   ○ **D.** NVRAM

10. What does the ipbase portion of the Cisco IOS file named c2600-ipbase-1.122-1.T.bin represent?

    ○ **A.** Hardware platform

    ○ **B.** Feature set

    ○ **C.** Train identifier

    ○ **D.** IOS version

Answers to Review Questions

1. A GBIC interface module can be inserted into the Gigabit Ethernet slot to allow for different media connections to that port. The physical media can range from copper to single-mode fiber. A GBIC is also hot swappable, so it can be installed without interrupting service to that switch.

2. Basic Rate Interface (BRI)

   BRI is an ISDN line that consists of two 64Kbps bearer (B) channels and one 16Kbps data (D) channel. Voice, video, and data traffic can be carried over the B-channels. Signals between tele-phone company switches use the D-channel.

Synchronous serial

A synchronous serial interface synchronizes clocks for the bit stream of both the sending and receiving end of a serial link. This enables the data rate to be adjusted if necessary to ensure that both ends of a serial link are functioning at the same speed.

Asynchronous serial

An asynchronous serial interface does the opposite of a synchronous serial interface. It does not synchronize the clocks for the bit stream of the sending and receiving end of a serial link.

High-Speed Serial Interface (HSSI)

High Speed Serial Interfaces offer up to 52Mbps transmission rates to the WAN from a Cisco router.

T1 controller card

A T1 controller card can be installed in a router's T1 slot to communicate with and control the 24 DS0 channels.

3. Data Circuit-Terminating Equipment (DCE) or Data Communications Equipment is the term used to identify a device that connects the Data Terminal Equipment (DTE) to a service provider's communications line. DCE equipment may consist of a modem, CSU/DSU, or BRI NT-1.

DTE is the term used to identify a device at the user end of a network and is connected to the service provider via the DCE device. DTE equipment may consist of a router, PC, or server.

4. Cisco IOS software is developed and maintained by Cisco to support a full array of system functions, applications (including Internet applications), and network hardware in a single software package. IOS software is installed on each Cisco router or switch and can accommodate network growth and provide for secure data transfers. The command-line interface (CLI) for routers and switches defines the commands that are used to communicate with the IOS.

5. Power over Ethernet (PoE) enables an end device to receive power over a copper ethernet cable. End devices that might use PoE include IP telephones, video cameras, and card scanners. This technology was originally developed by Cisco and called "inline power." IEEE has since standardized PoE with 802.3af.

Answers to Exam Questions

1. **A.** BRI consists of two 64Kbps B channels and one 16Kbps D channel. Answer B is incorrect because synchronous serial synchronizes clocks for the bit stream of both the sending and receiving end of a serial link. Answer C is incorrect because asynchronous serial does not synchronize the clocks for the bit stream of the sending and receiving end of a serial link. Answer D is incorrect because HSSI offers up to 52Mbps transmission rates to the WAN from a Cisco router.

2. **B.** Synchronous serial synchronizes clocks for the bit stream of both the sending and receiving end of a serial link. Answer A is incorrect because BRI consists of two 64Kbps B channels and one 16Kbps D channel. Answer C is incorrect because asynchronous serial does not synchronize the clocks for the bit stream of the sending and receiving end of a serial link. Answer D is incorrect because HSSI offers up to 52Mbps transmission rates to the WAN from a Cisco router.

3. **D.** HSSI offers up to 52Mbps transmission rates to the WAN from a Cisco router. Answer A is incorrect because BRI consists of two 64Kbps B channels and one 16Kbps D channel. Answer B is incorrect because synchronous serial synchronizes clocks for the bit stream of both the sending and receiving end of a serial link. Answer C is incorrect because asynchronous serial does not synchronize the clocks for the bit stream of the sending and receiving end of a serial link.

4. **B, C, D.** Modems, CSU/DSUs, and BRI NT-1s are all Data Circuit-Terminating Equipment. Answer A is incorrect because routers are considered Data Terminal Equipment.

5. **A, C, D.** Answers A, C, and D are correct because routers, PCs, and servers are all Data Terminal Equipment. Answer B is incorrect because modems are Data Circuit-Terminating Equipment.

6. **A.** ROM contains the basic code for booting a device and maintaining POST, ROMmon, bootstrap, and RXBOOT. Answer B is incorrect because Flash memory contains the Cisco IOS image. Answer C is incorrect because RAM is used for short-term storage of a machine's running IOS and running configuration. Answer D is incorrect because NVRAM stores the startup configuration.

7. **B.** Flash memory is nonvolatile and contains the Cisco IOS image. Answer A is incorrect because ROM contains the basic code for booting a device and maintaining POST, ROMmon, bootstrap, and RXBOOT. Answer C is incorrect because RAM is used for short-term storage of a machine's running IOS and running configuration. Answer D is incorrect because NVRAM stores the startup configuration.

8. **C.** RAM contains the running IOS and the running configuration (active configuration) that is used after a machine is booted. Answer A is incorrect because ROM contains the basic code for booting a device and maintaining POST, ROMmon, bootstrap, and RXBOOT. Answer B is incorrect because Flash memory contains the Cisco IOS image. Answer D is incorrect because NVRAM stores the startup configuration.

9. **D.** NVRAM stores the startup configuration. Answer A is incorrect because ROM contains the basic code for booting a device and maintaining POST, ROMmon, bootstrap, and RXBOOT. Answer B is incorrect because Flash memory contains the Cisco IOS image. Answer C is incorrect because RAM is used for short-term storage of a machine's running IOS and running configuration.

10. **B.** The term *ipbase* refers to the IP Base feature set. Answer A is incorrect because the hardware platform is c2600 or the Cisco 2600 router. Answer C is incorrect because the train identifier is T for Technical. Answer D is incorrect because the IOS version is represented by 122 or version 12.2.

Suggested Readings and Resources

The following are some recommended readings on network components, Cisco devices, and terminology:

1. "Serial Connectivity Network Modules," http://www.cisco.com/en/US/products/hw/ routers/ps274/products_data_sheet09186a0080091b8b.html.

2. "White Paper: Cisco IOS Reference Guide," http://www.cisco.com/warp/public/620/1.html.

3. Boney, James. *Cisco IOS in a Nutshell*, first edition. O'Reilly, 2001.

4. "Loading and Maintaining System Images," http://www.cisco.com/en/US/products/sw/iosswrel/ps1835/1026071.

5. "Cisco Router Guide," http://www.cisco.com/application/pdf/en/us/guest/products/ ps5855/c1031/cdccont_0900aecd8019dc1f.pdf.

7

Foundation Cisco IOS Operations

Objectives

This chapter covers the following Cisco-specified objectives for the "Configure, verify, and troubleshoot basic router operation and routing on Cisco devices" section of the CCNA 640-802 exam:

▶ **Manage Cisco IOS**

▶ **Describe the operation of Cisco routers (including: router bootup process, POST, router components)**

Outline

Study Strategies

▶ Read the information presented in the chapter, paying special attention to tables, Notes, and Exam Alerts.

▶ This chapter serves as a foundation for all configurations that are to come. It is not enough to just grasp these concepts. You should feel completely comfortable with the navigation of the IOS before tackling advanced configurations in future chapters.

▶ If possible, practice the syntax of every command discussed throughout this chapter (and book) with real or simulated Cisco equipment.

▶ Complete the Challenge Exercises and the Exercises at the end of the chapter. These exercises are designed to give you practical experience using the utilities discussed.

▶ Complete the Exam Questions at the end of the chapter. They are designed to simulate the type of questions you will be asked in the CCNA exam.

Introduction

Unfortunately, Cisco devices are not yet at the point where they can automatically configure themselves. With that being said, each Cisco device that contains an IOS (internetwork operating system) must have some interface in which you, the expert Cisco administrator, can interact with the operating system to perform any administration, configuration, and troubleshooting services.

This chapter explores the options available for interacting with Cisco IOS using the command-line interface (CLI). In Chapter 9, "Understanding the Cisco SDM," you will see that Cisco has simplified some Cisco device administration by creating a graphical user interface (GUI) in which many configuration and verification commands can be performed using a web browser. Granted this is a great tool for many tasks; however, you will inevitably need to access the CLI of Cisco IOS to perform tasks outside of the GUI's capabilities. As a consequence, you will need to understand the command hierarchy of the IOS CLI to accurately navigate your way around to achieve your administrative goal.

This chapter also looks into the multiple boot-up steps that occur when a Cisco router or switch is powered on, and how you can manipulate that startup sequence.

Terminal Options

After starting a router configuration using the Console Port or Auxiliary Port, you can choose from among several options to gain access to Cisco IOS Software. These access methodologies are commonly referred to as EXEC sessions. Assuming that the device model and IOS supports them, certain Cisco devices can support up to five means of gaining an EXEC session to the IOS, which are discussed in the following subsections.

Console Port

Several Cisco devices do not have a default IP address that can be utilized to gain access to the IOS. Therefore, administrators gain initial out-of-band terminal access to Cisco devices via the console port. After an EXEC access is gained, you can configure the device via the CLI of IOS.

> **NOTE**
>
> The term *out-of-band* simply refers to the fact that the console is a management port that is separate from interfaces that are used for networking data transmissions. Conversely, *in-band* management signals traverse over the same networking paths and interfaces as the data stream. This implies that you have IP connectivity to the devices that you are managing.

To connect to a console port, Cisco supplies you with a flat rollover cable. As illustrated in Figure 7.1, the pins in a rollover cable are reverse images of each other when the cable is viewed with both sides of the tabs in the same orientation. Cisco console cables either come with two RJ-45 connectors in which a DB-9 adapter is required for connection to the PC, or come with the DB-9 connector attached to one end of the cable. The 9-pin connector of the console cable connects to your terminal PC's COM port. Keep in mind that this management connection is for initial terminal access only and should not be confused with an actual networking ethernet cable of any sort.

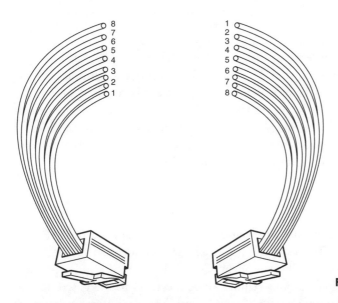

FIGURE 7.1   Cisco console cable pinouts.

EXAM ALERT

It is imperative to be able to recognize and differentiate between the pin configurations and the usage of a straight-through ethernet cable versus a cross-over ethernet cable versus a rollover console cable.

An ASCII terminal emulation software program must be running on your management PC if it is to interact with the Cisco IOS. There are several different terminal programs available, such as HyperTerminal, TeraTerm, SecureCRT, and others. The terminal setup of the COM port connected to the rollover console cable must be set to the following default console parameters: 9600 baud, 8 data bits, no parity bits, 1 stop bit, and no flow control. After the terminal is set up correctly and you have powered on the Cisco device, you should see the output from your console EXEC session in the terminal window.

Auxiliary Port

Certain Cisco models may contain another out-of-band management port called an auxiliary (AUX) port. This port is very similar to the console port in that it uses a rollover cable and has an RJ-45 connection to the Cisco device. The difference between the auxiliary and the console port is that the auxiliary port has flow control capability, which is useful for analog modem connectivity. By connecting an external modem to this management port, you can dial into the modem remotely and gain an EXEC session without being physically next to the Cisco device.

Telnet

As discussed in Chapter 1, "Standard Internetworking Models," Telnet is an Application layer protocol of the TCP/IP protocol suite that uses TCP port 23 to gain virtual terminal emulation to a device. Telnet is considered in-band management because it is required to have IP connectivity to the Cisco device into which you are trying to Telnet. Most Cisco devices allow at least 5 Telnet EXEC sessions to be connected for remote terminal access. For the sake of security, there is some configuration involved to allow Telnet access into the Cisco devices. Telnet is discussed in further detail in Chapter 8, "Foundation Cisco Configurations."

HTTP and HTTPS

Similar to Telnet, HTTP and HTTPS are also Application layer protocols of the TCP/IP protocol suite. HTTP uses TCP port 80 to establish a management connection to the Cisco device. HTTPS is a secure version of HTTP over Secure Socket Layer (SSL) and uses TCP port 443. HTTP and HTTPS terminal sessions require IP connectivity to the Cisco device, making it an in-band management communication methodology. The key difference between HTTP/HTTPS and Telnet is that when you use HTTP or HTTPS, you can have a graphical interface to the configuration and administration features of the Cisco IOS.

The HTTP EXEC session is made possible by an HTTP server service that can run if configured on the Cisco device. For security purposes, some Cisco routers do not have this functionality enabled by default. If this functionality is not going to be utilized, it is recommended that you disable this service to avoid any security vulnerabilities.

> **NOTE**
>
> HTTP and HTTPS are utilized in the Security Device Manager (SDM) configuration utility which will be discussed in greater detail in Chapter 9, "Understanding the Cisco SDM."

SSH

Imagine you have Telntetted into a Cisco device and it is prompting you for a password. If an attacker has the capability to eavesdrop on that Telnet terminal session, he could very well detect the password because the Telnet communications are in clear text.

With SSH (Secure Shell), you are provided a secure terminal EXEC connection through the use of encrypted communications between your terminal client and the Cisco device. Your terminal application must support SSH to connect securely to your Cisco device. Some terminal programs that support SSH are SecureCRT and Putty. In addition, the version and feature set of the Cisco IOS must support SSH. Similar to its brother in-band protocols, SSH also requires initial configurations before gaining access to an EXEC session. Granted, this additional configuration may seem tedious; however, the benefit of having secure remote terminal connections to the Cisco device outweighs the work involved.

REVIEW BREAK

Table 7.1 quickly reviews the five means of gaining EXEC sessions to Cisco Devices.

TABLE 7.1 Cisco EXEC Session Summary

	In-band Versus Out-of-band	Cabling	IP Connectivity Required	Notes
Console	Out-of-band	Rollover	No	Requires physical connectivity.
Auxiliary	Out-of-band	Rollover	No	Requires external modem for remote connectivity.
Telnet	In-band	Network cable	Yes	Can support at least five connections to most Cisco devices.
HTTP/HTTPS	In-band	Network cable	Yes	Must be enabled on Cisco routers. Should be disabled if not utilized.
SSH	In-band	Network cable	Yes	Requires SSH-compliant terminal emulation program and specific Cisco IOS version and feature set.

EXAM ALERT

Successfully initiating a Telnet, HTTP/HTTPS, or SSH session to a Cisco device is an excellent way to test that you have Application layer connectivity to that device.

Router/Switch Startup Procedures

Objective:

▶ Describe the operation of Cisco routers (including: router bootup process, POST, router components)

Now that you have an understanding of how to connect to the Cisco IOS, you can now look at the startup procedures for a Cisco router or switch to determine how the IOS is loaded and running in the first place when you power on those devices. Additionally, these devices would be doing us a huge administrative injustice if they did not load the configurations that you have toiled over in previous EXEC sessions (despite the obvious level of job security). Thus, you also need to look into how a saved configuration is applied after the IOS is loaded. As you will see, each of the memory components that were discussed in Chapter 6, "Introduction to Cisco Routers and Switches," performs a pivotal part in the storing, loading, and running of the IOS and the configuration.

Router and switch startup procedures are extremely similar to a computer's boot-up process. For instance, when you turn on a computer, the computer utilizes ROM (read-only memory) chips to perform a POST (power-on self-test) to check the critical hardware initially for start-up. Then it consults the BIOS (basic input/output system) settings to determine the order in which to search the hard drives, floppy drives, or CD drives to locate the operating system. After the operating system is loaded, it applies any custom configurations you have made in the past and utilizes those settings toward its normal operation.

Similarly, when you turn on a Cisco router and a switch, ROM chips perform a POST and then load the IOS process. You can manipulate the location sources of the IOS similar to specifying the boot drive in the BIOS settings on a computer. After the IOS is loaded, your saved configuration is loaded and applied to the device's operating functions. The next sections delve further into the specific processes that are occurring at each stage.

POST

When you first apply power to a Cisco router or switch, a specialized ROM performs a series of tests of the critical hardware components that are pertinent for startup and basic operation such as Flash memory, CPU, and interfaces. It makes sense to utilize ROM chips for this service because they are already hard-coded with their programs and they do not require constant power to keep those programs stored in the memory. If a failure occurs during this stage of the startup process, you may encounter one of several outcomes, ranging from a non-functioning interface all the way to complete device failure. In any case, your equipment should be under warranty or you have an active support contract in place to fix the failing hardware.

Bootstrap

After the hardware passes all its tests (if only the CCNA was that easy), another ROM seeks out the operating system in accordance to its programming routines. The code that is run in the ROM is commonly referred to as the bootstrap code. If a failure occurs at this stage of the boot-up process, your Cisco device could very likely enter what is known as ROM Monitor or commonly called ROMmon.

ROMmon

In your travels, if you or someone else has ever coined the phrase "hit rock bottom" you have a general idea of what purpose ROMmon serves. The ROM Monitor is a very limited codeset that enables you to perform elementary functions to manually get the router or switch back to a functioning state. You can perform low-level diagnostics and even copy a new IOS file to the Cisco device over the console port or configure TFTP information so the device can download the IOS image off of a TFTP server.

> **TIP**
>
> Keep in mind that your default console speed is 9600bps, and a typical IOS file exceeds 16 megabytes. If you need to re-copy a working IOS to the Cisco device in ROMmon mode over the console, I recommend changing the default console speed in ROMmon to a higher speed or taking a long lunch or dinner break.

ROMmon is also utilized during password recovery on a Cisco router to make it possible to tell the device manually to ignore any saved configurations (including the passwords). It is possible to force your Cisco device to go directly to ROMmon on boot by sending a break sequence in your terminal session in the first 60 seconds of bootup. You can tell you are in ROMmon mode if you are presented with a command prompt that looks like rommon 1 >. Any time you type a command in ROMmon, the number at the prompt increments by one (rommon 2 >, rommon 3 >, and so on).

IOS Loading

Up to this point, the Cisco router or switch has performed only initial diagnostics. With that being said, the IOS itself still has not been located or loaded. The bootstrap's programming has a specific search order which it typically follows to locate and load the IOS. I say "typically" because you can alter the natural order of things with the router or switch's startup process if you manipulate something called the configuration register.

Located in NVRAM, the configuration register is a 16-bit (4 hexadecimal characters) value that specifies how the router or switch should operate during initialization. For instance, 0x2102 (0x signifies all characters that follow are hexadecimal) is a common configuration register that specifies that the router or switch should boot in its typical fashion. However, if you manipulate certain characters in the configuration register, you can manually modify the startup process to load the IOS from locations other than the default. Specifically, the last hexadecimal character in the configuration register, known as the boot field, is the value that dictates where the bootstrap code can find the IOS. The possible boot field values are as follows:

- **0x2100**—When the boot field is a zero, the configuration register instructs the bootstrap to boot directly into ROM and load ROMmon.

- **0x2101-0x210F**—When the last field in the configuration register is 1-F, the router or switch boots normally.

TIP

In older router and switch models, a configuration register of 0x2101 (if the boot field has a value of one), the router or switch would boot a mini IOS located in ROM and commonly referred to as RxBoot. RxBoot looks very similar to the normal IOS; however, it does not provide the majority of the IOS's services. This mini IOS provides just enough functionality to reach a TFTP server and download a working IOS to the Cisco device. You can easily determine you are in RxBoot if the prompt looks like Router(boot)> in a router or Switch(boot)> in a switch.

Assuming the configuration register is 0x2102 (the default configuration register), the next step for initialization is to have the bootstrap search the configuration located in NVRAM to see whether the Cisco administrator has placed a command telling the router or switch specifically where to boot. The tools to do this are known as `boot system` commands. For example, if you have previously configured your device and put in the `boot system tftp c2600-do3s-mz.123-5.T1 172.16.1.1` command, you have instructed the bootstrap to load the IOS file c2600-do3s-mz.123-5.T1 from a TFTP server located at 172.16.1.1.

NOTE

Do not confuse this step with loading the configuration. This is just a step in the IOS loading process that enables the bootstrap code to implement any configuration specifications you previously saved that told the device where to boot. The configuration itself is not loaded until after the IOS is located and running.

If the default configuration register is utilized and you have not configured the device with any `boot system` commands, the default action of the bootstrap is to load the first IOS file in Flash memory. After the file is found, it is decompressed and loaded into RAM. At this point, the IOS is successfully loaded and running on your Cisco device.

What would happen if the IOS image were corrupted or missing? As with many functions of Cisco devices, a couple of failsafes are put in place to keep the device in an operating state or a mode in which you can get it back to an operating state. Specifically, if the Cisco router or switch cannot locate a working IOS file, it broadcasts out all interfaces in the hopes that a backup IOS file is stored on a TFTP server on its connected segments. If there isn't a TFTP server or the TFTP server does not contain a valid IOS file, the next failsafe for the IOS is to boot to ROMmon where you can copy the IOS over via the console or TFTP.

Configuration Loading

With the IOS loaded, the router or switch is now able to apply any saved configuration parameters. NVRAM is the first location where the device searches for the configuration. Here, a file called `startup-config` contains all the previous configurations that were present the last time an administrator saved the configuration. As the name states, this is the configuration that is loaded each time the Cisco device starts up. Similar to the IOS, after this configuration file is found, it is loaded into RAM as well. After the configuration is loaded and running at this point, it is conveniently referred to as `running-config`.

> **EXAM ALERT**
>
> The running-config is the active configuration running in RAM.

Cisco devices do not ship with a complete startup configuration, which is why you might have to initially configure your Cisco device through some means of out-of-band management such as the console or auxiliary port. So the question begs, what happens when you initially turn on a new Cisco router or switch, or if someone erases the startup configuration?

Many Cisco devices attempt to do an autoinstall by downloading a configuration file from an active TFTP server (similarly to the IOS) when they detect that the `startup-config` is not located in NVRAM. Typically, these files contain enough configuration parameters (such as IP addresses for interfaces) for you to Telnet into the device and configure the remaining parameters. If the Cisco device finds an autoinstall configuration file from a TFTP server, the device loads the file and makes that the `running-config`. On the chance that you were not proactive enough to have an autoinstall configuration on your TFTP server, the router or switch prompts you for something called *Setup Mode*.

> **EXAM ALERT**
>
> It is imperative that you can identify the steps that a switch or router follows during initialization, the memory or device architectures where these steps occur, and the fallback sequences when a failure has occurred in the boot-up sequence.

Setup Mode

With non-CCNA technicians in mind, Cisco created Setup Mode so you can build a working configuration on a device without having to memorize the nuances of the CLI of the IOS. Setup Mode is a friendly interactive dialog in which the IOS asks the administrator questions about common configuration parameters that enable the Cisco device to have basic operations. Illustrated in Figure 7.2, the Setup Mode dialog initially asks you whether you wish to continue with Setup Mode. If you answer "no" to this question, you exit out of Setup Mode and are brought immediately to a CLI EXEC session. In addition, if you want to cancel at any point in the Setup Mode and get to the command prompt, you can use Ctrl+C to terminate the setup dialog. After you complete all questions, Setup Mode displays the parameters that you specified and asks you whether you want to use this configuration. If you answer "yes," the Cisco device saves your configuration and applies the settings to the device's operations.

```
      --- System Configuration Dialog ---
Would you like to enter the initial configuration dialog? [yes/no]: yes

At any point you may enter a question mark '?' for help.
Use ctrl-c to abort configuration dialog at any prompt.
Default settings are in square brackets '[]'.

Basic management setup configures only enough connectivity
for management of the system, extended setup will ask you
to configure each interface on the system

Would you like to enter basic management setup? [yes/no]: yes
Configuring global parameters:

  Enter host name [Router]: CCNA
```

FIGURE 7.2   Setup Mode dialog.

> **TIP**
>
> Throughout the configuration with the IOS, you may encounter several different types of interactive dialogs similar to Setup Mode. To save yourself from unnecessary typing, you can use the default value that is located in the brackets to answer any single-answer question by simply hitting the Enter key. For example, notice in Figure 7.2, the `Enter host name` prompt contains the word `Router` in brackets. If you were to press the Enter key at that prompt, this Cisco router would have a host name of Router.

Password Recovery

As the next chapter explains, you can secure access to your Cisco devices in several ways. In times where you inherit a pre-configured device or accidentally forgot or mis-configured a password, you need some loophole in the boot-up process that enables you to regain access to the device. Once again, the configuration register plays a pivotal part in the quest to manipulate the natural order of Cisco device initialization.

The third character in the configuration register enables you to tell the device to ignore any configurations that might be saved in NVRAM. If this field is changed from a 0 to a 4, the device inevitably boots into Setup Mode because the router or switch is fooled that there is no startup configuration. Now, with the configuration register changed to 0x2142, you can reconfigure the Cisco device creating your own unique passwords and save that configuration for future device startups.

CAUTION

Don't Forget the Natural Order   Do not forget when performing password recovery to set your configuration register back to 0x2102. Failing to do so forces your router to constantly ignore your configurations, causing your router or switch to repeatedly enter Setup Mode.

EXAM ALERT

Be sure to recognize that a configuration register of 0x2142 is a typical setting for performing password recovery.

REVIEW BREAK

To solidify the startup process, the following is a recap of the stages of the boot-up, any fallback procedures, and the memory locations involved:

1. POST, located in ROM, tests hardware.

2. Bootstrap, located in ROM, looks at the boot field in the configuration register to locate IOS. 0x2100 boots to ROMMON located in ROM.

3. 0x2101-0x210F prompts bootstrap to parse startup-config in NVRAM for any boot system commands. If it finds any commands, it does what they say.

4. If no boot system commands are found, the first file in Flash is loaded. If no file is found in Flash, TFTP boots. If no IOS file is found from TFTP, the device goes to ROMmon in ROM.

5. After IOS is loaded, the configuration register is checked. If it is 0x2142, ignore startup-config in NVRAM. If it is 0x2102, load startup-config in NVRAM. If there is no startup-config, TFTP autoinstall. If no TFTP autoinstall configuration is found, enter Setup Mode.

Challenge

As you read in this chapter, be aware that many operations are occurring behind the scenes when you gain access to a Cisco device and turn it on. In this challenge, I want you to logically think through what is occurring at each stage of the boot-up process and identify the memory architectures that are involved given the following scenario:

Your night administrator planned to upgrade the IOS on your company's router last night. When you came in to work the next morning, you saw a written note from the night admin frantically explaining how he began the IOS upgrade, but he accidentally kicked out the power cord mid-upgrade and does not know what to do. Unfortunately, the IOS upgrade had to erase the IOS image file in Flash memory to make room for the new IOS. You do not have any TFTP servers on your network.

1. You must initially gain access to the device. Because the IOS cannot be loaded, what is the most logical way to gain an EXEC session?

2. When you turn on the device, what is the first thing your router will do and what memory is involved?

3. The default configuration register is configured, so where will the bootstrap look first to locate the IOS?

4. If you have not made any previous configurations telling the router how to boot, where will it look next?

5. Because the file isn't complete here, what is the first fallback failsafe?

6. Knowing that will fail, in what mode will you be and in what part of memory is that located?

7. What will the prompt look like?

Challenge Answer

To gain access to a non-functioning device, you will need to use some means of out-of-band management such as the console or the auxiliary port. When the device is powered on, the POST in ROM tests the hardware. Because the configuration register is 0x2102 (the default), the router searches for boot system commands in the startup-config. Because there are no configurations stating where to boot, the router looks into Flash. Unfortunately, the Flash memory does not have a complete IOS because the upgrade process was interrupted. With that being said, the router tries to locate an IOS file on a TFTP server. Because the scenario mentioned that there are no TFTP servers on the network, the router falls back to ROMmon in ROM, which displays a prompt similar to rommon 1 >.

Navigating the IOS

Objective:

▶ Manage Cisco IOS

By now, you have a new-found love and respect for your Cisco equipment after knowing all the work that occurs when you turn on your router or switch. What better way to prove that love and respect but by mastering the IOS that the Cisco devices have so painstakingly found and loaded for your administration and configuration pleasure? This section looks at the hierarchical levels of the IOS and what type of interactivity you can encounter at each level.

> **EXAM ALERT**
>
> You will be able to eliminate several distracting incorrect answers in the exam by recognizing the level of the IOS hierarchy the commands will be found.

User EXEC

At your organization, you may have Level 1 technicians who are not strong in Cisco fundamentals; thus, you want to ensure only that they have access to basic troubleshooting and statistics without worrying that they might change the configuration or cause some other network catastrophe. Because a multitude of administrators might need to gain access to these Cisco devices, it makes sense to ensure that the first level of IOS hierarchy they encounter is somewhat limited in the extent of what can be done. This is the nature of User EXEC.

In User EXEC, you are limited in the number and type of commands that are available to you. For instance, the majority of show commands are available at this level of the IOS hierarchy because they do not detrimentally affect the router or the switch to perform these commands. In addition, you can test IP connectivity to other devices with ping as well as remotely administer other devices or troubleshoot all the way up to Layer 7 with Telnet. The Cisco IOS prompt for User EXEC is signified by the greater than sign (>) following the hostname of the Cisco device. For example, a Cisco router and switch with their default hostnames would look like Router> and Switch>, respectively. Figure 7.3 displays the commands that you have available at User EXEC.

```
Router>?
Exec commands:
  access-enable     Create a temporary Access-List entry
  access-profile    Apply user-profile to interface
  call              Voice call
  clear             Reset functions
  connect           Open a terminal connection
  crypto            Encryption related commands.
  disable           Turn off privileged commands
  disconnect        Disconnect an existing network connection
  enable            Turn on privileged commands
  exit              Exit from the EXEC
  help              Description of the interactive help system
  lock              Lock the terminal
  login             Log in as a particular user
  logout            Exit from the EXEC
  modemui           Start a modem-like user interface
  mrinfo            Request neighbor and version information from a multicast
                    router
  mstat             Show statistics after multiple multicast traceroutes
  mtrace            Trace reverse multicast path from destination to source
  name-connection   Name an existing network connection
  pad               Open a X.29 PAD connection
  ping              Send echo messages
  ppp               Start IETF Point-to-Point Protocol (PPP)
  release           Release a resource
  renew             Renew a resource
  resume            Resume an active network connection
  rlogin            Open an rlogin connection
  set               Set system parameter (not config)
  show              Show running system information
  slip              Start Serial-line IP (SLIP)
  ssh               Open a secure shell client connection
  systat            Display information about terminal lines
  tclquit           Quit Tool Command Language shell
  telnet            Open a telnet connection
  terminal          Set terminal line parameters
  traceroute        Trace route to destination
  tunnel            Open a tunnel connection
  udptn             Open an udptn connection
  where             List active connections
  x28               Become an X.28 PAD
  x3                Set X.3 parameters on PAD
```

FIGURE 7.3 User EXEC command display.

Privileged EXEC

Assuming you need to acquire more functionality from your Cisco devices beyond basic troubleshooting and statistical displays, you have to have another layer of the Cisco IOS hierarchy in which you have access to all commands. Happily named, Privileged EXEC is the next level of the IOS, in which you have the same commands as you do in User EXEC, as well as some commands that can alter the Cisco device's functionality.

For example, in Privileged EXEC, you can perform debug commands that can show you hundreds of real-time routing and switching functions and report them to the console. Because this can cause quite a processing strain on the device, these commands are reserved for only those who can access Privileged EXEC. Additionally, some show commands such as show startup-config and show running-config can be seen only by those who should be able (privileged) to see the configuration of the devices (including passwords). Some other new and dangerous commands available in Privileged EXEC include delete, clear, erase, configure, copy, and reload (reboots the device), to name a few.

To gain access to Privileged EXEC, type the command **enable** from User EXEC. After you press Enter, the prompt changes from > to #, signifying that you are now in Privileged EXEC mode. Because anybody can read this section and learn how to get to these commands, it makes sense to have some way for the IOS to prompt for a password to authorize those who truly should be granted access. The next chapter discusses how to apply these passwords to restrict who gains access from User EXEC to Privileged EXEC. To return back to User EXEC, the reverse command is disable.

Global Configuration

One of the commands that you can access through Privileged EXEC is `configure`. This means that we have to enter yet another level of the Cisco IOS to make any configuration changes to the Cisco device. By typing the **`configure terminal`** command, you are telling the Cisco IOS that you are going to configure the Cisco device via your terminal window. The new level you enter after you complete this command is called Global Configuration. You can recognize it by looking at the command prompt, which will reflect `Router(config)#` for routers and `Switch(config)#` for switches.

Figure 7.4 displays a partial output of just some of the commands that are available in Global Configuration. Note that the commands `delete`, `debug`, `clear`, `configure`, and `copy` do not show up in the list of commands. You have a different set of commands available to you at this level of the IOS versus Privileged and User EXEC. This means that you must exit Global Configuration to use these commands as well as `show`, `reload`, and other Privileged EXEC-specific commands.

Of equal note, after you enter a command in the IOS, it is immediately applied to `running-config` and applied to the device's operation. The configurations are not listed and then applied later like batch files or executed compiled programs. Configuration help is shown in Figure 7.4.

```
Router>enable
Router#configure terminal
Enter configuration commands, one per line.  End with CNTL/Z.
Router(config)#?
Configure commands:
  aaa                          Authentication, Authorization and Accounting.
  aal2-profile                 Configure AAL2 profile
  access-list                  Add an access list entry
  alias                        Create command alias
  appfw                        Configure the Application Firewall policy
  application                  Define application
  archive                      Archive the configuration
  arp                          Set a static ARP entry
  async-bootp                  Modify system bootp parameters
  backhaul-session-manager     Configure Backhaul Session Manager
  banner                       Define a login banner
  bba-group                    Configure BBA Group
  boot                         Modify system boot parameters
  bridge                       Bridge Group.
  buffers                      Adjust system buffer pool parameters
  busy-message                 Display message when connection to host fails
  call                         Configure Call parameters
  call-history-mib             Define call history mib parameters
  call-manager-fallback        SRST for Cisco Call Manager fallback. For Call
                               Manager Express configuration use the
                               'telephony-service' command
  carrier-id                   Name of the carrier associated with this trunk
                               group
  ccm-manager                  Call Manager
  cdp                          Global CDP configuration subcommands
  chat-script                  Define a modem chat script
  class-map                    Configure QOS Class Map
  clns                         Global CLNS configuration subcommands
  clock                        Configure time-of-day clock
  cns                          CNS agents
  config-register              Define the configuration register
  configuration                Configuration access
  connect                      cross-connect two interfaces
  control-plane                Configure control plane services
  crypto                       Encryption module
  default                      Set a command to its defaults
  default-value                Default character-bits values
  define                       interface range macro definition
  dial-control-mib             Define Dial Control Mib parameters
  dial-peer                    Dial Map (Peer) configuration commands
```

FIGURE 7.4 Partial Global Configuration command display.

EXAM ALERT

Newer releases of Cisco IOS are making it possible to utilize some of these commands across the levels of the Cisco IOS hierarchies. However, for exam purposes, put on a pair of Cisco horse blinders to this new functionality and focus on the original levels and syntaxes described throughout this book.

As the name states, any configuration that is applied in this level applies globally to the Cisco router or switch. Here we can perform configuration tasks such as changing the hostname of the router or switch, creating a login banner, creating a password to prompt users trying to gain access to Privileged EXEC, and many others. It is also at this level of the Cisco IOS hierarchy that you can enter several different sub-configuration modes to apply specific configurations for things such as interfaces, routing protocols, and EXEC lines (which are discussed throughout this book).

Interface Configuration

Directly from Global Configuration, you can configure interface-specific commands that apply only to interfaces specified in the configuration. Now you can enable the interfaces, assign IP addresses, set speeds, and configure other interface commands. Once again, the commands that are available at this sub-configuration level of the IOS are not applicable at Global Configuration or Privileged EXEC and User EXEC.

To configure an interface, you must specify the interface you want to configure. If the device has fixed (non-modular) interfaces, you simply specify the type of interface followed by the interface number (and remember Cisco routers start their numbering schema with 0). For example, the 1600 series router has a fixed ethernet interface that cannot be removed from the router. To configure that interface, you type `interface Ethernet 0` from Global Configuration. Most devices today utilize the modular configuration in which you have to specify the module number as well as the interface number because these devices can change functionality depending on the type of module inserted into them. For example, to configure the second WAN serial interface on the first module on a 2800 series router, you would `input` `interface serial 0/1` where 0 is the module number (first module starts with 0) and 1 is the interface. The prompt in Interface Configuration Mode is displayed as `Router(config-if)#`, regardless of the interface type. This means you must keep track of what interface you are configuring because the prompt does not specify the type.

Line Configuration

Also accessed from Global Configuration, line configurations are specific to those EXEC lines through which a user can gain access to the Cisco device. Specifically, you can configure options such as logins and passwords for a user trying to gain User EXEC access to the console and auxiliary ports, as well as the 5 vty (virtual teletype) Telnet lines into a router or switch. From Global Configuration, you must utilize the keyword, `line`, followed by the

EXEC line you want to configure. For example, to configure console-specific commands, you would type **line console 0** from Global Configuration. The prompt changes to Router(config-line)#, regardless of the line you are configuring.

Context-Sensitive Help

Even though the Cisco IOS is a command-line interface, it is not without its help features to help you through your navigation of the IOS. Specifically, to see what commands are available at any level of the IOS, you can use the help feature of the IOS, the question mark. By typing ? (no Enter keystroke necessary) at any level of the IOS, you get a listing of all the commands available and a brief description of the command, such as you saw in Figures 7.3 and 7.4.

Quite often, the list of available commands may extend beyond one terminal screen. This is apparent because the string —More— is displayed at the bottom of the list on the screen. To see the next page of listed commands, you can press the space bar and the command list scrolls another terminal screen's length. If you prefer to see the commands line by line, you can keep hitting the Enter key and it displays only the next command each time you press it. On the chance that you have found the command you were looking for in the list, you can hit any key (pause for inevitable "where's the any key?" joke) to get back to the command prompt.

In some instances, you may not recall the command that you are looking for, but you do remember the first letter of the command. Let's say, for example, the command is in Global Configuration and starts with the letter *l*. You could use the question mark and scroll through all the commands; however, the IOS enables you to see the commands starting with *l* if you type the letter, followed immediately by the question mark (no space in between), as demonstrated below. Similarly, if you remembered that the command started with *log*, you can type those characters, followed immediately by the question mark, to see the commands logging and login-string.

```
Router>enable
Router#configure terminal
Enter configuration commands, one per line.  End with CNTL/Z.
Router(config)#l?
l2tp-class  lane   li-view      line
logging     login  login-string
Router(config)#l
```

Keep in mind that many commands in the IOS require a string of keywords to comprehend what you are trying to achieve with the command. For instance, if I was searching for the command logging and hit the Enter key, the IOS would report back an error to the terminal screen that the command was incomplete because it does not understand where I want to send my logging information. If you are unsure of the commands available, once again, you use the question mark for command help. In this case, you must put a space after the first keyword followed by the question mark. The IOS then displays a list of commands that are valid after the keyword logging, as displayed here:

```
Router(config)#logging ?
  Hostname or A.B.C.D  IP address of the logging host
  buffered             Set buffered logging parameters
  buginf               Enable buginf logging for debugging
  cns-events           Set CNS Event logging level
  console              Set console logging parameters
  count                Count every log message and timestamp last occurrence
  exception            Limit size of exception flush output
  facility             Facility parameter for syslog messages
  filter               Specify logging filter
  history              Configure syslog history table
  host                 Set syslog server IP address and parameters
  monitor              Set terminal line (monitor) logging parameters
  on                   Enable logging to all enabled destinations
  origin-id            Add origin ID to syslog messages
  queue-limit          Set logger message queue size
  rate-limit           Set messages per second limit
  reload               Set reload logging level
  server-arp           Enable sending ARP requests for syslog servers when
                       first configured
  source-interface     Specify interface for source address in logging
                       transactions
  trap                 Set syslog server logging level
  userinfo             Enable logging of user info on privileged mode enabling

Router(config)#logging
```

EXAM ALERT

In the simulations on the Cisco exam, you can use ? for help when configuring or troubleshooting the Cisco device. If you get stuck in a simulation, utilize the help feature extensively because you do not get docked points for using this feature.

Abbreviations

To make things easy for administration, the Cisco IOS enables you to abbreviate commands as long as you type enough characters for the IOS to interpret the command that you want to input. For instance, the previous example involved trying to locate the command that started with *l* in Global Configuration. Because there were several commands that started with *l*, you would need to type in more characters to find the logging command. Specifically, you would need to type **logg**, which is just enough characters for the IOS to understand that you want to use the logging command. If you want the IOS to complete typing the command for you, you can hit the Tab key and it autocompletes the command when you provide enough characters.

EXAM ALERT

The simulations on the exam support some of the abbreviations; however, not all of them are supported. With that being said, it is a good idea to be able to type the entire command in case it is not supported for abbreviation. The Tab autocomplete, however, is not supported on the exam simulations.

EXAM ALERT

Some multiple-choice questions and answers may show you the completed command, whereas others may show you the abbreviated one. Do not discount a valid answer if the full command syntax is not used.

Shortcut Keys

To make terminal editing simpler and faster, Cisco has created several shortcut keystrokes that can speed up IOS navigation. The most useful of these shortcuts enables you to cycle through your command history to re-use or edit previously typed commands. You can use both the up and down arrow keys or Ctrl+N and Ctrl+P (if arrow keys are not supported at your terminal) to cycle through the last 10 commands in the history buffer relative to the level of the IOS you are currently located. Table 7.2 lists some other useful terminal editing keystrokes that will help you navigate within a command line.

TABLE 7.2 Cisco IOS Terminal Editing Keystrokes

Keystroke	Function
Ctrl+A	Move the cursor to the beginning of the command line.
Ctrl+E	Move the cursor to the end of the command line.
Ctrl+B	Move the cursor back one character.
Ctrl+F	Move the cursor forward one character.
Esc+B	Move the cursor back one word.
Esc+F	Move the cursor forward one word.

The terminal editing keys discussed so far are very useful for moving within a particular level of the IOS. However, you need to know how to navigate back from those different levels of the Cisco IOS. Namely, if you need to go back one level of the IOS, simply type the command exit. For instance, if you are in the Interface Configuration mode of the IOS and you need to go back to Global Configuration, just type **exit**, and your prompt display should change from Router(config-if)# to Router(config)#.

Suppose you are back in the interface configuration and you need to `ping` or `traceroute` to your neighbor or do a `show` command to verify that the interface is working. Recall that this variety of commands can be performed only in Privileged EXEC or User EXEC. To return to these levels of the IOS hierarchy, you can type **exit** until you are all the way back. You can also use the keystroke Ctrl+Z or the keyword `end`, which will automatically take you back to Privileged EXEC, regardless of how deep in the configuration levels you happen to be.

Common Syntax Errors

As mentioned before, the IOS reports back error messages if you have not provided the correct syntax for a command. The three syntax error messages that you may encounter are as follows:

- **Ambiguous Command**—This error is displayed when you have not typed enough characters for the IOS to distinguish which command you want to use. In other words, several commands start with those same characters, so you must type more letters of the command for the IOS to recognize your particular command.

- **Incomplete Command**—The IOS has recognized your keyword syntax with this error message; however, you need to add more keywords to tell the IOS what you want to do with this command.

- **Invalid Input**—Also known as the "fat finger" error, this console error message is displayed when you mistype a command. The IOS displays a caret mark (^) at the point up to which the IOS could understand your command.

Below is an example for each of these three error console messages. Also notice that this configuration snapshot now includes abbreviations to get into Privileged EXEC and Global Configuration.

```
Router>
Router>en
Router#conf t
Enter configuration commands, one per line.  End with CNTL/Z.
Router(config)#r
% Ambiguous command:  "r"
Router(config)#router
% Incomplete command.
Router(config)#routre rip
                 ^
% Invalid input detected at '^' marker.
```

STEP BY STEP

7.1 Navigating the IOS

1. Go into Privileged EXEC by typing **enable** or **en** (or any abbreviation you feel comfortable with).

2. Enter Global Configuration by typing **configure terminal** or **config t**.

3. Enter the Line Configuration mode for the console by typing **line console 0** or **line con 0**.

4. Look at the list of commands available by using **?**.

5. Press the space bar to cycle page by page or Enter to cycle line by line.

6. Return back to Global Configuration by typing **exit**.

7. Enter the interface configuration for serial 0/0 by typing **interface serial 0/0** or **int ser 0/0**.

8. Exit back to Privileged EXEC by typing **Ctrl+Z** or **end**.

Use the output below as a loose reference of what the output might look like:

```
! Step 1
Router>
Router>en
! Step 2
Router#conf t
Enter configuration commands, one per line.  End with CNTL/Z.o
! Step 3
Router(config)#line con 0
! Step 4
Router(config-line)#?
Line configuration commands:
  absolute-timeout          Set absolute timeout for line disconnection
  access-class              Filter connections based on an IP access list
  activation-character      Define the activation character
  autocommand               Automatically execute an EXEC command
  autocommand-options       Autocommand options
  autohangup                Automatically hangup when last connection closes
  autoselect                Set line to autoselect
—More—
! Step 5
  buffer-length             Set DMA buffer length
***Output Removed for Brevity
! Step 6
Router(config-line)#exit
! Step 7
Router(config)#int ser 0/0
! Step 8
Router(config-if)#end
Router#
*Sep 26 23:40:41.019: %SYS-5-CONFIG_I: Configured from console by console
```

Chapter Summary

This chapter delved into the many intricacies surrounding the Cisco internetwork operating system. Specifically, you learned at least five ways to gain access to IOS. The two out-of-band methods are through the console and auxiliary interface. In-band methods such as Telnet, HTTP, HTTPS, and SSH require some level of configuration of the Cisco devices before you can remotely manage them.

To load the IOS, Cisco routers and switches have to complete a series of systematic stages. Initially, the device tests the hardware and loads the bootstrap code, both located in ROM. If the configuration register boot field has not been manipulated (values 0x1-0xF), then the bootstrap queries the `startup-config` in NVRAM for any `boot system` commands. If no commands are present, the first file in Flash memory is loaded into RAM. If the file in Flash is missing or corrupt, the Cisco router or switch broadcasts for help to any local TFTP servers. If that fallback fails, the router or switch returns back to ROM and loads ROMmon. After the IOS is loaded, the Cisco device can load the startup configuration in NVRAM (assuming you didn't change the configuration register to 0x2142 for password recovery). If the startup configuration is not present, the router or switch tries to autoinstall from a TFTP server. If that fails, the device enters the configuration dialog, Setup Mode.

If you were to cancel out of Setup Mode by answering "no" or typing **Ctrl+C**, you would give yourself the opportunity to conquer the mighty mountain of the Cisco IOS navigation hierarchy because you would immediately enter into User EXEC mode. In User EXEC, you have limited functionality (the majority of `show` commands, `ping`, `traceroute`, `Telnet`, and so on) and would need to use the command `enable` to enter Privileged EXEC to gain access to all the commands at that particular level. From here, you can enter Global Configuration by typing **configure   terminal** to configure parameters that apply to the entire device. Global Configuration can then be utilized as a jumping-off point to enter sub-configuration modes, such as for interfaces, EXEC lines, routing protocols, and many other sub-configuration modes.

At any point in IOS, you can see the commands available by using ? at the command prompt. If you were to get an ambiguous command error, Cisco IOS requires that you enter more characters to a keyword because multiple commands might share those beginning characters. You can easily discover the commands that start with certain characters by immediately typing ? after those letters. Incomplete Command errors signify that the command string required more keywords to know what to do with the command keyword. To see the commands available after a specific keyword, you can also use the ? preceded by a space to see what commands are valid. Invalid input errors indicate that the command was mistyped somewhere. In these situations, you can cycle through the previous commands by using the up and down arrows or Ctrl+P and Ctrl+N. After you find the mistyped command, you can use other terminal editing keys to navigate the cursor to the point where the mistake was made. To exit configuration modes, you can type **exit** to go back a level at a time. To go directly to Privileged EXEC, type Ctrl+Z or **end**.

Key Terms

- configuration register
- boot field
- POST
- ROMmon
- console port
- auxiliary port
- SSH
- bootstrap
- User EXEC

- Privileged EXEC
- Setup Mode
- `running-config`
- `startup-config`
- interface configuration
- line configuration
- terminal editing keys
- in-band
- out-of-band

Apply Your Knowledge

Exercise

7.1 Navigating a New Router

You have just received a new router that you will have to install at a customer's location in two days. To ensure you appear confident in your installation, you decide to take the router out for a test drive so you can be comfortable with the IOS navigation before arriving onsite.

This exercise assumes you have a router to utilize that is not in production.

> **NOTE**
>
> If you do not have an actual router, you can always follow along by using simulated software such as SemSim (www.semsim.com) or Boson's NetSim (www.boson.com). If your budget is tight, open up Notepad and type the commands as you would if you were in the router itself. Practicing these commands and understanding the level of IOS at which they should be typed are critical to your success in the CCNA exam and as a CCNA technician.

Estimated Time: 15 minutes

1. Plug the router into the power outlet and connect your console cable between your PC's COM port and the console port on the router.

2. Open your terminal program and set the settings for 9600 baud, 8 data bits, no parity bits, 1 stop bit, and no flow control.

3. Power on the router and notice bootstrap and IOS decompression from Flash output similar to Figure 7.5.

```
System Bootstrap, Version 12.3(8r)T9, RELEASE SOFTWARE (fc1)
Technical Support: http://www.cisco.com/techsupport
Copyright (c) 2004 by cisco Systems, Inc.

Correcting the backup nv_flash
PLD version 0x10
GIO ASIC version 0x127
c1841 processor with 262144 Kbytes of main memory
Main memory is configured to 64 bit mode with parity disabled


Readonly ROMMON initialized
program load complete, entry point: 0x8000f000, size: 0xc100

Initializing ATA monitor library.......
program load complete, entry point: 0x8000f000, size: 0xc100

Initializing ATA monitor library.......

program load complete, entry point: 0x8000f000, size: 0x17d0954
Self decompressing the image :
#####################################################################
#####################################################################
#####################################################################
############################## [OK]
```

FIGURE 7.5 IOS bootstrap and IOS decompression.

4. Because this is the first time the router has been turned on, a startup-config is not present in NVRAM, so you will inevitably go to Setup Mode. Exit Setup Mode by answering "no" to the question, Would you like to enter the initial configuration dialog? [yes/no]:

5. In User EXEC, type **enable** to enter into Privileged EXEC.

6. Enter Global Configuration by typing **configure terminal**.

7. See what commands are available in this mode by using the question mark for help.

8. Type **l** and press Enter to see the ambiguous command error.

9. Type **li** to see the incomplete command error.

10. Type **line consoul 0**, purposely misspelling the word *console* to see the invalid command error.

11. Press the up arrow or Ctrl+P to cycle to the previous command.

12. Enter Ctrl+A to go to the beginning of the command.

13. Enter Esc+F to move the cursor forward one word.

14. Move the cursor forward, using Ctrl+F, until you are at a point where you can correct the spelling to *console*.

15. Exit back to Privileged EXEC by entering Ctrl+Z or type the command **end**.

16. Exit out of Privileged EXEC by typing **disable** or the keyword **exit**.

Review Questions

1. What is the effect of changing the configuration register?

2. Why would a Cisco administrator use `boot system` commands?

3. What are the memory components in a router and what purpose do they have in the booting process?

4. What cabling and terminal settings are required for out-of-band management?

5. What is the significance of having User EXEC mode in addition to Privileged EXEC mode?

Exam Questions

1. What type of cable would you connect to manage your Cisco device from the COM port of your PC?

   ○ **A.** Cross-over cable

   ○ **B.** Straight-through cable

   ○ **C.** Patch cable

   ○ **D.** Rollover cable

2. Which are two methods of exiting out of Setup Mode? (Choose 2.)

   ○ **A.** Ctrl+C

   ○ **B.** Ctrl+Z

   ○ **C.** Answer no

   ○ **D.** Type end

3. You have just been given a router that will not save its configuration. As you boot up the router, you confirm that despite saving the configurations several times, the router enters Setup Mode consistently. What might be a possible cause?

   ○ **A.** Flash memory is corrupt.

   ○ **B.** TFTP Server is down.

   ○ **C.** The configuration register is 0x2100.

   ○ **D.** The configuration register is 0x2142.

4. What and where are the commands that can alter the location for the bootstrap IOS process?

   ○ **A.** `boot system` command, NVRAM memory

   ○ **B.** `boot enable` command, NVRAM memory

   ○ **C.** `boot strap` command, Flash memory

   ○ **D.** `boot system` command, Flash memory

5. Assuming no `boot` commands, what is the default location of the IOS and what is the order of the two fallbacks?

   ○ **A.** NVRAM, TFTP then ROM

   ○ **B.** Flash, TFTP then ROM

   ○ **C.** ROM, Flash then TFTP

   ○ **D.** TFTP, Flash then ROM

6. Which of the following is considered a typical default configuration register?

   ○ **A.** 0x2100

   ○ **B.** 0x2142

   ○ **C.** 0x2101

   ○ **D.** 0x2102

7. Which of the following are in-band management EXEC methods? (Choose 2.)

   ○ **A.** SSH

   ○ **B.** FTP

   ○ **C.** Console

   ○ **D.** Telnet

   ○ **E.** Auxiliary

8. Which of the following valid commands assign an IP address to an interface from Interface Configuration mode?

   ○ **A.** `Router(config)#ip address 192.168.1.1 255.255.255.0`

   ○ **B.** `Router(config-if)#ip address 192.168.1.1 255.255.255.0`

   ○ **C.** `Router#ip address 192.168.1.1 255.255.255.0`

   ○ **D.** `Router>ip address 192.168.1.1 255.255.255.0`

   ○ **E.** `Router(config-line)#ip address 192.168.1.1 255.255.255.0`

9. If your network does not have a TFTP server and your router's configuration was erased, what will the prompt look like when you reboot?

   ○ **A.** `rommon 1 >`

   ○ **B.** `Router(boot)>`

   ○ **C.** `Would you like to enter the initial configuration dialog? [yes/no]:`

   ○ **D.** The router would not be able to boot.

10. Which two commands will return you to Privileged EXEC? (Choose 2.)

   ○ **A.** Ctrl+Z

   ○ **B.** end

   ○ **C.** disable

   ○ **D.** Ctrl+C

11. Which three components are located in ROM? (Choose 3.)

   ○ **A.** bootstrap

   ○ **B.** POST

   ○ **C.** `startup-config`

   ○ **D.** IOS file

   ○ **E.** ROMmon

   ○ **F.** `running-config`

Answers to Review Questions

1. By changing any of the values in the configuration register from its default value of 0x2102, you are altering how the router or switch operates during initialization. The last hexadecimal field in the configuration register is the boot field. This value determines whether the device boots to ROM and loads ROMmon (0x0). Values of 0x1-0xF indicate that the device parses the startup configuration in NVRAM for any `boot system` commands. If the third hexadecimal character in the configuration register is a 0x4, the device ignores the startup configuration in NVRAM and enters the Setup Mode dialog.

2. The `boot system` commands provide flexible means of specifying from where to load an IOS. This is especially useful if you require specifying a specific IOS file to load in Flash (if multiple files exist) or on a TFTP server.

3. ROM contains the POST program and the bootstrap code for the initial stages of the booting process. Flash memory stores the IOS files. The configuration register is stored in NVRAM along with the startup configuration that contains any `boot system` commands.

4. The console and AUX ports both use the rollover cable. The terminal settings should reflect the following parameters: 9600 baud, 8 data bits, no parity bits, 1 stop bit, and no flow control.

5. User EXEC is useful if you have to give access to technicians who need rights to basic verification commands. Privileged EXEC enables access to the remaining command modes, including those commands that can affect the router or switch's operations.

Answers to Exam Questions

1. **D.** The cable to connect your terminal to the Cisco device's console or auxiliary port is a rollover cable. Answers A, B, and C are cables that are used for ethernet networking.

2. **A, C.** To exit out of Setup Mode, you must answer "no" to the `Would you like to enter the initial configuration dialog? [yes/no]:` question, or enter Ctrl+C at any prompt. Ctrl+Z and the End key are shortcuts to exit back to Privileged EXEC.

3. **D.** When the third hexadecimal character in the configuration register is a 4, the `startup-config` is ignored. This is a useful utility if you are doing password recovery; however, it is important that you remember to change it back to 0x2102. A is incorrect because the configuration is not stored in Flash. B is not viable because the Cisco device looks for a config on the TFTP only if the `startup-config` is missing. C will force the router or switch into ROMmon mode, which means the configuration never gets loaded because the IOS needs to be loaded first.

4. **A.** The `boot system` commands located in the `startup-config` in NVRAM can manually force the router or switch to boot the IOS from somewhere other than its default locations.

5. **B.** When no `boot system` commands are used, the bootstrap loads the first file in Flash memory. If that file is missing or corrupt, it tries to load an IOS from a TFTP server first. If there is no network connectivity or TFTP server present, the device enters ROMmon in ROM.

6. **D.** A normal configuration register is 0x2102. A forces the router or switch into ROMmon. B ignores the `startup-config`. C would load the first file in Flash; however, it is not the default configuration register.

7. **A, D.** The three in-band management session methods are SSH, Telnet, and HTTP. Answers C and E are out-of-band; B is not a management session method.

8. **B.** Without even discussing the actual configuration of the command, the question stated that it must be in Interface Configuration mode, which means the command prompt will look like `Router(config-if)#` or `Switch(config-if)#`.

9. **C.** Without a TFTP for autoinstall and with the startup-config missing, the router or switch enters Setup mode, which prompts you with `Would you like to enter the initial configuration dialog? [yes/no]:`. Answer A is the ROMmon prompt and D is the prompt for RxBoot mode.

10. **A, B.** Ctrl+Z and End return you to Privileged EXEC, no matter in which level of the configuration hierarchy you are. C returns you to User EXEC from Privileged EXEC mode. D is used to exit out of Setup Mode.

11. **A, B, E.** POST, bootstrap code, and ROMmon all reside in ROM. Startup-config is located in NVRAM, and running-config is located in RAM. The IOS file is typically located in Flash memory.

Suggested Readings and Resources

1. Boney, James. *Cisco IOS in a Nutshell*. O'Reilly Publishing, 2001.

2. "Using the Command-Line Interface," www.cisco.com.

3. "Rebooting" for an explanation of the booting process, www.cisco.com.

CHAPTER EIGHT

Foundation Cisco Configurations

Objectives

This chapter covers the following Cisco-specified objectives for the "Configure, verify, and troubleshoot basic router operation and routing on Cisco devices" section of the 640-802 CCNA exam:

▶ **Access and utilize the router to set basic parameters (including: CLI/SDM)**

▶ **Connect, configure, and verify operation status of a device interface**

▶ **Verify device configuration and network connectivity using ping, traceroute, telnet, SSH or other utilities**

▶ **Manage IOS configuration files. (including: save, edit, upgrade, restore)**

▶ **Manage Cisco IOS**

▶ **Verify router hardware and software operation using SHOW & DEBUG commands.**

▶ **Implement basic router security**

▶ **Configure, verify and troubleshoot DHCP and DNS operation on a router (including: CLI/SDM)**

▶ **Implement static and dynamic addressing services for hosts in a LAN environment**

Outline

Study Strategies

▶ Read the information presented in the chapter, paying special attention to tables, Notes, and Exam Alerts.

▶ As you are reading through each section, keep in mind on which level of Cisco IOS Software these commands exist.

▶ If possible, practice the syntax of every command discussed throughout this chapter (and book) with real or simulated Cisco equipment.

▶ Pay close attention to the functionality associated with these commands. It is tempting to focus too hard on the command syntax itself, which ultimately makes you lose focus on the reason you are learning about the command in the first place. The CCNA, ICND1, and ICND2 exams test you on both why you are typing the command and how to type it.

▶ Complete the Challenge Exercises throughout the chapter and the Exercises at the end of the chapter. The exercises will solidify the concepts that you have learned in the previous sections.

▶ Complete the Exam Questions at the end of the chapter. They are designed to simulate the type of questions you will be asked in the CCNA, ICND1, and ICND2 exams.

Introduction

Now that you have a firm understanding how to navigate Cisco IOS Software, it is time to put that knowledge to the test by exposing yourself to the huge number of commands that are available for configuration and verification. This chapter is specifically arranged to ensure that you understand on which layer of Cisco IOS navigation hierarchy each command resides. With the chapter divided into these sections, you will learn to apply these commands correctly if presented with a Cisco configuration objective for the exam and the real world. Additionally, you should notice similarities and form an association between the syntax and functionality of the commands and the level of IOS to which they can be applied and utilized. Having this knowledge at your fingertips will prove invaluable when configuring simulations or eliminating distracting answers on the CCNA, ICND1, and ICND2 exams.

Global Configuration

Objectives:

▶ Access and utilize the router to set basic parameters (including: CLI/SDM)

▶ Manage Cisco IOS

As mentioned in Chapter 7, "Foundation Cisco IOS Operations," Global Configuration commands affect the entire router or switch's operations. Recall also that you enter Global Configuration by typing `configure terminal` from Privileged EXEC, which changes the prompt to `Router(config)#`. This section looks at the syntax and functions of some basic Global Configuration parameters that you can configure in a switch or a router.

> **NOTE**
>
> The majority of configuration commands discussed throughout this entire book can be negated or removed if you type the keyword **no**, followed by the command again. The same syntax rules must apply when removing the command (you must type the command correctly and you must be in the correct level of the IOS hierarchy where the original command exists).

Altering the Boot Sequence

The previous chapter discussed two means of altering the default boot sequence of a router. Namely, you learned that by changing certain fields in the configuration register, you can force the Cisco device to perform actions such as booting from ROM and ignoring the startup configuration. In Global Configuration, the `config-register` command enables you to manipulate those fields and ultimately change the normal default operations of the router or switch.

For example, if you wanted to manipulate the configuration register to enter ROMmon on the next reboot, the Global Configuration command would look like this on a router:

```
Router(config)#config-register 0x2100
```

On the next boot, this router instructs the bootstrap to immediately boot into ROMmon in ROM. The prompt displays rommon 1 >, signifying that the manipulation was successful and you are indeed in the mini-IOS.

CAUTION

Don't Change Configuration Register Fields Unless Necessary   In this book, we mention only a couple of the boot field values and the configuration field values. Do not randomly experiment with the configuration register to see the outcome. You could very well change a configuration parameter that will cause the router or switch to boot abnormally, change the console speed (leaving you guessing what speed you need to use to get terminal connectivity), or not boot at all.

If you accidentally change these settings, you can try to change the configuration register back by forcing the device to go directly to ROMmon mode on boot-up. From a console connection, turn on the device and send a break sequence (Ctrl+Break Key in HyperTerminal) from your terminal window in the first 60 seconds. You see the rommon 1 > prompt, indicating that you are in ROM Monitor. From here, enter the following command:

```
rommon 1 >confreg 0x2102
```

You should see a response similar to the following:

```
You must reset or power cycle for new config to take effect
rommon 2 >
```

At this point, you can recycle the power on the device or type the ROMmon-specific command, **reset**, to reboot the device because you have restored the default configuration register to ensure normal operations.

The second Global Configuration command to globally affect the startup sequence that was mentioned in the previous chapter is the boot system command. With this command, you can optionally instruct the bootstrap to boot from specific locations, and even tell it which file to load if there are multiple IOS files at that location. Two different examples of the boot system commands are as follows:

```
Router(config)#boot system tftp c2600-do3s-mz.120-5.T1 172.16.1.1
Router(config)#boot system flash c2600-do3s-mz.120-5.T1
```

The first command instructs the bootstrap to locate the IOS on the TFTP server located at 172.16.1.1. The second boot system command configures the bootstrap to specifically load the IOS file c2600-do3s-mz.120-5.T1 in the possible event that Flash has multiple IOS image files on it. In examples where you have multiple boot system commands in a sequence, such as the example just given, the bootstrap tests each command in successive order until it successfully locates and loads an IOS.

Changing the Hostname

Throughout this and the last chapter, you saw that the default prompt for a router starts with the hostname Router. You should change the hostname to uniquely identify the Cisco device in your internetwork. This is especially useful if you are using Telnet to remotely manage multiple devices and you need to identify to which device you are connected. The syntax for the command to change the hostname of the Cisco device is hostname, followed by the name you have chosen (up to 25 characters) as illustrated here:

```
Router(config)#hostname CCNA2811
CCNA2811(config)#
```

Notice that once we type the hostname command, the prompt immediately is changed to its new hostname (in this case, CCNA2811).

Creating a Login Banner

It is advisable to display a login banner as a means to provide notice of acceptable use or as a warning to anyone attempting to gain unauthorized access to your Cisco device. In Cisco terms, this is known as the message of the day. This message is displayed to any user attempting to gain an EXEC session on all terminal lines in the IOS. An example configuration for the message of the day is as follows:

```
CCNA2811(config)#banner motd # This is a private system and may be accessed only by
authorized users.  Unauthorized access is strictly prohibited and will be enforced to
the full extent of the law.#
```

Notice that the banner motd (message of the day) command example contains a # character before and after the message. This is known as a delimiting character and is used to inform the IOS where your banner begins and ends. This can be any character, so it makes sense to use a character that is not present in the banner itself. For instance, if the delimiting character were "v", the banner would be displayed as This is a pri.

> **EXAM ALERT**
>
> Remember that the command to configure a login banner is banner motd.

> **CAUTION**
>
> **No Need for a Warm Welcome**   Be extremely careful of the message that you choose in your login banner. A login banner can be useful if you need to seek legal action against an intruder to your Cisco device. On the flip side, however, the wrong login banner can work against you. For example, if your login contains the word "welcome" or similar inviting words, this can be used as grounds for defense for an unauthorized user to gain access because it can be considered as invitation to your device.

Assigning a Password for Privileged EXEC Mode

Objective:

► Implement basic router security

Gaining access to Privileged EXEC essentially means you have access to all the functionality of the IOS, including those commands that can detrimentally affect the router or switch. With that being said, it makes sense to secure access to Privileged EXEC to ensure those who gain access are indeed skilled and authorized to do so. This is achieved in Global Configuration with the creation of an enable password, which prompts anyone attempting to access Privileged EXEC with a password that is known only by those who truly are privileged.

The command to assign a password to gain access to Privileged EXEC can be achieved with one of the following two commands:

```
CCNA2811(config)#enable password myenablepassword
CCNA2811(config)#enable secret mysecretpassword
```

> **TIP**
>
> Be careful not to accidentally put the additional keyword *password* after the **enable secret** command. Otherwise, your secret password would be "password," followed by your actual password. In addition, the commands are case sensitive, so make sure you don't accidentally put the wrong case in the command.

So what is the difference between the two commands? The enable secret password is secure because it utilizes a non-reversible one-way MD5 (Message Digest 5) cryptographic hash of the password so it cannot be deciphered by anybody who can see the configuration. On the other hand, the enable password command is in clear text and can be seen by anyone that gains access to that configuration. In practice, it is customary to utilize the enable secret command for the security that it provides over the enable password command. The following configuration demonstrates a secure enable password configuration, and the resulting prompt that occurs when you try to re-enter Privileged EXEC:

```
CCNA1841>enable
CCNA1841#configure terminal
Enter configuration commands, one per line.  End with CNTL/Z.
CCNA1841(config)#enable secret giforgot
CCNA1841(config)#end
CCNA1841#
*Aug 12 21:46:38.055: %SYS-5-CONFIG_I: Configured from console by console
CCNA1841#disable
CCNA1841>enable
Password:
```

> **EXAM ALERT**
>
> When the `enable password` command and the `enable secret password` command are used in the same configuration, the `enable secret` command overrides the `enable password` command. For example, using the preceding configuration examples above, the password would be "mysecretpassword" to enter Privileged EXEC.

It is possible to encrypt the password used in the `enable password` command by using the following Global Configuration command:

```
CCNA2811(config)#service password-encryption
```

This command actually encrypts all clear text passwords in your configuration, including passwords you assign to the EXEC lines (discussed later). This is useful in case anyone happens to actually see your configuration because the password cannot be distinguished visually upon initial sight. Be advised, however, that the encryption used is a Cisco proprietary encryption, which is easily broken to reveal the actual password. When choosing between this method and the `enable secret` method for secure Privileged EXEC, use `enable secret` because its encryption is exponentially stronger.

> **EXAM ALERT**
>
> The `service password-encryption` command encrypts all clear text passwords in the configuration with a Cisco proprietary encryption.

Domain Name–Specific Commands

Objective:

▶ Configure, verify and troubleshoot DHCP and DNS operation on a router (including: CLI/SDM)

Quite often, you have to test connectivity or connect to a multitude of devices from your router or switch. Unless you have all their IP addresses memorized or you have a trusty topology map with you wherever you go, you might find it difficult to accurately recall their IP address information. To assist you when such challenges arise, the Cisco IOS can statically or dynamically support domain name resolution on the Cisco device. This way, you can refer to the devices by a recognizable hostname versus an IP address.

The command to create a static entry in the IOS configuration file is `ip host`. For example, given the following command:

```
CCNA2811(config)#ip host corerouter 172.16.1.1
```

The IOS automatically forms a name-to-IP association in a host table so that every time you refer to *corerouter*, it translates that hostname to the IP of 172.16.1.1.

In instances where there are far too many devices to create individual static host entries, you might be better suited to have a DNS server keep the hostname-to-IP records. With that infrastructure in place, you can have your Cisco device use these servers for the name translation. The command to specify the DNS sever(s) (up to 6) is the `ip name-server` command as shown here:

```
CCNA2811(config)#ip name-server 172.16.1.254 172.16.1.100 172.16.1.2
```

Given the previous `ip name-server` command, when referencing a device by its hostname, the router will query the DNS servers with the IP addresses of 172.16.1.254, 172.16.1.100, and 172.16.1.2 to resolve that hostname to an IP address.

Domain resolution is automatically enabled on your Cisco device. If you have not configured a DNS server, it tries to resolve hostnames by sending a broadcast out all its active interfaces. This can be irksome when you accidentally type a command in User or Privileged EXEC and the IOS attempts to resolve the command thinking that it is a hostname. To disable this feature, use the following command:

```
CCNA2811(config)#no ip domain lookup
```

One final domain-specific command is to assign your Cisco device to an IP domain. This command has several purposes in a Cisco networking environment; however for our purposes, it will be crucial in enabling SSH connectivity to our Cisco device as discussed in the next section. The command to assign a default domain name to a Cisco device is `ip domain-name` as demonstrated here:

```
CCNA2811(config)#ip domain-name examprep.com
```

Enabling SSH

Objective:

▶ Implement basic router security

As mentioned in Chapter 7, SSH is a secure (and Cisco preferred) method of remote access to Cisco devices because of the terminal connection which uses RSA public key cryptography for authentication and encryption of the data sent over the terminal connection. Because this terminal connection utilizes encryption, two prerequisites for configuring SSH are to have IPsec (DES or 3DES) IOS feature-set on the Cisco device and have an SSH-supported terminal client such as Putty and SecureCRT.

Assuming your Cisco device meets the prerequisites for SSH, the first step in enabling SSH connectivity to the Cisco IOS is to configure a hostname (other than its default) and assign the device to a domain as previously discussed. The only remaining step in the SSH process is to generate an RSA key for the encryption. The default key length is 512 bits, however, it is recommended to have a key of at least 1024 bits in length for additional security strength. The command to generate this key is `crypto key generate rsa` as demonstrated here:

```
CCNA2811(config)#crypto key generate rsa
The name for the keys will be: CCNA2811.examprep.com
Choose the size of the key modulus in the range of 360 to 2048 for your General Purpose
Keys. Choosing a key modulus greater than 512 may take a few minutes.

How many bits in the modulus [512]: 1024
Generating RSA keys ...
[OK]
7w1d: %SSH-5-ENABLED: SSH 1.5 has been enabled
```

Notice how the key generating process uses the hostname and domain name of the device when generating the key; therefore, those configuration steps must be performed first. Also notice that at the completion of the key generation, SSH is automatically enabled.

> **NOTE**
>
> Starting with Cisco IOS Software Release 12.3(4)T, Cisco IOS devices support SSH version 2. Version 2 is more flexible and addressed some active attack vulnerabilities from version 1.

One final element to the SSH configuration is to define a username and password for authentication. This username/password pair will be used when you configure your SSH client to connect to the IOS. The command to define this username and password pair is `username` *username* `password` *password* in Global Configuration. For instance, if you want to use *SSHusername* as your username and *SSHpassword* as our password, the configuration would look like the following:

```
CCNA2811(config)#username SSHusername password SSHpassword
```

Line Configurations

This chapter previously discussed how to secure access to Privileged EXEC by using the `enable password` or `enable secret` command. However, this assumes that any administrators can still gain User EXEC to the Cisco device. The problem with this configuration is that you can send excessive pings or Telnet to another device from your router or switch in User EXEC. Because the ping and Telnet traffic are coming from your private router or switch, they might not be blocked by a security device such as a firewall. This section looks into how to secure access to the User EXEC by assigning a password on the EXEC lines into the Cisco device.

Securing Console Access to User EXEC

Objective:

▶ Implement basic router security

Console access necessitates that an admin have physical access to the device itself. If your Cisco router or switch is physically accessible to non-authorized personnel (not highly recommended), you should take preventative measures to add another level of security by having the devices prompt anybody trying to get to User EXEC via the console port for a password. The following three commands ultimately achieve that goal:

```
CCNA2811(config)#line console 0
CCNA2811(config-line)#login
CCNA2811(config-line)#password myconsolepassword
```

The first command navigates the IOS to a sub-configuration mode for the console port. The second command instructs the IOS to prompt anybody connecting to this EXEC line for a login, using the password chosen in the third command.

TIP

It does not matter if you type the `password` command before the `login` command. The important factor is that both commands are configured.

To add yet another additional level of security comfort, it is also advisable to have the IOS close the console session after so much time of inactivity (no typing) in the session. After the EXEC session is closed, the admin has to enter the console password (assuming the above console configuration was in place) to get into User EXEC again. This is generally useful for those emergency bathroom breaks that arise after a couple cups of coffee or those unscheduled fire drills.

By default, the console session closes after 10 minutes of inactivity which, unfortunately, is plenty of time for someone to jump on to your terminal and change passwords and lock you out if you are not present. To change that setting, use the `exec-timeout` command followed by the number of minutes and seconds the IOS should wait to time out. For example, if you want the console to close after 1 minute and 30 seconds of inactivity, the command should reflect the following:

```
CCNA2811(config-line)#exec-timeout 1 30
```

EXAM ALERT

The `exec-timeout` command identifies how long the EXEC terminal session will remain active when no commands are being typed. The syntax specifies the minutes followed by the seconds.

TIP

The IOS sends all alerts and notification messages to the console port by default. Unfortunately, this sometimes interrupts the command you are typing. To make your Cisco device more polite and stop interrupting you, use the `logging synchronous` command. After it is configured, IOS still send a notification to the terminal session, but returns a new line to the user with the information already entered.

Securing Auxiliary Access to User EXEC

Objective:

▶ Implement basic router security

If your organization has decided to allow remote terminal access to your Cisco device through an external modem or terminal server connected to the auxiliary port, you have added another means of getting to User EXEC that you must secure. The auxiliary port is slightly easier to connect than the console port because physical access is no longer a mandate. As long as you know the phone number to dial into the modem, you can gain access to a User EXEC session. This ease of access should be counterbalanced with security measures to ensure authorized users are connecting to this EXEC line.

Conveniently, the commands are practically identical to those used to secure a console connection. The only major difference is the navigation to the auxiliary port as opposed to the console:

```
CCNA2811(config)#line auxiliary 0
CCNA2811(config-line)#login
CCNA2811(config-line)#password myauxpassword
CCNA2811(config-line)#exec-timeout 1 30
```

Securing Telnet and SSH Access to User EXEC

Objectives:

▶ Implement basic router security

▶ Verify device configuration and network connectivity using ping, traceroute, telnet, SSH or other utilities

Telnet and SSH are by far the most insecure methods of establishing an EXEC session because any user with IP connectivity to the device can initiate a Telnet or SSH session to it. For this reason, the default state of these lines is to require that a vty password be set for anyone to achieve access to User EXEC. Otherwise, you will receive an error similar to the following:

```
Password required, but none set
```

In addition, if you do not have an enable password set on the device, you are not able to enter Privileged EXEC mode. The error you receive in this situation is the following:

```
% No password set
```

EXAM ALERT

Remember, by default a password must be set on the vty lines to give SSH and Telnet access to this device. An enable password must be set to access Privileged EXEC over a Telnet or SSH session.

Once again, the configuration is similar to those of the console and the auxiliary port; however, the navigation of the Telnet lines is slightly different than what you find with the rest. To assign a login password to all the vty lines into the device, you must specify the range of those vty lines in your navigation. For instance, most routers allow five Telnet or SSH sessions into them. To encompass all the vty lines, you have to identify them starting with the first line (remembering that numbering begins with 0), followed by the last (0-4 is a total of 5 lines), as shown here:

```
CCNA2811(config)#line vty 0 4
CCNA2811(config-line)#login
CCNA2811(config-line)#password mytelnetpassword
CCNA2811(config-line)#exec-timeout 1 30
```

The question usually begs, "What would happen if you configured only `line vty 0` or you put a different password on each vty line?" To answer the first part of the question, if you configure only `line vty 0`, the router prompts the first user for a password. If another user tries to connect with that first Telnet session still running, he cannot log in to the router (remembering that the default state is that a password must be set as mentioned in the earlier Exam Tip).

On the other hand, if you assign different passwords to each of the vty lines, you can connect on all the lines; however, you have no means of choosing or knowing to which vty line you are connected. You would have to guess the password within three tries (IOS only allows three attempts).

EXAM ALERT

Be sure you are easily able to supply a configuration to any number of the EXEC lines depending on the scenario given.

Challenge

Securing access to your router or switch is an inevitable challenge that you will face on the exam as well as throughout your Cisco career. In this challenge, you apply the configurations you just learned to ensure that you also secure access from User EXEC to Privileged EXEC.

1. Through your console, connect an EXEC session and enter into Privileged EXEC, followed by Global Configuration.

2. Configure your console port to prompt for a login and use the password **captnstubing**.

3. Reduce the default inactivity console session timeout to 2 minutes and 10 seconds.

4. Configure your auxiliary port to prompt for a login and use the password **bartenderisaac**.

5. Reduce the default inactivity console session timeout to 3 minutes.

6. Configure all five Telnet lines to prompt for a login and use the password **yeomangopher**.

7. Change the default hostname to **TheLoveRouter**.

(continues)

(continued)

8. Configure the default IP domain to be **comeaboard.com**.

9. Enable SSH by generating a 1024-bit RSA key.

10. Create a username **jmcoy** and password **cruisedirector** for SSH.

11. Secure Privileged EXEC by using a command that displays the password **theloveboat** in clear text.

12. Secure Privileged EXEC by using a command that performs the strongest encryption on the enable password, **something4every1**.

13. Which command will allow you to enter Privileged EXEC with them both configured?

14. Encrypt all the clear text passwords in the configuration using a Cisco proprietary encryption.

Your configuration should look like the following (with possible variation on the abbreviation of the commands):

```
! Step 1
Router>enable
Router#configure terminal
Enter configuration commands, one per line. End with CNTL/Z
! Step 2
Router(config)#line console 0
Router(config-line)#login
Router(config-line)#password captnstubing
! Step 3
Router(config-line)#exec-timeout 2 10
Router(config-line)#exit
! Step 4
Router(config)#line aux 0
Router(config-line)#login
Router(config-line)#password bartenderisaac
! Step 5
Router(config-line)#exec-timeout 3 0
Router(config-line)#exit
! Step 6
Router(config)#line vty 0 4
Router(config-line)#login
Router(config-line)#password yeomangopher
Router(config-line)#exit
! Step 7
Router(config)#hostname TheLoveRouter
! Step 8
TheLoveRouter(config)#ip domain-name comeaboard.com
! Step 9
TheLoveRouter(config)#crypto key generate rsa
The name for the keys will be: TheLoveRouter.comeaboard.com
```

```
Choose the size of the key modulus in the range of 360 to 2048 for your General Purpose
Keys. Choosing a key modulus greater than 512 may take a few minutes.
How many bits in the modulus [512]: 1024
Generating RSA keys ...
[OK]
7w1d: %SSH-5-ENABLED: SSH 1.5 has been enabled
! Step 10
TheLoveRouter(config)#username jmcoy password cruisedirector
! Step 11
TheLoveRouter(config)#enable password theloveboat
! Step 12
TheLoveRouter(config)#enable secret something4every1
! Step 14
TheLoveRouter(config)#service password-encryption
```

In this configuration, anyone connecting to the console port needs to enter the password *captnstubing* before gaining an EXEC session via the console port. After 2 minutes and 10 seconds of inactivity, the sessions close and users have to enter in the password again to return to User EXEC. Likewise, anyone accessing the router from the auxiliary port needs to enter the password *bartenderisaac* at the login prompt and has to re-enter that password after 3 minutes of inactivity. Up to five administrators can Telnet or SSH into this router, at which point they all have to enter the password *yeomangopher* at the login prompt. RSA was enabled by using the crypto key generate rsa command and specifying the key length as 1024. The key generated used our configured IP domain, comeaboard.com, and the default hostname of Router (since that was unchanged).

Because the enable password command and the enable secret command are used in this configuration, the password *something4every1* inevitably will be used to enter Privileged EXEC because the enable secret command overrides the enable password. The final command, service password-encryption, encrypts the enable, vty, aux, and console passwords so they are not visible to anyone who can see the configuration.

Router Interface Configurations

Objective:

▶ Connect, configure, and verify operation status of a device interface

Because a primary purpose of Cisco routers and switches is to transfer data between their interfaces, the configuration parameters that you apply to these interfaces dramatically affect how these devices operate in an internetwork. These interface configurations vary depending on the type of interface you are configuring and even which Layer 2 frame encapsulation you are utilizing for WAN interfaces. This section looks specifically at some of the basic configurations that you can apply to LAN and WAN interfaces on a router.

Assigning an IP Address

Recall from Chapter 1, "Standard Internetworking Models," that the basic functionality of a router is to forward packets from one network to another, using logical addressing. If you configure an IP address on an interface, that router systematically assumes that all packets that are destined for that IP address's network should be routed out that specific interface. For instance, if you assign the IP address of 192.168.1.1 with a subnet mask of 255.255.255.0 on a serial interface, the router automatically assumes when that interface is enabled that all packets destined for 192.168.1.x are to be sent out the WAN serial interface.

As you can see, assigning an IP address to an interface plays a pivotal role in a router's primary routing operation. The command to help fulfill that role on a given interface is ip address, followed by the assigned IP address for that interface and the subnet mask. For instance, if you wanted to assign the IP address of 192.168.1.1 with a subnet mask of 255.255.255.0 to the serial 0/0 interface of the 2600 modular router, the configuration would look like this:

```
Router(config)#interface serial 0/0
Router(config-if)#ip address 192.168.1.1 255.255.255.0
```

> **NOTE**
>
> Remember, if this was a router with a fixed interface (not modular), the command might look something like this:
>
> ```
> Router(config)#interface serial 0
> Router(config-if)#ip address 192.168.1.1 255.255.255.0
> ```

The first line in the configuration navigates you to the appropriate interface that you wish to configure. In this case, it is the first serial interface in the first module on the 2600 router (serial 0/0). The second command assigns the IP address of 192.168.1.1 to this interface. After this interface is enabled (discussed in next section), this router forwards any packets destined for 192.168.1.x 255.255.255.0 out its serial 0/0 interface.

> **TIP**
>
> Because a router needs to forward packets between networks, you cannot configure two interfaces with IP addresses that are part of the same subnet. For example, you cannot configure serial 0 for 192.168.1.1 255.255.255.0 and interface ethernet 0 with an IP of 192.168.1.2 255.255.255.0. Because both IPs exist on the 192.168.1.0 network, the router cannot distinguish to which interface to send packets destined for 192.168.1.x. When a configuration error such as this is attempted, the router informs you that the IP network overlaps with another interface and does not let you assign the second IP address.

For documentation and reference, you can assign a description to this interface by using the description command on the interface:

```
Router(config-if)#description This is my first interface description.
```

Enabling the Interface

All router interfaces are in a disabled (shutdown) state by default. It is the duty of the configuring administrator to enable the interface by using the no shutdown command. If properly configured and connected to the network, the interface comes up and begins routing data in and out that interface. An example of administratively enabling the interface with the no shutdown command is as follows:

```
Router(config)#interface serial 0/0
Router(config-if)#no shutdown
```

TIP

If your interface is not connected to any other devices to communicate at Layer 2, you can use the no keepalives command on the interface to keep your interface active. A keepalive is a mechanism that the IOS uses to send messages to itself or to the other end to ensure a network interface is alive.

LAN-Specific Commands

Many of the LAN interfaces on a router have auto-sensing capabilities such as duplex and speed. For instance, a Fast Ethernet interface can run at speeds of 10mbps or 100mbps at half- or full-duplex. It is generally a good idea to manually assign an interface's duplex and speed in case your connected device does not support auto negotiation. The configuration to manually set the speed and duplex on an interface is fairly straightforward, as follows:

```
Router(config)#interface FastEthernet 0/0
Router(config-if)#speed 100
Router(config-if)#duplex full
```

WAN-Specific Commands

When configuring synchronous serial interfaces, you may discover that you have to configure some additional parameters to ensure proper functionality of your Wide Area Network (WAN) interfaces. For instance, when you have a serial cross-over cable between two routers' serial interfaces in a lab environment, the serial interface with the DCE cable attached to it has to provide timing for the network for data to be recognized on this link. The command to provide this synchronous timing on the network is clock rate, followed by the speed in bits per second.

Additionally, WAN serial interfaces automatically assume that the circuit connected to them is of T1 speed (1.54mbps). In instances where you have set a lower clock rate or you are connecting to a WAN service that is using sub-T1 speeds or virtual circuits (discussed later in Chapter 22, "Wide Area Network Connection"), it is imperative to redefine the bandwidth that is connected to the interface for accurate operation of routing decisions. You can achieve this redefinition by using the bandwidth command followed by the speed of the circuit in kilobits per second.

The following configuration demonstrates both of these commands in action for a router in a lab simulating a 64kbps circuit:

```
Router(config)#interface Serial 0/0
Router(config-if)#clock rate 64000
Router(config-if)#bandwidth 64
```

Saving Configurations

Objective:

▶ Manage IOS configuration files (including: save, edit, upgrade, restore)

If you are like me, you like living on the edge by configuring your devices during scheduled brown-outs in a room full of people with size 15 feet who are prone to accidentally kick the power cord out of your Cisco device. The problem with that lifestyle is that when the power returns to your router or switch, the hard work you put into your configuration is gone because all your configurations were made to the running configuration stored in volatile RAM. This is unfortunately true, unless of course, you save your configuration file into NVRAM and make that your startup configuration.

The versatile command that deserves all this credit for saving your hides is the copy command. With this command, you are telling the IOS to copy a file from one file system to another. Some options you have after the copy command are running-config, startup-config, flash, and tftp. The last two are discussed later in this chapter; the Global Configuration command to save the configuration in a switch or router IOS is as follows:

```
Router(config)#copy running-config startup-config
```

EXAM ALERT

Cisco advises that you do not need to save the configuration in a simulation. Despite my danger-seeking lifestyle, I highly recommend you err on the safe side by saving your configuration in case this policy changes in the future.

TIP

After performing the `copy running-config startup-config`, later IOSs ask you for the filename that you want to call the configuration file with [`startup-config`] in brackets. If you hit the Enter key, it saves it as the startup-config that will be loaded on next reboot. Saving it with a different filename saves the configuration, but that configuration will not be the one that is loaded.

EXAM ALERT

If you want to return your router or switch to its default configuration, you can use the Privileged EXEC command, `erase startup-config`, and reboot the device with the `reload` command. After the router or switch reboots, you should enter into Setup Mode because the configuration in NVRAM was erased.

STEP BY STEP

8.1 Configuring Router Interfaces

1. Go into Privileged EXEC by typing **enable**.

2. Enter Global Configuration by typing **configure terminal**.

3. Go into the Fast Ethernet interface 0/0 and configure the IP address of 172.16.1.1 /16 by typing **ip address 172.16.1.1 255.255.0.0**.

4. Enable the interface using the no shutdown command.

5. Type **exit** and go into the Serial interface 0/0 and configure the IP address of 192.168.1.1 /24 by typing **ip address 192.168.1.1 255.255.255.0**.

6. Enable the interface by using the no shutdown command.

7. Type **end** or press Ctrl+Z to go back to Privileged EXEC, and save the configuration by using **copy running-config startup-config**.

THE RESULT SHOULD LOOK SIMILAR THE FOLLOWING:

```
! Step 1
Router>enable
! Step 2
```

```
Router# configure terminal
Enter configuration commands, one per line. End with CNTL/Z
! Step 3
Router(config)# interface fastethernet 0/0
Router(config-if)# ip address 172.16.1.1 255.255.0.0
! Step 4
Router(config-if)# no shutdown
! Step 5
Router(config-if) #exit
Router(config)# interface serial 0/0
Router(config-if)# ip address 192.168.1.1 255.255.255.0
! Step 6
Router(config-if)# no shutdown
! Step 7
Router(config-if)# Router(config-if)#end
00:04:48: %SYS-5-CONFIG_I: Configured from console by console
Router# copy running-config startup-config
Destination filename [startup-config]?
```

Using the show Command to Get Information

Objective:

▶ Verify router hardware and software operation using SHOW & DEBUG commands.

As an administrator of Cisco routers and switches, it is inevitable that you will have to get information and statistics to verify the functionality of those devices and the networks that are connected to them. The crux of every command to view these statistics is the show keyword. This section explains what information you can gain from several of these show commands and tells you how to interpret outputs of those commands.

TIP

Some of the show commands will have quite a lot of extraneous output that may not be pertinent to what you are trying to discover. In some extreme cases, this can go on for pages and pages of output and you could spend quite a bit of time weeding through all the information. To assist you finding specific information, the Cisco IOS now gives you the ability to filter the output by adding a pipe symbol (|) followed by the keyword include, exclude, or begin and the expression you want to filter. Include will only show you outputs that include the expression that you define in the command. Exclude provides the exact opposite service in that it will show you all the output except for the expression you specify. Finally, begin will show you the full output beginning at the point the expression is found.

Verifying Your Configurations

Without a doubt, verifying your configurations is one of the most widely used show functions in the Cisco IOS. What better way to double-check or troubleshoot your configuration could there be besides seeing it displayed right in front of you? One caveat to these particular show commands, however, is that you must be in Privileged EXEC to see the configurations. This makes logical sense because you don't want anybody from User EXEC to see your passwords in the configurations.

To see the active configuration that is running in RAM (that is, running-config), simply type **show running-config**. Similarly, the command show startup-config displays the configuration that will be loaded after you reboot the router or switch. The following example shows the show running-config command, and the output of some of the router configurations discussed in this chapter, performed on an 1720 router with a fixed Fast Ethernet interface:

```
CCNA1720#show running-config
Building configuration...
Current configuration:
!
version 12.4
service timestamps debug uptime
service timestamps log uptime
service password-encryption
!
hostname CCNA1720
!
enable secret 5 $1$nLCr$gNidpLSZvMnm2wFW6ACLm0
enable password 7 14120A0A0107382A29
!
boot-start-marker
boot-end-marker
!
!
memory-size iomem 15
no aaa new-model
ip subnet-zero
ip host corerouter 172.16.1.1
ip name-server 172.16.1.254
!
!
ip cef
!
interface FastEthernet0
 ip address 172.16.1.1 255.255.0.0
 no ip directed-broadcast
 full-duplex
!
interface Serial0/0
```

```
 bandwidth 64
 ip address 192.168.1.1 255.255.255.0
 no ip directed-broadcast
 no fair-queue
!
ip classless
ip http server
!
banner motd ^C This is a private system and may be accessed only by authorized users.
3Unauthorized access is strictly prohibited and will be enforced to the full
3 extent of the law.^C
!
line con 0
 exec-timeout 1 30
 password 7 045802150C2E
 login
line vty 0 4
 exec-timeout 1 30
 password 7 02050D480809
 login
!
End
```

NOTE

Notice that in the output of the show running-config command there are commands such as
service timestamps debug uptime, ip subnet-zero, and so on that have not been discussed. These are all configurations that are created by default by the IOS, and may vary depending on the
version of the IOS that is loaded. On that same note, some configurations do not even show up in the IOS
configuration even though they are configured on the router or switch. For instance, both interfaces were
administratively enabled in this configuration despite the lack of the command no shutdown being displayed on each interface configuration.

EXAM ALERT

One of your best resources on a simulation that has a troubleshooting scenario is the show running-
config command. By looking at the configuration and recognizing incorrect or missing entries, you can
determine what items must be fixed in a particular device to regain connectivity in the simulated network.

Viewing Interface Statuses and Statistics

Beyond a doubt, the next four show commands will serve as the most useful tools in determining interface functionality and the performance of the network connected to those interfaces. Some of the outputs for these interface-specific show commands display similar statistics;
nevertheless, each command serves a unique purpose depending on what facet of the interfaces
you are trying to investigate.

show interfaces Command

The most detailed show command that displays statistics about the status of the interfaces and the network traffic for that interface is the show interfaces command. This command shows you statistics for all interfaces on the router or switch; however, if you wish to view information about only a single interface, you can specify that interface in the command (for example, show interfaces serial 0/0). The output that follows illustrates the show interface output for a Fast Ethernet interface:

```
Router#show interfaces FastEthernet 0/0
FastEthernet0/0 is up, line protocol is up
  Hardware is Gt96k FE, address is 001a.2f66.fa1a (bia 001a.2f66.fa1a)
  Internet address is 172.16.0.1/16
  MTU 1500 bytes, BW 100000 Kbit, DLY 100 usec,
     reliability 255/255, txload 1/255, rxload 1/255
  Encapsulation ARPA, loopback not set
  Keepalive not set
  Full-duplex, 100Mb/s, 100BaseTX/FX
  ARP type: ARPA, ARP Timeout 04:00:00
  Last input 00:00:10, output 00:00:10, output hang never
  Last clearing of "show interface" counters never
  Input queue: 0/75/0/0 (size/max/drops/flushes); Total output drops: 0
  Queueing strategy: fifo
  Output queue: 0/40 (size/max)
  5 minute input rate 0 bits/sec, 0 packets/sec
  5 minute output rate 0 bits/sec, 0 packets/sec
     322 packets input, 70336 bytes
     Received 322 broadcasts, 0 runts, 0 giants, 0 throttles
     0 input errors, 0 CRC, 0 frame, 0 overrun, 0 ignored
     0 watchdog
     0 input packets with dribble condition detected
     343 packets output, 72188 bytes, 0 underruns
     0 output errors, 0 collisions, 3 interface resets
     0 babbles, 0 late collision, 0 deferred
     0 lost carrier, 0 no carrier
     0 output buffer failures, 0 output buffers swapped out
```

A common statistic of most of the interface show commands is the actual status of the interface itself. This is identified in the first line of output of the show interfaces commands. The first part of the status identifies the Layer 1 information of the interface, followed by the Layer 2 line protocol status.

If you understand the interface statuses you are ultimately building a solid foundation to accurately troubleshoot any malfunctioning interface. For example, if your interface is in an "up/line protocol up" state, you have eliminated Layer 1 and Layer 2 malfunctions for that interface. From this point, you can determine whether the problem on the interface is perhaps a Layer 3 problem (IP addressing, routing, and so on). Table 8.1 lists the possible values of this command.

TABLE 8.1 Interface Status Values

Layer 1	Layer 2 (line protocol)	Possible Symptoms
Up	Up	None. Interface is functional.
Up	Down	Encapsulation mismatch, lack of clocking on serial interfaces, missing keepalives.
Down	Down	Cable is disconnected or attached to a shutdown interface on the far-end device.
Administratively Down	Down	Local interface was not enabled with the no shutdown command.

EXAM ALERT

Be able to recognize the interface status meanings and determine the possible reasons for that status.

The rest of the output of the show interfaces command is also extremely useful for gaining information about the interface and the network. Of course, you won't be expected to know all the elements listed in this output; however, Table 8.2 displays some of the valuable common statistics descriptions.

TABLE 8.2 Show Interface Output Descriptions

Output	Description
Hardware is AmdFE, address is 0003.e32a.4080	The MAC address of the ethernet interface.
Internet address	Assigned IP address.
MTU 1500 bytes, BW 100000 Kbit, DLY 100 usec, reliability 255/255, txload 1/255, rxload 1/255	The Maximum Transmission Unit (frame size) for this interface, logical bandwidth (default or set with bandwidth command), cumulative delay, interface reliability, inbound and outbound load.
Encapsulation ARPA	Layer 2 frame encapsulation on interface.
Half-duplex, 100Mb/s, 100BaseTX/FX	Duplex and speed of interface.
Received 0 broadcasts, 0 runts, 0 giants	The number of broadcasts, runts (below minimum frame size), and giants (above maximum frame size).
0 collisions	The number of collisions that occurred on that segment.
0 late collision	Late collisions occur when your interface is set for half-duplex and you are connected to a full-duplex interface.

show ip interface brief Command

If the goal of your `show` command is to get a condensed output of the interfaces' status and their IP addresses, the `show ip interface brief` command conveniently shows you a minimal display of these statistics as illustrated here:

```
Router#show ip interface brief
Interface            IP-Address      OK? Method Status                Protocol
FastEthernet0/0      192.168.100.154 YES DHCP   up                    up
FastEthernet0/1      unassigned      YES unset  administratively down down
Serial0/0            unassigned      YES unset  administratively down down
```

show controller Command

Although the output of the `show controller` command is unintelligible to everyone except for the Cisco TAC (Technical Assistance Center), one particularly useful extract from this output is in the `show controller serial` command. The needle in this haystack of statistics is the line of output that identifies whether a DTE or a DCE cable is attached to the serial interface. This is useful if you are connecting to your router remotely and you are not sure whether your router should be providing the clocking (if you are the DCE interface). The following excerpt example illustrates this useful output:

```
Router>show controller serial 0/1
Interface Serial0/1
Hardware is PowerQUICC MPC860
V.35 DCE cable, clockrate 64000
...output omitted...
```

IOS File Version show Commands

The following section discusses how to back up your IOS to a TFTP server or download a new version of the IOS to your router or switch. Tasks of this magnitude, however, cannot be performed unless you do some initial legwork. Namely, you must perform some essential steps such as identifying the amount of Flash memory, the IOS filename located in Flash, and the current IOS version that is running on the device.

Different Cisco IOS versions and feature sets will ultimately dictate the size of the IOS file and the amount of Flash and DRAM memory required to run the IOS. If you are planning to upgrade to a new IOS, you must make sure that you have enough memory (the more, the better) in your device. To see the amount of Flash you have and the current IOS file stored in Flash memory, utilize the show flash command as follows:

```
Router>show flash
System flash directory:
File  Length   Name/status
   1   5510192   c2600-is-mz.120-3.T3.bin
[5510256 bytes used, 2878352 available, 8388608 total]
8192K bytes of processor board System flash (Read/Write)
```

Typically, the filename of the IOS file in Flash correctly reflects the actual IOS version running currently on the device. However, an administrator can easily change the filename to his or her own purposes, or there could be multiple IOS files stored on the Flash and you are not sure which one is running currently. To ensure the correct version of IOS, use the widely practical show version command.

As the following output demonstrates, the show version command displays a plethora of information well beyond the version of IOS running. Table 8.3 explains some of the useful output of this multifaceted command.

```
Router#show version
Cisco IOS Software, 1841 Software (C1841-ADVIPSERVICESK9-M), Version 12.4(3g), RELEASE
SOFTWARE (fc2)
Technical Support: http://www.cisco.com/techsupport
Copyright  1986-2006 by Cisco Systems, Inc.
Compiled Mon 06-Nov-06 01:23 by alnguyen

ROM: System Bootstrap, Version 12.3(8r)T9, RELEASE SOFTWARE (fc1)

CCNA1841 uptime is 8 hours, 35 minutes
System returned to ROM by power-on
System image file is "flash:c1841-advipservicesk9-mz.124-3g.bin"


This product contains cryptographic features and is subject to United
States and local country laws governing import, export, transfer and
use. Delivery of Cisco cryptographic products does not imply
third-party authority to import, export, distribute or use encryption.
Importers, exporters, distributors and users are responsible for
compliance with U.S. and local country laws. By using this product you
agree to comply with applicable laws and regulations. If you are unable
to comply with U.S. and local laws, return this product immediately.

A summary of U.S. laws governing Cisco cryptographic products may be found at:
http://www.cisco.com/wwl/export/crypto/tool/stqrg.html

If you require further assistance please contact us by sending email to
export@cisco.com.
```

```
Cisco 1841 (revision 6.0) with 236544K/25600K bytes of memory.
Processor board ID FTX1046W1X1
2 FastEthernet interfaces
1 Serial(sync/async) interface
2 Virtual Private Network (VPN) Modules
DRAM configuration is 64 bits wide with parity disabled.
191K bytes of NVRAM.
62720K bytes of ATA CompactFlash (Read/Write)

Configuration register is 0x2102
```

TABLE 8.3 show version Output Descriptions

Output	Description
Cisco IOS Software, 1841 Software (C1841-ADVIPSERVICESK9-M), Version 12.4(3g), RELEASE SOFTWARE (fc2)	The IOS feature set, version, and release.
ROM: System Bootstrap, Version 12.3(8r)T9,RELEASE SOFTWARE (fc1)	The version of the bootstrap code in ROM.
Router uptime is 8 hours, 35 minutes	The length of time the device has been running.
System returned to ROM by power-on	How the device was started.
System image file is "flash:c1841-advipservicesk9-mz.124-3g.bin"	The name of the IOS file that was loaded and the location of that file.
with 236544K/25600K bytes of memory	The amount of RAM in the system allocated to the device's processor, followed by memory allocated for packets. The total RAM is calculated by adding the two values together (236544K+25600K=49144K, or 48MB).
191K bytes of NVRAM..	The amount of NVRAM for the startup-config.
62720K bytes of ATA CompactFlash (Read/Write)	Total amount of Flash memory.
Configuration register is 0x2102	The current configuration register.

EXAM ALERT

Be able to rattle off all the information that you can extract from the show version command, including the current loaded IOS version, configuration register, and total memory of RAM, NVRAM, and Flash.

REVIEW BREAK

Table 8.4 reviews the show commands discussed in this chapter, including their functions and whether they are in User EXEC or both User EXEC and Privileged EXEC.

TABLE 8.4   show Command Review

Command	User EXEC/ Privileged EXEC	Output
show running-config	Privileged EXEC	Current configuration in RAM.
show startup-config	Privileged EXEC	Configuration in NVRAM to be loaded at next boot.
show interfaces	Both	Interface status, IP address, encapsulation, bandwidth, reliability, load, MTU, duplex, network statistics.
show ip interface brief	Both	IP address and status of interfaces.
show controller serial	Both	Microcode of interface, including whether DTE or DCE cable is attached.
show flash	Both	IOS filename and amount of used and available Flash memory.
show version	Both	IOS version, IOS filename, uptime, memory amounts, configuration register.

Troubleshooting Commands

Objectives:

▶ Verify device configuration and network connectivity using ping, traceroute, telnet, SSH or other utilities.

▶ Verify router hardware and software operation using SHOW & DEBUG commands.

Troubleshooting a Cisco device and the networks to which it is connected is an integral part of being a Cisco administrator. Most of your troubleshooting can be solved by verifying your configurations and the device's operations, using the show commands mentioned in the previous section. However, at times you may need to use additional commands to help identify and troubleshoot faults in the network.

Specifically, the clear command in Privileged EXEC resets statistical information that is being stored for the outputs of your show commands. For example, if you saw the output of the show interfaces serial 0/0 command and noticed excessive late collisions, how do you know whether those are recent statistics or collisions that occurred last week? Using the clear counters command resets those statistics so you can view up-to-date information from the show interfaces output.

One of the most widely utilized commands for troubleshooting is the ping command. ping uses ICMP echo and echo reply messages to verify connectivity to IP devices. To ping a specific device from User EXEC or Privileged EXEC, enter ping followed by the IP address or hostname of the device you are trying to verify, as follows:

```
Router#ping 192.168.1.1
Type escape sequence to abort.
Sending 5, 100-byte ICMP Echos to 192.168.1.1, timeout is 2 seconds:
.!!!!
Success rate is 80 percent (4/5)
```

Notice that the ping response contains a period (.) followed by four exclamation marks (!). An exclamation mark character is indicative of a successful receipt of a reply to the ping. The period character indicates that a timeout has occurred for that particular ICMP echo packet. In some instances, you may receive a U character, which signifies a Destination Unreachable ICMP message. These messages are indicative that a router along the packet's path to the destination did not know how to reach the destination network. When this occurs, the router sends a Destination Unreachable message back to the packet's source.

> **EXAM ALERT**
>
> ICMP Destination Unreachable messages are sent by a routing device when it does not know how to reach the destination network. The router sends this ICMP message back to the packet's source.

> **EXAM ALERT**
>
> Notice that in the output of the ping command, the first ping packet timed out. This actually is quite normal when pinging a device on a LAN because the router or switch might have to resolve the MAC address on the data link segment with an ARP request. Any successive pings shortly after should receive 100% of replies.

Similar to other operating systems, you can manipulate some of the options in a ping echo request, such as the datagram size and the timeout period in the Cisco IOS. To specify these options, you need to use an extended ping command. This command requires you to be in Privileged EXEC and is used by typing **ping** followed by the Enter key (no IP address). From there, you can change the default parameters such as the datagram sizes, timeout, and the number of packets sent, as shown in the following example:

```
Router#ping
Target IP address: 192.168.1.1
Repeat count [5]: 10
```

```
Datagram size [100]: 200
Timeout in seconds [2]: 5
Extended commands [n]: y
Source address or interface:
Type of service [0]:
Set DF bit in IP header? [no]:
Validate reply data? [no]:
Data pattern [0xABCD]:
Loose, Strict, Record, Timestamp, Verbose[none]:
Sweep range of sizes [n]:
Type escape sequence to abort 192.168.1.1, timeout is 5 seconds:
!!!!!!!!!!
Success rate is 100 percent (10/10)
```

EXAM ALERT

The extended `ping` must be entered in Privileged EXEC. The command is `ping` followed by the Enter key.

Another useful ICMP utility is the `traceroute` command. As the name states, `traceroute` sends ICMP messages and receives a reply from every routing device along the path to the destination. This is useful in situations where you suspect a router on the route to an unreachable network is failing. The command syntax for `traceroute` is similar to the `ping` command. In fact, you can also perform an extended `traceroute` by using the `traceroute` command in lieu of the `ping` keyword.

```
Router#trace 192.168.1.1
Tracing the route to 192.168.1.1
1 192.168.100.1 4 msec 0 msec 4 msec
2 10.1.1.3 4 msec 4 msec 0 msec
3 192.168.1.1 0 msec 0 msec 4 msec
```

EXAM ALERT

`traceroute` is an ICMP utility that tests the connectivity to a device by receiving responses from each routing device along the path to the destination. It is especially useful when you suspect a router on the route to an unreachable network is failing.

The final troubleshooting command (for now) is another exclusive Privileged EXEC command that should be used only when all other troubleshooting has failed. The `debug` command displays real-time information on such things as routing updates, packet forwarding, and interface keepalives, to name a few. The reason behind the cautionary tone of this explanation is because the `debug` command is very processor intensive and can generate a lot of information on your terminal screen. For this reason, it is highly recommended that you use these commands only in emergency situations or in a lab environment. If you must troubleshoot on a production router, be sure to issue the show processes command as follows:

```
RouterA#show processes
CPU utilization for five seconds: 0%/0%; one minute: 0%; five minutes: 0%
...Output Omitted...
```

The majority of the output will not make sense; however, the top of the output lists the CPU utilization up to the last 5 minutes. If any of these values exceeds 60%, do not use the debug commands. If you do, your router is likely to seize up from over-utilization.

> **EXAM ALERT**
>
> It is recommended to use the show processes command before using any debug commands to verify the router's current CPU utilization.

When you are finished troubleshooting, you can turn off debugging by putting a **no** in front of the command, or you can turn off all debugging by typing **no debug all** or **undebug all**. Specific debugging commands are discussed throughout the course of this book.

> **EXAM ALERT**
>
> If your device is seizing up from too much debug processing, turn it off by using the no debug all or undebug all commands.

> **TIP**
>
> To see accurate timestamps for your debug messages, it is highly recommended that you configure the clock to reflect the correct date and time by using the clock command in Privileged EXEC. In addition, to add a timestamp to the debug output, use the service timestamp command in Global Configuration.

Backing Up and Restoring Configurations and IOS Using TFTP

Objective:

Manage IOS configuration files. (including: save, edit, upgrade, restore)

Recall from the "Saving Configurations" section that you used the copy command to copy the running config in RAM to the startup config in NVRAM. By using this command, you are basically copying this configuration file from one filesystem component to another. Such is the case if you want to back up and restore configurations and IOSs to and from a TFTP server.

EXAM ALERT

The TFTP server is used to back up and restore configurations and IOS images.

A fair amount of setup and preparation is required to achieve this functionality, but the rewards of being able to back up and restore these files are well worth it. Specifically, the following preparations need to be in place for your switch or router to transfer these files to and from a TFTP server:

1. The TFTP server must have the TFTP service running. You can search the Internet for evaluation TFTP servers from companies such as SolarWinds and FutureSoft.

2. Your device must be cabled correctly. If you're using a switch, plug the TFTP server into the switch with a straight-through ethernet cable. If you're going directly between a router and the TFTP server, use a cross-over cable.

3. You must have IP connectivity to the server. In other words, your interface should be on the same subnet as the server.

4. There must be enough room on the TFTP server and your device's memory to store these files. If your Flash memory cannot store two files, the IOS erases the old file from Flash memory before copying the new one.

After all the preparations are in place, and you have verified connectivity between the TFTP server and your Cisco router or switch, you can use the copy command again to transfer files. Remember, the copy command instructs the IOS to copy from somewhere to somewhere. The available keywords, once again, are startup-config, running-config, tftp, and flash. When the tftp keyword is used, the IOS follows up with a few subsequent questions to help the IOS identify the IP address of the server, and the filenames of the source and destination files.

For example, to copy the IOS from a TFTP server to the Flash memory of the router, your command would look something like the following:

```
Router#copy tftp flash
Address or name of remote host []? 172.16.1.254
Source filename []? c2600-is-mz.120-3.T3.bin
Destination filename [c2800-is-mz.123-3.T3.bin]?
Copy 'c2800-is-mz.123-3.T3.bin' from Flash to server
as 'c2800-is-mz.123-3.T3.bin'? [yes/no]y
!!!!!!!!!!!!!!!!!!!!!!!!!!!!!!!!!!!!!!!!!!!!!!!!!!!!!!!!!!!!!!!!!!!!!!!!!!!!!
...output omitted...
Upload to server done
Flash device copy took 00:01:24 [hh:mm:ss]
```

> **NOTE**
>
> Similar to utilities such as ping and **traceroute**, successful copying of files to and from a TFTP server is displayed with an exclamation mark (!).

Similarly, if you wanted to upgrade your IOS to a new version or you want to restore a previously backed up IOS from your TFTP server, the command would be `copy tftp flash`. Remember, if your flash memory does not have enough space for your current IOS file and the new one, the process erases your old IOS file to make room for the new one. If you accidentally lose power during the file transfer, you inevitably end up in ROMmon. At that point, you can download the IOS again from the TFTP server or copy the image over the console.

After the IOS image is loaded to your Flash memory, you have to reboot the device for that IOS to run (because your current IOS is still decompressed and running in RAM). To reboot a Cisco device, use the `reload` command from Privileged EXEC. Do not forget to save any configuration changes that you made with the `copy running-config startup-config` command before rebooting the device because the router or switch uses the contents of your startup configuration when it reinitializes. In many current IOS versions, the IOS reminds you that your configuration has modified and asks you whether you want to save it. Answering "**yes**" to this prompt saves your configuration to NVRAM.

```
Router#reload
System configuration has been modified. Save? [yes/no]: yes
Building configuration...
[OK]
Proceed with reload? [confirm]
04:31:02: %SYS-5-RELOAD: Reload requested
```

> **EXAM ALERT**
>
> The `reload` Privileged EXEC command reinitializes the router or switch. The content in the startup configuration is loaded on boot-up.

The `copy` command can also be used to back up and restore your configurations. For example, to back up your current configuration, you can type **copy running-config flash**. Alternatively, you can always save your configuration to a text file by capturing the text output of your terminal program and doing the **show running-config** command. If you want to paste the configuration back into the Cisco device, just go into Global Configuration and paste the text back into the terminal program window.

Cisco Integrated File System

With DOS and UNIX command navigation in mind, the Cisco IOS has adopted a command structure that can be used regardless of what router platform you are on. These Integrated File System (IFS) commands use URL syntax to specify files in either the device's local memory or on network servers that you would like to see or copy. The commands such as `show` and `copy` are still the same; however, when specifying file locations, you use a URL to indicate the location and file name. This syntax also helps you perform commands like in our TFTP section without requiring the IOS to ask us questions because we are indicating all the information in the command line. For instance, in the previous section, we used the `copy tftp flash` command to download a new IOS to our router. This was followed by a subset of questions to identify the file names and IP address of the TFP server. With the IFS, we could do all that in one command such as the following:

```
Router# copy tftp://172.16.1.254/c2600-is-mz.120-3.T3.bin flash:c2600-is-mz.
120-3.T3.bin
```

Table 8.5 shows some of the keywords we recently learned and shows what they would be using the IFS.

TABLE 8.5   Integrated File System Keywords

Traditional Command Keyword	Integrated File System Keyword
flash	flash:filename
tftp	tftp://tftp_IP/filename
running-config	system:running-config
startup-config	nvram:starup-config

Neighbor Discovery with CDP

Imagine it is your first day at work and your boss wants you to create a topology map of the network, including model numbers, IPs, and IOS versions of all the Cisco equipment. Eager to impress the boss, you want to get this task done as soon as possible. The problem is that the equipment isn't allocated in the same building and your security badge won't allow you into other buildings. Thus, console access isn't possible and you don't know the IP addresses of the other devices to use SSH or Telnet into them. Instead of spending that free time looking in the want ads because you are afraid you are going to get fired, you can call upon a very useful protocol called Cisco Discovery Protocol (CDP) to gather information of directly connected Cisco neighbors.

As the name indicates, CDP is a Cisco proprietary protocol that operates at the Data Link layer. One unique feature about operating at Layer 2 is that CDP functions regardless of what Physical layer media you are using (UTP, fiber, and so on) and what Network layer routed protocols you are running (IP, IPX, AppleTalk, and so on). CDP is enabled on all Cisco devices by default, and is multicast every 60 seconds out of all functioning interfaces, enabling neighbor Cisco devices to collect information about each other. Although this is a multicast message, Cisco switches do not flood that out to all their neighbors as they do a normal multicast or broadcast.

EXAM ALERT

Remember the defining characteristics of CDP are that it is a proprietary Layer 2 protocol that can run regardless of the Layer 1 and Layer 3 configuration. It also is enabled by default and sent as a multicast to directly connected Cisco neighbors only.

The amount of information you can display ultimately depends on the command you use. For instance, the following example illustrates the output of the show cdp neighbors command:

```
CCNA2811>show cdp neighbors
Capability Codes: R - Router, T - Trans Bridge, B - Source Route Bridge
                  S - Switch, H - Host, I - IGMP, r - Repeater
Device ID         Local Intrfce    Holdtme    Capability  Platform    Port ID
Bldg1-3550        Fas 0            128         S I        WS-C3550-2  Fas 0/22
Engineering1801   Ser 0/1          134         R          1801        Ser 0/0
```

Table 8.6 explains the output depicted in the preceding example.

TABLE 8.6 show cdp neighbors Output Explanation

Output	Explanation
Device ID	Neighbor's configured hostname.
Local Intrfce	Local interface in which you received this information.
Holdtme	CDP hold-down timer to keep track of how long it has been since you received information from that neighbor and how many seconds to wait until you consider that neighbor dead.
Capability	The capabilities of the Cisco devices as explained in the legend at the top of the output.
Platform	The model number of the Cisco device.
Port ID	The interface in which the neighbor device sent out this CDP information.

By using the show cdp neighbors detail command or the show cdp entry * command, you can gain even more information about your neighbor Cisco devices. Specifically, you can see all the information from the show cdp neighbors output in addition to the Layer 3 information and the IOS version of your directly connected neighbors. Figure 8.1 illustrates the detailed output of these commands.

```
CCNA2621>show cdp neighbor detail

Device ID: Bldg1-3550
Entry address(es):
Platform: cisco WS-C3550-24,  Capabilities: Switch IGMP
Interface: FastEthernet0/0,  Port ID (outgoing port): FastEthernet0/22
Holdtime : 143 sec

Version :
Cisco Internetwork Operating System Software
IOS (tm) C3550 Software (C3550-I9Q3L2-M), Version 12.1(13)EA1a, RELEASE SOFTWARE (fc1)
Copyright (c) 1986-2003 by cisco Systems, Inc.
Compiled Tue 25-Mar-03 23:21 by yenanh

advertisement version: 2
Protocol Hello:  OUI=0x00000C, Protocol ID=0x0112; payload len=27, value=00000000FFFFFFFF010221FF00000000000000
0D65D04E00FF0000
VTP Management Domain: 'ThirteenBlack'
Native VLAN: 1
Duplex: full

-------------------------
Device ID: Engineering1601
Entry address(es):
   IP address: 192.168.100.5
Platform: cisco 1601,  Capabilities: Router
Interface: Serial0/1,  Port ID (outgoing port): Serial0
Holdtime : 145 sec

Version :
Cisco Internetwork Operating System Software
IOS (tm) 1600 Software (C1600-NY-L), Version 12.0(6), RELEASE SOFTWARE (fc1)
Copyright (c) 1986-1999 by cisco Systems, Inc.
Compiled Wed 11-Aug-99 01:13 by phanguye
```

FIGURE 8.1 `show cdp neighbors detail` or `show cdp entry *` output.

Based upon this information, you can already begin to see the topology layout of these three devices, as illustrated in Figure 8.2.

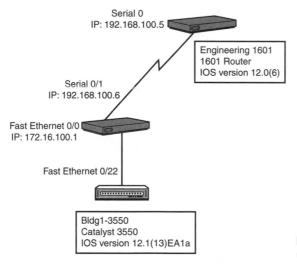

Serial 0
IP: 192.168.100.5

Engineering 1601
1601 Router
IOS version 12.0(6)

Serial 0/1
IP: 192.168.100.6

Fast Ethernet 0/0
IP: 172.16.100.1

Fast Ethernet 0/22

Bldg1-3550
Catalyst 3550
IOS version 12.1(13)EA1a

FIGURE 8.2 Example topology derived from CDP output.

At this point, I am sure you are completely in awe of the wonders that CDP can bring to your administrative duties; however, there are times you may wish to disable CDP. As mentioned before, CDP is a Cisco proprietary protocol enabled by default on all Cisco devices. So what happens when you are not connected to a Cisco device? Although the bandwidth usage is minimal, it still serves no purpose to continue sending CDP advertisements to non-Cisco devices that cannot interpret this protocol. In addition, it is a good idea to disable CDP for security reasons because you can gain so much useful information that could prove fatal in the wrong hands.

You can disable CDP in one of two ways: globally on the Cisco device or on an interface-by-interface basis. To disable CDP for the entire device, you have to configure the no cdp run command in Global Configuration. Otherwise, you can specify on which interfaces to disable CDP advertisement by navigating to those specific interfaces and using the no cdp enable command in the interface configuration.

EXAM ALERT

Keep in mind for the exam that the two commands to disable CDP are no cdp enable and no cdp run.

Challenge

Imagine that the lead engineer has asked you to install a new router in the lab rack. You connect the serial interfaces together with a v.35 cross-over cable and install the router in the rack. Complete the following steps to get the two devices to communicate:

1. Through your console, connect an EXEC session.

2. The cross-over cable is not labeled. What command can you type to verify if your end is the DCE or the DTE connector?

3. To get the two routers to communicate with each other, you have to assign an IP address in the same subnet as the old router's serial interface. You know the lead engineer uses /30 subnets on his serial interfaces, but you need to figure out what IP address he used. What command can you type to find this information from your local router?

4. Enter the serial configuration.

5. The IP address he used was 192.168.40.41. Configure the only available IP address left in that subnet.

6. You have the DCE connection, so provide clocking for a 128K network.

7. Exit back to Privileged EXEC and save your configuration.

To see whether you have a DTE or DCE cable attached to your serial interface, you should type the show controllers serial command. Because the interface is already enabled, CDP information should be mulitcast between your routers. To see the neighbor's configured interface IP address, type **show cdp neighbors detail** or **show cdp entry ***.

The configuration should look like the following (with possible variation on the abbreviation of the commands):

```
Router>enable
Router#configuration terminal
Router(config)#interface s0/0
Router(config-if)#ip address 192.168.40.42 255.255.255.252
Router(config-if)#clock rate 128000
Router(config-if)#end
Router#copy runnig-config startup-config
```

Using Telnet for Virtual Terminal Access

Objective:

▶ Verify device configuration and network connectivity using ping, traceroute, telnet, SSH or other utilities

Telnet is widely used as an in-band management protocol today for remotely administering Cisco devices. As long as you have IP connectivity to the Cisco device and have configured a password on the vty lines, you can remotely administer your Cisco switches and routers. However, it is possible to limit the devices that can Telnet into your devices based upon their IP addresses, which is discussed later in Chapter 19, "Using Cisco Access Lists."

In User EXEC and Privilege EXEC of the IOS, it is possible to Telnet from your Cisco device to another device. By typing telnet followed by the IP address that you are trying to reach, you initiate a Telnet session from your local router or switch. In all actuality, you do not even need to use the telnet keyword. If you just type an IP address or a hostname (assuming name resolution), the IOS automatically assumes you are attempting to Telnet to that host.

For example, if you Telnet from the 28111 router to the remote 1801, the output would look similar to the following:

```
CCNA2811>telnet 192.168.100.5
Trying 192.168.100.5 ... Open
User Access Verification
Password:
Engineering1801>
```

At this point, you can configure the Engineering1801 router as if you were directly consoled into it. However, there may be a time where you need to jump back to your original router to incorporate additional configurations, verify connectivity, or Telnet into other devices. While connected to the remote device, you can suspend your Telnet session temporarily and return to the origin of the Telnet session (CCNA2811 in our example). The useful, but strangely awkward keystroke to suspend a Telnet session in **Ctrl+Shift+6** followed by hitting the **x** key. Keep in mind that this only suspends the Telnet session; the session is still connected and running in a background process.

EXAM ALERT

Know that the keystroke combination Ctrl+Shift+6, *x* suspends a Telnet session.

As shown in Figure 8.3, you can verify the Telnet sessions that have originated from the local device by using the show sessions command. This example initiates and suspends two separate Telnet sessions from the CCNA2811 router.

```
CCNA2621>telnet 192.168.100.5
Trying 192.168.100.5 ... Open


User Access Verification

Password:
Engineering1601>
CCNA2621>telnet 172.16.1.100
Trying 172.16.1.100 ... Open


User Access Verification

Password:
Bldg1-3550>
CCNA2621>show sessions
Conn Host            Address          Byte  Idle Conn Name
   1 192.168.100.5   192.168.100.5       0     0 192.168.100.5
*  2 172.16.1.100    172.16.1.100        0     0 172.16.1.100
```

FIGURE 8.3 Multiple Telnet session example.

Notice that each session connection is numbered and there is an asterisk next to connection 2. This is the last Telnet session that was suspended and it is the session that will be resumed if you hit the Enter key without typing a command. You can also choose which Telnet session to resume by typing **resume**, followed by the connection number.

Ctrl+Shift+6, **x** suspends the Telnet session, but how do you actually close the Telnet session when you are finished? The answer is twofold. You can close a Telnet session from the originating local device by typing the keyword **disconnect** followed by the connection number. From the device into which you are Telnetted, you can also type **exit** or **logout** from User EXEC or Privileged EXEC.

EXAM ALERT

Be familiar with the multiple ways you can resume and disconnect a Telnet session.

Terminal Monitor

By default, your Cisco devices send their notification messages such as debug outputs, interface alerts, and system error messages to the console port. This means that you cannot send these notifications over a Telnet session to another device by default.

To have these messages copied to the vty lines, you need to use the terminal monitor command in Privileged EXEC mode of the device to which you are telnetted. For instance, in the configuration shown, Router A Telnets into Router B and enters Privileged EXEC mode to type the terminal monitor command. debug outputs, notifications, and errors messages are then sent over the vty lines to be viewed by the remote terminal.

```
RouterA>telnet 10.1.1.1
Trying 10.1.1.1 ... Open
User Access Verification
Password:
RouterB>enable
Password:
Router#terminal monitor
```

> **EXAM ALERT**
>
> The `terminal monitor` command copies debug outputs and error messages to the vty terminal lines.

STEP BY STEP

8.2 Telnet Practice

1. Telnet into your neighbor router by typing **telnet**, followed by the IP address.

2. Suspend that Telnet session by using the Ctrl+Shift+6, x keystroke.

3. Verify that suspended Telnet session by typing **show sessions**.

4. Disconnect the Telnet session by typing **disconnect**, followed by the connection number (should be 1).

IOS DHCP

Objectives:

▶ Configure, verify and troubleshoot DHCP and DNS operation on a router (including: CLI/SDM)

▶ Implement static and dynamic addressing services for hosts in a LAN environment

One of Cisco's many goals is to make their routers more versatile than simply just routing packets. Case in point, Cisco has incorporated security, switching, wireless, and/or voice in their line of Integrated Service Routers to provide multi-functionality out of a single device. In that same vein, the Cisco IOS has some convenient features that can provide services to small-to-medium size businesses minimizing the reliance on other devices and servers. One of those services that the Cisco router can provide is to act as DHCP server for a LAN to assign DHCP-enabled devices an IP address, address of the default gateway, domain name, and the DNS server address.

To start the configuration for this service, you have to configure your ethernet interface and make sure that it is up, administratively enabled, and assigned an IP address as described in this chapter. This makes logical sense since this is the interface that is connected to the DHCP-enabled clients. The next step is to logically define the DHCP address pool using the **ip dhcp pool** *poolname* command. Once you enter this command, the router prompt will indicate that you have entered a DHCP sub-configuration mode that looks like the following:

```
CCNA2811(config)#ip dhcp pool examprep
CCNA2811(dhcp-config)#
```

Once in dhcp-config, you can specify the parameters that will be passed to the requesting clients. For instance, to define the IP network scope that the router will use when leasing IPs, you use the **network** command followed by the subnet (not single IP) and the subnet mask in decimal form:

```
CCNA2811(dhcp-config)#network 172.16.0.0 255.255.0.0
```

You can also use CIDR notation for the subnet mask as demonstrated here:

```
CCNA2811(dhcp-config)#network 172.16.0.0 /16
```

Now, when devices with DCHP enabled come online and send a DHCP request for an IP, the Cisco router will receive that information and respond with an IP from the 172.16.0.0 network. In addition it can also be configured to assign the default gateway (which is probably the router), the address of the DNS server, the domain name of the LAN, and specify the length of time the IP is leased by the client. The configurations for these parameters are as follows:

```
CCNA2811(dhcp-config)#default-router 172.16.100.1
CCNA2811(dhcp-config)#dns-server 172.16.100.50
CCNA2811(dhcp-config)#domain-name examprep.com
CCNA2811(dhcp-config)#lease 7 2 45
CCNA2811(dhcp-config)#exit
```

Given the preceding configuration, DHCP-enabled clients will be assigned to the examprep.com domain and have a default gateway of 172.16.100.1, use 172.16.100.50 as a DNS server to resolve domain names to IP, and DHCP lease of this information will last for 7 days, 2 hours, and 45 minutes.

Since we already statically assigned the IP address of 172.16.100.1 to our default gateway and 172.16.100.50 to our DNS server, we want to make sure the router does not assign these IP addresses to device or else it would cause an IP conflict in our network. To exclude an IP address or an IP address range, use the `ip dhcp excluded-address` *ip-address* in Global Configuration for a single IP or define a range of IPs using the same command but defining a start IP an end IP.

In our example, we want to exclude the IP's 172.16.100.1 and 172.16.100.50, so our configuration would look like:

```
CCNA2811(config)#ip dhcp excluded-address 172.16.100.1
CCNA2811(config)#ip dhcp excluded-address 172.16.100.50
```

If we used that 172.16.100.x range for other statically assigned devices, we could simply just exclude all IP addresses from 172.16.100.1 through 172.16.100.254 like this:

```
CCNA2811(config)#ip dhcp excluded-address 172.16.100.1 172.16.100.254
```

To verify what devices are assigned IP's from our router's address scope, use the **show ip dhcp binding** command:

```
CCNA2811#show ip dhcp binding
Bindings from all pools not associated with VRF:
IP address        Client-ID/          Lease expiration       Type
                  Hardware address/
                  User name
172.16.100.2      01e0.041f.a632.a2   Dec 27 2007 11:59 PM   Automatic
```

> **CAUTION**
>
> **DHCP Can Cause Router Amnesia**   When I say router amnesia, I am referring to the loss of memory that can occur when you enable DHCP, especially in larger networks. Since this service requires maintaining all the IP leases it administers, it is possible to consume all of your router's memory resources if your network is too large and you have a lengthy lease time. In other words, use this service sparingly if your network fits the small-to-medium sized mold. In addition, if you have not done so already, upgrade the router's memory to whatever level or whatever budget you can afford to help unburden some of the information it will need to retain when DHCP is enabled.

Some of you may be reading this DHCP functionality and realize that you do not need it because you already have a configured and fully functional DHCP server. The Cisco IOS also gives you the option to configure your router's interfaces to be a DHCP client as well; allowing you to use your existing DHCP server and have it assign an IP address to your interface. The command to do this is similar to statically assigning an IP address to your interface, except you specify the keyword dhcp instead of an actual IP address:

```
CCNA2811(config)# interface FastEthernet 0/0
CCNA2811(config-if)# ip address dhcp
```

The address that is assigned to the router's interface cannot be seen by using the show running-config command since it is a temporary address. Instead, you can verify it by using the show dhcp lease command:

```
CCNA2811#show dhcp lease
Temp IP addr: 172.16.100.2 for peer on Interface: FastEthernet0
Temp  sub net mask: 255.255.0.0
   DHCP Lease server: 172.16.1.1, state: 3 Bound
   DHCP transaction id: 1967
   Lease: 16000 secs,  Renewal: 3000 secs,  Rebind: 16000 secs
Temp default-gateway addr: 172.16.1.1
   Next timer fires after: 00:00:32
   Retry count: 0    Client-ID: cisco-0019.e86a.6fc0-Vl1
   Hostname: CCNA2811
```

Chapter Summary

This chapter dealt with a plethora of commands and their respective syntaxes and outputs. In Global Configuration, you learned how to manipulate the startup process using either the `config-register` or `boot system` commands. Additionally, you saw how to use the `hostname` command to name your router or switch and how to create a message-of-the-day login banner with the `banner motd` command. To secure Privileged EXEC, you saw that the `enable password` command displays the password in clear text; however, the `enable secret` command encrypts the password using a one-way MD5 hash and overrides the `enable password` command if both are configured. For DNS-specific functions, you discovered that you can create static DNS entries with the `ip host` command or specify DNS servers using the `ip name-server` command.

In the line configuration for console, Telnet, and the aux port, you saw that you can configure a layer of security by having administrators enter a password to get into User EXEC. This was achieved by using the `login` and the `password` combo in the line configuration of each EXEC line. Additionally, you saw the utility of the `exec-timeout` command for changing the default timeout for an inactive EXEC session. Because these passwords are all in clear text, you can encrypt them in Global Configuration, using the `service password-encryption` command.

The configuration of interfaces entails assigning an IP address to a physical interface using the `ip address` command followed by the IP address and subnet mask or the keyword `dhcp` for dynamically assigned IPs by a DHCP server. One final imperative interface configuration step entails using the `no shutdown` command to administratively enable the interface.

You know from this chapter that the `copy` command can be used to meet several objectives such as saving the configuration, backing up and upgrading your IOS from a TFTP server, and backing up and restoring your configurations. You learned that the syntax of the `copy` command is copy from a source to a destination. The keywords you can use to identify the source and destination are `startup-config`, `running-config`, `tftp`, and `flash`.

To see your configurations, you now know that the `show running-config` command can show you the active configuration in RAM, and that `show startup-config` displays the configuration booted from NVRAM that you saved with the `copy running-config startup-config` command. For verification and viewing statistics of interfaces, you discovered that the `show interfaces` or the `show ip interface brief` command show you that the interface statuses can be one of the following: up/line protocol up (active), up/line protocol down (Layer 2 down), down/line protocol down (Layer 1 down), administratively down/line protocol down (interface requires `no shutdown` command). What's more, the `show controller serial` command can show you whether the interface has the DTE or the DCE cable connected to it in a lab environment with a cross-over serial cable.

You can sleep better at night knowing now that your Cisco devices, by default, receive Layer 2 proprietary CDP multicast messages from directly connected Cisco devices that advertise the hostname, local and remote interfaces, capabilities, device model, and its hold-down time. You saw these statistics by using the `show cdp neighbors` command; however, you also saw the IOS revision and the Layer 3 address of your neighbors by using the `show cdp neighbors detail` or `show cdp entry *` command. Disabling this useful utility was demonstrated with the `no cdp run` command in Global Configuration or `no cdp enable` in the interface configuration.

In this chapter, you also learned that you can Telnet into other devices from your Cisco router or switch. You suspended the Telnet session by using the `Ctrl+Shift+6, x` keystroke and verified that Telnet session by typing **show sessions**. Closing the Telnet session was achieved by typing **exit** or **logout** while in the active Telnet session, or **disconnect** followed by the connection number in the device where the Telnet originated.

Finally, we saw how Cisco routers have expanded their functionality beyond routing packets to include providing DHCP services for small-to-medium sized LANs. When DHCP-enabled clients send a DHCP request to the router, it responds with an IP address from its configured scope of IPs. In addition, the router can provide the address of the DNS server, default gateway, and the domain name of the LAN. To configure these parameters, you have to define the logical DHCP pool using the `ip dhcp pool` *pool_name* command which will take you into a `dhcp-config` mode where you define the network and other parameters that will be passed to the clients.

Key Terms

- `config-register` *register*
- `boot system` *location filename*
- `hostname` *hostname*
- `banner motd` *delimiting_char banner delimiting_char*
- `enable password` *password*
- `enable secret` *password*
- `service password-encryption`
- `ip host` *hostname IP*
- `ip name-server` *dns_server_IP*
- `ip domain-lookup`
- `login`
- `password` *password*
- `exec-timeout` *minutes seconds*

- `ip address` *address subnet_mask*
- `clock rate` *speed(bps)*
- `bandwidth` *speed(kbps)*
- `no shutdown`
- `copy` *from* to
- `erase startup-config`
- `show interfaces`
- `show ip interface brief`
- `show controller`
- `show flash`
- `show version`
- `show cdp neighbors`
- `show cdp neighbors detail`

▶ cdp run

▶ cdp enable

▶ telnet *IP_address*

▶ Ctrl+Shift+6, x

▶ show sessions

▶ resume *conn#*

▶ disconnect *conn#*

▶ terminal monitor

▶ ping

▶ Destination Unreachable

▶ extended ping

▶ debug

▶ ip dhcp pool

▶ show ip dhcp bindings

▶ ip address dhcp

▶ show dhcp lease

Apply Your Knowledge

Exercise

8.1 Configuring a New Router

You are now onsite at the customer's location and it is time to prove your configuration skills by setting up their router with the following parameters. This exercise assumes you have a router that is not in production to utilize.

Estimated Time: 25 minutes.

1. In Global Configuration, assign the hostname, CstmrARtr, create an appropriate login banner, and use the strongest encryption for access to Privileged EXEC with the password, giforgot.

2. In line configuration, secure Telnet and console access by using the password imnotsure.

3. For the LAN interface, assign the IP address of 172.16.31.17 /28 and enable the interface.

4. For the serial interface, assign the IP address of 192.168.1.17 /30 and enable the interface.

5. Verify the status of your interfaces by using the **show interfaces** and **show ip int brief**.

6. Verify your active configuration and save it to NVRAM.

   That configuration should look similar to the following 2811 configuration.

   ```
   Current configuration:
   !
   version 12.3
   service timestamps debug uptime
   service timestamps log uptime
   no service password-encryption
   ```

```
!
hostname CstmrARtr
!
enable secret 5 $1$PHvQ$Gouu3MIDqY9G5d9hq9tr7/
!
boot-start-marker
boot-end-marker
!
memory-size iomem 15
no aaa new-model
ip subnet-zero
!
!
ip cef
!
!
interface FastEthernet0
 description /28 is 255.255.255.240 in decimal notation
 ip address 172.16.31.17 255.255.255.240
 no ip directed-broadcast
!
interface FastEthernet1
 no ip address
 no ip directed-broadcast
 shutdown
!
interface Serial0/0
 description /30 is 255.255.255.252 in decimal notation
 ip address 192.168.1.17 255.255.255.252
 no ip directed-broadcast
 no fair-queue
!
ip classless
!
banner motd ^C This is a private system and may be accessed only by authorized
users.
3 Unauthorized access is strictly prohibited and will be enforced to the full
3 extent of the law.^C
!
line con 0
 exec-timeout 0 0
 password imnotsure
 login
 transport input none
line vty 0 4
 password imnotsure
 login
!
end
```

Review Questions

1. What is the purpose of configuring passwords on the line configurations?

2. What are the available keywords for the copy command?

3. How is CDP useful to a Cisco administrator?

4. What ICMP protocol commands can help you determine whether you have IP connectivity to a device?

5. What is the significance of x and y in the output of the show interfaces stats output: x/line protocol is y?

Exam Questions

1. You wish to assign the password Cisco to only the first Telnet line. What series of commands will achieve this?

   ○ **A.** `line vty 0 4, login, password Cisco`

   ○ **B.** `line vty 0, login, password cisco`

   ○ **C.** `line telnet 0, login, password Cisco`

   ○ **D.** `line vty 0, login, password Cisco`

2. You just issued the `show ip interface brief` command. You noticed that interface serial 0 is down/line protocol is up. What can be determined by this output?

   ○ **A.** Physical layer is up.

   ○ **B.** Data Link layer is down.

   ○ **C.** You cannot have a down/line protocol is up status.

   ○ **D.** The interface is active.

3. What are two commands that you can use to encrypt the password that allows you access into Privileged EXEC? (Choose 2.)

   ○ **A.** `service password-encryption`

   ○ **B.** `enable secret password`

   ○ **C.** `enable password password`

   ○ **D.** `encrypt enable password`

4. You copied and pasted a known working configuration from a text file into your new router via the terminal window; however, you do not have connectivity out all your interfaces. Why?

○ **A.** You have to use TFTP to copy a configuration.

○ **B.** The font in your text file was not Courier New.

○ **C.** You have to do a **no shutdown** on the interfaces.

○ **D.** The baud rate of your terminal program needs to be set to 38800.

5. What command shows you the configuration register?

○ **A.** `show version`

○ **B.** `show config-register`

○ **C.** `show interfaces`

○ **D.** `show flash`

6. You entered the following configuration in global config:

```
Router(config)#enable password cisco
Router(config)#enable secret giforgot
Router(config)#no enable secret giforgot
```

What will happen when you log out and try to re-enter Privileged EXEC?

○ **A.** There will be no password.

○ **B.** The password will be *cisco*.

○ **C.** The password will be *giforgot*.

○ **D.** Both passwords will work.

7. Which of the following commands does not close a Telnet session?

○ **A.** `exit`

○ **B.** `disconnect`

○ **C.** Ctrl+Shift+6, *x*

○ **D.** `logout`

8. Given the partial configuration output,

```
interface FastEthernet0
 description /28 is 255.255.255.240 in decimal notation
 ip address 172.16.31.17 255.255.255.240
 shutdown
```

Which of the following would you see when you issue the **show ip interface brief** command?

○ **A.** FastEthernet 0   172.16.31.17... up   up

○ **B.** FastEthernet 0   172.16.31.17... up   down

○ **C.** FastEthernet 0   172.16.31.17... down   up

○ **D.** FastEthernet 0   172.16.31.17... administratively down down

9. Given the following output, what can be determined about this interface? (Choose 2.)

```
FastEthernet0/0 is up, line protocol is up
   Hardware is AmdFE, address is 0003.e32a.4080 (bia 0003.e32a.4080)
   Internet address is 172.16.1.1/16
   MTU 1500 bytes, BW 100000 Kbit, DLY 100 usec,
      reliablility 255/255, txload 235/255, rxload 235/255
   Encapsulation ARPA, loopback not set
   Keepalive set (10 sec)
   Half-duplex, 100Mb/s, 100BaseTX/FX
   ARP type: ARPA, ARP Timeout 04:00:00
   Last input never, output 00:00:10, output hang never
   Last clearing of "show interface" counters never
   Queueing strategy: fifo
   Output queue 0/40, 0 drops; input queue 0/75, 0 drops
   5 minute input rate 0 bits/sec, 0 packets/sec
   5 minute output rate 0 bits/sec, 0 packets/sec
      0 packets input, 0 bytes
      Received 0 broadcasts, 0 runts, 0 giants, 0 throttles
      0 input errors, 0 CRC, 0 frame, 0 overrun, 0 ignored
      0 watchdog, 0 multicast
      0 input packets with dribble condition detected
      31 packets output, 2673 bytes, 0 underruns
      0 output errors, 0 collisions, 1 interface resets
      0 babbles, 156848 late collision, 0 deferred
      0 lost carrier, 0 no carrier
      0 output buffer failures, 0 output buffers swapped out
```

○ **A.** There is a duplex mismatch.

○ **B.** The administrator needs to do a no shutdown on this interface.

○ **C.** The bandwidth is incorrect.

○ **D.** This link is congested.

10. Given the following output, how can you reconnect to Telnet session 2? (Choose 2.)

```
CCNA2811#show sessions
Conn    Host                   Address          Idle   Conn Name
 1      131.108.100.152        131.108.100.152   0      131.108.100.152
*2      126.102.57.63          126.102.57.63     0      126.102.57.63
```

○ **A.** disconnect 2

○ **B.** Enter

○ **C.** Ctrl+Shift+6, *x*

○ **D.** resume 2

○ **E.** logout

11. Which of the following is not a necessary step in copying configuration and IOS files to and from your Cisco router and switch and a local TFTP server?

○ **A.** The TFTP server software must be running.

○ **B.** Your router should be directly connected with a straight-through cable.

○ **C.** Your interface must be on the same subnet as the TFTP server.

○ **D.** You should test whether you have IP connectivity by pinging the server from your router.

12. What command assigns the last IP address in the 10th subnet of the network 192.168.100.0/29? Zero subnets are allowed.

○ **A.** ip address 192.168.100.80 255.255.255.240

○ **B.** ip address 192.168.100.79 255.255.255.248

○ **C.** ip address 192.168.100.70 255.255.255.240

○ **D.** ip address 192.168.100.73 255.255.255.248

○ **E.** ip address 192.168.100.78 255.255.255.248

13. Given the following output,

```
Router>show flash
System flash directory:
File  Length    Name/status
  1   5510192   c2800-is-mz.123-3.T3.bin
[5510256 bytes used, 2878352 available, 8388608 total]
8192K bytes of processor board System flash (Read/Write)
```

What is the command used and what will be the outcome of upgrading to a 7KB IOS file from a TFTP server?

○ **A. copy tftp ios**, the current IOS file will be erased.

○ **B. copy flash tftp**, the current IOS will be unchanged.

○ **C. copy tftp flash**, the current IOS file will be erased.

○ **D. copy tftp flash**, the new IOS file is too large and it will go into ROMmom.

Answers to Review Questions

1. The password configurations on the terminal lines serve as a way to protect your router or switch from anyone gaining access to User EXEC.

2. The **copy** command tells the Cisco device to copy a file from somewhere to somewhere. The available keyword options for the copy command are **startup-config, running-config, tftp,** and **flash**.

3. CDP enables Cisco administrators to gain information from directly connected Cisco devices without requiring that they be connected with a terminal session. The **show cdp neighbors detail** or **show cdp entry *** command displays the Layer 3 address and the IOS version of the neighbors.

4. **ping** and **traceroute** use ICMP to test IP connectivity. **ping** tests if one device has connectivity to another device. **traceroute** displays the path the packets take to reach the destination. **traceroute** is useful for determining faulty routers along the path to the destination.

5. Given the show interfaces output x/line protocol is y, x represents the Physical layer status of the interface. y represents the Data Link layer status.

Answers to Exam Questions

1. **D.** To assign a login prompt and password for only the first vty line, you have to navigate to line vty 0. Answer A is incorrect because `line vty 0 4` is configuring all 5 vty lines. B has the correct navigation; however, the password is case sensitive. C is incorrect because the navigation to enter the Telnet lines is `line vty 0`.

2. **C.** The first part of the `show ip interface brief` command represents the status of the Physical layer, followed by the Data Link layer status. It is impossible to have this output because you cannot have Layer 2 without Layer 1 functionality. Answer A is incorrect because the Physical layer represented on the left side of the forward slash is down. B is also false because the Data Link layer represented on the right side of the forward slash is up. D is incorrect because an active interface is up/line protocol is up.

3. **A, B.** The `enable secret` command encrypts the password with a one-way MD5 hash. The `service password-encryption` encrypts the `enable password` command and all other clear text passwords. C is incorrect because the command does not encrypt the password. D is not a valid command.

4. **C.** The configuration was saved to Notepad through the use of the `show running-config` command and copied from the terminal window into the file. The problem that occurs is that the `no shutdown` command does not display in the configuration, which means when the configuration is pasted back into a new router, the interfaces are still administratively shut. A is incorrect because you do not require TFTP to copy configurations that are saved in a text file on your computer. B is false because the font is not essential. D is incorrect because the baud rate does not need to be changed.

5. **A.** `show version` displays the current configuration at the bottom of the command output. Answer B is incorrect because the command does not exist. Answers C and D are valid commands, but they will not display the configuration register.

6. **B.** If the `enable secret` and `enable password` command are in the same configuration, `enable secret` overrides `enable password`. However, the example removed the `enable secret` command, leaving only `enable password` left in the configuration. Thus, the password to get into Privileged EXEC is *cisco*. A is incorrect because the `enable password` command was not removed. C and D are incorrect because the `enable secret` password was removed from the configuration.

7. **C.** `Ctrl+Shift+6, x` suspends the Telnet session. Answers A, B, and D are incorrect because those commands will actually disconnect the Telnet session.

8. **D.** Because the interface configuration is configured in a shutdown state, the interface status should report the fast ethernet interface as administratively down/line protocol is down. Answers A, B, and C are incorrect because a shutdown interface does not have the Physical layer or the Data Link layer in an up state.

9. **A, D.** Because there is an excessive number of late collisions in the output, it is safe to assume that there is a duplex mismatch. Also, the link is 92% congested as indicated by the load statements (235/255). B is incorrect because the interface status is up/line protocol is up. C is incorrect because the bandwidth is accurate for a FastEthernet interface.

10. **B, D.** You can resume the suspended Telnet sessions in this device by hitting the Enter key or typing the keyword, `resume`. Answers A and E disconnect the Telnet session and C suspends it.

11. **B.** If connecting directly to a TFTP server from a router, you must use a cross-over cable. Answers A, C, and D are necessary steps to copy files to and from a TFTP server.

12. **E.** With a /29 or 255.255.255.248 subnet, the increment of these subnets is 8. Starting with 0, counting 10 networks gives you a Network/Subnet identifier of 192.168.100.72 (0,8,16,24,32,40,48,56,64,72). The last IP address in that subnet is 192.168.100.78. Answer A is a network ID and the wrong subnet mask. Answer B is the broadcast address for that subnet. Answer C is that last IP address in ninth subnet with the wrong subnet mask. D is the first valid IP address in that subnet.

13. **C.** The command to upload your IOS from a TFTP server is `copy tftp flash`. Given the `show flash` output, there is not enough space for another 7KB file, so the current IOS file will be erased during the copy process, after which the actual download of the new IOS will occur. Answer A is incorrect because the `ios` keyword does not exist. B is false because there is not enough room in Flash for both files, so the current IOS is will be erased.

Suggested Readings and Resources

1. Odom, Wendell. *CCENT/CCNA ICND1 Official Exam Certification Guide (CCENT Exam 640-822 and CCNA Exam 640-802), 2nd Edition*, Cisco Press Publishing, 2007.

2. Boney, James. *Cisco IOS in a Nutshell*, O'Reilly Publishing, 2001.

3. "Configuration Fundamentals Command Reference," www.cisco.com.

CHAPTER NINE

Understanding the Cisco SDM

Objective

This chapter covers the following Cisco-specified objective for the "Configure, verify, and troubleshoot basic router operation and routing on Cisco devices" section of the 640-802 CCNA exam:

▶ **Access and utilize the router to set basic parameters (including: CLI/SDM)**

Outline

Study Strategies

▶ Practice using the SDM in a lab environment.

▶ Learn how to set up basic router operation on an SDM-capable device.

Introduction

The Cisco Security Device Manager (SDM) is a web-based tool that was developed by Cisco for its IOS software-based routers. The SDM tool gives users the option to configure and monitor a router without using CLI. Chapter 8, "Foundation Cisco Configurations," covers a large number of CLI commands. This chapter reviews how to use the SDM tool for router configuration, verification, and monitoring from a web browser.

Getting Started

Only certain router models with more current IOS versions support SDM. For a complete list of router models and supported IOS versions, check http://www.cisco.com. This chapter demonstrates the SDM using a Cisco 851W router. This model router comes from Cisco with a "Cisco Router and Security Device Manager" CD. Cisco SDM Express is also installed on the router flash. If you are uncertain whether SDM is installed on the router flash, you can open a web browser and enter http://*insert router IP address here* in the address field to see if the SDM page loads. Note that a prerequisite to using SDM is an IP-configured interface that is in an administratively up/up state. This means that you need to manually configure that interface with an IP address and subnet mask and perform a `no shut` command before SDM will work. While you are logged into the router manually, also add the command `ip https` to allow for browser connectivity. Finally, ensure that the router does not have an access list in place that blocks the incoming HTTPS connection. Other outside factors might also prevent SDM from loading properly, such as services or Java plugins on the connected computer.

Figure 9.1 shows the welcome page that loads when you open the Cisco Router and Security Device Manager CD.

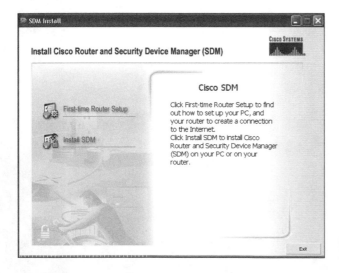

FIGURE 9.1 Install Cisco Router and Security Device Manager (SDM).

From this screen you can choose First-time Router Setup or Install SDM. Figure 9.2 explains First-time Router Setup. If SDM is not already installed, you go through the step in First-time Router Setup and then choose Install SDM.

FIGURE 9.2 Install Cisco Router and Security Device Manager (SDM): First-time Router Setup.

If you click First-time Router Setup, you are routed to an HTML file with detailed connection instructions. There is also a drop-down box where you may select the router model for more specific model details, as shown in Figure 9.3. The drop-down box shows models 831, 836, and 837, but selecting this option also works for the 851 model router.

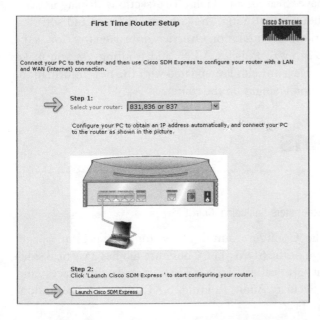

FIGURE 9.3 First-time Router Setup: Select your router.

After you have successfully connected to the SDM, a separate window opens, as shown in Figure 9.4.

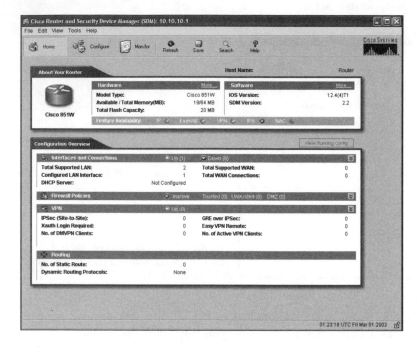

FIGURE 9.4 Cisco Router and Security Device Manager (SDM): Home.

As you can see in Figure 9.4, the SDM home page has clickable buttons across the top labeled Home, Configure, Monitor, Refresh, Save, Search, and Help. Two sections display general router information. The top section, About Your Router, shows basic hardware and software details about the router. The bottom section, Configuration Overview, is broken into four subcategories: Interfaces and Connections, Firewall Policies, VPN, and Routing. As you make configuration changes to the router, the relevant fields are updated with the new information. Let's move on and make some configuration changes on the router.

Global Configurations

Objective:

▶ Access and utilize the router to set basic parameters (including: CLI/SDM)

To begin router configurations, click the Configure button at the top of the Home page. Figure 9.5 shows the main Configure page of the SDM. The Configure tab has a vertical sidebar with more clickable options that are called Tasks. They include Interfaces and Connections, Firewall and ACL, VPN, Security Audit, Routing, NAT, Intrusion Prevention, Quality of Service, NAC, and Additional Tasks.

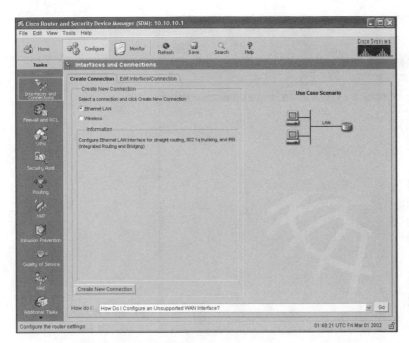

FIGURE 9.5 Configure Interfaces and Connections.

Changing the Hostname, Banner, Domain Name, and Secret Password

From the Configure page, click Additional Tasks in the left vertical sidebar. The Additional Tasks page opens, as shown in Figure 9.6. It has a list of additional tasks and a list of device properties. When expanded, Router Properties shows a few configurable items, including hostname, domain name, banner, and the enable secret password.

Double-click any of the item names to open a new window, as shown in Figure 9.7. Here you can change the router's hostname, domain name, banner, and secret password all in one window.

This window has two tabs. On the Device tab, click in each field and enter the desired Host (hostname), Domain (domain name), and Banner (message of the day). Figure 9.8 shows a sample configuration.

Click the Secret Password tab, shown in Figure 9.9, and enter a new password twice. Note that the window represents your password with asterisks.

FIGURE 9.6 Configure, Additional Tasks.

FIGURE 9.7 The Device Properties window.

FIGURE 9.8 Hostname, domain, and banner configuration.

FIGURE 9.9 Secret password configuration.

After you have entered a new hostname, domain name, banner, and enable secret password, click OK at the bottom of the window. The SDM automatically sends the new configuration commands to the router, as shown in Figure 9.10. Click OK again to close that window and return to the Additional Tasks page.

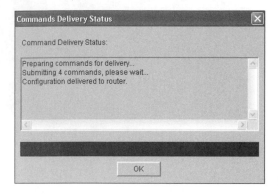

FIGURE 9.10   Commands Delivery Status window.

If you return to the Home page at this point, you see your router's new hostname in the top-right corner, as shown in Figure 9.11. You can also click the View Running Config button to see the current configuration of your router.

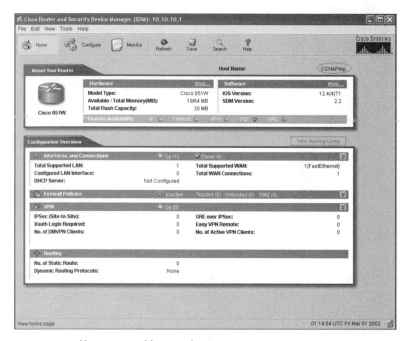

FIGURE 9.11   Home page with a new hostname.

Challenge

From the Cisco SDM, configure the following information on the router:

Host: CCNAPrep

Domain: examprep.com

Banner: This is a private system and may be accessed only by authorized users. Unauthorized access is strictly prohibited and will be enforced to the full extent of the law.

Secret Password: mysecretpassword

NOTE

After you click OK, the router prompts you to enter the new secret password information. Leave the username field blank, and enter your secret password to keep the SDM session connected.

Router Access

There is another way to configure username and password information using the SDM. On the Additional Tasks page, click Router Access to see what options can be configured using this tool, as shown in Figure 9.12.

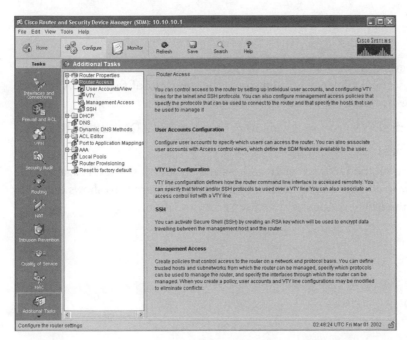

FIGURE 9.12 Configure, Additional Tasks, Router Access.

Click User Accounts/View. You see a line item with the secret password entry you created in the preceding section with a privilege level of 15 and a username of cisco. If the line item is highlighted, click the Edit option in the top right of the window. You now have the option to change the username, password, and privilege level of this account, as shown in Figure 9.13.

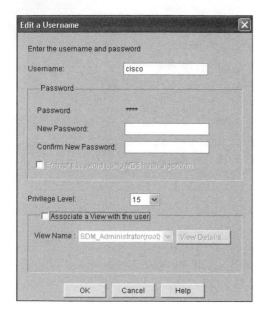

FIGURE 9.13   Edit a username.

DNS

To configure DNS server information in the SDM, click DNS on the Additional Tasks page. In the DNS Properties section, click the Edit button at the top right of the page. A separate DNS Properties window opens, as shown in Figure 9.14.

Click the Add button in the DNS properties window to open the Add a DNS server IP address window, shown in Figure 9.15.

In this window you can input the DNS server IP address and click OK. Click OK again in the DNS properties window to add the configurations to the router. Figure 9.16 shows the DNS properties section with the newly configured DNS server information.

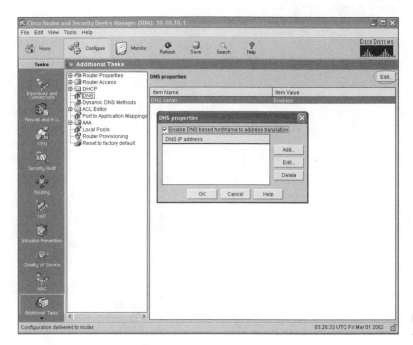

FIGURE 9.14 Configure, Additional Tasks, DNS.

FIGURE 9.15 Add a DNS server IP address window.

FIGURE 9.16 DNS properties with a new DNS server.

DHCP

From the Additional Tasks page you can also add a DHCP pool to the router. Click DHCP to see the two options for DHCP configurations: DHCP Pools and DHCP Bindings (see Figure 9.17).

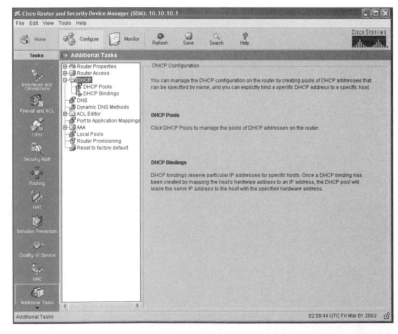

FIGURE 9.17 Configure, Additional Tasks, DHCP.

In the DHCP drop-down menu, click DHCP Pools, and then click the Add button at the top right of the page. A separate window called Add DHCP Pool opens, as shown in Figure 9.17. The DHCP Pool Name, DHCP Pool Network, Subnet mask, Starting IP, and Ending IP fields are mandatory. The Lease Length section is automatically filled in by the SDM, but you can change it to meet your individual requirements. The remaining fields are optional. Figure 9.18 shows the Add DHCP Pool with the fields filled in for a sample configuration.

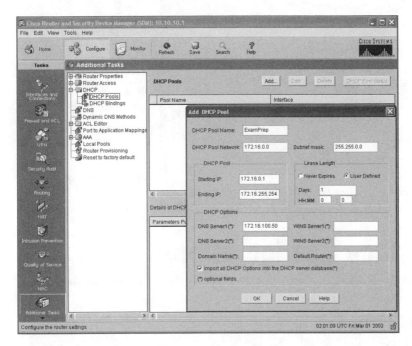

FIGURE 9.18 Add DHCP Pool window.

As soon as all of the parameters are filled in to your business specifications, click the OK button to configure the router. Figure 9.19 shows the DHCP Pools section with the newly configured DHCP pool properties.

FIGURE 9.19 DHCP Pools with a new DHCP pool configuration.

Router Interface Configurations

Objective:

▶ Access and utilize the router to set basic parameters (including: CLI/SDM)

To configure router interfaces, you must be in the Configure tab of the SDM. On the left vertical sidebar, click Interfaces and Connections. This is the first option listed under Tasks. The two tabs on this page are Create Connection and Edit Interface/Connection. Click Edit Interface/Connections to see all of the interfaces that are set up on the router and their current status, as shown in Figure 9.20.

Assigning an IP Address

To assign an IP address to another interface, you can double-click the interface name to open another configuration window. On interfaces where an IP address assignment is applicable, this window includes tabs for Connection, Association, NAT, General, and QoS. The Connection tab shows the current IP address information (if any) of the interface, which you can change. Figure 9.21 shows the configuration window for interface Fast Ethernet 4. The router is configured with a static IP address of 10.10.10.1 and a subnet mask of 255.255.255.0.

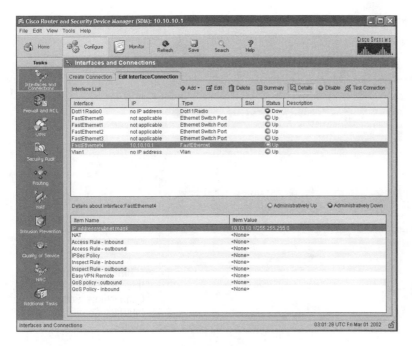

FIGURE 9.20 Configure, Interfaces and Connections, Edit Interface/Connection.

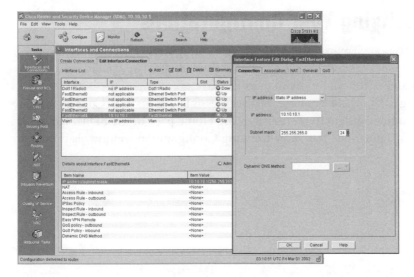

FIGURE 9.21 Interface Feature Edit Dialog - FastEthernet4.

Enabling the Interface

If you look back at the top right of Figure 9.20, you see an option to Disable interface Fast Ethernet 4. If you click an interface where the status is currently Down, such as the highlighted interface in Figure 9.22, you can Enable the interface from the SDM.

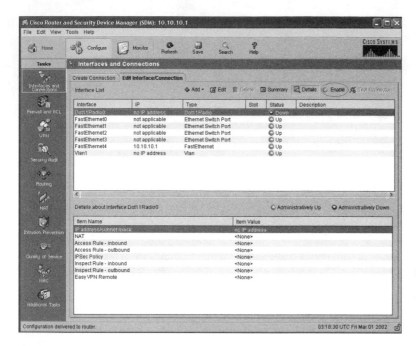

FIGURE 9.22 Configure, Interfaces and Connections, Edit Interface/Connection, Enable.

Saving and Verifying Your Configurations

After any router configuration changes, you *must* save the configuration by clicking the Save button. The SDM asks if you are sure about the save and then sends a `copy running-config startup-config` command to the router. As soon as the save is complete, the bottom of the SDM shows this message: "Running config copied successfully to Startup Config of your router." To verify your router configuration, return to the Home page of the SDM. Click the View Running Config button to open the Show Running Configuration window, as shown in Figure 9.23.

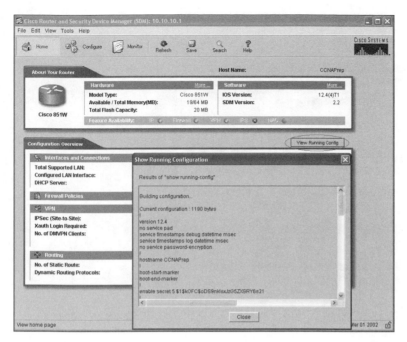

FIGURE 9.23 Show Running Configuration window.

Monitoring

Cisco SDM also offers device monitoring, which you can access by clicking the Monitor tab at the top of the page. The sidebar shows seven monitoring options (see Figure 9.24): Overview, Interface Status, Firewall Status, VPN Status, QoS Status, NAC Status, and Logging. As we discussed in Chapter 4, "General Network Security," logging is an important security feature on a network device. CPU, Memory, and Flash usage are shown in this view.

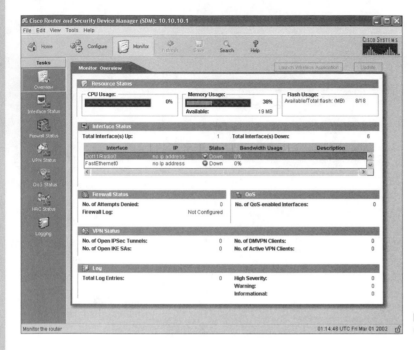

FIGURE 9.24   Monitor Overview page.

Chapter Summary

Now that you've seen a general overview of the Cisco SDM, for supported router models you can choose to use the SDM versus Cisco CLI. In my opinion, and for the CCNA exam, you should know both CLI and SDM configuration and verification methods. I encourage you to continue navigating the different pages and Tasks in the SDM to familiarize yourself with all available tools. If you are uncertain how to use an SDM Task, try the Help button for additional details and tutorials.

Key Terms

- ► Security Device Manager (SDM)
- ► Command-line interface (CLI)

Apply Your Knowledge

Exercise

9.1 SDM Configuration

The best way to learn SDM is to keep practicing the configurations on a test router. In this Exercise, configure the WAN interface on your router for the following IP address and subnet mask:

IP address: 192.168.1.1

Subnet mask: 255.255.255.0

Be sure to log back into the SDM with your new IP address!

Estimated Time: 5 minutes

Review Questions

1. What is the Cisco SDM?

2. What are the ten tasks listed in the vertical sidebar of the SDM?

3. What four properties can be configured in the Router Properties section of the SDM?

4. What options can be configured in the Router Access portion of the SDM?

5. What steps would you take to configure the WAN IP address on a router using SDM?

Exam Questions

For questions 1 through 5, refer to Figure 9.25.

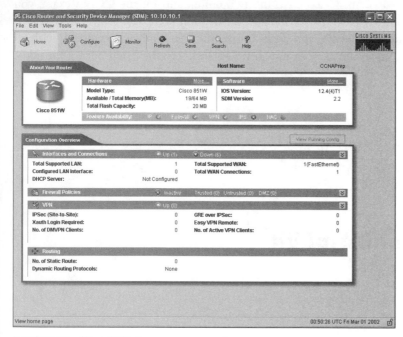

FIGURE 9.25 Cisco SDM: home page example.

1. What is the router's hostname?

  ○ **A.** Router

  ○ **B.** CCNA

  ○ **C.** CCNAPrep

  ○ **D.** CCNA851

2. From the home page of the Cisco SDM, what would you click to see the router's running configuration?

  ○ **A.** Configure

  ○ **B.** View Running Config

  ○ **C.** Monitor

  ○ **D.** Search

3. Which feature is not available on the router shown in Figure 9.25?

   ○ **A.** IP

   ○ **B.** Firewall

   ○ **C.** VPN

   ○ **D.** IPS

4. From the home page of the Cisco SDM, what would you click to configure the router's hostname?

   ○ **A.** Configure

   ○ **B.** View Running Config

   ○ **C.** Monitor

   ○ **D.** Search

5. To send a `copy running-config startup-config` command to the router with the SDM, which button would you click?

   ○ **A.** Configure

   ○ **B.** Monitor

   ○ **C.** Refresh

   ○ **D.** Save

6. How would you navigate the SDM to find and enable an interface?

   ○ **A.** Configure, Interfaces and Connections

   ○ **B.** Configure, Additional Tasks, Router Properties

   ○ **C.** Configure, Additional Tasks, Router Access

   ○ **D.** Configure, Interfaces and Connections, Edit Interface Connections

7. The Monitor screen on the SDM gives statistics for what three types of usage?

   ○ **A.** Memory

   ○ **B.** CPU

   ○ **C.** Disk Activity

   ○ **D.** Flash

8. Which of the following is configured from Router Properties?

   ○ **A.** IP Address

   ○ **B.** DHCP

   ○ **C.** SNMP

   ○ **D.** Secret Password

9. What privilege level is assigned to an account that is given a secret password?

   ○ **A.** 15

   ○ **B.** 10

   ○ **C.** 5

   ○ **D.** 0

10. User accounts can be added and edited in which section of the SDM?

    ○ **A.** Router Properties

    ○ **B.** Router Access

    ○ **C.** ACL Editor

    ○ **D.** DHCP

Answers to Review Questions

1. The Cisco Security Device Manager (SDM) is a web-based tool that Cisco developed for its IOS software-based routers. SDM allows users to configure and monitor a router without using CLI.

2. Interfaces and Connections
   Firewall and ACL
   VPN
   Security Audit
   Routing
   NAT
   Intrusion Prevention
   Quality of Service
   NAC
   Additional Tasks

3. Host Name
   Domain Name
   Banner (Message of the Day)
   Secret Password

4. User Accounts
   VTY Line Configuration
   SSH
   Management Access

5. From the Home page, select Configure, Interfaces and Connections, Edit Interface/Connection and then double-click the WAN interface. On the Connection tab, select static or dynamic IP address and enter the IP address and subnet mask.

Answers to Exam Questions

1. **C.** The hostname of the router shown is CCNAPrep.

2. **B.** To see the running configuration of your router, click View Running Config.

3. **D.** IPS has a red circle with an X next to it, indicating that it is unavailable on this router. Answers A, B, and C are incorrect because they have a green circle with a check mark, indicating that these are available features on the router.

4. **A.** To get to router configuration options, the best answer to this question is to click the Configure button. Answer B is incorrect because it shows the router's running configuration. Answers C and D are incorrect because they do not allow for device configuration.

5. **D.** With SDM, you click the Save button to send a `copy running-config startup-config` command to the router.

6. **D.** To find and enable an interface, you need to select Configure, Interfaces and Connections, Edit Interface Connections. Answer A is incorrect because it does not continue to the Edit Interface Connections tab. Answers B and C are incorrect because they refer to sections of the SDM that are used for general router properties or router access configurations.

7. **A, B, D.** The Monitor screen gives statistics on memory, CPU, and flash usage.

8. **D.** The secret password is configured in the Router Properties section of the SDM. Answer A is incorrect because the IP address is configured in the Interfaces and Connections section. Answers B and C are incorrect because they are not configured from Router Properties.

9. **A.** A secret password is given a privilege level of 15.

10. **B.** User accounts can be added and edited in the Router Access section of the SDM. Answer A is incorrect because it can only be used to add a secret password on the router. Answers C and D are also incorrect because they are not used to configure user accounts.

Suggested Readings and Resources

The following is recommended reading for general network security and related terminology:

1. "Cisco Router and Security Device Manager Q&A," http://www.cisco.com/en/US/products/sw/secursw/ps5318/products_qanda_item0900aecd800fd11b.shtml

CHAPTER TEN

Introduction to Routing and Routing Protocols

Objectives

This chapter covers the following Cisco-specified objectives for the "Describe how a network works," and "Configure, verify, and troubleshoot basic router operation and routing on Cisco devices" sections of the 640-802 CCNA exam:

▶ **Determine the path between two hosts across a network**

▶ **Describe basic routing concepts (including: packet forwarding, router lookup process)**

▶ **Perform and verify routing configuration tasks for a static or default route given specific routing requirements**

▶ **Compare and contrast methods of routing and routing protocols**

▶ **Verify device configuration and network connectivity using ping, traceroute, telnet, SSH or other utilities**

▶ **Verify network connectivity (including: using ping, traceroute, and telnet or SSH)**

▶ **Verify router hardware and software operation using SHOW & DEBUG commands**

Outline

Study Strategies

▶ Read the information presented in the chapter, paying special attention to tables, Notes, and Exam Alerts.

▶ Because routing is a method of passing IP packets along to Layer 3 forwarding devices, take the perspective of the routing devices as it receives the packet and try to determine the information required to send it on to the next forwarding device.

▶ Complete the Challenge and the Exercises at the end of the chapter. The exercises will solidify the concepts that you have learned in the previous sections.

▶ This chapter involves several mathematical challenges that are based on the subnetting foundations learned in Chapter 5, "Implementing IP Addressing." If necessary, review those concepts before tackling this chapter.

▶ Complete the Exam Questions at the end of the chapter. They are designed to simulate the types of questions you will be asked on the CCNA, ICND1, and ICND2 exams.

Introduction

So far, we have delved into many configurations of our routers that cover the administrative aspects of managing the device and providing basic connectivity. Don't forget, however, that the routers were originally designed and created to do one main function. To give you a hint, the function is in its name.

Recall that Layer 3 is responsible for determining the best path to a network, using logical addressing such as IP addresses. This chapter discusses the fundamentals of how Layer 3 devices such as routers and Layer 3 switches develop the routing logic to determine where to forward IP packets to reach a destination network.

The Default Gateway

Objective:

▶ Determine the path between two hosts across a network

To fully comprehend the routing of data, it helps to start where much of the data in a network originates: the computer. As application data is sent down the protocol stack, the source and destination IP addresses are added to the IP header. If the destination IP address is located on the same IP subnet as that on which the computer is, the computer adds the destination MAC address of that device at Layer 2 and sends it on the wire.

In instances where the destination IP address is on a remote network, it must send that traffic to a router on its segment that can forward the packet toward the destination network. Although you will forward traffic to this default gateway, the destination IP address remains unchanged. However, at Layer 2, the destination MAC address of the Ethernet frame reflects the default gateway's MAC address because this is the forwarding device on the local data link segment.

In the example illustrated in Figure 10.1, the PC sends traffic to the server on the remote 10.1.34.0 network. The source IP address and MAC address are those matching the PC. On the other hand, the Layer 3 destination IP address of the IP packet reflects the IP address of the server (10.1.34.101). Because the destination IP address does not exist on the PC's local subnet of 192.168.1.0, the PC encapsulates the router's Fast Ethernet 0/0 MAC at Layer 2 because that is the configured default gateway for this segment. The switch in this scenario is operating as only a Layer 2 switch. Thus, despite having an IP address for management, this is not the default gateway for this segment because it is only forwarding frames at Layer 2.

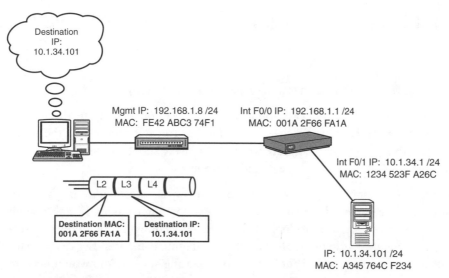

FIGURE 10.1 Default gateway example.

When the router receives the frame addressed to its interface MAC, it processes the Layer 3 information and consults its routing logic to determine whether it knows where to route the packet. Because the destination network is attached to the router, it knows to send the packet out its Fast Ethernet 0/1 interface. A new Ethernet frame using its Fast Ethernet 0/1 MAC address (1243 523F A26C) for the source MAC address and the server's MAC address (A345 764C F234) as the destination MAC are added to the original IP data as it is sent out to the destination segment.

Verifying and Troubleshooting the Default Gateway

Objective:

▶ Verify network connectivity (including: using ping, traceroute, and telnet or SSH)

Suppose that in Figure 10.1 the traffic was a ping packet to test connectivity to the remote computer. If for some reason that ping failed, you would need to determine where the problem occurred. One method of testing the failure would be to make sure that you have connectivity to and from the originating PC and the default gateway.

The default gateway on a computer can be assigned manually in the operating system or dynamically from a DHCP server. To ensure that the local computer has its IP and default gateway configured correctly, you need to look at the local PC's configuration. This step differs depending on the operating system installed on the originating computer. Let's assume for this example that the computer is using Windows as its operating system. You would need to go to a command prompt and enter **ipconfig** to see how the computer's interface(s) are configured for IP. In Figure 10.2, you can see from the output on the computer that the computer has been dynamically assigned an IP address of 192.168.1.2 and a subnet mask of 255.255.255.0. Notice also that the default gateway is also configured correctly, pointing to the local router's Fast Ethernet 0/0 IP address of 192.168.1.1.

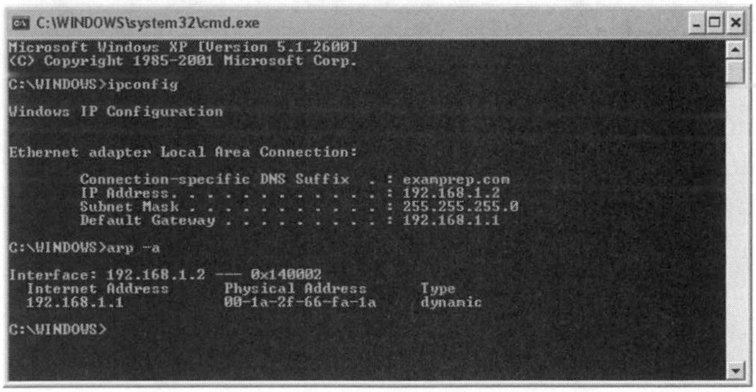

FIGURE 10.2 Windows computer gateway verification.

To seal the troubleshooting deal, notice that we went so far as to verify that the computer has a correct IP-to-MAC address binding for the default gateway by issuing the arp -a command from the command prompt to display the computer's ARP table. You can see from the output that the default gateway's IP address of 192.168.1.1 does correspond to its Fast Ethernet 0/0 MAC address. This ARP entry will continue to remain in the computer's volatile memory as long as it keeps getting used. If no packets are sent to this address for five minutes (default), the ARP entry is removed. If you want to manually clear your ARP table on your computer (useful in cases where you recently changed your default gateway), the command is arp -d followed by the IP address or a wildcard asterisk (*) to delete all the ARP entries.

Seeing that the configuration of the originating PC is correct, next we should see if we have IP connectivity to the router's Fast Ethernet interfaces. Because this is a small network, we can simply ping those IP addresses. In larger networks with many routers in between, it might be administratively easier to do a traceroute (the `tracert` command in Windows) to discover at what point along the routed path the ICMP packet fails.

So what happens if we can ping the two interfaces? At this point, we know that a packet can traverse our network, reach the default gateway, and exit the router's remote network interface. The only culprit left is the remote PC. It is a pretty sure bet that the remote computer must have an interface problem or configuration error. Keep in mind that it too must return that packet to our network. Therefore, the remote computer must also have a default gateway configured so that it can return that packet to its remote network. Using the same steps as we used for the originating computer, we should be able to determine exactly what is causing this computer to not successfully return packets to our computer.

Routing Sources

Objective:

▶ Describe basic routing concepts (including: packet forwarding, router lookup process)

Routers are methodical, tactless devices in that they do not necessarily care about the individual IP addresses that exist on a subnet. Their sole obsession is to maintain their routing logic by keeping track of the networks that exist and which interfaces to use to send the traffic if an IP packet is destined for that network. By using routing devices to relay packets out of their interfaces to other forwarding devices or the destination network, the IP packet eventually reaches the destination.

At the heart of the routing logic for Layer 3 devices is the routing table. This table, located in volatile RAM, contains a mapping of all the best routes to networks that the router is aware of and the interfaces to exit to reach those networks. So how is the router aware of these networks? Generally, three routing sources can feed the routing table with this information:

▶ **Connected interfaces:** As soon as you assign an IP address to a working (up/line protocol up) interface, the router associates the entire subnet of the interface's IP address in the routing table.

▶ **Static routes:** These are manual entries that an administrator enters into the configuration to specify the destination network and the next hop (router along the destination path).

▶ **Routing protocols:** Protocols exchanged between routing devices to dynamically advertise networks.

Connected interfaces remain in the routing tables as long as the interface is active and has a valid IP address assigned to it. Static routes remain in the table as long as you do not remove the static route configuration and the next hop is valid (the interface to the next hop is up). Networks learned from dynamic routing protocols remain in the routing table as long as the next hop is valid and the routing devices do not stop hearing the network(s) being advertised from the neighbor routers.

Administrative Distance

Now that you are aware of the multiple sources of routing information, you must consider a feasible anomaly that could occur with your routing sources. Namely, if you have several sources of information such as connected interfaces, static routes, and multiple routing protocols, which one are you to trust when more than one source advertises the same network? For example, if a router learns about the 192.168.1.0/24 network from a routing protocol and a static route, how does the router decide which entry to place into its routing table?

The answer lies within a program logic in the IOS called the *administrative distance*. The administrative distances are values between 1 and 255 that are assigned to routing information sources. These values represent a level of trustworthiness of the information source, in which lower administrative distances are preferred over higher ones.

> **NOTE**
>
> The administrative distance applies only when multiple sources are advertising exactly the same subnet.

Table 10.1 lists the Cisco IOS default administrative distances for some of the routing sources.

TABLE 10.1 Default Administrative Distances

Routed Source	Default Distance
Connected	0
Static route	1
EIGRP (internal)	90
OSPF	110
RIPv1 and v2	120
EIGRP (external)	170

It should come as no shock that connected interfaces are the most trustworthy sources because they are connected directly to the local router. Static routes have a low administrative distance of 1 because the Cisco IOS assumes that you are competent administrators and any manual entry of a routable network is trusted over any dynamic routing protocols such as EIGRP, OSPF, and RIP.

Static Routes

Objective:

▶ Perform and verify routing configuration tasks for a static or default route given specific routing requirements

When you interconnect routers, as shown in Figure 10.3, they are aware of only their directly connected networks. Unless you configure a static route or use routing protocols, the routers will never know about their neighbors' other networks, because they are not connected. In other words, Router A is unaware of Router B's 172.17.0.0 network, and Router B is unaware of Router A's 172.16.0.0 network.

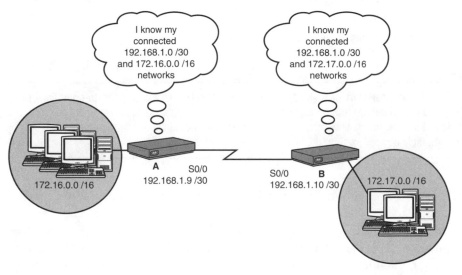

FIGURE 10.3 Static route exhibit.

So when do you use static routes as opposed to routing protocols? As mentioned before, static routes are manual configuration entries in which you tell the router how to get to destination networks that are not locally attached. This is useful in simple networks such as the one shown in Figure 10.3, in which there is a single link in or out of the networks, known as a *stub network*. Because there is only one link to get to the neighbor network, you don't need to worry about reacting dynamically if the path fails because there are no alternate paths to that network.

Additionally, if you want to have complete control of your routing path decisions or you want to conserve bandwidth on your links (routing protocols consume bandwidth), static routes can provide you authoritative control without requiring any link bandwidth or resources because they require only a local configuration.

> **EXAM ALERT**
>
> Keep in mind that static routes are used when you have a stub network, want control of your routing decisions, or want to conserve bandwidth on links.

Configuring Static Routes

The general idea behind the static route is to tell the router how to get to a destination network that is not attached to it by going through another router's interface. It is similar to telling someone, "To go outside, go through that door." The syntax to configure a static route in global configuration mode is `ip route` followed by the destination network, destination subnet mask, and the next-hop IP address of the neighbor's interface. For example, to configure a route to the 10.0.0.0/8 network through the neighbor's serial interface of 192.168.2.5, the command would look like this:

```
Router(config)# ip route 10.0.0.0 255.0.0.0 192.168.2.5
```

> **NOTE**
>
> It is possible to specify the local interface instead of using a next-hop IP address on point-to-point links (a link with only two routers connected to it on each side). On multi-access links such as Ethernet or Frame Relay, you should not use the interface because the local router does not know to which router to forward the information if multiple devices exist on the link.

In the stub network example shown in Figure 10.4, a static route to Router A and one to Router B were added, telling them about their neighbors' Ethernet networks. These entries are placed in their routing tables, specifying any packets that are destined for those respective networks must go to the IP of the neighbor's serial 0/0 interface. From that point, the packets are routed out Router A and Router B's Ethernet interface because those destination networks are directly connected to the router. This entry remains in the routing table as long as the next-hop address remains valid (the serial network does not go down) or the configuration is not removed.

For several reasons such as security, processor resources, and routing path control, you can force the static route to remain in the routing table even if the next-hop interface goes down. This is easily achieved by adding the keyword `permanent` at the end of the `ip route` command.

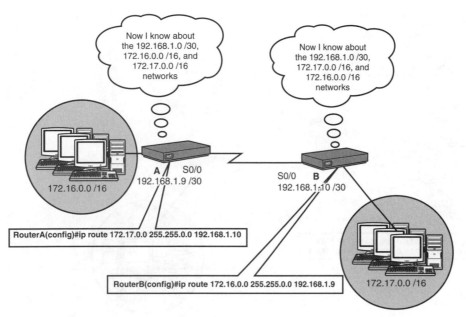

FIGURE 10.4 Static route configuration example.

Floating Static Routes

At the end of an `ip route` static route command, it is possible to add a parameter to assign this particular static route a higher administrative distance than the default administrative distance of 1. These entries, known as *floating static routes*, are not placed in the routing table if the subnet is being advertised by a routing source with a lower administrative distance. Floating static routes are useful when you have a standby redundant link to another network that will activate in the event of a primary link failure.

For example, consider the example configured in Figure 10.5. Because you have redundant point-to-point links, you can configure the primary static route as usual and include a floating static route to be used if the primary link fails. The 2 at the end of the second static route identifies that route as the floating static route. This entry does not show up in the routing table because the primary route advertises the same subnet with a lower administrative distance (if not specified, the default is 1). If one of the serial 0/0 interfaces on the primary link goes down, the next hop is no longer valid and is removed from the routing table. Because the floating static route has the next lowest administrative distance, that entry is put in the routing table and that link is used until the primary link returns.

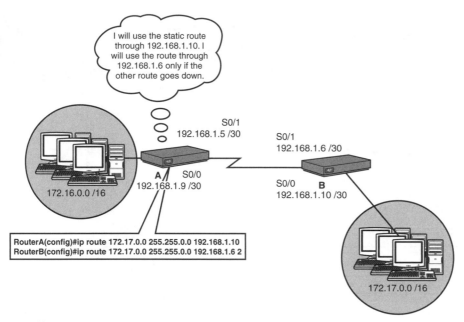

FIGURE 10.5 Floating static route configuration example.

Default Routes

Objective:

▶ Perform and verify routing configuration tasks for a static or default route given specific routing requirements

Static routes have proved their usefulness in situations where you want to add a network entry in a routing table when the network is reachable via a single path. This can turn into a daunting administrative task when there are a large number of networks in which you must configure static routes. This is especially true when you are connecting to your ISP because you do not want to configure a static route for every network on the Internet.

In these situations, you might be better served using something called a *default route*, as illustrated in Figure 10.6. This entry is a gateway of last resort for routers in that if a destination IP address does not have a network entry in the routing table, this route is used. The syntax for a default route is similar to a static route except that the destination and subnet mask are both 0.0.0.0:

```
Router(config)#ip route 0.0.0.0 0.0.0.0 192.168.1.10
```

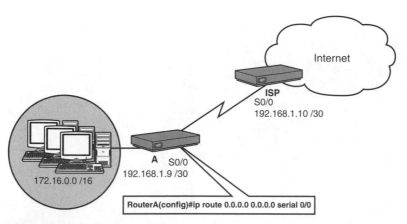

FIGURE 10.6 Default route configuration example.

Again, you can specify the local interface as opposed to the next-hop IP address on a point-to-point link.

Be sure to look closely at the wording in a question regarding a default route (gateway of last resort). When used in a router, the command is `ip route 0.0.0.0 0.0.0.0`; however, to configure a default route in a Layer 2 switch, it is `ip default-gateway` because Layer 2 switches do not have Layer 3 routing entries.

In some situations a default route may appear dynamically in a routing table. Specifically, if you have configured your interface to dynamically be assigned an IP address and default gateway from a DHCP server using the ip address dhcp command, the router automatically places a default route in its routing table using the default gateway as the next hop.

Configuring Static and Default Routes with SDM

Using the Security Device Manager web-based configuration interface, you can easily configure static and default routes with just a few clicks of the mouse. Specifically, from the Configure screen, select the Routing task to display routing configuration options. At the top of the screen shown in Figure 10.7 is a section dedicated to Static Routing. Here, when you click the Add button, a pop-up window displays the parameters that you can configure for static or default routes.

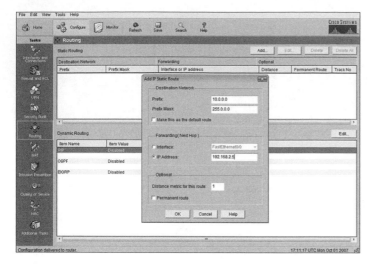

FIGURE 10.7 SDM static route configuration.

In the pop-up window, you specify the destination network and subnet mask, as you did for the IOS CLI command. The next hop defaults to a drop-down box that lists the interfaces, but you can select the IP Address option and specify the next-hop address. Also notice that there is a checkbox to make this route a default route, as well as a checkbox to make this a permanent static route entry. If you wanted to make this route a floating route, you could also put the distance metric for this route to an administrative distance value other than 1. After you click the OK button, the route is added to the running configuration of the IOS.

Verifying Static and Default Routes

The best way to verify a static or default route configuration is by checking that the route is evident in the routing table. The command to view the IP routing table is show ip route. If you want to see the routing entry for a specific network, you can append that subnet to the show ip route command (for example, show ip route 192.168.23.0). The following example displays the output of the show ip route command:

```
Router> show ip route
Codes: C - connected, S - static, I - IGRP, R - RIP, M - mobile, B - BGP
       D - EIGRP, EX - EIGRP external, O - OSPF, IA - OSPF inter area
       N1 - OSPF NSSA external type 1, N2 - OSPF NSSA external type 2
       E1 - OSPF external type 1, E2 - OSPF external type 2, E - EGP
       i - IS-IS, L1 - IS-IS level-1, L2 - IS-IS level-2, * - candidate default
       U - per-user static route, o - ODR, P - periodic downloaded static route
       T - traffic engineered route

Gateway of last resort is not set

S    172.17.0.0/16 [1/0] via 192.168.1.10
```

```
C    172.16.0.0/16 is directly connected, FastEthernet0/0
     192.168.1.0/30 is subnetted, 1 subnets
C       192.168.1.8 is directly connected, Serial0/0/0
S*   0.0.0.0/0 [1/0] via 192.168.1.10
```

Notice that the beginning of the output has a legend identifying the possible codes that can be listed in the routing table. In the table itself, you can see the two directly connected networks signified by the letter C. In addition, you can also see the static route to 172.17.0.0 and the static default route entries (indicated by the letter S), using 192.168.1.10 as the next hop. Also notice that the routing table identifies that the gateway of last resort (192.168.1.10) is set on this router because a default route was configured with the next hop to that address.

NOTE

You can clear out an entry in your routing table by using the `clear` command followed by the network or * for all networks in privileged EXEC mode. For example, to clear the 192.168.1.0 network from your routing table, you would enter the following:

Router# **clear ip route 192.168.1.0**

Dynamic Routing Protocols

Objective:

▶ Compare and contrast methods of routing and routing protocols

When complex networks contain multiple interconnections, static routes are no longer a practical solution because they cannot adapt or react to changes in the topology. Not to mention, the configuration complexity can grow exponentially as you add more devices to the network.

EXAM ALERT

Do not confuse routing protocols with routed protocols on the exam. Routed protocols are protocols such as those in the IP protocol suite that are used to carry the data across our network. Routing protocols are exchanged between routing devices to determine the optimal path to route the routed protocols.

For example, given the network design shown in Figure 10.8, Router A knows only the three directly connected networks attached to the router. For IP packets to reach the 172.17.0.0 network via static routes, you would have to configure Router A to go through one of its neighbor routers, such as Router B. However, Router B also requires a static route to 172.17.0.0 because that network is not directly connected to it. Supposing that the router is using Router F as its next hop, that router does not require a static route because it is directly connected. Unfortunately, our configuration undertaking does not stop there because we have to configure a static route in Router F and Router B back to the 172.16.0.0 network.

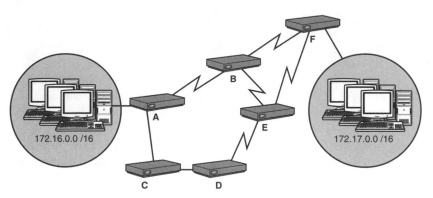

FIGURE 10.8 Complex internetwork design.

Granted, the configuration scenario shown in Figure 10.8 is not drastically difficult or strenuous, but imagine if the network contained 20 more routers. More importantly, consider what would happen if the link between A and B went down. Because the routes are statically configured in the routers, you must now go back and remove the static routes in Routers A and B and redirect the traffic by configuring static routes to go through Routers C, D, and E. Not to mention, you must remove and reconfigure static routes back to the 172.16.0.0 network in Routers F, E, D, and C.

To alleviate the administrative calamity you might have to encounter with static routes in complex networks, you can use dynamic routing protocols. If you configure routing protocols, the routers advertise their connected networks to the rest of the routers in the network, thus minimizing the amount of configuration required. In addition, routing protocols can detect and adapt to topology changes in the internetwork.

Routing Metrics

Because one of the core responsibilities of routing protocols is to build routing tables to determine optimal routing paths, you need to have some means of measuring which routes are preferred when there are multiple pathways to a destination. Routing protocols use some measure of metrics to identify which routes are optimal to reach a destination network. The lowest cumulative metric to a destination is the preferred path and the one that ultimately enters the routing table. Different routing protocols use one or several of the following metrics to calculate the best path:

▶ **Hop count:** The number of routing devices that the packet must travel to reach a destination network.

▶ **Bandwidth:** The cumulative bandwidth of the links to the destination in kilobits per second.

- ▶ **Delay:** The length of time (measured in microseconds) a packet takes from source to destination.

- ▶ **Reliability:** The consistency of the links and paths toward the destination based on error rates of the interfaces.

- ▶ **Load:** The cumulative amount of congestion or saturation of the links toward the destination.

- ▶ **MTU:** The maximum frame size that is allowed to traverse the links to the destination.

- ▶ **Cost:** An arbitrary number typically based on the bandwidth of the link.

Classful and Classless Routing Updates

As you will see in the following sections, routing protocols are categorized into several different classifications based on common characteristics and properties that they share. The first of these classifications revolves around the contents of routing updates that Layer 3 devices advertise to their neighbors. Specifically, if the routing updates do not contain the subnet mask along with their respective advertised networks, they are said to be *classful routing protocols*. Conversely, if the subnet mask is transmitted along with the network information, it is characterized as a *classless routing protocol*. This may seem like a trivial characteristic to define routing protocols, but as you will see, the results of the subnet mask being present or not in routing updates can affect the routing protocols you choose and how efficiently you can design your entire network.

With classful routing protocols, you assume that your network's design conforms to the class boundaries of IP subnets. In other words, major networks in your design use their default classful subnet masks as described in Chapter 5, "Implementing IP Addressing" (for example, Class A uses 255.0.0.0, Class B uses 255.255.0.0, and Class C uses 255.255.255.0). If you happen to subnet a major network into smaller subnets, classful routing protocols are disadvantageous, because they do not receive the revised subnet mask. For this reason, classful routing protocols process updates in one of two ways:

- ▶ If the network in the updates matches the same major classful network on the interface through which it was received, it uses the subnet mask of the interface and places it in the routing table.

- ▶ If the router advertises a network to a different major network out an interface that is not in the same major network, it automatically summarizes the network to its classful boundary.

For example, when Router B in Figure 10.9 sends an update to Router A using a classful rout-ing protocol (RIPv1 in this example), it summarizes the 172.17.30.0/24 to a default Class B 172.17.0.0 network because it is going out the serial 0/0 interface, which does not contain a subnet in that major network. The 192.168.1.60 network, on the other hand, is in the same major network, so it does not automatically summarize that subnet. When Router A receives that update, it adds the 172.17.0.0 network to its routing table, specifying Router B's serial interface IP (192.168.1.10) as the next hop to reach that network. In addition, it adds the 192.168.1.60 network as well, using its interface mask because it is in that same major network.

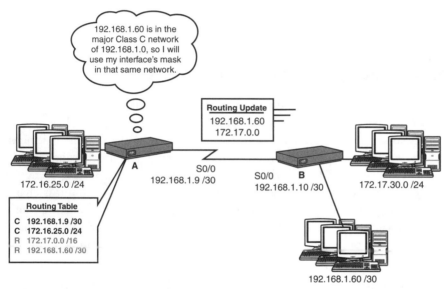

FIGURE 10.9 Classful routing update scenario.

Now consider if the Ethernet segment of Router B's 192.168.1.60 network had a /29 subnet mask. The end result would still be the same as before in that Router B would advertise the 192.168.1.60 subnet and Router A would use its interface's subnet mask of /30. In these instances, classful routing protocols are not the optimal choice because Router A has a route to only a third of the 192.168.1.60 /29 subnet. For this reason, when you subnet a major net-work, you must be sure that you use the same subnet mask throughout your network design with classful routing protocols. This same subnet design is commonly referred to as a *Fixed-Length Subnet Mask (FLSM)* network design.

Classful routing protocols can also be problematic when major classful networks are subnetted and are haphazardly dispersed throughout the network, as illustrated in Figure 10.10. When Routers A and C summarize their networks to Router B, Router B thinks that the 172.16.0.0 network is out both of its serial interfaces. This could easily result in traffic destined for 172.16.10.0 and 172.16.50.0 being load balanced out each interface, resulting in 50% packet loss because the packets are sent in a round robin fashion between both interfaces.

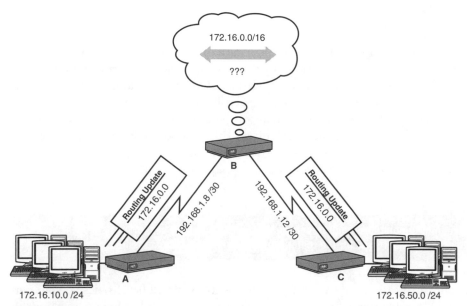

FIGURE 10.10   Discontiguous network example.

Because classless routing protocols advertise the subnet masks in their routing updates, discontiguous networks are no longer an issue because routing devices are aware of the subnetted networks. In addition, the requirement of using the same subnet mask throughout the network ceases to apply because the routers do not automatically summarize the networks to a classful boundary. No longer inhibited by these constraints, you are free to use different subnet masks, known as *Variable-Length Subnet Masks (VLSMs)* in your network design. In addition, you now have full autonomy to manually summarize networks as you wish to help keep routing tables small to conserve resources. VLSM and route summarization are described in greater detail in the following sections.

VLSM

Using classless routing protocols affords you the luxury of having support for a VLSM network design. This is advantageous in your network planning because you can allot the appropriate number of IP addresses required for each link. Not to mention, by assigning the minimal number of IP addresses required for a given link, you conserve IP addresses. For example, you can use a /30 subnet mask for point-to-point links because you need only two available IP addresses and a /27 subnet mask on an Ethernet segment to accommodate 30 hosts. If you were using classless routing protocols, you would have to use a /27 for all links, which would inevitably waste 28 IP addresses on the point-to-point links.

> **EXAM ALERT**
>
> Remember that point-to-point links require only a /30 (255.255.255.252) subnet mask because you need only two usable IP addresses for the router's interfaces on each side of the link.

Throughout your certification and career, it is quite possible you will have to design your network given a usable subnet and host requirements for all your links. When tackling this designing task, be sure to adhere to the following guidelines:

1. If possible, start with the larger subnets first.

2. Write out the ranges that you have assigned to ensure that you do not accidentally overlap subnets.

3. Make sure your networks start on incremental boundaries (128, 64, 32, and so on).

> **EXAM ALERT**
>
> Be prepared to use VLSM to assign subnets to links given the subnettable network and host requirements.

Challenge

Given the design shown in Figure 10.11, determine how you can use VLSM to ensure that you are using the appropriate subnets given a design scenario. In this example, the zero subnets are available for use.

1. Remember to add 2 to each network to accommodate the network ID and broadcast address.

2. Calculate the network and subnet mask for Network D (the largest network).

3. Given the remaining IP addresses, calculate the network and subnet mask for Network C.

4. Given the remaining IP addresses, calculate the network and subnet mask for Network B.

5. Given the remaining IP addresses, calculate the network and subnet mask for Network E.

6. Given the remaining IP addresses, calculate the network and subnet mask for the four point-to-point links.

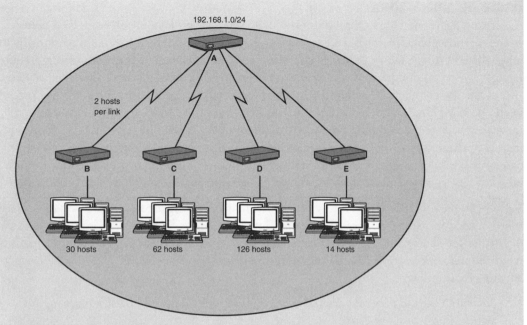

FIGURE 10.11 VLSM design scenario.

Challenge Answer

Network D needs to have a subnet that accommodates 128 addresses. A subnet mask of 255.255.255.128 or /25 provides enough hosts for that network. The next subnet for Network C begins at 192.168.1.128 (because you just took 128 IPs) and use a subnet mask of 255.255.255.192 or /26 to accommodate the 64 IP addresses. Network B is assigned the network of 192.168.1.192 with a subnet mask of 255.255.255.224 or /27 to give you 32 IPs. A subnet mask of 255.255.255.240 or /28 with a network ID of 192.168.1.224 is assigned to Network E for the 16 IPs required for that link. The four point-to-point links all use a 255.255.255.252 or /30 subnet mask using the last four networks: 192.168.1.240, 192.168.1.244, 192.168.1.248, 192.168.1.252. To summarize:

- ▶ **Network D:** 192.168.1.0 /25

- ▶ **Network C:** 192.168.1.128 /26

- ▶ **Network B:** 192.168.1.192 /27

- ▶ **Network E:** 192.168.1.224 /28

- ▶ **Point-to-point links:** 192.168.1.240 /30, 192.168.1.244 /30, 192.168.1.248 /30, and 192.168.1.252 /30.

Route Summarization

As already mentioned, classful routing protocols automatically summarize advertised networks to the classful subnet boundaries. Classless routing protocols, on the other hand, require you to manually control the networks being summarized to your neighbors in the router configuration. By aggregating a contiguous set of networks into an advertised summarized route, you keep the size of the routing tables to a minimum. Neighbors that receive the summarized route do not need to know about the individual subnets you create behind your router because they inevitably have to go through your router to get to them. The additional offshoot of this summarized picture is that your classless routing protocols do not need to notify those neighbors if one of those subnets goes down because they do not even have that subnet in their routing tables. Thus, you can isolate topology changes to be contained behind that summarizing router.

Because you are required to manually specify the networks you are to advertise, you must learn how to accurately summarize smaller subnets into one or several larger networks, or supernets. The rules for supernetting are similar to subnetting, except in this case, you are stealing bits from the network portion of an IP network to create a larger network. The rules for supernetting are as follows:

1. Be sure that the networks are contiguous (otherwise you would be summarizing networks that you do not have behind the router).

2. Count the number of networks you want to summarize.

3. Determine an increment that is equal to or less than the number of networks.

4. Make sure your base networks start on incremental boundaries (128, 64, 32, and so on) for the number of networks you are summarizing.

5. Calculate the subnet mask by the number of bits you need to steal from the original subnet to equal that incremental value.

The beauty of supernetting is that the resultant network and subnet mask will designate many IP address networks in a single entry. The fact that you are stealing bits from the network portion of an IP address could quite easily violate the traditional barriers of classful addressing, known as *Classless Interdomain Routing* (CIDR).

For instance, it would not be uncommon to see a summary entry look like the following: 192.168.16.0 /20. This single entry used to be a Class C (/24), but four bits were stolen from the network portion to represent 16 networks ($2^4 = 16$). When you advertise this supernet to neighbors, they know that they must go through your router to get to networks 192.168.16.0 through 192.168.31.0 (16 total networks).

EXAM ALERT

Be prepared to determine the networks being advertised in a given supernet or determine the summary network, given the networks to be summarized.

Figure 10.12 illustrates a typical route summarization example in which Router B is summarizing all its subnetted networks to Router A as one supernetted network. Following the steps outlined previously, you can determine the aggregate network entry to advertise, as follows:

▶ The networks are all contiguous, so you can summarize them accurately.

▶ A total of 32 networks need to be summarized.

▶ 32 conveniently falls on an incremental boundary.

▶ Because the network is 192.168.64.0, 64 is an increment of 32 so we can use that as the base network for the summary route.

▶ You must steal 5 bits (2^5 = 32) from the /24 network, so /19 (24 − 5 = 19).

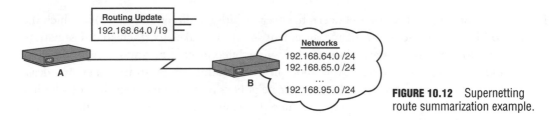

FIGURE 10.12 Supernetting route summarization example.

By creating the summary route 192.168.64.0 /19, Router A is required to maintain only that one entry in its routing table as opposed to the individual 32 subnets. If a topology change occurs in one of the subnets behind Router B, there is no need to advertise that change to Router A because it knows about only the summarized network.

> **NOTE**
>
> The number of summarized networks or the base network do not always conveniently fall on incremental boundaries. In those instances, it may take several summary network entries to encompass all the networks you want to summarize.

Interior and Exterior Gateway Routing Protocols

Routing protocols can fall under two major categories depending on the autonomy of the network on which the routing protocol exists. The identifying characteristic of the category to which the routing protocol belongs ultimately depends on whether the routing protocol exchanges updates within a network that is under your administrative control. When the network is under your control in your own administrative domain, it is known as an *autonomous system*. Routing protocols used to disseminate information to maintain routing tables and establish pathways inside an autonomous system are categorized as Interior Gateway Protocols (IGPs).

Conversely, the other category of routing protocols is designed to route in between these autonomous systems. For instance, Border Gateway Protocol (BGP) is a routing protocol that is used by ISPs for routing traffic over the Internet. Because the Internet comprises thousands of networks, each under different administrative control, you need to use an Exterior Gateway Protocol such as BGP to route in between these autonomous systems.

Distance Vector Routing Protocols

In addition to being an IGP/EGP or classful/classless, routing protocols can also fall into one of three classes. Again, the functionality and characteristics of the routing protocol dictate under which class it falls. The most long-standing of these classes is *distance vector routing protocols*.

Distance vector routing protocols concern themselves with the direction (vector) in which the destination lies and some means of measurement (metric) it takes to reach that destination. Distance vector routing protocols inform their directly connected neighbors of all the connected and learned networks they know about in their routing tables. In fact, they broadcast the contents of the entire routing table to their neighbors periodically, regardless of whether there is a change in the network topology. When the neighbors receive that routing information, they identify and add any new networks to their routing tables and update the metric before eventually passing it on to their neighbors. Because the routing table information is updated before it is sent on to neighbors, downstream routers do not learn that information first hand. For this reason, distance vector routing protocol update processing is often referred to as "routing by rumor." Distance vector routing protocols are discussed in greater detail in Chapter 11, "Distance Vector Routing Protocols."

Link-State Routing Protocols

As the name states, *link-state routing protocols* advertise the state of the links in the network. In fact, they advertise the states and metrics (cost) of all the links they know about for the entire topology to their neighbors, as opposed to just the best routes in your routing table. This detailed overview of the entire routing domain enables each router to calculate and make a decision on the best route from this first-hand information, rather than listen to what its neighbor believes is the best route. In fact, link-state routing protocols keep three tables: a neighbor table of all discovered neighbors, a topology table of all the possible routes to reachable networks learned, and a routing table that contains the best route based on the lowest metric calculated from the topology table.

At first, this may sound like a lot of information to be exchanged between routers; however, link-state routing protocols initially discover their neighbors when they first boot up and synchronize their topology tables. After the neighbor discovery and topology synchronization, they send only periodic hello messages to let their neighbors know they are still functioning.

This is significantly different from distance vector routing protocols that periodically exchange the entire routing table, which can contain a large amount of information, depending on the size of the network.

In addition, link-state routing protocols react much faster when a topology change occurs in the network. In fact, these protocols were initially created in response to the slow convergence issues that you typically encounter with distance vector routing protocols. The downfall to these routing protocols is the resources they consume in the router. Namely, maintaining and processing three tables consume quite a bit of memory and processor power. Link-state routing protocols are discussed in greater detail in Chapter 12, "Link-State and Hybrid Routing Protocols."

Advanced Distance Vector/Hybrid Routing Protocols

They say it usually takes three tries to get something absolutely right. The truth behind this saying is that you learn from the mistakes of the previous two attempts. Such is the case with advanced distance vector, often referred to as *hybrid* or *balanced hybrid* routing protocols. Because they take the best features and avoid the pitfalls of both distance vector and link-state routing protocols, hybrid routing protocols are a more proficient breed of routing protocols than their predecessors.

The Routing Table Revisited

Now that you have learned about the several types of routing sources, including static routes and dynamic routing protocols, it's time to revisit the routing table and solidify how network entries are added and used in routing decisions. To help illustrate this process, refer to the following show ip route output :

```
RouterA> show ip route
Codes: C - connected, S - static, I - IGRP, R - RIP, M - mobile, B - BGP
       D - EIGRP, EX - EIGRP external, O - OSPF, IA - OSPF inter area
       N1 - OSPF NSSA external type 1, N2 - OSPF NSSA external type 2
       E1 - OSPF external type 1, E2 - OSPF external type 2, E - EGP
       i - IS-IS, L1 - IS-IS level-1, L2 - IS-IS level-2, * - candidate default
       U - per-user static route, o - ODR, P - periodic downloaded static route
       T - traffic engineered route

Gateway of last resort is not set

R     172.17.0.0/16 [120/1] via 192.168.1.10, Serial0/0/0
C     172.16.0.0/16 is directly connected, FastEthernet0/0
      10.0.0.0/8 is variably subnetted, 4 subnets, 3 masks
D        10.2.0.0/16 [90/2297856] via 192.168.1.10, Serial0/0/0
D        10.3.0.0/16 [90/2297856] via 192.168.1.10, Serial0/0/0
```

```
R        10.0.0.0/8 [120/2] via 192.168.1.6, Serial0/0/1
D        10.1.0.0/16 [90/2297856] via 192.168.1.10, Serial0/0/0
D        10.4.0.0/16 [90/2297856] via 192.168.1.10, Serial0/0/0
O        10.4.0.1/32 [110/65] via 172.16.0.1, FastEthernet0/0
    192.168.1.0/30 is subnetted, 2 subnets
C        192.168.1.8 is directly connected, Serial 0/0/0
C        192.168.1.4 is directly connected, Serial 0/0/1
```

Notice that there are now several entries for directly connected networks, a static route, and several dynamic routing protocol entries from EIGRP, RIP, and OSPF. For each dynamic routing protocol, the network and subnet mask are being advertised by neighbor routers, followed by two numbers in brackets separated by a slash (/). The number to the left of the forward slash is the administrative distance of the routing protocol. The number to the right of the forward slash represents the metric that is being used by the routing protocol to determine the best path to the destination network. This information is immediately followed by the router from which it learned this information (thus, the next-hop address). The last item in the routing entry represents the interface packets must exit to reach those networks.

EXAM ALERT

You must be adept at deciphering the output of a routing table.

Assuming that several of the routing protocols advertised the same networks, how did these specific network entries come to be in the routing table? The obvious answer is that the interfaces, a static route, and multiple routing protocols were configured and the resultant table just appeared. However, to answer the question more specifically, each routing protocol determined which routes should be entered in the routing table based on the lowest metric to those destinations. In the chance that one or more routing sources is trying to place a network entry in the routing table for exactly the same subnet, the routing protocol with the lowest administrative distance is chosen because it is the most trustworthy.

After the routing table is built, packets are routed to their destinations by examination of the destination IP address in an IP packet and associating the network in the routing table with that IP address. If there isn't a match for the network lookup, the packet is forwarded to its default route. If the gateway of last resort is not set (as in this show ip route output), the packet is dropped, and an ICMP destination unreachable message is sent back to the source to indicate that the destination cannot be reached.

EXAM ALERT

Routing of packets is based on the destination IP address in a packet. If the router does not have an entry for the packet's associated network or does not have a default route, it sends an ICMP destination unreachable message back to the source.

In the `show ip route` output, several entries for the 10.0.0.0 network are listed in the routing table. Interestingly, there is a RIP entry for the 10.0.0.0 /8 network to go out serial 0/0/1 and four EIGRP-learned networks for 10.1.0.0 /16, 10.2.0.0 /16, 10.3.0.0 /16, and 10.4.0.0 /16, all destined for interface serial 0/0/0. Because the EIGRP networks are subnets of the major 10.0.0.0 network, which interface will the router use to route a packet destined, for example, for 10.1.0.3?

Cisco's routing logic answers this question by using a rule called the *longest match*. The longest match rule states that when a packet has multiple possible network entries to use, the more specific subnet is used over the less specific. In other words, the longer the number of bits in the subnet mask (thus the smaller subnet), the more chance it has of being the chosen network. In the routing table example, a packet destined for 10.1.0.3 would use the subnet with the longest prefix (subnet mask), which is the EIGRP route for 10.1.0.0/16 exiting interface Serial 0/0/0.

Routing Redistribution

You are likely to encounter in your Cisco travels certain situations in which you must run multiple routing protocols in your network. For instance, your company is in the process of merging with another company's network, and their routers are running a different routing protocol than yours. In addition, you may have to connect your Cisco router network to a non-Cisco routing infrastructure and you are using Cisco proprietary routing protocols.

In instances where you are running multiple routing protocols, it may be necessary to have networks advertised in one routing protocol injected into the other. Unfortunately, because routing protocols are so diverse in nature, they do not inherently interact or exchange information with each other when multiple routing protocols are running in the network. The transferal of network information from one routing protocol into another is a manual configuration called *redistribution*.

The redistribution configuration is typically done at one or a couple of routers that sit on the boundary between each routing protocol, as illustrated in Figure 10.13. These devices run both routing protocols and must be manually configured to inject the networks learned from one routing protocol into the next. Redistribution can occur in one of two fashions:

- ▶ **One-way redistribution:** Networks from an edge protocol are injected into a more robust core routing protocol, but not the other way around. This method is the safest way to perform redistribution.

- ▶ **Two-way redistribution:** Networks from each routing protocol are injected into the other. This is the least preferred method because it is possible that suboptimal routing or routing loops may occur because of the network design or the difference in convergence times when a topology change occurs. Figure 10.13 is an example of two-way redistribution.

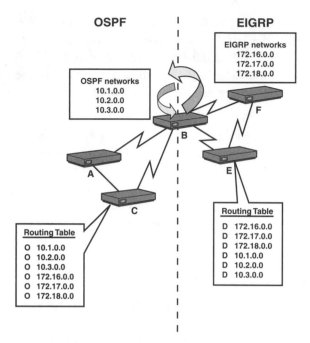

FIGURE 10.13 Two-way redistribution example.

EXAM ALERT

Remember that one-way redistribution translates networks from one routing protocol in another, but not vice versa. Two-way routing redistribution dispenses networks from each routing protocol into the other.

Chapter Summary

This chapter looked more closely at the operations involved in routing packets with Layer 3 devices such as routers and Layer 3 switches. You send packets from workstations on the local network to routing devices by configuring those devices with a default gateway IP address that matches the IP of your router. When the packet arrives at the router, it consults its routing table to determine whether the destination IP address in the IP packet has a match for the destination's network. If it does not have a matching entry, it looks to see whether the routing table has a default route. If no gateway of last resort is set, it drops the packet and sends an ICMP destination unreachable message back to the source. In instances where there are several matches for the destination network, it uses the entry that has the longest match.

The entries in the routing table can come from several routing sources. When the interface is operational and an IP address is assigned, they show up in the routing table as connected interfaces. Manual static route entries that were manually configured show up as an S. Routing protocols choose their best network paths by calculating the lowest metric for their respective routing protocols. If multiple routing sources advertise the same subnet, the source with the lowest administrative distance is placed in the routing table.

The routing protocols can fall into several categories, based on the characteristics that the protocols utilize. For instance, if a routing protocol does not advertise the subnet mask in its routing updates, it is a classful routing protocol. Classful routing protocols require the network design to have the same subnet mask in the design known as FLSM. In addition, these routing protocols cannot support discontiguous networks and automatically summarize network entries to the classful boundary when crossing interfaces in other major networks. When subnet masks include the routing advertisements, these updates are said to be classless. Classless routing protocols support VLSM network designs, discontiguous networks, and require manual summarization of networks.

If the routing protocol is designed to route inside an autonomous system, that routing protocol is an IGP. EGP routing protocols, on the other hand, are designed to route between autonomous systems.

Finally, routing protocols can belong to one of the following three classifications:

- ▶ **Distance vector:** The entire routing table is periodically sent to directly connected neighbors regardless of a topology change. These routing protocols manipulate the routing table updates before sending that information to their neighbors and are slow to converge when a topology change occurs.

- ▶ **Link-state:** All possible link states are stored in an independent topology table in which the best routes are calculated and put into the routing table. The topology table is initially synchronized with discovered neighbors followed by frequent hello messages. These routing protocols are faster to converge than distance vector routing protocols.

- ▶ **Hybrid:** By using the best characteristics from both link-state and routing protocols, these advanced routing protocols efficiently and quickly build their routing information and converge when topology changes occur.

Key Terms

- Default gateway
- Routing table
- Connected interface
- Hop
- Routing protocols
- Administrative distance
- Static routes
- Stub networks
- Floating routes
- Default route
- Classful routing protocols
- Classless routing protocols
- FLSM
- Discontiguous networks

- VLSM
- Route summarization
- Supernet
- CIDR
- Autonomous system
- IGP
- EGP
- Distance vector routing protocols
- Link-state routing protocols
- Advanced distance vector/hybrid routing protocols
- Longest match rule
- Redistribution

Apply Your Knowledge

Exercises

10.1 Create a Static and Default Route

This exercise tests your configuration skills in configuring a static and default route.

Estimated Time: 5 minutes

1. Enter privileged EXEC mode.

2. Enter global configuration mode.

3. Configure a static route for the 10.23.5.0/24 network using 192.168.64.2 as the next-hop address.

4. Configure a floating static route for the 10.23.5.0/24 network using 192.168.60.3.

5. Configure a default route to exit out of your serial interface.

10.2 Create a Summary Route

This exercise ensures that you can accurately supernet smaller subnets into one summary route.

Estimated Time: 5 minutes

Given the following networks, what is the summary route you can use to advertise these individual subnets to your neighbor router as an aggregate entry?

> 172.16.0.0 /16
>
> 172.17.0.0 /16
>
> 172.18.0.0 /16
>
> 172.19.0.0 /16

1. Count the number of networks you want to summarize.

2. Determine an increment that is equal to or less than the number of networks.

3. Make sure your base networks start on incremental boundaries (128, 64, 32, and so on) for the number of networks you are summarizing.

4. Calculate the subnet mask by the number of bits you need to steal from the original subnet to equal that incremental value.

Review Questions

1. What are the Layer 2 and Layer 3 characteristics of a packet destined for a network on a remote segment?

2. Why would you use a static route versus a routing protocol?

3. What are the characteristics of distance vector routing protocols?

4. What are the characteristics of link-state routing protocols?

5. What is the difference between classful and classless routing protocols?

Exam Questions

1. Given the following output, on which interface will a packet destined for 192.168.1.34 /24 be routed?

```
RouterA> show ip route
Codes: C - connected, S - static, I - IGRP, R - RIP, M - mobile, B - BGP
       D - EIGRP, EX - EIGRP external, O - OSPF, IA - OSPF inter area
       N1 - OSPF NSSA external type 1, N2 - OSPF NSSA external type 2
       E1 - OSPF external type 1, E2 - OSPF external type 2, E - EGP
       i - IS-IS, L1 - IS-IS level-1, L2 - IS-IS level-2, * - candidate default
       U - per-user static route, o - ODR, P - periodic downloaded static route
```

```
        T - traffic engineered route

Gateway of last resort is not set

C    10.0.0.0/8 is directly connected, Serial0/1
R    172.17.0.0/16 [120/1] via 192.168.1.10, Serial0/0
C    172.16.0.0/16 is directly connected, FastEthernet0/0
     192.168.1.0/30 is subnetted, 1 subnets
C       192.168.1.8 is directly connected, Serial0/0
```

- ○ **A.** Serial 0/1

- ○ **B.** Serial 0/0

- ○ **C.** Fast Ethernet 0/0

- ○ **D.** None of the above

2. Your network designer subnetted the major classful network of 192.168.2.0 into varying-sized subnets throughout your network. Which routing protocol category should not be your choice of routing protocol?

- ○ **A.** Classful

- ○ **B.** IGP

- ○ **C.** Link-state

- ○ **D.** ODR

3. Which of the following is not a characteristic of link-state routing protocols?

- ○ **A.** Fast convergence

- ○ **B.** Broadcasts routing table

- ○ **C.** Keeps track of neighbors in table

- ○ **D.** Knows all possible routes

4. Which of the following is not a subnet in the CIDR summary route 192.168.16.0 /21?

- ○ **A.** 192.168.16.0 /24

- ○ **B.** 192.168.20.0 /24

- ○ **C.** 192.168.24.0 /24

- ○ **D.** 192.168.23.0 /24

5. What is the consequence of using the following command?

   Router(config)# **ip route 0.0.0.0 0.0.0.0 192.168.10.2**

   ○ **A.** The entry will show up in the routing table signified with an R.

   ○ **B.** This entry is configured in a Layer 2 switch to send traffic to a Layer 3 routing device.

   ○ **C.** 192.168.10.2 is the IP address of the router that advertised this network in the routing protocol update.

   ○ **D.** If there is not an exact match in the routing table, packets will be sent to 192.168.10.2.

6. What is the consequence of using the following command? (Choose two)

   Router(config)# **ip route 192.168.20.4 255.255.255.0 10.1.1.1 3**

   ○ **A.** The 3 at the end of the command signifies that it is a floating static route.

   ○ **B.** The 3 at the end of the command signifies the hops to get to the destination.

   ○ **C.** The destination network is incorrect, so this command will not work.

   ○ **D.** The default administrative distance for this command is 120.

7. The network entry for 192.168.2.0 /24 is being advertised by RIP and OSPF. Which routing protocol displays the subnet in the routing table, and why?

   ○ **A.** OSPF because it has a lower metric

   ○ **B.** RIP because it is classful

   ○ **C.** OSPF because it has a lower administrative distance

   ○ **D.** RIP because it has a higher administrative distance

8. Which of the following is not a reason to use static routes?

   ○ **A.** To minimize configuration in complex networks.

   ○ **B.** To get finer control of routing decisions.

   ○ **C.** Destination networks are stubs.

   ○ **D.** To conserve bandwidth.

9. Given the following entries in a routing table, on which interface will a packet destined for 10.4.0.1 exit?

```
RouterA> show ip route
Codes: C - connected, S - static, I - IGRP, R - RIP, M - mobile, B - BGP
       D - EIGRP, EX - EIGRP external, O - OSPF, IA - OSPF inter area
       N1 - OSPF NSSA external type 1, N2 - OSPF NSSA external type 2
       E1 - OSPF external type 1, E2 - OSPF external type 2, E - EGP
       i - IS-IS, L1 - IS-IS level-1, L2 - IS-IS level-2, * - candidate default
       U - per-user static route, o - ODR, P - periodic downloaded static route
       T - traffic engineered route

Gateway of last resort is not set

C    172.16.0.0/16 is directly connected, FastEthernet0/0
     10.0.0.0/8 is variably subnetted, 4 subnets, 3 masks
I       10.0.0.0/8 [100/8976] via 172.17.0.2, FastEthernet0/1
D       10.1.0.0/16 [90/2297856] via 192.168.1.10, Serial0/1
D       10.4.0.0/16 [90/2297856] via 192.168.1.10, Serial0/1
O       10.4.0.0/30 [110/65] via 192.168.2.10, Serial0/0
```

  ○ **A.** Fast Ethernet 0/0

  ○ **B.** Serial 0/1

  ○ **C.** Serial 0/0

  ○ **D.** None of the above

10. Given the following entries in a routing table, which of the following are true? (Choose two)

```
RouterA> show ip route
...Ouput Omitted...

Gateway of last resort is 192.168.2.10 to network 0.0.0.0

C    172.16.0.0/16 is directly connected, FastEthernet0/0
     10.0.0.0/8 is variably subnetted, 4 subnets, 3 masks
I       10.0.0.0/8 [100/8976] via 172.17.0.2, FastEthernet0/1
D       10.1.0.0/16 [90/2297856] via 192.168.1.10, Serial0/1
D       10.4.0.0/16 [90/2297856] via 192.168.1.10, Serial0/1
S*      0.0.0.0/0 [1/0] via 192.168.2.10, Serial0/0
```

  ○ **A.** A packet destined for 192.168.100.2 will exit Serial 0/0.

  ○ **B.** The metric for network 10.4.0.0/16 is 90.

  ○ **C.** The metric for network 10.0.0.0/8 is 8976.

  ○ **D.** The routing protocol for network 10.1.0.0 has an administrative distance of 100.

Answers to Review Questions

1. When a packet is destined for a remote network, the Layer 3 source address is the workstation or device that is sending the traffic. The destination Layer 3 address is the IP address of the destination device. At Layer 2, the source address is the MAC address of the sending workstation or device. The destination Layer 2 address, however, is the MAC address of the default gateway. The default gateway is the routing device on the local segment that is responsible for forwarding packets from the local segment to remote networks.

2. Static routes are used primarily in stub networks or when the administrator wishes to have complete control over the routing decisions of their routing devices. Routing protocols are used in complex networks with multiple paths to a destination. Unlike static routes, routing protocols can dynamically react to topology changes in the internetwork.

3. Distance vector routing protocols periodically send routing table updates to their directly connected neighbors regardless of whether there is a change in the topology. These routine routing updates contain the contents of the entire routing table.

4. Link-state routing protocols initially discover their neighbors and retain that information in a neighbor table. Information about all possible routes is exchanged between these neighbors and stored in a router's topology table. After the initial exchange of information, link-state routers periodically send hello messages as opposed to full routing updates. With the knowledge of all possible routes in the topology, the routers calculate the best route to each destination and place them in the routing table.

5. Classful routing protocols do not contain the subnet mask in the routing updates. Networks using classful routing protocols require that a FLSM design does not support discontiguous networks. Classless routing protocols updates contain the subnet mask that enables the network design to support VLSM and discontiguous networks.

Answers to Exam Questions

1. **D.** A packet destined for 192.168.1.34 /24 would require a network entry for 192.168.1.0 in the routing table. Because there isn't an exact match for that network, the router sends it out the interface specified in a default route. This router does not have a default route configured, so the packet is dropped, and an ICMP destination unreachable is sent to the source. Answer A is incorrect because packets destined for the 10.0.0.0 /8 exit the serial 0/1 interface. Answer B is incorrect because packets destined for the 172.17.0.0 /16 exit the serial 0/0 interface. Answer C is incorrect because packets destined for the 172.16.0.0 /16 exit the Fast Ethernet 0/0 interface.

2. **A.** Because the network is designed with variable-length subnet masks, you should not use a classful routing protocol. B is incorrect because IGP routing protocols should be utilized inside your network. C is incorrect because link-state routing protocols support classless routing updates. D is incorrect because classless routing protocols support VLSM designs.

3. **B.** Link-state routing protocols do not broadcast their entire routing tables. They synchronize their topology table containing all possible routes with the neighbors they initially discover. Answers A, C, and D are all characteristics of link-state routing protocols.

4. **C.** Because the summary route stole three bits from the default Class C (/24), you are summarizing 2^3 or eight networks. 192.168.16.0 is in an increment of 8, so that is the base network. The range of networks that are summarized extend to network 192.168.23.0 for a total of 8 networks. Answers A, B, and D all fit in the range of networks that are summarized by the 192.168.16.0 /21 summary route.

5. **D.** The default route configured specifies that packets should be routed to the 192.168.10.2 next hop if there is not a specific match in the routing table. Answer A is incorrect because static route entries show up with the letter S in the routing table. Answer B is incorrect because by default this is a routing command that can be configured only in Layer 3 devices. `IP default gateway` is the command to configure a gateway of last resort for Layer 2 switches. Answer C is false because static routes are not advertised to other routers.

6. **A, C.** The 3 at the end of the static route command overrides the default administrative distance of 1 for a static route. This is probably being used to create a floating static route in a redundant network. The command, however, does not work because you have an inconsistent subnet mask with the destination network. The network ID should reflect 192.168.20.0 or the subnet mask should be 255.255.255.252. Answer B is incorrect because the 3 represents the administrative distance. Answer D is incorrect because static routes have a default administrative distance of 1.

7. **C.** OSPF has a lower administrative distance than RIP (110 vs. 120), so that entry shows up in the routing table because the lower administrative distance is preferred over higher ones. Answer A is incorrect because the metric of OSPF applies only if the OSPF routing protocol has multiple pathways to the 192.168.2.0 network. Answer B is false because classful or classless is not a factor in decisions between routing sources. Answer D is incorrect because routing protocols with lower administrative distances are trusted over routing protocols with higher administrative distances.

8. **A.** Static routes require more configurations in a complex network because you have to configure a static route for each destination in every router. Answers B, C, and D are all valid reasons to use static routes.

9. **C.** Because the OSPF entry has the longest match for the 10.4.0.1 network, you use that route out Serial 0/0. The interfaces in answers A and B conceivably could be used; however, the longest match rule states that when a packet has multiple possible network entries to use, the more specific subnet is used over the less specific. Because the serial interface has the longest match (the most specific subnet), that is the interface the packet destined for 10.4.0.1 will use.

10. **A, C.** This routing table indicates that a default route is configured. Because there isn't a match for 192.168.100.2 in the routing table, it is sent out Serial 0/0 as specified in the default route. The numbers in the brackets represent the administrative distance followed by the metric. Thus, the remaining correct statement is that the metric for the IGRP route for 10.0.0.0/8 is 8976. Answer B is false because the metric for the 10.4.0.0 /16 network is 2297856. Answer D is incorrect because the 10.1.0.0 /16 network is learned via EIGRP which has an administrative distance of 90.

Suggested Readings and Resources

1. Alex Zinn. *IP Routing: Packet Forwarding and Intra-domain Routing Protocols*. Addison Wesley Professional, 2002.

2. Keith Kruepke, Paul Cernick, and Mark Degner. *Cisco IP Routing Handbook*. Hungry Minds, 2000.

3. "Routing Protocols," www.firewall.cx.

4. "IP Routing," technology support on www.cisco.com.

11

Distance Vector Routing Protocols

Objectives

This chapter covers the following Cisco-specified objectives for the "Describe how a network works," and "Configure, verify, and troubleshoot basic router operation and routing on Cisco devices" sections of the 640-802 CCNA exam:

▶ **Configure, verify, and troubleshoot RIPv2**

▶ **Compare and contrast methods of routing and routing protocols**

▶ **Troubleshoot routing issues**

▶ **Verify router hardware and software operation using SHOW & DEBUG commands**

Outline

Study Strategies

▶ Read the information presented in the chapter, paying special attention to tables, Notes, and Exam Alerts.

▶ Keep in mind the characteristics of distance vector routing protocols and how those characteristics apply to RIP and RIPv2.

▶ Complete the Challenges and the Exercises at the end of the chapter. The exercises will solidify the concepts that you have learned in the previous sections.

▶ This chapter builds on the concepts discussed in Chapter 10, "Introduction to Routing and Routing Protocols." If you are not completely confident in your comfort with the fundamentals of routing protocols and their metrics, review Chapter 10 before proceeding with this chapter.

▶ Complete the Exam Questions at the end of the chapter. They are designed to simulate the types of questions you will be asked on the CCNA, ICND1, and ICND2 exams.

Introduction

The preceding chapter looked at distance vector routing protocols from a sort of high-altitude overview. This chapter brings you closer so that you can see the specific protocols that belong to this routing protocol class and explore the unique characteristics and functionality they provide. You will also learn how to configure those routing protocols to meet your administrative needs and how to verify and troubleshoot their operation.

Distance Vector Operations

Objective:

▶ Compare and contrast methods of routing and routing protocols

To recap, distance vector routing protocols are legacy routing protocols that help routing devices determine the networks that are present in a topology. Using a routing algorithm, known as the Bellman-Ford algorithm, distance vector routing protocols periodically broadcast routing updates consisting of the routing table to directly connected neighbors on adjacent data links, regardless of whether a change has occurred in the topology. When those devices receive that update, they compare it with their existing routing table information. If the distance vector metric for an entry in the routing update is greater (higher) than a current entry in the routing table, it is discarded. If the metric is equal or less, it is added to the routing table with an updated metric to include the path to the advertising neighbor. This entry eventually is passed to the next routing device where the process occurs over again.

> **NOTE**
>
> Many routing protocols, when the metrics on more than one route received by an update are equal, put both entries in the routing table and perform load balancing (transferring packets over both alternate paths).

Because these neighbors base their decisions on information that is not learned firsthand, distance vector routing protocol operations are often referred to as *routing by rumor*. In addition, each router in a distance vector routing topology has the same responsibility and function as the next router. In other words, distance vector routers contain flat relationships with each other.

> **EXAM ALERT**
>
> Distance vector routing protocols use the Bellman-Ford algorithm by broadcasting the entire routing table to directly connected neighbors regardless of whether a topology change occurs or not. The information in the update is added and recalculated before being sent to other neighbors.

Consider the example shown in Figure 11.1, which uses a classful distance vector routing protocol such as RIP version 1. Each router contains its directly connected networks in its routing table. Because the routing protocol is classful, the subnetted 192.168.1.0 network has a Fixed-Length Subnet Mask (FLSM) design. In addition, the routing table entries contain the metric (hop count for this particular example) indicated by "0" because they are all connected. This is also followed by the interface that packets will exit to reach those networks. Without the use of static routes or routing protocols, the routers can never reach the networks that lie beyond their neighbor routers.

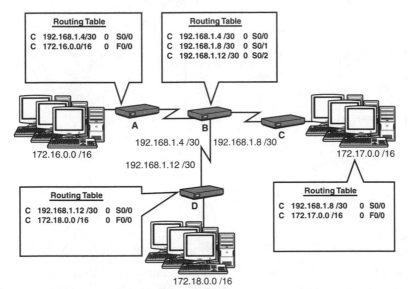

FIGURE 11.1 Distance vector routing initiation.

After you configure and enable a distance vector routing protocol, it advertises the networks in the routing table to its adjacent neighbors. For example, Router A broadcasts a routing update containing the 192.168.1.4 network as well as the 172.16.0.0 network to Router B. As soon as Router B receives that update, it compares the entries in its routing table with the information learned from Router A. Router B already knows about 192.168.1.4 as a directly connected network, so it disregards that entry because the directly connected network has a lower administrative distance than the routing protocol. Because the 172.16.0.0 network is new information, it adds that to its routing table with an updated metric of 1. The 172.16.0.0 network is one hop away through Router A. Similarly, when that entry is advertised to Routers C and D, the metric is updated again to 2 because it is two hops away (through Router B and then Router A).

Likewise, Routers A, C, and D receive an update from Router B containing two new networks that will be added to their routing table as two hops away. This process continues until each router has an accurate depiction of all the networks in the domain, as shown in Figure 11.2. In other words, the network will be converged. Despite having achieved full convergence, the routes will still advertise their routing table to their neighbors periodically, even if there isn't a change in the topology.

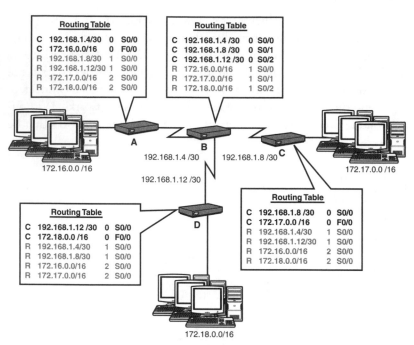

FIGURE 11.2 Distance vector routing converged scenario.

Routing Loops

One of the major concerns with routing protocols is the possible occurrence of a routing loop. Routing loops are hard to find these days because routing protocols have implemented many measures to mitigate them, but it is still important to examine the plausible historic events that necessitated the need for such measures. Additionally, there still is a slim possibility that these loops can occur regardless of the countermeasures in place.

To demonstrate a routing loop scenario, I will use the existing converged topology and introduce a link failure on Router A, as illustrated in Figure 11.3. Notice that the routing table in Router A changed to reflect only the remaining connected interface left since its serial link failed. Because the next hop to the protocol-learned networks is down, those entries are removed too. Likewise, Router B removes the connected interface as well as the network entry for 172.16.0.0 because that link and consequently the next hop to that network is down.

Imagine in this scenario that Router D sends its periodic update to Router B before Router B can advertise the topology change in its update. When Router B receives the update, it compares the information with its own routing table as distance vector routing protocols typically do. The new subnet information learned in the routing update is added to the routing table. In this unfortunate case, Router B learns (again) about the 172.16.0.0 and the 192.168.1.4 networks and believes they can be reached through Router D (despite Router D originally having learned those routes via Router B). What's more, Router B adds its metric to get to Router D to reach the networks that don't even exist, as shown in Figure 11.4.

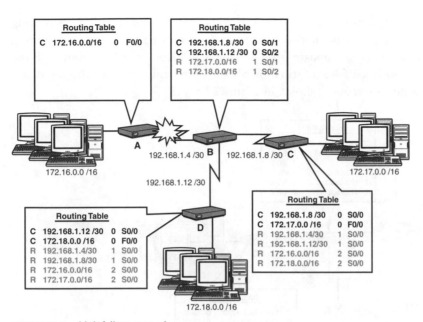

FIGURE 11.3 Link failure scenario.

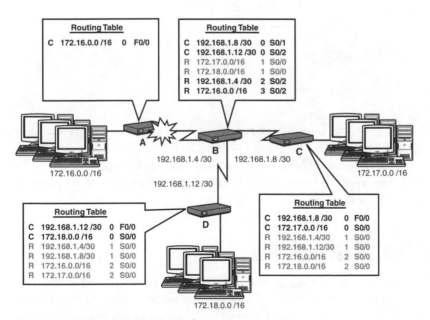

FIGURE 11.4 Incorrect update scenario.

Router B continues to update its neighbor routers periodically with the entries in its routing table. Unfortunately, the unreachable networks appear to be moving away because the hop count inevitably increases with each update from Router B and Router D for infinity. All the while, poor Router C also is fed false information about these networks from Router B and also has to keep adjusting its metrics as shown in Figure 11.5.

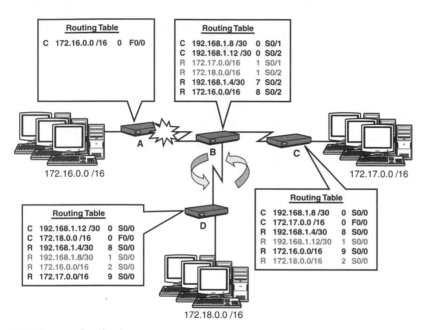

FIGURE 11.5 Routing loop.

With all three routers containing false information regarding those networks, any packets destined for the 172.16.0.0 and the 192.168.1.4 network are sent to Router D, who in turn, sends them right back to Router B, and so on. These packets will continue to bounce back and forth in the routing loop until the time to live field in the IP packets expire or the link becomes so saturated, traffic cannot flow between the two routers.

Routing Loop Mitigation

To avoid routing loops, distance vector routing protocols have implemented several counter-measures within the routing protocol operations. The following sections describe the preventative measures that have been put in place to mitigate routing loops. For obvious reasons, the majority of these are integrated within the routing protocol and cannot be disabled.

Counting to Infinity

As demonstrated earlier, when routers are continuously passing updates to unreachable networks between each other, the metric continues to increase forever, which is known as *counting to infinity*. The easiest way to mitigate this routing protocol side effect is to incorporate a ceiling on the maximum hop count in the design of the routing protocol. Using this tactic, routers can determine a network to be unreachable after it reaches the maximum hop count allowed for that protocol. Table 11.1 lists the routing protocols and their maximum hop count values.

TABLE 11.1   Maximum Hop Counts

Protocol	Distance Vector/Link State/Hybrid	Maximum Hop Count
RIPv1	Distance vector	15
RIPv2	Distance vector	15
EIGRP	Hybrid	224
OSPF	Link state	Infinite

Notice that RIP version 1 and 2 both have a maximum hop count of 15, which drastically limits the size of the allowed RIP network. EIGRP, because it is has some distance vector routing protocol features, has a maximum hop count value of 224. OSPF is a link-state routing protocol that does not use or require a maximum hop count, so it can have an infinite number of hops.

Split Horizon

Split horizon is similar to that old saying, "Don't ride out on the horse you rode in on." After hearing this little tidbit, if you were to turn around and say back to me that split horizon is similar to that old saying, "Don't ride out on the horse you rode in on," it would get redundant, confusing, and annoying pretty quickly. Such is the case with routing updates.

As you saw earlier, you can get into trouble when routers advertise networks back to the router from which they learned them. Split horizon fixes this dilemma by suppressing those networks in the routing updates being sent back to the source. In other words, split horizon does not advertise networks out the same interface as that from which it learned them.

Take the example shown in Figure 11.6. Because Router D learned about the 192.168.1.4, 192.168.1.8, 172.16.0.0, and 172.17.0.0 subnets from Router B, it does not advertise those networks back to Router B out Serial 0/0. In addition, because it heard Router B advertising the 192.168.1.12 network as well, it does not advertise that back out that interface either. Thus, the only network that Router D will still advertise to Router B is the 172.18.0.0 network because that subnet was not learned via serial 0/0. Now when the link fails on Router A, Router B will not receive a misleading update about the 192.168.1.4 and the 172.16.0.0 networks because Router D and Router C do not advertise those networks back to Router B.

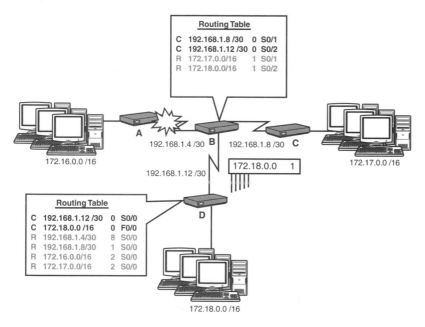

FIGURE 11.6 Split horizon updates.

> **NOTE**
>
> Contrary to what you might think, when a router advertises a network in a routing update to its neighbors, it adds the metric automatically, as shown in Figure 11.6.

> **EXAM ALERT**
>
> Be sure you understand the operations involved in split horizon.

Route Poison, Poison Reverse, and Hold-Down Timers

To avoid count-to-infinity routing loops, a maximum hop count is defined for a routing protocol so the metrics do not increment indefinitely in the event of a routing loop. With route poisoning, the router that recognizes the link failure poisons the affected networks by setting them to an infinite metric for that routing protocol. When that router sends this update to its neighbors, they are notified of the link failure and can update their routing table accordingly.

To illustrate the route poisoning concept, refer to Figure 11.7. Notice in this topology that a redundant route has been added between Router D and Router A. The resultant routing table for Router D now has a route to the 172.16.0.0 network through Router A because it is only one hop count as opposed to two hops through Router B. In addition, notice that Router D has equidistant hops to reach network 192.168.1.4. In this case, Router D keeps both routes in the routing table and load balances between both links for packets destined for that network. When the link fails between Router A and Router B, Router A and Router B set the affected networks to an infinite metric. In this example, because I am using RIP, the maximum hop count is 15, so 16 is an infinite metric.

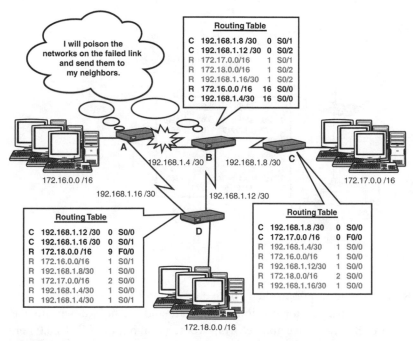

FIGURE 11.7 Route poisoning.

When Routers C and D receive these updates from their neighbors, they can advertise the poisoned network out all their interfaces. With poison reverse, the routers override the split horizon rule and even send the update back to the source, which proves useful as an acknowledgment that those devices are aware of the topology change. At the same time, when Routers C and D receive the poisoned update, they put that network in a "possible down" state in their routing table, as illustrated in Figure 11.8. This is the work of the hold-down timer.

Hold-down timers are activated when a router receives a poisoned update from a neighbor indicating that a known network is now inaccessible. To ensure that the router does not hastily listen to alternate routes causing yet another routing loop, the router ignores updates with a poorer metric than the original until the hold-down timer expires. This gives the rest of the topology ample time to react to the link change. However, if an update is received with a *better* metric than the original route entry, the router discontinues the hold-down timer and uses that entry in its routing table.

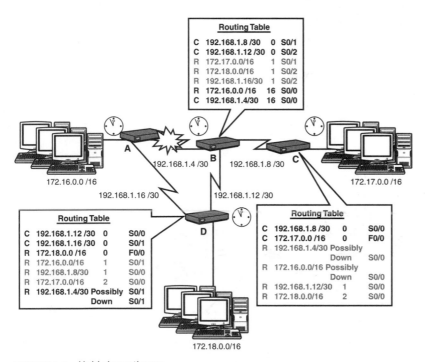

FIGURE 11.8 Hold-down timers.

In Figure 11.8, when Routers A and B poison their route entries and pass them to Routers C and D, those poisoned networks are put in a possible down state and the hold-down timer is activated. In that time, Router B may receive updates from Router D about the 172.16.0.0 network because Router D has an alternate route. However, Router B must wait for the hold-down timer to expire before using the alternate path. For this reason, distance vector routing protocols are considered the slowest routing protocols to converge.

Triggered Updates

One way distance vector routing protocols speed up their convergence while helping avoid routing loops at the same time is something called *flash* or *triggered updates*. Because one of the contributing causes of routing loops is the lack of update information reaching all devices quickly enough, triggered updates enable the router to send the update immediately after a link fails, as opposed to waiting for its periodic update time.

Invalid/Dead Timers

In place of a link failure, what do you suppose would happen if Router A had some operational failures or you removed or changed the routing protocol configuration or networks? Other routers in the domain would not be aware of this change because it isn't a link failure that they can detect and react to. To ensure that these networks are not circulating indefinitely in a routing system, routing protocols have invalid, or dead, timers. If a router stops receiving updates from a router after a set amount of time, that router is considered to be dead and the networks that learned from that router are invalid. Likewise, if a particular network stops advertising with a routing protocol, that entry becomes invalid after the dead timer ages out. This timer is reset every time an update is received from a neighbor for each network in the routing table. When the timer expires, the router poisons the route and advertises that topology change to its neighbors.

> **TIP**
>
> You can clear out aged entries in the routing table quickly by using the `clear ip route` command followed by the network you want to remove, or use the wildcard, *, to remove all entries.

RIP

The first distance vector routing protocol that is discussed here is coincidentally one of the oldest routing protocols that is still used today. Circa 1988, Routing Information Protocol (RIP) for IP was defined in RFC 1058; however, its roots stem back to the 1970s at Xerox Corporation's Palo Alto Research Center. The following sections look at the characteristics and configurations involved with this resolute routing protocol.

RIP Characteristics

RIP is a fairly simple routing protocol in both characteristics and implementation. You already know that RIP uses hop count as its only metric, in which it can support up to 15 as a maximum. In instances where the metric is identical (for example, equal hop count) for a subnet, it load balances up to six equal paths (four by default). Like other distance vector routing protocols, RIP sends the contents of its routing table to its directly connected neighbors, regardless of whether there is a change in the topology. Particularly, RIP's update interval is every 30 seconds and its invalid timer is for 180 seconds. Thus, RIP (version 1) broadcasts its routing table every 30 seconds and considers a neighbor or a network to be dead after six missed updates.

Because RIP does not advertise subnet masks in its routing updates, it is also a classful routing protocol. Recall that this requires every subnet of a major network to have the same (fixed-length) subnet masks. In addition, RIP automatically summarizes subnetted networks to their default classful boundaries when sending the update over a different major network which, in turn, nullifies any support for a discontiguous network design.

As with many routing protocols, RIP requires manual redistribution if you want to advertise networks from a different routing source other than connected interfaces and other RIP-learned networks. This is also the case for default routes. If you configure a static default route in a router that is running RIP, you must use the `default-information originate` command in the routing process to redistribute that default route in its routing updates to its neighbors without any additional configuration. The neighbors receive these updates and set that router as their gateway of last resort, assuming that a static default route is not configured with a lower administrative distance. The routing table subsequently displays the learned 0.0.0.0/0 subnet as a RIP-learned network.

> **EXAM ALERT**
>
> Although version 1 of RIP is considered outdated by the CCNA, ICND1, and ICND2 exams, it is important to know its characteristics and configuration because RIPv2 shares many characteristics and is similar in configuration.

RIP Configuration

The configuration for RIP is seamless as long as you remember these two simple rules:

▸ Advertise only your directly connected networks.

▸ Advertise only the classful network.

The first rule is imperative to keep in mind when configuring routing protocols. Remember that the point of the routing protocols is to advertise their known networks to each other so they can build their routing tables. With that being said, do not confuse the configuration of routing protocols with static routes. You do not specify a destination network with routing protocols as you would a static route. Instead, you specify local networks and let the routing protocols advertise them to each other.

Because RIP is a classful routing protocol and does not advertise subnet masks in its updates, the second rule is self-explanatory. Regardless of whether you subnetted major networks into smaller subnets, you have to specify only the subnet to its classful boundary. In other words, you specify the network portion of the IP address and use zeros for the host bits. To recap, the classful boundaries are listed in Table 11.2, in which N represents the network and H represents the host.

EXAM ALERT

It is imperative to know and practice the two rules for configuring RIP.

TABLE 11.2   Classful Network Boundaries

Class	First Octet	Network
A	1 to 126	N.H.H.H
B	128 to 191	N.N.H.H
C	192 to 223	N.N.N.H

To configure RIP and advertise the directly connected classful networks, you must enter the configuration mode for routing protocols, using the `router` keyword in global configuration mode followed by the routing protocol you want to configure. After you are in the routing protocol configuration mode (signified by the `(config-router)#` prompt), you specify the directly connected classful networks by using the `network` command. If you need to remove a specific network from being advertised, you need to enter the RIP routing process again and enter `no` followed by the keyword `network` and the network number you want to remove.

Using Figure 11.9 as an example, Routers A, C, and D each have two directly connected networks while Router B has three. To configure RIP to advertise the routing protocols, the configuration for Router A would look like the following:

```
RouterA(config)#router rip
RouterA(config-router)#network 172.16.0.0
RouterA(config-router)#network 192.168.1.0
```

TIP

If you accidentally configure a network at the incorrect classful boundary, the IOS configuration automatically changes your configuration statement(s) to reflect the classful network.

EXAM ALERT

Be prepared to configure a routing protocol given a network topology. Even though there is IOS support to autocorrect your mistakes when entering the networks, as mentioned in the preceding Tip, do not rely on the exam to allow that as a correct answer.

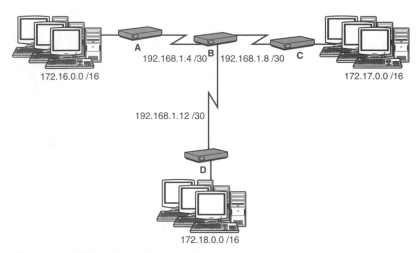

172.16.0.0 /16

192.168.1.4 /30   192.168.1.8 /30

172.17.0.0 /16

192.168.1.12 /30

172.18.0.0 /16

FIGURE 11.9 RIP configuration scenario.

Because Router A has the 172.16.0.0 network and the 192.168.1.4 network attached to it, the classful networks that are advertised are 172.16.0.0 because it is a Class B, and 192.168.1.0 because that network is a Class C. You do not need to include any other network statements because the routers will advertise each others' networks. After you define the networks with the `network` command, RIP begins to advertise and listen for updates on those interfaces that are contained in that classful network. For instance, if you did not configure the `network 192.168.1.0` statement in Router A, you would never be able to send and receive updates on the serial interface, which would entail that Router B would never learn of the 172.16.0.0 network and Router A would never learn of the other networks in the topology.

> **EXAM ALERT**
>
> Keep in mind that the routing protocol does not listen to or learn from advertisements on an interface unless you include their respective networks in the routing protocol process with the `network` command.

Router B has three directly connected 192.168.1.x networks, so how many statements do you think you must configure for Router B to participate in RIP updates? Despite having three networks, you must advertise the classful networks in the RIP configuration; thus, you require only one statement for the 192.168.1.0 network that will, in essence, encompass all three subnets. Figure 11.10 shows the configurations for each router in this topology.

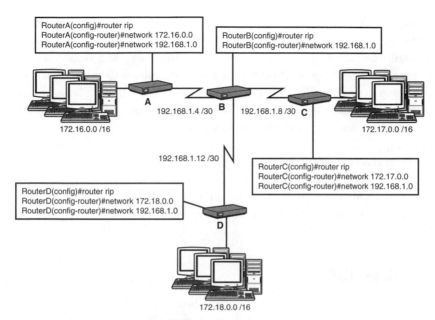

FIGURE 11.10 Completed RIP configuration scenario.

If you want to change the number of allowed equal paths to load balance with RIP, you can use the `maximum-paths` command in the routing process. For example, if you wanted to change the maximum paths to six equal paths, the configuration would look like the following:

```
RouterA(config)#router rip
RouterA(config-router)#maximum-paths 6
```

> **TIP**
>
> To disable load balancing over multiple equal paths, set the maximum paths to 1.

Passive Interfaces

Some of you may have looked at these configurations and noticed a strange flaw in our logic. Namely, we've established that when we configure each network to be advertised in the routers, updates begin being sent and received on the interfaces attached to those networks. But do we really need to be sending updates on LANs that do not connect to RIP routers? For instance, the Ethernet interface on Router A from Figure 11.10 that connects to the 172.16.0.0 network does not have a router on that LAN segment. In essence, we are wasting good bandwidth and processor cycles by broadcasting these RIP update every 60 seconds to a bunch of computers who do not need to receive them. To solve this dilemma for RIP and all other routing protocols, Cisco created a handy configuration option for routing protocols called *passive interface*.

With this additional configuration command, you specify an interface or interfaces to the routing protocol process that will no longer send routing updates. What is interesting, however, is that the interfaces will still receive and process updates on that interface. As a result, passive interfaces are useful not only for saving bandwidth, but also can be used to manipulate our routing policies by allowing us to determine whether or not we send routing updates to certain routers. The command to achieve this marvelous feat is `passive-interface interface` in the routing process configuration, such as shown here for RIP:

```
RouterA(config)#router rip
RouterA(config-router)#passive-interface fastethernet 0/0
```

With this command in place, updates are no longer sent out of Fast Ethernet 0/0. However, if for some reason an update was received on that interface, it would still process it and put it in its routing table.

RIPv2 Characteristics

In an attempt to keep up with modern needs from a routing protocol, RIP version 2 was created in 1994 to address many of the shortcomings of its predecessor. Many of the characteristics are similar to RIPv1; nonetheless, RIPv2 had some significant improvements:

▶ **Multicast updates:** Rather than broadcast its routing updates, RIPv2 uses a reserved multicast address of 224.0.0.9 to communicate with other RIPv2 neighbors. By using a multicast address, it does not waste the processing resources of non-RIP devices because only RIPv2 devices process messages to that address.

▶ **Classful or classless support:** RIPv2 is classful by default, but can be configured as a classless routing protocol, which allows for subnet masks to be sent in the routing updates. The implication of this enhancement entails that RIPv2 can support VLSM and discontiguous network designs.

▶ **Authenticated updates:** To ensure the origin of the routing update and protect from attackers spoofing routing updates, RIPv2 allows update authentication in which the passwords must match in all routers to validate the routing update.

EXAM ALERT

Be sure to remember the enhancements that RIPv2 holds over RIPv1.

RIPv2 Configuration

Objective:

▶ Configure, verify, and troubleshoot RIPv2

The configuration for RIPv2 is practically identical to RIPv1. In other words, you still must enter the RIP routing process with the `router rip` command and still must advertise the directly connected classful networks. To enable RIPv2, you have to enter the command `version 2` in the routing process:

```
RouterA(config)#router rip
RouterA(config-router)#version 2
RouterA(config-router)#network 172.16.0.0
RouterA(config-router)#network 192.168.1.0
```

By default, RIPv2 is classful. To configure this enhanced routing protocol to support classless routing updates, the only entry you need to configure is the `no auto-summary` command in the routing process:

```
RouterA(config)#router rip
RouterA(config-router)#no auto-summary
```

After you configure this command, the RIP version 2 updates being multicast to 224.0.0.9 are no longer be considered classful, because the subnet mask is advertised in the updates along with the network.

TIP

By default, RIP is configured to send version 1 and accept version 1 and 2 received updates. This means that routers that have not been changed to version 2 will still accept version 2 updates but will process them as version 1 (ignoring any subnet mask or authentication). Be sure to keep this in mind if you decide to revert your RIP configuration to version 1 by using the `version 1` command. This command instructs the router to receive only version 1 updates, which causes version 2 updates to be treated as an illegal version and be ignored. To revert to the default RIP configuration, a better command to use is `default version` in the RIP routing process.

EXAM ALERT

If a router is explicitly configured to run as version 1, RIP version 2 updates are considered an illegal version and are ignored.

RIPv2 Update Authentication

As previously mentioned, RIPv2 provides update authentication to help protect from rogue devices or attackers injecting false routing information into your routing table by authenticating the routing updates. This authentication is achieved by defining a key and attaching a key string (password) to it. This key string must match on both routers, or the updates will be rejected.

To define the authentication key, use the `key chain` command followed by a name for the key chain in global configuration mode. After you enter that command, you are put into `config-keychain` subconfiguration mode:

```
RouterA(config)#key chain luckyrabbitsfoot
RouterA(config-keychain)#
```

Here you can configure several keys if you want, with different key string passwords. To create a key, use the `key` keyword and a number identifier for that key. You are put into another subconfiguration mode for that specific key, as shown by the `config-keychain-key` prompt:

```
RouterA(config-keychain)#key 1
RouterA(config-keychain-key)#
```

Now we finally get to define our password, using the `key-string` command followed by the password that will match on each side:

```
RouterA(config-keychain-key)#key-string whataRIPoff
```

With our key chain defined, we have to apply it to interfaces that connect to neighboring RIPv2 routers with matching authentication configurations. The command to assign the key chain to the interface is `ip rip authentication key-chain` followed by the key chain you defined a moment ago:

```
RouterA(config-keychain-key)#exit
RouterA(config-keychain)#exit
RouterA(config)#interface serial 0/0/0
RouterA(config-if)#ip rip authentication key-chain luckyrabbitsfoot
```

This key chain is sent over the link in clear text by default. This defeats the point of securing links, because the key chain can be seen if the link is being eavesdropped. To secure the key using an MD5 hash of the password, use the following command:

```
RouterA(config-if)#ip rip authentication mode md5
```

Configuring RIP with SDM

RIP configurations using SDM are relatively similar and just as easy as configuring default and static routes. Select **Configuration**, **Routing**. Focus on the bottom of the screen for our dynamic routing protocols. When you click the **Edit** button, you see the pop-up window shown in

Figure 11.11, in which you can specify your routing protocol parameters. You can enable RIP by checking the checkbox and specifying which version you want to run. Below that, you add the networks you want to advertise. Be sure that you specify each network that is directly attached to the router. This ensures that they are included in the routing updates and that the updates are sent and received on the interfaces associated with those networks. Finally, in the bottom of the window, you can check the checkboxes for the interfaces that you want to make into passive interfaces to save bandwidth or control which routers will have updates sent to them.

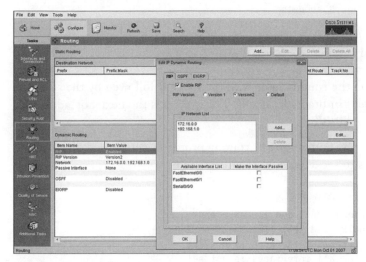

FIGURE 11.11 SDM RIP configuration.

RIP Verification

Objective:

▶ Verify router hardware and software operation using SHOW & DEBUG commands

To verify RIP, you can use an assortment of show commands, each equally contributing to a wealth of information about the RIP routing protocol you configured. For instance, show running-config is an easy pick to show your configuration for RIP and the networks that you have configured. It is also a useful starting point if you are troubleshooting an existing implementation of RIP and you suspect missing or misconfigured network statements.

To ensure that RIP updates are being received from neighbors, show ip route proves the network configuration is functioning, because you will see RIP entries appear in the routing table:

```
RouterA#show ip route
Codes: C - connected, S - static, I - IGRP, R - RIP, M - mobile, B - BGP
       D - EIGRP, EX - EIGRP external, O - OSPF, IA - OSPF inter area
       N1 - OSPF NSSA external type 1, N2 - OSPF NSSA external type 2
       E1 - OSPF external type 1, E2 - OSPF external type 2, E - EGP
```

```
      i - IS-IS, L1 - IS-IS level-1, L2 - IS-IS level-2, * - candidate default
      U - per-user static route, o - ODR, P - periodic downloaded static route
      T - traffic engineered route

Gateway of last resort is not set

R    172.17.0.0/16 [120/2] via 192.168.1.6, Serial0/0/0
C    172.16.0.0/16 is directly connected, FastEthernet0/0
R    172.18.0.0/16 [120/2] via 192.168.1.6, Serial0/0/0
     192.168.1.0/30 is subnetted, 3 subnets
R       192.168.1.8 [120/1] via 192.168.1.6, Serial0/0/0
R       192.168.1.12 [120/1] via 192.168.1.6, Serial0/0/0
C       192.168.1.4 is directly connected, Serial0/0/0
```

The RIP entries are identified in the routing table with the letter R followed by the administrative distance and the hop count in brackets. The IP 192.168.1.6 is the next-hop address to reach those networks out of Serial 0/0/0.

Finally, to see detailed information about all the IP routing protocols configured on a routing device, use show ip protocols to see a plethora of information:

```
RouterA#show ip protocols
Routing Protocol is "rip"
  Sending updates every 30 seconds, next due in 24 seconds
  Invalid after 180 seconds, hold down 180, flushed after 240
  Outgoing update filter list for all interfaces is not set
  Incoming update filter list for all interfaces is not set
  Redistributing: rip
  Default version control: send version 2, receive version 2
    Interface           Send  Recv  Triggered RIP    Key-chain
    FastEthernet0/0       2    2                      ____
    Serial0/0/0          2    2                      luckyrabbitsfoot_
  Automatic network summarization is in effect
  Maximum path: 4
  Routing for Networks:
    172.16.0.0
    192.168.1.0
  Routing Information Sources:
    Gateway         Distance    Last Update
    192.168.1.6        120      00:00:11
  Distance: (default is 120)
```

In this output, you can see the timers involved with the routing protocol, including the update interval of 30 seconds and the invalid and hold-down timers. The show ip protocols output also lists the interfaces participating in RIP and the version that they are configured to send and receive (in this case, version 2). On our serial 0/0/0 interface, you can also see that we have configured RIP authentication and that the key chain *luckyrabbitsfoot* is assigned to this interface. In addition, you can see which networks you are routing using RIP. This is useful for administrators who do not have access to privileged EXEC mode (and who therefore cannot use the show running-config command) to verify which networks are being advertised.

Troubleshooting RIP

Objective:

▶ Troubleshoot routing issues

Troubleshooting routing protocols always begins with verification of the routing configuration and status by using the show commands discussed in the last section. You can also test whether you have IP connectivity by pinging or you can test the route packets will take by using the traceroute command. However, if you need to get into the trenches, so to speak, and verify the updates as they are being sent and received, you need to use real-time troubleshooting tools entailing the debug command.

> **TIP**
>
> If you forget which debug processes you have running, you can issue the show debug command to list all the processes you are currently debugging.

To actively see real-time updates as they are being sent and received for RIP, use the privileged EXEC command debug ip rip, as demonstrated here:

```
RouterA#debug ip rip
RIP protocol debugging is on
RouterA#
*Aug  6 22:33:21.002: RIP: received packet with MD5 authentication
*Aug  6 22:33:21.002: RIP: received v2 update from 192.168.1.6 on Serial0/0/0
*Aug  6 22:33:21.002:      172.17.0.0/16 via 0.0.0.0 in 2 hops
*Aug  6 22:33:21.002:      172.18.0.0/16 via 0.0.0.0 in 2 hops
*Aug  6 22:33:21.006:      192.168.1.8/30 via 0.0.0.0 in 1 hops
*Aug  6 22:33:21.006:      192.168.1.12/30 via 0.0.0.0 in 1 hops
```

In this section of the debug output, the router receives an update from a neighbor with the IP address 192.168.1.6. This update is a version 2 update and has been authenticated using MD5. If any new subnets are learned from this update, they ultimately are placed in the routing table, using 192.168.1.6 as the next-hop address and Serial 0/0/0 as the exiting interface, because that is where this information was learned. Notice in this section that subnet masks are received in the update, solidifying the fact that you are running a classless routing protocol, RIPv2.

The next bit of output that follows is the local router sending its v2 multicast (224.0.0.9) update out its Fast Ethernet 0/0 interface. Most important, notice how the router increments the hop count by 1 before sending it to any neighbors on its LAN:

```
*Aug  6 22:33:23.598: RIP: sending v2 update to 224.0.0.9 via FastEthernet0/0
(172.16.0.1)
*Aug  6 22:33:23.598: RIP: build update entries
*Aug  6 22:33:23.598:    172.17.0.0/16 via 0.0.0.0, metric 3, tag 0
*Aug  6 22:33:23.598:    172.18.0.0/16 via 0.0.0.0, metric 3, tag 0
*Aug  6 22:33:23.598:    192.168.1.0/24 via 0.0.0.0, metric 1, tag 0
*Aug  6 22:33:23.598: RIP: ignored v2 packet from 172.16.0.1 (sourced from one of our
addresses)
```

Also, take note of the 192.168.1.0 entry that is being advertised out this Fast Ethernet 0/0 interface. Because the interface has an IP address of 172.16.0.1, which is not in the same major network, this router automatically summarized its subnetted entries to 192.168.1.0. Therefore, we can surmise by this debug output that we have not configured the no auto-summary on Router A. If this were the case, the entry would remain classless and look more like this:

```
*Aug  6 22:33:23.598:    192.168.1.4/30 via 0.0.0.0, metric 1, tag 0
```

The final output that follows is proof that split horizon is enabled and working on this router. This is evident because the router does not send any entries that it received on serial 0/0/0 from the first output explanation. Recall that split horizon keeps a router from advertising networks back out the interface from which it received that information. Because the 192.168.1.8, 192.168.1.12, 172.17.0.0, and 172.18.0.0 networks were received in the router's Serial 0/0/0 interface, they cannot be sent back out that interface.

```
*Aug  6 22:33:23.822: RIP: sending v2 update to 224.0.0.9 via Serial0/0/0 (192.168.1.5)
*Aug  6 22:33:23.822: RIP: build update entries
*Aug  6 22:33:23.822:    172.16.0.0/16 via 0.0.0.0, metric 1, tag 0
```

EXAM ALERT

Be sure you can decipher the output of a debug ip rip command.

Challenge

Given the following design in Figure 11.12, configure RIP on Router A to be able to communicate with the remainder of the preconfigured network.

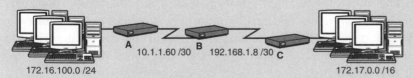

FIGURE 11.12 RIP configuration challenge.

1. Remember to remove any existing static routes. Why?

2. Enter the configuration process for RIP.

3. Advertise Router A's networks.

   What will Router B do with the update from Router A?

   What will the networks look like when Router B sends them on to Router C?

4. Configure Router A to run RIP version 2.

5. Configure Router A to be classless.

   What will the update from Router A look like now?

6. Configure RIP authentication using an MD5 hash of the password on Routers A and B.

Challenge Answer

You must first remove any static routes because they have a lower administrative distance than RIP. The configuration in steps 2 and 3 would look like the following:

```
RouterA(config)#router rip
RouterA(config-router)#network 172.16.0.0
RouterA(config-router)#network 10.0.0.0
```

Despite having subnetted the major networks in our topology, you must advertise the directly connected classful networks. When Router B receives that update, it adds the 172.16.0.0 entry into its routing table (because 10.1.1.60 is already directly connected) with a metric of 1 and uses Router A's serial interface as the next hop. The entry is not 172.16.100.0 because Router A auto-summarizes that network when exiting its WAN interface because that is on a different major network. When Router B sends that entry to Router C, it is sent as 172.16.0.0 with a metric (hop count of 2).

To configure Router A for RIPv2 and make it classless, you must add the following configurations:

```
RouterA(config)#router rip
RouterA(config-router)#version 2
RouterA(config-router)#no auto-summary
```

With this configuration, Router A does not automatically summarize the 172.16.100.0 network and it sends the subnet mask along to Router B. If B is running RIPv2 also, it keeps the network in its subnetted form of 172.16.100.0/24.

To assign RIP update authentication, we have to create matching keys on each router and apply them to the serial interfaces of each router:

(continues)

(continued)

```
RouterA(config)#key chain RtrAKey
RouterA(config-keychain)#key 1
RouterA(config-keychain-key)#key-string perfectmatch
RouterA(config-keychain-key)#exit
RouterA(config-keychain)#exit
RouterA(config)#interface serial 0/0/0
RouterA(config-if)#ip rip authentication key-chain RtrAKey
RouterA(config-if)#ip rip authentication mode md5

RouterB(config)#key chain RtrBKey
RouterB(config-keychain)#key 1
RouterB(config-keychain-key)#key-string perfectmatch
RouterB(config-keychain-key)#exit
RouterB(config-keychain)#exit
RouterB(config)#interface serial 0/0/0
RouterB(config-if)#ip rip authentication key-chain RtrBKey
RouterB(config-if)#ip rip authentication mode md5
```

Notice that the names of the key chains do not have to match, but the actual key strings inside the key chains do.

Chapter Summary

This chapter discussed the distance vector routing protocols, RIP and RIPv2. Both routing protocols are susceptible to routing loops and have several countermeasures in place to help mitigate these anomalies. For instance, both routing protocols have a maximum hop count to ensure that routing loops do not cause routers to increment the metric for infinity, and define a reasonable limit on the size of the network to which the routing protocol can scale. Split horizon contributes in the mitigation of routing loops by ensuring that routers do not advertise networks out the same interface as that on which those networks were learned. When a link fails, distance vector routing protocols poison the affected routes by setting them to an infinite metric and immediately shoot them out as a flash or triggered update. The split horizon rule is overridden in this instance to send a notice that the link is possibly down. The link remains in that state (unless it receives an update that has a better metric than the original network entry) until the hold-down timer expires. After the hold-down timer lapses, the router can use routes with less favorable metrics than the original.

Table 11.3 summarizes the characteristics of RIPv1 and RIPv2.

TABLE 11.3   RIP and RIPv2 Comparison

	RIPv1	RIPv2
Classful/classless	Classful	Both
Algorithm	Bellman-Ford	Bellman-Ford
Metric	Hops	Hops
Maximum hop count	15	15
Infinite metric	16	16
Update/invalid	30/180	30/180
Updates	Broadcast	Multicast (224.0.0.9)
Load balancing	Equal paths	Equal paths

To configure RIP, you must enter the routing process first with the `router` keyword in global configuration mode followed by the routing protocol. After you are in the routing process, you advertise the networks with the `network` command followed by the directly connected classful networks.

To enable RIPv2, you must add the command `version 2` in the RIP routing configuration process. When you enable version 2, updates are no longer broadcast to neighbors, but rather are sent as multicasts to 224.0.0.9. In addition, because RIPv2 can be classless in addition to classful, you can disable automatic summarization of networks with the `no auto-summary` command. Additionally, RIPv2 supports update authentication. This is achieved by defining matching key strings in a key chain and applying that key chain to the interfaces connected to RIP-enabled routers with update authentication configured.

To verify the routing process for RIP, you can use the `show ip route` command to view the IP routing table and examine whether networks have been learned from the routing protocol. In addition, `show ip protocols` displays the networks you are advertising in the local router, as well as the timers for each IP routing protocol.

When performing real-time troubleshooting, you can use the `debug ip rip` command. Be sure that you do not use these commands on a production router that is reporting high CPU utilization from the `show processes` output.

Key Terms

▶ Bellman-Ford algorithm

▶ Counting to infinity

▶ Route poison

▶ Poison reverse

▶ Hold-down timers

▶ Triggered updates

▶ RIP

▶ Passive interface

▶ RIPv2

Apply Your Knowledge

Exercises

11.1 Configure RIPv2 Router A

In this exercise and the next, you will configure RIP between two routers.

> **NOTE**
>
> This exercise assumes you have two nonproduction routers with a DCE to DTE serial cable or simulated software. If you do not have these on hand, write down what the configurations would look like.

Estimated Time: 20 minutes

   1. Enter privileged EXEC mode on Router A.

   2. Enter global configuration mode.

   3. Configure and enable the Fast Ethernet interface on Router A to have an IP address of 192.168.1.1/24.

   4. Configure and enable the serial interface on Router A to have an IP address of 10.1.1.1/30.

   5. Configure the clock rate (if this is the DCE) for 64000 bits per second.

   6. Enter the routing process for RIP.

   7. Advertise the directly connected classful networks.

   8. Enable version 2 of RIP.

   9. Disable automatic summarization.

 10. Exit to global configuration mode and create a key and key string for RIP authentication.

 11. Apply the key chain to the serial interface using an MD5 hash of the password.

11.2 Configure RIPv2 Router B

Now that Router A is configured, you must configure its neighbor, Router B, to send and receive routing updates.

Estimated Time: 20 minutes

   1. Enter privileged EXEC mode on Router B.

   2. Enter global configuration mode.

   3. Configure and enable the Fast Ethernet interface on Router B to have an IP address of 172.16.30.1/24.

   4. Configure and enable the serial interface on Router B to have an IP address of 10.1.1.2/30.

   5. Configure the clock rate (if this is the DCE) for 64000 bits per second.

   6. Enter the routing process for RIP.

   7. Advertise the directly connected classful networks.

   8. Enable version 2 of RIP.

   9. Disable automatic summarization.

 10. Exit to global configuration and create a key and key string that matches Router A for RIP authentication.

 11. Apply the key chain to the serial interface using an MD5 hash of the password.

11.3 Verify Routing

If configured correctly, you should be able to verify your RIP routing in this exercise.

Estimated Time: 10 minutes

1. In both Router A and Router B, do a `show ip protocols` to verify the networks that you are advertising.

2. Do a `show ip route` and verify that you have a RIP entry in your routing table from your neighbor.

3. If statements are missing, troubleshoot the routing process by using `debug ip rip`.

Review Questions

1. What are the mitigation methods distance vector routing protocols use to avoid routing loops?

2. What are the characteristics of RIP?

3. What additional features are present in RIPv2 that are not present in RIP?

4. What is the purpose of the `passive-interface` command?

5. What are the fundamental configuration steps for RIPv2?

Exam Questions

1. Given the following output, which of the following is a true statement?

```
CstmrARtr#show ip route
Codes: C - connected, S - static, I - IGRP, R - RIP, M - mobile, B - BGP
       D - EIGRP, EX - EIGRP external, O - OSPF, IA - OSPF inter area
       N1 - OSPF NSSA external type 1, N2 - OSPF NSSA external type 2
       E1 - OSPF external type 1, E2 - OSPF external type 2, E - EGP
       i - IS-IS, L1 - IS-IS level-1, L2 - IS-IS level-2, * - candidate default
       U - per-user static route, o - ODR

Gateway of last resort is not set

R    1.0.0.0/8 is possibly down, routing via 192.168.1.9, Serial0
C    172.17.0.0/16 is directly connected, Ethernet0
R    172.16.0.0/16 [120/1] via 172.17.0.2, 00:00:19, Ethernet0
     192.168.1.0/30 is subnetted, 1 subnets
C       192.168.1.8 is directly connected, Serial0
```

   ○ **A.** The 172.16.0.0 has an administrative distance of 1.

   ○ **B.** The 1.0.0.0 network is in a hold-down state.

    ○ **C.** The configuration for this router to advertise RIP should have a network 172.16.0.0 and a network 1.0.0.0 statement.

    ○ **D.** None of the above

2. Given the following output, which of the following statements is false regarding the 0.0.0.0/0 network?

```
CstmrARtr#show ip route
Codes: C - connected, S - static, I - IGRP, R - RIP, M - mobile, B - BGP
       D - EIGRP, EX - EIGRP external, O - OSPF, IA - OSPF inter area
       N1 - OSPF NSSA external type 1, N2 - OSPF NSSA external type 2
       E1 - OSPF external type 1, E2 - OSPF external type 2, E - EGP
       i - IS-IS, L1 - IS-IS level-1, L2 - IS-IS level-2, * - candidate default
       U - per-user static route, o - ODR

Gateway of last resort is 192.168.1.9 to network 0.0.0.0

R    1.0.0.0/8 [120/1] via 192.168.1.9, 00:00:21, Serial0
C    172.17.0.0/16 is directly connected, Ethernet0
R    172.16.0.0/16 [120/1] via 172.17.0.2, 00:00:02, Ethernet0
     192.168.1.0/30 is subnetted, 1 subnets
C       192.168.1.8 is directly connected, Serial0
R*   0.0.0.0/0 [120/1] via 192.168.1.9, 00:00:21, Serial0
```

    ○ **A.** The 0.0.0.0 network was statically configured in this router.

    ○ **B.** The gateway of last resort is the 192.168.1.9 router.

    ○ **C.** The default route was advertised to the local router via RIP.

    ○ **D.** The default route was automatically redistributed in Router 192.168.1.9.

3. Based on the following output, which network may not show up in the routing table?

```
RouterA#debug ip rip
RIP protocol debugging is on
RouterA#
00:26:27: RIP: received v1 update from 192.168.1.6 on Serial0/0
00:26:27:        192.168.1.8 in 12 hops
00:26:27:        192.168.1.12 in 15 hops
00:26:27:        172.17.0.0 in 14 hops
00:26:27:        172.18.0.0 in 16 hops
```

    ○ **A.** 172.17.0.0

    ○ **B.** 192.168.1.8

    ○ **C.** 192.168.1.12

    ○ **D.** 172.18.0.0

4. Which two commands enable a distance vector routing protocol to be classless?

- ○ **A.** `version 2`
- ○ **B.** `passive-interface`
- ○ **C.** `no auto-summary`
- ○ **D.** `router classless`

5. Which of the following is a possible reason for the following `debug ip rip` output?

```
*Aug 10 02:02:24.023: RIP: sending v2 update to 224.0.0.9 via Serial0/0/0
(192.168.1.5)
*Aug 10 02:02:24.023: RIP: build update entries
*Aug 10 02:02:24.023:    172.16.0.0/16 via 0.0.0.0, metric 1, tag 0
*Aug 10 01:57:50.823: RIP: received packet with MD5 authentication
*Aug 10 01:57:50.823: RIP: ignored v2 packet from 192.168.1.6 (invalid
authentication)
```

- ○ **A.** The interface that received the update is running as a passive interface.
- ○ **B.** Both routers are not configured for RIPv2.
- ○ **C.** The key strings do not match.
- ○ **D.** Split horizon will not allow the update to be received because that same network was sent on the same interface.

6. Which of the following is not a mechanism to avoid routing loops?

- ○ **A.** Split horizon
- ○ **B.** Update authentication
- ○ **C.** Hold-down timers
- ○ **D.** Route poisoning

7. Given the following output of a `show ip protocols`, which of the following commands was not configured on this router?

```
Router#show ip protocols
Routing Protocol is "rip"
  Sending updates every 30 seconds, next due in 24 seconds
  Invalid after 180 seconds, hold down 180, flushed after 240
  Outgoing update filter list for all interfaces is not set
  Incoming update filter list for all interfaces is not set
  Redistributing: rip
  Default version control: send version 2, receive version 2
    Interface            Send  Recv  Triggered RIP     Key-chain
    FastEthernet0/0       2     2
    Serial0/0/0           2     2                       shorty
```

```
Automatic network summarization is in effect
Maximum path: 6
Routing for Networks:
  172.16.0.0
  192.168.1.0
Routing Information Sources:
  Gateway          Distance      Last Update
  192.168.1.6         120        00:00:11
Distance: (default is 120)
```

○ **A.** version 2

○ **B.** ip rip authentication key-chain shorty

○ **C.** maximum-paths 6

○ **D.** network 192.168.0.0

8. Which command should you implement before doing any debug commands?

○ **A.** show running-config

○ **B.** show processes

○ **C.** undebug all

○ **D.** copy running-config startup-config

9. Given the following output of a debug ip rip, which of the following is true?

```
00:57:27: RIP: received v2 update from 192.168.1.6 on Serial0/0
00:57:27:     192.168.1.8/30 via 0.0.0.0 in 1 hops
00:57:27:     192.168.1.12/30 via 0.0.0.0 in 1 hops
00:57:27:     172.17.0.0/16 via 0.0.0.0 in 1 hops
00:57:27:     172.18.0.0/16 via 0.0.0.0 in 1 hops
```

○ **A.** The routing updates are broadcast to their neighbors.

○ **B.** The router automatically summarizes these networks.

○ **C.** Networks 172.17.0.0 and 172.18.0.0 have an infinite metric.

○ **D.** The no auto-summary command is used in RIPv2.

10. Which characteristic does not go with its respective routing protocol?

○ **A.** Multicasts updates—RIP

○ **B.** 180 invalid timer—RIP

○ **C.** Classful—RIPv2

○ **D.** Classless—RIPv2

Answers to Review Questions

1. Because distance vector routing protocols are susceptible to routing loops, they have incorporated several countermeasures to help mitigate any routing loop anomalies. For instance, all distance vector routing protocols have a maximum hop count to avoid counting to infinity. In addition, split horizon prevents routers from advertising networks out the same interface in which they were learned. Upon learning about a failing network, routers poison the route by setting it to an infinite metric and send a triggered update to the router's neighbors. The router will not process new inferior information about the failed network until the hold-down timer expires to ensure that the failed network does not get accidentally reinstated.

2. RIP is a classful distance vector routing protocol that uses hop count as its metric (maximum of 15). RIP broadcasts the contents of the routing table to its directly connected neighbors every 30 seconds.

3. RIPv2 supports classless routing updates if the `no auto-summary` command is used. In addition, RIPv2 updates are sent as multicasts and can be authenticated using an MD5 password.

4. The `passive-interface` command indicates that the specified interface will not send routing updates; however, the interface can still receive and process updates. This is useful to control which routers are sent updates and to save wasted bandwidth and processing of broadcasts or multicasts on LAN segments.

5. To enable RIP, you must enter the routing process by using the keyword `router` followed by the routing protocol. When you are in the routing configuration process, you must advertise the directly connected classful networks attached to the router by using the `network` command followed by the classful network. To enable RIPv2, you have to add the command `version 2` in the routing configuration.

Answers to Exam Questions

1. **B.** Because the routing table update shows the 1.0.0.0/8 network as possibly down, it is currently in a hold-down state and waiting for the hold-down timer to expire before accepting a route with a higher metric. Answer A is incorrect because the AD is 120 and the hip count is 1. C is false because those network entries were learned via RIP, not advertised. D is incorrect, because B is correct.

2. **A.** Because the default route has an R statement next to it, it was redistributed automatically by the neighbor at 192.168.1.9. If it was statically configured, it would have an S indication next to the route. Answers B, C, and D are true because the 0.0.0.0 route was redistributed and advertised via RIP by the router with the IP address of 192.168.1.9.

3. **D.** Because the 172.18.0.0 has an infinite metric for RIP being advertised, it is most likely a poisoned route or a router that is not showing up in the routing table. Answers A, B, and C will show up in the routing table because their hop count does not exceed the maximum hop count for RIP (15).

4. **A, C.** The only distance vector routing protocol that can be classless is RIPv2. The command to enable RIPv2 is `version 2`. To make it classless, you use the `no auto-summary` command. Answer B is incorrect because the `passive-interface` command is used to keep updates from being sent out that specific interface. Answer D is not a valid command.

5. **C.** Because the output indicated that the update that was received was ignored because of authentication failure, the logical choice is that the key strings in the update authentication are not matching. Answer A is incorrect because a passive interface would not ignore incoming updates since it suppressed only outgoing updates. Answer B is incorrect because the output shows the updates as version 2 and only version 2 uses authentication. Answer D is incorrect because split horizon does not ignore incoming updates.

6. **B.** Update authentication is not a mechanism to avoid routing loops. Split horizon, hold-down timers, and router poisoning are all mechanisms to avoid routing loops so answers A, C, and D are incorrect.

7. **D.** The network statement is incorrect. The correct network command would be `network 192.168.1.0`. Answer A is incorrect because the output shows that version 2 is being sent and received. Answer B is incorrect because the output shows that the *shorty* key chain is applied. Answer C is incorrect because the output shows that the maximum paths have been increased from 4 to 6.

8. **B.** Before running any `debug` commands, you should check your router's current and past utilization with the `show processes` command. Answer A does not have any effect on the debug process. Answer C will turn off any debugging after the debugging process has been initiated. Answer D does not have any effect on the debugging process.

9. **D.** The update is indicative of a RIPv2 update that has been configured as classless with the `no auto-summary` command. This is true because the updates contain the subnet masks. Answer A is false because RIPv2 multicasts its updates to 224.0.0.9. B is false because the `no auto-summary` command disables automatic summarization. C is incorrect because an infinite metric for RIPv2 is 16.

10. **A.** RIPv2 sends its updates as multicasts, not version 1. Answer B is true because RIP has an invalid timer of 180 seconds. Answers C and D are also true because RIPv2 is classful by default but can be configured as classless.

Suggested Readings and Resources

1. Alex Zinn. *IP Routing: Packet Forwarding and Intra-domain Routing Protocols*. Addison Wesley Professional, 2002.

2. Keith Kruepke, Paul Cernick, and Mark Degner. *Cisco IP Routing Handbook*. Hungry Minds, 2000.

3. Anthony Bruno and Jacqueline Kim. *CCDA Exam Certification Guide*. Cisco Press, 2004.

4. "Routing Protocols," www.firewall.cx.

5. RIP and RIPv2 technology support on www.cisco.com.

12

Link-State and Hybrid Routing Protocols

Objectives

This chapter covers the following Cisco-specified objectives for the "Configure, verify, and troubleshoot basic router operation and routing on Cisco devices" section of the 640-802 CCNA exam:

▶ **Configure, verify, and troubleshoot OSPF**

▶ **Configure, verify, and troubleshoot EIGRP**

▶ **Compare and contrast methods of routing and routing protocols**

▶ **Troubleshoot routing issues**

▶ **Verify router hardware and software operation using SHOW & DEBUG commands**

Outline

Study Strategies

▶ Read the information presented in the chapter, paying special attention to tables, Notes, and Exam Alerts.

▶ The concepts mentioned in this chapter are the essentials to understand for the CCNA and ICND2 exams. Additional features and configurations entailed with these routing protocols are covered in the Building Scalable Cisco Internetworks exam for the CCNP. If you're researching them in other information sources, be sure not to get too engrossed in these additional features.

▶ This chapter requires a firm understanding of subnetting. Review Chapter 5, "IP at the Network Layer," and ensure that you have mastered this topic before tackling wildcard masks in this chapter.

▶ Complete the Challenges and the Exercises at the end of the chapter. The exercises will solidify the concepts that you have learned in the previous sections.

▶ This chapter makes mention of the concepts discussed in Chapter 10, "Introduction to Routing and Routing Protocols." If you are not completely comfortable with the fundamentals of routing protocols and their metrics, review Chapter 10 before proceeding with this chapter.

▶ This chapter revisits route summarization, which was discussed in Chapter 10. Be sure you are familiar with supernetting before reading this chapter.

▶ Complete the Exam Questions at the end of the chapter. They are designed to simulate the types of questions you will be asked on the CCNA and ICND2 exams.

Introduction

Distance vector routing protocols are ideal for small networks that have routers with slow processing power and limited memory resources. Today's enterprises require significantly larger networks that can scale way beyond the limits of distance vector routing protocols. As networks grow larger, routing protocols must also be able to react to topology changes faster to ensure that all devices are aware of a change in a reasonable amount of time. Link-state and balanced hybrid/advanced distance vector routing protocols were designed to overcome the scalability and convergence speed restrictions that hindered distance vector routing protocols. This chapter looks at how the innovators of these two classes of routing protocols, OSPF and EIGRP, achieve these feats and shows you how to implement and customize them in your configurations.

Link-State Operations

Objective:

▶ Compare and contrast methods of routing and routing protocols

Recall that distance vector routing protocols use the Bellman-Ford algorithm, which entails routing devices advertising directly connected networks that are sent to any neighbor listening on adjacent segments. When they receive the updates, they manipulate their routing tables and advertise the subsequent information to their directly connected neighbors. One of the major downfalls of this algorithm is that the updates contain secondhand information from other routers, and the best pathway is chosen according to another device's perception of the network. This is similar to following directions to a destination based on your friend's sister's boyfriend's recollection of getting to that destination over his preferred roads and highways.

Link-state routing protocols use the Dijkstra Shortest Path First (SPF) algorithm, which is a complex and processor-intensive mathematical calculation for determining optimal paths. It's different from distance vector routing algorithms because the calculations are actually done based on all possible routes to a destination that link-state routing protocols store in their topology tables. The best route that is chosen from the topology table for any given network is placed in the router's routing table.

Routers receive this topology information from the neighbors they discovered by listening for Link-State Advertisements (LSAs) from other routers. In fact, link-state routing protocols establish a relationship with these neighbors and track them in yet another table, called the *neighbor table*, before even sending update information.

The updates that are exchanged between the routers contain not only the subnets that their neighbors know about, but all the information about their link states, including the status of the links and the metrics for each subnet they are aware of. Knowing all the possible links and their associated metrics to reach them, the router can make firsthand decisions about which is the best path for it to take to reach each destination. Returning to the preceding analogy, now you would learn about all the possible paths to the destination from your friend, your friend's sister, her boyfriend, MapQuest, and so on. You would base your decision on the best path using all that information.

After a router sends that topology information to its neighbors, it does not need to continuously send them that information repeatedly, as distance vector routing protocols require. Instead, link-state routing protocols send small hello LSAs every so often just to reassure neighbors that the router is still alive and ticking.

In the event of a topology change, a link-state update (LSU) is flooded to all routers, immediately alerting them of the topology change. In fact, link-state routers that receive this topology change notification flood the link-state update to their neighbors before processing and recalculating the change to update their own routing tables with the new information. Thus, there is no need for loop-prevention measures, as you witnessed with distance vector routing protocols, because link-state routing protocols propagate this information and converge exponentially faster.

Because link-state routing protocols can scale to such large sizes, they can segment the routing domain into smaller systems, known as areas, so that devices do not have to maintain an excessive amount of information in their topology tables. What's more, the routers that send information between these divisions summarize the subnets located inside the area connected to them to the rest of the autonomous system (AS). By minimizing the routing update traffic and overhead, you can speed up convergence and confine instability to a single area. Because the routers that perform this route summarization have a special function over the rest of the routers in the autonomous system, link-state routing protocols are hierarchical by design.

OSPF

Objective:

▶ Configure, verify, and troubleshoot OSPF

The most widely used link-state routing protocol today is an IETF standard routing protocol called Open Shortest Path First (OSPF). Developed in 1988, this routing protocol was created to overcome the limitations that RIP presented for large-scale networks. The following sections look at the fundamentals of OSPF and show you how to apply them in your configuration.

OSPF Characteristics

OSPF is unique among the routing protocols that are discussed in this book. This is true from its operations all the way down to the configuration. Notably, one of the more intriguing aspects of this routing protocol is that it is completely classless. With the subnet masks accompanying the networks in the routing updates, routers are aware of all the individual subnets that exist. The upside of this knowledge is that you do not have to concern yourself too much with discontiguous network designs, and you can implement VLSM addressing throughout the topology. The downside of knowing all the subnets is that the topology database can grow to be quite large, depending on the size of the autonomous system. Not only does this knowledge exhaust the memory resources in your routers, but any change in the links associated with those subnets causes a flood of updates, consequently causing each router to run the SPF algorithm again. If your autonomous system consists of 1,000 routers, each one has to expend the processing resources to flood the update and rerun its algorithmic calculations based on the residual topology. If the link is continuously going up and then down (known as *flapping*), each of the 1,000 routers continually floods updates and reruns its Dijkstra SPF algorithm, which could exhaust a router's resources and detrimentally affect the router's capacity to function.

OSPF Areas

OSPF mitigates the need for excessive topology databases and update traffic overhead by segmenting an OSPF autonomous system into smaller areas. As mentioned before, routers that transmit information from one area to another can be configured to summarize the subnets being advertised to other areas. In this situation, routers in other areas need to keep only summarized entries in their topology table, minimizing the amount of memory required. If a link goes down within the area, only devices within that area need to be notified, because the rest of the OSPF autonomous system is aware of only the summarized route. With that update confined within that area, other routers in different areas do not receive an update and do not have to flood and recalculate the information in the update.

For instance, Figure 12.1 shows an OSPF autonomous system in which you have created three areas. Routers C and E have the responsibility of summarizing the subnets in their areas to the rest of the OSPF autonomous system. This hierarchy in routing ensures that any link failure that occurs in the areas they are summarizing does not go beyond those routers. Because these hierarchical routers are sitting on the border between two areas, they are called Area Border Routers (ABRs).

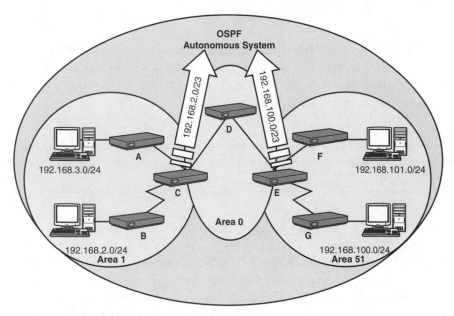

FIGURE 12.1 OSPF AS with areas.

Backbone Area

Notice that at the center of the OSPF autonomous system in Figure 12.1 is Area 0, to which Area 1 and Area 51 are attached. This is not by coincidence, but rather by design. Area 0, also known as the *backbone area*, is an essential part of an OSPF design because, as the name states, this is the area in which traffic from one area must transit to reach another area. If your network design requires only a single area, that area must be Area 0.

Any area that is created must somehow be connected to the backbone area. Because this area is truly an information highway interconnecting all other areas, it typically consists of robust routers called *backbone routers* that are either completely inside or have an interface that connects to Area 0. Traffic originating in one area is sent to the backbone ABR for that area, which in turn ultimately passes the traffic to the destination backbone ABR and finally to the destination router inside the remote area. Because these links inside the backbone carry excessive traffic, the backbone routers typically are interconnected with high-speed interlinks such as Fast Ethernet or Gigabit Ethernet.

EXAM ALERT

Remember that Area 0 is also commonly called the backbone area. All areas that are created must connect back to Area 0.

Stub Area

Recall that the term *stub* in networking refers to networks that contain a single pathway in or out. Accordingly, a stub area is an area that contains only one pathway in or out of that area. The IETF created this concept of a stub area as a measure to decrease the topology database even further for routers that are inside a stub area.

NOTE

Because the backbone area is a transit area that interconnects other areas, it can never be configured as a stub.

Again, the ABR router takes the credit for this reduction in OSPF overhead, as shown in Figure 12.2. If the area is configured on all routers inside that area as a stub area, the ABR replaces all the networks it learns from the rest of the OSPF autonomous system with a default route. It also advertises that route to the routers inside the stub area. This makes sense, because the routers inside the stub area are using that ABR as a gateway of last resort to leave their area.

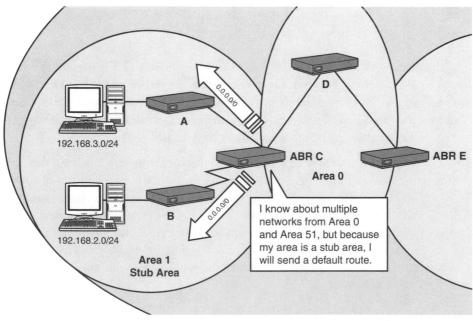

FIGURE 12.2   Stub area.

OSPF Metrics

When OSPF routers run the Dijkstra algorithm to calculate the best route to reach destination subnets, they use the lowest cumulative cost to reach that network. The path cost is calculated by taking 10^8 divided by the bandwidth in bps. Table 12.1 lists some of the common path costs associated with their respective bandwidths.

TABLE 12.1   Cost Values Based on Bandwidth

Bandwidth	OSPF Cost
56kbps	1785
64kbps	1562
T1 (1.544Mbps)	64
E1 (2.048Mbps)	48
Ethernet (10Mbps)	10
Fast Ethernet (100Mbps)	1
Gigabit Ethernet (1000Mbps)	1

EXAM ALERT

Be prepared to calculate the cost for any given link speed.

Notice that when you reach and exceed Fast Ethernet speeds of 100Mbps, the cost is still 1. For that reason, you can configure OSPF to use a different reference for the bandwidth that is higher than 10^8 to account for links of that magnitude.

Router ID

Unlike most routing protocols, OSPF routers identify each other with something known as a *router ID*. The router ID is a 32-bit unique number in which the router is known to the OSPF autonomous system. This ID is determined in the following order:

1. The highest IP address assigned to an active logical interface at the start of the OSPF process.

2. If no logical interface is present, the highest IP address of an active physical interface at the start of the OSPF process.

NOTE

When I say "highest IP address," I am talking about the numerical value of the IP address, not the class of the IP address.

> **EXAM ALERT**
>
> Be sure to know how to determine a router's router ID based on the IP addresses of the router's interfaces.

Note that if there is a logical interface, the IP address overrides any physical IP address for the router ID, even if it is a lower value. What do I mean by a logical interface? Cisco routers let you create logical or virtual interfaces called *loopback interfaces*. The advantage of using these virtual interfaces is that, unlike physical interfaces, loopback interfaces cannot go down unless the router is malfunctioning or turned off.

> **EXAM ALERT**
>
> For the exam, keep in mind that loopback interfaces are logical interfaces that cannot go down unless the router is malfunctioning or turned off.

OSPF Topologies

The environment in which OSPF operates varies greatly depending on the type of topology to which an OSPF interface is connected. Such operations as hello and dead timers, neighbor discovery methods, and OSPF update overhead reduction ultimately are dictated by the OSPF interface's topology. Here are the three main types of topologies:

- ▶ **Broadcast multiaccess:** These topologies denote multiple devices accessing a medium in which broadcasts and multicasts are heard by all devices sharing that medium (such as Ethernet).

- ▶ **Nonbroadcast multiaccess:** NBMA topologies are similar to broadcast multiaccess topologies (multiple devices accessing a medium), except that devices cannot hear each others' broadcasts because the medium is separated by other routers, such as with Frame Relay.

- ▶ **Point-to-point:** A point-to-point link has only two devices on a shared network link.

To demonstrate the point, consider how OSPF timers operate in different topologies. For instance, in broadcast multiaccess and point-to-point links, the hello and dead intervals are 10 and 40 seconds, respectively. Remember, these hello messages are not full routing updates like distance vector routing protocols. The hello messages contain minimal information to identify the sending device to other neighbor routers to ensure that their dead timers do not expire and cause a topology change.

Because NBMA network topologies such as Frame Relay typically comprise slower links, the default timers for these topologies are 30 seconds for hello messages and 120 seconds for the dead timer. The hello messages are not sent as often in NBMA topologies to ensure that OSPF routers do not needlessly consume bandwidth on the WAN links.

DR/BDR Elections

Another significant topology-related function of OSPF is the election of a Designated Router (DR) and a Backup Designated Router (BDR) in broadcast and nonbroadcast multiaccess topologies. Routers in these topologies undergo these elections to reduce the amount of update overhead that can be incurred when a link state changes.

For example, in Figure 12.3, all the routers in Area 7 are connected to a switch, which indicates a broadcast multiaccess topology.

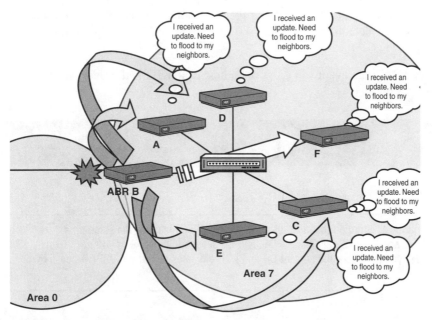

FIGURE 12.3   Broadcast multiaccess topology updates.

If the link connected to Area 0 on ABR Router B were to fail, OSPF protocol dictates that it flood the update to all the neighbors in its neighbor table. When Router B sends that update to all the routers in the topology, all devices hear it because they are all connected to the same switch. However, recall that after the other routers receive that update, they have to alert all their neighbors—again, all the routers connected to the switch. This time, multiple routers send the update and cause excessive traffic on the switched network to devices that are already aware of the update. If you have a large number of routers in the topology, this update traffic can consume quite a bit of unnecessary bandwidth and processor utilization. In point-to-point links, it is not necessary to have a DR or BDR election, because only two routers are on the segment, and there is no threat of excessive update traffic.

EXAM ALERT

Remember that DRs and BDRs are elected only on broadcast and nonbroadcast multiaccess networks.

When a DR and BDR are elected (in case the DR fails), routing updates are minimized, because the update is sent only to the DR and the BDR. The DR then is responsible for updating the rest of the topology. The election is determined by the following:

1. **Highest interface priority:** An arbitrary number you can configure on an interface-by-interface basis. The default is 1. A value of 0 renders the device ineligible for DR and BDR election.

2. **Highest router ID:** In the event of a tie, the highest router ID is the tiebreaker.

EXAM ALERT

Remember that a 0 value for an interface priority makes it ineligible to become a DR or BDR for that segment.

TIP

This election is based on the assumption that all devices start the OSPF process at the same time. Realistically, the first router that comes online is the DR, and the second is the BDR. If you need to set another router as the DR, you must take the current DR and BDR offline or restart the OSPF process to force the election.

Figure 12.4 shows the election process between several routers in a broadcast multiaccess topology. Because Router D's interface priority is highest, that router becomes the DR for that segment. Router F, with the second-highest priority, becomes the BDR if Router D is turned off or crashes. Now if a link fails, the update is sent to Router D, which in turn updates the rest of the topology.

EXAM ALERT

Be able to determine which routers will be elected the DR and BDR on each segment (decided by the highest interface priority, followed by the highest Router ID in the event of a tie). Also, keep in mind that DR and BDR elections can vary on an interface-by-interface basis. In other words, a router may be a DR on one segment and a BDR or neither on another interface segment.

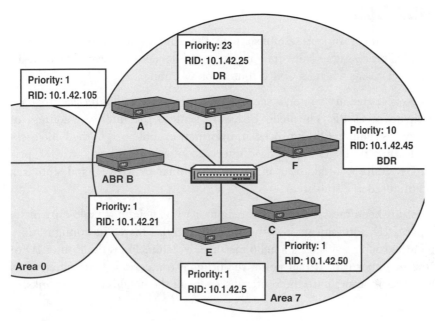

FIGURE 12.4 DR and BDR elections.

One missing piece of this OSPF puzzle is how the devices manage to send updates to the DR and BDR routers only if they are all connected in the same topology. The answer lies in the manner in which OSPF routers propagate LSAs and LSUs. Rather than broadcast this information as RIPv1 does, OSPF sends updates to two different reserved multicast addresses. The multicast address, 224.0.0.6, is reserved for the DR and BDR. When a router needs to send an update in a broadcast or nonbroadcast topology, it sends the LSU to 224.0.0.6, which only the DR and BDR process. The DR then sends the LSU to the multicast address of 224.0.0.5, which is the address to which all OSPF routers listen for updates and hello messages.

So now when Router B detects the link failure, it multicasts its LSU to 224.0.0.6, which only Router D and Router F process. Because Router D is the DR, it disseminates the update to everyone else in the topology by sending the update to 224.0.0.5.

OSPF Initialization

Recall that link-state routing protocols establish who the router's neighbors are before exchanging updates. This process is actually quite intricate and depends on several factors. To clarify, let's look at what happens when an OSPF router comes online.

After the OSPF process is started in a router, it sends a hello message out all interfaces that are configured to participate in OSPF. The hello LSAs are sent to the multicast address of 224.0.0.5 so that all devices running OSPF process it. Information contained in the hello messages includes the following: router ID, hello/dead intervals, known neighbors, area ID, priority, DR address, BDR address, authentication password (similar to RIPv2), and stub area flags (if the area is configured as a stub area).

A router that receives this hello message adds that neighbor to its neighbor table only if the hello/dead intervals, area ID, authentication password, and stub flag match its configuration. If these values match, the router sends back a hello message, which includes the Router ID of the new router in the neighbor list. At that point, the original router adds that router to its neighbor table. This process occurs until the router discovers all the neighbors on its links.

> **EXAM ALERT**
>
> Remember that the hello/dead intervals, authentication password, stub flag, and area ID must match in the hello LSAs to form a neighbor relationship.

It is important to note that no update information has been exchanged at this point. If the topology has a DR elected (indicated in the hello messages it received), it synchronizes its topology table with that router because the DR always has the most current information. If the topology is a point-to-point connection, the two routers synchronize with the neighbor on the other side of the link. After the topology tables are synchronized, it is said that the devices have formed an adjacency. Now that the router has all possible routes in the topology table, it can run the Dijkstra algorithm to calculate the best routes to each subnet.

Introduction to Configuring OSPF

One of the first steps you should take when configuring OSPF is to configure loopback interfaces to ensure that your Router ID matches the IP address of the loopback interface when the OSPF routing process is started. To create a virtual loopback interface, you configure it like a normal interface:

```
Router(config)#interface loopback 0
Router(config-if)#ip address 10.1.42.1 255.255.255.255
```

The interface number for the loopback interface is arbitrary because the interface is virtual. Also, notice that the subnet mask used in the loopback interface is 255.255.255.255 or a /32. This is known as a *host mask*. Typically it is used on loopback interfaces because there is no need to use an entire subnet on a virtual interface that doesn't connect to anything.

> **EXAM ALERT**
>
> Keep in mind for the exam that loopback interfaces typically have a subnet mask of 255.255.255.255, known as a host mask.

To start the OSPF process for configuration, you use the **router** keyword followed by **ospf**, just as you have in the past with other routing protocols. In the case of OSPF, however, you must specify a process ID after the `router ospf` keywords. The process ID is an arbitrary number ranging from 1 to 65535, in which the router can track whether you have multiple instances of OSPF running in your router. Because this process ID is only known on the local router that you configure, the process ID does not need to match in all router configurations.

> **EXAM ALERT**
>
> Remember that the process ID is a locally significant number between 1 and 65535 that is used to track multiple instances of OSPF that might be running on the router. It does not have to match in all other router configurations.

Wildcard Masks

Before we go further with the explanation of the OSPF configuration, you need to understand the means by which OSPF advertises the classless networks in the configuration. Because you no longer have the luxury of putting a classful subnet in the `network` statement, you need to have some way of telling the router what specific IP subnets are to be applied to the OSPF routing process. OSPF (as well as EIGRP and access lists) uses something called a *wildcard mask* to tell the IOS how much of an IP address should be applied to a criteria in a configuration statement. That criteria differs depending on which configuration statements the wildcard mask is using.

> **NOTE**
>
> Wildcard masks are revisited with access lists in Chapter 19, "Using Cisco Access Lists."

In the case of OSPF, the wildcard mask is used to define what portion of the IP in a `network` statement is to be associated with the routing process. If the IP addresses assigned to interfaces match the scope of the addresses defined with the IP address and wildcard mask criteria in the `network` entry, OSPF is enabled on those interfaces, and their subnets are advertised in routing updates.

Wildcard masks are represented as 32-bit numbers separated into four octets, just like IP addresses and subnet masks. Each bit in the wildcard mask corresponds to the same bit position in the IP address to identify whether that bit should be applied to the criteria. Specifically, if the bit value in a wildcard mask is a 0, the corresponding bit in the IP address is checked and applied to the criteria. Conversely, a 1 in a wildcard mask bit signifies that the corresponding bit in the IP address can be ignored. Using these 0s and 1s, you are basically telling the IOS to perform pattern matching against the IP address that precedes the wildcard mask and to apply the portion that matches the conditions in the configuration statement.

For example, if you wanted to apply a wildcard mask to a specific IP address, every bit in the wildcard mask must be a 0 (0000000.0000000.0000000.0000000), because each corresponding bit in the IP address is being applied to the criteria. So, for example, if you wanted to specify the IP address of 10.1.4.2, the corresponding wildcard mask for that specific IP would be 0.0.0.0 in decimal. On the contrary, if you wanted to apply the criteria to any IP (therefore, you do not care whether any of the corresponding bits match), you would need to have a wildcard mask composed of all 1s (11111111.1111111.11111111.11111111, or 255.255.255.255 in decimal). Technically, it does not matter which IP address precedes this wildcard mask, because you are applying any value, so it is common to use an IP address of 0.0.0.0 with the 255.255.255.255 wildcard mask.

In cases such as those with OSPF, you need to use wildcard masks to specify a specific IP subnet. For instance, given an IP subnet of 192.168.1.0 /24, you know that you want to apply the criteria to the first 24 bits in the IP address. Because the last octet of the IP subnet can be any value from 0 to 255, you don't want to apply any of those bits to your criteria. The resultant wildcard mask ultimately is composed of the first three octets in the wildcard mask, containing all 0s to match the 192.168.1, and the last octet, containing all 1s. Thus, the 192.168.1.0 /24 subnet would be identified as 192.168.1.0 0.0.0.255 in the configuration statement.

That may seem fairly cut and dried, but how do you apply a wildcard mask to a subnet such as 192.168.1.4 /30? You know that the first three octets will have all 0s, but you can't say you don't care about all 8 bits in the last octet, because you want to apply this criteria to only the IPs in the 192.168.1.4 255.255.255.252 subnet (192.168.1.4 to 192.168.1.7). As shown in Figure 12.5, by breaking the last octet into binary, you can see how to align the corresponding bits in the wildcard mask. Namely, the first 6 bits in the last octet must be exactly the same values that are in the IP address to give you a decimal value of 4. The last 2 bits can be any combination of 1s or 0s, because they will ultimately give you the values of 192.168.1.4, 192.168.1.5, 192.168.1.6, and 192.168.1.7. Because the first 6 bits must match, and the last two do not matter, the wildcard mask in binary for the last octet is 00000011, or 3 in decimal. So, to specify the 192.168.1.4 /30 subnet, your statement would look like 192.168.1.4 0.0.0.3.

	. 128	64	32	16	8	4	2	1
IP: 192 168.1.4	. 0	0	0	0	0	1	0	0
SM:255.255.255.252	. 1	1	1	1	1	1	0	0
WCM: 0.0.0.3	. 0	0	0	0	0	0	1	1

FIGURE 12.5 Wildcard mask breakdown.

TIP

An easier way to determine a wildcard mask for an entire subnet is to subtract the subnet mask from 255.255.255.255. For example, 255.255.255.255 – 255.255.255.252 = 0.0.0.3. In addition, the wildcard mask is always 1 less than the increment of the subnet in the octet where the subnet falls. For instance, a subnet of 255.255.255.252 has an increment of 4. So the wildcard mask in the last octet (because the /30 subnet falls in the last octet) is 1 less than the increment, or 0.0.0.3.

Notice in Figure 12.5 that the wildcard mask happens to be the inverse of the subnet mask. For this very reason, the wildcard mask is sometimes called the *inverse mask*. This is the case for all wildcard masks that correspond to an entire subnet.

EXAM ALERT

You will be expected to be able to determine a wildcard mask given an IP address or an entire subnet for several concepts throughout the CCNA and ICND2 exams. It is imperative that you practice and master these calculations and be able to recognize an incorrect configuration if presented with a troubleshooting scenario.

OSPF Network Configuration

Reverting to the matter of configuring OSPF, you left off with entering the OSPF routing process by entering something similar to the following:

```
Router(config)#router ospf 4
```

Recall that the number 4 in this example is the process ID and does not have to match in all routers. Because you are in the routing process (indicated by the `Router(config-router)#` prompt) for OSPF, you are ready to specify the classless networks that are to participate in OSPF. As you do with other routing protocols, you start by using the keyword `network`, but from there you go a different direction. At this point, you need to specify an IP address or IP subnet, followed by the *wildcard mask* to identify which interfaces are participating in the

OSPF process. Immediately following the IP and wildcard mask is the keyword area, followed by the OSPF area number where the router's interface is located. For example, if you have an IP address of 192.168.1.1 with a subnet mask of 255.255.255.0 connected to area 0, you would configure it something like this:

```
Router(config)#router ospf 4
Router(config-router)#network 192.168.1.0 0.0.0.255 area 0
```

> **EXAM ALERT**
>
> Be sure you understand the syntax involved in starting the OSPF process and assigning networks to that process.

Because you use the wildcard mask in the OSPF configuration, you actually have multiple ways to specify an interface and its subnet in the OSPF routing process. Using the same example, you could use any of the configurations shown in Table 12.2 to place that interface in area 0.

TABLE 12.2   Alternative network Statements

Command	Description
Router(config-router)#network 192.168.1.1 0.0.0.0 area 0	The interface with the IP address of 192.168.1.1 and its subnet are advertised in OSPF.
Router(config-router)#network 192.168.0.0 0.0.255.255 area 0	Interfaces and their subnets starting with 192.168 are advertised in OSPF.
Router(config-router)#network 192.0.0.0 0.255.255.255 area 0	Interfaces and their subnets starting with 192 are advertised in OSPF.
Router(config-router)#network 0.0.0.0 255.255.255.255 area 0	All interfaces and their subnets are advertised in OSPF.

> **EXAM ALERT**
>
> Because there are so many ways you can advertise the networks with OSPF, the exam looks for one specific way. If it isn't otherwise specified, specify the entire subnet for each interface.

Figure 12.6 shows the configuration for two of the routers in the multiarea OSPF autonomous system. First, notice that Router B and Router D do not have matching Router IDs. These values are significant locally only to those routers to keep track of multiple instances of OSPF that might be running. Router D has both interfaces in the backbone area, so you specify each subnet, using the appropriate wildcard mask, and identify the networks to be in Area 0. Notice that the configuration parameters are similar in Router B, except the interface that has the 192.168.1.8 subnet assigned to it is in Area 51. With that network placed in a different area, that router is now configured to be an ABR.

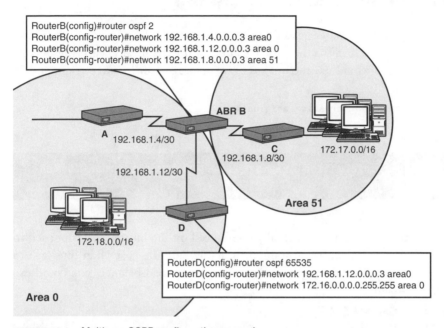

FIGURE 12.6 Multiarea OSPF configuration example.

Additional OSPF Commands

As you know, OSPF is loaded with additional features and capabilities that make this routing protocol extremely adaptable. Throughout the course of your Cisco career, you may find yourself needing to configure additional parameters to fit the needs of your network. This section covers a few of the many configurations that OSPF offers.

For instance, in instances where you want to designate your area as a stub to decrease the amount of routing information stored in the topology database, you can use the `area` command in the routing process to identify that area as a stub:

```
Router(config-router)#area 51 stub
```

EXAM ALERT

Remember, the stub flag was one of the required fields to form a neighbor relationship, so be sure you configure this for all routers that touch that area.

Because OSPF does not have automatic summarization, you have to configure these routers manually to summarize a set of networks. For example, if you wanted to summarize the 192.168.1.4 /24 to 192.168.1.7 /24 subnets in Area 51, you would use the range keyword in the area configuration, as in the following:

```
Router(config-router)#area 51 range 192.168.1.4 255.255.252.0
```

Similar to RIP, suppose your local router has a default route configured, and you want to redistribute that default route into OSPF so that other routers will dynamically learn the default route via OSPF updates. You would use the default-information originate command in the routing configuration:

```
Router(config-router)#default-information originate
```

> **EXAM ALERT**
>
> Remember that the default-information originate command is used to generate a default route into OSPF updates.

OSPF also has several commands that are actually configured on the interfaces as opposed to in the routing process. For example, if you wanted to manipulate the cost of an interface to make a network favorable over another or to force the router to load-balance, you could use the ip ospf cost command:

```
Router(config)#interface serial 0/0
Router(config-if)#ip ospf cost 2
```

On interfaces that are connected to broadcast and nonbroadcast multiaccess topologies, it is highly recommended that you change the priority in the routers in which you want to force the DR and BDR election. By default, the priority is 1, but you can change that manually by using the ip ospf priority command as follows:

```
Router(config)#interface serial 0/0
Router(config-if)#ip ospf priority 3
```

Configuring OSPF with SDM

With all these configuration commands for OSPF we have encountered so far (which are only the tip of the iceberg), it is a relief to have some of these configurations simplified by the web-based SDM GUI. To begin, we should take similar steps as we did with the CLI configuration, which is to create a loopback interface. You can do this by selecting **Configuration**, **Interface** and **Connections**. From there, select the **Edit Interface/Connection** tab, and choose the Add tool at the top of the window. Choose **New Logical Interface**, **Loopback**, as shown in Figure 12.7, to bring up the loopback configuration pop-up window.

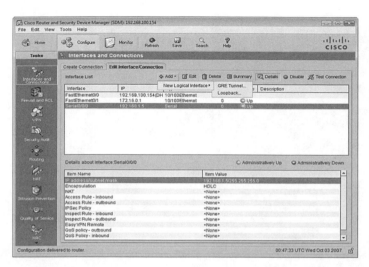

FIGURE 12.7 OSPF SDM logical interface creation.

Here you need to select Static IP Address from the pull-down menu. This allows you to input your IP address and subnet mask for this logical interface, as shown in Figure 12.8, which will inevitably become the router ID for your OSPF routing process.

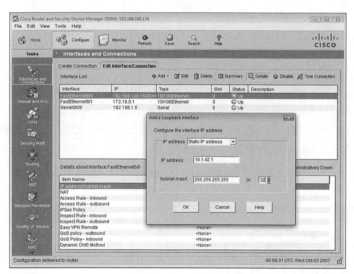

FIGURE 12.8 OSPF SDM loopback interface configuration.

With our loopback interface in place, it is time to configure the OSPF routing protocol parameters. Select **Configure**, **Routing**. Click the **Edit** button in the Dynamic Routing section. In the Edit IP Dynamic Routing dialog box, shown in Figure 12.9, choose the **OSPF** tab. Identify your process ID for OSPF, and click the **Add** button to add networks to the Network List. The Add an OSPF dialog box asks for the networks, wildcard masks, and area IDs for that OSPF process. As soon as all the networks have been advertised, the configurations are added to the running-config after you click **OK**.

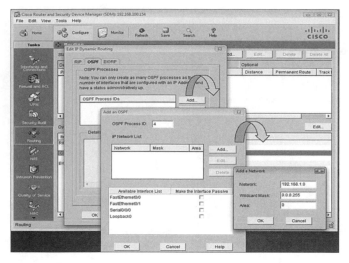

FIGURE 12.9   OSPF SDM configuration.

Verifying OSPF

Objective:

▶ Verify router hardware and software operation using SHOW & DEBUG commands

Because there are so many aspects to OSPF, you have a considerable number of show commands at your disposal to verify OSPF operations. As before, you can use show running-config to verify the local configuration of your routing protocol. In the case of OSPF, this is useful to ensure that you configured the network and wildcard mask correctly, as well as associated the network with the correct area. In addition, show ip protocols again shows you information about the networks you are advertising with OSPF.

Recall that OSPF maintains three separate tables in its routing process: the routing table, the neighbor table, and the topology table. You are already familiar with the show ip route command to view the routing table and verify whether you are receiving OSPF networks from the neighbors:

```
RouterA>show ip route
Codes: C - connected, S - static, I - IGRP, R - RIP, M - mobile, B - BGP
       D - EIGRP, EX - EIGRP external, O - OSPF, IA - OSPF inter area
       N1 - OSPF NSSA external type 1, N2 - OSPF NSSA external type 2
       E1 - OSPF external type 1, E2 - OSPF external type 2, E - EGP
       i - IS-IS, L1 - IS-IS level-1, L2 - IS-IS level-2, * - candidate default
       U - per-user static route, o - ODR

Gateway of last resort is not set
O IA 172.17.0.0/16 [110/74] via 192.168.1.6, Serial0/0
C    172.16.0.0/16 is directly connected, FastEthernet0/0
O       172.18.0.1/16 [110/65] via 192.168.1.6, Serial0/0
     10.0.0.0/32 is subnetted, 1 subnets
```

```
C        10.1.42.1 is directly connected, Loopback0
         192.168.1.0/30 is subnetted, 1 subnets
C        192.168.1.4 is directly connected, Serial0/0/0
```

The 172.17.0.0 and 172.18.0.0 networks in this example were learned via OSPF through the Serial 0/0/0 interface. Notice that the 172.17.0.0 entry has an IA (interarea) indicator. It signifies that this network was learned from an ABR and that the network resides in another area.

To see a listing of the neighbors that were discovered through LSA hello advertisements, you can look in your router's neighbor table by using the show ip ospf neighbor command:

```
RouterA>show ip ospf neighbor
Neighbor ID     Pri  State       Dead Time   Address       Interface
10.1.42.100      10  FULL/DR     00:00:39    192.168.1.6   Serial0/0
```

The Neighbor ID is actually the Router ID of the neighbor that is being advertised in the neighbor's hello messages. The Pri field indicates the priority configured on your neighbors' interfaces. Because the default priority is 1 and this neighbor has a priority of 10, that router happens to be the DR for that segment, as shown in the State field. The other possible values for this state are BDR and DROTHER (not DR or BDR), depending on whether those routers won the election on that segment.

The show ip ospf database command shows the third table that OSPF maintains: the topology table. This table lists all the network entries and the advertising routers for those entries. From this table, the SPF algorithm is run, and the routes with the lowest cumulative cost are put in the routing table. Here you can see the output of the show ip ospf database summary command, because the information is presented in a more intelligible output:

```
RouterA>show ip ospf database summary

        OSPF Router with ID (10.1.42.1) (Process ID 1)

                Summary Net Link States (Area 51)

  Routing Bit Set on this LSA
  LS age: 537
  Options: (No TOS-capability, DC)
  LS Type: Summary Links(Network)
  Link State ID: 172.17.0.0 (summary Network Number)
  Advertising Router: 10.1.42.100
  LS Seq Number: 80000001
  Checksum: 0x7863
  Length: 28
  Network Mask: /16
        TOS: 0  Metric: 10
```

You can see the 172.17.0.0 network you learned from the neighbor router, 10.1.42.100, and the cost of the link associated with that network.

> **NOTE**
>
> In a larger-scale example, there could be hundreds of these networks that have been learned from other routers in the OSPF area and in other areas as well.

The final show command for OSPF is actually extremely useful when you want to gather information about the network topologies that are connected to the router's interfaces. The show ip ospf interface command yields a wealth of information, such as the local router's Router ID, interface topology type, link cost and priority, router ID for the DR and BDR on the segment, hello/dead intervals, and a count of how many neighbors and adjacencies formed:

```
RouterA#show ip ospf interface
FastEthernet0/0 is up, line protocol is up
  Internet Address 172.16.0.1/16, Area 51
  Process ID 4, Router ID 10.1.42.1, Network Type BROADCAST, Cost: 1
  Transmit Delay is 1 sec, State DR, Priority 1
  Designated Router (ID) 10.1.42.1, Interface address 172.16.0.1
  No backup designated router on this network
  Timer intervals configured, Hello 10, Dead 40, Wait 40, Retransmit 5
    oob-resync timeout 40
    Hello due in 00:00:03
  Supports Link-local Signaling (LLS)
  Index 2/2, flood queue length 0
  Next 0x0(0)/0x0(0)
  Last flood scan length is 0, maximum is 0
  Last flood scan time is 0 msec, maximum is 0 msec
  Neighbor Count is 0, Adjacent neighbor count is 0
  Suppress hello for 0 neighbor(s)
Serial0/0/0 is up, line protocol is up
  Internet Address 192.168.1.5/30, Area 0
  Process ID 4, Router ID 192.168.100.155, Network Type POINT_TO_POINT, Cost: 64
  Transmit Delay is 1 sec, State POINT_TO_POINT,
  Timer intervals configured, Hello 10, Dead 40, Wait 40, Retransmit 5
    oob-resync timeout 40
    Hello due in 00:00:07
  Supports Link-local Signaling (LLS)
  Index 1/1, flood queue length 0
  Next 0x0(0)/0x0(0)
  Last flood scan length is 0, maximum is 0
  Last flood scan time is 0 msec, maximum is 0 msec
  Neighbor Count is 0, Adjacent neighbor count is 0
  Suppress hello for 0 neighbor(s)
```

> **EXAM ALERT**
>
> The show ip ospf neighbor and show ip ospf interface commands can show you which router is the DR and which is the BDR.

Troubleshooting OSPF

Objective:

▶ Troubleshoot routing issues

At the risk of sounding like a broken record, you should begin your troubleshooting by using the show commands discussed in the preceding section to ensure that your configurations are correct. Some of the more common problems that occur with OSPF configurations are simple mistakes such as those that occur with incorrect network statements (incorrect network ID, wildcard mask, or area) and forgetting to configure each router as a stub in a stub area.

In cases where the configuration checks out, OSPF also can debug routing information in real time if you use the debug ip ospf events command. This command is useful if you are trying to troubleshoot occurrences such as routers that cannot form a neighbor relationship. In the following example, you can see that a hello message has been received from 10.1.42.100. Notice that no real routing information is shown in these hello messages, because OSPF does not send entire routing updates in its hello LSAs.

```
RouterA#debug ip ospf events
OSPF events debugging is on
00:57:13: OSPF: Rcv hello from 10.1.42.100 area 51 from Serial0/0 192.168.1.6
00:57:13: OSPF: End of hello processing
```

Challenge

It is time to test your OSPF configuration skills. In this challenge, you configure a new OSPF router given the following parameters:

Fast Ethernet interface IP: 172.16.100.65 /27 Area 0

Serial interface IP: 192.168.100.9 /30 Area 1

Router ID: 10.1.1.1 /32

1. Ensure that the Router ID is configured before you configure the OSPF router process.

2. Configure the OSPF router process using an ID of 65535.

3. Advertise the entire Fast Ethernet subnet, and place it in the backbone area.

4. Advertise the entire Serial subnet, and place it in Area 1.

5. Configure Area 1 as a stub.

6. Navigate to the Fast Ethernet interface, and make sure your router becomes the DR by setting the priority to 2.

(continues)

(continued)

Challenge Answer

Based on the parameters specified, your router configuration should resemble the following:

```
!Step 1
interface Loopback0
 ip address 10.1.1.1 255.255.255.255
 exit
!Step 2
router ospf 65535
!Step 3
 network 172.16.100.64 0.0.0.31 area 0
!Step 4
 network 192.168.100.8 0.0.0.3 area 1
!Step 5
 area 1 stub
exit
!Step 6
interface FastEthernet0/0
 ip ospf priority 2
```

To configure the router ID, you have to assign the IP address of 10.1.1.1 with a host mask of 255.255.255.255 to a virtual loopback interface so that it is chosen over the physical interfaces. After the OSPF process has begun, you need to advertise both subnets attached to the interfaces. The network ID for the Fast Ethernet interfaces is 172.16.100.64. The wildcard mask for a subnet of 255.255.255.224 is 0.0.0.31 (255.255.255.255 to 255.255.255.224). Likewise, the network ID for 192.168.100.9 is 192.168.100.8 with a wildcard mask of 0.0.0.3 (255.255.255.255 to 255.255.255.252).

Balanced Hybrid Operations

Objective:

▶ Compare and contrast methods of routing and routing protocols

Balanced hybrid routing protocols are sometimes called *advanced distance vector routing protocols*. The rationale behind this logic is that these routing protocols use similar metrics and have a maximum hop count as distance vector routing protocols. However, balanced hybrid routing protocols discover neighbors and put them in a neighbor table before exchanging routing information, as well as keep lists of all possible routes in a topology table, just as link-state routing protocols do. By taking the best attributes from both classes of routing protocols, they have the pick of the litter, so to speak. This enables these routing protocols to be considered some of the more elite routing protocols.

EIGRP

The biggest contender for routing protocol stardom is a Cisco-proprietary routing protocol called Enhanced Interior Gateway Routing Protocol. As the name states, EIGRP is an enhanced version of the (now-defunct) Cisco distance vector routing protocol, IGRP. The next sections look at exactly how this routing protocol is actually one of the fastest-converging protocols that exist today.

EIGRP Characteristics

Objective:

▶ Compare and contrast methods of routing and routing protocols

One of the most notable features that EIGRP offers is the use of a robust 32-bit composite metric. Specifically, EIGRP uses bandwidth and delay (each multiplied by 255 to make them 32-bit) as its default metrics to determine the best routing path to a destination. In addition, you can configure EIGRP to include additional metrics such as reliability, load, and MTU. By using this more robust composite metric (as opposed to using hop count or cost based on bandwidth), routers can accurately determine the best path to take to a destination. For example, in Figure 12.10, RIPv2 would take the T1 link as the best route to reach 172.17.0.0, because it has the fewest hops. EIGRP, on the other hand, considers the links' bandwidth and determines that the bottom path is the optimal route, because the Fast Ethernet links combined are still faster than a single TI of 1.54Mbps.

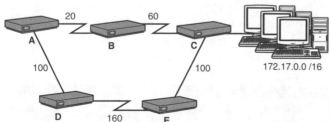

FIGURE 12.10 EIGRP composite metric in action.

Because EIGRP metrics can vary considerably depending on the bandwidth and delay of the links to the destination, EIGRP also can support load balancing up to six *unequal* paths (as opposed to RIP's and OSPF's equal paths). What's more, EIGRP can support larger networks than RIP, because its maximum hop count is 244 as compared to RIP and RIPv2's 15 hops. EIGRP still requires a maximum hop count, because it shares some characteristics of distance vector routing protocols and uses mechanisms to avoid routing loops.

Because EIGRP is a true hybrid routing protocol, it has taken some of the best features of link-state routing protocols too. For instance, EIGRP discovers its neighbors and builds a topology table by sending hello messages as a multicast to the reserved multicast address of 224.0.0.10. After the neighbors are discovered, they synchronize their topology databases and send hello messages afterwards to keep their dead timers from expiring. The timers differ depending on the topology, just as you saw with OSPF. Specifically, point-to-point and broadcast topologies have a 5-second hello interval and 15-second dead timer, whereas nonbroadcast multiaccess topologies such as Frame Relay have a 60-second hello interval and 180-second dead timer.

Cisco, however, did not stop there with the features of this balanced hybrid routing protocol. It developed a new routing algorithm called the Diffusing Update Algorithm (DUAL) that ensures a 100% loop-free routing environment that can converge in the face of a topology change in a split second. EIGRP also can route not only IP, but also IPX and AppleTalk routed protocols in your network if you have an older Novell or Macintosh environment.

> **EXAM ALERT**
>
> It is important to remember that EIGRP can route IP, IPX, and AppleTalk routed protocols.

> **NOTE**
>
> If you are routing IP, IPX, and AppleTalk with EIGRP, it keeps a routing, neighbor, and topology table for each routed protocol. This means it has to maintain nine tables, which consumes a lot of memory and processor resources.

Another additional useful characteristic of EIGRP is its capability to distinguish between internally learned networks and networks that were redistributed into EIGRP. External networks get tagged when being redistributed, so EIGRP knows not to trust those networks over native EIGRP networks. EIGRP assigns the external networks an administrative distance (AD) of 170 and the internal networks an administrative distance of 90.

> **EXAM ALERT**
>
> Be sure to remember that internal networks have an AD of 90 and that external networks have an AD of 170.

Last but not least, EIGRP is classful by default but can be configured to be classless, similar to RIPv2. By disabling automatic summarization, you can support VLSM designs and discontiguous networks, as well as manually summarize networks at any bit boundary you want.

The only significant downfall of this routing protocol is that all your routers must be Cisco routers (not that this is a bad thing) to support this proprietary routing protocol.

Successor and Feasible Successor Routes

The secret of EIGRP's rapid convergence is found in its topology table. Just like OSPF, EIGRP stores all possible routes in the database and calculates the best path to each subnet, based on the lowest cumulative composite metric. Those best routes are known as the *successor routes*.

EIGRP keeps track of the composite metric for every subnet that is being advertised to it by neighbor routers, known as the *advertised distance*. The router also tracks that advertised distance plus the composite metric to reach that advertising router from the local router, known as the *feasible distance*. The lowest feasible distance to a particular subnet becomes the successor route and is the path that is also placed in the routing table.

Where EIGRP sets itself apart from OSPF is that it keeps an ace up its sleeve, so to speak. If the conditions are correct, EIGRP keeps a backup route in its topology table known as the *feasible successor*. In the event that a successor route fails, the feasible successor becomes the successor route and is placed in the routing table in about one second.

The feasible successor route is chosen only if the route will not cause a loop when activated and if the advertised distance from a neighbor is less than the existing successor route's feasible distance. In other words, the feasible successor must have an advertised metric that is less than the metric of the route in the routing table. For example, to reach Network X, imagine your local router's successor route might have a feasible distance of 8000. If any neighbor propagated an advertised distance for it to reach Network X of 7999 or less, its route is a feasible successor. If the advertised distances are 8000 or more, the route is in the topology table but is not a candidate for a feasible successor.

DUAL Algorithm in Action

You already know that the feasible successor route in the topology table is used if the primary successor route fails. So what happens if there isn't a feasible successor, as illustrated in Figure 12.11? In this figure you see a glimpse of Router D's topology table for the 172.17.0.0 /16 subnet. The P next to the network stands for passive state, which in EIGRP terms is actually a good thing. Underneath, you see two possible routes through Router A and Router B with numbers in parentheses separated by a slash. The number on the left represents the advertised distance from the neighbor router, and the number on the right represents the feasible distance to reach that subnet through that advertising router. Because the path through Router B has the lowest feasible distance, that is the successor route, which is also placed in the routing table. The route through Router A has an advertised distance of 9700, which is not less than the successor route's feasible distance (3700), so it cannot be a feasible successor.

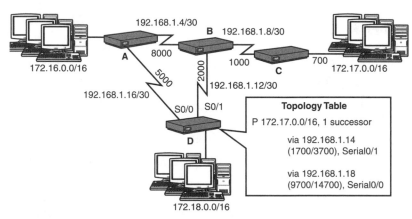

FIGURE 12.11 Passive EIGRP topology.

Now let's see what happens when the successor route to Router B fails, as shown in Figure 12.12. Without a feasible successor route to 172.17.0.0, Router D puts that network into an active state. The network is active because the router begins to actively query its directly connected neighbors about whether they have a route to the affected network. This is considerably different from and less resource-intensive than OSPF, because the router only asks its neighbors, as opposed to flooding the update throughout the area.

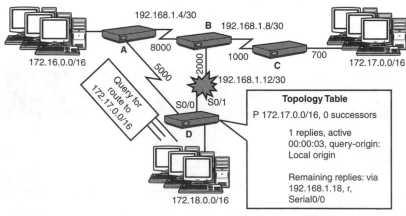

FIGURE 12.12 Active EIGRP topology.

When Router A responds to Router D's query, it adds that entry to its topology table, which in turn becomes the new successor route and is placed in the routing table. To ensure a loop-free environment, Router D has to wait for all queries to come back before implementing the new route. That is why EIGRP routers start what is known as a *Stuck in Active (SIA)* timer, which is how long it waits for a response from a query. The default SIA timeout is 180 seconds.

EIGRP Stub Routing

It should come as no surprise that EIGRP borrowed another link-state concept to improve routing convergence and save router resources. Similar to an OSPF stub area, EIGRP allows you to configure what is known as EIGRP *stub routing*. This configuration is most useful in instances where the network is designed in a hub-and-spoke topology, as shown in Figure 12.13.

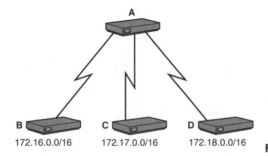

172.16.0.0/16   172.17.0.0/16   172.18.0.0/16   **FIGURE 12.13**   Hub-and-spoke EIGRP topology.

Because each of the remote routers (Routers B, C, and D) all have to pass data through the central Router A to reach the remotes, it does not make sense for EIGRP devices to act as they normally would when a topology change occurs. For example, if the 172.16.0.0 network connected to Router B goes down, what good does it do for the routers to go into an active state for that link and query its neighbors for an alternate route? There is only one way in and out of that network (because that is the defining characteristic of a stub network). By configuring the remote routers as stub routers (the central, or hub, router does not need to be configured), the routers immediately respond to the query as "inaccessible" and speed up the time it takes to converge the network.

EIGRP Configuration

Objective:

▶ Configure, verify, and troubleshoot EIGRP

One of the greatest aspects of EIGRP is that you get all this advanced functionality with minimal configuration effort. EIGRP essentially follows the same configuration guidelines as RIPv2. Namely, it must advertise the directly connected networks. Because EIGRP is also classful by default, the networks configured must be at a default classful boundary. A key element that differs in the RIPv2 configuration is the inclusion of an AS number in the routing process configuration. This AS number is an arbitrary number between 1 and 65535 that you or your network administrator assigns to your network. It is imperative that you make this number match in all your router configurations, or the routers will ignore the routing updates.

> **EXAM ALERT**
>
> Do not confuse the autonomous system number with OSPF's process ID. Autonomous system numbers with EIGRP must match in every router that you configure, or the updates are ignored.

In the routing process, you use the network keyword followed by the directly connected classful networks, because EIGRP is classful by default. The following sample configuration demonstrates adding the 172.16.0.0 and 10.0.0.0 networks to the EIGRP process for autonomous system 100:

```
Router(config)#router eigrp 100
Router(config-router)#network 172.16.0.0
Router(config-router)#network 10.0.0.0
```

You can change EIGRP into a classless routing protocol by entering the no auto-summary command, just as you did with RIPv2. And to round out EIGRP's hybrid configuration characteristics, you can also specify the wildcard mask after the network ID, as you did with OSPF, to indicate specific subnets such as this configuration:

```
Router(config)#router eigrp 100
Router(config-router)#no auto-summary
Router(config-router)#network 172.16.30.0 0.0.0.255
Router(config-router)#network 10.100.0.0 0.0.255.255
```

After you configure the routing protocol to be classless, you can support VLSM, discontiguous networks, and route summarization at any bit level. With automatic summarization turned off, however, you must manually configure EIGRP route summaries. The command to do this is ip summary-address eigrp, which is actually configured on the interface on which the summarized route will be advertised:

```
Router(config)#interface serial 0/0/0
Router(config-if)#ip summary-address eigrp 192.168.4.0 255.255.254.0
```

The Bandwidth Bandwagon

Because EIGRP uses bandwidth as one of its metrics to determine the best path to a destination, it is imperative that the routers accurately depict the bandwidth that is currently on their interfaces. Because Fast Ethernet and Gigabit interfaces automatically define the bandwidth of their interfaces, you do not have to worry about any additional configurations on the LAN interfaces.

WAN interfaces, such as serial, asynchronous serial, and HSSI, can have varying speeds, depending on the WAN circuits to which they are connected. For instance, it is possible to have a 64kbps link connected to one serial interface and T1 connected to another. By default, Cisco IOS software automatically assumes that any circuit connected to a serial interface is T1 (1544kbps) speed, so how can you tell EIGRP about a link speed that is less than T1? The answer is by using the bandwidth interface command followed by the bandwidth in kbps, as discussed in Chapter 8, "Foundation Cisco Configurations." By specifying the actual bandwidth on the interface, EIGRP incorporates that information in its metrics and can make accurate routing decisions based on the proper speeds of the links.

Unequal-Path Load Balancing

One of the outstanding features of EIGRP is its capability to load-balance up to six unequal paths (four by default). To achieve this remarkable feat, you must configure a multiplier based on the lowest composite metric to a destination. The command for this multiplier is variance, which is configured in the EIGRP routing process.

For instance, Figure 12.14 illustrates a simplified topology with the composite metrics to reach 172.17.0.0. In its default state, EIGRP chooses the router through Router B because it has the lowest cumulative composite metric to reach the destination network. Because the path through B and C has a metric of 80, and the path through D and E has a metric of 110, you can specify a variance of 2, which acts as a multiplier of the lowest metric (80 in this case). The configuration for this would look like the following:

```
RouterA(config)#router eigrp 100
RouterA(config-router)#variance 2
```

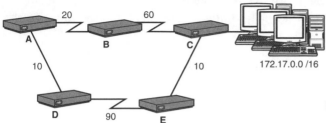

FIGURE 12.14 Unequal-path load balancing with the `variance` command.

> **TIP**
>
> The variance multiplier does not have to be an exact multiplication. If the multiplied value happens to go over the highest composite metric to a destination, it still load-balances over any path that is included in the range.

IP Default Network

Like other routing protocols, EIGRP does not automatically redistribute default routes to downstream neighbors in its routing updates. As an alternative, you can configure a default network that tells downstream neighbors to reach the network specified as a gateway of last resort. This does not, however, configure a default route or a gateway of last resort in the router in which it is configured.

The syntax to configure a default network is the `ip default-network` command in global configuration mode. The network that you specify must already be a subnet that is present in the routing table. Downstream neighbors will set that specified network as their gateway of last resort and determine the fastest way to reach it via their routing protocol. For example, if you wanted to use the 192.168.1.0 network in your routing table as a gateway of last resort for downstream neighbors receiving your EIGRP updates, the configuration would resemble the following:

```
RouterA(config)#ip default-network 192.168.1.0
```

EIGRP Stub Routing Configuration

Recall that stub routing is a way to reduce convergence time in hub-and-spoke networks that are using EIGRP. The stub routing configuration occurs only on the remote routers and is achieved by using the `eigrp stub` command in routing configuration mode:

```
RouterA(config)#router eigrp 100
RouterA(config-router)#eigrp stub
```

As soon as this command is enabled, the router advertises summary routes that are connected to the router. This is important to keep in mind, because you either need to have automatic summarization kept on or create manual summary routes using the `ip summary-address eigrp` command.

EIGRP Configuration Using SDM

Let's round out our SDM routing capabilities by seeing the simplicity of configuring EIGRP in the SDM interface. As with OSPF, these configurations take place in the Configure, Routing task in the Dynamic Routing properties; however, this time you choose the **EIGRP** tab in the Edit IP Dynamic Routing dialog box, as shown in Figure 12.15. In the Add a EIGRP dialog box, you identify what autonomous system number this router will use for EIGRP and click the **Add** button to add networks to the network list. Similar to the OSPF configuration, when you click the **Add** button, you see the Add a Network dialog box, asking for the networks and optional wildcard mask of the network(s) to be added to the EIGRP process.

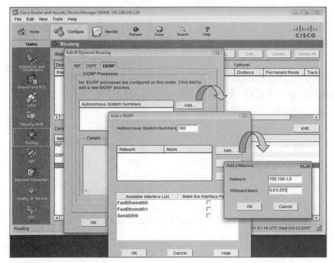

FIGURE 12.15 EIGRP SDM configuration.

EIGRP Verification

Objective:

▶ Verify router hardware and software operation using SHOW & DEBUG commands

As with all the routing protocols, the show ip protocols command displays the networks being advertised, the administrative distance of the routing protocol, and the routing sources for EIGRP-learned networks:

```
RouterA#show ip protocols
Routing Protocol is "eigrp 100"
  Outgoing update filter list for all interfaces is
  Incoming update filter list for all interfaces is
  Default networks flagged in outgoing updates
  Default networks accepted from incoming updates
  EIGRP metric weight K1=1, K2=0, K3=1, K4=0, K5=0
  EIGRP maximum hopcount 100
```

```
EIGRP maximum metric variance 1
Redistributing: eigrp 100
Automatic network summarization is in effect
Automatic address summarization:
  192.168.1.0/24 for FastEthernet0/0
    Summarizing with metric 2169856
  172.16.0.0/16 for Serial0/0
Routing for Networks:
  172.16.0.0
  192.168.1.0
Routing Information Sources:
  Gateway         Distance      Last Update
  (this router)          5      00:00:07
  192.168.1.6           90      00:00:01
Distance: internal 90 external 170
```

As with OSPF, you can look at the three tables that EIGRP maintains for each routed proto-col. To see the IP routing table, as before, use the show ip route command to verify that you are receiving EIGRP entries, which are signified by the letter D:

```
RouterA#show ip route
Codes: C - connected, S - static, I - IGRP, R - RIP, M - mobile, B - BGP
       D - EIGRP, EX - EIGRP external, O - OSPF, IA - OSPF inter area
       N1 - OSPF NSSA external type 1, N2 - OSPF NSSA external type 2
       E1 - OSPF external type 1, E2 - OSPF external type 2, E - EGP
       i - IS-IS, L1 - IS-IS level-1, L2 - IS-IS level-2, * - candidate default
       U - per-user static route, o - ODR, P - periodic downloaded static route
       T - traffic engineered route

Gateway of last resort is not set

D    172.17.0.0/16 [90/2195456] via 192.168.1.6, Serial0/0
C    172.16.0.0/16 is directly connected, FastEthernet0/0
D EX 172.19.0.0/16 [170/2169856] via 192.168.1.6, Serial0/0
D    172.18.0.0/16 [90/2297856] via 192.168.1.6, Serial0/0
     10.0.0.0/32 is subnetted, 1 subnets
C       10.1.42.1 is directly connected, Loopback0
     192.168.1.0/24 is variably subnetted, 2 subnets, 2 masks
C       192.168.1.4/30 is directly connected, Serial0/0
```

Notice the entry for 172.19.0.0 with an EX indicator next to it. You may have already guessed by looking at the administrative distance in the brackets (170) that this is an external EIGRP route that was learned through another routing source being redistributed into EIGRP. Because it is not native to EIGRP, it is trusted less than an internally learned route.

To see a listing of your EIGRP neighbors that were discovered through listening to the 224.0.0.10 multicast address, enter the show ip eigrp neighbors command:

```
RouterA#show ip eigrp neighbors
IP-EIGRP neighbors for process 100
H    Address             Interface    Hold Uptime    SRTT   RTO  Q  Seq
                                      (sec)          (ms)        Cnt Num
0    192.168.1.6         Se0/0         11 00:16:27    36   216  0  7
```

You can view the final table, the topology table, using the show ip eigrp topology command. Here you can see all the possible routes, determine the successor routes, learn whether you have any feasible successors for each subnet, and learn whether those subnets are in an active or passive state:

```
RouterA#show ip eigrp topology
IP-EIGRP Topology Table for process 100

Codes: P - Passive, A - Active, U - Update, Q - Query, R - Reply,
       r - Reply status
P 192.168.1.4/30, 1 successors, FD is 2169856
        via Connected, Serial0/0
P 172.16.0.0/16, 1 successors, FD is 28160
        via Connected, FastEthernet0/0
P 172.17.0.0/16, 1 successors, FD is 2195456
        via 192.168.1.6 (2195456/281600), Serial0/0
P 172.18.0.0/16, 1 successors, FD is 2297856
        via 192.168.1.6 (2297856/128256), Serial0/0
P 172.19.0.0/16, 1 successors, FD is 2169856
        via 192.168.1.6 (2169856/256), Serial0/0
```

> **NOTE**
>
> Notice that the syntax for viewing the topology table for EIGRP is show ip eigrp topology as opposed to OSPF's show ip ospf database.

EIGRP Troubleshooting

It wouldn't be a troubleshooting section unless I reminded you that verifying the routing protocol configuration and process should be the first step before entering any debug commands. With that said, EIGRP can perform real-time debugging with the debug ip eigrp command:

```
RouterA#debug ip eigrp
03:43:46: IP-EIGRP: Processing incoming UPDATE packet
03:43:46: IP-EIGRP: Int 172.17.0.0/16 M 2195456 - 1657856 537600 SM 281600 - 256000
25600
03:43:46: IP-EIGRP: Int 172.18.0.0/16 M 2297856 - 1657856 640000 SM 128256 - 256 128000
03:43:46: IP-EIGRP: Int 172.19.0.0/16 M 2169856 - 1657856 512000
?SM 256 - 256 0
03:43:46: IP-EIGRP: Int 172.17.0.0/16 metric 2195456 - 1657856 537600
03:43:46: IP-EIGRP: Int 172.18.0.0/16 metric 2297856 - 1657856 640000
03:43:46: IP-EIGRP: Int 172.19.0.0/16 metric 2169856 - 1657856 512000
```

Chapter Summary

This chapter rounded out your routing protocol classes as you delved into the modern link state and balanced hybrid routing protocols. Table 12.3 summarizes the characteristics of the link-state routing protocol, OSPF, and the balanced hybrid routing protocol, EIGRP.

TABLE 12.3 OSPF and EIGRP Comparison

	OSPF	EIGRP
Classful/classless	Classless	Both
Algorithm	Dijkstra SPF	DUAL
Metric	Cost (10^8/bandwidth bps)	32-bit composite
Maximum hop count	None	224
Areas or autonomous system configuration	Areas	Autonomous systems
Hello/dead time	10/40, 30/120	5/15, 60/180
Cisco or IETF	IETF	Cisco
Updates	Multicast (224.0.0.5, 224.0.0.6)	Multicast (224.0.0.10)
Load balancing	Equal paths	Unequal paths
Routed protocols	IP	IP, IPX, AppleTalk

Because the OSPF Router ID is determined by the highest virtual IP address followed by the highest physical IP, it is recommended that the first step you should take when configuring OSPF is to create a loopback interface. To start the OSPF routing process, use the router keyword in global configuration mode, followed by the routing protocol and the OSPF process ID. This process ID is a locally significant number between 1 and 65535 that does not need to match in all router configurations. After you are in the routing process, you advertise the networks with the network command, followed by the network ID and the wildcard mask for that classless subnet. This is immediately followed by the area keyword and the area to which you want to associate that network.

By using areas, you can minimize topology and routing tables by creating route summaries on the ABR routers that are between two areas. This also helps contain any topology changes to that area, because other areas are unaware of those individual subnets. You can also create a stub area that instructs the ABR to send a default route to the routers inside the stub area instead of the subnets from other areas. Because Area 0 is the transit backbone area to which all other areas must connect, it cannot be a stub area.

OSPF also performs elections in broadcast and nonbroadcast topologies to reduce update overhead. The DR and BDR are elected based on the highest interface priority followed by the router ID as a tiebreaker. Updates are sent to the DR and BDR, which listen on the 224.0.0.6 reserved multicast address. The update is then propagated to the rest of the segment with the 224.0.05 multicast address, to which all OSPF devices are listening.

EIGRP configuration consists of specifying the autonomous system number in the `router eigrp` command, which must match in all routers. When in the routing process for EIGRP, the directly connected classful networks are advertised. You can make EIGRP classless by using the `no auto-summary` command.

OSPF and EIGRP can be verified with the `show ip protocols` and `show ip route` commands, as with other routing protocols. In addition, you can view the neighbor table by using `show ip ospf neighbor` for OSPF and `show ip eigrp neighbors` for EIGRP. You can view all the possible networks learned via OSPF's neighbors by looking at its topology table with the `show ip ospf database` command. EIGRP, on the other hand, shows you all the routes as well as the successor and any feasible successor routes in the topology table if you use the `show ip eigrp topology` command. The successor route is the primary route, which is placed in the routing table. The feasible successor route is viable only if the advertised distance to a subnet is less than the feasible distance for the local router.

Finally, you also can see real-time updates and hello messages in your routing protocols if you use the `debug ip ospf` command for OSPF and `debug ip eigrp` for EIGRP.

Key Terms

- Dijkstra SPF algorithm
- Topology table
- LSA
- Neighbor table
- Area
- LSU
- Flapping
- ABR
- Backbone area
- Backbone router
- Router ID
- Loopback interface
- Broadcast multiaccess topology
- Nonbroadcast multiaccess topology
- Point-to-point topology

- DR
- BDR
- OSPF priority
- Adjacency
- Host mask
- Process ID
- Wildcard mask
- DUAL
- Successor route
- Advertised distance
- Variance
- Feasible distance
- Feasible successor route
- SIA timer
- Stub routing

Apply Your Knowledge

Exercises

12.1 Configure EIGRP Router A

In this exercise and the next, you will configure EIGRP between two routers.

> **NOTE**
>
> This exercise assumes you have two nonproduction routers with a serial cross-over cable or simulated software. If you do not have these on hand, write out what the configurations would look like.

Estimated Time: 20 minutes

1. Enter privileged EXEC mode on Router A.

2. Enter global configuration mode.

3. Configure and enable the Fast Ethernet interface on Router A to have an IP address of 192.168.1.1/24.

4. Configure and enable the Serial interface on Router A to have an IP address of 10.1.1.1/30.

5. Configure the clock rate (if this is the DCE) for 64000 bits per second.

6. Configure a `bandwidth` statement to reflect this speed on the serial interface.

7. Enter the routing process for EIGRP, using 102 as the AS number.

8. Advertise the directly connected classful networks.

9. Make EIGRP classless by using the `no auto-summary` command.

12.2 Configure EIGRP Router B

Now that Router A is configured, you must configure its neighbor, Router B, to send and receive routing updates.

Estimated Time: 20 minutes

1. Enter privileged EXEC mode on Router B.

2. Enter global configuration mode.

3. Configure and enable the Fast Ethernet interface on Router B to have an IP address of 172.16.30.1/24.

4. Configure and enable the Serial interface on Router B to have an IP address of 10.1.1.2/30.

5. Configure the clock rate (if this is the DCE) for 64000 bits per second.

6. Configure a bandwidth statement to reflect this speed on the serial interface.

7. Enter the routing process for EIGRP, using 102 as the AS number.

8. Advertise the directly connected classful networks.

9. Make EIGRP classless by using the no auto-summary command.

10. Because there is only one way into and out of Router B's network, configure it to use stub routing.

12.3 Verify Routing

If the routers were configured correctly, you should be able to verify your EIGRP routing in this exercise.

1. In both Router A and Router B, enter show ip protocols to verify the networks that you are advertising.

2. Enter show ip route and verify that you have an EIGRP entry in your routing table from your neighbor.

3. Verify that the neighbor was discovered by using the show ip eigrp neighbors command.

4. Make sure your route is the feasible successor and that it is in a passive state in the topology table by using show ip eigrp topology.

Review Questions

1. What is the OSPF router ID, and how is it determined?

2. What is the significance of a designated router, and what circumstances are necessary for a router to become a DR?

3. What is the purpose of an OSPF area?

4. How does the DUAL algorithm use the contents of the topology table to ensure rapid convergence?

5. What are the basic configuration steps for using OSPF and EIGRP routing protocols?

Exam Questions

1. David, your Cisco coworker, shows you the following output from a debug ip ospf events command:

```
RouterA#debug ip ospf events
OSPF events debugging is on
00:30:53: OSPF: Rcv hello from 10.1.42.100 area 51 from Serial0/0 192.168.1.6
00:30:53: OSPF: Mismatched hello parameters from 192.168.1.6
00:30:53: Dead R 40 C 120, Hello R 10 C 30  Mask R 255.255.255.252 C
255.255.255.252
```

He knows that the Rs stand for received and the Cs stand for configured. However, he can't figure out why he cannot get OSPF to work. What should you tell him?

- ○ **A.** OSPF needs to have the classful networks advertised.
- ○ **B.** Area 51 is an invalid area number.
- ○ **C.** Check the OSPF timers.
- ○ **D.** 10.1.42.100 needs to be a DR.

2. Given the following output, which of the following statements is false?

```
RouterA>show ip ospf interface
FastEthernet0/0 is up, line protocol is up
  Internet Address 172.16.0.1/16, Area 51
  Process ID 1, Router ID 10.1.1.1, Network Type BROADCAST, Cost: 1
  Transmit Delay is 1 sec, State DR, Priority 1
  Designated Router (ID) 10.1.42.1, Interface address 172.16.0.1
  No backup designated router on this network
  Timer intervals configured, Hello 10, Dead 40, Wait 40, Retransmit 5
    Hello due in 00:00:04
  Index 1/1, flood queue length 0
  Next 0x0(0)/0x0(0)
  Last flood scan length is 0, maximum is 0
  Last flood scan time is 0 msec, maximum is 0 msec
  Neighbor Count is 0, Adjacent neighbor count is 0
```

- ○ **A.** This router will listen for updates on multicast address 224.0.0.6.
- ○ **B.** 10.1.1.1 is not a loopback IP address.
- ○ **C.** The router interface is not connected to the backbone area.
- ○ **D.** This router will listen for LSA hellos on 224.0.0.5.

3. Given the following customer requirements, which routing protocol would you recommend?

Requirements: fast convergence, IP only, large network, VLSM support needed, Cisco and Nortel routers.

- ○ **A.** RIPv2
- ○ **B.** RIPv1
- ○ **C.** EIGRP
- ○ **D.** OSPF

4. Based on the following output, which of the following statements are true? (Choose two)

```
RouterA#show ip eigrp topology
IP-EIGRP Topology Table for process 100

Codes: P - Passive, A - Active, U - Update, Q - Query, R - Reply,
       r - Reply status
P 172.17.0.0/16, 1 successors, FD is 2195456
        via 192.168.1.6 (2195456/281600), Serial0/0
        via 192.168.1.31 (2297856/128256), Serial0/1
```

- ○ **A.** The route for 172.17.0.0 is down and is being queried.
- ○ **B.** Router 192.168.1.31 has a composite metric of 2297856 to get to 172.17.0.0.
- ○ **C.** Router 192.168.1.6 has an administrative distance of 2195456.
- ○ **D.** There is no feasible successor to 172.17.0.0.

5. Given the following output, why is OSPF not working correctly?

```
RouterA#show running-config
interface FastEthernet0/0
 ip address 172.16.0.1 255.255.0.0
!
interface Serial0/0
 ip address 192.168.1.5 255.255.255.252

RouterA#configure terminal
RouterA(config)#router ospf 9
RouterA(config-router)#network 172.16.0.0 0.0.255.255 area 0
RouterA(config-router)#network 192.168.1.0 0.0.0.4 area 0
```

- ○ **A.** The network ID and wildcard mask are incorrect.
- ○ **B.** The area needs to be configured as a stub area.
- ○ **C.** You need the no auto-summary command to make OSPF classless.
- ○ **D.** The autonomous system number doesn't match other router configurations.

6. Given the following output, what will the OSPF router ID be for this router if you configure it for OSPF?

```
RouterA>show ip interface brief
Interface            IP-Address      OK? Method Status
Protocol
FastEthernet0/0      172.16.0.1      YES NVRAM  up                        up
Serial0/0            192.168.1.5     YES NVRAM  up                        up
Loopback0            10.1.42.1       YES NVRAM  administratively down down
```

   ◯ **A.** OSPF does not require a router ID because this router has a broadcast topology.

   ◯ **B.** 172.16.0.1

   ◯ **C.** 10.1.42.1

   ◯ **D.** 192.168.1.5

7. What is the cost of a 512kbps link for OSPF?

   ◯ **A.** 156

   ◯ **B.** 195

   ◯ **C.** 10

   ◯ **D.** 64

8. What is the effect of the following configuration?

```
RouterA#show running-config
interface FastEthernet0/0
 ip address 10.1.0.1 255.255.0.0
 !
interface Serial0/0/0
 ip address 10.100.25.2 255.255.255.252
 !
interface Serial0//01
 ip address 10.10.45.102 255.255.255.252
 !
router ospf 234
 network 10.0.0.0 0.255.255.255 area 10
```

   ◯ **A.** Only interface Fast Ethernet 0/0's subnet will be associated into OSPF area 10.

   ◯ **B.** Only interface Serial 0/0/0's subnet will be associated into OSPF area 10.

   ◯ **C.** Only interface Serial 0/0/1's subnet will be associated into OSPF area 10.

   ◯ **D.** None of the above

9. Which command enables unequal load balancing over all three links with the metrics Network A-234, Network B-23, and Network C-601?

   ◯ **A.** variance 10

   ◯ **B.** variance 3

   ◯ **C.** variance 30

   ◯ **D.** variance 25

10. What would be the result of the following two configurations?

```
RouterA(config)#router EIGRP 200
RouterA(config-router)#no auto-summary
RouterA(config-router)#network 172.17.0.0 0.0.255.255
RouterA(config-router)#network 192.168.34.0 0.0.0.255

RouterB(config)#router EIGRP 100
RouterB(config-router)#no auto-summary
RouterB(config-router)#network 172.18.0.0 0.0.255.255
RouterB(config-router)#network 192.168.34.0 0.0.0.255
```

○ **A.** Router A adds the 172.18.0.0 network to its routing table.

○ **B.** Router B does not add the 192.168.34.0 network, because it is advertising it to Router A.

○ **C.** The routing updates do not contain the subnet masks.

○ **D.** Router A and Router B ignore each other's updates.

11. Which of the following characteristics does *not* apply to EIGRP and OSPF?

○ **A.** The timers for hello/dead differ depending on the topology.

○ **B.** Both routing protocols support VLSM, router summarization, and discontiguous networks by default.

○ **C.** Both routing protocols have a routing table, neighbor table, and topology table.

○ **D.** Both routing protocols discover neighbors by sending hellos to a multicast address.

Answers to Review Questions

1. The router uses the OSPF router ID to know the rest of the OSPF routing domain. The highest IP address of the logical loopback interfaces is used at the startup of the OSPF routing process to determine the OSPF router ID. If no loopback interfaces are configured or enabled, the router uses the highest IP address of an active physical interface.

2. The designated router is elected by broadcast and nonbroadcast multiaccess networks to minimize the amount of routing update overhead. On each network segment, the router with the highest interface priority (default is 1) is elected as the DR, and the router that has the interface with the second-highest priority is the BDR. In cases where the interface priorities are tied, the highest router ID is used as a tiebreaker.

3. OSPF areas are a way to segment an OSPF routing domain into smaller routing systems to reduce the amount of routing overhead and to confine topology changes. Area 0 is known as the backbone area, to which all other areas must connect.

4. The DUAL algorithm keeps track of the advertised distance and the feasible distance for each net-work in the topology table. The lowest feasible distance to a destination is known as the successor route and is the network that is put in the routing table. If the router receives an update that has an advertised distance less than the successor route's feasible distance, that entry becomes the feasi-ble successor, which is used if the successor route fails.

5. To configure OSPF and EIGRP, you must enter the routing process using the `router` keyword fol-lowed by the routing protocol. In the case of OSPF, you must also specify a process ID to locally identify the instance of OSPF. The valid range of OSPF process IDs is between 1 and 65535 and does not need to match in all router configurations. On the other hand, EIGRP requires that you specify an autonomous system number that does have to match in all router configurations.

After you are in the routing process, you advertise the connected networks with the `network` command. EIGRP configurations require that you enter the directly connected classful network(s) after the `network` keyword. Conversely, OSPF configurations require that you specify the network ID followed by the wildcard mask. Following the wildcard mask, you must also use the `area` key-word, followed by the area to which that network belongs.

Answers to Exam Questions

1. **C.** For OSPF to form a neighbor relationship, the hello/dead timers, stub flag, authentication pass-word, and area ID must match. Because the output shows that the received timers are different from those that were configured, the timers must be misconfigured. Answer A is incorrect because OSPF is a classless routing protocol. Answer B is incorrect because Area 51 is an area within the acceptable ranges of 0 to 65535. Answer D is incorrect because 10.1.42.100 does not need to be a DR to send hello messages.

2. **B.** The router ID is chosen based on the highest active virtual loopback address. If no loopback is present, the highest physical IP address is chosen when the OSPF process starts. Answer A is true because the output indicates that this router's interface is the DR, which listens to 224.0.0.6. Answer C is also true because this interface is connected to Area 51, not Area 0. Answer D is true because all OSPF routers (including the DR and BDR) listen to hellos on 224.0.0.5.

3. **D.** Given the customer requirements, Answer D is the only viable option. Answers A and B aren't good choices because they require fast convergence. Answer C is tempting, but the fact that the customer has Nortel routers cancels out EIGRP and IGRP, because they are Cisco-proprietary.

4. **B, D.** The topology table shows that 192.168.1.31 is advertising (advertised distance) a metric of 2297856. Because that advertised distance is larger than the feasible distance of the successor route (281600), it cannot be a feasible successor. Answer A is incorrect because the subnet is not in an active state. Answer C is tricky, because the number with the slash is not the administrative distance, as you would see in a routing table. It is the advertised distance followed by the feasible distance.

5. **A.** The network ID for Serial 0/0's subnet should be 192.168.1.4, and the wildcard mask for a 255.255.255.252 subnet mask is 0.0.0.3. Answer B is incorrect because the type of area has no bearing on this configuration. Answer C is incorrect because OSPF does not require a command to make it classless. Answer D is incorrect because OSPF does not use autonomous system numbers.

6. D. Typically, the 10.1.42.1 address would be the correct router ID for OSPF. However, the output shows it as administratively down. Because that interface isn't active, the highest active physical IP address is used (192.168.1.5). Answer A is incorrect because all OSPF routers use a Router ID. Answer B is incorrect because it is not the highest active IP address. Answer C would be correct if the interface were not administratively shut down.

7. B. To calculate OSPF cost, you take 10^8/bandwidth in bps. Thus, 100000000/512000 = 195. Answer A is the cost of a link speed of 640kbps. Answer C is the cost of 10Mbps Ethernet. Answer D is the cost of a T1.

8. D. Because the wildcard mask is configured to allow any network starting with 10.x.x.x to be in the OSPF routing process, all interfaces are applied in this configuration. Answers A, B, and C are incorrect because the wildcard mask encompasses all three of the networks assigned to the interfaces.

9. C. Because the lowest metric to the destinations is 23, and the highest is 601, a multiplier of 30 enables metric values from 23 to 690 (30×23). Answer A is incorrect because the multiplier only load-balances over links with a metric up to 230. Answer B is incorrect because the multiplier only load-balances over links with a metric up to 69. Answer D is incorrect because the multiplier only load-balances over links with a metric up to 575.

10. D. The autonomous system number must match in both devices, or the routers ignore each other's updates. Answer A is incorrect because Router A is not advertising the 172.18.0.0 network. Answer B is incorrect because Router B already has the 192.168.34.0 network in its routing table because Router B is advertising this directly connected network. Answer C is incorrect because EIGRP is configured as classless because the no auto-summary command is used.

11. B. EIGRP is not classless by default. You must configure the no auto-summary command for EIGRP to support VLSM, router summarization, and discontiguous networks. Answer A is true because OSPF and EIGRP both have different hello/dead intervals, depending on the topology to which the interfaces are connected. Answer C is true because EIGRP and OSPF both have routing, topology, and neighbor tables. Answer D is true because OSPF and EIGRP both discover neighbors by sending hello messages to a multicast address.

Suggested Readings and Resources

1. Alex Zinn. *IP Routing: Packet Forwarding and Intra-domain Routing Protocols*. Addison Wesley Professional, 2002.

2. Keith Kruepke, Paul Cernick, and Mark Degner. *Cisco IP Routing Handbook*. Hungry Minds, 2000.

3. Anthony Bruno and Jacqueline Kim. *CCDA Exam Certification Guide*. Cisco Press, 2004.

4. Ravi Malhotra. *IP Routing*. O'Reilly, 2002.

5. Mark Sportack. *IP Routing Fundamentals*. Cisco Press, 1999.

6. "Routing Protocols," www.firewall.cx.

7. "OSPF, EIGRP," technology support on www.cisco.com.

CHAPTER THIRTEEN

Foundation Switching Operations

Objectives

This chapter covers the following Cisco-specific objectives for the "Configure, verify and troubleshoot a switch with VLANs and interswitch communications" and "Implement a small switched network":

▶ **Explain basic switching concepts and the operation of Cisco switches**

▶ **Perform and verify initial switch configuration tasks including remote access management**

▶ **Verify network status and switch operation using basic utilities (including: ping, traceroute, telnet, SSH, arp, ipconfig), SHOW & DEBUG commands**

▶ **Identify, prescribe, and resolve common switched network media issues, configuration issues, auto negotiation, and switch hardware failures**

▶ **Interpret the output of various show and debug commands to verify the operational status of a Cisco switched network**

Outline

Study Strategies

▶ Read the information presented in the chapter, paying special attention to tables, Notes, and Exam Alerts.

▶ One of the best practices when reading about switching functions is to visualize the information contained in the Ethernet frames and imagine how a switch uses that information to build its forwarding table and forward frames to other network segments.

▶ Complete the Challenge and the Exercises at the end of the chapter. They will solidify the concepts that you have learned in the previous sections.

▶ After you have read about and understood Spanning Tree Protocol, try to draw your own LAN design and determine the STP elections and port roles that will result from your design.

▶ Complete the Exam Questions at the end of the chapter. They are designed to simulate the types of questions you will be asked on the CCNA and ICND1 exams.

Introduction

You have already learned in Chapter 3, "Data Link Networking Concepts," that you can use bridges and switches to segment a LAN into smaller collision domains. This chapter looks in close detail at the operations of bridges and switches. Specifically, you will investigate the transparent functionality that occurs when a switch is building and utilizing its frame forwarding logic, as well as the peculiar nature of Spanning Tree Protocol (STP) in redundant switched networks.

Switching Functionality

Objective:

▶ Explain basic switching concepts and the operation of Cisco switches

Switches forward frames based on the Layer 2 Ethernet MAC addresses. These devices receive Ethernet frames transmitted from other devices and dynamically build a MAC address table based on the source MAC address inside those frames. This MAC address table is commonly referred to as a Content Addressable Memory (CAM) table.

These dynamic entries in the CAM table are not permanent, however. After the switch or bridge stops receiving frames from a certain MAC address (this varies, but it's typically five minutes), the entry is removed from the CAM table to save memory and processor resources. The exceptions to this are static MAC entries that have been manually configured on a port-by-port basis for security and control purposes.

When deciding to which port to forward the Ethernet frame, a switch consults this CAM table and forwards the Ethernet frame based on the destination MAC address of the Ethernet header. In instances where the destination MAC address is not in the table, it copies and forwards the frame out every port except the one at which it was received. This action is commonly known as flooding.

> **EXAM ALERT**
>
> It is important to remember that switches build their MAC address tables using the source address in an Ethernet frame header. In addition, they base their forwarding decisions on the destination MAC address in an Ethernet frame header.

Recall that switches segment LANs into collision domains; however, they still are in a single broadcast domain. Switches do not have entries for broadcast addresses (FFFF.FFFF.FFFF) or multicast addresses (0100.5E00.000-0100.5E7F.FFFF) in their CAM tables. As previously mentioned, when a bridge or a switch receives a frame with a destination MAC address not in its table, it floods that frame out every port.

For instance, consider the switched topology example illustrated in Figure 13.1. When Computers A, B, and C and Printer D originally sent an Ethernet frame, the switch recorded the source MAC address of that frame and the associated port in its CAM table. If Computer A sends an Ethernet frame destined for Printer D's MAC address of 1111.2222.3333, the switch forwards only that frame out to its Fast Ethernet 0/14 interface. If Computer A sends a broadcast with a destination of FFFF.FFFF.FFFF, that entry does not exist in the CAM table, so that frame is flooded out all interfaces except for Fast Ethernet 0/1.

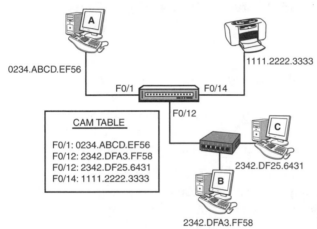

FIGURE 13.1 Switch address learning and forwarding.

Notice that Computers B and C are plugged into a hub. So what happens when Computer B sends an Ethernet frame to Computer C? The frame hits the Layer 1 hub, which regenerates the signal out all ports except the one it came in on (regardless of the MAC address because it is a Physical layer device). When the frame reaches the switch, the switch realizes that the source and destination MAC addresses reside on the same interface, so it does not send that frame on to any other ports. This process is also commonly known as *filtering*.

Frame Transmission Methods

Switches are often classified based on the method in which they process and forward frames in and out of their interfaces. This classification differs depending on the device's processing capabilities and manufacturer. The three transmission methods that a bridge or switch may use are discussed in the following sections.

Store-and-Forward

Properly named, the store-and-forward method of frame transmission involves the switch, which buffers (stores temporarily in a small memory location) the entire Ethernet frame and performs a cyclic redundancy check (CRC) of that frame to make sure it is not a corrupted frame (damaged or abnormally changed in the frame's transmission). If the frame calculation detects a bad frame, it is dropped at that point. Thus, the frame is forwarded only if the CRC calculation results in a normal frame.

Because the entire frame is checked, store-and-forward switching is said to be latency (delay) varying. In other words, depending on the payload inside the frame, the switch takes varying processing times to buffer the entire frame and perform the CRC before sending it to its destination. Although this method sounds like a lengthy process, this is the most widely used method of switching in Cisco Catalyst switches because the hardware processors for the interfaces are so advanced and robust that the switch hardly works up a sweat.

Cut-Through

Cut-through transmissions are practically the antithesis of store-and-forward frame transmission. In fact, instead of processing the entire frame, cut-through switching entails the switch buffering just enough information to know where to forward the frame before sending it on to another segment. In other words, it looks only up to the destination MAC address in the Ethernet header and sends it on regardless of whether the frame contains errors.

This hot-potato method of frame transmission was once appealing for devices with low processing power. Because it has to inspect only the beginning of an Ethernet frame header, latency is not a factor with this method. The downside of cut-through switching, however, is that it still passes bad frames on to other segments because it does not perform CRC calculations of any kind.

Fragment-Free

In a true Goldilocks fashion, if cut-through is too hot and store-and-forward is too cold, fragment-free may be just right for you. Fragment-free is a hybrid of the two transmission methods because it buffers up to the first 64 bytes of a frame (all collisions occur within the first 64 bytes). This obviously is not as fast as cut-through; nevertheless, it ensures that many of the invalid frames in the LAN are not transmitted on to other segments. Figure 13.2 illustrates how much of an Ethernet frame is buffered and processed with each of the three transmission methods discussed.

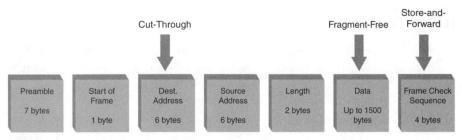

FIGURE 13.2   Frame transmission comparison.

Half- and Full-Duplex Connections

Data communication on switch ports can occur in either half- or full-duplex transmissions. Half-duplex connections are unidirectional in that data can be sent in only one direction at a time. This is similar to two-way radios or walkie-talkies, in which only one person can speak at one time. With half-duplex communication in an Ethernet network, CSMA/CD (carrier sense multiple access with collision detection) is enabled, which results in 50 to 60% of the bandwidth on the link being available to be used.

Full duplex, on the other hand, is indicative of two-way communication in which devices can send and receive information at the same time. With these connections, CSMA/CD is automatically disabled, allowing for theoretically 100% of the bandwidth in both directions. In fact, it uses the two wires that typically are used for detecting collisions to simultaneously transmit and receive. Because CSMA/CD is disabled, that means the connection has to be in an environment where collisions cannot occur. In other words, it must be connected to a switch or directly connected with a cross-over cable.

> **EXAM ALERT**
>
> If you are connected to a hub, the connection must be half-duplex with CSMA/CD. When running full duplex, you must be directly connected to a switch.

> **NOTE**
>
> Because full duplex allows 100% in both directions, it is sometimes advertised at twice the speed. For instance, a 100Mbps interface might be marketed as achieving 200Mbps. Although it is advertised as 200Mbps, in reality, you are receiving 200Mbps of *throughput*.

Switching Design

You have already seen how switches operate when connected to end-user devices such as PCs, printers, and servers. However, when switches are connected to other switches to form a redundant network, a switching loop can occur. Figure 13.3 illustrates a scenario in which a switching loop can occur.

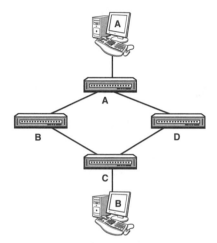

FIGURE 13.3 Redundant switch design.

In this design, redundant links interconnect the switches. Although it is a good idea to have redundancy in the network, the problem arises when a computer sends out a frame with a broadcast, multicast, or unknown unicast destination MAC address. Recall that any of these three transmissions causes a switch to copy and flood that frame out all ports except for the one on which it came in. So if Computer A sends a broadcast, Switch A floods that out to Switches B and D. Again, if this is a broadcast message, Switches B and D flood that frame out to Switch C. Staying true to its design, Switch C floods the frame back to Switches B and D, and so on. Broadcasts continuously circle the switched network until ultimately the amount of broadcast traffic consumes the switched network's bandwidth and all traffic ceases to flow. This unsettling scenario just described is called a *broadcast storm* and can be avoided completely by using a Layer 2 protocol sent among switches called the *Spanning Tree Protocol*.

Spanning Tree Protocol

Once a proprietary protocol from DEC, Spanning Tree Protocol (STP) was standardized and blessed by the IEEE specification, 802.1d. STP allows networks to maintain a level of redundancy while disabling the detrimental side effects that can occur such as broadcast storms. Enabled by default on most switches, STP forms noncircular (no looping) paths throughout the internetwork by performing an election and basing calculations on that election. These calculations dictate which ports should remain in a nonforwarding (known as blocking) state to eliminate redundant loops that can cause broadcast storms. STP also can react to changes in the switched network to ensure that the redundant links may be used in the event of a topology change such as a link going down. The following sections explain exactly how this remarkable protocol operates behind the scenes in a LAN.

> **EXAM ALERT**
>
> **Remember that STP is standardized by the IEEE 802.1d specification and is used to prevent switching loops in a switched network.**

Root Bridge

As previously mentioned, STP performs an election in the switched topology. The winner of this election serves as the base of all calculations and ultimately becomes the root to the spanning tree. Conveniently, this elected bridge or switch is called the *root bridge*. From the root bridge, noncircular branches extend throughout the switched network like those of a tree—a spanning tree.

> **NOTE**
>
> Don't let the term "root bridge" confuse you. When the 802.1d specification was drafted for STP, it was referred to as a "root bridge" because bridges were the prominent devices at the time. In modern times, it can just as easily be a switch.

So how does this election take place? You can rule out voting because each bridge or switch believes itself to be the root bridge at startup. The deciding factor on who becomes the root bridge is something referred to as the Bridge ID. The Bridge ID comprises two components:

▸ **Priority:** This is an arbitrary number from 0 to 61440, which can be administratively set in increments of 4096. The default value for priority is 32768, or 8000 in hex.

▸ **MAC address:** The 48-bit MAC address of the switch itself.

The device with the lowest Bridge ID becomes the root bridge. If a new switch or bridge is added with a lower Bridge ID to the switched network, a new election takes place, and that switch ultimately becomes the new root bridge for the switched network.

Consider the example shown in Figure 13.4. Notice that all switches have their default priority value of 32768 in their Bridge IDs. Thus, the lowest MAC address ultimately dictates who will win the election. Because Switch A has the lowest MAC address in the switched network, it will be the root bridge.

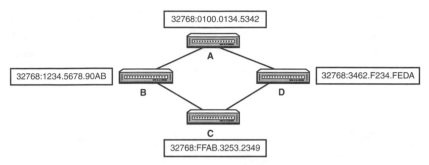

FIGURE 13.4   Root bridge election.

Because this election process occurs automatically with bridges and switches, it is highly advised that you change your priority in a robust and reliable switch in your internetwork as opposed to letting this election occur by chance. This is especially true because manufacturers choose the MAC address, and a lower MAC address could very well mean an old or low-end switch or bridge, which might not be the best choice for your root bridge. How to manually set the priority is discussed later in this chapter.

These Bridge IDs are advertised to each other through *Bridge Protocol Data Units (BPDUs)*. These messages are sent as multicasts every two seconds by the root bridge out its interfaces to other switches on adjoining segments who, in turn, forward them on to other connected switches. In addition, these messages also contain the Bridge ID of the root bridge in every update that is sent. As long as you are receiving BPDUs that contain a higher Bridge ID than your Bridge ID, you will remain the root bridge (because all devices assume they are the root at startup).

Root Ports

In addition to the local bridge ID and the root bridge ID, BPDUs contain information that helps switches perform calculations to decide which ports should be forwarding and which should be blocking to create a loop-free switched network. The key to this calculation lies within the cumulative cost back to the root bridge. Although it sounds as if these Cisco switches are keeping track of how much you paid for them, this is not what is meant when you use the term "cost." The cost is actually an inverse of the bandwidth for each link segment. Because it is the inverse, the lower the cumulative cost back to the root bridge, the faster the path is. Table 13.1 lists the standard costs used today in switches. It is possible to change these values administratively if you want to control which link becomes the best path to the root bridge.

TABLE 13.1   Port Cost Values

Interface	Cost
10Gbps	2
1Gbps	4
100Mbps	19
10Mbps	100

After the root bridge is determined, each nonroot switch or bridge forms an association back to the root bridge based on the lowest cumulative path cost back to the root. Whichever interface has the fastest route to the root bridge automatically becomes a forwarding port called the *root port*.

> **NOTE**
>
> The root port is determined for the entire switch. Thus, each switch should contain only one root port back to the root bridge.

The root bridge advertises a root path cost of 0 to Switches B and D. As the BPDU enters their interfaces, they add the cost value of that interface and advertise that to any adjacent switches on other segments. Every nonroot bridge determines its fastest path back to the root by looking at these BPDUs that it receives from other switches. For instance, Switch B knows that going out of the top segment back to the root has a cost of 4, and going through Switch C has a cost of 42. Because the top segment has the lowest cumulative cost, that becomes the root port for Switch B.

What would happen if there were a tie in the root path cost? For instance, Switch C has two equal-cost paths of 23 back to the root bridge through Switch B and Switch D. In the event of a tie, the following are calculated to determine the root port:

1. The port with a switch advertising the lowest Bridge ID.

2. If the same Bridge ID (parallel links to the same switch), the lowest port priority is used. The port priority is an arbitrary number assigned to an interface that can be administratively set to choose one link over another. The default value is 128.

3. If the same port priority, the ultimate tiebreaker is the lowest interface number—for example, Fast Ethernet 0/1 over Fast Ethernet 0/6, because the links are identical.

> **EXAM ALERT**
>
> In the event of equal path costs, the lowest Bridge ID is the first tiebreaker.

Figure 13.5 expands on the switched networking example to include the path costs.

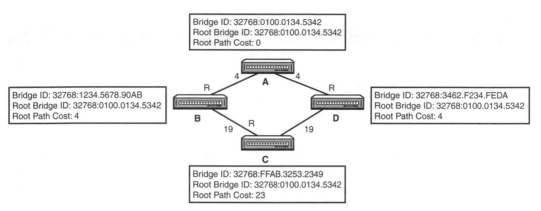

FIGURE 13.5 Root port calculation.

Designated Ports

After every switch has determined its root port, the switches and bridges determine which port is to become the designated port for every segment that connects the two switches. As the name states, the designated port is the port on each interconnecting segment that is designated to forward traffic from that segment to another segment back to the root bridge. This too is determined through a calculation of the fastest way back to the root port. In the case of a tie, the same decision criteria applies to designated ports as root ports as described earlier.

In Figure 13.6, the designated ports have been calculated based on which switch is advertising the lowest cumulative cost back to the root on each segment. For instance, the BPDUs from Switch B to Switch C are advertising a root path cost of 19, whereas the BPDU being sent from Switch C to Switch B is advertising 38. Because Switch B has the lower root path cost, that is the designated port for that segment.

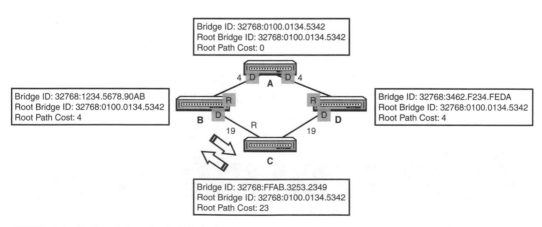

FIGURE 13.6 Designated port calculation.

Blocked Ports

To this point, the discussion has focused on how to determine which ports will be forwarding traffic in a switched network. Yet to be addressed is the original point of STP, which is to remove any potential switching loops. To remove potential switching loops, switches and bridges keep any port that is not a root or designated port in a blocked state. Keep in mind that a blocked state is not disabled (shut down); the interface is just not participating in forwarding any data. Blocked interfaces still receive BPDUs from other switches to react to any changes in the topology.

> **EXAM ALERT**
>
> Keep in mind for the exam that a blocked interface still receives BPDUs from other switches.

In Figure 13.7, notice that all the root ports have been elected, as well as the designated ports for each segment. Notice on the segment between Switch C and Switch D that a port connected to Switch C is not a root port or a designated port. This port blocks user data to ensure that a switching loop does not occur and expose the network to broadcast storms. This also means that any devices connected to Switch C sending Ethernet data to any device connected to Switch D will ultimately go through Switch B, and then Switch A, to finally arrive at Switch D.

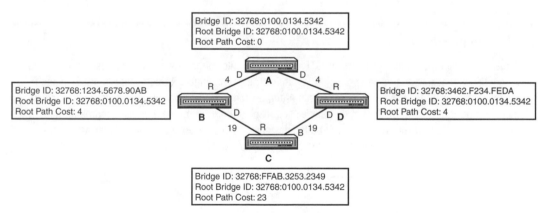

FIGURE 13.7 Blocked port calculation.

Challenge

To ensure your understanding of STP, this challenge steps you through the scenario illustrated in Figure 13.8.

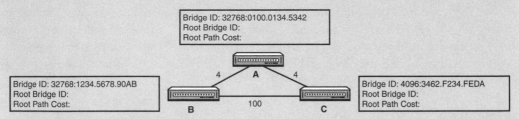

FIGURE 13.8 STP challenge scenario.

1. All switches believe themselves to be the root bridge at startup. After sending their BPDUs, which switch remains the root bridge, and why?

2. Every *nonroot* bridge determines its root ports. Which interfaces become root ports based on the election result?

3. Every segment must have a designated port to use to forward traffic onto other segments. Which interfaces on the three segments will be designated ports?

4. One port should remain that is not designated or a root port. In what state will this port be?

Challenge Answer

Figure 13.9 displays the end result of the STP election and calculation. Switch C becomes the root bridge in this design because the default priority was administratively changed in this design to 4096, giving Switch C the lowest Bridge ID. Because Switch A and Switch B are nonroot bridges, they must calculate their root ports based on the lowest cumulative cost back to the root bridge. For each segment, the switch with the lowest root path cost will be the designated port. Because Switch C's interface on the lower segment is not a root or designated port, that interface will be blocking.

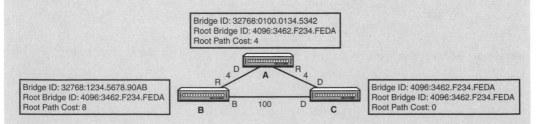

FIGURE 13.9 STP challenge scenario answer.

Port State Transitions

You now know how STP removes switching loops in your switched LAN by electing a root bridge and calculating which ports should forward based on the lowest root path cost. However, as explained earlier, STP must be able to react to topology changes, such as a segment or switch going down, to ensure the redundant design is put to good use. When this type of change occurs, ports that were once in a blocking state could quite possibly transition to a forwarding state.

If devices were to immediately transition from a blocking state to a forwarding state, they could easily cause loops in the network because the topology change did not have a chance to propagate throughout the entire switched network. To remedy this dilemma, STP transitions into two intermediate states before moving to a forwarding role. In these transitionary states, the switch ensures that enough time has transpired to propagate the changes, and it undergoes a pre-forwarding routine to ensure that it will know where to forward the data when the interface is forwarding. Table 13.2 displays, in order, the possible STP states, their functions, and the time it takes to transition out of each state.

TABLE 13.2 STP Port States

State	Function	Transition Time
Disabled	Interface is administratively shut down or inoperative as a result of a security violation.	N/A
Blocking	Does not forward any user data. All ports start out in this state. Does not send, but still can receive BPDUs to react to topology changes.	0 to 20 seconds
Listening	Begins to transition to a forwarding state by listening and sending BPDUs. No user data sent.	15 seconds
Learning	Begins to build MAC addresses learned on the interface. No user data sent.	15 seconds
Forwarding	User data forwarded.	

It may initially take the switch 20 seconds to start the transition process to the listening stage because that is the default time limit that STP uses to consider a neighbor switch to be down. In other words, if a switch stops hearing 10 BPDUs (equal to 20 seconds) from an adjoining switch or bridge, it considers that device to be dead and must react to the new topology. This 20-second timer is known as the *max age timer*.

When a topology change occurs in the network, a nonroot switch sends a specific BPDU called a Topology Change Notification (TCN) out its root port back to the root bridge. This BPDU is one of the only times that a BPDU does not originate from the root bridge. As soon as the root bridge finally receives that notification, it broadcasts a special BPDU to all the switches in the network to start aging out old MAC entries in their CAM tables after about eight times faster (default is 300 seconds). At that point, the switches start rebuilding their CAM tables to reflect the new topology and forward frames accordingly.

The listening and learning states wait 15 seconds each by default, but can be administratively changed if you have a relatively small switched network. These 15-second intervals are commonly referred to as *forward delays* because they delay the transition to a forwarding state. It is important to consider that it could take up to 50 seconds for an interface to transition to a forwarding state when the topology changes. Consequently, no data is transferred in those 50 seconds—which in the networking world is about 10 phone calls of complaining end users.

> **EXAM ALERT**
>
> An STP topology change could take up to 50 seconds.

The max age and forward delay timers are based on a default network diameter of seven switches including the root bridge. Diameter (in switching terms) refers to the number of bridge or switches between any two hosts. If your network is, for instance, only a diameter of 2, you can decrease these timers because it doesn't take as long to propagate a change in the topology. Another benefit of STP is that these timers are ultimately dictated by the root bridge. Thus, to change the timers, you have to configure the change on only the root bridge, and it gets propagated to the other switches. This change could possibly backfire and cause switching loops in instances when you add more switches to the network and forget to change the timers. The next section discusses some safer alternatives to speed up the convergence time of STP when a topology change occurs.

Initial Switch Configurations

Objective:

▶ Perform and verify initial switch configuration tasks including remote access management

Catalyst switches, for the most part, are designed so that the default state of the switch allows for basic Layer 2 functionality without requiring any configuration from the administrator. For example, the physical interfaces on the switch are already enabled, which means that you can plug a cable in the switch and the interface operates without requiring you to perform a no shutdown on that interface. Does that mean you don't have to learn about Catalyst switch commands? No such luck.

> **NOTE**
>
> Switch Ethernet interfaces are commonly referred to as *ports*.

The majority of the administrative configurations such as configuring hostnames, login banners, passwords, and Telnet/SSH access are identical to the configurations of the router IOS, as described in Chapter 7, "Foundation Cisco IOS Operations." These next sections look at a few commands and configurations that are specific to Catalyst switches.

Assigning a Management IP Address to a Switch

Cisco Layer 2 switches forward frames solely based on MAC addresses. On the other hand, Layer 3 switches and routers use IP addresses in their data forwarding decisions. So why assign an IP address to a Layer 2 switch?

Chapter 8, "Foundation Cisco Configurations," mentions that to remotely manage a device via SSH, Telnet, or HTTP, you need to have IP connectivity to the switch. Likewise, if you were to manage the switch using SNMP, you would also have to program your management server to use its IP address to gather statistics from the switch. All these management functions assume that an IP address is assigned to the device, which in the Catalyst switch's case does not have an IP address in its default configuration.

Unlike Cisco routers, Layer 2 switches do not assign IP addresses on all the physical interfaces. In fact, the interface to which you assign an IP address on a Layer 2 Catalyst switch is actually a virtual interface called VLAN 1 (Chapter 15, "Virtual LANs," discusses the significance of VLAN 1). To assign an IP address to the entire switch, you use exactly the same syntax as a router's physical interface to configure the VLAN 1 interface:

```
Switch(config)#interface VLAN1
Switch(config-if)#ip address 172.16.1.100 255.255.0.0
Switch(config-if)#no shutdown
01:35:19: %LINK-3-UPDOWN: Interface Vlan1, changed state to up
```

Defining a Default Gateway

If you were to Telnet into the switch from the terminal on the far network, the Telnet traffic would traverse through the local router, across the WAN link, through the remote router, and finally to the switch. To return the Telnet traffic back to the terminal, the switch would have to send it to a routing device, because the terminal is on another network. To instruct the switch to send any traffic destined for another network to that router, you have to define a default gateway (also known as a gateway of last resort) as shown in Figure 13.10.

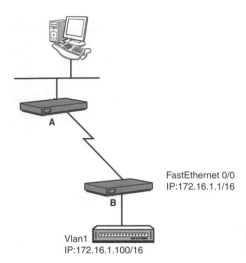

FastEthernet 0/0
IP:172.16.1.1/16

Vlan1
IP:172.16.1.100/16

FIGURE 13.10 Remote management requirement for default gateway.

The command to configure a default gateway is **ip default-gateway**, followed by the IP address of the router that is on the switch's segment in Global Configuration. Using the example in Figure 13.10, the configuration would look like the following:

```
Switch(config)#ip default-gateway 172.16.1.1
```

> **EXAM ALERT**
>
> The **ip default-gateway** switch command is used when a switch needs to send or return traffic to a remote network segment. The IP address specified after the **ip default-gateway** command is the router on the local segment that will route the traffic to the remote network.

IP Assignment Using DHCP

Similar to router interfaces, the IP assigned to the VLAN 1 interface and the default gateway can be dynamically assigned using a DHCP server. The configuration is also similar to DHCP-assigned router interfaces except that the configuration is applied to the logical VLAN 1 interface as opposed to a physical port on the switch:

```
Switch#configure terminal
Enter configuration commands, one per line. End with CNTL/Z.
Switch(config)#interface vlan 1
Switch(config-if)#ip address dhcp
Switch(config-if)#no shutdown
00:58:49: %LINK-3-UPDOWN: Interface Vlan1, changed state to up
Interface Vlan1 assigned DHCP address 172.16.1.100, mask 255.255.0.0
```

After the `ip address dhcp` command is applied, the switch sends a DHCPDISCOVER broadcast out on all switch ports assigned to VLAN1 (by default, all switch ports are assigned to VLAN1). If a configured DHCP server exists on those segments, it replies with the IP address for the VLAN 1 interface and default gateway for the switch. As such, there is no required configuration of an IP address or default gateway in the switch configuration. It must be said, however, that despite the fact that this does simplify some of the administration configuration or reconfiguration tasks that are necessary to manage a switch, it is not practical because you need to readily know the IP address of the switch to effectively manage it.

Verifying the IP address and default gateway assigned by the DHCP server cannot be achieved by showing the running or startup configuration. Instead, you can use output from the `show dhcp lease` command to verify the IP address and default gateway:

```
Switch#show dhcp lease
Temp IP addr: 172.16.1.100 for peer on Interface: Vlan1
Temp  sub net mask: 255.255.0.0
   DHCP Lease server: 172.16.1.1, state: 3 Bound
   DHCP transaction id: 1967
   Lease: 16000 secs,  Renewal: 3000 secs,  Rebind: 16000 secs
Temp default-gateway addr: 172.16.1.1
   Next timer fires after: 00:00:32
   Retry count: 0   Client-ID: cisco-0019.e86a.6fc0-Vl1
   Hostname: Switch
```

Configuring Multiple Switch Interfaces

By design, switches may have a plethora of interfaces that may require a similar configuration. For instance, if the first 20 ports of your switch need to be set to a speed of 100mbs and full duplex, you would be undertaking quite an administrative task of typing the same commands into each interface configuration for all 20 interfaces. To save time, the Catalyst switch's IOS contains a navigation and configuration command shortcut called `interface range` that enables you to define a range of switch ports and configure them simultaneously. The configuration can be condensed to something like this:

```
Switch(config)#interface range FastEthernet 0/1 - 20
Switch(config-if)#speed 100
Switch(config-if)#duplex full
```

TIP

Note that the syntax of the `interface range` command requires you to put a space between the starting and ending interfaces in the range separated by a hyphen.

> **NOTE**
>
> You can manually override the default autonegotiating speed and duplex settings for each interface as demonstrated.

Configuring and Verifying Spanning Tree Protocol

Objective:

▶ Verify network status and switch operation using basic utilities (including: ping, traceroute, telnet, SSH, arp, ipconfig), SHOW & DEBUG commands

STP is enabled by default on all Cisco Catalyst switches. In fact, if you are running multiple VLANs (virtual LANs) on your switch (discussed in Chapter 15), Cisco switches run an instance of STP on each VLAN configured. With that being said, no configuration is required unless you want to alter the default parameters of STP or manually define optimal switching paths or designate certain switches as root bridges.

Changing Priority and Port Cost

One of the common configurations you might encounter in your travels is to change the default priority of a switch to ensure that it will win the election for root bridge. To configure this option, you have to define which VLAN's priority you want to change and give a value in increments of 4096. For instance, if you wanted your switch to be the root bridge for VLAN 1, you would configure the following in global configuration:

```
Switch(config)#spanning-tree vlan 1 priority 4096
```

Cisco also created a command that automatically changes the switch's priority to become the root bridge for a given VLAN:

```
Switch(config)#spanning-tree vlan 4 root primary
```

If you wanted to change the default cost calculations for a specific interface to ensure that a port becomes a forwarding interface, you could change the spanning tree cost on any interface by entering interface configuration mode and using the following commands:

```
Switch(config)#interface FastEthernet 0/1
Switch(config-if)#spanning-tree cost 1
```

Verifying Spanning Tree Protocol

Objective:

▶ Interpret the output of various show and debug commands to verify the operational status of a Cisco switched network

To verify spanning tree operation in your switch, you can issue the show spanning-tree command to see a display of the STP operations for each VLAN. If you want to see specific information regarding a particular VLAN or interface, you can also add additional keywords after the command to see the output for only those items. The following output from **show spanning-tree** displays the STP statistics for VLAN 1:

```
Switch#show spanning-tree vlan 1

VLAN0001
  Spanning tree enabled protocol ieee
  Root ID    Priority    32769
             Address     000d.65d0.4e00
             This bridge is the root
             Hello Time   2 sec  Max Age 20 sec   Forward Delay 15 sec

  Bridge ID  Priority    32769    (priority 32768  sys-id-ext 1)
             Address     000d.65d0.4e00
             Hello Time   2 sec  Max Age 20 sec   Forward Delay 15 sec
             Aging Time 15

Interface        Role Sts Cost      Prio.Nbr Type
---------------- ---- --- --------- -------- --------------------------------
Fa0/1            Desg LIS 19        128.1    P2p
Fa0/23           Desg FWD 19        128.24   P2p
Fa0/24           Back BLK 19        128.23   P2p
```

Notice in this output that you can see the MAC address and the priority of the root bridge and the local switch (which happens to be the root bridge for this VLAN). In addition, you can see the timers using 802.1d for port state transitions, including the max age and forward delay. Finally, this useful show command displays the interfaces that are active and participating in STP and their associated roles and states in the spanning tree network.

Troubleshooting Basic Switch Connectivity

Objectives:

▶ Verify network status and switch operation using basic utilities (including: ping, traceroute, telnet, SSH, arp, ipconfig), SHOW & DEBUG commands

▶ Identify, prescribe, and resolve common switched network media issues, configuration issues, auto nego-tiation, and switch hardware failures

As always, when troubleshooting connectivity issues, use a layered approach and eliminate pos-sibilities at each layer to home in on the possible cause of the problem. Over time, you will begin to develop a sixth sense about these problems and decrease the amount of effort it takes to accurately pinpoint a connectivity problem. In the meantime, let's look at some possible connectivity scenarios and walk through some possible deductions as to what might cause the problem.

In instances where you cannot gain console connectivity to the switch, you should ask the fol-lowing questions:

1. Is the switch powered on and running? Although this seems like common sense, it is still valid to check to make sure the switch is powered on and successfully completed its bootup process. Catalyst switches all have LEDs (light-emitting diodes) on the switch face to signify that it is operating correctly. The system and status lights for the switch should both be a steady green if the device is powered on and operating normally.

2. Are your terminal connections correct? Verify that you have configured your terminal application correctly by setting the speed, flow control, and start and stop bits and ensure that you have the console (rollover) cable connected between your PC and the switch.

3. Did you or someone else change the console password? If you are gaining access to IOS but cannot log in, you may need to perform password recovery on the switch. Consult the switches' manual or look online at cisco.com for switch-specific steps to recover your password.

In instances where you cannot gain remote connectivity to the switch, you should ask the fol-lowing questions:

1. Is the switch powered on and running? If possible, console into the switch or have some-one check that the switch is powered on and successfully completed its bootup process.

2. Do you have IP connectivity to the switch? You can utilize troubleshooting commands from the switch such as `ping` to test connectivity between the switch and the management computer you are remotely connecting from. If your pings fail, verify that you have con-figured the default gateway for the switch and continue troubleshooting using the `tracer-oute` command to identify where along the forwarding data path the packets are failing.

3. Did you or someone else change the vty password or SSH login and password? If you are gaining access to IOS but cannot log in, you may need to reconfigure the SSH and Telnet passwords via the console to regain access to these remote management protocols.

In instances where the switch is not forwarding frames, you should ask yourself these questions:

1. Is the switch powered on and running? This would be fairly evident because all devices connected to the switch would be unable to communicate with each other. If possible, check that the switch is powered on and successfully completed its bootup process.

2. Does the switch have Layer 1 connectivity to the device(s)? The LEDs above the port may give you a quick indication if there is a problem with that port.

   To verify your cabling, ensure you are using a straight through Ethernet cable if connecting to a PC, router, or other end device. If connecting to another switch, you should have a cross-over Ethernet cable attached to those interfaces. What's more, you can also verify that the interfaces are not administratively shut down and are in an up/up state using the show `interfaces interface-id` command.

   Keep in mind that if you just connected the end device to the switch, it will take at least 30 seconds to transition to a forwarding state, as dictated by spanning tree protocol.

3. Does the output of the `show interfaces interface-id` command show you incorrect speed or duplex? An interface that does not become active or is constantly bouncing up and down may indicate duplex and/or speed mismatches from autonegotiation. This will be evident if the `show interfaces interface-id` output is displaying excessive collisions or the interface is in an up/down state. To remedy this problem, ensure that the switch and the end device are set for autonegotiation. To eliminate all doubt, manually set the speed and duplex parameters on the switch port(s) and the end device.

4. Does your switched internetwork intermittently stop forwarding frames? Recall that when new switches are added to a switched internetwork, it may take up to 50 seconds to have the switches converge to the new STP topology. If you are not adding switches to the network, verify that there isn't a faulty switch causing re-elections of the STP topology by using the `debug spanning-tree` command. This command shows real-time events of the spanning tree process and indicates whether a switch might have an interface that is going up and down causing re-elections in the STP topology.

Chapter Summary

This chapter has explored the mysteries behind Ethernet switching. Namely, it showed how switches build their MAC address table (also known as a CAM table), using the source MAC address of Ethernet frames, and forward, filter, or flood those frames based on the destination MAC. The method in which it forwards the frames differs from switch to switch. Specifically, the switch might use the latency varying store-and-forward transmission method, which buffers the entire frame and calculates the CRC before forwarding the frame. Cut-through switching looks at only the destination MAC address in an Ethernet frame, whereas fragment-free looks at up to the first 64 bytes, in which most collisions occur.

Switch connections can communicate in half duplex or full duplex, depending on the device to which they are connected. For instance, half-duplex connections are unidirectional and must be used when connecting to a hub because collisions must be detected. Full duplex can be used only when no possibility of collision exists, because it disables the collision detection circuitry to allow simultaneous bidirectional traffic. To ensure a collision-free environment for full-duplex connections, you must be directly connected to a switch.

When multiple switches are connected in a redundant design, STP (IEEE 802.1d) removes the possibility of switching loops, which can cause broadcast storms. It achieves this by electing a root bridge based on the lowest Bridge ID (priority + MAC) being advertised in BPDUs. After the root bridge is elected, every nonroot bridge forms an association to the root bridge by determining the port with the best path (lowest cumulative cost), which becomes the root port. For every segment, a designated port is also elected based on the fastest route back to the root bridge. In the event of a tie, the Bridge ID is used, followed by the lowest port priority, and finally the lowest port ID.

STP ports start in a blocking state, in which no data or BPDUs are being sent. If the port can forward frames, it transitions to a listening state for 15 seconds (forward delay), where it begins to exchange BPDUs. The learning stage follows for another 15 seconds to learn the MAC address on the interface and then finally transitions to a forwarding state.

Key Terms

- ▶ CAM table
- ▶ Store-and-forward
- ▶ Cut-through
- ▶ Fragment-free
- ▶ Half duplex
- ▶ Full duplex

▶ STP

▶ Root bridge

▶ BPDUs

▶ Bridge ID

▶ Root port

▶ Cost

▶ Designated port

▶ Blocking

▶ Listening

▶ Learning

▶ Forwarding

▶ Max-age timer

▶ Forward-delay timer

▶ `ip default-gateway` *`gateway_IP`*

▶ `interface range` *`media port_range`*

Apply Your Knowledge

Exercises

13.1 Basic Switch Configuration

This exercise reinforces the configurations involved in an initial setup of a Catalyst Switch. You may need to look back to Chapter 7 as a reference for some of the commands.

Estimated Time: 5 minutes

1. Power on your switch and enter user EXEC mode through the console.

2. In global configuration, assign the hostname, CstmrASwtch, create an appropriate login banner, and use the strongest encryption for access to privileged EXEC, using the password, giforgot.

3. Create a username of ccent with ssh4me as the password for SSH connectivity (requires cryptographic software image from Cisco.com).

4. In line configuration, specify Telnet and SSH as valid transport input protocols and to use the local username and password as the login on the first five vty lines.

NOTE

Catalyst switches may have more than the typical five vty lines you saw in router configurations.

---

5. Assign a management IP address of 172.16.31.30 /28.

6. Create the domain name of the switch to examcram.com.

7. Generate the RSA key for SSH.

8. Set the default gateway to be a hypothetical router address of 172.16.31.17 /28.

9. Using the **interface range** command, set the first three Fast Ethernet interfaces to be hard-coded as full duplex.

10. Verify your active configuration and save it to NVRAM.

The configuration should look similar to the following Catalyst 3550 configuration:

```
Current configuration : 1819 bytes
!
version 12.2
no service pad
service timestamps debug uptime
service timestamps log uptime
no service password-encryption
!
hostname CstmrASwtch
!
enable secret 5 $1$ueGU$jTruyGB16bJKo9AIa8kkO/
!
username ccent password ssh4me
ip subnet-zero
!
!
ip domain name examcram.com
ip ssh time-out 60
ip ssh authentication-retries 2
!
!
spanning-tree mode pvst
spanning-tree extend system-id
!
!
interface FastEthernet0/1
 no ip address
 duplex full
!
interface FastEthernet0/2
```

```
 no ip address
 duplex full
!
interface FastEthernet0/3
 no ip address
 duplex full
!
!!!Output omitted...
!
interface GigabitEthernet0/1
 no ip address
!
interface GigabitEthernet0/2
 no ip address
!
interface Vlan1
 ip address 172.16.31.30 255.255.255.240
!
ip default-gateway 172.16.31.17
ip classless
ip http server
!
!
banner motd ^C This is a private system and may be accessed only by authorized users.
Unauthorized access is strictly prohibited and will be enforced to the full
extent of the law.^C
!
line con 0
line vty 0 4
login local
 transport input telnet ssh
line vty 5 15
login
!
end
```

13.2 Force the Election

This exercise entails connecting two switches and watching the election with STP.

Estimated Time: 10 minutes

1. Power on both switches without connecting the two together.

2. Console into one switch and navigate to user EXEC.

3. Connect the two switches with a cross-over cable.

4. Verify which switch is the root bridge from the **show spanning-tree** output.

5. On the switch that is not the root bridge, force the election by changing the priority to 4096.

13.3 Witness the Wonders of STP

This exercise forces the STP election by changing the priority in a switch.

Estimated Time: 5 minutes

1. Power on both switches without connecting the two together.

2. Console into one switch and navigate to user EXEC.

3. Connect the two switches with a cross-over cable.

4. Issue the **show spanning-tree** command immediately after connecting to watch the port state change to listening.

5. Issue the **show spanning-tree** command within another 15 seconds to see the state change to learning.

6. Issue the **show spanning-tree** command after another 15 seconds to see the state change to forwarding.

Review Questions

1. What do switches do when a frame with a new source and destination MAC address is received?

2. What is the purpose of Spanning Tree Protocol?

3. How is a root bridge elected?

4. How do you configure IP connectivity to a Layer 2 switch?

5. When is it appropriate to run a switch interface in half duplex versus full duplex?

Exam Questions

1. What two components make up a Bridge ID? (Choose two)

    ○ **A.** IP address

    ○ **B.** Port priority

    ○ **C.** MAC address

    ○ **D.** Bridge priority

2. Considering the following output:

```
Switch>show spanning-tree

VLAN0001
  Spanning tree enabled protocol ieee
  Root ID    Priority    32768
             Address     000c.418f.6542
             Cost        19
             Port        23 (FastEthernet0/23)
             Hello Time   2 sec  Max Age 20 sec  Forward Delay 15 sec

  Bridge ID  Priority    32769  (priority 32768 sys-id-ext 1)
             Address     000d.65d0.4e00
             Hello Time   2 sec  Max Age 20 sec  Forward Delay 15 sec
             Aging Time 300
Interface          Role Sts Cost      Prio.Nbr Type
---------------- ---- --- -------   -------- -------------------------------
Fa0/23             Root FWD 19        128.23   P2p
```

which of the following is false?

- ○ **A.** This switch is the root bridge.
- ○ **B.** The forward delay times have been changed.
- ○ **C.** The max age timer has been changed.
- ○ **D.** The priority has been changed.

3. Given the following output:

```
Switch>show spanning-tree

VLAN0001
  Spanning tree enabled protocol ieee
  Root ID    Priority    32768
             Address     000c.418f.6542
             Cost        19
             Port        23 (FastEthernet0/23)
             Hello Time   2 sec  Max Age 20 sec  Forward Delay 15 sec
...Ouput Omitted...
```

what speed is the interface?

- ○ **A.** 10Mbps
- ○ **B.** 1Gbps
- ○ **C.** 10Gbps
- ○ **D.** 100Mbps

4. Which of the following can be determined from the following output?

```
Switch>show spanning-tree
...Output Ommitted...
Interface        Role Sts Cost      Prio.Nbr Type
---------------- ---- --- --------- -------- --------------------------------

Fa0/5            Root LRN 19        128.5    P2p
```

○ **A.** This port has the slowest connection back to the root bridge.

○ **B.** The port priority has been administratively changed.

○ **C.** This interface is learning MAC addresses.

○ **D.** Data is being forwarded.

5. Based on Figure 13.11, which of the following STP roles will Switch A and Switch D have on their shared link? (Choose two)

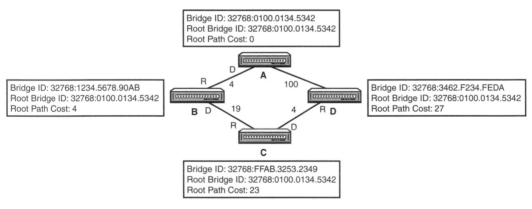

FIGURE 13.11 STP topology exhibit.

○ **A.** Switch A will have a root port.

○ **B.** Switch D will have a designated port.

○ **C.** Switch D will have a blocking port.

○ **D.** Switch A will have a designated port.

6. Which frame transmission method is latency varying?

○ **A.** Store-and-forward

○ **B.** Cut-through

○ **C.** Fragment-free

○ **D.** All of the above

7. Why is the following output false?

```
Switch#show mac-address-table
          Mac Address Table
-------------------------------------------

Vlan    Mac Address     Type       Ports
----    -----------     --------   -----
...Output Omitted...
   1    0300.3E9E.07E9  DYNAMIC    Fa0/3
   1    FFFF.FFFF.FFFF  DYNAMIC    Fa0/1
   1    0300.3E3E.531A  DYNAMIC    Fa0/3
```

- ○ **A.** There are no static MAC address entries.

- ○ **B.** There cannot be two MAC addresses learned on the same interface.

- ○ **C.** No multicast entries are shown.

- ○ **D.** A broadcast address should not be present in the CAM table.

8. What is the purpose of configuring a default gateway in a Catalyst switch?

- ○ **A.** To have the switch act as the default gateway for end devices connected to it.

- ○ **B.** To enforce all STP ports to a forwarding state so all switching traffic goes through the switch.

- ○ **C.** To enable Layer 3 routing in the switch.

- ○ **D.** To specify the IP address of the router that will forward requests made to the management IP address of the switch from devices on other subnets.

9. Which of the following are likely to occur when a switch with a higher Bridge ID is added to the switched topology? (Choose two)

- ○ **A.** A re-election will occur, and the new switch will become the root bridge.

- ○ **B.** The new switch will determine the fastest path back to the root bridge and make that its root port.

- ○ **C.** If the added switch creates a redundant path, at least one switch port in all of the interconnected switches will be in a blocking state.

- ○ **D.** The switch will immediately begin forwarding frames sent to it by end devices connected to it.

10. You just connected your interface to a hub. Which of the following must be true?

- ○ **A.** Your speed must be 10Mbps.

- ○ **B.** Your duplex must be full.

- ○ **C.** Your duplex must be half.

- ○ **D.** CSMA/CD must be disabled.

Answers to Review Questions

1. When a switch receives an Ethernet frame that contains an unknown source MAC address, it associates that MAC address with the receiving interface in the CAM table. When the switch receives an Ethernet frame with an unknown unicast destination MAC address, the switch floods that frame out every port except the one on which it was received.

2. Spanning Tree Protocol eliminates switching loops in environments when multiple switches are connected in a redundant design.

3. The root bridge is elected based on the switch that has the lowest advertised Bridge ID in the switches' BPDUs. The Bridge ID is composed of the priority plus the switch's MAC address. If another switch with a lower Bridge ID is added to the STP topology, a re-election occurs, and that switch becomes the new root bridge.

4. To gain IP connectivity to a Layer 2 switch, you must configure its management VLAN1 interface either manually with `ip address` *`ip-address mask`* command or dynamically using the `ip address dhcp` command. If you are connecting to the device remotely from another network, the switch must also have a gateway of last resort configured statically using the **ip default-gateway** *`ip-address`* command or dynamically from a DHCP server.

5. When you connect to a hub, collision detection must be enabled; thus, you must run the interface as half duplex. Full-duplex interfaces have collision detection disabled and can be enabled only when the switch port is connected to another switch or an end device.

Answers to Exam Questions

1. **C, D.** The Bridge ID comprises the bridge priority plus the MAC address of the switch. Answer A is incorrect because Layer 2 switches do not use IP addresses for Bridge IDs. Answer B is incorrect because the port priority is used as a tiebreaker only when determining the root or designated ports.

2. **A.** The output displays the Root Bridge ID with a different MAC address than the local switch. So, this switch is not the root bridge. The timers and priority are all still their default values. B is incorrect because the forward delay timers are at their default value of 15 seconds. Answer C is incorrect because the max age timer is at its default value of 20 seconds. D is incorrect because the switch's priority is at its default value of 32768.

3. **D.** A port cost of 19 is 100Mbps. Answers A, B, and C are incorrect because 10Gbps has a port cost of 2, 1Gbps has a port cost of 4, and 10Mbps has a port cost of 100.

4. **C.** Because the interface is in the learning state, it is beginning to learn the MAC addresses on that interface. Answer A is incorrect because the port is the root port, indicating that it is the fastest back to the root bridge. Answer B is incorrect because the port priority has not changed from its default value of 128. Answer D is false because the port is in the learning state; it still is not able to forward traffic.

5. **C, D.** Switch A has the fastest way back to the root (itself) on that segment, so it will be designated. Because Switch D's interface is not a root or a designated port, it must be blocking. Answer A is incorrect because only nonroot switches and bridges have root ports. Answer B is incorrect because Answer D has the slowest path back to the root for that particular segment.

6. **A.** Only the store-and-forward are latency varying because they have to buffer frames of different sizes. Answers B, C, and D are incorrect because cut-through looks at only the destination MAC address, and fragment-free looks at the first 64 bytes, so their latency will not vary.

7. **D.** The source MAC address in an Ethernet frame should not be a broadcast (only destination addresses), so a switch should never have that entry in its CAM table. Answer A is insignificant because static entries are not mandatory. Answer B is incorrect because a switch can learn multiple MAC addresses on a single interface. Answer C is incorrect because multicast addresses should not be present in a CAM table by default.

8. **D.** The default gateway is the IP address of the Layer 3 routing device that is used when devices are issuing Telnet, SSH, HTTP, and SNMP requests to the switch. To respond to these requests, the switch must send the responses to the router who in turn will route them back to the end device. Answer A is false because the switch itself is not the Layer 3 gateway for other devices despite the fact that the Layer 2 frames are switched through it. The default gateway for end devices is still the router of the LAN. Answer B is incorrect because the default gateway is not related to STP. Answer C is incorrect because the `ip default-gateway` command does not enable Layer 3 routing in switches. The command to achieve Layer 3 routing is `ip routing` and is useful only if you have a Layer 3 switch.

9. **B, C.** Because this switch has a higher Bridge ID, it does not become the root bridge. It elects the fastest port back to the root bridge as its root port. If the added switch creates a redundant loop in the switched network, STP blocks one of the ports to avoid broadcast storms. Answer A is incorrect because the BridgeID must be lower than the current root bridge to force an election. Answer D is incorrect because the switch will still transition into the listening and learning states before forwarding frames.

10. **C.** When connecting to a hub, you have to be able to detect collisions; thus, you must be running half duplex. The speed doesn't matter, so Answer A is incorrect. Answers B and D are incorrect because setting the port to full duplex disables CSMA/CD.

Suggested Readings and Resources

1. David Barnes and Basir Sakandar. *Cisco LAN Switching Fundamentals*. Cisco Press, 2004.

2. Matthew J. Castelli. *LAN Switching First-Step*. Cisco Press, 2004.

3. "Spanning-Tree Protocol," www.cisco.com.

CHAPTER FOURTEEN

Enhanced Switching Operations

Objectives

This chapter covers the following Cisco-specific objectives for the "Configure, verify and troubleshoot a switch with VLANs and interswitch communications" section of the 640-802 CCNA exam:

▶ **Describe enhanced switching technologies (including: VTP, RSTP, VLAN, PVSTP, 802.1q)**

▶ **Interpret the output of various show and debug commands to verify the operational status of a Cisco switched network**

Outline

Study Strategies

▶ Read the information presented in the chapter, paying special attention to tables, Notes, and Exam Alerts.

▶ Rapid Spanning Tree Protocol requires a solid understanding of Spanning Tree Protocol. If you do not feel like you have a firm grasp of Spanning Tree Protocol, reread those sections from Chapter 13, "Foundation Switching Operations."

▶ Complete the Challenge and the Exercises at the end of the chapter. These exercises will solidify the concepts you have learned in the previous sections.

▶ As with most technologies discussed in this book, it is always beneficial to visualize the data's path and how the Cisco devices respond to the data depending on the technology in use and the device's configuration.

▶ Complete the Exam Questions at the end of the chapter. They are designed to simulate the types of questions you will be asked on the CCNA and ICND1 exams.

Introduction

The 802.1d Spanning Tree Protocol was created with very few design flaws; however, as with most great things, there is always room for improvement. The biggest grievance the networking community had with Spanning Tree Protocol was the slow convergence when a topology change occurred in the network. Recall that it could take up to 50 seconds for the switched internetwork to converge and forward data frames again when a topology change occurred. What's more, it took roughly 30 seconds for an individual access port to become active when you plugged a device into it, because it had to transition from the listening and learning STP states before forwarding frames.

Cisco found several proprietary ways to improve the convergence lag of traditional Spanning Tree Protocol. In addition, the IEEE adopted many of the ideas from Cisco and created a much faster converging Spanning Tree Protocol which is happily named Rapid Spanning Tree Protocol (RSTP). As these switching technologies evolved and improved over the years, they became more and more adopted in switched internetworks. With this in mind, you too must evolve and improve your understanding of these enhanced switching technologies. This chapter looks at the creative enhancements that were created over the years and demonstrates how they improve the speed limitation of Spanning Tree Protocol.

Cisco Enhancements to Spanning Tree Protocol

The steps to transition to a forwarding state in STP are critical to ensure that the switched network has enough time to propagate a change in the topology. However, in the networking world, 50 seconds is a lot of downtime. In some instances, this 50 seconds may be detrimental because of the disruption of data traffic and should be avoided if it is safe to do so. In light of these scenarios, Cisco has created some enhancements to normal STP operation that can decrease the time it takes for the switched network to converge (have a consistent perspective of network), as discussed in the next sections.

PortFast and BPDU Guard

Imagine you just plugged your server, IP phone, or just a normal PC into your switch. Because STP is running on all ports on the Catalyst switches by default, the interface into which you plug your server transitions from a blocking state to the listening state, followed by the learning, and finally the forwarding. In that 30 seconds, devices such as IP phones and computers cannot use those services that the server provides because no data transfer can occur until spanning tree is in a forwarding state.

To speed up the spanning tree process for end devices, you can configure your first STP enhancement, called *PortFast*. If you configure this feature on an interface, it skips the listening and learning states and transitions immediately to the forwarding state to enable instant data transfer.

If you enable PortFast on an interface, it is imperative that you never plug a switch or hub into it. This could easily cause a loop in your switched network. In fact, Cisco has added a function to PortFast called BPDU Guard that acts as a loop-preventive detector for BPDUs on a PortFast-enabled interface. When a BPDU is received on a PortFast-configured interface with BPDU Guard enabled, the port is disabled automatically and must be enabled by an administrator to ensure that a switching loop will not occur.

> **EXAM ALERT**
>
> **PortFast immediately transitions from a blocking to a forwarding state on ports connected to end devices. BPDU Guard is a feature that disables the PortFast-enabled interface if a BPDU is received on that port.**

UplinkFast

In an optimal redundant switching design, you would have redundant high-end distribution layer switches in your network, with your access layer switch having an uplink to both, as shown in Figure 14.1. With this design, if your root port were to fail, it would still take at least 30 seconds to transition the backup link to a forwarding state. With a feature called UplinkFast, you can bypass the listening and learning states for this redundant uplink to ensure faster recovery.

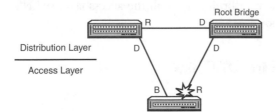

FIGURE 14.1 UplinkFast switching design scenario.

> **NOTE**
>
> For UplinkFast to work, the access layer switch must have direct knowledge of link failure (a link that is connected to the switch), it must have one port in a blocking state, and the link failure must be on the root port.

BackboneFast

BackboneFast is similar to UplinkFast, in which a redundant link transitions faster than normal to a forwarding state. The difference is that the transition occurs without having direct knowledge of the link failure. Consider the scenario shown in Figure 14.2. The failure actually occurs on the link between the two distribution layer switches. When that link fails, the distribution switch on the left begins to have delusions of grandeur and believe it is the root bridge, and it advertises that to the access layer switch. Because this access switch still has connectivity to the actual root bridge, it disregards the left distribution switch's false BPDUs (referred to as *inferior* BPDUs). By design, it must wait the max age (20 seconds) before transitioning to a learning state on its backup link and send a BPDU to the distribution switch, informing it of access to the actual root bridge.

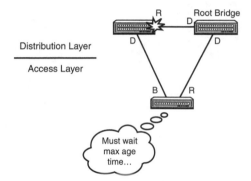

FIGURE 14.2 BackboneFast switching design scenario.

With BackboneFast, the access layer switch bypasses the max age time and immediately transitions from blocking to listening. After the distribution switch receives that BPDU from the access layer switch, it realizes it has a path to the root bridge through the access layer switch, and that corresponding interface becomes its root port.

Configuring Cisco STP Enhancements

Objective:

▶ Interpret the output of various show and debug commands to verify the operational status of a Cisco switched network

To enable the Cisco enhancements on a Catalyst switch, you can configure PortFast with BPDU Guard on an interface-by-interface basis. Conversely, UplinkFast and BackboneFast are configured globally on the switch, as demonstrated in the following configuration:

```
Switch(config)#interface FastEthernet 0/3
Switch(config-if)#spanning-tree portfast
%Warning: PortFast should only be enabled on ports connected to a single
 host. Connecting hubs, concentrators, switches, bridges, etc... to this
 interface when PortFast is enabled, can cause temporary bridging loops.
 Use with CAUTION
Switch(config-if)#spanning-tree bpduguard enable
Switch(config-if)#exit
Switch(config)#spanning-tree uplinkfast
Switch(config)#spanning-tree backbonefast
```

> **NOTE**
>
> You can also enable BPDU Guard globally as opposed to on a port-by-port basis by using the `spanning-tree portfast bpduguard` default command in global configuration mode:
>
> Switch(config)# **spanning-tree portfast bpduguard default**

To verify that PortFast, UplinkFast, and BackboneFast are enabled on your switch, use the show spanning-tree summary command:

```
Switch#show spanning-tree summary
Root bridge for: none.
PortFast BPDU Guard is enabled
UplinkFast is enabled
BackboneFast is enabled
Spanning tree default pathcost method used is short


Name                 Blocking Listening Learning Forwarding STP Active
-------------------- -------- --------- -------- ---------- ----------
  1 VLAN                    0         0        0          1          1
```

EtherChannel

Objective:

▶ Interpret the output of various show and debug commands to verify the operational status of a Cisco switched network

Although it isn't an actual enhancement to Spanning Tree Protocol, EtherChannel proves to be a useful feature in Cisco switches to help overcome wasted bandwidth that might result from STP. For instance, consider the two switches illustrated in Figure 14.3. Because these switches have multiple redundant links between them, Spanning Tree Protocol ultimately blocks three of the links to avoid a loop. If these were Gigabit Ethernet interfaces, 3 gigabits of throughput would be wasted.

FIGURE 14.3 EtherChannel implementation.

EtherChannel solves this dilemma by bundling the individual links into a single virtual interface. In this manner, the switch does not block the other ports in the bundle and load-balances data across the individual links to aggregate the bandwidth. What's more, if one of the individual links fails, EtherChannel detects the failure and redistributes the data traffic load over the remaining links in a matter of milliseconds.

EtherChannel is a hardware feature present on most Cisco Catalyst switches today. Before configuring EtherChannel, you must connect all the interfaces (up to eight), and they must be configured identically (speed, duplex, and so on). To assign them to an EtherChannel logical bundle, you have to navigate into each interface or use the **interface range** command and assign them to the same group number with the channel-group command:

```
Switch(config)#interface range FastEthernet0/1 - 8
Switch(config-if-range)#speed 100
Switch(config-if-range)#channel-group 3 mode on
```

This configuration places the first eight Fast Ethernet interfaces in logical EtherChannel bundle number 3. By adding these interfaces to the EtherChannel bundle, the Cisco IOS creates a logical interface called a port-channel interface. This logical interface simplifies configurations that need to affect the entire bundle (for instance, the duplex) because any configuration that is configured on this interface gets applied to all the individual interfaces in the bundle:

```
Switch(config)#interface Port-channel 3
Switch(config-if)#duplex full
Switch(config)#show running-configuration
Building configuration...
!
version 12.2
service timestamps debug uptime
service timestamps log uptime
no service password-encryption
!
hostname Switch
!
!!!Output Omitted
!
interface Port-channel 3
 no ip address
 duplex full
 speed 100
!
interface FastEthernet 0/1
 no ip address
 duplex full
```

```
 speed 100
 channel-group 3 mode on
!
interface FastEthernet 0/2
 no ip address
 duplex full
 speed 100
channel-group 3 mode on
!
interface FastEthernet 0/3
 no ip address
 duplex full
 speed 100
channel-group 3 mode on
!
!!!Output Omitted
```

Rapid Spanning Tree Protocol

Objective:

▶ Describe enhanced switching technologies (including: VTP, RSTP, VLAN, PVSTP, 802.1q)

One of the greatest drawbacks of PortFast, UplinkFast, and BackboneFast is that they require an all-Cisco network because they are Cisco-proprietary functions. Luckily, the IEEE made its own revised version of Spanning Tree Protocol to incorporate these functions while incorporating an updated algorithm for faster topology convergence. Enter Rapid Spanning Tree Protocol (RSTP), IEEE specification 802.1w.

TIP

To help remember that the 802.11w designation is for RSTP, think of Elmer Fudd: The wascally wabbit wuvs Wapid STP (802.1w).

Spanning Tree Similarities

Aside from the fact that 802.1w Rapid Spanning Tree Protocol and 802.1d Spanning Tree Protocol are both defined by an IEEE 802.1 specification, RSTP shares some core functional principles with STP, making them similar in several ways. Namely, RSTP adopts the same switch and port election process in determining the root bridge, root ports, and designated ports. In other words, the switch with the lowest Bridge ID advertised in its BPDUs becomes the root bridge, and every nonroot switch chooses its root port back to that root bridge based on the lowest cumulative root path cost. In case of a tie in the root path cost, the Bridge ID is used, followed by the definitive tiebreaker, the port priority. And again, for each segment, a designated port is chosen for each segment to forward frames from one segment to the next.

Because RSTP and STP share these core elements, Rapid Spanning Tree Protocol is completely backward-compatible with Spanning Tree Protocol. The only caveat is that you will not be able to enjoy the radical improvements that are incorporated with Rapid Spanning Tree Protocol on switches that are running traditional 802.1d STP. And with that segue, we will now explore the differences between the two spanning tree algorithms and how these changes dramatically improved the convergence issues with Spanning Tree Protocol.

> **EXAM ALERT**
>
> Make sure that you understand and can explain the similarities between 802.1d Spanning Tree Protocol and 802.1w Rapid Spanning Tree Protocol.

RSTP Port States and Roles

RSTP adopted the 802.1d port states with a slight difference. Because the blocking and listening states were essentially nonoperational in terms of actively discovering the network's topology, RSTP has redefined these to be a *discarding* state. Discarding ports are similar to blocking ports in that they do not forward frames or learn MAC addresses but still can receive BPDUs from other switches. Learning and forwarding states are still active spanning tree transition states and maintain the same functionality in RSTP-enabled LANs.

As previously mentioned, RSTP still uses the concepts of a root port and designated ports. To incorporate additional functionality that is specific to popular redundant LAN designs, RSTP created two more port roles, as illustrated in Figure 14.4. Based on the principle of UplinkFast, the following two new port roles were created:

 ▶ **Alternate port**: A blocking (or I should say *discarding*) port that becomes the *root* port if the active root port fails. In other words, this is a nonforwarding root port that has the second-best path back to the root switch.

 ▶ **Backup port**: A discarding port that becomes the *designated* port if the active designated port fails. The backup port occurs when you have two or more ports connected to the same LAN segment and provides a redundant backup to the segment (but not necessarily back to the root).

> **EXAM ALERT**
>
> Keep in mind that despite alternate ports and backup ports having specific roles, they are still discarding interfaces.

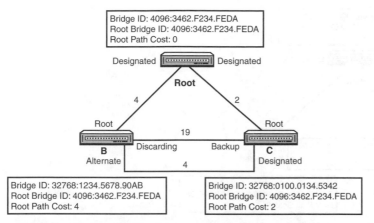

Bridge ID: 4096:3462.F234.FEDA
Root Bridge ID: 4096:3462.F234.FEDA
Root Path Cost: 0

Designated   **Root**   Designated

4   2

Root   19   Root

B   Discarding   Backup   **C**
Alternate   4   Designated

Bridge ID: 32768:1234.5678.90AB
Root Bridge ID: 4096:3462.F234.FEDA
Root Path Cost: 4

Bridge ID: 32768:0100.0134.5342
Root Bridge ID: 4096:3462.F234.FEDA
Root Path Cost: 2

FIGURE 14.4 Alternate and backup port switching design scenario.

Notice that the election has occurred in this topology and the top switch has been elected the root switch based on its low Bridge ID. Each nonroot switch chose its root ports based on the fastest path back to the root switch. Similarly, the designated ports were chosen for each LAN segment based on the lowest root path cost. Where RSTP shines can be witnessed in the redundant links between Switches B and C.

In traditional 802.1d, the parallel links between Switches B and C would result in three of the four ports being blocked to avoid a possible loop. If a topology change occurred, one of the blocking ports would transition to the listening state, followed by the learning state, before forwarding again, which could take anywhere from 30 to 50 seconds. With Rapid Spanning Tree, the three ports are still technically discarding frames. However, Switch B's bottom link port has been given the RSTP alternate role because that port would become the root port if Switch B's root port went down. In addition, Switch C's top link port has been named the backup port for that specific segment because that port would be elected the designated port if its current link connected to the designated port went down. To solidify the function of these roles, let's look at what happens in the event of a link failure.

If the link between Switch B and the root switch fails, as shown in Figure 14.5, the alternate port quickly becomes the new root port and begins forwarding frames.

In Figure 14.6, the link connected to the designated port fails, causing the backup port to become the active designated port for that segment. Because the bottom link has gone down, Switch B puts its alternate port into a discarding state, and its previously discarding port transitions to a forwarding state.

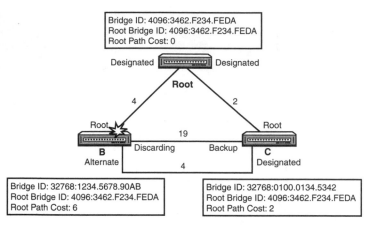

FIGURE 14.5 Alternate port transition.

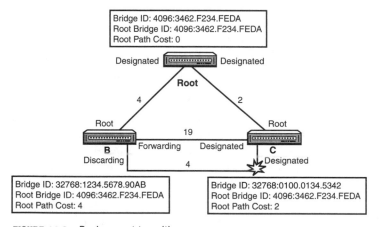

FIGURE 14.6 Backup port transition.

Now, let's see what happens when Switch C loses its link back to the root switch, as shown in Figure 14.7. Because Switch C has lost its root port, it now must find a new root port based on the fastest way back to the root switch (in this case, the port connected to the bottom link). In the event that Switch C's new root port fails, the port connected to the top link becomes the new root port, so this interface is elected as an alternate port. Now the roles are reversed for Switch B because its alternate port is now the designated port for that LAN segment because it has the fastest port back to the root. In addition, the port that was once in a discarding state for Switch B is now transitioned to a backup state, because that will become the designated port if the current designated port fails. It is important to keep in mind that although these roles have different names, they are still in a discarding state and are not forwarding frames or learning MAC addresses.

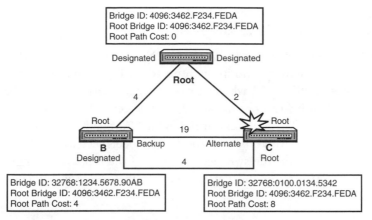

FIGURE 14.7 RSTP topology role reversal example.

RSTP Link and Edge Types

Another interesting difference between Spanning Tree Protocol and Rapid Spanning Tree Protocol is RSTP's distinction between the links between switches and connections to end devices. For instance, RSTP considers any connection between switches running in full duplex (directly connected to each other) as *link-type point-to-point*. If the switch interface is running in half duplex (connected to a hub), the link is called *link-type shared* because it is probably connected to a shared network. Finally, nonswitch or hub end devices such as computers are *edge-type* connections according to RSTP.

Rapid Spanning Tree Protocol actually reacts to topology changes and converges faster depending on these distinctions. Specifically, link-type point-to-point and edge-type connections play a specific role in how fast RSTP adapts to network topology transitions. Because the use of hubs is rather insignificant these days, RSTP does not put any effort into increasing convergence speed for link-type shared connections.

BPDUs and Topology Changes

Rapid Spanning Tree Protocol uses BPDUs to communicate information throughout the topology with one major distinction: each switch generates its own BPDUs and advertises them to neighboring switches. This is significantly different from traditional STP, in which the root bridge generates the BPDUs (except when a topology change is detected), and each switch passes that information to the next switch. What's more, RSTP takes a chapter out of our routing protocol's book and uses these BPDUs as keepalives to let neighboring switches know that the switches are still active in the topology. When a switch fails to hear three BPDU keepalives from its neighbor, it considers that neighbor as dead and immediately reacts to the change. That is considerably more aggressive than traditional STP switches, which would wait a max age (20 seconds) before considering the switch dead. If an RSTP switch receives a BPDU from an 802.1d STP switch, it sends STP BPDUs only to that switch to allow for backward-compatibility.

Recall that STP switches send a topology change notification (TCN) back to the root bridge if that change has occurred. This is followed by a notification broadcast from the root bridge to age out old MAC address entries. With RSTP, when a topology change occurs, the TCN still occurs. However, it is sent to all switches from the switch that detects the anomaly, and switches immediately start aging out their MAC address entries in the CAM table. This is similar to the flash flood of updates that occurs with link-state routing protocols such as OSPF. By not having to rely on the root bridge to alert the switched topology of the topology change, the switches can age out their old MAC entries and start adapting to the new topology considerably faster than 802.1d STP.

Rapid Transition

By now you should recognize that the most unique function of RSTP is its capability to converge in an expedient manner. The core ingredient of this feature is that it no longer reactively relies on conservative timers to transition to a forwarding state.

For instance, on edge ports that are connected to end devices, the interface takes on the same functionality as PortFast with BPDU Guard in that it immediately transitions to a forwarding state. In fact, the way to configure the port as an edge port on a switch is to configure PortFast on the interface. When an edge port receives a BPDU, however, it immediately transitions to a point-to-point link type.

Where the connection between two switches is a full-duplex point-to-point link, RSTP takes a rather unique approach to converging. When a point-to-point link comes up between two switches, a handshake occurs between the two switches using BPDUs to establish what role their local ports will play for that link. Because there is no reliance on conservative timers to transition the ports to a forwarding state, the exchange occurs rather quickly.

We've already established that switches use traditional STP algorithms to determine their root port and designated ports. However, the process used when ports transition to a forwarding state is a proposal/agreement handshake. Specifically, when a switch receives a BPDU and calculates that its local port will become the *designated port* for that segment after connecting to a switch, it immediately sends a proposal to its neighbor to begin forwarding. When RSTP switches receive proposals to forward and determine that the port that received the proposal will become a root port, they put all *nonedge* ports in a discarding state (if they aren't already) to avoid any possibility of a loop occurring. You can think of this as similar to getting a marriage proposal. You would want to discontinue any other relationships to avoid confusion before accepting the proposal. This process of blocking all nonedge point-to-point links before sending a proposal is called *synchronization* or *sync* for short. It is so named because the switch ensures that these new links to a root switch and the resulting topology will be accurately synchronized with all other ports.

When the RSTP switch has successfully synced all its ports, it sends an agreement back to the switch that sent the proposal to allow forwarding. It begins to forward out its root port and starts learning MAC addresses itself. When the original switch receives the agreement message on its designated port, it too immediately begins forwarding and learning MAC addresses.

Consider the example shown in Figure 14.8. Suppose Switch A was just added to the topology. After an initial exchange of BPDUs, Switch A realizes that it will be the root switch because it has the lowest Bridge ID, and its local interface will be the designated port for that new segment. Switch A sends a proposal to forward to Switch B. Switch B receives that proposal and knows its local port will be a root port. It begins syncing by blocking all nonedge ports (in this case they are all already discarding because no other switches are attached). Switch B replies to Switch A with an agreement BPDU and immediately begins learning MAC addresses and forwarding on that port. Likewise, Switch A receives the agreement back and transitions its designated port to a forwarding state and begins learning MAC addresses as well.

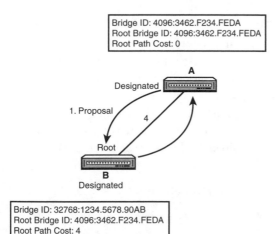

FIGURE 14.8 RSTP synchronization convergence.

Let's complete your understanding of RSTP's rapid transition to forwarding states by looking at what happens when the switching topology changes and we add another switch and a redundant connection, as shown in Figure 14.9. The initial BPDUs are exchanged, and Switch A recognizes that its port connected to Switch C will be a designated port. Again, Switch A sends a proposal to transition to a forwarding state to Switch C. When Switch C receives this proposal on its soon-to-be root port, it begins its syncing process. It puts the interface between Switch C and Switch B into a discarding state before sending an agreement back to Switch A to avoid a possible loop. It does not put the port connected to the PC into a discarding state, though, because it is an edge port and does not participate in RSTP. After the agreement is sent, Switch C begins forwarding on its root port. Likewise, Switch A begins forwarding on its designated port after it receives the agreement.

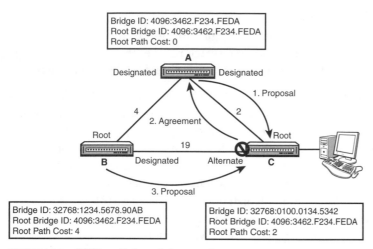

FIGURE 14.9 RSTP multiple-switch scenario.

After all this handshaking occurs between Switches C and A, Switch B also realizes that its link will become a designated port for the link between Switch B and C. One more time, a proposal is sent from Switch B to Switch C to begin forwarding. This time, however, Switch C's port is not the optimal port back to the root bridge, so it does not become a root port. Thus, no agreement is ever sent back to Switch B, and that port stays in a discarding state (technically an alternate state, because that is an alternate route to the root switch). Switch B continues to send proposals until a forward-delay timer expires. At this point it assumes that it is a designated port and starts forwarding.

Here is a summary of the steps involved in this synchronization process:

1. After switches are connected to a point-to-point link, they exchange BPDUs.

2. If a switch determines that its port will become a designated port, it sends a proposal to start forwarding to its neighbor.

3. The neighboring switch receives the proposal. If its port is a root port, it synchronizes the change by putting all nonedge ports into a discarding state and sends an agreement back to the original switch. If its port is a discarding port, it does not respond to the proposal.

4. The original switch immediately transitions to a forwarding state if it receives an agreement or eventually transitions to a forwarding state after a forward-delay occurs.

Although this sounds as if there are many steps, the process happens relatively quickly. Interestingly enough, the topology would end up in the same state (with the same ports blocking and forwarding) as traditional STP. The key difference is that it can take several seconds to have all switches converge (even in larger networks) as opposed to several minutes with 802.1d STP (because each switch would take 30 to 50 seconds to reach a forward state).

> **NOTE**
>
> The configuration and verification of Rapid Spanning Tree Protocol is beyond the scope of this book and certification level. If you're interested in pursuing the implementation of an enterprise RSTP network, continue with the Cisco Certified Network Professional (CCNP) certification track after completing your CCNA.

Challenge

To solidify all the novel terminology and processes we covered in this section, let's put that new knowledge to the test by considering the topology illustrated in Figure 14.10.

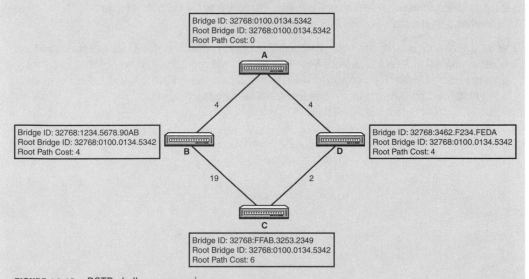

FIGURE 14.10 RSTP challenge scenario.

Imagine that you are the proud new owner of Switch C, and you just added it to the RSTP topology. Knowing what you know now, answer the following questions about what transpires in the RSTP network:

1. Which port is the root port, and why?

2. What state is the other port in?

3. Is there a backup port? Why or why not?

4. What does Switch D do when it detects Switch C?

5. How does Switch C respond?

6. What does Switch B do when it detects Switch C?

7. How does Switch C respond?

(continues)

(continued)

Challenge Answer

The port connected to Switch D is the root port because it has the fastest path back to the root switch. Switch C's other port gets put into a discarding state because it has the least optimal path to the root. Specifically, RSTP puts this port into an alternate state because that port will become the root if its current root goes down. There is no backup port in this scenario because there are no parallel links in the design to the same LAN segment.

When Switch D detects Switch C, it discovers that its port will become a designated port and sends a proposal to forward to Switch C. When Switch C receives that proposal, it immediately begins syncing by blocking all nonedge ports. It then sends an agreement back to Switch D and begins forwarding and learning MAC addresses. When Switch D receives that agreement, it too begins forwarding frames on its designated port and starts learning MAC addresses.

When Switch B detects the new link to Switch C, it too realizes that its port will be a designated port and sends a proposal to Switch C. Because Switch C's port is a suboptimal port, it remains discarding and does not reply to Switch B's proposal. After a forward delay occurs, Switch B transitions its designated port to a forwarding state and begins forwarding and learning MAC addresses.

Chapter Summary

Cisco has created some proprietary means to speed up STP transitions that can be configured on Catalyst switches. PortFast allows the switch port to go immediately to a forwarding state for end devices such as servers. To protect these interfaces from forming a switching loop (by accidentally connecting a hub or switch to the PortFast interface), Cisco created BPDU Guard, which disables the interface if a BPDU is received on the interface. UplinkFast also skips the listening and learning transitions when a direct failure occurs on a switch with redundant uplinks to its distribution switch. BackboneFast speeds up convergence by skipping the max age time when switches learn of a failure indirectly.

802.1w Rapid Spanning Tree protocol was created to speed up convergence by incorporating many of the Cisco-proprietary enhancements as well as developing an algorithm that no longer reactively converges based solely on timers. Table 14.1 outlines some of the similarities and differences between 802.1d and 802.1w.

TABLE 14.1 STP and RSTP Compared

Function	802.1d Spanning Tree Protocol	802.1w Rapid Spanning Tree Protocol
BPDUs	✓	✓
Root bridge/switch	✓	✓
Root and designated ports	✓	✓
Listening state	✓	
Learning state	✓	✓
Discarding state		✓
Alternate and backup ports		✓
Edge ports		✓
Rapid transition		✓
Synchronization		✓

Key Terms

▸ RSTP

▸ PortFast

▸ BPDU Guard

▸ UplinkFast

▸ BackboneFast

▸ EtherChannel

▸ Discarding

▸ Synchronization

Apply Your Knowledge

Exercises

14.1 Time Flies with PortFast

This exercise forces the STP election by changing the priority in a switch.

Estimated Time: 5 minutes

1. Power on your switch.

2. Console into one switch, and navigate to user EXEC.

3. Configure an interface for PortFast.

4. Plug a device into that interface.

5. Issue the show spanning-tree command within 15 seconds to see the state change immediately to forwarding.

14.2 Imagine the Wonders of RSTP

In this exercise, you draw your existing switched network and imagine what transpires when it runs RSTP. If you do not have a switched network, create or design your own topology, and draw how you imagine the switches would be implemented and what links should exist between the switches.

Estimated Time: 10 minutes

1. Draw a new or your existing STP switched topology.

2. Imagine that you are running RSTP in the network, and determine the root switch, root ports, designated ports, and discarding ports (they should be the same as the STP topology now).

3. Identify any switch ports that might be an alternate or backup port.

4. Consider the proposal/agreement exchanges that occur in each switch and if syncing occurs in them.

5. For the ultimate practice exercise, add a switch to your design with a lower Bridge ID so that it becomes the root switch. Determine how this change gets propagated to other switches in the RSTP design.

Review Questions

1. Why would you use PortFast with BPDU Guard?

2. What is the advantage of using UplinkFast?

3. What is the advantage of using BackboneFast?

4. In what circumstances would you have a backup or alternate port state in RSTP?

5. What is the primary purpose of synchronization?

Exam Questions

1. You've connected your switches together with a crossover cable. What would be a possible reason for a switching loop to occur?

   ○ **A.** Because STP is disabled by default, you need to enable it on both switches.

   ○ **B.** You configured one of the interfaces as PortFast.

   ○ **C.** You need to use a straight-through cable.

   ○ **D.** The forward delay timers were set to 15 seconds.

2. Which of the following is actively participating (forwarding frames) in the RSTP topology?

   ○ **A.** Ports in a learning state

   ○ **B.** Alternate ports

   ○ **C.** Connected edge ports

   ○ **D.** Backup ports

3. Which of the following is not a similarity between STP and RSTP?

   ○ **A.** Root bridge elections

   ○ **B.** Use of BPDUs to communicate topology information to other switches

   ○ **C.** Learning state

   ○ **D.** BPDUs originate only from the root switch.

4. After connecting your switch to another switch, you notice that your interface immediately gets shut down. Which of the following is a possible reason for this occurrence?

   ○ **A.** BPDU Guard

   ○ **B.** Duplicate MAC addresses

   ○ **C.** UplinkFast

   ○ **D.** BackboneFast

5. Given the following output:

```
Switch#show spanning-tree

VLAN0001
 Spanning tree enabled protocol rstp
 Root ID  Priority  1
          Address   0011.92cc.fc00
          Cost    19
          Port    3 (FastEthernet1/0/1)
          Hello Time  2 sec Max Age 20 sec Forward Delay 15 sec

  Bridge ID Priority  4097  (priority 4096 sys-id-ext 1)
          Address   0011.92cd.0280
          Hello Time  2 sec Max Age 20 sec Forward Delay 15 sec
          Aging Time 300

Interface      Role Sts  Cost    Prio.Nbr  Type
---------------- ---- --- --------- -------- ----------------
Fa 0/2         Root FWD  19     128.4    P2p
Fa 0/10         Desg FWD  19     128.12   Edge P2p
```

   what is the significance of port Fa 0/10?

   ○ **A.** It is connected to another switch.

   ○ **B.** An end device is connected to this interface.

   ○ **C.** It is in a discarding state.

   ○ **D.** MAC addresses are not learned on this interface.

6. Given the following output:

```
Switch#show spanning-tree

VLAN0001
 Spanning tree enabled protocol rstp
 Root ID  Priority  1
          Address   0011.92cc.fc00
          Cost    19
```

```
        Port    5 (FastEthernet1/0/3)
        Hello Time   2 sec Max Age 20 sec Forward Delay 15 sec

  Bridge ID Priority  12289 (priority 12288 sys-id-ext 1)
        Address    0011.92cc.f080
        Hello Time   2 sec Max Age 20 sec Forward Delay 15 sec
        Aging Time 300

Interface       Role  Sts Cost    Prio.Nbr  Type
---------------- ---- --- --------- -------- ---------------
Fa 0/2          Altn  BLK 19       128.4     P2p
Fa 0/3          Root  FWD 19       128.5     P2p
```

which of the following is not true?

- ○ **A.** Fa 0/3 has the fastest path to the root switch.

- ○ **B.** Fa 0/2 has a viable path back to the root switch.

- ○ **C.** If Fa 0/3 goes down, Fa 0/2 transitions to a listening and learning state before forwarding.

- ○ **D.** This switch can interoperate with 802.1d STP.

7. Which of the following occurs when a link fails in an EtherChannel bundle?

- ○ **A.** STP becomes active on the remaining links.

- ○ **B.** The bundle redistributes the traffic over the remaining active links.

- ○ **C.** The entire bundle is shut down, and an administrator needs to reenable it.

- ○ **D.** Another interface is automatically added to the bundle to compensate.

8. Given the following output:

Switch#**show spanning-tree**

```
VLAN0001
 Spanning tree enabled protocol rstp
 Root ID  Priority  1
        Address    0011.92cc.fc00
        Cost    19
        Port    5 (FastEthernet1/0/3)
        Hello Time   2 sec Max Age 20 sec Forward Delay 15 sec

  Bridge ID Priority  12289 (priority 12288 sys-id-ext 1)
        Address    0011.92cc.f080
        Hello Time   2 sec Max Age 20 sec Forward Delay 15 sec
        Aging Time 300

Interface       Role  Sts Cost    Prio.Nbr  Type
```

```
- - - - - - - - - - - - - - - - -  - - - -  - - -  - - - - - - - - - -  - - - - - - - -  - - - - - - - - - - - - - - - -
Fa 0/1        Desg  FWD 19     128.1     P2p
Fa 0/2        Bckp  BLK 19     128.4     P2p
Fa 0/3        Root  FWD 19     128.5     P2p
```

which of the following is true?

- ○ **A.** If Fa 0/1 goes down, Fa 0/2 is the new root port.

- ○ **B.** Fa 0/1 and Fa 0/2 are connected to separate segments.

- ○ **C.** If Fa 0/2 goes down, Fa 0/1 transitions to a listening and learning state before forwarding.

- ○ **D.** If Fa 0/1 goes down, Fa 0/2 is the new designated port.

9. Which of the following is not necessary for UplinkFast to occur?

- ○ **A.** The switch must hear an inferior BPDU from a neighbor.

- ○ **B.** Failure must occur on the root port.

- ○ **C.** The switch must have direct knowledge of the link failure.

- ○ **D.** The switch must have one blocked port.

10. Which of the following is not part of the proposal/agreement handshake for RSTP rapid transition?

- ○ **A.** The switch with the designated port sends the proposal to forward.

- ○ **B.** The switch with the root port must sync before agreeing to the proposal.

- ○ **C.** As soon as the handshake is complete, each port immediately forwards frames and learns MAC addresses.

- ○ **D.** As soon as the proposal is received, it is forwarded to the root bridge.

Answers to Review Questions

1. PortFast is a Cisco-proprietary enhancement to STP that enables a switch port to bypass the listening and learning STP states for end devices such as workstations and servers. BPDU Guard protects PortFast interfaces from switching loops by disabling an interface if a BPDU is received from another switch.

2. UplinkFast is useful when you have redundant uplinks to its distribution switch. If the root port to the distribution switch fails, UplinkFast skips the listening and learning states and immediately begins forwarding on the redundant link.

3. BackboneFast speeds up convergence by skipping the max age time when switches learn of a failure indirectly through an inferior BPDU from a neighboring switch.

4. Alternate ports are redundant root ports placed in a discarding state in which they immediately transition to a forwarding state if the primary root port fails. Backup ports are also discarding ports that provide a redundant connection to the designated port for a specific LAN segment. If the designated port for a given segment were to fail, the backup port would immediately transition to a forwarding state.

5. The purpose of RSTP synchronization is to ensure that a switch synchronizes new root information accurately to all other ports without causing a loop. It achieves this by putting all nonedge ports in a discarding state before agreeing to forward on the new root link.

Answers to Exam Questions

1. **B.** When PortFast is enabled, you must not connect a switch, bridge, or hub to that interface, or loops may occur. Answer A is false because STP is enabled by default. Answer C is incorrect because you must use cross-over cables when connecting two switches together. Answer D is incorrect because the forward delay timers are set to 15 seconds by default.

2. **C.** Edge ports connected to end devices immediately transition to forwarding states and actively forward frames. Answer A is incorrect because the learning state is learning MAC addresses but is still not in a forwarding state. B and D are incorrect because alternate and backup ports are both in discarding states.

3. **D.** In RSTP, BPDUs originate from each switch and act as a keepalive. STP BPDUs originate from the root bridge and are forwarded by other switches. Root bridge elections, learning states, and BPDUs as communication all exist in both STP and RSTP, so answers A, B, and C are incorrect.

4. **A.** If an interface is configured for PortFast with BPDU Guard, it immediately puts the switch in a disabled state if it detects a BPDU from another switch. Answer B is incorrect because there would not be duplicate MAC addresses in a switched network. Answers C and D are incorrect because UplinkFast and BackboneFast would not disable a port if connected to another switch.

5. **B.** Because the output indicates that the interface is an edge interface, this means an end device is connected to it. A is incorrect because another switch cannot be connected to an edge port. Answer C is incorrect because the port is a designated port and is forwarding frames. Answer D is incorrect because this interface is forwarding; thus, it is forwarding frames and learning MAC addresses.

6. **C.** Alternate ports immediately transition to a forwarding state if the root port goes down. A is true because Fa 0/3 is the root port. Answer B is true because the alternate port must have a viable path to the root to become the alternate port. D is also true because RSTP is backward-compatible with 802.1d STP.

7. **B.** When a link fails in an EtherChannel bundle, the traffic is redistributed over the remaining links. Answer A is incorrect because STP treats the entire bundle as a single link and would not be activated if the bundle remained. Answer C is incorrect because the bundle remains active. Answer D would be nice if it were true, but it is also incorrect because the EtherChannel links are applied only to those interfaces that you have configured to be part of the bundle.

8. **D.** The backup port automatically starts to forward and becomes the new designated port if the current designated port fails. Answer A is incorrect because it will not become a root port. Answer B is incorrect because a backup port exists only if two ports are connected to the same segment. Answer C is incorrect because the link immediately transitions to a forwarding state.

9. **A.** Inferior BPDUs are not necessary for UplinkFast to work; they are specific to BackboneFast. Answers B, C, and D are true because a switch must have one blocked port, a failure on the root port, and direct knowledge of that failure for UplinkFast to work correctly.

10. **D.** It is not necessary for RSTP switches to forward any notifications back to the root switch like STP. Answer A, B, and C are true because the handshake entails the designated switch sending a proposal. The other switch receives the proposal, blocks all ports connected to point-to-point links, and sends an agreement. When the switches are finished with the handshake, they immediately begin forwarding frames.

Suggested Readings and Resources

1. Richard Froom, Balaji Sivasubramanian, and Erum Frahim. *Building Cisco Multilayer Switched Networks (BCMSN) (Authorized Self-Study Guide)*, 4th Edition. Cisco Press, 2007.

2. "Spanning Tree Enhancements," www.cisco.com.

3. "Rapid Spanning-Tree Protocol," www.cisco.com.

CHAPTER FIFTEEN

Virtual LANs

Objectives

This chapter covers the following Cisco-specified objective for the "Configure, verify and troubleshoot a switch with VLANs and interswitch communications" section of the 640-802 CCNA exam:

▶ **Describe enhanced switching technologies (including: VTP, RSTP, VLAN, PVSTP, 802.1q)**

▶ **Describe how VLANs create logically separate networks and the need for routing between them**

▶ **Configure, verify, and troubleshoot VLANs**

▶ **Configure, verify, and troubleshoot trunking on Cisco switches**

▶ **Configure, verify, and troubleshoot interVLAN routing**

▶ **Configure, verify, and troubleshoot VTP**

Outline

Study Strategies

▶ Read the information presented in the chapter, paying special attention to tables, Notes, and Exam Alerts.

▶ Complete the Challenge Exercises and the Exercises at the end of the chapter. The exercises will solidify the concepts that you have learned in the previous sections.

▶ Complete the Exam Questions at the end of the chapter. They are designed to simulate the type of questions you will be asked in the CCNA exam.

Introduction

One of the underlying problems with Layer 2 switches is that excessive broadcast and multi-cast traffic can affect other devices in a switched network because bridges and switches flood these types of messages. If you are a receiver of all this excessive traffic, you have to waste processing utilization and endure wasted bandwidth even if those devices are not in your department. This chapter explores how VLANs solve your broadcast concerns by segmenting broadcast domains at Layer 2 and how they affect your switched network design.

Overview of VLANs

Objectives:

▶ Describe enhanced switching technologies (including: VTP, RSTP, VLAN, PVSTP, 802.1q)

▶ Describe how VLANs create logically separate networks and the need for routing between them

In your company, you may have several departments connected to the same Layer 2 switch or switched network. Quite often, departments may be running applications and protocols that are unique to users within their own group. Unfortunately, if this traffic consists of multicasts and broadcasts (or unknown unicasts, for that matter), that traffic hits all users connected to that switched network.

For instance, imagine that the Not-So-Human Resources department is running a developed program that helps them track employee lunch break times. Unfortunately, this traffic relies heavily on broadcasts to communicate with other applications being used by personnel in that department. The broadcast and multicast traffic from the Not-So-Human Resources depart-ment continues to be flooded out to everyone else in the network because they are all con-nected to the same switched network. Because this is the only department that uses this soft-ware, ideally it would be convenient to separate the Not-So-Human Resources group into their own separate switched LAN so their traffic doesn't affect any other department.

To this point, the only way you could segment this network into smaller broadcast domains is by using a router because routers do not forward broadcasts or multicasts by default. The problem with this solution is that routers can be expensive, considering you need an interface for each department to keep the traffic separate. In addition, because routers have to process all the way into the Layer 3 information of a packet before sending the traffic to a different segment, throughput is considerably slower than that of a switch. Not to mention, if you have users within departments physically dispersed all throughout your network, the broadcast and multicast traffic would never reach them because the router does not forward them onto other interfaces.

The answer to all these problems lies within the magic of virtual LANs (VLANs). VLANs enable you to segment broadcast domains at Layer 2 without a router. Each VLAN created in a switch represents a logical grouping of devices into their own broadcast domain. Thus, each department can have its own VLAN that separates traffic from one department from that of other departments. In fact, devices in one VLAN cannot communicate with other devices in another VLAN without the help of a router, even if those devices are plugged into the same switch. What's more, VLANs can span multiple switches, so the geographic location of the devices is no longer a limiting factor. As members of a specific department are added or moved, you simply need to assign their switch interface to the department's VLAN.

What is also remarkable about VLANs is that because each VLAN represents a broadcast domain in which devices can communicate only with other devices in that same VLAN, there must be a separate instance of Spanning Tree Protocol (STP) running for each VLAN. In other words, if you have 20 VLANs running in your switched network, you will have 20 instances of STP running, each with its own root bridge. The term for this ability to have a separate instance of Spanning Tree Protocol for each VLAN is called *PVST (per VLAN Spanning Tree)*. It is for this very reason that the configuration for the STP priority (discussed in Chapter 13, "Foundation Switching Operations") required that the VLAN be specified in the command syntax.

> **EXAM ALERT**
>
> Unless VLANs are specifically mentioned in an exam question or answer choices, routers segment broadcast domains and switches segment collision domains.

VLAN Membership Methods

After the VLANs are created, they have to be associated with the users or departments connected to the switches. The most common way to associate VLANs is statically on a port-by-port basis. When the VLAN is associated with the switch port, it is referred to as an *access port*. When a single VLAN is assigned on the interface, traffic is sent to and received by only devices connected to interfaces with the same VLAN.

For instance, consider the typical single-switch VLAN configuration exhibited in Figure 15.1. All these switches are access ports that have a single VLAN assigned to them. On Fast Ethernet interfaces 0/1 and 0/3, they are assigned to VLAN 1. Our Not-So-Human Resources VLAN (VLAN 3) has been assigned to Fast Ethernet interfaces 0/2, 0/4, and 0/5. The devices connected to these interfaces can communicate only with other interfaces that also contain that VLAN. So in the example, the printer and the computer on the right can communicate with each other and the computer connected to interface Fast Ethernet 0/2. Even though they are connected to the same switch, these devices cannot communicate with the computers connected to interfaces assigned to VLAN 1 because they are in a completely different broadcast domain.

An alternative to static VLANs is to have the VLANs dynamically associated with the frames entering a switch. To achieve this, you must configure a VLAN Membership Policy Server (VMPS). The VMPS is a device, such as a server or even a high-end Catalyst switch, that has an association of every MAC address with a VLAN. When the frame enters a port, the switch acts as a client and queries the VMPS for the VLAN assigned to that MAC. This is appealing because you don't have to configure VLANs on every interface; however, it does require a good deal of initial setup on the actual server.

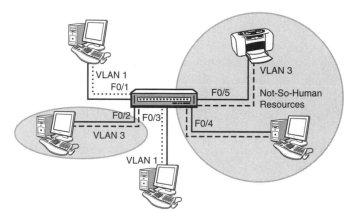

FIGURE 15.1 Single-switch VLAN scenario.

The Management VLAN

Conveniently enough, your switch is already configured with a default VLAN that is used for management on access ports. This is used for a management communication channel because the IP address, CDP, and VTP (discussed later in this chapter) all exist in the management VLAN for ethernet, VLAN 1. This VLAN is created by default in all Cisco Catalyst switches and assigned to all interfaces. Because it is applied to all switch ports, it still holds true that all devices connected to a switch are in the same broadcast domain.

Recall from Chapter 13 that to assign a management IP address to a switch, you configure the IP on interface VLAN 1. This means that your management workstation must have access to VLAN 1 to remotely manage the Catalyst switch. If you change the VLAN on the port in which your management station or your router (if managing it remotely) is connected, you lose the ability to manage the switch with Telnet, SSH, HTTP, or SNMP.

Configuring and Verifying VLANs

Objective:

▶ Configure, verify, and troubleshoot VLANs

All interfaces are already assigned to VLAN 1. To create smaller broadcast domains in your switch, you must create those VLANs for each department you want to segment and assign them to their respective interfaces. Specifically, the configuration steps for VLANs are as follows:

1. Create the VLAN, using a number between 2 and 1001.

2. Name the VLAN. If you do not assign it a name, it uses VLAN*xxxx*, where *xxxx* is the VLAN number.

3. Assign it to a switch port.

EXAM ALERT

Know the three steps involved in configuring VLANs.

VLAN-specific configurations are permanently stored in Flash memory in a special file called the VLAN database (vlan.dat). To configure VLANs on the Catalyst switch, you must navigate to a VLAN configuration mode from global configuration referred to as config-VLAN Mode.

To navigate to this configuration mode, you type the command **vlan** followed by the VLAN ID you want to create. At this point, the prompt changes to **Switch(config-vlan)#**, signifying that you are in the config-VLAN mode. At this stage of the VLAN configuration, you have the option to assign a unique name to the VLAN you just created by typing the keyword **name** followed by the custom name of your VLAN. If you do not specify a name, the switch will automatically assign the name using the VLAN ID. For instance, if you chose the number 4 for the VLAN ID, the VLAN name defaults to VLAN0004.

In the following example, we are creating two VLANS; one we named NSHR and the other we left to its default VLAN name based on the VLAN ID:

```
Switch#configure terminal
Enter configuration commands, one per line.  End with CNTL/Z.
Switch(config)#vlan 3
Switch(config-vlan)#name NSHR
Switch(config-vlan)#exit
Switch(config)#vlan 4
Switch(config-vlan)#exit
Switch(config) #
```

A VLAN is useful only if it is assigned to an interface; thus, our next logical step is to assign VLAN 3 and VLAN 4 to switch ports to segment those devices connected to those interfaces into their own VLAN broadcast domain. To statically assign the VLANs to a switch port, you must navigate to the interface and use the `switchport access vlan` command as demonstrated here:

```
Switch(config)#interface FastEthernet 0/2
Switch(config-if)#switchport access vlan 3
Switch(config-if)#exit
Switch(config)#interface FastEthernet 0/7
Switch(config-if)#switchport access vlan 4
```

Because these VLAN configurations are stored in the VLAN database, they will not be displayed in the running or startup configs. Instead, to verify your VLAN configuration, use the `show vlan` command to observe the VLANs that you created and the interfaces to which they are applied, as demonstrated in Figure 15.2.

```
Switch#show vlan

VLAN Name                             Status    Ports
1    default                          active    Fa0/1, Fa0/3, Fa0/4, Fa0/5, Fa0/6, Fa0/8, Fa0/9, Fa0/10
                                                Fa0/11, Fa0/12, Fa0/13, Fa0/14, Fa0/15, Fa0/16, Fa0/17, Fa0/18
                                                Fa0/19, Fa0/20, Fa0/21, Fa0/22, Fa0/23, Fa0/24, Gi0/1, Gi0/2
3    NSHR                             active    Fa0/2
4    VLAN0004                         active    Fa0/7
1002 fddi-default                     active
1003 token-ring-default               active
1004 fddinet-default                  active
1005 trnet-default                    active

VLAN Type  SAID    MTU   Parent RingNo BridgeNo Stp  BrdgMode Trans1 Trans2
1    enet  100001  1500  -      -      -        -    -        0      0
3    enet  100003  1500  -      -      -        -    -        0      0
4    enet  100004  1500  -      -      -        -    -        0      0
1002 fddi  101002  1500  -      -      -        -    -        0      0
1003 tr    101003  1500  -      -      -        -    srb      0      0
1004 fdnet 101004  1500  -      -      -        ieee -        0      0
1005 trnet 101005  1500  -      -      -        ibm  -        0      0

Remote SPAN VLANs
------------------------------------------------------------------------

Primary Secondary Type          Ports
```

FIGURE 15.2   `show vlan` output.

EXAM ALERT

The previous version of the exams tested your knowledge on configuring VLANs using the VLAN Database Configuration Mode from privileged EXEC. The current exams no longer test your configuration knowledge using this mode but rather using the config-VLAN Mode as described in this chapter.

VLAN Trunking

One of the most remarkable features of VLANs is that they can span multiple interconnected switches. VLAN traffic is carried from switch to switch over interfaces called *trunks*. These trunk links must be at least 100Mbps because the traffic must carry all the VLAN traffic from the access ports.

Just as access ports have a single VLAN assigned to them, trunk ports essentially have all VLANs assigned to them. As frames traverse a trunk link, the VLAN identifier is added to the ethernet frame. The receiving switch uses the VLAN identifier and sends the frames out only the access ports that have that VLAN assigned to them. As the frame is sent out the interface, the VLAN identifier is removed, which gives the illusion to the end devices that the entire process is transparent.

EXAM ALERT

Remember that a trunk carries traffic for all the VLANs that are present on the switch by default.

NOTE

All VLAN traffic traverses a trunk link by default; however, it is possible to configure a trunk link to allow only traffic from certain VLANs.

Similar to VLANs in a single switch, traffic is contained to only those devices that are members of the same VLAN. For example, Figure 15.3 displays a typical scenario in which VLANs span multiple switches over a trunk link. Tagged frames from VLANs 1 and 3 are multiplexed (multiple messages combined over a single channel) over the trunk between the switches. However, traffic from VLAN 3 goes out to only those access interfaces that have VLAN 3 assigned to them; likewise, traffic from VLAN 1 is passed out only to the ports with VLAN 1 assigned.

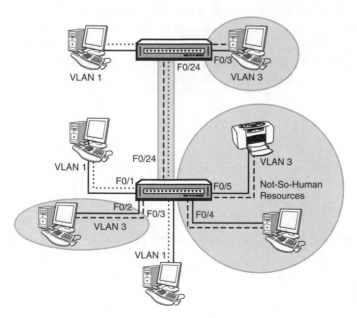

FIGURE 15.3 Multiple-switch VLAN scenario.

> **EXAM ALERT**
>
> Be prepared to identify which devices can communicate with each other given a VLAN configuration in one or several switches.

ISL Trunks

The VLAN identification is added to Layer 2 ethernet frames differently, depending on the type of trunk that is configured. Cisco's proprietary method of adding VLAN IDs to an ethernet frame is called Inter Switch Link (ISL). ISL trunking entails the original ethernet frame being encapsulated by ASIC chips with the VLAN information. The ISL encapsulation has a 26-byte header and an additional 4-byte CRC trailer at the end. Because an additional 30 bytes are added to the ethernet frame, the size of the frame can exceed a typical ethernet frame size of 1518 bytes. If the interface isn't configured as an ISL trunk, it drops the giant frame because it violates the MTU limit of a typical ethernet frame. For this reason, ISL requires a direct point-to-point (no intermediate devices) trunk connection between the switches.

802.1q Trunks

The IEEE created its own standard VLAN tagging method standardized as 802.1q. 802.1q differs from ISL because the VLAN ID is not encapsulated, but actually inserted in the originally ethernet frame. The VLAN identifier is contained within the four extra bytes inserted in the ethernet frame after the source address. Because the original frame size is manipulated when these four bytes are added to the frame, a new CRC must be calculated for the original ethernet Frame Check Sequence (FCS) field. Because only four bytes are added to the ethernet frame, these frames are known as baby giant frames and may be passed by other intermediary Layer 2 devices that are not configured as a trunk.

Native VLANs

Another unique feature of 802.1q trunks is the concept of a native VLAN. Traffic originating from access ports that shares the same VLAN as the trunk's native VLAN goes untagged over the trunk link. Similarly, any untagged frame that is received on an 802.1q trunk port is considered destined for the native VLAN assigned to the trunk port. For this reason, it is imperative that each side of the IEEE 802.1q link be configured with the same native VLAN, or the traffic from one VLAN leaks into another VLAN as illustrated in Figure 15.4. By default, the native VLAN for trunk ports is the same as the management VLAN, VLAN 1.

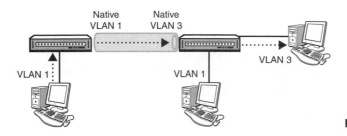

FIGURE 15.4 Native VLAN leakage.

Configuring and Verifying ISL and 802.1Q Trunks

Objective:

▶ Configure, verify, and troubleshoot trunking on Cisco switches

The first step to configuring a trunk link is deciding which type of trunk you want to use. For instance, if you are connecting to a non-Cisco switch, you have to use a standard trunk VLAN tagging method such as IEEE 802.1q. In addition, certain models of Cisco switches (such as the Catalyst 2950 and 2960) support only 802.1q trunking, so make sure you research the capabilities of your switch model before configuring the interfaces.

To configure a trunk port, navigate to the interface that is connected to the other switch. On models that support ISL and 802.1q trunking, you must first specify which VLAN tagging you want to use with the `switchport trunk encapsulation` command, as shown here:

```
Switch(config)#interface FastEthernet 0/24
Switch(config-if)#switchport trunk encapsulation dot1q
```

Notice the syntax starts with `switchport trunk` instead of `switchport access` (from the VLAN configurations) because this interface is being configured as a trunk to carry all VLANs.

With the trunk encapsulation configured, you are ready to enable the interface to begin forwarding all VLAN traffic. The port, however, is still operating as an access port until you specifically configure the interface to switch to trunking mode. To set this interface into a permanent trunking state, you must also type the following command:

```
Switch(config-if)#switchport mode trunk
```

EXAM ALERT

Be prepared to configure an interface as a trunk port.

Dynamic Trunking with DTP

Cisco switches can dynamically enable trunking on an interface through the use of a Cisco proprietary protocol called Dynamic Trunking Protocol (DTP). For instance, the default dynamic trunking state is called *desirable*, which actively tries to negotiate trunking as long as the other side of the trunk uses a compatible DTP condition.

The possible trunking modes are as follows:

▸ **Access**—The port does not trunk because it is an access port with a single VLAN.

▸ **Trunk**—The port permanently trunks and tries to negotiate the far-end to trunk with DTP.

▸ **Dynamic Desirable**—The port negotiates to trunk if the other side is set to trunk, desirable, or auto.

▸ **Dynamic Auto**—The port negotiates to trunk if the other side is set to trunk or desirable.

▸ **Nonegotiate**—The port permanently trunks, but disables DTP negotiation (for connecting to non-Cisco switches).

To verify the trunk configuration and status, use the show interface trunk command:

```
Switch>show interface trunk
Port       Mode          Encapsulation  Status        Native vlan
Fa0/24     on            802.1q         trunking      1

Port       Vlans allowed on trunk
Fa0/24     1-4094

Port       Vlans allowed and active in management domain
Fa0/24     1-4

Port       Vlans in spanning tree forwarding state and not pruned
Fa0/24     1-4
```

The output lists the ports that are configured to trunk and the encapsulation and VLANs that are allowed to traverse the trunk (all VLANs by default). In addition, because the interface is now set up as a trunk, you no longer see interface Fast Ethernet 0/24 listed in the **show vlan** output because it is no longer an access port.

EXAM ALERT

If the output of the show vlan command is displayed, know that missing interfaces are set up as a VLAN trunk and are not listed.

VLAN Trunking Protocol

Imagine you just configured 50 VLANs in your local switch. If you want to have these VLANs span your five switches in your network, you have to configure each switch with those exact VLANs. That is at least 200 more configurations that you have to perform before you can even begin to assign the VLANs to their respective ports.

To minimize the administrative overhead involved in replicating VLAN configurations on the remaining switches in your internetwork, Cisco has created a proprietary protocol called VLAN Trunking Protocol (VTP). With VTP, you have to make the initial VLAN configuration on only a single switch. This switch has a special role to propagate any VLAN revisions (additions, changes, or deletions) to the rest of the switches that want to receive these updates, known collectively as a VTP domain. These messages are sent as multicasts to a unique MAC address that only Cisco devices participating in VTP will hear (01-00-0C-CC-CC-CC).

VTP Modes

A VTP domain is similar to a large corporation in that there are specific job responsibilities and functions that everyone must perform in accordance to a job role. The switches inside a VTP domain also have a hierarchy in the roles that they can perform and the responsibilities of the switches that result from that role. These roles are dictated by the VTP mode in which they operate and ultimately define the level of VLAN configuration allowed on the switches and whether the VLAN information is stored and propagated. The three VTP modes in which a switch can operate are server, client, and transparent mode, which are discussed in the following sections.

> **NOTE**
>
> VTP only advertises the VLANs that are configured. It does not advertise the VLAN interface assignments because switches can contain different hardware.

Server Mode

In the corporation analogy, a switch operating in server mode would be considered the CEO of the network. It is responsible for maintaining the VLAN information for the rest of the network by telling everyone else what to do. In server mode, you have complete autonomy and are able to make any additions, deletions, or changes to the VLAN configurations. Because this functionality seems to be a reasonable function of all switches, server is the default VTP mode of all switches.

After you make a revision to the VLAN information in the VLAN database, the changes are propagated across trunk links to other switches in the VTP domain to synchronize their VLAN databases with the server's configuration. Each VTP advertisement from the VTP server contains a revision number in the message. When other switches receive this information, they compare the revision number of the new message to the last revision received. If the information is new (higher revision number), the switches apply those changes to their VLAN configurations. If the revision number is the same as the advertisement, the switches know that they have the latest information and ignore the update. In instances when the revision number advertised is lower than the current one in the database, they send an update to the sender because the sender's information is older than what they contain in their VLAN databases.

Client Mode

Imagine the chaos your company would have if everyone in the organization was the CEO. You would have everybody trying to tell each other what to do and nothing would ultimately get done. At some point, you need to have faithful workers who follow every word that the CEO tells them. In other words, you need yes-men.

The yes-men in the VTP domain are those switches that operate in client mode. Their sole purpose is to take the configuration revision from server switches and incorporate them into their operations. These switches also propagate those changes to other switches to ensure that the advertisement is heard across the entire VTP domain. Unlike switches in server mode, however, client mode switches do not permanently store their VLAN information in the VLAN database. Thus if switches in client mode reboot, they do not contain any VLAN information until they receive an update from the VTP server.

Because they receive their configuration from the VTP server, switches in VTP client mode cannot add, change, or delete VLANs. In fact, the IOS reports back an error similar to the following:

```
VTP VLAN configuration not allowed when device is in CLIENT mode.
```

This lack of functionality is actually quite useful when new switches are added to an existing VTP domain so they do not accidentally advertise incorrect VLAN information to switches in the VTP domain (assuming their revision number is higher).

Transparent Mode

To round out the corporation analogy, the inevitable third type of worker in large corporations is the disgruntled employee. These employees believe they know how to run the company better than the CEO, so they do things their way. However, to ensure that they keep their jobs, they don't let anyone know about their delusions.

Similarly, switches running in transparent mode also do their own thing in the sense that they are allowed to add, change, and remove VLAN configurations. In addition, they store those VLAN configurations in their VLAN database so they are present when the switch reboots. The key difference between server and transparent mode switches is that transparent mode switches do not advertise their configurations to other switches. In addition, they also do not use any configuration revisions being advertised by server switches. They do, however, send those advertisements out their trunk ports to other switches in case there are client mode switches downstream from them. In other words, the switch is transparent because the advertisements from the server seem to pass right through them.

So why have transparent mode in the first place? Basically, transparent mode enables you to create your own VLAN configurations that are contained within a single switch. This is useful if you have VLANs connected to that switch that are not used by any other switches in the domain.

The obvious follow-up question to this is, "Why use VTP on this switch if it does not listen to the VTP server revisions or advertise its own VLANs?" To answer this question, take a look at the exhibit in Figure 15.5. When the switch in server mode sends its VTP revision to the switch operating in transparent mode, that switch ignores the advertisement and passes it to the client switches below. If the transparent switch did not participate in VTP, it would drop those advertisements from the server and the client switches would never receive the configuration revisions.

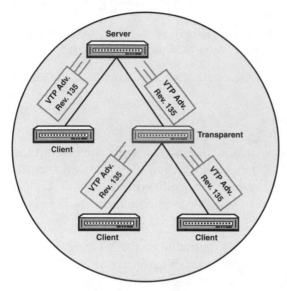

FIGURE 15.5 VTP domain with transparent switch.

Transparent mode is full of quirks above its normal VTP responsibilities. For instance, when running in VTP transparent mode, you have the ability to use extended-range VLANs. When using normal-range VLANs, you are limited to using 1-1005 as your VLAN ID. When running VTP in transparent mode (and using 802.1q trunks), your range of VLAN IDs can be extended to 1006-4094. Be advised, however, since switches in transparent mode do not advertise their VLANs, VTP does not recognize VLANs above 1005.

Furthermore, transparent mode stores the VLANs that you configure in the running and startup configurations as opposed to the VLAN database; therefore, you will see the VLANs you configured when you show the running or startup configurations in the IOS. Following this logic, it makes sense why other switches do not receive advertisements of VLANs from switches in transparent mode since it is actually the VLANs stored in the VLAN database that are advertised in VTP.

EXAM ALERT

Make sure you understand the functions of each VTP role. Also, remember that you must be in either server or transparent mode to make any VLAN configuration changes in a switch.

CAUTION

VTP Revision Mayhem   Recall that when adding a new switch to an existing VTP domain, it is highly recommended that you put the switch in client mode. If you left your switch in the default server mode, you could possibly have a higher revision number than the existing server of the domain. If you add that switch to the domain and you do not have any VLANs configured, when you advertise that to the rest of the VTP domain, the client and the other server use that configuration because it has a higher number. That would cause all the VLANs to be removed in all switches because your VLAN database does not contain any VLAN configurations.

To reset your revision number, you can either change the name of your VTP domain to a bogus domain name and set it back to the existing domain name or set your switch to transparent mode followed by returning it to server or client mode.

VTP Pruning

VLAN traffic is being sent over trunk links to other switches no matter whether or not the VLAN is active on an interface. In other words, if a user connected to VLAN 2 sends a broadcast, that message is replicated to all switches in the domain regardless of whether VLAN 2 is assigned to a switch port. This could consume unnecessary bandwidth on the trunk links connecting the switches.

To minimize the traffic overhead, you can configure VTP pruning on the VTP server of the domain. When enabled, switches advertise to each other which VLANs are active. With this information, the switch can limit VLAN traffic to other switches that do not have the VLAN active on an interface, minimizing the amount of unnecessary traffic that is sent to other switches on the trunk link.

Configuring and Verifying VTP

Objective:

▶ Configure, verify, and troubleshoot VTP

Similar to the VLAN configurations, VTP is stored in the VLAN database. From global configuration mode, you can easily change the VTP mode of the switch from server to transparent or client mode. In addition, you can define your VTP domain name as well as assign an MD5 password for VTP updates. The domain name (and password if configured) are case sensitive and must match in all switches in the VTP domain or the VTP updates will be ignored from other switches and VTP will not function.

To configure VTP-specific properties, use the vtp command followed by the VTP parameter you want to configure as illustrated in the following configuration example:

```
Switch#configure terminal
Enter configuration commands, one per line.  End with CNTL/Z.
Switch(config)#vtp domain CCNA
Changing VTP domain name from NULL to CCNA
Switch(config)#vtp password imustmatch
Setting device VLAN database password to imustmatch
```

To communicate with other switches in the VTP domain, the VTP domain name has to be CCNA as shown in this switch. In addition, the VTP password must also match in all configurations to ensure VTP updates are authenticated from each other.

> **NOTE**
>
> The default VTP domain is Null. If you connect your switch to an existing VTP domain while running in server or client mode, the switch will inherit the VTP domain name from a VTP server's summary advertisement.

To change the default VTP mode from server to client or transparent, you simply need to use the **vtp mode** command in global configuration followed by the mode you wish the switch to participate in:

```
Switch(config)#vtp mode transparent
Setting device to VTP TRANSPARENT mode.
```

> **EXAM ALERT**
>
> Be prepared to configure VTP parameters in a switch.

The show vtp status command is a critical command for verifying your VTP configuration. As demonstrated in Figure 15.6, the **show vtp status** command displays the revision number of the VTP updates from the server, the operating mode, domain name, pruning status, and the MD5 digest of the password.

```
Switch>show vtp status
VTP Version                     : 2
Configuration Revision          : 0
Maximum VLANs supported locally : 1005
Number of existing VLANs        : 8
VTP Operating Mode              : Transparent
VTP Domain Name                 : CCNA
VTP Pruning Mode                : Enabled
VTP V2 Mode                     : Disabled
VTP Traps Generation            : Disabled
MD5 digest                      : 0x6B 0xC0 0x7F 0x02 0xCB 0xE9 0xBA 0xA4
Configuration last modified by 192.168.100.2 at 3-1-93 00:31:16
```

FIGURE 15.6 show vtp status output.

> **EXAM ALERT**
>
> Given the output(s) of the show vtp status command, be able to identify the operating mode and what functionality the switch has because of that VTP mode. In addition, be able to troubleshoot VTP inconsistencies such as non-matching VTP domain and MD5 passwords.

Challenge

The concepts and configurations are very critical to comprehend for the CCNA exam. The following challenge tests your comprehension of the concepts and configuration of VLANs, trunks, and VTP.

1. How many broadcast domains are present in the switch by default and what VLAN(s) are present?

2. Enter global configuration and change your VTP domain to VTPMaster.

3. Create the VTP password for the domain to be allhailme.

4. Change the VTP mode to client.

5. You need to create two separate broadcast domains in your local switch for the ExamCram and the ExamPrep departments. Configure them with VLAN numbers 100 and 200, respectively, and apply the configuration.

   Why will this fail?

6. Change your VTP mode back to the default, add the VLANs, and exit the VLAN database.

7. Apply VLAN 100 to interface Fast Ethernet 0/1.

8. Apply VLAN 200 to interface Fast Ethernet 0/2.

9. Make Fast Ethernet 0/24 an interface to carry all VLAN traffic to a neighboring switch, using the IEEE standard VLAN tagging.

Challenge Answer

In solving this Challenge the switch is configured, by default, for a single broadcast domain in the management VLAN 1. The configuration for steps 1–4 is as follows:

```
Switch#configure terminal
Enter configuration commands, one per line.  End with CNTL/Z.
Switch(config)#vtp domain VTPMaster
Changing VTP domain name from NULL to VTPMaster
Switch(config)#vtp password allhailme
Setting device VLAN database password to allhailme
Switch(config)#vtp client
Setting device to VTP CLIENT mode.
```

Any VLAN creation will fail at this point because you cannot add, change, or delete VLANs in VTP client mode. The remaining configuration steps are demonstrated here:

```
Switch(config)#vtp server
Setting device to VTP SERVER mode.
Switch(config)#vlan 100
Switch(config-vlan)#name ExamCram
Switch(config-vlan)#exit
Switch(config)#vlan 200
```

```
Switch(config-vlan)#name ExamPrep
Switch(config-vlan)#exit
Switch(config)#interface FastEthernet 0/1
Switch(config-if)#switchport access vlan 100
Switch(config-if)#exit
Switch(config)#interface FastEthernet 0/2
Switch(config-if)#switchport access vlan 200
Switch(config-if)#exit
Switch(config)#interface FastEthernet 0/24
Switch(config-if)#switchport trunk encapsulation dot1q
Switch(config-if)#switchport mode trunk
```

InterVLAN Routing

Objective:

▶ Configure, verify, and troubleshoot interVLAN routing

One of the remarkable features about VLAN segmentation with a Layer 2 switch is that the traffic from one VLAN remains separate from all other VLANs. Quite often, however, devices need to communicate or access services with another device that is in another VLAN. Because the VLANs are in separate networks (broadcast domains), you need a device that is capable of routing in between networks. In other words, you need a router or a Layer 3 switch.

Each broadcast domain that is created in a switch is associated with an IP subnet. Devices in the same VLAN share the same subnet so they can use IP to communicate with each other. Routers and Layer 2 switches route between the logical subnets to allow traffic from one VLAN to reach another VLAN. This is known as interVLAN routing.

Router on a Stick

One method of routing between VLANs is to use a router. Because each VLAN is associated with its own subnet, a router needs to have an interface for each VLAN (IP subnet) so it can route in between them. This can become a costly and unscalable solution if you have a large number of VLANs in your switched network.

The most effective manner of using a router to perform interVLAN routing is something commonly referred to as "router on a stick." The gist behind this solution is to produce a configuration in which the router can see all the VLAN traffic over a single link. In other words, the router trunks to a switch over a single link, hence the term "router on a stick." Despite the router being able to see all the VLAN traffic, however, it still requires interfaces with IP subnets assigned to them to route in between these VLANs. The answer for this is something called *subinterfaces*.

Subinterfaces are virtual interfaces that are created on a single physical interface. When a physical interface is divided into these virtual interfaces, the router still considers them to be directly connected interfaces with subnets assigned to them and can route in between them. To create the subinterfaces, you navigate in the IOS as you would to a physical interface; however, you add a decimal followed by the logical subinterface number. The IOS prompt changes to reflect Router(config-subif)#, signifying you are in the subinterface configuration mode, as demonstrated here:

```
Router(config)#interface FastEthernet 0/1.1
Router(config-subif)#
```

The decimal number you assign to an interface does not have to be in any sequential order. In fact, for good design practices, you should use the same number of the VLAN for which you created the subinterface. In addition, because these are logical interfaces, if one subinterface goes down, it does not affect the rest of the subinterfaces. However, if the physical interface happens to go down, then logic follows that all your subinterfaces go down with the ship, so to speak. Additionally, you do not need to enable no shutdown on each subinterface; this is required only on the physical interface itself.

After you create a subinterface for a VLAN on your Fast Ethernet or Gigabit interface (remember trunks must be at least 100Mbps), you can assign the IP address to the interface for that VLAN's subnet. This IP address is the default gateway for all the devices in that VLAN because the default gateway is the IP address to which devices send their traffic destined for another network. To assign the VLAN to each subinterface, you must use the **encapsulation** command and signify which method of VLAN tagging you have configured on the trunk, followed by the VLAN assigned to that subinterface.

> **EXAM ALERT**
>
> To use a router-on-a-stick solution for interVLAN routing, you must trunk between the router and the switch. In addition, the interface must be at least Fast Ethernet and contain subinterfaces for each VLAN.

For instance, given a scenario similar to Figure 15.7, you would create a subinterface in the router for each VLAN. The IP address assigned to these interfaces acts at the default gateway for the PCs. When the computer in VLAN 1 wants to send traffic to the computer in VLAN 3, it sends the traffic over the switch trunks to the router that is to route and re-encapsulate the ethernet frame to have a VLAN ID of VLAN 3. When the switches receive the frame, they forward it out of only access ports that have VLAN 3 assigned to it.

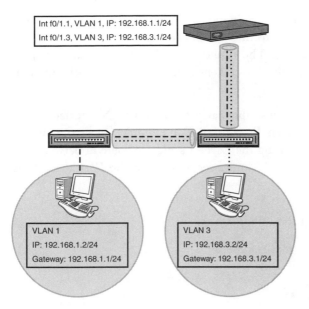

Int f0/1.1, VLAN 1, IP: 192.168.1.1/24
Int f0/1.3, VLAN 3, IP: 192.168.3.1/24

VLAN 1
IP: 192.168.1.2/24
Gateway: 192.168.1.1/24

VLAN 3
IP: 192.168.3.2/24
Gateway: 192.168.3.1/24

FIGURE 15.7   Router-on-a-stick scenario.

The router configuration for Figure 15.7 would look like the following, assuming you are using 802.1q trunks:

```
Router(config)#interface FastEthernet 0/1.1
Router(config-subif)#ip address 192.168.1.1 255.255.255.0
Router(config-subif)#encapsulation dot1q 1
Router(config)#interface FastEthernet 0/1.3
Router(config-subif)#ip address 192.168.3.1 255.255.255.0
Router(config-subif)#encapsulation dot1q 3
```

Switched Virtual Interfaces

An alternative to trunking to an external router is to use a Layer 3 switch to route in between the VLANs. Layer 3 switches combine the logical routing functionality of a router with the hardware speed of a switch because it uses ASICs to do some of the routing operations. So if the Layer 3 switch is faster than a router, why use routers? The answer is that Layer 3 switches do not have all the routing functionality that a router has. Specifically, you cannot purchase the Layer 3 switches with serial interfaces that can connect to a WAN. The Layer 3 switches are designed more to have routing functionality between VLANs in an ethernet LAN.

If you have a Layer 3 switch in your enterprise (certain models of the Catalyst 3550/60, 4500, and 6500 series of switches), you need to trunk to that switch and configure a different set of virtual interfaces to allow interVLAN routing. The result is called *switched virtual interfaces (SVI)*. The interfaces that you configure in the Layer 3 switches are, conveniently enough, VLAN interfaces.

To configure the switched virtual interfaces, you simply navigate to the VLAN interface number that matches your VLAN and assign it an IP address. For example, given the similar interVLAN scenario in Figure 15.8, you are using the Layer 3 switch to route in between the two VLANs. You just need to create the VLAN interfaces and assign the IP addresses, as demonstrated in the following configuration:

```
Switch(config)#interface Vlan 1
Switch(config-if)#ip address 192.168.1.1 255.255.255.0
Switch(config)#interface Vlan 3
Switch(config-if)#ip address 192.168.3.1 255.255.255.0
```

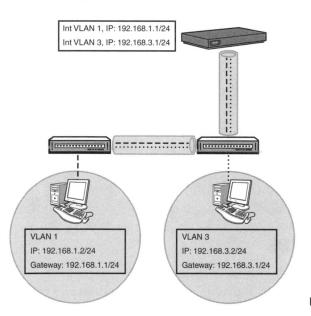

FIGURE 15.8 SVI interVLAN scenario.

Voice VLANs

We've established earlier in this chapter that access ports are ports that only have one VLAN assigned to them. That is typically the case unless you want to assign Voice VLANs, sometimes referred to as auxiliary VLANs, to an interface. In these cases, the access VLAN is actually the VLAN assigned for normal data and the voice VLAN is a separate VLAN for Voice over IP (VoIP) from a Cisco IP Phone.

Cisco IP Phones, such as the 7960, connect to switches and send the IP traffic that contains the voice payloads over the LAN and eventually to the gateway device that connects it to the traditional voice network. In addition to having the responsibility of breaking down speech and sound into data packets, these IP Phones also have an internal LAN switch with a data port on them that you can use to connect your PC or other end-device to minimize unnecessary cabling and the amount of ports needed on the Catalyst switch.

By configuring the switch port connected to these phones, you have the ability to logically separate the voice traffic from the phone and the data traffic traversing through the phone's internal switch into separate broadcast domains. This is useful for management purposes because you can essentially configure all IP Phones to be in their own subnet because the phones will be assigned to the same voice VLAN. But even more important than that, you can configure the Catalyst switch to use QoS and instruct the IP Phone (using CDP no less) to classify the voice traffic differently from the data. By giving the voice traffic higher priority over the data traffic, you are minimizing the possibility that your data traffic will impede the voice packets from reaching their destination (at least from the Catalyst switch) and deteriorate voice quality. To illustrate the process entailed with Cisco IP Phones and voice VLANs, refer to Figure 15.9.

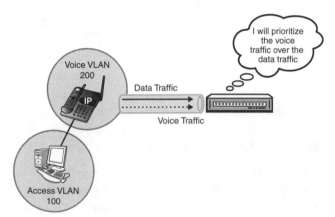

FIGURE 15.9   Voice and access VLAN with IP Phone.

In this illustration, the PC connected to the IP Phone is sending data traffic that is switched through the phone and is assigned to the access data VLAN 100 on the Catalyst switch. Voice traffic coming from the IP Phone is tagged with the voice VLAN ID of 200 and is given a higher QoS priority over the data traffic. If there is contention for sending the voice and data traffic, the switch will choose the voice traffic to ensure optimal voice quality.

To configure a voice VLAN, the syntax is relatively the same as access VLANs except it uses the keyword voice instead of access. For instance, assuming the IP Phone in Figure 15.9 was connected to the Catalyst switch's Fast Ethernet 0/20 interface, the configuration would look like the following:

```
Switch(config)#interface FastEthernet 0/20
Switch(config-if)#switchport access vlan 100
Switch(config-if)#switchport voice vlan 200
```

Troubleshooting VLAN

Objectives:

▶ Configure, verify, and troubleshoot VLANs

▶ Configure, verify, and troubleshoot trunking on Cisco switches

▶ Configure, verify, and troubleshoot interVLAN routing

▶ Configure, verify, and troubleshoot VTP

I am sure by this point you recognize the usefulness of segmenting your LAN into separate broadcast domains using VLANs. Unfortunately, this valuable Layer 2 technology is not without its share of problems that can (and typically do) arise when implementing VLANs in a switched environment. By logically narrowing down the possible causes based upon the symptoms and using the verification commands learned in this chapter, you should be able to tackle the majority of anomalies that occur in a small-to-medium sized switched network with VLANs.

One of the most common symptoms that may arise when implementing VLANs is the inability to have end-devices able to communicate with each other. The list of possible causes for this can be endless; however, the following questions and solutions will address the most prevalent problems:

1. Is this one of the design requirements of implementing VLANs in the first place? Recall that a major benefit of VLANs is to logically separate traffic into separate broadcast domains. If devices are in separate VLANs and do not have a router or Layer 3 switch to route in between the VLANs, then this is the result that is supposed to occur.

2. Are the trunks operating correctly between the switches? Assuming that you have multiple switches, verify the configuration and the status of the switch trunks by using the **show interfaces trunk** command. If the trunk link is not operating correctly, use the OSI model as a guide and begin with the Physical layer by verifying the cable between the switches is a cross-over ethernet cable. Once that is verified, move up to the Data Link layer and check your trunk configuration. Specifically, make sure trunk negotiation was successful, especially if your network is not an all-Cisco switched network. When in doubt, manually configure each side of the link to trunk by using the **switchport mode trunk** command.

3. Are the end-devices assigned to the correct VLANs? If they are designed to be in the same VLAN, verify the VLAN names match and they are assigned to the correct interfaces by using the **show vlans** command. If they are on separate VLANs, verify your configuration and the status of the interfaces on your router or your Layer 3 switch. In addition, ensure that the end-devices are utilizing the IP address of the subinterface or switched virtual interface as their default gateway.

4. If using 802.1q trunks, are both switches sharing the trunk using the same native VLAN? Recall that VLAN leakage can occur if both sides of the trunk are not configured with the same VLAN. Verify the native VLAN on both switches by utilizing the `show interfaces trunk` command.

The next troubleshooting scenario we will look at revolves around the possibility that output of the `show vlan` command reveals that your VLANs in your switch are missing or are inconsistent with what you originally configured in the rest of your switches:

1. Is your switch in VTP transparent mode? Mismatched VLANs is not only possible in transparent mode, but it is actually one of the reasons to use transparent mode. In addition, it might also explain why you do not see your VLANs since they will not show up in the VLAN database, but they can be found in your running or startup configuration.

2. Are the VTP configuration revision numbers incrementing along with the other switches in the network? It is plausible that the switch has lost a connection to the rest of the switched network. Verify the trunk is configured and operating as mentioned in the first scenario. Secondly, it may be possible that the management VLAN (VLAN 1 by default) is being blocked from propagating between the trunks (we will look into how to change the management VLAN and only allow certain VLANs over trunks in Chapter 16, "Implementing Switch Security.") Recall that the management IP, CDP, and VTP advertisements all are advertised using the management VLAN between switches. As a result, if the management VLAN is being blocked, VTP advertisements are consequently being blocked as well. Finally, there may be a switch that was added to your network between you and the VTP server that is configured for a different VTP domain. When the VTP server sends its VTP advertisements to the interjector switch, it will discard the VTP advertisement because it is not in the same VTP domain. The end result is that your switch never receives those VTP advertisements and your VTP configuration revisions will not increase.

3. Is there another VTP server in your switched internetwork? It is common to have several VTP servers in a network for redundancy; however, if another administrator is adding, changing, and/or removing VLANs on other VTP server switches, it will increment its configuration revision and all other switches in client and server mode will follow suit. If a VTP server is added and does not have any VLANs configured, that would explain it if all of your configured VLANs have suddenly disappeared as well. You can verify this by issuing the `show vtp status` command which will show you the IP address of the last VTP updater if known.

4. Has there been any configuration changes to the VTP domain or VTP passwords? If your switch does not have matching VTP domain names or VTP passwords, the switch will not accept VTP advertisements. This can be verified using the `show vtp status` command on each switch. If you suspect the password is not matching, use the `show vtp password` command from privileged EXEC.

Chapter Summary

VLANs are convenient for segmenting broadcast domains at Layer 2. The departments of an enterprise can be assigned their own logical VLAN to ensure traffic in one VLAN does not affect other VLANs. In fact, VLAN traffic cannot go from one VLAN to another VLAN without the assistance of an external router or a Layer 3 switch.

VLANs can be statically assigned to switch access ports, or a VMPS can be used to assign them dynamically. By default, all interfaces are assigned to the management VLAN, VLAN 1. To configure a VLAN, enter global configuration and create the VLAN and name it. After the VLANs are created, you must assign them to your switch ports by using the `switchport access vlan` command.

VLANs can span multiple switches by using ISL or 802.1q trunks. This makes it simple to move users throughout a switched network with no geographic restrictions. ISL is a Cisco proprietary VLAN tagging that encapsulates the original ethernet frame with a 26-byte header and a 4-byte CRC. Because this exceeds a typical frame MTU, the trunk must be point-to-point (directly connected). 802.1q is an IEEE standard of frame tagging that inserts the VLAN ID in the original ethernet frame and calculates a new CRC. 802.1q also uses the concept of native VLANs, which are VLANs that are not tagged as they traverse a trunk. To configure a trunk, you must first define the encapsulation method with the `switchport trunk encapsulation` command, and then set the interface to trunk with the `switchport mode trunk` command.

To minimize the amount of VLAN administration in switches, Cisco created VTP, which entails a VTP server sending advertisements with revision numbers containing the VLANs in the VTP domain. VTP clients use that information from the server; however, they cannot create, modify, or delete any VLANs. Transparent mode does not use the information sent from VTP servers; conversely, they can create, modify, or delete (but not advertise) their VLANs. VTP configuration also transpires from global configuration, in which you can switch the switch's operating mode, define the domain name, and assign a VTP password for update authentication.

To allow traffic from one VLAN to another, you must configure interVLAN routing. If you use an external router (router on stick), you must trunk to the interface and configure subinterfaces to route in between the VLANs. If your switched network has a Layer 3 switch, you can use that as the routing device between VLANs by creating a switched virtual interface (SVI) and assigning an IP to it.

Key Terms

- ▶ VLANs

- ▶ access ports

- ▶ PVST

- ▶ VMPS

- ▶ management VLAN

- ▶ trunk

- ▶ multiplexing

- ▶ ISL

- ▶ 802.1q

- ▶ native VLANs

- ▶ DTP

- ▶ VTP

- ▶ VTP Domains

- ▶ server mode

- ▶ client mode

- ▶ transparent mode

- ▶ VTP pruning

- ▶ port security

- ▶ interVLAN routing

- ▶ router on a stick

- ▶ subinterfaces

- ▶ SVI

- ▶ Voice VLAN

Apply Your Knowledge

Exercises

15.1 Create Your VTP Domain

In this exercise you establish your own VTP domain and ensure that your switch propagates the VLANs you will create in Exercise 15.2.

> **NOTE**
>
> These exercises assume that you have two Cisco Catalyst switches. As always, if you do not have the equipment, mentally go through the configuration and practice typing the commands as you would if you were configuring the switches.

Estimated Time: 10 minutes

1. Enter global configuration.

2. Configure your switch for VTP server mode (default, but for redundancy's sake).

3. Name the VTP domain GoldiLocks (remember domain name is case-sensitive).

4. Create a VTP password for VTP updates to be 3Bears (remember password is case-sensitive).

5. Exit global configuration and verify the configuration with the **show vtp status** command.

15.2 VLAN Creation and Assignment

In this exercise you create the VLANs that will be propagated by the VTP domain created in Exercise 15.1 and forwarded by the trunks in Exercise 15.3.

Estimated Time: 15 minutes

1. Enter global configuration.

2. Create VLAN 100 with the name 2hot.

3. Create VLAN 200 with the name 2cold.

4. Create VLAN 300 with the name justright.

5. Exit global configuration.

6. Assign VLAN 100 to interface Fast Ethernet 0/1.

7. Assign VLAN 200 to interface Fast Ethernet 0/2.

8. Assign VLAN 300 to interface Fast Ethernet 0/3

9. Verify VLAN configuration with the show vlan command.

15.3 802.1q Trunking

This exercise enables the VLAN traffic to span multiple switches with IEEE 802.1q trunking.

Estimated Time: 5 minutes

1. Connect the switches together with a cross-over ethernet cable using interface 0/12.

2. Configure Fast Ethernet 0/12 to 802.1q encapsulation.

3. Set the interface mode to trunking.

4. Verify your trunk with the `show interface trunk` command.

15.4 InterVLAN Routing

This exercise enables traffic to be routed from one VLAN to another with an external router.

Estimated Time: 15 minutes

1. Connect the switch to the router's Fast Ethernet interface with a straight-through cable.

2. Configure the switch port to become an 802.1q trunk (see Exercise 15.3).

3. Configure a subinterface for VLAN 100, 200, and 300 (set their encapsulation to dot1q and assign their respective VLANs).

4. Assign an IP address to each subinterface (from different subnets).

Review Questions

1. What are the characteristics of VLANs?

2. What are trunks and how do they work?

3. What is the purpose of VTP?

4. What are the characteristics of the three VTP modes?

5. Why is router-on-a-stick sometimes necessary in switched environments?

Exam Questions

1. Given the following output, which two facts can be determined? (Choose 2.)

```
Switch>show vtp status
VTP Version                    : 2
Configuration Revision         : 45
Maximum VLANs supported locally : 1005
Number of existing VLANs       : 10
VTP Operating Mode             : Client
VTP Domain Name                : CCNA
VTP Pruning Mode               : Enabled
VTP V2 Mode                    : Disabled
VTP Traps Generation           : Disabled
MD5 digest                     : 0xCC 0x69 0x27 0x01 0xC8 0xA8 0x59 0xD7
```

   ○ **A.** This switch will save VLAN information into NVRAM.

   ○ **B.** This switch will synchronize its VLAN database with updates starting with number 46 or above.

   ○ **C.** This switch can add, change, and delete VLANs.

   ○ **D.** This switch passes VTP advertisements from the server.

2. Considering the following output:

```
Switch>show vlan

VLAN Name                          Status    Ports
---- ------------------------      ------    ------
1    default                       active    Fa0/1, Fa0/2, Fa0/3, Fa0/4,
     Fa0/5,Fa0/6, Fa0/7, Fa0/8, Fa0/9
2    VLAN0002                      active
100  ExamCram                      active
200  ExamPrep                      active
```

   Which of the following is false?

   ○ **A.** Interfaces Fast Ethernet 0/1–0/9 are in the management domain.

   ○ **B.** Interfaces above Fast Ethernet 0/10 could be configured as a trunk.

   ○ **C.** Interface Fast Ethernet 0/10 is an access port.

   ○ **D.** VLAN 2 was not configured with a custom name.

3. Which of the following VTP modes save their VLAN information to NVRAM? (Choose 2.)

   ○ **A.** Transport

   ○ **B.** Client

   ○ **C.** Server

   ○ **D.** Transparent

4. Which is not a characteristic of VLANs?

○ **A.** Users can be moved easily because VLANs span multiple switches.

○ **B.** Users can be logically grouped according to their departments.

○ **C.** There is a separate instance of STP for each VLAN.

○ **D.** Broadcasts are not forwarded over trunks.

5. You want to connect your Cisco Catalyst switch to a Nortel switch. Which of the following is true?

○ **A.** 802.1q trunks should be used.

○ **B.** ISL trunks should be used.

○ **C.** VLAN configurations will be accepted by the Nortel switch if it is in VTP client mode.

○ **D.** Cisco is the only switch that can configure VLANs.

6. Which of the following would cause VLAN leakage?

○ **A.** Incorrect ISL configuration.

○ **B.** Native VLAN mismatch.

○ **C.** VTP passwords don't match.

○ **D.** Saggy VLAN diapers.

7. Given the following output from two switches, why are the VLAN databases not synchronized?

```
SwitchA>show vtp status
VTP Version                      : 2
Configuration Revision           : 45
Maximum VLANs supported locally  : 1005
Number of existing VLANs         : 10
VTP Operating Mode               : Server
VTP Domain Name                  : Examprep
VTP Pruning Mode                 : Enabled
VTP V2 Mode                      : Disabled
VTP Traps Generation             : Disabled
MD5 digest                       : 0xCC 0x69 0x27 0x01 0xC8 0xA8 0x59 0xD7
SwitchB>show vtp status
VTP Version                      : 2
Configuration Revision           : 45
Maximum VLANs supported locally  : 1005
Number of existing VLANs         : 10
VTP Operating Mode               : Client
VTP Domain Name                  : ExamPrep
VTP Pruning Mode                 : Enabled
VTP V2 Mode                      : Disabled
VTP Traps Generation             : Disabled
MD5 digest                       : 0xCC 0x69 0x27 0x01 0xC8 0xA8 0x59 0xD7
```

○ **A.** VTP versions are incorrect.

○ **B.** Passwords do not match.

○ **C.** Both devices should be set to server mode.

○ **D.** VTP domains do not match.

8. What can be determined from the following output?

```
Switch>show interface trunk

Port        Mode         Encapsulation Status       Native vlan
Fa0/24      on           802.1q        trunking     1

Port       Vlans allowed on trunk
Fa0/24      1-4094

Port       Vlans allowed and active in management domain
Fa0/24      1-4,100,200

Port       Vlans in spanning tree forwarding state and not pruned
Fa0/24      1-4,100,200
```

○ **A.** The trunk is proprietary to Cisco.

○ **B.** Ethernet frames from VLAN 1 will not be tagged over the trunk.

○ **C.** This trunk will create giant frames that will be dropped by non-Cisco devices.

○ **D.** Ethernet frames are being encapsulated with a 30-byte VLAN ID.

9. How do you associate VLANs to an interface in a router-on-a-stick configuration?

○ **A.** By creating a VLAN interface in the switch.

○ **B.** By creating the subinterface number to match the VLAN.

○ **C.** By having a separate physical interface for each VLAN.

○ **D.** By using the **encapsulation** command.

10. Which of the following is not a characteristic of router-on-a-stick?

○ **A.** The interface must be 10Mbps or higher.

○ **B.** The link must be a trunk.

○ **C.** Subinterfaces are used to route in between the VLANs.

○ **D.** The IP address assigned is used as the VLAN's default gateway.

Answers to Review Questions

1. VLANs are created in switches to segment broadcast domains at Layer 2. Departments in your organization can be assigned their own VLAN, which provides a logical segmentation in which traffic from one department does not interfere with that of another department. VLANs can span multiple switches, which simplifies administration when users need to move throughout the switched network.

2. Trunks are used to carry VLAN traffic from one switch to another switch. Frames are tagged with a VLAN identifier as they traverse the trunk link and are removed on the receiving switch. ISL is a Cisco proprietary method of trunking in which the original frame is encapsulated with a 26-byte header and a 4-byte CRC. IEEE 802.1q trunks insert a 4-byte VLAN identifier inside the ethernet frame.

3. VTP is a convenient Cisco proprietary Layer 2 protocol that enables switches to advertise VLAN configuration information to other switches in a VTP domain.

4. Server mode is the default VTP mode in which VTP advertisements are sent to other switches in the VTP domain. VLAN configurations in server mode are saved to the VLAN database. Client mode processes and forwards VTP advertisements from the VTP server. You cannot change any VLAN configurations or save the VLAN configuration in client mode. Transparent mode also forwards VTP advertisements from the VTP server; however, switches in transparent mode do not process the VTP advertisements. In transparent mode, you can configure VLANs and save them to NVRAM; however, these local VLANs are not advertised to other switches in the VTP domain.

5. Router-on-a-stick is used when you want to allow traffic from one VLAN to be routed into another VLAN. Router-on-a-stick requires a switch to trunk to a Layer 3 router. The router uses subinterfaces to logically separate the VLANs into virtual interfaces in which the router can route in between.

Answers to Exam Questions

1. **B, D.** Because this switch is operating in client mode, it synchronizes with updates received from the VTP server as long as the revision number is greater than its current revision number. It passes the advertisements from the VTP server to other switches in the VTP domain. Answer A is incorrect because client mode switches do not save their VLAN information into NVRAM. Answer C is incorrect because you cannot add, change, or delete VLANs in client mode.

2. **C.** Interface Fast Ethernet 0/10 could not be an access port, or it would be included in the list of interfaces assigned to a VLAN. Answer A is true because they are all assigned to VLAN 1. Answer B is true because the interface number does not show up in the `show vlan` output if it is a trunk. D is true because the VLAN name is VLAN0002, which is the default naming convention the IOS uses when a name isn't configured for a specific VLAN.

3. **C, D.** Server and Transparent VTP modes are the only modes that save their VLAN configuration to NVRAM. Answer A is incorrect because Transport is not a VTP mode. Answer B is incorrect because switches operating in Client mode do not save their VLAN information in NVRAM.

4. **D.** Broadcasts will still be forwarded over trunks to other switches in the same VLAN. Broadcasts in one VLAN, however, do not affect other VLANs. Answers A, B, and C are all characteristics that apply to VLANs.

5. **A.** Because you are connecting to a Nortel switch, you must use a standard method of trunking (IEEE 802.1q). ISL and VTP are Cisco proprietary functions. Answer B is incorrect because ISL is a Cisco proprietary trunk encapsulation. Answer C is incorrect because VTP is a Cisco proprietary protocol. Answer D is false because other switch manufacturers support VLAN configurations.

6. **B.** VLAN leakage occurs when there is a VLAN mismatch on a trunk link with 802.1q. Answer A is incorrect because ISL does not use native VLANs. Answer C is incorrect because VTP does not affect VLAN leakage. Answer D is incorrect because switches don't wear diapers.

7. **D.** The domain names are case sensitive. If they do not match, the switches cannot synchronize their VLAN database information. Answer A is incorrect because both switches are operating in the same VPT version. Based upon the fact that the MD5 digest of the VTP password is identical, Answer B is incorrect. Answer C is incorrect because both switches do not need to be in server mode in order for the switches to exchange VLAN configurations via VTP.

8. **B.** Because the trunk is 802.1q with a native VLAN of 1, ethernet frames originating from VLAN 1 going over this trunk are not tagged. Answers A, C, and D are incorrect because they are characteristics of ISL.

9. **D.** The `encapsulation` command is used to assign VLANs to a subinterface. Answer A is incorrect because SVIs are in Layer 3 switches, not external routers. Answer B is a good design practice, but does not assign the VLANs to the subinterface. Answer C is incorrect because router-on-a-stick is over one interface.

10. **A.** Because the interface must be a trunk, the speed of the link should be 100Mbps or greater. Answers B, C, and D are all characteristics of router-on-a-stick.

Suggested Readings and Resources

1. Barnes, David and Sakandar, Basir. *Cisco LAN Switching Fundamentals*. Cisco Press, 2004.

2. Castelli, Matthew J. *LAN Switching first-step*. Cisco Press, 2004.

3. "Virtual Local Area Networks," www.firewall.cx.

4. "Configuring VLANs," Catalyst 3560 Configuration Guide on www.cisco.com.

16

Implementing Switch Security

Objectives

This chapter covers the following Cisco-specific objectives for the "Configure, verify and troubleshoot a switch with VLANs and interswitch communications" section of the 640-802 CCNA exam:

▶ **Implement basic switch security (including: port security, unassigned ports, trunk access, management vlan other than vlan1, etc.)**

▶ **Interpret the output of various show and debug commands to verify the operational status of a Cisco switched network**

Outline

Study Strategies

▶ Part of being thorough in securing your switched network is to think like an attacker. With that in mind, try to consider ways in which your network is vulnerable and how you would go about gaining access if you were the attacker.

▶ Many of the topics discussed in this chapter can also be applied to securing your router. Keep that in mind when reading these topics as a refresher on how to secure your Cisco devices.

▶ Read the information presented in this chapter, paying special attention to tables, Notes, and Exam Alerts.

▶ Complete the Challenge and the Exercises at the end of the chapter. The exercises will solidify the concepts that you have learned in the previous sections.

▶ Complete the Exam Questions at the end of the chapter. They are designed to simulate the types of questions you will be asked on the ICND1, ICND2, and CCNA exams.

Introduction

Securing a network is an endless task. Every day there are new scripts and exploits, new vulnerabilities, and new methods to gain access to your network. Our job as Cisco administrators is to stay ahead of the game as much as possible and make it as difficult as possible to gain access.

As discussed in Chapter 4, "General Network Security," the basis of any good security implementation is a thorough security policy. Switched networks must be a pivotal piece of that security policy; however, they are typically the most overlooked. The fact that the LAN is tucked away inside your network provides a false sense of security, especially because some of your biggest threats might be the users attached to the switched network. This chapter examines how to secure access to the Cisco devices in your LAN as well as the traffic that flows through it.

Securing Physical Access to the Catalyst Switch

Similar to troubleshooting, our first layer of defense for securing the switched network should start at the Physical layer. Specifically, we need to secure access to the physical switch itself and the cables that are connected to it. It doesn't take a skilled attacker to physically destroy a switched network to which he or she has complete access.

With that being said, the first and probably most critical step of securing your network is to ensure that the switches themselves are secured in a cool room in which only you or those authorized have access. If users have physical access to the switches, they can easily console into the switch and perform a password-recovery exercise (easily found on the Internet) just by repowering the switch and holding down a button during power-up. Even unintentional attacks such as custodial staff unplugging your switches to run the vacuum can occur easily if not secured correctly. If you can, also make sure that the Ethernet cabling between the switches and end devices is not in plain sight and therefore can't be easily damaged. You don't want the last act by a fired employee to be taking down your entire network by ripping out your existing wiring.

> **EXAM ALERT**
>
> Physically securing Cisco devices is an integral step in implementing a secure Cisco network.

Securing Terminal Access to the Catalyst Switch

After we have ensured that the switch is physically secured, the next layer of defense to implement is securing terminal access to the switch so that attackers cannot perform reconnaissance or manipulate configurations. Because there are several ways to gain access to the Cisco IOS, due diligence is required to ensure that all terminal connections are secured.

To start, the first logical terminal access to secure is the console and auxiliary port. Many might ask why, because we already physically secured the switch. To answer a question with a question, would you have an account at a bank that leaves your money out on a table because they have an alert security guard standing at the door? A layered defensive approach entails having security measures at each step of the way so that attackers will have many obstacles in their way in achieving their objective.

To secure access to the console and aux port, the simplest defense you can use is securing them with a password. Just as in router configurations, this is achieved in the line configuration using the `password` command. It is also a good idea to make sure that your passwords are strong passwords containing at least eight characters and that they have a combination of numbers, symbols, and lower and uppercase letters:

```
Switch(config)# line console 0
Switch(config-line)# login
Switch(config-line)# password EggsAmKr@m
Switch(config-line)# exit
Switch(config)# line auxiliary 0
Switch(config-line)# login
Switch(config-line)# password EggsAmPr3p
```

What's more, you can create a local username and password combination that is stored in the configuration. This username and password will be required to be entered when someone attaches to the console and gets an EXEC prompt. The only difference in the configuration is that you no longer need to specify a password in the line configuration, because you achieved that in defining the username and password combination, and you also must use the keyword `local` in the `login` command. This keyword tells the IOS to use the local username and password combination that can be found in the configuration:

```
Switch(config)# username jchambers password Sysco-Prez
Switch(config)# line console 0
Switch(config-line)# login local
Switch(config-line)# exit
Switch(config)# line auxiliary 0
Switch(config-line)# login local
```

Now, when someone attaches to the console or aux port, he or she is prompted for a username and password, such as the following:

```
Press RETURN to get started.
User Access Verification

Username:jchambers
Password:
Switch>
```

> **NOTE**
>
> If you configure the console and aux login to use the username and password using the `login local` command and a password configuration is present on the line as well, the IOS uses the username and password over the password line configuration.

> **TIP**
>
> You can use a special username and password command that encrypts the password similarly to the `enable secret` command. Conveniently enough, the command is `username` *username* `secret` *password*. This applies an MD5 hash of the password so that it cannot be easily acquired if the configuration is accessed.

To Telnet or Not to Telnet

Recall that although Telnet is a convenient way to gain EXEC access to the Cisco device, it also is extremely dangerous, because everything that is sent using Telnet is in clear text and can be intercepted by anyone eavesdropping on the session. With that being said, whenever possible, use SSH for remote terminal connectivity to the Cisco device. Recall that the configuration for enabling SSH on a Cisco device is as follows:

1. Change the default hostname of the Cisco device.
2. Configure a domain name with the `ip domain-name` command.
3. Generate the RSA key with at least a 1024-bit key with the `crypto key generate rsa` command.
4. Create a username and password.

A recommended third step in this process, however, is to limit the vty lines on the Cisco device to accept only SSH as an input protocol. In other words, this step entails disallowing Telnet into the vty lines. The command to limit the terminal input on the vty lines is `transport input SSH` on the vty line configuration:

```
Switch(config)# line vty 0 15
Switch(config-line)# transport input SSH
```

When you exclude the keyword `telnet` in the `transport input` command, only SSH is allowed as a terminal input protocol on all the vty lines.

> **EXAM ALERT**
>
> To specify SSH as the only secure terminal input, use the transport input SSH command.

Whether you are using SSH or are only left with using Telnet, make sure you have properly secured user EXEC access through the vty lines using the same methods as the aux and console. Specifically, configure a password on the vty lines or use the `login local` command to prompt for a username and password.

As a final defensive measure on these vty lines, you can also specify an IP or IP subnet that is permitted to gain access to these vty lines. If the source IP address of the Telnet or SSH session is not from the permitted IP(s), the session will not be allowed to connect. This command is the `access-class` command; it is discussed in detail in Chapter 19, "Using Cisco Access Lists."

Additional IOS Security Practices

In addition to securing access to Cisco IOS, it is also a good idea to secure the contents of the configuration using some practical and simple configuration steps that we have discussed. This list is not exhaustive by any means, but it is a good beginning point:

▶ Encrypt your enable password to privileged EXEC using the `enable secret` command.

▶ Encrypt all other clear-text passwords in the configuration using `service password-encryption`.

▶ Create a login banner that warns against unauthorized access attempts to the EXEC prompt.

▶ Disable EXEC access on unused terminal access ports (such as aux ports) using the `no exec` command in the line configuration.

▶ Limit how long the terminal session stays idle to not exceed one minute with the `exec-timeout` command (`exec-timeout 1 0`).

Challenge

Now that you have a basic checklist of security dos and don'ts for physical security and connectivity to a switch, it is time to evaluate your existing switched network and consider if your switches are secured. If you do not have a switch network, imagine that you just received a switch, and think about what you should do to secure it. Then check yourself with the following questions:

1. Are the switch and its cables physically secured?

2. Are the console and auxiliary port secured?

3. If your switch has a supported IOS, are you running SSH for remote management?

4. If you do not have SSH, have you fully secured your vty lines for Telnet?

5. Are all passwords encrypted?

Layer 2 Security

Feeling satisfied with securing access to the physical switch and cables as well as access to the Catalyst switch IOS, our next step on our secure ladder is to get to the core of our switching functions and secure the possible vulnerabilities that occur at the Data Link layer.

The transparent functions that our switches perform, such as MAC address learning and forwarding, as well as VLAN broadcast domain segmentation, are taken for granted because they are just that: transparent. Consequently, these are the most overlooked aspects of switch security today, because we naturally assume that the default behavior of the switch's design is how it should be. Any thought of securing that behavior goes against the switch's basic operations. In the following sections, you will see that although the extra configuration steps might involve slightly more work, the end result is that you won't lose sleep wondering when the next attack might cause your cell phone to go off.

Port Security

Objective:

▶ Implement basic switch security (including: port security, unassigned ports, trunk access, management vlan other than vlan1, etc.)

Anybody who has physical access to the ports of your switches can easily attach another switch or hub to enable more devices to be on the switched network. If you want to limit the number of MAC addresses that can be dynamically learned on a switch port (for environments such as college campuses and hotels), you can enable the port security feature on your switch ports that are accessible to end users. With the `switchport port-security` commands, you can define the maximum number of MAC addresses to be learned on an access port. If this maximum number is exceeded, the switch port is put in an error-disabled state (by default) in which you have to reenable the interface by administratively shutting it down (with the `shutdown` command) and reenabling the port with the `no shutdown` command. Although this is a bit drastic, it is a surefire way to ensure that switch administrators know where the violation occurred and help identify the users who might be responsible.

To configure this port security functionality, you must enable this port security on each interface, followed by the maximum MAC count allowed on the interface (the default is 1). For example, if you wanted to restrict the number of MAC addresses allowed to 10, you would use the following configuration on the port:

```
Switch(config-if)# switchport port-security
Switch(config-if)# switchport port-security maximum 10
```

Furthermore, you can change the default action when a violation occurs on the secured port with the `switchport port-security violation` command:

```
Switch(config-if)# switchport port-security violation {protect ¦ restrict ¦ shutdown}
```

The default action is shutdown, which puts the port in the error-disabled state, as mentioned earlier. You can also choose to have the port increase a violation counter and alert an administrator using an SNMP trap with the `restrict` keyword. The `protect` keyword only allows traffic from the secure port; it drops packets from other MAC addresses until the number of MAC addresses drops below the maximum.

> **EXAM ALERT**
>
> The `switchport port-security` maximum command restricts how many MAC addresses can be learned on a switch interface. The `switchport port-security violation shutdown` command instructs the switch to disable the port when a violation occurs.

Static MAC with Port Security

The default state of Cisco Catalyst switches is to learn MAC addresses dynamically. For security purposes, you can assign static MAC addresses to an interface to ensure that a MAC address is recognized on only a specific interface. For instance, if you want to make sure that no one tries to connect to your switch and spoof (falsely assume the identity of) your server's MAC address of FA23.239B.2349, you could use the following port security command to statically assign that MAC address to the Fast Ethernet 0/2 interface:

```
Switch(config)# interface fastethernet 0/2
Switch(config-if)# switchport port-security
Switch(config-if)# switchport port-security mac-address FA23.239B.2349
```

This configuration leaves the maximum secure MAC address at its default of 1. If the switch receives another MAC address on Fast Ethernet 0/2, or the MAC address FA23.239B.2349 is seen entering a port other than Fast Ethernet 0/2, the port is disabled.

Port security also can save you some configuration by learning *sticky* secure MAC addresses. With the command `switchport port-security mac-address sticky`, the switch automatically configures the addresses already dynamically learned on the interface, as well as any new MAC addresses (up to the maximum) to be secure MAC addresses. These sticky addresses actually get added as sticky secure MAC configuration line entries in the running configuration. If you save the configuration and reboot the switch, those secure MAC addresses won't need to be relearned.

> **EXAM ALERT**
>
> Sticky addresses are secure MAC addresses that are dynamically learned on the interface.

Verifying Port Security

Objective:

▶ Interpret the output of various show and debug commands to verify the operational status of a Cisco switched network

To verify the port security configuration parameters on the interface, as well as the number of security violations that have occurred on that interface, use the `show port-security interface` *interface* command:

```
Switch# show port-security interface fa0/2
Port Security                   : Enabled
Port Status                     : Secure-up
Violation Mode                  : Shutdown
Aging Time                      : 0 mins
Aging Type                      : Absolute
SecureStatic Address Aging      : Disabled
Maximum MAC Addresses           : 1
Total MAC Addresses             : 1
Configured MAC Addresses        : 1
Sticky MAC Addresses            : 0
Last Source Address             : fa23.239b.2349
Security Violation Count        : 0
```

Based on this output, you can see that port security is enabled and is not in a disabled state. The default actions for violations (shutdown) and maximum MAC addresses are configured on Fast Ethernet 0/2, with a configured MAC address of fa23.239b.2349.

To verify your configured port security addresses, use the `show port-security address` command:

```
Switch# show port-security address
            Secure Mac Address Table
-----------------------------------------------------------------
Vlan    Mac Address     Type              Ports   Remaining Age
                                                     (mins)

----    -----------     ----              -----   ------------
   1    fa23.239b.2349  SecureConfigured   Fa0/2      -

-----------------------------------------------------------------
Total Addresses in System (excluding one mac per port)    : 0
Max Addresses limit in System (excluding one mac per port) : 1024
```

Here you can see that your statically configured secure MAC address is configured on Fast Ethernet 0/2. Compare that output to a dynamically learned sticky MAC address, which shows the type as SecureDynamic as opposed to SecureConfigured:

```
Switch# show port-security address
          Secure Mac Address Table
-----------------------------------------------------------------
Vlan    Mac Address        Type          Ports   Remaining Age
                                                    (mins)
----    -----------        ----          -----   -------------
   1    fa23.239b.2349     SecureDynamic  Fa0/2      -
-----------------------------------------------------------------
Total Addresses in System (excluding one mac per port)    : 0
Max Addresses limit in System (excluding one mac per port) : 1024
```

VLAN Security

Objective:

▶ Implement basic switch security (including: port security, unassigned ports, trunk access, management vlan other than vlan1, etc.)

Considering that the default VLAN assigned to every interface is VLAN 1, and that the default management VLAN that houses CDP, VTP, and the switch's IP address is also VLAN 1, what VLAN would you choose if you wanted to attack a switched network? All you would essentially have to do is get connected to an unconfigured interface and start determining the switch's IP address and gaining access to that switch.

The way to mitigate this is actually simple and can be achieved in three ways:

1. Administratively shut down all unused interfaces. Even though this would be an administrative pain, it would ensure that no one gets access to the switched network unless you or another authorized administrator grants them access.

2. Configure a different VLAN to act solely as the management VLAN and remain separate from user data. VLAN 1 is typically used because older switches could only assign an IP to this interface. Newer IOS versions allow you to configure any VLAN you choose as the management VLAN by configuring the IP address on another created VLAN such as this:

```
Switch(config)# interface vlan 99
Switch(config-if)# ip address 172.16.1.100 255.255.0.0
Switch(config-if)# no shutdown
```

   This VLAN should be assigned only to access ports that have management stations connected to them that require remote connectivity to the switch.

3. Assign all unused ports to an unused VLAN other than VLAN 1. If you create a dummy VLAN and assign it to all interfaces, anyone who gains access won't be able to gain access to VLAN 1.

EXAM ALERT

Remember that the three ways to secure unassigned ports are to shut them down, change the management VLAN, and assign another VLAN besides VLAN 1 to them.

These steps will secure your access ports with VLANs assigned to them, but what about the interfaces that carry all the VLAN traffic? To this point, you have to consider trunk links a prime target for attacks as well, because they carry all the VLAN traffic. In essence, why buy the cow when you can break into the dairy farm?

To secure the trunk links, you can manually configure which VLANs are allowed to traverse the trunk links. Specifically, if you have changed your management VLAN, as mentioned previously, you can be sure that only switches that need access to that management VLAN receive that traffic over their trunks. Recall that by default, all VLANs are allowed over trunk links. By manually configuring which VLANs are allowed over each trunk, you limit the amount of data an attacker has access to. The command `switchport trunk allowed vlan vlan_list` on a trunk interface manually specifies which VLANs are allowed to traverse the trunk. The `vlan_list` is similar to the `interface range` command, where the list is either a single VLAN, a comma-separated list of VLANs, or a hyphenated list of VLANs. For example, to allow only VLANs 1 to 50 and VLANs 60 and 70, the configuration would look like this:

```
Switch(config)# interface fastethernet0/1
Switch(config-if)# switchport mode trunk
Switch(config-if)# switchport trunk allowed vlan 1-50,60,70
```

To verify the VLANs that are allowed over the trunk, use the `show interfaces trunk` command:

```
Switch#show interfaces trunk
Port      Mode        Encapsulation  Status        Native vlan
Fa0/1     desirable   802.1q         trunking      1

Port      Vlans allowed on trunk
Fa0/1     1-4094

Port      Vlans allowed and active in management domain
Fa0/1     1-50,60,70

Port      Vlans in spanning tree forwarding state and not pruned
Fa0/1     1-50,60,70
```

Notice that the first section of the output does not specify the VLANs that are specifically allowed. That is because this first output illustrates which VLANs are allowed on the trunk. The management domain and spanning tree VLANs actually reflect the specific VLANs that we configured to traverse the link.

Cisco has also made these configurations simpler by adding some keywords that might simplify the VLAN list. For example, with the add and remove keywords, you can specify if you want to append or delete any VLANs in the current list of allowed VLANs. For example, if you wanted to add VLAN 75 to the preceding configuration and remove VLAN 70 from the allowed list, you would configure it like the following:

```
Switch(config-if)# switchport trunk allowed vlan add 75
Switch(config-if)# switchport trunk allowed vlan remove 70
```

Notice how this change affects the VLAN list when we enter the show interfaces trunk command now:

```
Switch# show interfaces trunk
Port      Mode         Encapsulation Status        Native vlan
Fa0/1     desirable    802.1q        trunking      1

Port      Vlans allowed on trunk
Fa0/1     1-4094

Port      Vlans allowed and active in management domain
Fa0/1     1-50,60,75

Port      Vlans in spanning tree forwarding state and not pruned
Fa0/1     1-50,60,75
```

Finally, Cisco also added the keyword except, which can be translated as "all VLANs except the VLANs in this list." For example, if you wanted all VLANs except VLANs 60 to 70, you would enter this command:

```
Switch(config-if)# switchport trunk allowed vlan except 60-70
```

Again, notice the changed VLAN list when you enter the show interfaces trunk command now:

```
Switch# show interfaces trunk
Port      Mode         Encapsulation Status        Native vlan
Fa0/1     desirable    802.1q        trunking      1

Port      Vlans allowed on trunk
Fa0/1     1-4094

Port      Vlans allowed and active in management domain
Fa0/1     1-59,80-4094

Port      Vlans in spanning tree forwarding state and not pruned
Fa0/1     1-59,80-4094
```

VTP Passwords

In our discussions of routing protocols in earlier chapters, we discussed how to authenticate the updates sent by other routers so that attackers cannot inject false routes into a routing table and hijack traffic or disrupt normal routing. This is just as important with VTP updates between switches. An attacker can inject false VLAN information in VTP updates and bring down a switched network quite easily as long as he or she knows the VTP domain and has the highest revision number in the VTP update. To keep this from happening, be sure you take the extra step and configure passwords for switches participating in the VTP domain with the `vtp password` command:

```
Switch(config)# vtp password examprep
Setting device VLAN database password to examprep
```

"See"DP

This might sound like Cisco sacrilege, but you should consider disabling CDP on switch interfaces that do not need it, such as edge ports connected to end devices. If you consider the information someone can learn from CDP, you'll realize the major security liability it can be. From just a single CDP multicast, an attacker could learn the hostname, the local port on the switch that sent the CDP message, and the switch's IP address. With this information and strong motivation, it is only a matter of time before your switch and its networks are infiltrated.

Recall that to disable CDP on individual interfaces, you must configure `no cdp enable` on each interface. If you have no need for CDP, disable it globally on the switch with the `no cdp run` command.

Chapter Summary

Securing a switched network entails trying to protect all Layer 1 aspects of the switch, including access to the IOS itself. In addition, it is imperative to secure the switch's Layer 2 operations so that an attacker doesn't interrupt or damage the switched network.

Securing the Physical layer entails ensuring that the switch and its cables are in a secure environment where users cannot inflict damage on them. This step also gives added protection from users gaining console access to the switch to gain information to attack the network or attack or manipulate the switch itself. Leveraging the IOS's internal security measures such as logins and passwords for terminal access is also ideal in building a layered defense. When possible, it is also recommended that you use SSH instead of Telnet for remote access to the IOS, because the communications between the management computer and the switch are secured.

Data Link layer security involves securing individual ports using port security. Port security protects ports by defining a maximum number of MAC addresses that are allowed to be dynamically learned on an individual port. You can also manually specify the MAC address(es) that are allowed to be present in the source address of the Ethernet frame when entering that port. This can be a single static configured MAC address, or you can configure sticky learning, and the addresses will be dynamically added to the configuration. When a port security violation occurs, the default action is to disable the interface. When this occurs, you have to shut down the interface and administratively bring it back up. You can configure the switch port to just report the violation (restrict), or you can reject frames from nonsecure MAC addresses until the number of MAC addresses falls under the limit (protect).

You should also secure unassigned ports that are automatically assigned to the default management VLAN (VLAN 1) by either administratively shutting down the interface, changing the management VLAN, or assigning a dummy VLAN to the unused interfaces. Trunks can be secured by allowing only specific VLANs (such as the management VLAN) to traverse to switches that specifically require access to those VLANs.

VTP should be secured using VTP passwords so that switches that receive the VTP update can authenticate it. In addition, CDP reveals potentially dangerous information in its multicasts; thus, it is recommended that you disable CDP globally or on interfaces that do not require it.

Key Terms

- ▶ Port security
- ▶ Error-disabled
- ▶ Restrict
- ▶ Protect
- ▶ Sticky secure MAC addresses
- ▶ switchport trunk allowed vlan

Apply Your Knowledge

Exercises

16.1 The Impregnable IOS

Now it is time to take the security features you learned about in this chapter and apply them to our switch. To start, we will walk through an exercise of securing access to the IOS and the passwords in the configuration.

Estimated Time: 15 minutes

1. Console into your switch.

2. Configure a username and password. If supported, make the password secured with an MD5 hash.

3. Change the default hostname, and configure a domain name for the switch.

4. Generate a 1024-bit RSA key.

5. Configure the console's login to prompt for the username and password.

6. Disable the auxiliary port from getting EXEC access.

7. Configure the login of the vty lines to prompt for a username and password.

8. Allow SSH only on the vty lines (remove Telnet).

9. Limit the timeout for EXEC sessions to 45 seconds.

10. Assign an MD5 hashed enable password.

11. Encrypt all clear-text passwords.

Your configuration should be similar to the following:

```
! Step 2
Switch(config)# username artvandelay secret Imp0rt3xp0rt
! Step 3
Switch(config)# ip domain-name examprep.com
Switch(config)# hostname Swtch2950
! Step 4
Swtch2950(config)# crypto key generate rsa
The name for the keys will be: Swtch2950.examprep.com
Choose the size of the key modulus in the range of 360 to 2048 for your General
Purpose Keys. Choosing a key modulus greater than 512 may take a few minutes.

How many bits in the modulus [512]: 1024
Generating RSA keys ...
[OK]
7w1d: %SSH-5-ENABLED: SSH 1.99 has been enabled
! Step 5
Swtch2950(config)# line console 0
```

```
Swtch2950(config-line)# login local
Swtch2950(config-line)# exit
! Step 6
Swtch2950(config)# line auxiliary 0
Swtch2950(config-line)# no exec
Swtch2950(config-line)# exit
! Step 7
Swtch2950(config)# line vty 0 15
Swtch2950(config-line)# login local
! Step 8
Swtch2950(config-line)# transport input ssh
! Step 9
Switch(config-line)# exec-timeout 0 45
Switch(config-line)# exit
! Step 10
Swtch2950(config)# enable secret MD5p@ssw0rd
! Step 11
Swtch2950(config)# service password-encryption
```

16.2 Layer 2 Security To-Do

With our switch secured, it is time to secure the switch's Layer 2 operations.

Estimated Time: 10 minutes

1. Enable port security on ports 1 through 5 using the `interface range` command.

2. Set the maximum number of dynamically learned MAC addresses to 10.

3. Change the default action of violations to disallow traffic from any newly learned MAC addresses over our maximum.

4. Configure the sixth interface to have only a single MAC address of 1234.5678.ABCD.

5. Configure the seventh interface to have secure MAC addresses sticky-learned.

6. Disable CDP globally.

7. Create VLAN 50.

8. Make this VLAN your management VLAN by assigning an IP address to it.

9. Configure the twelfth interface as a trunk.

10. Allow all VLANs except VLAN 50 to traverse the trunk.

Your configuration should be similar to the following:

```
! Step 1
Swtch2950(config)# interface range fastethernet 0/1-5
Swtch2950(config-if)# switchport port-security
! Step 2
Swtch2950(config-if)# switchport port-security maximum 10
! Step 3
```

```
Swtch2950(config-if)# switchport port-security violation protect
Swtch2950(config-if)# exit
! Step 4
Swtch2950(config)# interface fastethernet 0/6
Swtch2950(config-if)# switchport port-security mac-address 1234.5678.ABCD
Swtch2950(config-if)# exit
! Step 5
Swtch2950(config)# interface fastethernet 0/7
Swtch2950(config-if)# switchport port-security mac-address sticky
Swtch2950(config-if)# exit
! Step 6
Swtch2950(config)# no cdp run
! Step 7
Swtch2950(config)# vlan 50
Swtch2950(config-vlan)# exit
! Step 8
Swtch2950(config)# interface vlan 50
Swtch2950(config-if)# ip address 172.16.1.100 255.255.0.0
Swtch2950(config-if)# no shutdown
Swtch2950(config-if)# exit
! Step 9
Swtch2950(config)# interface fastethernet 0/12
Swtch2950(config-if)# switchport mode trunk
! Step 10
Swtch2950(config-if)# switchport trunk allowed vlan except 50
Swtch2950(config-if)# exit
```

Review Questions

1. What is the significance of securing physical access to a switch?

2. How can you harden (make secure) the Cisco IOS?

3. How can you secure the management VLAN?

4. How can you ensure that only one specific end device is attached to a switch port?

5. Why could CDP be a potential security risk?

Exam Questions

1. Which of the following is not a violation action of port security?

   ○ **A.** Protect

   ○ **B.** Shut down

   ○ **C.** Notify

   ○ **D.** Restrict

2. Which is not a recommended way to secure unassigned ports?

   ○ **A.** Assign a dummy VLAN.

   ○ **B.** Change the native VLAN.

   ○ **C.** Change the management VLAN.

   ○ **D.** Shut down unused interfaces.

3. Which commands resulted in the following output? (Choose two)

```
Switch# show interfaces trunk
Port       Mode         Encapsulation Status        Native vlan
Fa0/1      desirable    802.1q        trunking      1

Port       Vlans allowed on trunk
Fa0/1      1-4094

Port       Vlans allowed and active in management domain
Fa0/1      1-100,102-4094

Port       Vlans in spanning tree forwarding state and not pruned
Fa0/1      1-100,102-4094
```

   ○ **A.** Switch(config-if)# **switchport trunk allowed vlan except 101**

   ○ **B.** Switch(config-if)# **switchport trunk disallowed vlan 101**

   ○ **C.** Switch(config-if)# **switchport trunk except vlan 101**

   ○ **D.** Switch(config-if)# **switchport trunk allowed vlan remove 101**

4. Which of the following is not a recommended security implementation for securing the Catalyst switch?

   ○ **A.** SSH

   ○ **B.** Disable the console port.

   ○ **C.** Configure the login and password for the vty lines.

   ○ **D.** Allow only specific management IP address(es) into the vty lines.

5. Which command produced the following output?

```
Switch# show port-security address
          Secure Mac Address Table
-------------------------------------------------------------------
Vlan    Mac Address        Type            Ports   Remaining Age
                                                       (mins)
----    -----------        ----            -----   ------------
```

```
   1     1234.5678.9ABF     SecureConfigured      Fa0/9         -
---------------------------------------------------------------------
Total Addresses in System (excluding one mac per port)     : 0
Max Addresses limit in System (excluding one mac per port) : 1024
```

- ○ **A.** Switch(config-if)# **switchport port-security sticky**

- ○ **B.** Switch(config-if)# **switchport port-security mac-address 1234.5678.9abf**

- ○ **C.** Switch(config-if)# **switchport port-security mac-address sticky**

- ○ **D.** Switch(config-if)# **switchport port-security 1234.5678.9abf**

6. Given the following:

```
Switch# show port-security interface fa0/6
Port Security                    : Enabled
Port Status                      : Err-disabled
Violation Mode                   : Shutdown
Aging Time                       : 0 mins
Aging Type                       : Absolute
SecureStatic Address Aging       : Disabled
Maximum MAC Addresses            : 1
Total MAC Addresses              : 2
Configured MAC Addresses         : 0
Sticky MAC Addresses             : 0
Last Source Address              : fa53.c39b.af34
Security Violation Count         : 1
```

which of the following is a possible cause of the output?

- ○ **A.** Fast Ethernet 0/6 is receiving traffic and working correctly.

- ○ **B.** A static MAC address has been configured on Fast Ethernet 0/6.

- ○ **C.** Fast Ethernet 0/6 is learning sticky MAC addresses.

- ○ **D.** Fast Ethernet 0/6 is shut down because a violation has occurred.

7. Why is the following output false?

```
Switch# show port-security interface fa0/2
Port Security                    : Enabled
Port Status                      : Secure-up
Violation Mode                   : Shutdown
Aging Time                       : 0 mins
Aging Type                       : Absolute
SecureStatic Address Aging       : Disabled
Maximum MAC Addresses            : 10
```

```
Total MAC Addresses                : 50
Configured MAC Addresses           : 0
Sticky MAC Addresses               : 0
Last Source Address                : de26.287b.2490
Security Violation Count           : 0
```

- ○ **A.** There are more MAC addresses than the maximum allowed and no violations.

- ○ **B.** You cannot have the violation action be shutdown unless static secure MAC addresses are configured.

- ○ **C.** Sticky addresses must be configured if there is more than one MAC address.

- ○ **D.** The maximum MAC addresses cannot be changed from the default value of 1.

8. After changing the management VLAN to a VLAN other than VLAN 1, you lose SSH access to the switch. Which of the following is not a valid reason why?

- ○ **A.** The new management VLAN interface was not administratively enabled.

- ○ **B.** The port of the management computer has to be assigned to the new management VLAN.

- ○ **C.** The Layer 3 gateway must have access to the new management VLAN if the switch is on a network other than the management PC.

- ○ **D.** The management station's ARP entry has not timed out for the old VLAN interface.

9. Which of the following is false regarding what happens when you use the `login local` command on line configurations?

- ○ **A.** The switch uses the username and password configured from the global configuration.

- ○ **B.** You are prompted for a login and password as long as you don't use the `password` command on the line configuration.

- ○ **C.** This command can be configured on vty lines, the auxiliary port, and the console port.

- ○ **D.** The password can be encrypted using the `username` *username* `secret` *password* command.

10. Which of the following is not a default state of switches?

- ○ **A.** VLANs allowed on the trunk are all but the management VLAN.

- ○ **B.** Port security violation action is shut down.

- ○ **C.** Maximum number of MAC addresses learned on port security-enabled interfaces is 1.

- ○ **D.** Management VLAN is VLAN 1.

Answers to Review Questions

1. An attacker can maliciously cause physical damage to the switch and/or the cables connected to the switch and ultimately bring down your network. If the attacker wants to covertly attack the network or gain unauthorized access to other devices or networks, he or she can also gain console access to the switch and perform password recovery to reconfigure the switch or discover other devices. For these reasons, it is imperative to ensure that the physical equipment and cables are secured from unauthorized users.

2. The first step to hardening the Cisco IOS is to secure all points of terminal entry to the IOS. This entails assigning passwords (or usernames/password combinations) to the console, aux, and vty lines. Additionally, if any of these services are not being used, you should disable EXEC access. For remote access, you should use SSH over Telnet if possible and allow SSH only on the vty lines.

   After terminal access is secured, you should ensure that all passwords are encrypted in the configuration, disable CDP on interfaces that do not require it, and decrease the amount of time an EXEC session can remain idle.

3. The best way to secure the management VLAN is to assign a different VLAN interface as the management VLAN. You can achieve this easily by assigning the IP address to a VLAN specifically created for management (other than VLAN 1). In addition, disallow that VLAN from traversing trunk links to other switches that do not require it.

4. To ensure that a single device is attached to a switch port, enable port security and allow only one MAC address as the maximum (the default). For additional security, manually or dynamically (using sticky learning) specify the device's MAC address.

5. CDP advertises pertinent information for discovery and troubleshooting. Information such as CDP-advertising ports, hostname, and IP addresses can be intercepted and used to attack the switch.

Answers to Exam Questions

1. **C.** Notify is not a valid action of port security. The three actions that can be configured are shut down, protect, and restrict.

2. **B.** Changing the native VLAN will not secure an unused port; in fact, it might cause VLAN leakage. Assigning a dummy VLAN, shutting down unused interfaces, and changing the management VLAN are all viable ways of protecting unassigned ports.

3. **A, D.** Based upon the output of the `show interfaces trunk` command, all the VLANs are allowed over the trunk except VLAN 101. Answer A is correct because that command tells the switch to allow all VLANs except VLAN 101. Answer D is also correct because it specifies that VLAN 101 should be removed from the list (which, by default, is all VLANs). Answers B and C are incorrect because they are not valid command syntax.

4. **B.** Answer B is not a recommended security implementation because you will always require console access as a failsafe to gain access to Cisco devices. SSH, login/passwords for vty lines, and specifying management IP address(es) of management station(s) are all recommended security implementations.

5. **B.** Because the output indicates that the MAC address is SecureConfigured, it must have been manually configured using the `switchport port-security mac-address 1234.5678.9abf` command. Answers A and D are not valid command syntax for port security. Answer C is valid syntax, but the output for the MAC address would show up as SecureDynamic.

6. **D.** The port status of the output indicates that it is in an error-disabled state, which means that a violation has occurred and that the default action (shutdown) has disabled the port. Because the maximum MAC addresses is configured as 1, and it has learned two MAC addresses, it is safe to say that this is the cause of the violation. Answer A is incorrect because the port is not in a Secure-Up (active) state. Answer B is incorrect because the count of configured MAC addresses is 0. Answer C is incorrect as well because the output indicates that the sticky MAC address count is also 0.

7. **A.** If the number of MAC addresses is exceeded, security violations should increase, and the configured action should take place (in this case, shutdown). Answer B is incorrect because you can have the violation be shutdown on dynamic, sticky-learned, or static MAC addresses. Answer C is incorrect because it is not required (although it might be more practical) to configure sticky addresses when there is more than one secure MAC address. Answer D is incorrect because the maximum MAC addresses can be configured to be more than 1.

8. **D.** Changing the management VLAN does not change the switch's MAC address. Thus, any device that has an ARP entry tying the IP address of the switch to its MAC address will not be different when moving that IP to another management VLAN, and SSH should still work. Answer A is incorrect because the new management VLAN must be administratively enabled. Answer B is incorrect because devices connected to the switch must have access to the new management VLAN. If the port connected to the management station is not in that VLAN, the port will not be able to reach the VLAN because it is in a separate broadcast domain. Similarly, answer C is incorrect because the router or Layer 3 switch must have access to the new management VLAN to route the SSH traffic between the remote network and the local switch.

9. **B.** You will still be prompted for a login and password, regardless of whether a password is configured. The switch uses the local username and password (which can be encrypted using the `username` *username* `secret` *password* command) and can be assigned to console, aux, and vty lines, so answers A, C, and D are incorrect.

10. **A.** By default, all VLANs (including the management VLAN) are allowed to traverse trunks. The default port security violation state is to shut down, so answer B is incorrect. Answer C is incorrect because the maximum number of MAC addresses for port security is 1. Answer D is also incorrect because the default management VLAN is 1.

Suggested Readings and Resources

1. Richard Froom, Balaji Sivasubramanian, and Erum Frahim. *Building Cisco Multilayer Switched Networks (BCMSN) (Authorized Self-Study Guide)*, 4th Edition. Cisco Press, 2007.

2. Wendell Odom. *CCNA ICND2 Official Exam Certification Guide (CCNA Exams 640-816 and 640-802)*, 2nd Edition. Cisco Press, 2007.

3. "Port Security," www.cisco.com.

17

Understanding Wireless Networking

Objective

This chapter covers the following Cisco-specific objective for the "Explain and select the appropriate administrative tasks required for a WLAN" section of the 640-802 CCNA exam:

▶ **Describe standards associated with wireless media (including: IEEE WI-FI Alliance, ITU/FCC)**

Outline

Study Strategies

▶ Read the information presented in this chapter, paying special attention to tables, Notes, and Exam Alerts.

▶ Spend some time soaking up how Wireless Radio Frequency operates. This understanding is key to an optimized wireless network deployment.

▶ The ICND1 and CCNA exams focus only on the concepts behind wireless technology rather than the configuration. The Exam Alerts in this chapter and Chapter 18, "Wireless Security and Implementation Considerations," will guide you to specific areas of study.

Introduction

It was one of those moments I'll never forget. I (Jeremy) had just installed my brand-new D-Link 802.11b wireless access point in my home and slid the new PCMCIA wireless card into my laptop. I sat on the couch in another room, held my breath, and opened Internet Explorer. I was so excited to see my home page appear, I jumped up off the couch and yelled to my wife, "Sue! I'm on the Internet! Look!" I held my laptop high in the air to show that there were no wires attached. "Wow…" came the not-as-excited reply (she had become used to my ultra-geekdom by this point). I then proceeded to run around the house, laptop in hand, yelling, "I'm still on the Internet! I'm still on the Internet!" as I went in and out of each room. Amazing. Network connectivity without wires!

Fast-forward two years from that monumental moment. I am standing in an office talking to the VP of Sales for the organization. "What do you *mean* the wireless is down?" he says to me. "The wireless access point went bad. We have one on order. It should be here early next week," I reply. "So what am I supposed to do until then?" he counters. He follows my gaze to the Ethernet wall jack, about three feet from the desk. "You're going to have to plug in," I mutter as I pull an Ethernet cable from my bag. From the look of utter annoyance on his face, I might as well have told him that he'll have to walk five miles, uphill, in the snow before he will get his Internet access back.

What happened to the excited people running through companies screaming, "I have Internet!" with their laptops held high above their heads? Convenience happened—and the ultimate convenience at that: solid network connectivity without wires. Yes, 802.11 wireless networking has taken over the world faster than nearly any other network technology ever created. It is now rare to find even a small business without a wireless access point sitting on a shelf somewhere. It doesn't matter if users are sitting at home, at work, or at Starbucks; they've all come to expect that they will always be connected to the great network power of the sky.

The Business Case

The funny thing about wireless LANs (WLANs) is that the technology was just so cool that network administrators started deploying it and making up the business case as they went along. Wireless networks were a new way of looking at infrastructure, and within a few years of mainstream deployment, the applications that used this infrastructure began to emerge. One of the first changes businesses began to realize was the increased use of laptops within the organization rather than their stationary desktop counterparts. In 2005, laptops outsold desktops for the first time, accounting for 53% of all PC sales. That figure continued to increase in the following years as vendors began including embedded wireless network cards in the devices. Companies are now purchasing laptops for their employees for two reasons.

Employees love laptops, because they get a "new computer" they can use at home, on vacation, and at the office. The companies love the laptop because the employee can now *work* while they are at home, on vacation, and at the office. Along with laptops, personal digital assistants (PDAs) began to support 802.11 wireless standards. These devices now allow employees to check email, voice mail, and the company intranet over a virtual private network (VPN), all while walking to a flight.

While a host of new wireless networking devices continue to emerge (including wireless VoIP phones), the most tangible benefit of wireless is found simply in not having wires. The IT cost of moving an employee from one cubicle to another ranges from $175 to $375, depending on the equipment present. When you realize that an average of 10 to 15% of staff moves every year, you can begin adding up the numbers for your organization. Likewise, eliminating cable runs in new or existing buildings can always provide traceable cost savings provided by wireless technology.

Finally, realize that wireless technology has moved to the point where even someone who knows nothing about networking can drive to a local electronics store and pick up a wireless access point requiring zero setup and configuration. Some users are so desperate to have wireless access at work that they bring in their own wireless network devices and build "mini-WLANs" in their cubicles, knowingly or unknowingly violating company policy. This can subject your organization to an enormous security risk that could have been minimized by using a centrally managed WLAN system.

The Players in the 802.11 Market

Objective:

▶ Describe standards associated with wireless media (including: IEEE WI-FI Alliance, ITU/FCC)

802.11 holds a host of standards that every vendor is scrambling to implement and every network admin is trying to keep straight. Three organizations play key roles in managing this wireless world:

- ▶ **International Telecommunication Union-Radiocommunication Sector (ITU-R):** Regulates the radio frequencies (RF) used for wireless transmission

- ▶ **Institute of Electrical and Electronic Engineers (IEEE):** Maintains the 802.11 wireless transmission standards

- ▶ **Wi-Fi Alliance:** Ensures certified interoperability between 802.11 wireless vendors

Entering the Radio Frequency World

Objective:

▶ Describe standards associated with wireless media (including: IEEE WI-FI Alliance, ITU/FCC)

Because of the simplicity associated with setting up 802.11 wireless networks in small office/home office (SOHO) environments, it can be easy to underestimate the task of deploying a wireless network on a corporate scale. Wireless access points (WAPs) use radio frequencies that are subject to interference and distortion. Likewise, when we move into the wireless network world, we take a step backward in our switch-based mind-set to the days of network hubs. Only one device attached to a wireless access point can send or receive at a time (half duplex). Understanding these facts is key to a successful WLAN deployment.

Understanding Wireless Transmission

Back in the day, the two competing LAN technologies were Ethernet and Token Ring. Many argued that Token Ring was the better technology because the users would never experience a collision of data on the network. This is because only one user could transmit data at a time due to the token-passing mechanism. Ethernet ended up winning the competition because its method of collision detection (CSMA/CD) allowed for higher transmission speeds.

When we move into the WLAN environment, we move our transmission methods to a collision avoidance (CSMA/CA) strategy because wireless devices have no collision detection mechanism. Likewise, because a wireless device that is sending data cannot receive data at the same time, WLAN devices run at half duplex as a rule. When you combine this limitation with signal degradation due to wireless range and interference, you'll find that wireless devices rarely run at the advertised speed (11Mbps for 802.11b, 54Mbps for 802.11b and 802.11a). Most of the time, the actual speed you are receiving is less than half of the maximum data rate!

Much of the wireless signal degradation is due to the nature of RF. Most of us are used to the land of Ethernet, where data signals travel cozily through a padded copper wire, free from most interference. Wireless RF signals are sent through the air using an antenna, and unfortunately, the air is an ugly place. The first challenge that the wireless signal faces is physical objects. Every object the signal must pass through can degrade the signal in some way. Reflective surfaces, such as metal or glass, cause RF waves to bounce off, shooting in a different direction. Uneven surfaces, such as a gravel road, piles of merchandise in a warehouse, a desk, or a cubicle can cause the signal to reflect and scatter in many directions. Finally, as wireless signals pass through physical objects, they are absorbed. This absorption rate differs depending on the type of material the signal passes through.

As if physical objects weren't enough, the wireless signal is also subject to interference. All 802.11 technology uses unlicensed wireless bands (discussed further in a moment). This means that they are not sanctioned by the United States Federal Communications Commission (FCC), and any wireless device can use them. In many ways, this is fantastic. Without unlicensed wireless bands, every new wireless network in the world would need approval from the FCC, along with all the licensing fees associated with the process! However, unlicensed RF bands also present the challenge of conflict. Cordless phones, Bluetooth, microwave ovens, and WLAN technology all share the same unlicensed RF band. Never before have network administrators faced the challenge of a Stouffer's Microwavable Macaroni Dish being responsible for a 1-minute network outage. It's a good thing this is reduced to 30 seconds in high-powered microwaves!

> **NOTE**
>
> The U.S. designates the FCC to manage the radio frequency bands. Other countries each have their own agency that manages radio frequencies. Often, these agencies mirror many of the rules that the FCC has specified. However, you may find differences as you move from country to country.

Unlicensed RF Bands

The FCC maintains three unlicensed RF bands called the Industrial, Scientific, and Medical (ISM) bands. Figure 17.1 shows where these RF bands fit in the entire wireless spectrum.

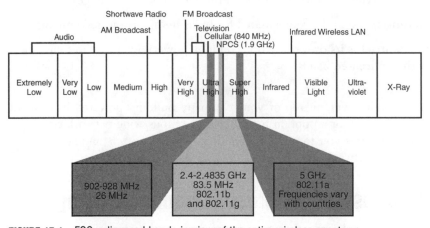

FIGURE 17.1 FCC unlicensed bands in view of the entire wireless spectrum.

The three specific bands are as follows:

- **900MHz band:** 902MHz to 928MHz

- **2.4GHz band:** 2.400GHz to 2.483GHz

- **5GHz band:** 5.150GHz to 5.3GHz and 5.725GHz to 5.825GHz

> **EXAM ALERT**
>
> You will want to know the two primary unlicensed RF bands used for wireless networking: 2.4GHz and 5GHz.

Keep in mind that these ranges of frequency are for the U.S. Other countries may support more frequencies, and others support fewer. Some countries may not allow unlicensed wireless transmission at all!

Every company that manufactures equipment that transmits wirelessly and that does not want to license frequencies from the FCC is forced to share these unlicensed bands. Combining different devices in the same area that are sharing the same frequencies results in interference. For our WLAN, that means impaired performance or potentially a completely unusable network, depending on the severity of the interference.

By far, more equipment uses the 2.4GHz band, making it more difficult to keep the airwaves free from interference. The more popular 802.11b, 802.11g, and 802.11n standards fit into this RF band. The 5GHz band is home to the 802.11a standard. On that note, let's also discuss some key facts about RF:

▶ **Fact #1:** The higher frequencies allow for higher data rates.

▶ **Fact #2:** The higher frequencies have shorter transmission distances (range).

▶ **Fact #3:** Shorter distances can be compensated for by using high-powered antennas.

▶ **Fact #4:** Every country has its own restrictions on how powerful your radio transmission can be for the unlicensed bands.

So, building a 500-foot-high tower on top of your company building powered by a small nuclear generator most likely is not an option for achieving campus-wide network coverage. The alternative solution requires you to purchase many small transmitters and strategically place them throughout your network.

The Key to Successful Wireless: Channel Surfing

Because government restrictions keep us from saturating our campus network with an ultra-powerful wireless signal, we are forced to deploy many transmitters (WAPs) that have a much smaller coverage radius. The problem with this solution is that these transmitters all use the same RF band. Because a good wireless design requires overlapping signals, we are stuck with a problem: the adjacent transmitters will interfere with each other.

Having a 10 to 15% overlap in signals, as shown in Figure 17.2, is a good design. With the right configuration, this overlap can allow clients to roam seamlessly between transmitters. However, the client will experience heavy interference and performance degradation within the overlapping coverage areas.

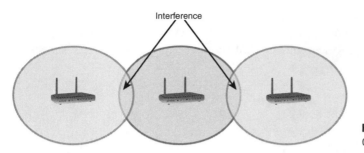

FIGURE 17.2 The problem with overlapping wireless signals.

The solution? Wireless channels. Just because a wireless access point uses the 2.4GHz range of RF doesn't mean it consumes the entire range. The 2.4GHz RF band is divided into different channels, as shown in Figure 17.3.

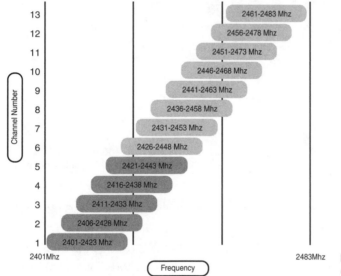

FIGURE 17.3 2.4GHz band wireless channels.

The 2.4GHz band supports up to 14 different channels (the FCC allows only channels 1 to 11 in the U.S.). Each channel consumes 22MHz of frequency bandwidth. When you walk through the setup wizard of a wireless access point, one of your options is a channel selector, typically populated with channels 1 to 11. Your goal is to put adjacent access points on separate channels. Be careful when doing this—it's not as simple as it looks! First, most of the wireless channels the FCC has sanctioned are overlapping. Figure 17.3 shows that Channel 1 (2401 to 2423MHz) overlaps with Channel 2 (2406 to 2428MHz), Channel 3 (2411 to 2433MHz), Channel 4 (2416 to 2438MHz), and Channel 5 (2421 to 2443MHz). Placing one access point on Channel 1 and an adjacent access point on Channel 3 would cause interference problems.

For this reason, it is commonly said that the 2.4GHz band supports only three channels: 1, 6, and 11. These three channels do not overlap with each other. With this in mind, we need to arrange our wireless access deployment into logical, nonoverlapping "cells," as shown in Figure 17.4.

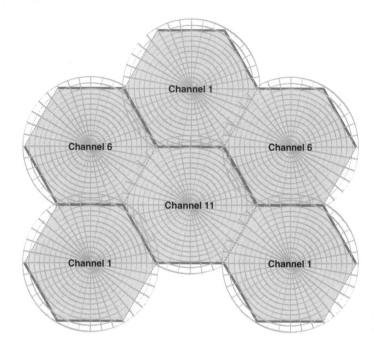

FIGURE 17.4   Arranging 2.4GHz channels into logical, adjacent cells.

Looking at Figure 17.4 should make you realize that, indeed, deploying an organization-wide wireless network does take planning.

One of the big advantages that the 5GHz band has over the 2.4GHz band is the number of channels supported. Depending on your locale and the channels you choose, you could have up to 23 nonoverlapping channels in the 5GHz range! This makes it much more viable to find a clear channel without interference. Remember our Stouffer's Macaroni Dish microwave issue? Using different channels can be one solution to help alleviate some of the microwave interference.

EXAM ALERT

Understanding the concept of wireless RF channels is key—not only for proper network design, but also for the ICND1 and CCNA exams.

The 802.11 Standards Family

Now that you have a foundational understanding of RF signaling, we can move to the 802.11 standard. When many network administrators hear of 802.11 technology, their mind immediately equates this with the three or four popular wireless networking standards: 802.11a, 802.11b, 802.11g, and the prestandard (at the time of this writing) 802.11n. However, 802.11 describes much more than this when dealing with wireless networks. For example, 802.11e describes quality of service (QoS) standards for 802.11, and 802.11i is an enhanced wireless security standard, to name just a couple. In a way, 802.11 is similar to TCP/IP in that it depicts a suite of protocols and standards.

Of course, in this suite of standards, the most popular are the common 802.11a, 802.11b, 802.11g, and 802.11n. Let's look at the evolution of these standards.

Party Like It's 1999: 802.11a and 802.11b

In 1999, two competing standards were released: 802.11a and 802.11b. As with most brand-new standards, vendors did not really begin implementing and releasing equipment that used 802.11a or 802.11b until about 2002. The two standards offered the following features:

	802.11a	802.11b
RF Band	5GHz	2.4GHz
Bandwidth	54Mbps	11Mbps
Channels	Up to 23	3 (nonoverlapping)
Outdoor Range	Approximately 75 meters	Approximately 100 meters
Indoor Range	Approximately 25 meters	Approximately 45 meters

It's an interesting story how these two standards competed. 802.11a was clearly the better standard. It offered faster speeds (54Mbps versus 11Mbps), more channels (23 versus 3), and an overall cleaner RF band (nowhere near as many devices use the 5GHz band as the 2.4GHz band). Alas, the 802.11b standard won the competition (for now) just because it was more available. The silicon used to make the 802.11a chips was in short supply, and the industry was hungry for wireless, so it gobbled up 802.11b instead.

2003 Delivers: 802.11g

After the newness of the 802.11b standard wore off, users and administrators alike demanded more speed. The IEEE answered with the 802.11g standard. This standard borrowed much of the 802.11a technology and implemented it in the 2.4GHz RF band. One of the major hurdles that was overcome was to achieve backward compatibility with 802.11b, thus allowing 802.11g access points to also support 802.11b clients. For this reason, most access points are labeled as 802.11b/g. Let's pull the same stats on 802.11g as we did for 802.11a and 802.11b:

802.11g	
RF Band	2.4GHz
Bandwidth	54Mbps
Channels	3 (nonoverlapping)
Outdoor Range	Approximately 95 meters
Indoor Range	Approximately 40 meters

The Next Generation: 802.11n

At the time of this writing, 802.11n is currently in prestandard state, set to become a standard in September 2008. Therefore, I will write about the basics of what we currently think the 802.11n standard will become. 802.11n adds multiple input, multiple output (MIMO) technology to wireless cards and access points. Simply put, you now have multiple antennas that can send or receive between devices. This can bring about increased range and throughput. The irony of the situation is that even though the 802.11n standard is not yet complete, vendors are releasing prestandard devices, placing their bets on what they believe the standard will be. This is quite a risk, because it has yet to be decided which RF band 802.11n will use; it could use the 2.4GHz and/or 5GHz bands. Perhaps by the time you read this the standard will have been decided. Here is what we currently know about 802.11n:

802.11n	
RF Band	2.4GHz and/or 5GHz
Bandwidth	248Mbps (with two receiving and two transmitting antennas, called "2×2")
Channels	Unknown
Outdoor Range	Approximately 160 meters
Indoor Range	Approximately 70 meters

> **NOTE**
>
> Many vendors are now supplying wireless network cards and wireless access points that support all three (802.11a/b/g) wireless standards. I would expect that the 802.11n standard will obtain similar support before long.

Chapter Summary

In less than a decade, 802.11 wireless technology has changed everything we thought a LAN environment to be. Many people believe that someday networks will become "a world without wires" as wireless technology becomes more developed and deployed. To successfully deploy a wireless network, it is essential to understand the basics of radio frequency (RF). The 802.11 wireless networking standards are designed to operate in the unlicensed bands of 2.4GHz (802.11b/g) and 5GHz (802.11a). These bands are subject to interference from a variety of devices, so care must be taken to choose the correct location, number of access points, and channels when deploying wireless networking devices. Many wireless spectrum analysis tools are available from the general market that can help with this process.

Because of interference and half-duplex operation, the actual throughput of a wireless device is typically half of the maximum specified by the standard. As new standards develop, the throughput and range of wireless technology will continue to increase.

Key Terms

- ▶ 802.11a, b, g, n
- ▶ Radio frequency (RF)
- ▶ ITU-R
- ▶ IEEE
- ▶ Wi-Fi Alliance
- ▶ 2.4GHz band
- ▶ 5GHz band
- ▶ Wireless channels
- ▶ CSMA/CA
- ▶ Multiple input, multiple output (MIMO)
- ▶ Wireless cells
- ▶ Wireless roaming

Apply Your Knowledge

Exercise

15.1 Designing a Wireless Network

Estimated Time: 15 minutes

This exercise helps you apply the knowledge of wireless design you have gained in this chapter. Figure 17.5 represents the design of a new office building you have acquired. Your organization would like to deploy 802.11g wireless that covers the entire building. It has seven Cisco wireless access points to use and would like to minimize the amount of wireless access available outside the building. Each access point provides 300 feet of unobstructed wireless coverage; however, each wall you pass through reduces this coverage by an average of 75 feet. The thicker walls surrounding the building reduce the coverage by 150 feet. Find the most effective location in which to place each wireless access point in the network. In addition, state what channel the wireless access point will use. The diagram scale is located at the bottom of Figure 17.5.

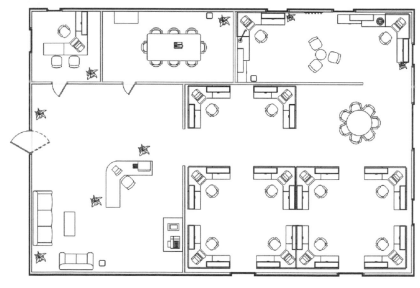

FIGURE 17.5 Wireless network schematic.

Review Questions

1. Three agencies manage the standards and frequencies of wireless networks. List the names of these agencies and briefly describe their functions.

2. 802.11b/g is the more popular wireless standard worldwide. One of your fellow network administrators on staff states that 11 separate RF channels are available for use across your corporate network. Is this true? Should you use all 11 channels? Justify your response.

3. List the three RF spectrums that are considered unlicensed bands. Which wireless standards are associated with each?

4. Higher and lower frequencies on the RF spectrum provide different benefits. What are the benefits of higher frequencies (such as 2.4GHz and 5GHz) over lower frequencies?

5. List at least three business benefits of using wireless networking.

Exam Questions

1. What Cisco-founded organization ensures compatibility between all 802.11 wireless vendor equipment?

   ○ **A.** 802.11

   ○ **B.** IEEE

   ○ **C.** ITU-R

   ○ **D.** Wi-Fi Alliance

2. Which of the following wireless standards use the 2.4GHz RF band? (Choose two)

   ○ **A.** 802.11a

   ○ **B.** 802.11b

   ○ **C.** 802.11g

   ○ **D.** 802.11i

3. 802.11 wireless standards use which of the following transmission methods?

   ○ **A.** CSMA/CD, half duplex

   ○ **B.** CSMA/CD, full duplex

   ○ **C.** CSMA/CA, half duplex

   ○ **D.** CSMA/CA, full duplex

4. How many wireless channels are available in the U.S.A. for the 2.4GHz band without overlapping frequencies?

   ○ **A.** 1

   ○ **B.** 3

   ○ **C.** 11

   ○ **D.** 23

5. When wireless technology uses a higher frequency, what factors must you consider? (Choose two)

   ○ **A.** The higher frequency will allow for higher throughput

   ○ **B.** The higher frequency will restrict throughput

   ○ **C.** The higher frequency has more range

   ○ **D.** The higher frequency has limited range

6. You are the network administrator for Widgets, Inc., a worldwide distributing organization. You are planning on setting up a new wireless network for the organization. Which of the following are considerations for the new wireless network?

   ○ **A.** The geographic location of the office

   ○ **B.** The radio frequencies currently in use at the office locations

   ○ **C.** The radio channels currently in use at the office locations

   ○ **D.** The wireless cell configuration on the access point

7. To provide for successful client roaming, how should wireless cells be configured?

   ○ **A.** Wireless cells should use the same RF band and channel

   ○ **B.** Wireless cells should use the same RF band but different channels

   ○ **C.** Wireless cells should use different RF bands but the same channel

   ○ **D.** Wireless cells should use different RF bands and channels

8. Which of the following are advantages of 802.11a over 802.11b? (Choose two)

   ○ **A.** Increased throughput

   ○ **B.** Increased range

   ○ **C.** More channel diversity

   ○ **D.** Support for more clients

9. You are deploying a wireless network at a new office location. The office happens to be located next to an apartment complex with many existing wireless access points using all available channels in the RF band. Which agency would handle this situation?

   ○ **A.** ITU-R

   ○ **B.** IEEE

   ○ **C.** Wi-Fi Alliance

   ○ **D.** None of the above

10. What is the largest cost savings that organizations typically find with wireless technology?

   ○ **A.** Elimination of stationary equipment

   ○ **B.** Minimized office space due to roaming users

   ○ **C.** Access to new cost-savings applications

   ○ **D.** Cable installation and management cost

Answers to Review Questions

1. The agencies that govern wireless networks are as follows:

   The International Telecommunication Union-Radiocommunication Sector (ITU-R) regulates the radio frequencies used for wireless transmission.

   The Institute of Electrical and Electronic Engineers (IEEE) maintains the 802.11 wireless transmission standards.

   The Wi-Fi Alliance ensures certified interoperability between 802.11 wireless vendors.

2. The short answer to this question is that yes, 11 channels are available for use. However, it is not a good idea to use all 11 channels, because many of them overlap RF signals. In the U.S., you should use only channels 1, 6, and 11, because these channels have no overlap in RF signal.

3. The three unlicensed RF bands are as follows:

   900MHz: No mainstream wireless network technologies use this spectrum.

   2.4GHz: 802.11b and 802.11g use this spectrum.

   5GHz: 802.11a uses this spectrum.

4. Higher frequencies provide more bandwidth than the lower frequencies, but they also have a more limited range.

5. There are many reasons why a business may be interested in wireless networking. Here are four:

   Elimination of stationary equipment

   Minimized office space due to roaming users

   Access to new cost-savings applications

   Cable installation and management cost

Answers to Exam Questions

1. **D.** The Wi-Fi Alliance was founded by Cisco to ensure vendor interoperability on the 802.11 wireless standard. A vendor can obtain Wi-Fi certification, which assures customers that the equipment will interoperate with any other Wi-Fi certified device. Answer A is incorrect because 802.11 represents the wireless standard. Answer B is incorrect because the IEEE only manages and approves the wireless standards. Answer C is incorrect because the ITU-R is focused on regulating the 802.11 RF bands.

2. **B, C.** 802.11b and 802.11g share the 2.4GHz band. This allows the newer 802.11g standard to be backward-compatible with 802.11b. 802.11a uses the 5GHz band, and 802.11i is a security standard that does not use a specific band.

3. **C.** 802.11 uses CSMA/CA (collision avoidance) with half-duplex transmission. Because of this, the maximum rate of transmission is rarely attained when communicating on an 802.11 wireless network.

4. **B.** In the U.S., only three nonoverlapping channels are available for the 2.4GHz band. Europe has four nonoverlapping channels, because access to other unlicensed RF bands is available. The moral of the story? If you're having trouble finding a free wireless channel in your area, move to Europe.

5. **A, D.** The benefit of using a higher frequency is the ability to obtain more bandwidth (throughput). The drawback is the limited range of the higher frequencies.

6. **A, B, C.** When deploying a new wireless network, you must take into account the geographic region, because government regulations dictate what unlicensed RF bands and channels are available for public use. Likewise, you must also see what wireless RF bands and channels are free (not in use) in your location to get a clean signal. Answer D is incorrect because wireless cells are not configured on access points; rather, they are a design concept.

7. **B.** To provide for client roaming, wireless cells should use the same RF band but different channels. This allows a client to move between wireless access points without interference caused by overlapping signals.

8. **A, C.** 802.11a has more bandwidth (54Mbps) compared to 802.11b (11Mbps) and more wireless channels available (up to 23). 802.11b does have more range than 802.11a because it uses the lower-frequency 2.4GHz band. Neither standard has any advantage as far as client support.

9. **D.** Although the ITU-R does manage the RF bands, it would not handle this specific situation. Both the 2.4GHz and 5GHz bands are considered unlicensed for a reason: no entity will manage them. The solution to the apartment situation would be to find out if the apartment wireless devices are transmitting at a higher-than-legal power or to change your company to the less-congested 5GHz band.

10. **D.** Although wireless provides many conveniences for businesses, the primary cost savings can be found in the elimination of cable installation and management.

Suggested Readings and Resources

1. Wikipedia 802.11 definitions, http://en.wikipedia.org/wiki/802.11

2. How WiFi Works, http://computer.howstuffworks.com/wireless-network3.htm

3. Chris Ward and Jeremy Cioara. *Exam Cram 2 CCNA Practice Questions*. Que Publishing, 2004.

4. Toby Velte and Anthony Velte. *Cisco 802.11 Wireless Networking Quick Reference*. Cisco Press, 2005.

CHAPTER EIGHTEEN

Wireless Security and Implementation Considerations

Objectives

This chapter covers the following Cisco-specified objectives for the "Explain and select the appropriate administrative tasks required for a WLAN" section of the 640-802 CCNA exam:

▶ **Identify and describe the purpose of the components in a small wireless network (including: SSID, BSS, ESS)**

▶ **Identify the basic parameters to configure on a wireless network to ensure that devices connect to the correct access point**

▶ **Compare and contrast wireless security features and capabilities of WPA security (including: open, WEP, WPA-1/2)**

▶ **Identify common issues with implementing wireless networks**

Outline

Study Strategies

▶ The ICND2 and CCNA exams are designed to test on a general understanding of wireless concepts rather than hands-on configuration of wireless devices

▶ Be sure to have an in-depth understanding of the different wireless security standards (WEP, WPA, and WPA2). Cisco considers these important since this represents the core of your wireless network security architecture

▶ When focusing on implementation, be sure to understand how to deploy close proximity 802.11b/g wireless access points without causing them to interfere with each other

Introduction

Okay. I admit it. I (Jeremy) drove to a friend's house and arrived a bit early, so I decided to spend a few minutes in the car checking my email. I pulled my laptop out of the back and did a quick wireless scan of the neighborhood. Two SSIDs appeared: Linksys and Netgear, both without security. I joined the Linksys network and checked my online web mail. (I prefer to think of this as "borrowing" the Internet connection rather than "stealing" wireless.) That's when a bearded man with a tattered shirt and loaded shotgun came out the front door. Sorry; I just needed a dramatic twist.

Harmless enough, right? *Wrong!* Imagine a strange individual walking into your front office with a laptop and saying, "Would you mind if I plugged into that wall jack over there?" Yes, I would mind. That would undermine every written security standard we have in our organization. But that's exactly what happens when you fail to properly understand and implement the security standards available for wireless networks. Keep in mind that not all wireless security is created equal. Some security standards (such as WEP) may give you a false sense of security, because many network intruders eat WEP security keys for breakfast. This is why a good comprehension of wireless security is absolutely necessary, even for the novice network administrator.

Understanding the Threats

Introducing wireless networking into your organization opens the door to three new types of attacks on your network: war driving, direct hacking, and employee ignorance. Let me explain each of these in detail.

War Driving

You know you've entered a new realm of network security when "driving" becomes one of the intrusion efforts. This term actually originated from the days of old, when a similar method known as war dialing was in place. In the 1980s, most businesses connected offices through dialup connections, typically using modems. War dialing would consist of a hacker randomly dialing through the phone number range in his local area (for example, setting up his modem to dial numbers 100-0000 through 999-9999 in the U.S.). The dialing itself was not the hacking attempt; rather, it was a scan for phone numbers responding to modem signals.

War driving uses a similar concept. An intruder mounts an 802.11-compatible wireless antenna on his vehicle and drives through the city, identifying available wireless networks. When combined with a Global Positioning System (GPS) device, war-driving software (such as KisMet or KisMac) can be very accurate in pinpointing the available wireless networks on a map of the city. When the intruder returns home, he can analyze the available networks and plot his next steps of attack.

Keep in mind that war driving can discover wireless networks even if they are encrypted, authenticated, and/or using a "hidden" (nonbroadcast) SSID.

Direct Hacking

The direct hacking effort typically begins after the war-driving scan of the area is complete. The intruder then identifies what network(s) he wants to attack. The hacking effort can come in many forms:

▶ **Breaking into the WLAN:** As soon as the intruder has identified available wireless networks, he can try to break the encryption and/or authentication system. Although this can be accomplished (with much effort) from the attacker's home, it is usually attempted within range of the wireless signal. For example, the attacker can sit in the parking lot and attempt to break into the building's wireless network. If he is successful, he joins the wireless network and begins scanning the internal network of your organization to find available resources.

▶ **Decrypting data:** Because wireless network communication is transmitted into the air, anything that your users access from a wireless device has the potential to be captured by an intruder's wireless sniffer software. If this data is sent unencrypted, the intruder can simply reassemble the packets to regenerate the original file (such as a Microsoft Word document, an Adobe Acrobat PDF file, or even a VoIP conversation). If the data is encrypted, the intruder captures the data and returns home to attempt to break the encryption keys. If he is successful, he can reassemble the original files and steal corporate data.

▶ **Attempting a wireless DoS attack:** The final effort that can be accomplished by direct hacking methods is to unleash a denial of service (DoS) attack on the wireless network. If the intruder is successful, the wireless access point that he attacks is rendered inoperable to your company. This type of attack is not as common in a WLAN environment, because most companies have not yet moved critical network services to the wireless network. The hacker's efforts would be seen as more of a temporary inconvenience than a major network issue.

Employee Ignorance

Employee ignorance was the best term I could come up with for this category of security threat. Depending on the individual employee, I suppose you could substitute "insolence," "rebellion," or "stupidity" for the word "ignorance." Here's the concept: Your company policy dictates that you will not run wireless networking because of security threats. However, the "ignorant" employee has a laptop he really wants to use with wireless technology, which gives him the freedom to roam between areas while remaining connected to the network. The employee takes networking into his own hands and connects a low-end wireless access point to the network jack in his cubicle. With the click of a Cat 5 cable, your network security has been reduced to nothing, and a gaping hole into the network is now broadcast to the outside world. This same issue can occur even if your company provides a WLAN network and the user is just outside the range of the wireless signal. If appropriate detection measures are not taken, this massive hole in your network security can go undiscovered for months!

Deploying a Secure Wireless Network

Although volumes could be (and have been) written on wireless security, I would just like to discuss the 10,000-foot view of wireless security. This will give you an idea of the areas of focus when you are considering using wireless networking technology in your organization. As soon as you understand these areas, you can begin digging deeper into the technology to find the right fit for your wireless design.

> **TIP**
>
> The CCENT and CCNA certifications require only a foundational understanding of wireless security topics, which are discussed in this book.

Wireless security can be broken into three major categories: encryption, authentication, and detection.

Wireless Encryption

Objective:

▶ Compare and contrast wireless security features and capabilities of WPA security (including: open, WEP, WPA-1/2)

When you're ready for a technology roller coaster ride, begin studying the history of wireless encryption standards. I mentioned in the preceding chapter that wireless networking technology is so amazing that companies began using it long before the security standards were heavily tested and proven to withstand attacks. So, fasten your seat belt, and let's ride through the evolution of wireless encryption standards, starting where it all began: with WEP.

Wired Equivalent Privacy (WEP)

The WEP standard was the first measure of security released for wireless networking. This encryption method was based on the simple concept of using preshared keys (PSKs) to generate an encryption algorithm. Here's an overview of how the WEP encryption algorithm works:

The WEP standard uses an encryption formula called RC4. This is essentially a mathematical formula that takes every piece of data you want to encrypt and scrambles it. The missing piece of this formula is the PSK, which you enter. This is visually demonstrated in Figure 18.1.

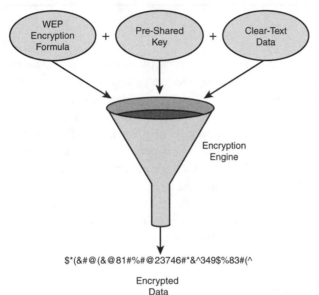

$*(&#@(&@81#%#@23746#*&^349$%83#(^

Encrypted
Data

FIGURE 18.1 The mechanics of WEP encryption.

When the wireless access point receives data, it uses the reverse formula to decrypt the data. So, for WEP to work successfully, you must manually enter the PSK on both the wireless client and the wireless access point.

When WEP was originally released (in 1997), it used 64-bit encryption, which is considered weak by today's standards. You can compare 64-bit encryption to a math formula with 64 steps. Each step scrambles the original data more and more.

NOTE

The more bits you use for encryption, the more complex your encryption algorithm, and the more difficult it is to break. However, the more bits you use for encryption, the harder it is for your network device to communicate because of the processing power needed. This may result in slower network communication.

Unfortunately, within a few years of WEP's initial release, *major* security vulnerabilities were found. The wireless standards groups improved the strength of the WEP algorithm by releasing a 128-bit version in 2002, which some people refer to as WEP2. Although it makes the algorithm slightly more difficult to break, many flaws in the underlying design of WEP caused this security standard to crumble.

Wireless security was suffering in a huge way when WPA was released.

> **TIP**
>
> Remember that WEP offers 64-bit and 128-bit encryption strengths. Also, keep in mind that the WEP standard allows only static, preshared keys.

Wi-Fi Protected Access (WPA)

The wireless networking industry faced a major issue. A newer encryption algorithm was needed to combat the weaknesses of WEP, but the more complex encryption algorithms would require more-powerful 802.11-compatible wireless hardware to process the algorithm. By this point, the industry had already purchased millions of wireless access points and wireless cards, so simply saying, "Sorry! Go ahead and scrap all that equipment and buy new stuff." was not an option. In 2003 the Wi-Fi Alliance (a group of extremely smart people sponsored by many organizations) stepped forward and proposed WPA. WPA used a new encryption algorithm called Temporal Key Integrity Protocol (TKIP). TKIP ran on the same wireless hardware that was originally created, and it used a 128-bit encryption algorithm. It was engineered to dramatically increase the number of encryption keys that could be used and virtually eliminated the attacks that were successful on WEP keys. Although WPA was not flawless, it was a tremendous step forward from the original WEP standard.

Wi-Fi Protected Access, Reloaded (WPA2 and 802.11i)

WPA was never meant to solve the world's wireless security problems. Although it was *much* more secure than WEP, it did have the weakness of using the same old hardware that WEP used. Inherent in that hardware were a few security weaknesses that simply could not be overcome by changing the encryption formula. For that reason, the Wi-Fi Alliance quickly (in 2004) proposed an alternative standard casually called WPA2 and officially called 802.11i.

WPA2 uses a completely different encryption standard known as Advanced Encryption Standard (AES). This encryption standard was standardized by the U.S. government and has been extensively analyzed and tested. The WPA2 standard left behind the old hardware and required that users purchase new wireless hardware (both cards and access points).

To ease the transition, WPA2 hardware can run in backward-compatibility mode to support the original WPA and even WEP standards. This allows an organization to upgrade its wireless access points to the new hardware and still support the older WEP- and WPA-compliant clients. As the clients upgrade to newer wireless devices, WPA2 (and thus AES encryption) can be used.

> **TIP**
>
> WPA uses TKIP encryption, and WPA2 uses AES.

Wireless Authentication (802.1x)

The wireless encryption we've discussed so far does indeed secure the data, but it has a couple of weaknesses. First, using a preshared key system means that you must go to every wireless device and accurately enter the PSK before the device can communicate on the network. Likewise, keeping the same PSK for an extended amount of time increases the chances of the encryption algorithm's being hacked, so it's a good idea to change the PSK on a regular basis. In a small network of 10 or so wireless devices, this may not be a big deal, but in a large network with hundreds or even thousands of wireless devices, this can be a full-time job. The second issue presented by a PSK system is the inability to remove access. For example, if you are using a PSK among your 50 laptop users on the network, and one of the users leaves the company, you must change the PSK for the 49 other wireless users to eliminate the security vulnerability from the former employee.

Simply relying on a shared PSK among all devices is not a secure or scalable solution for business. What was needed was a method of wireless authentication. This would allow you to have a system of granting or restricting access based on a variety of criteria, such as usernames and passwords or certificates. The industry responded with the ultimate authentication method, which we now know as 802.1x.

Usually when we think of network authentication, we think of accessing an operating system. For example, when you log into a Microsoft Windows domain, you must authenticate using a username and password to gain access to shared resources on the Windows-based servers. When you Telnet to a Cisco device, you must authenticate to gain access to manage the device using the Cisco IOS. 802.1x takes authentication to an entirely new level. Now, you must authenticate to gain access to the Layer 2 LAN network fabric. Now, to access the wireless access point and use the 802.11 network, you must authenticate. You can also apply 802.1x to LAN network switches. When a device plugs into an Ethernet port, it must authenticate before it gains access to that port and, thus, the network.

Think of the possibilities as soon as you begin using network authentication! When a user leaves the company, you can negate her user account on a Microsoft Windows server. This will cause her to lose the ability to log on to the Windows workstation and, at the same time, lose the ability to even plug into a switch port or attach to the wireless network! Talk about cutting off a user! Now, let me give you the basics of how this works.

802.1x designates three network devices that participate in network authentication: the supplicant, the authenticator, and the authentication server. Figure 18.2 shows the placement of these devices.

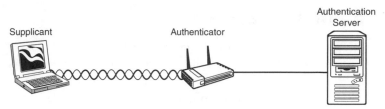

FIGURE 18.2 Equipment participating in 802.1x authentication.

When the user wants to access the network, he must first send his authentication credentials (such as a username and password) to the authenticator, which forwards them to the authentication server. When the authentication server receives the credentials, it checks them against its database and then tells the authenticator whether the device has passed authentication. If the device fails authentication, its access to the network is terminated or severely limited, depending on how you (as the administrator) decide to restrict the device. If the device passes authentication, the supplicant and authentication server generate a dynamic encryption key known as the session key. This provides the same security as the PSK but does not require you to enter a PSK on the client or wireless access point.

I could say much more about network authentication, but, as I said at the beginning of this section, this is a 10,000-foot overview of the concepts. You now know what network authentication is all about and what it is used for. It's now up to you to continue past the CCNA in your Cisco studies to determine the best method to implement network authentication. Proceed into that world with a grave warning: Don't let the EAP monsters eat you alive! Don't worry; you'll know what I mean when you get there.

> **TIP**
>
> Keep in mind that WPA and WPA2 standards allow for static PSKs or dynamic keys when used with 802.1x. WEP allows only static PSKs.

Wireless Intrusion Prevention System (IPS)

By using wireless network authentication and encryption, we have addressed the concerns of war driving and network hackers. But what about those pesky users who plug unauthorized wireless access points into the network? For that we have wireless IPS. You can think of IPS as introducing a variety of detection lasers into your network. I think back to the 1996 movie *Mission Impossible* with Tom Cruise. In one scene, Cruise (well, Ethan Hunt, to be exact) must retrieve a chip from a secured computer room by twisting and contorting his body through a variety of lasers projected around the room. In the same sense, deploying wireless IPS for your network sets up a variety of "sensors" that detect when a policy has been violated. The minute a rogue access point shows up in the network, the system can alert you, pinpointing the location of the access point on a map of your campus. Amazing!

Network-wide IPS can detect a variety of additional suspicious movements around the network, in both the wired and wireless worlds. However, discussing the rest of those detections is part of the Cisco Certified Security Professional (CCSP) certification.

Wireless Implementation Guidelines

Objectives:

▶ Identify and describe the purpose of the components in a small wireless network. (Including: SSID, BSS, ESS)

▶ Identify the basic parameters to configure on a wireless network to ensure that devices connect to the correct access point

Now that you've read an overview of the wireless security considerations, let's talk about planning to implement wireless technology. There's much more to planning a wireless LAN deployment than putting a few wireless access points in place. You need to understand how the topology, distance, and placement of wireless access points can affect the efficiency of your wireless LAN.

Understanding Wireless Topologies

Webster's Dictionary defines "topology" as a branch of mathematics concerned with properties of geometric configurations (such as point sets) that are unaltered by elastic deformations (as stretching or twisting) that are homeomorphisms. The CCENT and CCNA exams stop short of requiring a full understanding of homeomorphism (or elastic deformation, for that matter). However, the exams do require you to have some knowledge of the placement of wireless access points in your corporate network. The first piece to understand is that anyone can deploy a wireless network in one of two forms: ad hoc or infrastructure.

Ad hoc wireless networks technically use an Independent Basic Service Set (IBSS) topology. This means that each wireless device independently manages the wireless network. This type of wireless network originates from and includes the wireless device, as shown in Figure 18.3.

This type of network can be created by users on-the-fly to share files or services with others. For example, someone on an airplane might want to share a folder of files with the person next to her. She can create an ad hoc wireless network and allow the other person to join and access the shared files over a network connection.

Ad hoc networks typically are very limited in range and security capabilities. You may want to consider restricting laptops in your corporation from starting ad hoc wireless networks, because they could be considered a potential security vulnerability.

FIGURE 18.3 Ad hoc wireless networking.

Infrastructure wireless networks are a far more common topology. This involves using a dedicated piece of equipment (typically a wireless access point) to initiate and manage the wireless network. Wireless access points can be configured to use one of two infrastructure modes: Basic Service Set (BSS) or Extended Service Set (ESS). The BSS is the simplest form of wireless network. It includes a single wireless access point managing a group of clients, as shown in Figure 18.4.

An ESS is a wireless topology (note the word change from "network" to "topology") that includes two or more wireless access points providing extended wireless coverage across the network, as shown in Figure 18.5.

In Figure 18.5, notice that the wireless coverage overlaps. Wireless best practices state that you should have a 10 to 15% overlap in your wireless coverage. This allows you to implement seamless roaming, allowing a wireless client to move between access points with no service interruption. This is not as critical for data clients, such as laptops. Rather, real-time wireless clients such as 802.11-compatible cell phones, cordless VoIP phones, and some PDAs benefit from the overlapping coverage. Imagine dropping a phone call anytime you moved more than 300 feet in the network! More steps are involved in implementing seamless wireless roaming, but the 10 to 15% overlapping coverage is the starting point.

The second thing to notice in Figure 18.5 is that the channels are different on the two wireless access points. One of the wireless access points uses Channel 11, and the other uses Channel 6. This prevents the two wireless access points from interfering with each other. This channel concept is more fully discussed in Chapter 17, "Understanding Wireless Networking."

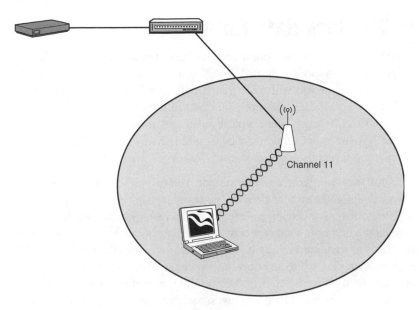

FIGURE 18.4   A single basic service set design.

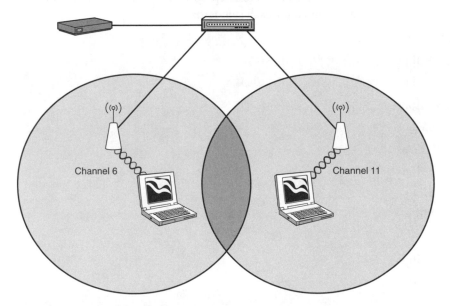

FIGURE 18.5   An extended service set design.

Understanding Wireless Data Rates

So you purchased a new 802.11g wireless access point and implemented it with clients running 802.11g cards. 54Mbps of pure wireless speed—right? Wrong! You may have purchased an access point capable of handling 54Mbps, but you will never reach that speed. *Never!* Repeated performance tests have revealed that actual data rates are about half of the theoretical data rate, on average. This means that your 802.11b access point typically averages about a 5Mbps actual data rate. 802.11g usually is in the 20Mbps range. You might be wondering why the standard says that you can handle 54Mbps when the actual throughput is much less. Well, there are many reasons.

Suppose you travel to the moon in an oxygen-free environment. You carry a single wireless access point and a single wireless card plugged into a single solar-powered laptop that does nothing but run the wireless card (no Bluetooth, no electrical interference). You sit with the wireless access point about 2 feet from the laptop and only send *or* receive data (never both). You *might* get close to the 54Mbps capability. But even that is stretching it. When you move from the world of cables into the world of wireless, you open yourself to an entirely different style of communication. One of the first considerations that you'll notice is the truth behind the range of the access point. Yes, in an obstruction-free environment, the 802.11b/g wireless signal can travel 300 feet. But couple that fact with the idea that higher data rates (11Mbps for 802.11b and 54Mbps for 802.11g) require stronger signals. You'll find that the data rates step down the farther you go from the access point. The following steps are defined for each standard:

- ▶ 802.11a and 802.11g:
  - ▶ Step 1: 54Mbps
  - ▶ Step 2: 48Mbps
  - ▶ Step 3: 36Mbps
  - ▶ Step 4: 24Mbps
  - ▶ Step 5: 18Mbps
  - ▶ Step 6: 12Mbps
  - ▶ Step 7: 9Mbps
  - ▶ Step 8: 6Mbps
- ▶ 802.11b:
  - ▶ Step 1: 11Mbps
  - ▶ Step 2: 5.5Mbps
  - ▶ Step 3: 2Mbps
  - ▶ Step 4: 1Mbps

So, when you picture wireless data rates coming from your wireless access point, think of them as a radial circle for each rate, with the rates continually decreasing the farther you go. This is represented in Figure 18.6.

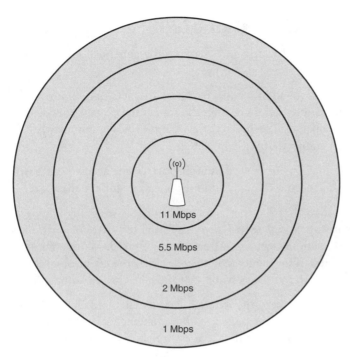

FIGURE 18.6 Wireless data rates.

You'll notice that no exact measurement is attached to each of the radial circles dictating speed around the wireless access point. That's because range is not the only criterion to consider when determining wireless data throughput. From Chapter 17, you'll remember that wireless shares the unlicensed FCC frequency bands with many other pieces of equipment. Bluetooth, other 802.11 wireless clients, cordless phones, and microwave ovens are just a few that can cause interference. Couple that with typical obstructions such as walls, cubicles, desks, and so on, and you have a wireless signal that varies from business environment to business environment. It is impossible to say just how far and "clean" the signal will be in your specific environment. Many companies make testing equipment that displays the signal strength and data rate to a laptop or PDA screen. This gives you a good idea of how wireless will fare in your environment.

> **NOTE**
>
> Because wireless technology uses a CSMA/CA mechanism, all clients adopt the speed of the slowest client on the access point. For example, if three wireless clients are attached to the wireless access point running at 24Mbps, and a wireless client some distance away attaches at 6 Mbps, all clients will run at the lowest speed!

The saving grace of wireless data rates is the fact that most users will not notice. Most devices that use a wireless signal are used for lower-bandwidth communication. For example, a wireless VoIP phone consumes about 100Kbps of bandwidth. Laptops used in wireless environments typically surf the net or check email. Most devices that handle large data file transfers or other high-bandwidth communication typically are hardwired.

General Wireless Implementation Steps

With all those considerations floating around your mind, here are the general steps to implement wireless:

1. **Ensure hardwired operation:** Before adding any wireless to the network, connect a device (such as a laptop) to the same switch port where you plan to connect your wireless access point. Ensure that it operates as expected, verifying VLAN assignment, DHCP operation, and Internet connectivity (if applicable).

2. **Install the wireless access point in your tested switch port:** Some access points will connect using straight-through Ethernet cabling, and others may require a cross-over cable.

3. **Configure a basic wireless network and test:** Keep this initial test extremely simple. Just implement a wireless SSID with no security. After it is configured, join the wireless network from a client, and test your connectivity. Ensure that the client obtains an IP address and can perform the same actions as when you use a hardwired connection.

4. **Add wireless security and test:** Implement the wireless security standard chosen for your network. It's usually best to begin with a preshared key system of security to keep it simple. After you have added the security, reconfigure the wireless client, and test again.

Working through these four steps, you have established a baseline for your wireless network. As you add more features or security standards on top of the existing foundation, you can return to a "last known good" configuration if something goes wrong.

Wireless Troubleshooting

Objective:

▶ Identify common issues with implementing wireless networks.

Wireless troubleshooting is far more complex than typical wired troubleshooting. Physical problems are much more elusive, because they deal primarily with interference rather than a simple cable break or failing switch port. For example, I recently deployed in a business a wireless network that worked great until 4 in the afternoon. As soon as we crossed the 4 p.m. barrier, all wireless connectivity was lost. After doing some spectrum analysis, we found that a nearby airport was using a device (we still aren't sure what it was) that completely flooded the 2.4GHz frequency range. The company decided to move to 802.11a (which was a fairly large network upgrade) to avoid this interference.

Likewise, wireless technology is fairly new to the industry. You may find that firmware for your access point has bugs and needs to be upgraded to a newer version to avoid persistent crashing (this happens far more often than you may realize). The following wireless troubleshooting checklist may be helpful as you attempt to diagnose the issue.

Client Troubleshooting

Most wireless issues are related to the client:

▸ **Verify that the wireless card is enabled:** Most new laptops have a button or switch that disables the wireless card to save battery life.

▸ **Move to a "known good" region of the building:** Do your testing in an area known to have a strong wireless signal. This may require using multiple wireless devices.

▸ **Verify that the client can identify the wireless network using the installed wireless utility:** If you are unable to identify wireless SSID(s) in your vicinity, the client's wireless card may be disabled, or the wireless access point may not be working.

▸ **Ensure that the wireless client has the correct wireless security information and supports your security standards:** You may need to re-enter the preshared key to ensure that you entered it correctly. Likewise, the wireless card may not support the wireless security on your network. Try connecting to an SSID that does not use security from the wireless device.

Wireless Access Point Troubleshooting

Most troubleshooting that deals with the wireless access point focuses on physical considerations:

▸ **Verify that the wireless access point is running the latest firmware version:** Nothing is worse than spending hours on a problem that is related to a bug in the wireless firmware.

▸ **Test the wireless reception radius at different times of the day:** Because of the varying degrees of interference that may occur over time, it is best to run multiple tests on your signal strength. You can do this simply and inexpensively by carrying around a laptop and observing the reception at differing locations.

▸ **Verify your wireless channel configuration:** If you have multiple wireless access points or are in an area where other access points may interfere, verify (using wireless software) the most saturated and unsaturated channels. For 802.11b/g, use channels 1, 6, or 11 in the U.S. For 802.11a, many more channels are available, and you should test for the cleanest frequency.

▸ **Consider the materials around and close to the access point:** Try to avoid installing the access point near metal objects, which reflect the signal. Realize that a concrete block wall will absorb much more signal than a drywall barrier.

Chapter Summary

All in all, deploying a wireless network is not for the fainthearted. Installing a wireless access point in the network essentially broadcasts and extends your network beyond the walls of your organization into treacherous territory. Wireless intruders can begin capturing data and breaking into the network without your ever knowing an attack is happening. This is why it is so critical to understand the security considerations before you attach wireless equipment in your environment.

When securing your wireless network, not all security standards are created equal. The initial WEP system of security offered only 64-bit encryption. It was easily broken because of the key strength as well as a number of flaws that plagued the initial WEP deployment. WEP2 increased the key strength to 128-bit encryption, but it still suffered many of the other weaknesses of WEP. WPA was released to address many of those weaknesses, but it was considered an interim solution while network users began migrating to new hardware. Modern networks employ WPA2 (aka 802.11i) to ensure up-to-date security standards in the world of wireless.

In addition to locking down the wireless network, many implementation considerations must be taken into account. Wireless is susceptible to RF interference. This adds many physical layers of troubleshooting that did not exist in the wired environment. Ensuring that your wireless cells include an acceptable amount of overlap and differing channels lays the foundation for ensuring adequate wireless coverage for your organization.

Key Terms

- 802.11a/b/g/n
- WEP 64-bit
- WEP 128-bit
- WPA
- WPA2 (802.11i)
- 802.1x
- Wireless Intrusion Prevention System (IPS)
- Basic Service Set (BSS)
- Extended Service Set (ESS)
- Radio Frequency (RF)
- 2.4GHz band
- 5GHz band
- Wireless channels
- Wireless cells
- Wireless roaming
- Wireless data rate

Apply Your Knowledge

Review Questions

1. List the three encryption standards you can currently use with wireless networking.

2. Describe the differences between WEP, WPA, and WPA2. What type of encryption does each use? What are their strengths and weaknesses?

3. List three potential vulnerabilities of a wireless network.

4. Because a wireless access point forces all clients to use the speed of the slowest client, how do you think you should ideally deploy your wireless access points?

5. What is the process for successfully installing a wireless access point?

Exam Questions

1. What is a rogue access point?

   ○ **A.** An unauthorized access point that has been placed on your LAN

   ○ **B.** An access point configured to broadcast the corporate SSID

   ○ **C.** An access point using WEP or WEP2 security

   ○ **D.** An access point that has been compromised by an intruder

2. When designing a wireless ESS system, how much cell overlap is recommended?

   ○ **A.** None. Cell overlap can cause interference.

   ○ **B.** 5 to 10%

   ○ **C.** 10 to 15%

   ○ **D.** 15 to 20%

3. What scenario would be an ideal case to implement WEP security?

   ○ **A.** You are running a small business network environment implementing the 802.11a wireless standard

   ○ **B.** You would like to implement the 802.1x security standard using a Windows RADIUS server to authenticate users

   ○ **C.** You would like to implement increased security instead of or in addition to the typical WPA or 802.11i standards

   ○ **D.** You are required to implement wireless using older equipment that does not support WPA or WPA2

4. You are sitting in a library and would like to share files with a coworker sitting across the table. To accomplish this, the coworker connects to a wireless SSID managed by your laptop. What type of network topology is this?

   ○ **A.** Unsecure

   ○ **B.** Ad hoc

   ○ **C.** Basic Service Set

   ○ **D.** Extended Service Set

5. You are using a Cisco 7921 wireless VoIP device. While speaking to your coworker on the phone, you are walking through multiple wireless cells. What type of network topology is this?

   ○ **A.** Unsecure

   ○ **B.** Ad hoc

   ○ **C.** Basic Service Set

   ○ **D.** Extended Service Set

6. Your organization uses a wireless security standard that requires people to authenticate to a back-end server with a valid active directory username and password before they are granted access to the wireless network. Upon successful authentication, the dynamic encryption keys are generated for use during the wireless session. What type of network security is in use?

   ○ **A.** WEP

   ○ **B.** WEP2

   ○ **C.** WPA

   ○ **D.** 802.11i

   ○ **E.** 802.1x (EAPOL)

7. Which of the following accurately describes the difference between WPA and WPA2?

   ○ **A.** WPA integrates with WEP encryption standards, whereas WPA2 is not backward-compatible.

   ○ **B.** WPA uses TKIP encryption, and WPA2 uses AES.

   ○ **C.** WPA uses preshared keys, and WPA2 allows for back-end user authentication.

   ○ **D.** WPA is used on 802.11a networks, whereas WPA2 is compatible with 802.11a/b/g networks.

8. You are troubleshooting a wireless laptop for a user in your organization. The wireless laptop cannot identify any available wireless SSIDs in the region. Your personal laptop can identify three SSIDs from the same location. The user has previously connected to the corporate network without issue. You have noticed increased interference from a neighboring company during different times of the day. What is the most likely cause of this issue?

    ○ **A.** The client wireless network card is disabled.

    ○ **B.** The RF interference has become too heavy for the client to view the available SSIDs.

    ○ **C.** The client wireless card is using the wrong frequency.

    ○ **D.** The signal is being absorbed before reaching the client laptop.

9. You suspect that one of your network users has violated the corporate security policy by plugging in a personal wireless access point in his cubicle. What Cisco security solution would allow you to detect this issue?

    ○ **A.** Cisco ACS Server

    ○ **B.** Cisco wireless IPS

    ○ **C.** Cisco wireless 802.1x

    ○ **D.** MAC address security

10. A network user has issued a trouble ticket stating that she is experiencing file transfers well below the 54Mbps speed that her wireless laptop claims to achieve. What are three valid reasons for this?

    ○ **A.** RF interference

    ○ **B.** CSMA/CA transmission method

    ○ **C.** Proximity to the access point

    ○ **D.** The duplex setting on the client's laptop

    ○ **E.** The client has not implemented 802.1x

Answers to Review Questions

1. The three encryption standards are WEP, WPA, and WPA2.

2. WEP uses the RC4 encryption algorithm. WPA uses the TKIP encryption method, which is more secure than WEP but not as secure as the WPA2 standard, which uses AES encryption. WEP does not have many strengths other than compatibility; all wireless devices can support the WEP standard. WPA has the strength of being interoperable with older WEP-compatible hardware, but it still has a few security weaknesses. WPA2 supports extremely strong encryption, but it is not backward-compatible with older wireless hardware.

3. Wireless networks are vulnerable to war driving, direct hacking, and employee ignorance.

4. Wireless access points should be deployed in a "tight configuration." This means that you should have many access points broadcasting smaller, more high-speed signals rather than a few access points broadcasting weaker signals that reach a larger radius.

5. First, ensure hardwire operation. Then, install the access point and test a basic network SSID with no security. Finally, add security and perform a final test.

Answers to Exam Questions

1. **A.** Rogue access points typically are brought in by internal corporate users with nonmalicious or malicious intent. Regardless of the intent, the rogue access point adds an enormous security liability to your network.

2. **C.** Wireless best practices recommend a 10 to 15% overlap of wireless cells. This allows for seamless roaming by wireless devices. Answer A is true only if the wireless access points are configured to use the same channel (frequency range). Because of this, you should never have adjacent access points using the same channel.

3. **D.** Both WEP (64-bit) and WEP2 (128-bit) encryption methods have been found to be insecure. The only time they should be used is in a network environment that uses older equipment and is unable to support the newer security standards.

4. **B.** Ad hoc networks are wireless networks generated from a participating device in the network, such as a laptop. These laptops can use many of the same security methods as BSS or ESS wireless topologies.

5. **D.** An Extended Service Set (ESS) wireless topology is the combination of two or more Basic Service Set (BSS) networks. This allows client roaming (between wireless cells) without service interruption.

6. **E.** 802.1x (less commonly known as Extensible Authentication Protocol over LAN [EAPOL]) adds a secure authentication system to a LAN environment. This technology can be used to secure both wired and wireless LAN connections. The other answers represent varying encryption standards.

7. **B.** WPA was released as an interim solution to improve the security of WEP. It uses an encryption method known as TKIP, which is more secure than WEP but not as secure as the WPA2 standard, which uses AES encryption.

8. **A.** The most likely cause of this issue is that the client wireless card is turned off. This happens frequently with laptops, because manufacturers commonly put a switch or button on the case of the laptop that easily turns the laptop on or off. The fact that it could not see any wireless networks while your personal laptop sat next to it reveals that wireless networks are reaching the location through the interference. The card cannot be the wrong frequency, because it previously connected to the corporate network without issue.

9. **B.** The Cisco wireless IPS system identifies rogue wireless access points added to the network. The 802.1x and the Cisco ACS Server are primarily responsible for user authentication and privileges. MAC address security can help disable a port with a rogue wireless access point, but it cannot detect the rogue's existence.

10. **A, B, C.** Wireless is susceptible to many types of RF interference. Likewise, the farther the client is from the access point, the lower her speed becomes. Finally, wireless uses a CSMA/CA transmission method, which causes the amount of bandwidth to diminish the more clients you add to the access point.

Suggested Readings and Resources

1. Wikipedia 802.11 definitions, http://en.wikipedia.org/wiki/802.11

2. How WiFi Works, http://computer.howstuffworks.com/wireless-network3.htm

3. Chris Ward and Jeremy Cioara. *CCNA Practice Questions*. Que Publishing, 2008.

4. Toby Velte and Anthony Velte. *Cisco 802.11 Wireless Networking Quick Reference*. Cisco Press, 2005.

CHAPTER NINETEEN

Using Cisco Access Lists

Objectives

This chapter covers the following Cisco-specific objectives for the "Implement, verify, and troubleshoot NAT and ACLs in a medium-size Enterprise branch office network" sections of the 640-802 CCNA:

▶ **Describe the purpose and types of ACLs**

▶ **Configure and apply ACLs based on network filtering requirements (including: CLI/SDM)**

▶ **Configure and apply ACLs to limit telnet and SSH access to the router (including: SDM/CLI)**

▶ **Verify and monitor ACLs in a network environment**

▶ **Troubleshoot ACL issues**

Outline

Study Strategies

▶ Read the information presented in the chapter, paying special attention to tables, Notes, and Exam Alerts.

▶ Spend plenty of time looking over the configuration examples. Understanding the configuration of access lists is paramount to understanding many of the upcoming chapters and exam objectives.

Introduction

A packet slides smoothly across the ethernet cable, gliding through a switch as it heads to its final destination: the company accounting server. Nobody in the network suspects that this is no normal packet. Behind all the source and destination header information lies a specially engineered code designed to unleash a denial of service attack when processed by the unsuspecting Windows 2003 Server platform. Just one more router to pass through and the deed will be done. Let's pick up the dialog here:

Incoming router Ethernet interface: bang, bang! (*a loud knock is heard*)

Router processor (*yelling*): "Source and destination please!"

Malicious packet (*in a scandalous voice*): "Yeah, I'm 10.6.9.2 headed to 10.56.100.10 on port 137...make it snappy."

* gunshot rings out, malicious packet falls to the ground *

Router processor (*scraping the crumpled bits into a bucket*): "Your type isn't welcome in these parts...punk."

You have just been witness to one of the most well-known uses of an access list: network traffic control. This function enables you to turn a common router into a fairly sophisticated firewall (the Dirty Harry dialog does require an IOS upgrade, however). As you might imagine, a cornerstone function like this is not only relevant for the CCNA exam, but also for Cisco network deployments worldwide.

Access List Concepts

Objective:

▶ Describe the purpose and types of ACLs

When you look at the term *access list*, the only word that stands out is *access*. Of course, this immediately causes any technology-minded person to conjure thoughts of controlling traffic, firewalls, and intrusion detection. Although this may have been Cisco's initial intention when they created the concept of access lists, nowadays access lists are used for a plethora of functions on any Cisco device. When you hear the term *access list*, don't focus on the word *access*; rather, focus on the word *list*.

An access list is nothing more than an ordered list of `permit` and `deny` statements. Every time the router needs to refer to the list for some reason, it reads it at the top and works its way down. You can picture it like a bouncer at an upscale drinking establishment. He may have the following list in his hand:

Deny Joshua Smith

Deny Benjamin Newport

Permit people with brown hair

The bouncer is then told to screen people as they attempt to enter the establishment. Now, when the first patron attempts to enter the building, the following transcript occurs:

Bouncer: "Is your name Joshua Smith?"

Patron: "No."

Bouncer: "Is your name Benjamin Newport?"

Patron: "No."

Bouncer: "Do you have brown hair?"

Patron: "Yes."

Bouncer: "You may enter our establishment."

The next person that attempts to enter the building is subjected to exactly the same list of questions in exactly the same order. Now this leads to a major question about this story: What if someone attempted to enter the building who did not have the name Joshua Smith or Benjamin Newport, but also did not have brown hair? That person is denied. No questions asked. This is one of the cornerstone facts of access lists on a Cisco device: *If you have not been explicitly permitted, you are implicitly denied.*

> **EXAM ALERT**
>
> Access lists always have an implicit deny statement at the end of the list. This statement is never displayed and cannot be seen through any show command. In an access list, if you have not been explicitly permitted, you are implicitly denied.

The implicit deny statement is hidden at the end of all access lists, and its order cannot be changed. However, the ordering of access lists elsewhere is of great importance. It can affect everything about your access list. For example, what if the question, "Do you have brown hair?" was listed first in the bouncer's access list? In that case, Joshua Smith or Benjamin Newport may have been permitted because they had brown hair, even though they were explicitly denied elsewhere in the list. A router stops processing an access list after an initial match statement is found. Let's leave the bouncer example behind for now and begin applying these concepts to networking.

Suppose you had defined the following access list (this is not correct syntax; rather, it is a conceptual view):

Permit host 192.168.1.50

Deny network 192.168.1.0/24

Permit host 192.168.1.100

<implicit deny>

This list would permit the host 192.168.1.50, as it intended. However, the host 192.168.1.100 would never be permitted because it is listed after the second statement in the list, which denies the entire Class C 192.168.1.0/24 subnet.

CAUTION

Depending on the IOS version you are using, there may be different ways the IOS formats access lists. In older IOS versions, the access list is arranged exactly as you enter it into the command line and cannot be reordered unless you completely erase the access list and re-create it. In modern IOS versions, the Cisco router can automatically reorder the list if you make an obvious mistake, as shown in the prior access list. In the newest versions of the IOS, the Cisco router assigns sequence numbers to each entry, allowing the addition, removal, and reordering of any line in the access list. (This is an awesome feature, which is covered later in the chapter during the discussion of named access lists.)

EXAM ALERT

For the CCNA exam, assume that the router is using an older version of the IOS that is arranged exactly as you enter it into the command line and cannot be reordered unless you completely erase the access list and re-create it.

Throughout the rest of this chapter, it is assumed that the IOS version is the same as it is on the CCNA exam. This means there is no automatic reordering of the list, lines cannot be individually removed, and the only additions that can be made are lines that are inserted at the end of the access list (this is the default when configuring the access list).

After all this, keep in mind that these are only the guidelines for creating an access list. Remember: An access list is just a list of `permit` and `deny` statements. The way in which you apply the access list defines the *function* of the access list. If you apply the access list inbound or outbound on a router interface, then the router begins to filter packets according to the instructions in the access list. If you apply the access list to your Network Address Translation (NAT) configuration, then the access list defines what IP addresses are permitted to be translated to an Internet-valid address. If you apply the access list to a dial-on-demand configuration, then the access list defines what devices or network traffic types are allowed to bring up a dial-up interface (such as a modem). I hope I am getting the point across: *An access list is nothing more than a list of* `permit` *and* `deny` *statements. How you apply it dictates what function the access list really serves.*

Functions of an Access List

Objective:

▶ Describe the purpose and types of ACLs

At this point, we have discussed a few access list uses in passing; however, the truth is that you will rarely encounter a major function of a Cisco router that does not require an access list in some way. For the CCNA exam, you should be aware of the following access list functions:

▶ Packet filtering

▶ Quality of service (QoS)

▶ Dial-on-demand routing (DDR)

▶ Network Address Translation (NAT)

▶ Route filtering

> **EXAM ALERT**
>
> **Although you may be required to understand some of the common applications of access lists on the CCNA exam, you will be required only to demonstrate proficiency in configuring access lists for packet filtering and NAT.**

Packet Filtering

Of course, packet filtering is the most well-known application of access lists. This access list application enables you to turn your router into a basic firewall. By using these foundation IOS features, you can begin filtering traffic inbound or outbound from any interface on your router. Depending on the type of access list you use, you can filter traffic based on the source address (standard access list) or based on the source and destination address, along with protocol and port number (extended access list).

> **CAUTION**
>
> As soon as you apply an access list for packet filtering inbound or outbound on an interface, the router must begin comparing every packet against the access list. Depending on the size and matching criteria of your access list, this can cause significant processor load.

Quality of Service

With the emerging technology of Voice over IP (VoIP), it has become necessary to give unequal treatment to network traffic. For example, if a router is receiving a considerable amount of Web surfing traffic (HTTP) and a VoIP telephone call attempts to come through, the VoIP conversation should receive prioritization over the HTTP traffic to ensure high-quality voice conversations; even if it means dropping a few of the HTTP packets. This is the concept of Quality of Service (QoS). The QoS matching methods rely extensively on access lists to define what types of traffic are prioritized over others. In this case, you see access lists in the view that they are *permitting* traffic to be prioritized and *denying* others from gaining network priority.

Now, not all QoS methods seek the good of the traffic they match. There is a QoS method called *traffic policing* that limits the bandwidth available to a certain application. For example, a network may have problems with users using peer-to-peer file sharing applications, such as Napster, Kazaa, or Morpheus, and depleting the Internet connection bandwidth. In this case, a QoS policing policy can be defined to limit the bandwidth available to these application types. Here's where the access list irony can be seen: The access list matches these applications (permits) and then restricts the amount of bandwidth they can use. The applications that are not matched (denied) do not have any bandwidth restrictions placed on them. In this access list function, from the application's point of view, it is better to be denied than permitted. Are you beginning to see that an access list is just a list of statements? How you apply that access list determines the effect it has on the network traffic.

Dial-on-Demand Routing

Dial-on-demand routing encompasses any type of temporary (not always on) connection. Despite their "legacy" stereotype, dial-up connections are here to stay because no other connection type has proved to be as reliable as the circuit switched technology. Although many people immediately think of modem connections, ISDN BRI and PRI services also fit this profile. In recent years in the United States, the number of ISDN BRI connections has dropped drastically because of the emergence of cheaper connections that use DSL and cable modem technology. However, the number of ISDN connections overseas is enormous.

Now you might wonder…what does dial-on-demand routing have to do with access lists? Well, in this case, access lists do not define what traffic is permitted across the dial-on-demand connection; rather, it defines what traffic is interesting enough to bring up the line. If you ever saw the movie *Wayne's World* in the early 90s, there is a moment where the singer Alice Cooper walks by Wayne and Garth. Immediately, they fall to the ground yelling, "We're not worthy!" In the same sense, you will create an access list that defines traffic that is "worthy" to dial the connection. Some ISDN connections charge a per-minute cost for being connected, so it may pay off to limit dial-up connections to certain traffic sources or packet types before the line is engaged.

Network Address Translation

Network Address Translation (NAT) has been in widespread use for over a decade, and yet still never ceases to amaze me. There is perhaps no other configuration that gives you as much satisfaction in "beating the system" as NAT (other than using your neighbor's wireless access point, of course). NAT theoretically allows more than 60,000 internal hosts to share a single, registered, public IP address to access the Internet. This has overcome the current public IP address shortage and extended the life of TCP/IP version four for years beyond what many thought possible.

> **EXAM ALERT**
>
> Because of the overwhelming popularity of NAT deployments, it is one of the newest topics to be added to the CCNA exam. You will be expected to configure NAT using the Cisco SDM for CCENT-level certification (covered in Chapter 20, "Enabling Internet Connectivity with NAT"). Configuring NAT from the command-line interface is required for CCNA-level certification (covered in Chapter 21, "Command-Line NAT Implementation").

The way access lists are used in NAT is similar to the way they were used in dial-on-demand routing. The access lists define what source addresses are "worthy enough" to be transmitted. A `permit` statement in the access list applied to a NAT configuration says, "This host (or subnet) is permitted to be translated with NAT." A `deny` statement in the same access list says, "This host (or subnet) is *not* permitted to be translated with NAT." A `deny` statement does not prevent traffic from being sent; rather, it denies it from being translated with NAT before it is sent.

Route Filtering

The final access list application covered in this text is route filtering. The routing protocols discussed so far, such as RIP, IGRP, EIGRP, and OSPF, all make it their mission to pass all known network routes to neighboring routers. In some network situations, this could cause a problem. Perhaps you don't want the router to pass *all* routes to *every* router on your network. For example, you might have some edge routers that connect to a partner company or an Internet-based peer. You could protect your network by using an access list to filter the routes that are sent and received to and from this peer.

A configuration known as a *distribute list* is used most often to apply the access list used for this function. In order to set this up, you would configure an access list permitting only the networks you would like to send or receive (or denying the networks you would not like to send or receive, depending on your strategy). As discussed before, creating the access list does absolutely nothing, functionally speaking; it must be applied to take action. In the case of route filtering, you would apply the access list under router configuration mode, `Router(config-router)`, for the routing protocol you would like to filter, by using the `distribute-list`

<access_list_number> <in/out> syntax. Access list numbers are used to identify the access list you are referencing. For example, if I wanted to keep my routing protocol from sending the routes I have listed as "deny" routes in access list #50, I would use the syntax:

```
Router(config-router)# distribute-list 50 out
```

If I wanted to keep my router from receiving the routes I had listed as "deny" routes in access list #50, I would use the syntax:

```
Router(config-router)# distribute-list 50 in
```

Standard Access Lists

Objective:

▶ Configure and apply ACLs based on network filtering requirements.

Cisco provides two primary categories of IP-based access lists: standard and extended. Standard access lists can permit or deny traffic based only on the source IP address. For example, I can set up an access list that says the host `192.168.1.1` is denied. However, if I use a standard access list to accomplish this, I can never say what destination the host is denied from reaching or what protocol it is denied from using; I can say only that they are denied. Period. Therefore, the interface on the router where you apply the standard access list can make all the difference. The benefits of using standard access lists are the simplicity and resource usage. Because the standard access lists filter based only on the source IP address, the router processor and memory resources are not as taxed as they are when you use an extended access list.

Configuration of Standard Access Lists

Whenever you decide to begin configuring any type of access list, remember this wisdom from the Cisco elders: Context-sensitive help is your friend. If you have not yet become accustomed to entering a question mark after each step of your configuration, now is the perfect chance to gain that familiarity. In these initial examples, the question mark is entered after each command to find out what arguments the router expects next.

The standard access list is created from Global Configuration mode with the `access-list` command, so that's where this example begins:

```
Neo(config)#access-list ?
  <1-99>            IP standard access list
  <100-199>         IP extended access list
  <1100-1199>       Extended 48-bit MAC address access list
  <1300-1999>       IP standard access list (expanded range)
  <200-299>         Protocol type-code access list
```

```
<2000-2699>        IP extended access list (expanded range)
<700-799>          48-bit MAC address access list
dynamic-extended  Extend the dynamic ACL absolute timer
```

Just by looking at the categories of access-list, you can tell what protocols this router supports. In this case, the router supports the IP-only feature set. Otherwise, you would see access list categories for each protocol (such as IPX/SPX, Appletalk, or Decnet). Notice the number ranges for each access list; the type of access list you are going to create depends on what number you type after the access-list command. If you were to type **access-list 25**, the syntax that followed would be that of a standard access list because you chose a number between 1 and 99. Likewise, if you were to enter the command **access-list 135**, the syntax that followed would be that of an extended access list because you chose a number between 100 and 199.

> **EXAM ALERT**
>
> Knowing that access list numbers 1–99 represent standard access lists and 100–199 represent extended access lists increases your chances of passing the CCNA exam by at least 1.2%.

In addition to dictating the type of access list that will be created, the access *list* number represents your access list as a whole. As the name "access *list*" implies, each access list number can contain many individual statements. For example, you could create access list 4, which contains 3000 specific lines dictating what source IP addresses are permitted and denied.

Even though each access list can contain many statements, if you have a router with an extremely complex configuration, you could run out of access lists. For this reason, Cisco created the expanded access list ranges for both standard (1300–1999) and extended (2000–2699) access lists, as shown in the prior syntax. This ensures that routers will never run out of IP access list numbers again. The configuration example continues by using access list number 25:

```
Neo(config)#access-list 25 ?
  deny    Specify packets to reject
  permit  Specify packets to forward
  remark  Access list entry comment
```

The first decision you need to make about this access list entry is whether the statement will permit or deny. Remember, at the bottom of every access list is the invisible implicit deny, so you need to permit at least one thing. Imagine that you want to permit the host 10.1.1.5:

```
Neo(config)#access-list 25 permit ?
  Hostname or A.B.C.D  Address to match
  any                  Any source host
  host                 A single host address
```

You are now given the option to either enter an IP address, use the any keyword to match any source host address, or to use the host keyword to match a single host address. You might ask the question at this point, "So do I enter the IP address 10.1.1.5 here, or the keyword host?" You can enter either one. Try entering the IP address first, and then the example returns to the host command:

```
Neo(config)#access-list 25 permit 10.1.1.5 ?
  A.B.C.D  Wildcard bits
  log      Log matches against this entry
```

Because the host keyword was not used, the router is now prompting for the correct wildcard bits. This may bring back bad memories of the OSPF routing protocol, which is another major router configuration that relies on wildcard masks (also called inverse masks) to specify OSPF interface(s). Just to review, a wildcard mask is exactly the opposite of a subnet mask. The zero bits (0) of a wildcard mask say, "Look at these," whereas the one bits (1) of a wildcard mask say, "I don't care." For example, if you entered the IP address 172.16.0.0 with a wildcard mask 0.0.255.255, the router would look at the 172.16 digits (because they matched the binary zeros in the wildcard mask) and would not care about the 0.0 digits (because they matched the binary ones in the wildcard mask). This means that the address 172.16.90.100 would match because all the router cares about is that the address starts with 172.16. This now brings us back to the configuration. You need to create a wildcard mask that matches exactly the IP address 10.1.1.5. It would be safe to say that you want the router to look at every single octet of that IP address, so the appropriate wildcard mask would be 0.0.0.0. Here's a look at the complete line of syntax:

```
Neo(config)#access-list 25 permit 10.1.1.5 0.0.0.0 ?
  log  Log matches against this entry
  <cr>
```

Notice that the only options context-sensitive help gives you is to enter the log command (which writes a record to the router log file anytime this entry is matched) or to press Enter. If you choose the latter, you enter your first line into an access list. Let's work through the syntax one more time to add a second statement to the access list. This time, you want to permit the entire 192.168.77.0/24 subnet:

```
Neo(config)#access-list ?
  <1-99>      IP standard access list
  <100-199>   IP extended access list
  <1000-1099> IPX SAP access list
  <1100-1199> Extended 48-bit MAC address access list
  <1200-1299> IPX summary address access list
  <1300-1999> IP standard access list (expanded range)
  <200-299>   Protocol type-code access list
  <2000-2699> IP extended access list (expanded range)
  <300-399>   DECnet access list
  <400-499>   XNS standard access list
  <500-599>   XNS extended access list
  <600-699>   Appletalk access list
  <700-799>   48-bit MAC address access list
  <800-899>   IPX standard access list
```

```
<900-999>   IPX extended access list
rate-limit  Simple rate-limit specific access list
```

Notice the IOS on the Neo router has been upgraded to a version that supports a few more protocols than the prior IOS version. You will now continue on through this configuration of permitting the entire 192.168.77.0/24 subnet, using context-sensitive help to guide you through each additional piece of syntax.

```
Neo(config)#access-list 25 ?
  deny    Specify packets to reject
  permit  Specify packets to forward

Neo(config)#access-list 25 permit ?
  Hostname or A.B.C.D  Address to match
  any                  Any source host
  host                 A single host address

Neo(config)#access-list 25 permit 192.168.77.0 ?
  A.B.C.D  Wildcard bits
  log      Log matches against this entry
  <cr>

Neo(config)#access-list 25 permit 192.168.77.0 0.0.0.255 ?
  log  Log matches against this entry
  <cr>

Neo(config)#access-list 25 permit 192.168.77.0 0.0.0.255
Neo(config)#
```

The second line has just been added to access list 25. Notice that the wildcard mask 0.0.0.255 tells the router to look at the 192.168.77 (the first three octets of zero bits in the wildcard mask), and to ignore the last octet (because of the one bit in the last octet of the wildcard mask). You can now use a couple of show commands to verify your work: show ip access-lists or show running-config.

```
Neo#show ip access-lists
Standard IP access list 25
    permit 10.1.1.5
    permit 192.168.77.0, wildcard bits 0.0.0.255


Neo@show running-config
Building configuration...
<…output omitted…>
access-list 25 permit 10.1.1.5
access-list 25 permit 192.168.77.0 0.0.0.255
```

Initially, it looks as if the router lost the wildcard mask that was added for the 10.1.1.5 host. The Cisco router removes the 0.0.0.0 because an IP address without the wildcard mask is assumed to be an individual host anyway.

EXAM ALERT

Some IOS versions completely remove the wildcard mask as shown in the text, whereas other, newer IOS versions insert the `host` keyword, such as in the following:

```
access-list 25 permit host 10.1.1.5
```

To be safe on the CCNA exam, always use either the wildcard mask or the `host` keyword when configuring your access list in a simulation. Never just type in an IP address and press Enter. Although this may work on real Cisco equipment, the test simulations may deduct points.

Placement of Standard Access Lists

As mentioned before, you can create access lists all day on your router and no functional change will ever occur. Access lists take effect only when you apply them in some way. This chapter focuses on applying access lists for security purposes. Access lists can be placed inbound or outbound on any router interface. When applying `access-list` for security, remember this mantra:

One access list...

> ...per protocol,

> > ...per interface,

> > > ...per direction

You must take these rules into account when deciding how to engineer the access list. Here is what the mantra means: You must design a single access list to include all the possible `permit` and `deny` statements you need for each protocol (such as TCP/IP or IPX/SPX, not sub-protocols such as TCP or UDP) on a single interface for the inbound or outbound direction. You are allowed to apply only one access list number inbound and one access list outbound.

Finally, keep this in mind before you apply an access list: The access list goes into effect *immediately* when applied. Before you apply the access list, check the access list thoroughly to make sure you have allowed enough traffic to pass through. The most common mistake made by network administrators is to create an access list and quickly list the items they want to deny. They then apply this to an interface, forgetting about the implicit deny at the end of the access list. The access list then acts as a "deny all" statement for the interface, effectively shutting down the communication on that interface. If this is done in a production network, it can have devastating effects.

The other common mistake is to make changes to an access list while it is applied to an interface. Although this can be done successfully, it is not recommended. The changes go into effect immediately after you press the Enter key, not giving you the time you need to take the entire access list into consideration.

NOTE

Many Cisco administrators create their access lists in a text editor such as Notepad, which enables you to reorder the statements as you see fit before the access list is created and applied.

With all these cautions in place, the syntax to apply the access list to the interface is simple. Use the following syntax from interface configuration mode:

```
Router(config-if)#ip access-group <access_list_number> <in/out>
```

The <in/out> keyword tends to be the most confusing portion of this syntax. The in keyword filters inbound traffic to the interface, whereas the out keyword filters outbound traffic from the interface. The easiest way to remember this is to picture yourself as a router. Seriously, stand up and say out loud, "I am a router." Now hold your arms out and picture them as router interfaces. Your left arm is a FastEthernet connection to a switch. Your right arm is a serial link to a remote office. If you apply an access list on your FastEthernet interface in the IN-bound direction, it filters traffic coming from the switch, up your arm, and into your body. If you apply it OUT-bound on your FastEthernet interface, you are filtering traffic leaving your body, and going out to the switch. By putting yourself in the place of the router, you will get the direction right every time.

EXAM ALERT

Cisco testing procedures do not currently restrict you from standing and waving your arms wildly in the testing center as long as you do not hit any other test takers.

For example, let's apply access list 25 that was created previously to a router's FastEthernet 0 interface in the inbound direction. Just as a refresher, I list the syntax used to create the access list first, and then apply it to the interface:

```
Trinity(config)#access-list 25 permit 10.1.1.5 0.0.0.0
Trinity(config)#access-list 25 permit 192.168.77.0 0.0.0.255
Trinity(config)#interface fastethernet 0
Trinity(config-if)#ip access-group 25 in
```

The access list is now applied and in effect. The router permits the host 10.1.1.5 and anyone from the network 192.168.77.0/24 to enter the router's FastEthernet 0 interface (inbound) from an attached switch. The implicit deny keeps any other devices from entering FastEthernet 0.

Standard Access List Examples

Now let's start putting this newfound knowledge into practice. Use the topology shown in Figure 19.1 to see a visual diagram for this example.

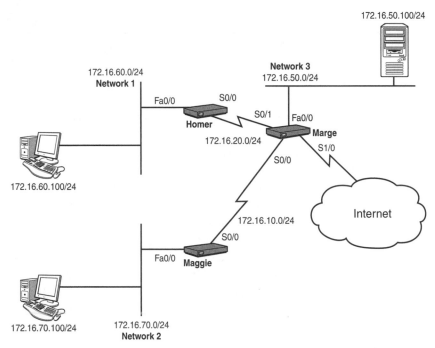

FIGURE 19.1 Standard access list deployment.

Isolating Networks

To keep devices on Network 3 from accessing devices on Network 1 the first thing you must determine is where in the network you want to create the access list. When configuring standard access lists, the best practice is to create and apply the access list on the router closest to the *destination*. Standard access lists cannot dictate what the source IP addresses are permitted or denied; they can say just that they are permitted or denied. By applying the access list close to the destination, you effectively limit the scope of effect that the access list has. If you apply it too close to the source, you may deny or permit too much. You will see more examples of this as you work through applying more access lists.

EXAM ALERT

Know that the best practice of standard access lists is to apply them on the interface closest to the destination.

When you look at the figure, you can see that the Homer router is closest to the destination (Network 1), so that is the place to begin configuration:

```
Homer>enable
Homer#configure terminal
Homer(config)#access-list 30 deny 172.16.50.0 0.0.0.255
```

A line has been added to the access list to block Network 1. If the access list is left like this, it will also deny all other traffic because of the implicit deny at the end, so you need to add a statement that permits all other networks to reach Network 1:

```
Homer(config)#access-list 30 permit any
```

TIP

The any keyword is a shortcut, just as the host keyword is. You could accomplish the same thing by using the statement:

```
access-list 30 permit 0.0.0.0 255.255.255.255
```

When you have a wildcard mask of all 255s, the router does not care what you enter for the IP address (which is all zeros in this case, but could have been anything). This is equivalent to a permit any statement. Use whichever one you feel more comfortable with.

You have created the access list; now it's time to apply it. Looking back at the figure, there are two possible places to apply this access list on the Homer router: inbound on the S0/0 interface, or outbound on the Fa0/0 interface. Using the best practice of applying closest to the destination, this is how to do the latter:

```
Homer(config)#interface fastethernet 0/0
Homer(config-if)#ip access-group 30 out
```

Voilà! This part of the example is accomplished. Now here's the complete code without the commentary:

```
Homer>enable
Homer#configure terminal
Homer(config)#access-list 30 deny 172.16.50.0 0.0.0.255
Homer(config)#access-list 30 permit any
Homer(config)#interface fastethernet 0/0
Homer(config-if)#ip access-group 30 out
```

Isolating a Network from Specific Hosts

You now need to prevent just two devices (the Network 1 and 2 hosts) from accessing Network 3. If you remember the rule of applying the standard access list closest to the destination, you know that the configuration should be performed on the Marge router:

```
Marge>enable
Marge#configure terminal
Marge(config)#access-list 45 deny host 172.16.70.100
Marge(config)#access-list 45 deny host 172.16.60.100
Marge(config)#access-list 45 permit any
```

Now that the access list has been created, you have to decide where to apply it. Initially, you might eye the S0/0 interface inbound. If you applied it there, the host 172.16.70.100 and 172.16.60.100 would be denied as soon as they tried to make their way into the S0/0 interface of Marge. Although this would prevent the hosts from reaching Network 3, it would also block them from accessing Network 1 and the Internet (because they cannot even enter the Marge router). Aha! Do you now see why it is so important to apply the standard access list close to the destination? In this case, you need to apply it to the FastEthernet 0/0 interface, outbound:

```
Marge(config)#interface fastethernet 0/0
Marge(config-if)#ip access-group 45 out
```

Perfect. This part of the example is complete.

Isolating the Internal Network from the Internet

The servers on Network 3 contain confidential information and should not be accessible from the Internet. Assuming your entire internal network uses 172.16.0.0/16 addresses, this configuration should maintain the isolation of Network 3 from Network 1 and 2 hosts. Wow! This requires a little thought. You have no idea what addresses may be trying to come in from the Internet, so you have to reverse your strategies. So far, you have been denying a host or network and permitting everything else. You must now permit what you know and deny everything else, still keeping in mind that you cannot allow the two hosts from the previous objective to access the server. Start on the Marge router in Global Configuration mode and remove the access list applied previously:

```
Marge(config)#no access-list 45
```

CAUTION

Removing the access list by using the no access-list <number> command does not remove the access-group command from the interface. The access list is still applied! Thankfully, an empty access list allows all traffic (this overrules the implicit deny statement). However, as soon as you add one line to the access list, the implicit deny statement is reapplied with all its fury. It is a very good idea to un-apply the access list from the interface while you make changes.

Whew! That caution popped up at just the right place. Let's follow that advice:

```
Marge(config)#interface fastethernet 0/0
Marge(config-if)#no ip access-group 45 out
```

Now you can start on a new access list. First, deny the specific hosts that should not be able to reach Network 3:

```
Marge(config)#access-list 45 deny host 172.16.70.100
Marge(config)#access-list 45 deny host 172.16.60.100
```

Super. Now that they're taken care of, you can permit the rest of the 172.16.0.0/16 subnet (all the internal networks):

```
Marge(config)#access-list 45 permit 172.16.0.0 0.0.255.255
```

Notice that the wildcard mask cares about only the first two octets of the IP address, thus permitting any IP address that begins with 172.16. This is why the `deny` statements for the hosts were listed first. Otherwise, this line would have permitted them. With the one `permit` statement added, you have finished creating the access list. The implicit `deny` should catch any other networks not specified (including those coming from the Internet). Finally, using best practices, you need to apply this list close to the destination:

```
Marge(config)#interface fastethernet 0/0
Marge(config-if)#ip access-group 45 out
```

Awesome! This just keeps getting better. Mission accomplished.

Restricting VTY Access

Objective:

▶ Configure and apply ACLs to limit telnet and SSH access to the router

Now here's a new application for an access list. So far, access lists have been applied inbound and outbound on interfaces, but access lists can also be applied to VTY lines (which are used for Telnet and SSH). This example will allow only the host on Network 2 to Telnet to the Marge router. The command syntax to do this differs slightly from applying an access list to an interface. Instead of using the `ip access-group` command, use the `access-class` command.

After referring back to the figure, you can see that the host on Network 2 has the IP address 172.16.70.100. Here's the configuration:

```
Marge(config)#access-list 55 permit host 172.16.70.100
Marge(config)#line vty 0 4cm
Marge(config-line)#access-class 55 in
```

That's it! The implicit `deny` blocks all other hosts from accessing your VTY lines. This brings up a huge tip.

> **CAUTION**
>
> If you are configuring access lists on your router remotely, be sure to allow your remote Telnet session access into the router in the access list. It is a very common mistake to create an access list that kills the remote Telnet session and requires the administrator to drive to the site (or contact someone on-site) to reconfigure the router through the console port. It is, therefore, a good practice to issue the following command before applying an access list remotely:
>
> ```
> Router# reload in 5
> ```
>
> This instructs the router to reboot itself in 5 minutes if there is no administrative intervention. This way, if you lock yourself out of the router, it reboots and sets its configuration back to what it was before you applied the access list. If the access list applies successfully without limiting remote access, be sure to issue the `reload cancel` command to stop the automatic reboot countdown.

Extended Access Lists

"Beware of the extended access list!" This grave warning comes from many CCNA testers who have gone before you. Out of all the topics on the CCNA exam, not one has come close to tripping up candidates more than the extended access list. With most things in Cisco, the difficulty comes in the concept and the syntax is quite simple. However, when it comes to the extended access lists, the concepts are fairly straightforward; it is the syntax that can be a monster. Fear not, my brave CCNA studier. After working through this section, you will feel quite comfortable with extended access lists.

Configuration of Extended Access Lists

After you have set up a few standard access lists, you'll have the configuration mastered. Standard access lists allow you to permit or deny network traffic based only on the source address. On the other hand, extended access lists allow you to permit or deny traffic based on the sub-protocol, source address, source port number, destination address, and destination port number—and that's just what is on the CCNA exam. An extended access list can even filter based on time of day or user authentication. Now if you imagine fitting all those parameters into a single line of syntax, you begin to understand why extended access list syntax can become quite long.

Before we get deep into each step of the syntax, let's take a step back and look at extended access list parameters from a distance. First off, extended access lists are identified by the numbers 100–199, as shown by context-sensitive help:

```
Neo(config)#access-list ?
  <1-99>           IP standard access list
  <100-199>        IP extended access list
  <1100-1199>      Extended 48-bit MAC address access list
  <1300-1999>      IP standard access list (expanded range)
  <200-299>        Protocol type-code access list
```

```
<2000-2699>       IP extended access list (expanded range)
<700-799>         48-bit MAC address access list
dynamic-extended  Extend the dynamic ACL absolute timer
```

From a broad view, an extended access list requires three major parameters: a protocol, source information, and destination information. The general syntax looks like this:

```
Access-list <100-199> <protocol> <source_information>
<destination_information>
```

Now let's walk through the creation of an extended access list, one piece at a time. This example uses access list 150, putting it smack in the middle of the access list range. For this example, web access should be allowed for one host, 10.1.1.5.

```
Neo(config)#access-list 150 ?
  deny     Specify packets to reject
  dynamic  Specify a DYNAMIC list of PERMITs or DENYs
  permit   Specify packets to forward
  remark   Access list entry comment
```

The first thing you notice is that you have the standard <permit/deny> option, but now a dynamic option has been added to the list. Although dynamic access lists are beyond the scope of the CCNA certification, the concept is pretty amazing: You can have an access list that allows minimal outbound or inbound access. If you have a user that needs access to a network through your router, you can authenticate that user to the router with a pre-determined username and password. If the authentication is successful, a dynamic entry is added to the access list allowing the device access for a certain amount of time, after which the access list entry is removed. Amazing stuff!

Because extended access lists have the same implicit deny statement as standard access lists, you must permit at least one type of packet or all traffic is denied. You can now continue on through this configuration of permitting web access for the host 10.1.1.5, using context-sensitive help to guide you through each additional piece of syntax.

```
Neo(config)#access-list 150 permit ?
  <0-255>  An IP protocol number
  ahp      Authentication Header Protocol
  eigrp    Cisco's EIGRP routing protocol
  esp      Encapsulation Security Payload
  gre      Cisco's GRE tunneling
  icmp     Internet Control Message Protocol
  igmp     Internet Gateway Message Protocol
  ip       Any Internet Protocol
  ipinip   IP in IP tunneling
  nos      KA9Q NOS compatible IP over IP tunneling
  ospf     OSPF routing protocol
  pcp      Payload Compression Protocol
  pim      Protocol Independent Multicast
  tcp      Transmission Control Protocol
  udp      User Datagram Protocol
```

Now the syntax is starting to look quite a bit different from the standard access list. You now have the choice of what protocol to permit or deny.

These protocols are roughly defined as the following (the applications are explained further during the discussion on port numbers):

▶ **IP**—Permits or denies source/destination addresses that use the entire TCP/IP protocol suite. Using this keyword permits or denies *all* access from a source to a destination.

▶ **TCP**—Permits or denies source/destination addresses that use TCP-based applications. The most common applications include FTP, Telnet, SMTP, and HTTP.

▶ **UDP**—Permits or denies source/destination addresses that use UDP-based applications. The most common applications include DNS and TFTP.

▶ **ICMP**—Permits or denies source/destination addresses that use ICMP-based applications. The most common applications include Echo, Echo-Reply, and Unreachables.

In this example, the access list needs to permit HTTP access, which uses the TCP protocol.

```
Neo(config)#access-list 150 permit tcp ?
  A.B.C.D  Source address
  any      Any source host
  host     A single source host
```

You are now prompted for the source IP address information. Just as with a standard access list, you have the option of entering a source IP address followed by a wildcard mask, using the host keyword to designate an individual host, or using the any keyword to designate all hosts. This example uses the host keyword to designate an individual PC.

```
Neo(config)#access-list 150 permit tcp host 10.1.1.5 ?
  A.B.C.D  Destination address
  any      Any destination host
  eq       Match only packets on a given port number
  gt       Match only packets with a greater port number
  host     A single destination host
  lt       Match only packets with a lower port number
  neq      Match only packets not on a given port number
  range    Match only packets in the range of port numbers
```

From this next context-sensitive help prompt, it looks as if there is a prompt to enter either a destination IP address or port information. BEWARE! This is where most extended access list mistakes are made! As you can see from the context-sensitive help, you can enter many forms of port information: a port equal (eq) to a certain number, greater than (gt) a certain number, less than (lt) a certain port number, a range of port numbers, and the list goes on and on. Initially, you might think that this is the place to permit the port for HTTP access (port 80). Unfortunately, that thought process is incorrect. This area is where you discover the strange and fascinating phenomena known as a source port number.

By this point, you most likely know the commonly used port numbers such as TCP port 21 for FTP, TCP port 80 for HTTP, and so on. However, most administrators never learn that these are actually destination port numbers. For any TCP/IP-based communication, there is always a destination *and* source port number. Here's how it works: imagine you have a PC connected directly to the Internet. You would like to use a web browser to access the latest news headlines; however, like most technology-based individuals, you also have 10 other web browser instances minimized at the bottom of your task bar. You open a new web browser (instance #11) and access the news website. Sure enough, the web browser window fills with text and pictures of all the latest news and events. Now how in the world did your computer know to fill *that* web browser window (#11) with the information rather than one of the other 10 you had minimized at the bottom of the screen? The answer is in the source port information. As soon as you opened the web browser #11, Windows (or whatever operating system you are using) generated a unique source port number for that window. Whenever it attempts to communicate with the destination host, it uses its unique source port number. The source port number that the operating system chooses is always above the range of "well known" ports (which range from 0–1023).

For example, imagine that the news website you want to communicate with is Fox News (www.foxnews.com), and your PC's IP address is 204.1.9.52. When the web browser opens, it generates a random source port of 3382. As shown in Figure 19.2, when the web request is sent from your PC to the Fox News web server, it is sent to the destination www.foxnews.com:80 (this is known as a socket—the combination of a destination IP address with a destination port number). It has a source of 204.1.9.52:3382. When the Fox News website communicates back to your PC, it uses a destination of 204.1.9.52:3382 with a source address of www.foxnews.com:80.

Back to the task at hand. If you enter port number information after the source IP address, you permit or deny *source* port information.

NOTE

You will rarely, if ever, know a network device's source port number information. This number is randomly generated by the host's operating system.

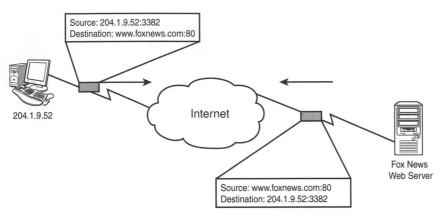

FIGURE 19.2 TCP communication using source and destination port numbers.

By omitting the any source port information and continuing on to the destination address specifications, the Cisco router assumes all source ports are permitted. This example allows web access. The destination address is the entire Internet address space. This can be easily summed up with the destination address keyword of any. The following code enters the any keyword and continues to use the context-sensitive help to guide you through each additional piece of syntax.

```
Neo(config)#access-list 150 permit tcp host 10.1.1.5 any ?
  ack           Match on the ACK bit
  dscp          Match packets with given dscp value
  eq            Match only packets on a given port number
  established   Match established connections
  fin           Match on the FIN bit
  fragments     Check non-initial fragments
  gt            Match only packets with a greater port number
  log           Log matches against this entry
  log-input     Log matches against this entry, including input interface
  lt            Match only packets with a lower port number
  neq           Match only packets not on a given port number
  precedence    Match packets with given precedence value
  psh           Match on the PSH bit
  range         Match only packets in the range of port numbers
  rst           Match on the RST bit
  syn           Match on the SYN bit
  time-range    Specify a time-range
  tos           Match packets with given TOS value
  urg           Match on the URG bit
  <cr>
```

Now you can see that you have a multitude of choices, some of which include the same port number options you were given before. Now that the destination IP address information has been specified (with the any keyword), you can now fill in the destination port number. Most of the time you will use the eq (equals to) port number syntax to designate a single port number. The following code enters the eq keyword and continues to use the context-sensitive help to guide you through each additional piece of syntax.

```
Neo(config)#access-list 150 permit tcp host 10.1.1.5 any eq ?
  <0-65535>    Port number
  bgp          Border Gateway Protocol (179)
  chargen      Character generator (19)
  cmd          Remote commands (rcmd, 514)
  daytime      Daytime (13)
  discard      Discard (9)
  domain       Domain Name Service (53)
  echo         Echo (7)
  exec         Exec (rsh, 512)
  finger       Finger (79)
  ftp          File Transfer Protocol (21)
  ftp-data     FTP data connections (20)
<…output omitted for brevity…>
  telnet       Telnet (23)
  time         Time (37)
  uucp         Unix-to-Unix Copy Program (540)
  whois        Nicname (43)
  www          World Wide Web (HTTP, 80)
```

Notice that the context-sensitive help now provides a list of commonly used port numbers. At the top of the list is the option <0-65536>, enabling you to enter any port number you choose. In this example, you can enter either the keyword www or port number 80 and the result will be the same.

EXAM ALERT

Although you can see the list of commonly used port numbers right now, the list may not be available to you in the CCNA exam. At a minimum, you should commit the following list of ports to memory:

TCP Ports:

      Port 21: FTP

      Port 23: Telnet

      Port 25: SMTP

      Port 53: DNS

      Port 80: HTTP

      Port 443: HTTPS

UDP Ports:

      Port 53: DNS

      Port 69: TFTP

To complete the access list, the necessary port information is added:

```
Neo(config)#access-list 150 permit tcp host 10.1.1.5 any eq 80
```

As before, for the access list to take effect, it must be applied. The same syntax is used to do this as is used for the standard access list: ip access-group <in/out>. Don't forget the best way to find the direction you should apply the access list: Imagine yourself as a router. Is the traffic going away from you (leaving one of your interfaces)? Apply the access list *out*bound. Is the traffic coming into you (received by one of your interfaces)? Apply the access list *in*bound.

Cisco recommends applying extended access lists closer to the source of the network traffic you are permitting or denying. This is completely opposite to what you do with standard access lists. The reason for the complete turnaround is that extended access lists enable you to specify source *and* destination requirements, whereas standard access lists allow you to specify only source requirements. With a standard access list, network traffic may have to cross an entire worldwide network just to find out that it has been denied. With extended access lists, you can designate that traffic is denied from a certain destination before that traffic ever leaves its local subnet.

EXAM ALERT

Standard access lists are always applied closest to the destination. Extended access lists are always applied closest to the source.

Practical Extended Access List Examples

Because of their flexibility, extended access lists are, by far, the most commonly used access lists in production networks. This section takes a look at a few real-world requirements and puts extended access lists into action. Figure 19.3 shows the network diagram used for the extended access list examples.

Blocking a Subnet

This example blocks the Network 2 subnet from reaching the intranet server using the FTP protocol. You must first decide what router to work with. Extended access list best practices recommend denying this traffic as close to the source as possible. This means that you need to access the Maggie router.

```
Maggie(config)#access-list ?
  <1-99>             IP standard access list
  <100-199>          IP extended access list
  <1100-1199>        Extended 48-bit MAC address access list
  <1300-1999>        IP standard access list (expanded range)
  <200-299>          Protocol type-code access list
  <2000-2699>        IP extended access list (expanded range)
  <700-799>          48-bit MAC address access list
  dynamic-extended   Extend the dynamic ACL absolute timer
```

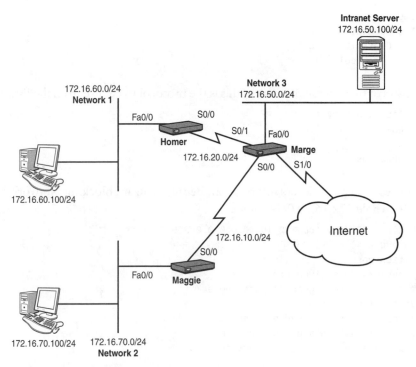

FIGURE 19.3 Extended access lists network diagram.

Because these are extended access lists, you must use access list numbers 100–199. This example uses 125.

```
Maggie(config)#access-list 125 ?
  deny      Specify packets to reject
  dynamic   Specify a DYNAMIC list of PERMITs or DENYs
  permit    Specify packets to forward
  remark    Access list entry comment
```

The objective requires you to deny FTP traffic, so you should use the deny keyword:

```
Maggie(config)#access-list 125 deny ?
  <0-255>  An IP protocol number
  ahp      Authentication Header Protocol
  eigrp    Cisco's EIGRP routing protocol
  esp      Encapsulation Security Payload
  gre      Cisco's GRE tunneling
  icmp     Internet Control Message Protocol
  igmp     Internet Gateway Message Protocol
  ip       Any Internet Protocol
  ipinip   IP in IP tunneling
  nos      KA9Q NOS compatible IP over IP tunneling
  ospf     OSPF routing protocol
```

```
pcp          Payload Compression Protocol
pim          Protocol Independent Multicast
tcp          Transmission Control Protocol
udp          User Datagram Protocol
```

The FTP application protocol runs on top of TCP, so this is the protocol to choose from the list:

```
Maggie(config)#access-list 125 deny tcp ?
  A.B.C.D  Source address
  any      Any source host
  host     A single source host
```

The access list now requires source IP address information. Because you are blocking Network 2, you should include the whole 172.16.70.0/24 range:

```
Maggie(config)#access-list 125 deny tcp 172.16.70.0 0.0.0.255 ?
  A.B.C.D  Destination address
  any      Any destination host
  eq       Match only packets on a given port number
  gt       Match only packets with a greater port number
  host     A single destination host
  lt       Match only packets with a lower port number
  neq      Match only packets not on a given port number
  range    Match only packets in the range of port numbers
```

Be careful, now. You can enter either the destination IP address information or port number information. Remember, this first prompt enables you to enter *source* port information. You will rarely, if ever, enter any source port restrictions. Of course, the CCNA exam constantly tries to trick you with this often confused fact. This example continues right on to the destination IP address information. The intranet server has the address 172.16.50.100.

```
Maggie(config)#access-list 125 deny tcp 172.16.70.0 0.0.0.255
3host 172.16.50.100 ?
  ack         Match on the ACK bit
  dscp        Match packets with given dscp value
  eq          Match only packets on a given port number
  established Match established connections
  fin         Match on the FIN bit
  fragments   Check non-initial fragments
  gt          Match only packets with a greater port number
  log         Log matches against this entry
  log-input   Log matches against this entry, including input interface
  lt          Match only packets with a lower port number
  neq         Match only packets not on a given port number
  precedence  Match packets with given precedence value
  psh         Match on the PSH bit
  range       Match only packets in the range of port numbers
  rst         Match on the RST bit
  syn         Match on the SYN bit
```

```
time-range    Specify a time-range
tos           Match packets with given TOS value
urg           Match on the URG bit
<cr>
```

Now you are given the option again to enter the port configurations. At this point, the router is requesting destination port information, which is what you need to use to block FTP. Before you can specify an individual port, you must first designate the eq (equal to) syntax:

```
Maggie(config)# access-list 125 deny tcp 172.16.70.0 0.0.0.255
3host 172.16.50.100 eq ?
  <0-65535>     Port number
  bgp           Border Gateway Protocol (179)
  chargen       Character generator (19)
  cmd           Remote commands (rcmd, 514)
  daytime       Daytime (13)
  discard       Discard (9)
  domain        Domain Name Service (53)
  echo          Echo (7)
  exec          Exec (rsh, 512)
  finger        Finger (79)
  ftp           File Transfer Protocol (21)
  ftp-data      FTP data connections (20)
<…output omitted for brevity…>
  telnet        Telnet (23)
  time          Time (37)
  uucp          Unix-to-Unix Copy Program (540)
  whois         Nicname (43)
  www           World Wide Web (HTTP, 80)
```

You are again given a laundry list of port numbers that you can enter. You can enter the exact port number or use the commonly used port names in the list.

```
Maggie(config)#access-list 125 deny tcp 172.16.70.0 0.0.0.255
3host 172.16.50.100 eq 21
```

The first line of the access list is now created, but don't forget that there is still an implicit deny at the end of the list. If you were to apply this list now, it would block the subnet from reaching anything. You must add at least one permit line; in this case, it is a permit any statement.

```
Maggie(config)#access-list 125 permit ?
  <0-255>   An IP protocol number
  ahp       Authentication Header Protocol
  eigrp     Cisco's EIGRP routing protocol
  esp       Encapsulation Security Payload
  gre       Cisco's GRE tunneling
  icmp      Internet Control Message Protocol
  igmp      Internet Gateway Message Protocol
  ip        Any Internet Protocol
```

```
ipinip     IP in IP tunneling
nos        KA9Q NOS compatible IP over IP tunneling
ospf       OSPF routing protocol
pcp        Payload Compression Protocol
pim        Protocol Independent Multicast
tcp        Transmission Control Protocol
udp        User Datagram Protocol
```

> **CAUTION**
>
> Remember that with extended access lists, the only protocol that encompasses *all* TCP/IP traffic is the IP protocol. Often, the TCP protocol is mistakenly chosen for the `permit any` statement, which results in only TCP-based applications working.

As mentioned before, the access list must permit all other traffic through. Thus, you must use the `ip` protocol selection followed by a source of any and a destination of any. This is accomplished in the following line:

```
Maggie(config)#access-list 125 permit ip any any
```

This line allows all TCP/IP traffic from any source to any destination. This is how to create a `permit any` (which overrules the implicit deny) in an extended access list.

The access list is now created, but before it can take effect, it must be applied—in this case, as close to the source as possible. Looking back at Figure 19.3, you can see that the FastEthernet 0/0 interface is as close to the source as you can get (directly connected), so that is the best option.

```
Maggie(config)#interface fastethernet 0/0
Maggie(config-if)#ip access-group 125 in
```

Just like that, the first objective is accomplished. All hosts on Network 2 are denied from using FTP to access the intranet server, but permitted to do anything else. Here is the complete configuration, without commentary:

```
Maggie(config)#access-list 125 deny tcp 172.16.70.0 0.0.0.255
3host 172.16.50.100 eq 21
Maggie(config)#access-list 125 permit ip any any
Maggie(config)#interface fastethernet 0/0
Maggie(config-if)#ip access-group 125 in
```

Restricting by Protocol

Allow the host on Network 1 to use only HTTP and HTTPS to access the intranet server. Do not restrict any other access to or from the Network 1 subnet.

This example allows the host on Network 1 to use HTTP and HTTPS only to access the intranet server. Do not restrict any other access to or from the Network 1 subnet. Now that you have seen a couple access list examples, you can do this with a little less commentary. The router closest to the source this time is the Homer router.

```
Homer(config)#access-list 130 permit tcp host 172.16.60.100
3host 172.16.50.100 eq 80
Homer(config)#access-list 130 permit tcp host 172.16.60.100
3host 172.16.50.100 eq 443
```

Now that you have added the lines to permit the HTTP and HTTPS protocols coming from the host on Network 1, you need to deny the host from using any other protocol or port to access the intranet server:

```
Homer(config)#access-list 130 deny ip host 172.16.60.100 host 172.16.50.100
```

Did you remember that you should use the ip keyword rather than tcp? That's an easy mistake to make. Now you must allow all other traffic to continue unhindered:

```
Homer(config)#access-list 130 permit ip any any
```

Finally, you must apply as close to the source as possible:

```
Homer(config)#interface fastethernet 0/0
Homer(config-if)#ip access-group 130 in
```

Objective, accomplished!

Restricting by Network

Now here's something new! In this example, your network should block all incoming Internet traffic unless an Internet host is fulfilling a request originating from the internal network. This is one of the most common requests for networks requiring Internet access. Executives want the network to be secure, so they want to block all incoming traffic from the Internet. However, if you plan on applying a deny ip any any-style access list to the Internet interface, you might as well unplug the cable. This is why Cisco came up with something known as the *TCP-established* access list command. Here's the concept:

When a web browser connects to a web server, it typically does so on TCP port 80. To be reliable, the TCP protocol initiates all its sessions using something known as a *TCP three-way handshake*. This process gets both the sending and receiving hosts on the same page and begins the data transfer. What the TCP-established command access list argument does is watch for this handshake to take place. It then opens return traffic ports to allow the contacted Internet host (and *only* that host) to communicate back to the internal machine requesting data.

To satisfy the objective, you can access the command prompt on the Marge router and enter the following line:

```
Marge(config)#access-list 110 permit tcp any any established
```

This access list is then applied to the interface connected to the Internet in the incoming direction:

```
Marge(config)#interface serial 1/0
Marge(config-if)#ip access-group 110 in
```

> **CAUTION**
>
> Although permitting only the TCP established sessions is very secure, it is not flawless. Cisco therefore created something known as Context Based Access Control (CBAC), implemented in firewall feature-set IOS versions. Although this is not on the exam, it is worth mentioning.

> **EXAM ALERT**
>
> Know how to implement a TCP-established access list and what effect this type of configuration has.

Named Access List

In recent years, Cisco has introduced a much better form of access list. As the name implies, a named access list transcends the typical access list number ranges, enabling you to assign a logical name to the access list. In addition to the logical name, these named access lists also allow some simple editing. You can remove individual access list lines without deleting and re-creating the entire access list. In very recent IOS versions, the named access lists have been enhanced to allow complete flexibility of inserting and even rearranging access list entries.

Named access lists are also configured from Global Configuration mode, but are prefaced with the `ip` command:

```
Marge(config)#ip access-list ?
  extended    Extended Access List
  log-update  Control access list log updates
  logging     Control access list logging
  resequence  Resequence Access List
  standard    Standard Access List
```

Because you have specified that you would like to create an IP access list (as opposed to IPX or Appletalk), the router would like to know whether you would like to create a standard or extended access list (and don't worry, I talk about that intriguing `resequence` keyword later). It's time to set up a standard access list:

```
Marge(config)#ip access-list standard ?
  <1-99>       Standard IP access-list number
  <1300-1999>  Standard IP access-list number (expanded range)
  WORD         Access-list name
```

At first, it doesn't look too different from the numbered access lists created thus far. However, look at that last option: Access-list name. You can enter the name of an access list. I'll name this one Jeremy's_List. Watch what happens:

```
Marge(config)#ip access-list standard Jeremy's_List
Marge(config-std-nacl)#
```

Now, instead of adding access list lines directly from Global Configuration mode, you are taken into an access list sub-configuration mode. From here, you can add permit and deny entries.

```
Marge(config-std-nacl)#?
Standard Access List configuration commands:
  <1-2147483647>  Sequence Number
  default         Set a command to its defaults
  deny            Specify packets to reject
  exit            Exit from access-list configuration mode
  no              Negate a command or set its defaults
  permit          Specify packets to forward
  remark          Access list entry comment
```

Notice the addition of the sequence number option! By default, the Cisco router inserts lines with sequence number increments of 10. That means that the first line you enter is sequence 10, the next will be 20, and so on. This is fantastic because you can squeeze lines in between just by choosing a sequence number in the range greater than 10 and less than 20. Here is a brief example of this:

```
Marge(config-std-nacl)#10 permit host 10.1.1.1
Marge(config-std-nacl)#20 permit host 10.2.2.2
Marge(config-std-nacl)#15 permit host 10.3.3.3
Marge(config-std-nacl)#^Z
Marge#show access-lists
Standard IP access list Jeremy's_List
    20 permit 10.2.2.2
    15 permit 10.3.3.3
    10 permit 10.1.1.1
```

Lines can be removed by entering no <sequence number>. This makes the old form of access list look rudimentary.

```
Marge (config)#ip access-list standard Jeremy's_List
Marge (config-std-nacl)#no 15
Marge (config-std-nacl)#^Z
Marge #show access-lists
Standard IP access list Jeremy's_List
    20 permit 10.2.2.2
    10 permit 10.1.1.1
```

Now, check out the command you saw in the context-sensitive help earlier:

```
Marge(config)#ip access-list resequence Jeremys_List ?
  <1-2147483647>  Starting Sequence Number
```

This `resequence` command makes it possible to move access list lines around! For example, if I wanted to move sequence number 10 to sequence number 35, I could enter

```
Marge(config)#ip access-list resequence Jeremys_List 10 35
```

> **NOTE**
>
> The sequence number feature was added to all access lists (named or otherwise) in IOS version 12.2(15)T and 12.3(2)T.

Verifying Access Lists

Objectives:

▶ Verify and monitor ACLs in a network environment

▶ Troubleshoot ACL issues

You can use three commands to verify your access list configuration. These commands are `show running-config`, `show ip interface`, and `show access-lists`.

show running-config

Although this command can be used to verify nearly any configuration on your Cisco router, it is especially useful when you are working with access lists. There is no other command that can quickly show you where access lists are applied without requiring you to weed through excessive amounts of output. The following output has been trimmed down for brevity.

```
Marge#sh running-config
Building configuration...
Current configuration : 1867 bytes
!
version 12.3
service telnet-zeroidle
service tcp-keepalives-in
service timestamps debug uptime
service timestamps log uptime
service password-encryption
!
hostname Marge
!
```

```
interface Serial 1/0
 ip address dhcp
 ip access-group 170 in
!
access-list 170 permit tcp any any established
```

show ip interface

This command shows you where your access lists are applied, as long as you are patient enough to weed through the excessive amounts of output. The following command views the access lists applied to interface serial 1/0. Pay particular attention to lines 10 and 11.

```
Marge#show ip interface serial 1/0
Serial0/1 is up, line protocol is up
  Internet address is 10.152.19.1/24
  Broadcast address is 255.255.255.255
  Address determined by non-volatile memory
  Peer address is 10.152.19.2
  MTU is 1500 bytes
  Helper address is not set
  Directed broadcast forwarding is disabled
  Outgoing access list is not set
  Inbound  access list is 170
  Proxy ARP is enabled
  Local Proxy ARP is disabled
  Security level is default
  Split horizon is enabled
  ICMP redirects are always sent
  ICMP unreachables are always sent
  ICMP mask replies are never sent
  IP fast switching is enabled
  IP fast switching on the same interface is enabled
  IP Flow switching is disabled
  IP CEF switching is enabled
  IP CEF Feature Fast switching turbo vector
  IP multicast fast switching is disabled
  IP multicast distributed fast switching is disabled
  IP route-cache flags are Fast, CEF
  Router Discovery is disabled
  IP output packet accounting is disabled
  IP access violation accounting is disabled
  TCP/IP header compression is disabled
  RTP/IP header compression is disabled
  Policy routing is disabled
  Network address translation is enabled, interface in domain outside
  WCCP Redirect outbound is disabled
  WCCP Redirect inbound is disabled
```

show ip access-lists

Initially, this command might look like a concise version of `show running-config`. However, it has one very handy feature that the other `show` commands lack: the capability to show how many packets have matched a given line in an `access-list`. This capability can be critical in times of troubleshooting and verification.

In the following example, you can see that there is a single access list (30) that has three lines. Next to each line, the number of packets that have matched those entries is displayed.

```
Marge#show ip access-lists
Standard IP access list 30
    permit 10.0.0.0, wildcard bits 0.255.255.255 (94 matches)
    permit 172.16.0.0, wildcard bits 0.0.255.255 (82 matches)
    deny   any (250 matches)
```

Chapter Summary

This chapter has given the theory and configuration of IP standard and extended access lists. A full understanding of these concepts is absolutely critical, not only for your network security, but also for a variety of additional configurations on your router such as NAT, QoS, and dial-on-demand routing (DDR) to name a few.

The two classifications of IP access lists give you all the flexibility you need in applying them to your network. Standard access lists filter based only on the source address. These are useful because they consume less processor and memory resources on your router when you require only simple `allow` and `deny` statements based on source addressing. Common uses of standard access lists include NAT, QoS, and restricting Telnet or Secure Shell (SSH) router access. On the other hand, extended access lists enable you to filter based on the source address, destination address, protocol, and port number. Although they may cost you significant processor resources, extended access lists give you the ultimate in flexibility when choosing the types of traffic to allow or deny in your network. Extended access lists have many uses, but are primarily used for security. The type of access list you create depends on the access list number you select when performing the configuration. For standard access lists, use numbers between 1–99; for extended access lists, use numbers between 100–199.

Access lists can be created without any effect to your router. For an access list to be put in action, it must be applied in some way. To apply an access list to an interface, use the `ip access-group <access_list_number> <in/out>` syntax. To determine the direction the access list should be applied, put yourself in the place of the router. Is the access list filtering traffic coming into you (*in*bound) or going away from you (*out*bound)? If you would like to use an access list to filter Telnet access to your router, the access list should be applied to your VTY ports. Under this line configuration mode, use the `access-class <access_list_number> in` command to apply the access list.

Modern IOS versions include the capability to support sequenced, named access lists. This feature offers the tremendous advantage of being able to assign a logical name to the access list, remove statements from the access list, and resequence entries in your access list.

Key Terms

- standard access list
- extended access list
- named access list
- IP `access-group`
- `access-class`
- inverse mask/wildcard mask
- TCP-established
- IP
- TCP
- UDP
- ICMP
- FTP
- HTTP
- HTTPS/SSL
- Telnet
- TFTP
- DNS

Apply Your Knowledge

Exercises

19.1 Configuring an Access List to Restrict Telnet Access

You are designing a corporate network and would like to implement tight security on all Cisco devices. The first concern is ensuring that only specific hosts can manage the Cisco routers. Figure 19.4 gives the corporate network layout.

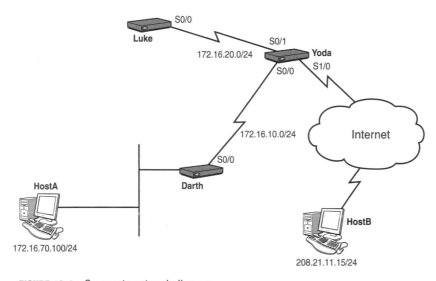

FIGURE 19.4   Corporate network diagram.

You are currently working on the Yoda router. Create and apply an access list that allows only HostA and HostB to manage the Yoda router remotely via Telnet, using the most efficient process.

Estimated Time: 5 minutes

TIP

Be careful when approaching these types of questions on the CCNA exam. You could use an extended access list and apply it to all interfaces of the Yoda router that blocks TCP port 23 (Telnet) from all hosts except HostA and HostB; however, this would not be the most efficient process. Telnet restrictions should be applied to the VTY lines of your device.

To complete this exercise, use the following steps:

1. Log on to the Yoda router and enter Global Configuration mode.

```
Yoda>
Yoda>enable
Yoda#configure terminal
Enter configuration commands, one per line.  End with CNTL/Z.
Yoda(config)#
```

2. Create a standard access list that permits only HostA and HostB. The implicit deny at the end of the list blocks all other users.

```
Yoda(config)#access-list ?
  <1-99>           IP standard access list
  <100-199>        IP extended access list
  <1100-1199>      Extended 48-bit MAC address access list
  <1300-1999>      IP standard access list (expanded range)
  <200-299>        Protocol type-code access list
  <2000-2699>      IP extended access list (expanded range)
  <700-799>        48-bit MAC address access list
  dynamic-extended Extend the dynamic ACL absolute timer

Yoda(config)#access-list 1 ?
  deny    Specify packets to reject
  permit  Specify packets to forward
  remark  Access list entry comment

Yoda(config)#access-list 1 permit ?
  Hostname or A.B.C.D  Address to match
  any                  Any source host
  host                 A single host address

Yoda(config)#access-list 1 permit host ?
  Hostname or A.B.C.D  Host address

Yoda(config)#access-list 1 permit host 172.16.70.100
Yoda(config)#access-list 1 permit host 208.21.11.15
```

3. Apply the access list to the VTY ports to restrict Telnet access.

```
Yoda(config)#line vty 0 4
Yoda(config-line)#access-class ?
  <1-199>     IP access list
  <1300-2699> IP expanded access list
  WORD        Access-list name

Yoda(config-line)#access-class 1 ?
  in   Filter incoming connections
  out  Filter outgoing connections

Yoda(config-line)#access-class 1 in
```

19.2 Configuring an Access List to Allow Basic Web Access

You have been contacted to set up a simple Cisco network to provide Internet access to a small, 20-person company. The owners of the company want to ensure that only basic Internet access (HTTP/HTTPS/FTP) is allowed for the internal employees. Refer to Figure 19.5 for a diagram of the network.

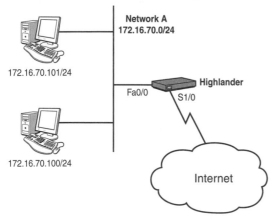

FIGURE 19.5 Small company network diagram.

Estimated Time: 10 minutes

> **TIP**
>
> Most people think that FTP uses only TCP port 21. However, port 21 negotiates only the FTP session. If that is the only port you open, users can log in to FTP servers, but as soon as they try to get a directory list or initiate a file transfer, the connection fails. The FTP Data channel is negotiated on TCP port 20, by default.

To provide the basic web access, perform the following steps:

1. Log in to the Highlander router and enter Global Configuration mode.

```
Highlander>enable
Highlander#configure terminal
Enter configuration commands, one per line.  End with CNTL/Z.
Highlander(config)#
```

2. Create the access list permitting the correct ports. HTTP uses TCP port 80, HTTPS uses TCP port 443, FTP uses port 21 and 20.

```
Highlander(config)#access-list ?
  <1-99>             IP standard access list
  <100-199>          IP extended access list
  <1100-1199>        Extended 48-bit MAC address access list
  <1300-1999>        IP standard access list (expanded range)
  <200-299>          Protocol type-code access list
  <2000-2699>        IP extended access list (expanded range)
  <700-799>          48-bit MAC address access list
  dynamic-extended   Extend the dynamic ACL absolute timer

Highlander(config)#access-list 135 ?
  deny     Specify packets to reject
  dynamic  Specify a DYNAMIC list of PERMITs or DENYs
  permit   Specify packets to forward
  remark   Access list entry comment

Highlander(config)#access-list 135 permit ?
  <0-255>  An IP protocol number
  ahp      Authentication Header Protocol
  eigrp    Cisco's EIGRP routing protocol
  esp      Encapsulation Security Payload
  gre      Cisco's GRE tunneling
  icmp     Internet Control Message Protocol
  igmp     Internet Gateway Message Protocol
  ip       Any Internet Protocol
  ipinip   IP in IP tunneling
  nos      KA9Q NOS compatible IP over IP tunneling
  ospf     OSPF routing protocol
  pcp      Payload Compression Protocol
  pim      Protocol Independent Multicast
  tcp      Transmission Control Protocol
  udp      User Datagram Protocol

Highlander(config)#access-list 135 permit tcp ?
  A.B.C.D  Source address
  any      Any source host
  host     A single source host

Highlander(config)#access-list 135 permit tcp 172.16.70.0 ?
  A.B.C.D  Source wildcard bits

Highlander(config)#access-list 135 permit tcp 172.16.70.0 0.0.0.255 ?
  A.B.C.D  Destination address
  any      Any destination host
  eq       Match only packets on a given port number
  gt       Match only packets with a greater port number
```

```
host     A single destination host
lt       Match only packets with a lower port number
neq      Match only packets not on a given port number
range    Match only packets in the range of port numbers

Highlander(config)#access-list 135 permit tcp 172.16.70.0 0.0.0.255 any ?
  ack           Match on the ACK bit
  dscp          Match packets with given dscp value
  eq            Match only packets on a given port number
  established   Match established connections
  fin           Match on the FIN bit
  fragments     Check non-initial fragments
  gt            Match only packets with a greater port number
  log           Log matches against this entry
  log-input     Log matches against this entry, including input interface
  lt            Match only packets with a lower port number
  neq           Match only packets not on a given port number
  precedence    Match packets with given precedence value
  psh           Match on the PSH bit
  range         Match only packets in the range of port numbers
  rst           Match on the RST bit
  syn           Match on the SYN bit
  time-range    Specify a time-range
  tos           Match packets with given TOS value
  urg           Match on the URG bit
  <cr>

Highlander(config)#access-list 135 permit tcp 172.16.70.0 0.0.0.255 any eq ?
  <0-65535>     Port number
  bgp           Border Gateway Protocol (179)
  chargen       Character generator (19)
  cmd           Remote commands (rcmd, 514)
  daytime       Daytime (13)
  discard       Discard (9)
  domain        Domain Name Service (53)
  echo          Echo (7)
  exec          Exec (rsh, 512)
  finger        Finger (79)
  ftp           File Transfer Protocol (21)
  ftp-data      FTP data connections (20)
  gopher        Gopher (70)
  hostname      NIC hostname server (101)
  ident         Ident Protocol (113)
  irc           Internet Relay Chat (194)
  klogin        Kerberos login (543)
  kshell        Kerberos shell (544)
  login         Login (rlogin, 513)
  lpd           Printer service (515)
  nntp          Network News Transport Protocol (119)
```

```
pim-auto-rp  PIM Auto-RP (496)
pop2         Post Office Protocol v2 (109)
pop3         Post Office Protocol v3 (110)
smtp         Simple Mail Transport Protocol (25)
sunrpc       Sun Remote Procedure Call (111)
syslog       Syslog (514)
tacacs       TAC Access Control System (49)
talk         Talk (517)
telnet       Telnet (23)
time         Time (37)
uucp         Unix-to-Unix Copy Program (540)
whois        Nicname (43)
www          World Wide Web (HTTP, 80)
```

```
Highlander(config)#access-list 135 permit tcp 172.16.70.0 0.0.0.255 any eq 80
Highlander(config)#access-list 135 permit tcp 172.16.70.0 0.0.0.255 any eq 443
Highlander(config)#access-list 135 permit tcp 172.16.70.0 0.0.0.255 any eq 21
Highlander(config)#access-list 135 permit tcp 172.16.70.0 0.0.0.255 any eq 20
```

3. Apply the access list. In this case, apply the list closest to the destination. Although this is not typical for extended access lists, it is necessary when providing Internet access because the destination must be specified as any.

```
Highlander(config)#interface serial 1/0
Highlander(config-if)#ip access-group 135 out
```

Review Questions

1. Your manager at the office asks you to explain the concept behind a standard access list. Using simple terms, explain these concepts.

2. It is critical that an access list is applied correctly when it is used on a router for security purposes. What mantra dictates the rules behind access list application?

3. Explain how a router processes an access list filtering traffic inbound from the Internet.

4. What filtering options does an extended access list give you that are not supplied by a standard access list?

5. One of the criteria an extended access list allows you to use in your filtering options is the source and destination port number. What is the difference between these? Why are two ports necessary for all communication?

Exam Questions

1. Which of the following are valid reasons to implement access lists? (Choose all that apply.)

   ○ **A.** QoS

   ○ **B.** Route filtering

   ○ **C.** Dial-on-demand routing

   ○ **D.** Console port security

2. Which type of access list can filter traffic based on the source port? (Choose all that apply.)

   ○ **A.** Standard

   ○ **B.** Extended

   ○ **C.** User-Based

   ○ **D.** Static

   ○ **E.** Named

   ○ **F.** Unnamed

3. You are filtering traffic to an FTP site and you want only FTP traffic to reach the server. You do not want additional traffic to reach the server. Which traffic should be allowed?

   ○ **A.** TCP on ports 20 and 21

   ○ **B.** UDP on ports 20 and 21

   ○ **C.** TCP on port 21

   ○ **D.** TCP and UDP on ports 20 and 21

4. What happens to a packet that does not meet the conditions of any access list filters?

   ○ **A.** The packet is routed normally.

   ○ **B.** The packet is flagged and then routed.

   ○ **C.** The packet is dropped.

   ○ **D.** The administrator is notified.

5. You have an IP address and wildcard mask of 10.0.20.5 255.255.0.0. Which of the following IP addresses will be affected by this access list? (Choose all that apply.)

○ **A.** 10.0.0.10

○ **B.** 192.168.20.5

○ **C.** 172.30.20.5

○ **D.** 10.2.1.1

6. You want to create an access list to filter all traffic from the 172.16.16.0 255.255.240.0 network. What wildcard mask is appropriate?

○ **A.** 0.0.7.255

○ **B.** 0.0.15.255

○ **C.** 0.0.31.255

○ **D.** 0.0.63.255

7. Regarding access lists, which of the following statements is correct?

○ **A.** Only one access list per protocol, per direction, per interface

○ **B.** Only one access list per port number, per protocol, per interface

○ **C.** Only one access list per port number, per direction, per interface

○ **D.** Only one access list per port number, per protocol, per direction

8. You need to temporarily remove access list 101 from one of your interfaces—which command is appropriate?

○ **A.** `no access-list 101`

○ **B.** `no ip access-group 101`

○ **C.** `access-list 101 disable`

○ **D.** `access-group 101 disable`

9. Which of the following creates a standard access list that allows traffic from the 172.16 subnet?

○ **A.** `access-list 1 permit 172.16.0.0 0.0.255.255`

○ **B.** `access-list 100 permit 172.16.0.0 255.255.0.0`

○ **C.** `access-list 1 permit 172.16.0.0 255.255.0.0`

○ **D.** `access-list 100 permit 172.16.0.0 0.0.255.255`

10. You want to create an access list that denies all outbound traffic to port 80 from the 10.10.0.0 network. Which access list entry meets your requirements?

    ○ **A.** `access-list 101 deny tcp 10.10.0.0 0.0.255.255 eq 80`

    ○ **B.** `access-list 91 deny tcp 10.10.0.0 0.0.255.255 any eq 80`

    ○ **C.** `access-list 101 deny tcp 10.10.0.0 0.0.255.255 all eq 80`

    ○ **D.** `access-list 101 deny tcp 10.10.0.0 0.0.255.255 any eq 80`

Answers to Review Questions

1. A standard access list is nothing more than a generic list of `permit` and `deny` statements. It chooses what devices are allowed through a router based on who they are (their source IP addresses).

2. One access list, per protocol, per interface, per direction.

3. Regardless of how an access list is applied, the router processes it the same: Statements are read from the top of the list down. If a packet matches one of the statements, the router executes the direction of the statement (permit or deny) and exits the access list processing. If the packet does not match any of the statements in the access list, it is implicitly denied.

4. An extended access list gives you the option of filtering based on the TCP/IP sub-protocol (such as TCP, UDP, or ICMP), the destination address, and the source/destination port number. Beyond the CCNA level, an extended access list also enables you to filter based on criteria such as time of day or QoS marking.

5. When communicating on a TCP/IP-based network, the destination port helps identify what server application your client is attempting to access. For example, sending data to TCP port 80 indicates the HTTP server service. The source port number is used to identify the client application to which the server should respond. These two ports are always necessary in any communication to identify the applications on both ends of the connection.

Answers to Exam Questions

1. A, B, C. Access lists can be used with QoS in implementing many forms of queuing and congestion avoidance techniques. Access lists can filter routing protocol updates. Access lists can also specify interesting traffic to trigger dial-on-demand routing. Answer D is incorrect because access lists aren't used for console port security.

2. B, E. Extended access lists can use source and destination information, including the source port, and named access lists can be either extended or standard, so they have the capability to filter based on the source port. Answer A is incorrect because standard access lists can filter on source address information, but not source port. Answer C is incorrect because there are no user-based access lists. Answer D is incorrect because there are no static access lists. Answer F is incorrect because there are no unnamed access lists.

3. **A**. FTP uses TCP and ports 20 and 21. Answer B is incorrect because FTP uses TCP. Answer C is incorrect because port 20 is required as well. Answer D is incorrect because UDP is not necessary.

4. **C**. A packet that does not meet any filters is dropped. Answer A is incorrect because the packet is discarded rather than routed. Answer B is incorrect because there is no mechanism to flag the packet. Answer D is incorrect because although it is conceivable that an administrator could be notified by default, the packet is simply dropped.

5. **B, C**. The significant bits are the last 16, indicated by the wildcard mask of 255.255.0.0. 192.168.20.5 and 172.30.20.5 match the last two octets, or 16 bits, of the 10.0.20.5 IP address. Answers A and D are incorrect because although the first portions of the IP address match, it is the last two octets that are significant.

6. **B**. 0.0.15.255 affects the 172.16.16.0 255.255.240.0 network. In the third octet, the first four bits are checked in binary, resulting in 00000000.00000000.00001111.11111111. Answer A is incorrect because this does not match the given problem, checking too many bits (five) in the last octet. Answer C is incorrect because this mask checks only three bits in the third octet. Answer D is incorrect because this mask checks only two bits in the third octet.

7. **A**. You may create only one access list per protocol, per direction, per interface. Answer B is incorrect because you can have multiple access lists for a single port number, and only one per direction. Answer C is incorrect because you may have only one access list per protocol, not per port number. Answer D is incorrect because you may not have more than one access list per interface.

8. **B**. The correct syntax is `no ip access-group 101`. This removes the access list from the interface. Answer A is incorrect because this line deletes the access list entirely. Answers C and D use invalid syntax.

9. **A**. This answer has the correct syntax of the `access-list` command followed by the list number, `permit`/`deny`, IP address, and a wildcard mask. Answers B and D are incorrect because they indicate an extended access list. Answer C is incorrect because the wildcard mask has been reversed.

10. **D**. Use the `any` keyword to specify all destinations. Answer A is incorrect because no destination is specified. Answer B is incorrect; this specifies a standard access list. Answer C is incorrect because `all` is not the proper keyword.

Suggested Reading and Resources

1. Cisco Online Documentation: Filtering IP Packets Using Access Lists, http://www.cisco.com/univercd/cc/td/doc/product/software/ios122/122cgcr/fipr_c/ipcprt1/1cfip.htm#wp1109098.

2. Ward, Chris and Cioara, Jeremy. *Exam Cram 2 CCNA Practice Questions*. Que Publishing, 2004.

3. Odom, Wendell. *CCNA Certification Library*. Cisco Press, 2003.

CHAPTER TWENTY

Enabling Internet Connectivity with NAT

Objectives

This chapter covers the following Cisco-specific objectives for the "Implement, verify, and troubleshoot NAT and ACLs in a medium-size Enterprise branch office network" section of the 640-802 CCNA exam:

▶ **Explain the basic operation of NAT**

▶ **Configure NAT for given network requirements using SDM**

▶ **Troubleshoot NAT issues**

Outline

Study Strategies

▶ Read the information presented in the chapter, paying special attention to tables, Notes, and Exam Alerts.

▶ Focus on the Network Address Translation terminology. Understanding these terms is paramount to understanding the NAT configuration as a whole.

▶ When studying, focus on the static NAT configurations first, because these are the simplest. After you master this configuration, move on to NAT overload, followed by dynamic NAT.

Introduction

I can still remember the very first time I saw Network Address Translation (NAT) in action. "This is the most amazing thing I have ever seen," I said, with the same awestruck feeling as the first time you walk up and look over the Grand Canyon. Okay, perhaps it wasn't that fantastic, but at the same time, NAT is definitely at the top of my list of configurations I love to set up.

Despite it being one of the most widely implemented concepts in the world of network technology, NAT is one of the newer topics added to the CCNA exam. This is most likely because of its configuration complexity: It requires a thorough understanding of standard access lists to successfully deploy. However, Cisco is very wise in adding it to the entry-level exam, because nearly every network in the world uses NAT in some shape or form. Even home networks using Linksys, D-Link, and Netgear routers use NAT.

NAT was originally developed through a combination of Cisco engineers and the Internet Engineering Task Force (IETF) group in 1994 to overcome the quickly approaching IP address shortage. With the Internet popularity growing at a rate far faster than expected, the remaining public IP addresses would soon be depleted. At that time, TCP/IP version 6 (IPv6, which would have solved the IP address shortage) had been created in a draft status, but it would require a worldwide upgrade of network devices and operating system software to successfully deploy. Rather than upgrading all network-capable devices, the focus was placed on creating a gateway device that could enable multiple network devices to share a single IP address.

As this concept materialized, NAT was born. Theoretically, a router running NAT is capable of allowing more than 60,000 devices to share a single Internet-valid IP address. Practically speaking, the router resources (processor and memory) and WAN bandwidth are depleted long before that limit is reached. With thousands of devices capable of using a single public IP address, the life of TCP/IP version 4 (IPv4) has been extended years beyond what was thought possible.

NAT also acts as a natural security boundary by eliminating end-to-end traceability. If your router has only a single IP address that is connected to the Internet, the public IP address, which is assigned to the outside interface, does not belong to any one internal host. For example, imagine that your router's public IP address is 209.1.5.9, and all your internal hosts come from the subnet 192.168.1.0/24. Whenever one of the internal hosts accesses the Internet, it is seen as 209.1.5.9. However, if anyone from the Internet attempts to access 209.1.5.9, the address maps to no individual host, which makes the internal network invisible to the Internet.

NAT Concepts

Objective:

▶ Explain the basic operation of NAT

Although the introductory discussion of NAT covers the most popular uses of the technology, NAT can be used for much more. Before you go deeper into the specific uses, though, you must understand the foundation concepts.

As its core function, Network Address Translation does just that: translate addresses. It can take any IP address and make it look like another. This is why the creative geniuses behind TCP/IP defined three ranges of "private IP addresses" in RFC 1918. The following is a list of the three private address ranges:

▶ **Class A:** 10.0.0.0 to 10.255.255.255

▶ **Class B:** 172.16.0.0 to 172.31.255.255

▶ **Class C:** 192.168.0.0 to 192.168.255.255

TIP

You need to know the private IP address ranges.

You might notice that a private address range is defined for each class of address. This gives a company more flexibility to use different ranges based on the company size. As a general statement, most small companies use the 192.168.X.X range, most medium-sized companies use the 172.16.X.X to 172.31.X.X ranges, and most large companies use the 10.X.X.X ranges. Remember, this is just a general statement, not a solid rule.

It is commonly stated that these private addresses are nonroutable, but this is untrue. Thousands of companies around the world use these addresses and route them throughout their private networks just fine. This misunderstanding came about because all Internet service providers (ISPs) use access lists to block these addresses from entering or leaving their networks. It is accurate to say that these private addresses are not *Internet* routable, because if they were, there would be thousands of duplicate IP address conflicts every day.

As shown in Figure 20.1, networks connected to the Internet typically use these private IP addresses internally and then translate them when attempting to access the Internet. This enables you to have many duplicate addresses around the world without any conflicts, because they never communicate directly. This can cause problems with overlapping IP addresses when companies merge, but NAT can even be engineered to solve these problems.

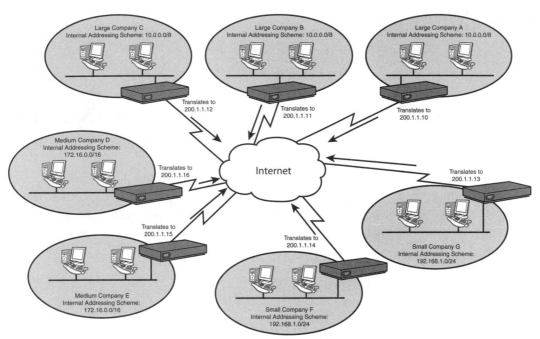

FIGURE 20.1   Network that uses a NAT configuration with private addressing.

With this foundation in place, you're ready to examine the styles of NAT.

Static NAT

Static NAT is the simplest form of NAT. It enables you to map one IP address to another in a one-to-one relationship. This is typically used to allow access to internal servers from the Internet that are using a private address space. In Figure 20.2, three servers are located on the internal network: a web server, an FTP server, and an email server. These three servers are assigned to a private IP address space (192.168.1.0/24) and would typically be inaccessible from the Internet. By using static NAT, you can map the private IP addresses to a public IP on a one-to-one basis, enabling these servers to be accessed from the Internet using the three public IP addresses shown in Figure 20.2.

This static NAT mapping goes both ways. When someone from the Internet accesses 200.1.1.1, it is translated to the internal address 192.168.1.1. Likewise, when the server 192.168.1.1 accesses the Internet, it is seen as 200.1.1.1. Although this form of NAT does not allow multiple internal hosts to share a single address, it does implement the security features of NAT by eliminating end-to-end traceability and enables servers that are sharing your private network to be accessed from the Internet.

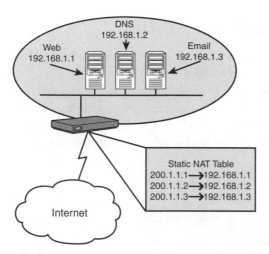

FIGURE 20.2 Static NAT address mappings.

Static NAT can also be configured to statically translate individual TCP or UDP ports. This awesome feature enables you to take a single IP address and translate one or many ports to either the same host or many different hosts. For example, you might have a router that has the external IP address 195.1.1.1. You can statically configure NAT so that when your router receives a request on 195.1.1.1, using TCP port 80 (HTTP), it redirects it to the internal address 192.168.1.50 on TCP port 80. However, when it receives a request on 195.1.1.1, using TCP port 21 (FTP), it redirects it to the internal address 192.168.1.100 on TCP port 21. In this way, NAT can act as a type of firewall (allowing only some ports through to specific hosts) and give you the flexibility of offering many services through the same IP address. Using static NAT with ports even makes it possible to redirect port numbers. For example, you might be using one of those scandalous DSL or cable Internet providers that block certain port numbers to keep you from running a web server from home. You can configure static NAT in such a way that when your router receives a request on TCP port 800 it redirects it to an internal IP address on TCP port 80.

Dynamic NAT

Static NAT is superb if you have a few hosts that need to be translated; however, if many hosts need to be translated, creating static entries for each one can be quite tedious. This is where dynamic NAT can help. Dynamic NAT enables you to define a pool of addresses to be translated along with a pool of addresses to which they are to be translated. The router then dynamically maps these IP addresses as the need arises. This is *not* the same thing as allowing multiple hosts to share the same IP address (known as NAT *overloading*). Dynamic NAT makes many one-to-one mappings without requiring you to configure them statically.

NAT Overload and Port Address Translation

Now we come to the form of NAT that made it famous. NAT overload, also known as Port Address Translation (PAT), enables a single IP address to support many internal clients. Whenever a host establishes communication with a server outside the NAT firewall, it tries to access a specific port number (known as the *destination port*). However, it also uses a source port number to allow for return traffic (this is discussed more thoroughly in Chapter 19, "Using Cisco Access Lists"). Figure 20.3 shows how NAT overload also incorporates this source port number into the translation.

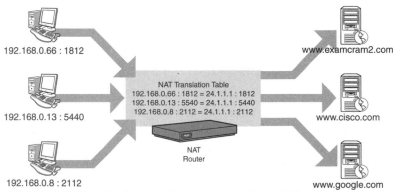

FIGURE 20.3 NAT overload uses port numbers to make translations unique.

The hosts communicating randomly generate the source ports. The NAT router then appends these to the public IP address to make the source *socket* (or IP address and port number combination) unique. When the Internet server replies to whatever request was made, it does so to the source IP and socket. When the NAT router receives the reply, it then can redirect it to the correct internal host by referring to its NAT translation table. Because hosts use random source ports, there is very little possibility that two hosts will choose the same source port number (one chance out of some 60,000). However, if two hosts do happen to choose the same port number, the NAT device causes one of the device sessions to reset and choose a different port number. By using unique port numbers, the router can originate thousands of requests from its single Internet IP address. This provides Internet access to the internal network clients while using just one Internet address.

To review, Table 20.1 shows the three forms of NAT and the styles of translation they perform.

TABLE 20.1   NAT Translation Forms and Types

NAT Configuration	Translation Type
Static NAT	One-to-one IP address translations
Dynamic NAT	Many-to-many IP address translations
NAT overload/PAT	Many-to-one IP address translations

NAT Terminology

Believe it or not, setting up NAT is not very difficult; it's learning the terminology used with NAT that can fry your brain. The first time you see these terms, it may make no sense to you, and that's just fine. It takes some time to soak in. Now, keep in mind that these are not "Cisco terms." Rather, they are an industry standard way of referring to the four different points in a NAT-based network. Before trying to understand four NAT address descriptions, you must understand the building blocks used to construct these terms:

▶ **Inside/outside:** These NAT descriptors refer to where a device is physically located. If a device is "inside," it is under your control; it is in your network. If a device is "outside," it is not under your control; it is outside your network.

▶ **Local/global:** These NAT descriptors refer to where an IP address is located *from the perspective of a NAT device*. The NAT device is a network device that has its address translated through a NAT router. It could be a PC, a server, an Xbox, or any other type of host that has a private address that is translated to a real address on the Internet. If the IP address is considered "local," it is seen as a device on the local subnet from the perspective of a NAT device (this may or may not be true). If the IP address is considered "global," it is seen as not on the local subnet from the perspective of a NAT device.

If that doesn't sound confusing, just wait until we start combining these terms for the four NAT address descriptions. Figure 20.4 shows a visual location of these address on the network.

▶ **Inside local addresses:** These addresses are the easiest to understand because they refer to everything inside your network. Remember the word *constructs* discussed just a moment ago: An address "inside" is physically located inside your network. From the perspective of the NAT device, it is "local," meaning it is seen on the internal network. If an inside local address were to communicate with another inside local address, that communication would be described as standard LAN connectivity. No routers would be needed.

▶ **Inside global addresses:** Now the terms begin to mix a little bit. Let's break this down into the individual pieces: First, the address is "inside," which means that it is physically located on your network; it is under your control. "Global" means that it is seen as an IP address not on the local subnet from the perspective of one of your NAT devices. Put all this together and you are left with the Internet valid IP address assigned to your router that is directly connected to the Internet. This is where a fundamental understanding of inside and outside can really help. If the address were an "outside global," it would not be under your control, meaning that it could be any of the millions of devices attached to the Internet.

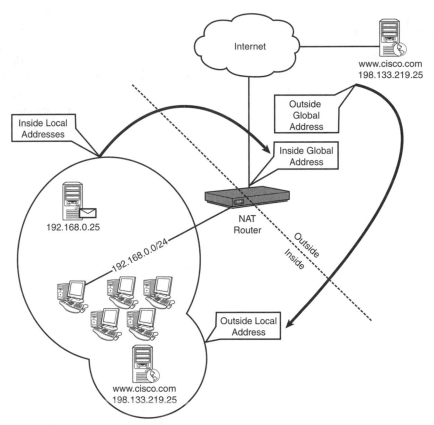

FIGURE 20.4 NAT terminology.

▶ **Outside global addresses:** Outside global addresses refer to devices that are physically "outside" your network—outside your control. These addresses are "global," meaning that the NAT devices on the inside of your network see these as nonlocal addresses. Put these two pieces together and you have a description of a standard Internet IP address.

▶ **Outside local addresses:** I saved the best for last. Outside local addresses confused me for quite some time until I fully understood the capabilities of NAT. First, let's look at the pieces: This address is physically "outside" your network, out of your control, out on the Internet. However, it appears to NAT devices as an IP address on the "local" subnet. What this describes is an Internet host translated as it comes through the NAT router *into* your local network. You can think of this as "reverse NAT," or just NAT in the other direction. As shown in Figure 20.4, when the cisco.com web server speaks to the internal hosts on the 192.168.0.0/24 network, they believe it to be co-located on the local subnet with them. They come to this conclusion because the NAT router translates the outside global address to something local (perhaps 192.168.0.1, the NAT gateway's address).

> **TIP**
>
> Understanding the four NAT address descriptors listed is useful not only for the ICND1, ICND2, and CCNA exams, but also for understanding any real-world NAT documentation.

Configuring NAT Using Cisco SDM

Objective:

▶ Configure NAT for given network requirements using SDM

Cisco gives you plenty of flexibility when setting up NAT on a Cisco router. Now, anytime you are reading technical documentation and come across the word "flexibility," your mind should naturally translate this to "complexity." Thankfully, Cisco hid many of the configuration details behind the beautiful SDM interface.

> **TIP**
>
> For the ICND1 exam, Cisco expects you to be able to configure NAT using the Cisco Security Device Manager (SDM) graphic interface. For the ICND2 and CCNA exams, Cisco expects you to be able to configure NAT using the command-line interface.

Configuring NAT Overload

NAT overload (also known as PAT) is required for just about any business that provides Internet access to its internal users. As discussed previously, this version of NAT allows you to share (overload) a single public IP address among many internal private IP addresses. Because of its common use, Cisco categorizes this as *Basic NAT* in the SDM interface. However, if you see the command-line equivalent to the Basic NAT overload configuration, you'll realize it's anything but "basic"! When we're done with the SDM, I'll show you the commands it generated as a "sneak peek" at the ICND2 exam.

To access the NAT configuration window in the SDM, click the **Configure** link and choose **NAT** from the Tasks sidebar. The window shown in Figure 20.5 appears.

To configure NAT overload, choose the **Basic NAT** radio button and click the **Launch the selected task** button. After the initial introductory screen, you're asked to select the outside and inside interfaces for NAT, as shown in Figure 20.6. The interface you select in the drop-down box should connect to your ISP. In this example, the Ethernet 1/0 interface connects to a local ISP. The range of IP addresses that you select using the checkbox represents internal IP address ranges. In this example, our internal network is represented by 172.30.2.0 to 172.30.2.255. If I were to translate the options shown in Figure 20.6 into a simple English statement, I would say, "Use NAT overload to translate any internal IP address starting with 172.30.2 to whatever IP address is assigned to the Ethernet 0/1 interface."

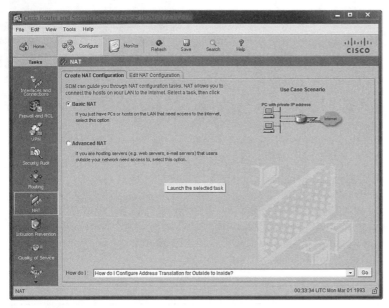

FIGURE 20.5   The NAT Configuration window in Cisco SDM.

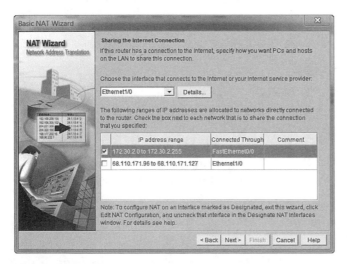

FIGURE 20.6   Selecting the outside and inside interfaces for NAT.

As soon as you click the Next button, you're done. Seriously! That's how simple Cisco makes the NAT overload configuration using the SDM GUI. The last thing you'll see is a summary screen verifying the options you've selected, as shown in Figure 20.7. When you click Finish, SDM delivers the configuration commands to the router, and your network should be NAT-enabled.

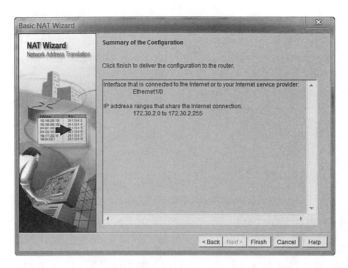

FIGURE 20.7 The Basic NAT configuration summary window.

I know you're thinking, "That was *way* too easy." Me too. Let's take a quick look at some select pieces of the running configuration just to make sure we really know what is happening behind the scenes:

```
NAT_ROUTER#show run
Building configuration...

Current configuration : 1160 bytes
!
interface FastEthernet0/0
 ip address 172.30.2.77 255.255.255.0
 ip nat inside
!
interface Ethernet1/0
 ip address 68.110.171.98 255.255.255.224
 ip nat outside
```

The first thing you'll notice is the `ip nat inside` and `ip nat outside` commands under the FastEthernet0/0 and Ethernet1/0 interfaces. The function of these commands is simple. They tell the router what interface connects to the outside world (your ISP) and what interface(s) connect to the inside world (your internal network). Keep in mind that you can have multiple inside interfaces without any difficulty. Having multiple outside interfaces can cause the router some confusion (which is why the Cisco SDM allows you to elect only a single outside interface). Let's move on a little further in the running configuration:

```
!
access-list 1 remark SDM_ACL Category=2
access-list 1 permit 172.30.2.0 0.0.0.255
!
ip nat inside source list 1 interface Ethernet1/0 overload
```

These commands are what I consider the "power commands" of NAT. Here's the idea: the first section represents an access list that allows the Cisco router to identify the internal network IP addresses (172.30.2.0/24 in this case). The access list is then utilized in the nat command below it. That one command is what puts this whole configuration in motion. The best way to understand that command is to imagine it as a conversation between you and the router. Trust me—the more you configure Cisco routers, the more conversations like this you will have:

You: I want to do NAT (ip nat).

Router: That's nice. Where would you like to NAT from?

You: The inside of my network to the outside (inside).

Router: Great! What interface would you like to use for the outside IP address?

You: I'd like to use Ethernet1/0 (interface Ethernet1/0).

Router: How would you like to use it?

You: I'd like all internal IP addresses to share the single IP address on Ethernet 1/0 (overload).

That's the story! As the router puts these commands into action, all users in the 172.30.2.0/24 range are provided with Internet access.

> **NOTE**
>
> Keep in mind that this is an introductory explanation of the NAT syntax. This configuration is discussed fully in Chapter 21, "Command-Line NAT Implementation."

Providing Internet access to the company through NAT overload is just one piece of the networking puzzle. Most companies have internal servers that need not only access *to* the Internet but access *from* the Internet. These are typically email servers, web servers, or FTP servers, to name just a few. Fortunately for your business, NAT provides a natural firewall between you and the Internet. Because private addresses are unreachable from the Internet, your internal network is protected from the outside world.

> **NOTE**
>
> Don't get a false sense of security by running NAT! Although NAT does protect your internal network from being reached directly from the Internet, it is not flawless network security. If one of the hosts on your internal network becomes infected with a virus or worm, it can initiate connections through the NAT gateway and allow return traffic (which could potentially be malicious) back into your network.

The problem with this natural firewall is that it also makes your internal servers unreachable from the Internet. To solve this, we can use static NAT mappings.

The SDM gives you a couple methods of setting up NAT mappings: configuring the mappings at the same time as NAT overload (using the **Advanced NAT** selection on the **Create NAT Configuration** tab) or adding them individually from the Edit NAT Configuration tab. We'll talk about both methods here, starting with the Advanced NAT selection.

Advanced NAT Wizard

The Advanced NAT configuration wizard, shown in Figure 20.8, is most useful when you are setting up NAT overload and static NAT mappings at the same time. This section assumes that you did not work through the Basic NAT wizard previously (although the Advanced NAT wizard will still function if you previously completed the Basic NAT wizard).

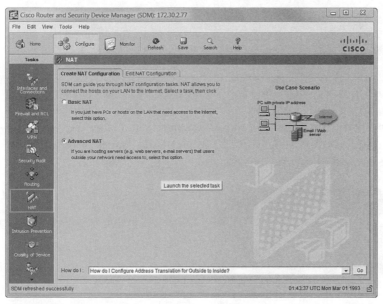

FIGURE 20.8 Beginning the Advanced NAT configuration.

To start the Advanced NAT wizard, simply select its radio button and click the **Launch the selected task** button. After you see the introductory page, the wizard asks you to identify the interface connected to your ISP, just as it did in the Basic NAT wizard. However, at this point you start to see something different: the wizard also asks if you are using any additional public IP addresses, as shown in Figure 20.9. Many organizations that run their own internal servers purchase additional, dedicated IP addresses for those servers. If your organization is using more IP addresses than what is assigned to the outside interface of your router, click the **Add** button and enter them one by one. If you do not have additional IP addresses, don't worry! We can do some really great stuff with the one IP address assigned to your router's outside interface (we'll talk about that in just a moment). In Figure 20.9, I have added the IP addresses 200.1.1.1 and 200.1.1.2 so that I can use them later in the configuration. We'll assume that our "virtual company" owns these two IP addresses.

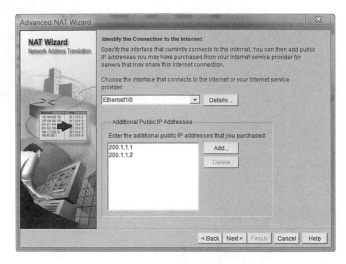

FIGURE 20.9 The Advanced NAT wizard asking for additional IP addresses.

After clicking the **Next** button, you're prompted to identify networks that connect to your internal network. In our case, we already went through the Basic NAT wizard and performed this step. Thankfully, Cisco SDM is smart enough to pick up on this and label the previously selected ranges as Designated, as shown in Figure 20.10. You can add ranges of IP addresses that are not listed by using the **Add Networks** button.

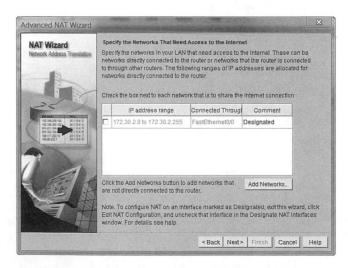

FIGURE 20.10 The Advanced NAT wizard identifying internal IP address ranges.

After clicking the **Next** button, we come to the window allowing us to configure our static NAT mappings. This is where the real action happens. We are initially given a blank window showing public-to-private IP address mappings. After you click the **Add** button, the Add Address Translation Rule window appears, as shown in Figure 20.11.

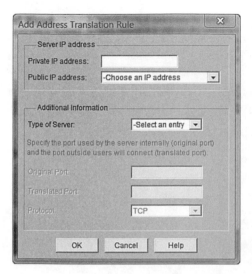

FIGURE 20.11 The Advanced NAT wizard's Add Address Translation Rule window.

From here, we can make our static NAT mappings. The simplest way to do this is to translate a single public IP address to a single private IP address. To accomplish this, you can type in the private IP address you would like to use and select the public IP address from the drop-down box, as shown in Figure 20.12.

FIGURE 20.12 Adding a static NAT mapping.

In Figure 20.12, I am planning on mapping the internal IP address 172.30.2.50 to the public IP address 200.1.1.1. However, before I do, I want you to notice the other option that is available: **IP address of Ethernet1/0**. If your organization has only a single IP address and that IP address is assigned to the router's outside interface, this selection allows you to use that IP address and map it to internal servers on your network. There are some restrictions when doing this, but we'll talk about those in just a moment. For now, I'll click the **OK** button, and the public-to-private mapping is made, as shown in Figure 20.13.

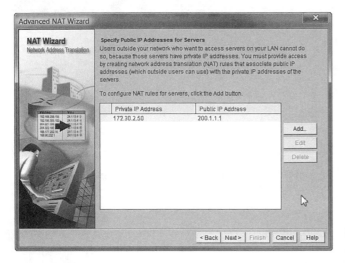

FIGURE 20.13 The first static NAT mapping is made.

I want to make a key statement at this point: Based on what I have just done, the *full* public IP address 200.1.1.1 is mapped to the private IP address 172.30.2.50. This means that if someone on the Internet accesses 200.1.1.1 on TCP port 80 (HTTP), that will forward into 172.30.2.50 on TCP port 80. Likewise, if someone on the Internet accesses 200.1.1.1 on TCP port 21 (FTP), that will forward into 172.30.2.50 on TCP port 21. It is a *full* mapping between the public address 200.1.1.1 and the private address 172.30.2.50. In contrast to a full mapping, I will configure a specific NAT port mapping.

Port mappings allow you to map individual ports on public IP addresses to individual ports on private IP addresses. This allows you to use each public IP address to its maximum potential. For example, my company might have an internal email server (which needs at least TCP port 25), an internal web server (needing at least TCP port 80), and an internal FTP server (needing at least TCP port 21). However, at this time my company has only a single public IP address of 200.1.1.2 (pretend that you never saw the other 200.1.1.1 IP address I just configured). I could use single-port mappings to map 200.1.1.2 TCP port 25 to the email server, 200.1.1.2 TCP port 80 to the web server, and 200.1.1.2 TCP port 21 to the FTP server! All with just one public IP address.

Here's how we can make it happen: Click the **Add** button to create a new NAT mapping. Just like before, enter the private IP address you'd like to map, and choose a public IP address from the drop-down menu. In this case, I'll use 172.30.2.10 as the internal email server and 200.1.1.2 as the public IP address (my final configuration window is shown in Figure 20.10). This time, we'll specify the service in the Additional Information section. Thankfully, Cisco SDM is so amazing that it already has a prebuilt mapping just for email servers! All I need to do is choose **E-mail server** from the Type of Server drop-down, as shown in Figure 20.14.

FIGURE 20.14   Mapping email services using port mappings.

The wizard also gives me the option to use an alternative port for receiving email. If my server is not using the standard TCP port 25 (SMTP) for receiving email, I can enter that here. Otherwise, I just need to click OK, and I'm good to go. The final mapping is displayed in the Advanced NAT wizard window, shown in Figure 20.15. Notice that port 25 is designated next to the public and private IP address. This is just a port mapping rather than a full IP address mapping.

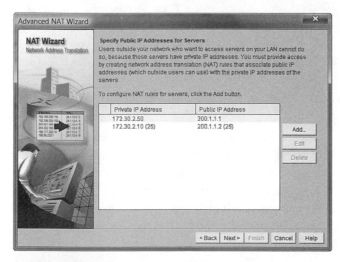

FIGURE 20.15   A full IP NAT mapping and an individual port NAT mapping.

NOTE

The Cisco router supports only individual NAT port mappings for the IP address assigned to the outside interface. You cannot fully map the outside interface IP address to an internal server because it is partially used for communication by the Cisco router.

We can now perform another two port mappings on the same 200.1.1.2 IP address, reusing it for the web and FTP servers. The Cisco SDM has built in **Web Server** selection under the Type of Server drop-down (just as it did for the email server previously). Rather than wasting space showing that configuration, let me show you something more interesting: the FTP server mapping. Again, I'll click the **Add** button to create a new mapping. I'll map the public IP address 200.1.1.2 to the internal FTP server address 172.30.2.11. This time, I'll choose **Other** under the Type of Server drop-down box (the Cisco SDM doesn't have a prebuilt FTP server mapping—yet). If you look at Figure 20.16, you'll notice that the SDM interface now gives us the opportunity to enter a value for the Original Port (received on the public IP address) and a value for the Translated Port (received on the private IP address). Most of the time, these values are the same, as shown in the Figure 20.16. Now, when 200.1.1.2 receives a request on TCP port 21, it translates it to 172.30.2.11 on TCP port 21.

FIGURE 20.16   Mapping specific NAT port numbers.

You could also perform port redirection by specifying a *different* port in either the Original Port or Translated Port fields. For example, if I entered 2100 in the Original Port field and kept 21 in the Translated Port field, the router would redirect (translate) requests received on 200.1.1.2 TCP port 2100 to 172.30.2.11 TCP port 21. You might be thinking, "Why on Earth would someone do this?!" There are plenty of reasons. Perhaps the network administrator did not want to use the well-known port number TCP 21 for the FTP server for security reasons. It could also be that port 21 on 200.1.1.2 was already used for another FTP server. Using TCP port 2100 would now allow you to run *two FTP servers off a single public IP address!* It doesn't get much better than that! Well, I suppose it could. Because 65,535 TCP ports are defined, we could theoretically run 65,535 FTP servers off a single IP address. Now we're talkin'!

> **NOTE**
>
> I (Jeremy) use this port redirection feature quite a bit for Microsoft's Remote Desktop Protocol (RDP). At my office, I have five servers running that I often need to access no matter where I am in the world. The RDP protocol allows me to access the desktop as if I were sitting directly at the server console. By default, RDP uses TCP port 3389. If I were to use only this port, it would require five public IP addresses to access each server. Instead, I set up the following port mappings:
>
> ▶ Public IP:3389 → Primary Server:3389
>
> ▶ Public IP:3390 → Email Server:3389
>
> ▶ Public IP:3391 → CallManager Server:3389
>
> ▶ Public IP:3392 → DNS Server:3389
>
> ▶ Public IP:3393 → FTP Server:3389
>
> By doing this, I can use just a single IP address, yet access any server using RDP just by specifying a different port number.

Take a look at Figure 20.17 for a final view of all our NAT mappings, including the web server. After we click the **Next** button, we see a configuration summary screen showing all the mappings we've set up. Click **Finish** to end the Advanced NAT wizard and deliver the configuration to the router.

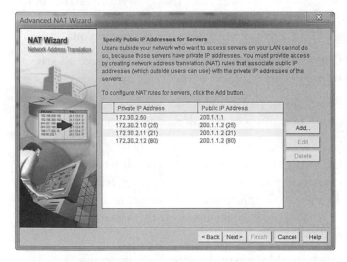

FIGURE 20.17 A combination of NAT rules.

Edit NAT Configuration

Now we come to the second way to configure static NAT mappings using SDM: through the Edit NAT Configuration tab, shown in Figure 20.18.

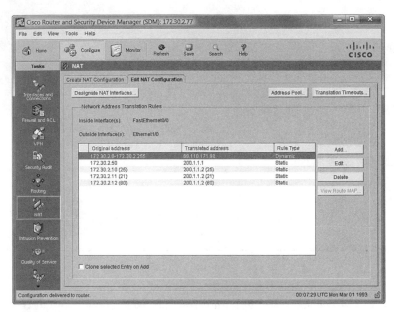

FIGURE 20.18 The Edit NAT Configuration window.

This window is most useful if you have already set up Basic NAT (NAT overload) on the router and want to make changes to your NAT configuration in some way. Just by glancing around the configuration window shown in Figure 20.18, you can see quite a few options at your disposal:

▶ **Designate NAT Interfaces:** Opens a configuration window allowing you to allocate or reallocate which interfaces on your router connect to the inside or outside networks.

▶ **Address Pool:** Allows you to create one or more pools of IP addresses that you can use for dynamic NAT (using NAT from one group of IP addresses to another; see the description earlier in this chapter).

▶ **Translation Timeouts:** Opens a configuration window that lets you set time limits for memory-resident idle NAT entries. For example, if someone opens a Telnet session through the NAT router and does not enter information, the router maintains the mapping in the NAT table for 86400 seconds by default. After this amount of time, the NAT entry is removed, and the Telnet session terminates.

▶ **Add:** Opens a window allowing you to add static or dynamic NAT mappings.

▶ **Edit:** Opens a window allowing you to edit the selected NAT mapping.

▶ **Delete:** Removes the selected NAT mapping.

You might also notice the **Clone selected Entry on Add** checkbox at the bottom of the window. If checked, this prepopulates the new NAT entry window (opened by clicking the **Add** button) with whatever entry you have selected. For example, let's say I wanted to create another static NAT mapping for our web server. I would like to map 200.1.1.2 TCP port 443 (HTTPS) to 172.30.2.12 port 443. Because I already have an entry mapping port 80 to this web server, I could check the **Clone selected Entry on Add** checkbox, select the current TCP port 80 mapping in the list, and click the **Add** button. The window shown in Figure 20.19 appears.

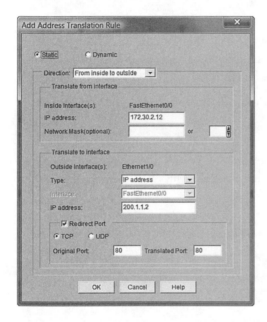

FIGURE 20.19 Adding a static NAT entry by cloning.

Nice! The **Static** radio button is already checked, the IP addresses have already been entered, and the correct interfaces are selected. All I have to do is change the Original Port and Translated Port fields to **443** and click **OK**. So easy a sea snail could do it! While we're here, let's talk about the configuration options in this window:

- ► **Static/Dynamic:** Choose the style of NAT you want to apply.

- ► **Direction:** This selector has caused plenty more confusion than it's worth. Your choices in the drop-down box are **From inside to outside** and **From outside to inside**. The common misunderstanding is that this selector makes the translation a one-way street. The truth is that regardless of the direction you choose, the mapping is always two-way. For example, let's say I create a map by choosing **From inside to outside** and map the inside IP address 172.30.2.12 to the outside IP address 200.1.1.2. When the server 172.30.2.12 accesses the Internet, it is seen as 200.1.1.2. Likewise, if someone on the Internet accesses 200.1.1.2, he or she reaches the server at 172.30.2.12. It's a two-way translation. The good news is that you can always choose which direction makes more sense to you—outside-in or inside-out. This selector also gives you more flexibility when performing dynamic NAT.

▶ **Inside IP Address/Network Mask:** The inside address or pool of addresses you want to translate.

▶ **Outside Interface(s)/Type:** Allows you to enter the individual IP address or interface you want to translate. If the **Type** drop-down box has the IP address selected (shown in Figure 20.15), the IP address field can be modified. If the **Type** drop-down box has the interface selected, the Interface field can be modified.

▶ **Redirect Port/Original Port/Translated Port:** Allows you to choose the protocol and port numbers you want to translate.

After I click the **OK** button, the new static NAT translation is added. As I mentioned earlier, the **Edit NAT Configuration** tab is the best place to make changes to an existing NAT setup.

Verifying NAT Configuration

Objective:

▶ Troubleshoot NAT issues

To verify that everything is working, we need to return to our command-line interface. (The SDM can verify that packets are passing through interfaces but is unable to show us the detailed NAT information we need.) The first thing I want to do when I get to the command line is issue the show ip interface brief command (by far, my favorite command in all of Cisco) to get my bearings:

```
NAT_ROUTER#show ip interface brief
Interface              IP-Address      OK? Method Status                Protocol
FastEthernet0/0        172.30.2.77     YES NVRAM  up                    up
Ethernet1/0            68.110.171.98   YES NVRAM  up                    up
Serial1/0              unassigned      YES NVRAM  administratively down  down
Serial2/0              unassigned      YES NVRAM  administratively down  down
```

We can see our internal IP address (172.30.2.77) and our external IP address (68.110.171.98). Let's start by ensuring that we can reach the Internet *without* involving NAT by issuing a ping command directly from the router. I typically ping the world's best-known public DNS server at 4.2.2.2 anytime I want to test Internet connectivity:

```
NAT_ROUTER#ping 4.2.2.2

Type escape sequence to abort.
Sending 5, 100-byte ICMP Echos to 4.2.2.2, timeout is 2 seconds:
!!!!!
Success rate is 100 percent (5/5), round-trip min/avg/max = 20/23/28 ms
```

Beautiful. Now I'll configure an internal client to use this router as its default gateway and do some Internet surfing. I'll spare you the screen captures of me surfing the Internet—you'll just have to trust that I'm really surfing. Yep, there's my Apple homepage (I've recently become quite the Apple enthusiast). I'll also surf over to www.CiscoBlog.com to see if there's anything new. Okay, I'm done surfing. Now let's verify that NAT is occurring from the Cisco router's perspective. You can use two major commands to do so. Here's the first:

```
NAT_ROUTER#show ip nat statistics
Total active translations: 38 (5 static, 33 dynamic; 37 extended)
Outside interfaces:
  Ethernet1/0
Inside interfaces:
  FastEthernet0/0
Hits: 1211  Misses: 121
Expired translations: 88
Dynamic mappings:
-- Inside Source
[Id: 1] access-list 1 interface Ethernet1/0 refcount 33
```

The show ip nat statistics command verifies NAT from a more global perspective. The primary information you can gather is the outside and inside interface configuration and the number of hits and misses. The number of hits defines how many packets match an existing NAT mapping. For example, I went to www.CiscoBlog.com while I was surfing the Internet. The very first packet that went through the Cisco router was considered a "miss" because no existing NAT translation was created. So, the Cisco router created the NAT translation, passing the traffic from my internal client (172.30.2.177) to the www.CiscoBlog.com website. The website then received my connection, created a TCP socket, and streamed many packets back to my web browsing application. All those packets were considered "hits" by NAT because they matched an existing NAT translation.

The second command you can use to verify that NAT is working is the more popular of the two:

```
NAT_ROUTER#show ip nat translations
Pro Inside global       Inside local       Outside local       Outside global
--- 200.1.1.1           172.30.2.50        ---                 ---
tcp 200.1.1.2:21        172.30.2.11:21     ---                 ---
tcp 200.1.1.2:25        172.30.2.10:25     ---                 ---
tcp 200.1.1.2:80        172.30.2.12:80     ---                 ---
tcp 68.110.171.98:49221 172.30.2.177:49221 17.149.160.10:80    17.149.160.10:80
```

```
tcp 68.110.171.98:49222 172.30.2.177:49222 17.149.160.10:80   17.149.160.10:80
tcp 68.110.171.98:49223 172.30.2.177:49223 17.149.160.10:80   17.149.160.10:80
tcp 68.110.171.98:49224 172.30.2.177:49224 17.149.160.10:80   17.149.160.10:80
tcp 68.110.171.98:49225 172.30.2.177:49225 17.149.160.10:80   17.149.160.10:80
tcp 68.110.171.98:49226 172.30.2.177:49226 17.149.160.10:80   17.149.160.10:80
tcp 68.110.171.98:49238 172.30.2.177:49238 17.149.160.10:80   17.149.160.10:80
tcp 200.1.1.2:443       172.30.2.12:443    ---               ---
tcp 68.110.171.98:49236 172.30.2.177:49236 66.151.152.126:80 66.151.152.126:80
tcp 68.110.171.98:49237 172.30.2.177:49237 206.16.21.35:80    206.16.21.35:80
tcp 68.110.171.98:49242 172.30.2.177:49242 69.89.31.87:80     69.89.31.87:80
tcp 68.110.171.98:49244 172.30.2.177:49244 69.89.31.87:80     69.89.31.87:80
tcp 68.110.171.98:49245 172.30.2.177:49245 69.89.31.87:80     69.89.31.87:80
tcp 68.110.171.98:49243 172.30.2.177:49243 209.85.171.167:80 209.85.171.167:80
udp 68.110.171.98:49308 172.30.2.177:49308 4.2.2.2:53         4.2.2.2:53
udp 68.110.171.98:49309 172.30.2.177:49309 4.2.2.2:53         4.2.2.2:53
udp 68.110.171.98:49310 172.30.2.177:49310 4.2.2.2:53         4.2.2.2:53
udp 68.110.171.98:49311 172.30.2.177:49311 4.2.2.2:53         4.2.2.2:53
udp 68.110.171.98:49312 172.30.2.177:49312 4.2.2.2:53         4.2.2.2:53
udp 68.110.171.98:49313 172.30.2.177:49313 4.2.2.2:53         4.2.2.2:53
udp 68.110.171.98:49314 172.30.2.177:49314 4.2.2.2:53         4.2.2.2:53
udp 68.110.171.98:49315 172.30.2.177:49315 4.2.2.2:53         4.2.2.2:53
tcp 68.110.171.98:49227 172.30.2.177:49227 208.46.174.96:80   208.46.174.96:80
tcp 68.110.171.98:49228 172.30.2.177:49228 208.46.174.96:80   208.46.174.96:80
tcp 68.110.171.98:49229 172.30.2.177:49229 208.46.174.96:80   208.46.174.96:80
```

Wow—look at that! These are all the NAT translations my router is currently maintaining. This is how you can really tell if NAT is working. If you look at the first few translations, you'll be able to verify the static NAT mappings that we entered through the SDM just a few moments ago. The IP address in the Inside global column represents the address on the interface connecting to the Internet. The IP address in the Inside local column represents the internal IP address on your LAN. Do you see now why it's so important to know that terminology mentioned at the beginning of the chapter? If it's a little fuzzy, now would be a good time to flip back a few pages and review.

The static mappings have no data in the Outside local and Outside global columns because they are not currently in use (no one is accessing those IP addresses from the Internet at this time). If they were being accessed, we would see the IP address of the device accessing them in those two columns.

Now take a look farther down; you see a *bunch* of mappings on the inside global IP address 68.110.171.98 and the inside local IP address 172.30.2.177. The global IP address represents my ISP-assigned Internet address that I am using for NAT overload (all the internal clients share this one). The local IP address represents the internal client I was surfing the Internet with. Next to each of those IP addresses is a colon, followed by a port number. These are the *source* UDP and TCP port numbers that my web surfing client uses to keep all its applications separate.

> **NOTE**
>
> We'll talk more about the specifics of the `show ip nat translations` command in Chapter 21.

In the two rightmost columns (Outside local and Outside global) you see the public IP addresses that my web surfing client was accessing. I know what you might be thinking: "Why do you have *so many* entries in the NAT table? I thought you accessed just two websites!" You're right! I did access only two websites. However, my laptop had to do DNS lookups to access both the websites, and those websites were supported by many other servers. For example, the Apple website might have one server that supplies the raw HTML pages, another server that supplies all the graphics, another for flash content, and so on. For each of those servers, the client may have to do another DNS lookup (which is why you see so many requests to the 4.2.2.2 DNS server IP address), and the Cisco router has to maintain another NAT mapping to allow data through. On top of it all, this is just one laptop surfing the Internet! Imagine what this table would look like in a large corporate network. Good thing the `show ip nat translation` command supports plenty of filtering options!

Troubleshooting NAT

When you use the SDM to configure NAT, not too much can go wrong, but you can follow some general troubleshooting steps if things don't seem to be working correctly. To start, enter the following modified `show running-config` commands:

```
NAT_ROUTER#show running-config interface fastEthernet 0/0
Building configuration...

Current configuration : 111 bytes
!
interface FastEthernet0/0
 ip address 172.30.2.77 255.255.255.0
 ip nat inside
NAT_ROUTER#show running-config interface Ethernet 1/0
Building configuration...

Current configuration : 100 bytes
!
interface Ethernet1/0
 ip address 68.110.171.98 255.255.255.224
 ip nat outside
```

This filters the large running configuration to just the interfaces you'd like to see. What you want to verify is that the interface connecting to your internal network is configured as the `ip nat inside` interface and that the interface connecting to the ISP is configured as the `ip nat outside` interface.

If things look good there, do a ping from the router itself. This will test your Internet connectivity without the NAT process getting in the way. The problem could be a simple routing issue (such as missing a default route to your ISP). If things check out in the router-originated ping, try the ping from an internal client. Be sure you're pinging an IP address rather than a hostname (such as www.examcram.com). You don't want a DNS problem getting in the way. If the client can ping successfully, NAT is operational.

Last, but not least, is a command that has saved me plenty of troubleshooting time: `clear ip nat translations *`. This command wipes out the NAT table maintained on the router. Sometimes, when we are setting up a network, we end up with NAT entries in the table that don't belong there. It could just be from changing a client's IP address before NAT timeouts are reached, it could be that your public or private IP address changes, or it could just be that the router doesn't feel like NATing today. It's always worthwhile to try entering `clear ip nat translations *` from the privileged prompt before you get too deep in troubleshooting other issues. Don't worry; it shouldn't cause any connectivity problems for existing clients using the Internet. The router will just create a new NAT mapping the next packet that comes through. I have seen this command cause Instant Messenger clients to log out and log back in again, but people don't really use Instant Messenger clients for anything productive anyway, right?

Chapter Summary

You'd be hard-pressed to find any corporate network in the world providing Internet access without using NAT. Because of this, Cisco has added it as one of the core competencies of both a CCENT and CCNA certified individual.

The big-picture concept of NAT is fairly simple: converting one IP address to another. However, the technical details behind NAT are where the complexity lies. Most of the challenge with NAT is learning the terminology that describes the different addresses on a network. Inside local addresses are internal to a network. The inside global address represents the public Internet address assigned to your router. Outside global addresses represent all the hosts outside your network attached to the Internet with Internet IP addresses. Finally, outside local addresses represent hosts outside your network as they are seen by the internal NAT hosts.

A company planning to use NAT will deploy one of the three private address ranges on its internal network, which are prevented from routing to the Internet. It then uses one of the three forms of NAT—static NAT, dynamic NAT, or NAT overload—to translate these private ranges onto the Internet. Most networks use a combination of NAT overload and static NAT to accomplish most major network objectives.

Key Terms

- ▶ Network Address Translation (NAT)
- ▶ Port Address Translation (PAT)
- ▶ Static NAT
- ▶ Dynamic NAT
- ▶ NAT overload
- ▶ Private IP addresses
- ▶ Public IP addresses
- ▶ Inside local address
- ▶ Inside global address
- ▶ Outside local address
- ▶ Outside global address
- ▶ Port redirection

Apply Your Knowledge

Review Questions

1. List the three private ranges of IP addresses typically used with NAT translations.

2. Three forms of NAT are used in networks today: static NAT, dynamic NAT, and NAT overload/PAT. What is the use of each of these forms of NAT?

3. You would like to see the current NAT translations passing through your router. What command would you enter?

4. You are troubleshooting NAT on your router. It appears as though some of the entries are mapped to incorrect IP addresses. How can you erase the current NAT translations and allow them to rebuild?

5. Your organization has an internal web server that it needs to make available to the Internet. What form of NAT will you use, and why?

Exam Questions

1. You have an internal web server that has the IP address 172.16.5.9. You need to enable this server to be accessed on TCP port 80 from the Internet. What would be the best solution for this situation?

   ○ **A.** Static NAT

   ○ **B.** Dynamic NAT

   ○ **C.** NAT overload

   ○ **D.** Standard routing

2. Which of the following forms of NAT incorporates the source IP address (inside local) along with the source port number to make every translation unique?

   ○ **A.** Static NAT

   ○ **B.** Dynamic NAT

   ○ **C.** NAT overload

   ○ **D.** NAT port mapping

3. Which of the following is *not* a task you can perform from the Edit NAT Configuration tab of SDM?

   ○ **A.** Configure access lists for use with dynamic NAT.

   ○ **B.** Select inside and outside interfaces of the router.

   ○ **C.** Adjust NAT timeout values.

   ○ **D.** Configure NAT overload capabilities.

Refer to the following figure for Questions 4 and 5.

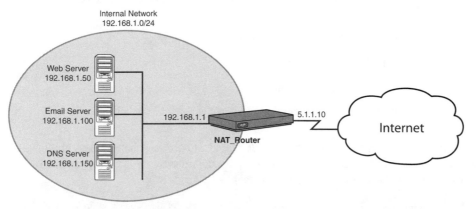

4. According to NAT terminology, the IP address 192.168.1.100 for the email server is considered an
   _____.

   ○ **A.** Inside local address

   ○ **B.** Inside global address

   ○ **C.** Outside local address

   ○ **D.** Outside global address

5. According to NAT terminology, the IP address 5.1.1.10 is considered an _____.

   ○ **A.** Inside local address

   ○ **B.** Inside global address

   ○ **C.** Outside local address

   ○ **D.** Outside global address

6. Which of the following represent a private IP address? (Choose two)

   ○ **A.** 192.168.5.205

   ○ **B.** 172.32.65.31

   ○ **C.** 10.168.5.205

   ○ **D.** 224.16.23.1

7. You are configuring a new router for NAT and would like to set up NAT overload and a single, static NAT mapping allowing access to an internal web server. What would be the most efficient way to accomplish this?

   ○ **A.** Basic NAT SDM wizard

   ○ **B.** Advanced NAT SDM wizard

   ○ **C.** Using the Edit NAT Configuration tab

   ○ **D.** Using the Basic NAT SDM wizard followed by the Edit NAT Configuration tab

8. You are using NAT overload on your company's Cisco router to provide Internet access to your internal network. The NAT process is overloading the IP address assigned to the router's outside interface. Which of the following statements are *not* true? (Choose two)

   ○ **A.** Multiple internal users cannot access the same website at the same time, because the website will see two requests coming from the same IP address.

   ○ **B.** Static NAT mappings can be added for the interface IP address, but only for specific ports.

   ○ **C.** Static NAT mappings can be added for the full interface IP address.

   ○ **D.** Cisco's NAT process will allow you to NAT not only to the interface IP address but also to other IP addresses not assigned to the interface.

9. You would like to see the active NAT translations that are happening on your router. Your primary interest is in the inside local IPs that are being translated. What command shows you this information?

   ○ **A.** `show ip nat statistics`

   ○ **B.** `show ip nat translations`

   ○ **C.** `show ip interface`

   ○ **D.** `show running-config`

10. You have just changed one of your internal computer's IP addresses, and it appears that it can no longer access the Internet. You have verified the correct subnet and gateway information. What commands should you perform on the router to ensure that cached information does not play a role in this failure? (Choose two)

   ○ **A.** `clear arp`

   ○ **B.** `clear ip route`

   ○ **C.** `clear ip nat translations*`

   ○ **D.** `clear startup-config`

Answers to Review Questions

1. The three private address ranges are as follows:

   Class A: 10.0.0.0 to 10.255.255.255

   Class B: 172.16.0.0 to 172.31.255.255

   Class C: 192.168.0.0 to 192.168.255.255

2. Static NAT is responsible for one-to-one translations. It is typically used to make private servers available on the Internet. Dynamic NAT is used to translate one pool of addresses to another. This is the least common form of NAT and is typically used to solve duplicate IP addresses when merging two networks. Last is NAT overload. This form of NAT is the most popular because it allows many internal hosts to share a common public IP address.

3. The correct command is `show ip nat translations` from privileged mode.

4. You can enter the command `clear ip nat translations` * to erase the current NAT table from memory. The table will naturally rebuild as users access the Internet.

5. Static NAT is most appropriate to make internal resources available to the outside world. This is because static NAT performs one-to-one translations allowing you to direct specific IP address requests to a public address to a privately addressed server.

Answers to Exam Questions

1. **A.** Static NAT provides the best solution when you need a 1:1 translation from a private address or port number to a public address or port number. Answer B is incorrect because dynamic NAT allows many hosts to be translated at the same time. Answer C is incorrect because NAT overload allows many internal hosts to share a single Internet IP address. Answer D is also incorrect. Standard routing does not work because private addresses are blocked from traversing the Internet.

2. **C.** NAT overload uses the source port number to send many unique requests out a single, public IP address. Answer A is incorrect because static NAT performs 1:1 translations from public to private IP addresses. Answer B is incorrect because dynamic NAT performs many 1:1 translations without requiring manual entries. Answer D is incorrect because NAT port mapping is not a valid form of NAT.

3. **A.** You cannot create access lists for use with dynamic NAT from the Edit NAT Configuration tab. All other tasks can be performed from this window.

4. **A.** Inside local addresses encompass any address on your internal network that is translated to the outside network via NAT. Answer B is incorrect because the inside global addresses are the IPs assigned to the outside interface of your router. Answer C is incorrect because the outside local addresses are outside (Internet) addresses as they appear to a NAT device. Answer D is incorrect because the outside global addresses are standard Internet-attached devices.

5. **B.** The inside global addresses are the IPs assigned to the outside interface of your router. Answer A is incorrect because inside local addresses encompass any address on your internal network that is translated to the outside network via NAT. Answer C is incorrect because the outside local addresses are outside (Internet) addresses as they appear to a NAT device. Answer D is incorrect because the outside global addresses are standard Internet-attached devices.

6. **A, C.** The private address ranges are 10.x.x.x, 172.16.x.x to 172.31.x.x, and 192.168.x.x. Answers B and D fall outside these ranges.

7. **B.** The Advanced NAT wizard allows you to configure NAT overload and static NAT mappings at the same time in the same wizard. If you use the Basic NAT wizard (Answer A), you would have to follow it up with the Edit NAT Configuration tab, which is not the most efficient way to configure NAT. This makes both Answers A and D incorrect. Answer C is incorrect because using the Edit NAT Configuration tab would require you to manually set up NAT overload and the static NAT mapping individually, which is not the most efficient process.

8. **A, C.** When using NAT overload, multiple users *can* access the same website at the same time because the router uses unique source port numbers to distinguish each request. Also, when using NAT with the IP address assigned to the outside interface, you cannot create a static NAT mapping for the entire IP address, because this would make local router services unavailable. Both of the other statements are true.

9. **B.** The `show ip nat translations` command shows you all active translations currently in place on your router. It includes the inside local and global and the outside local and global addresses for each translation. Answer A is incorrect because the `show ip nat statistics` command tells you only how many translations are currently happening. Answer C is incorrect because the `show ip interface` command does not give you any NAT statistics. Answer D is incorrect because the `show running-config` command tells you only the NAT configurations you have set up.

10. **A, C.** The `clear arp` command ensures that the router does not have the incorrect MAC address mapped to the computer's IP address. The `clear ip nat translations *` command ensures that the cached NAT translations are not pointed to the wrong IP address. Answer B is incorrect. The `clear ip route` is not necessary because the routing table did not change and could cause downtime for your router. Answer D is incorrect because the `clear startup-config` does not remove any cached configuration.

Suggested Reading and Resources

1. Cisco TAC NAT Configuration Syntax, http://www.cisco.com/univercd/cc/td/doc/product/software/ios122/122cgcr/fipr_c/ipcprt1/1cfipadr.htm#wp1042290

2. Chris Ward and Jeremy Cioara. *Exam Cram 2 CCNA Practice Questions*. Que Publishing, 2004.

3. How Network Address Translation Works, http://computer.howstuffworks.com/nat1.htm

21

Command-Line NAT Implementation

Objectives

This chapter covers the following Cisco-specific objectives for the "Implement, verify, and troubleshoot NAT and ACLs in a medium-size Enterprise branch office network" section of the 640-802 CCNA exam:

▶ **Explain the basic operation of NAT**

▶ **Configure NAT for given network requirements**

▶ **Troubleshoot NAT issues**

Outline

Study Strategies

▶ Read the information presented in the chapter, paying special attention to tables, Notes, and Exam Alerts.

▶ Focus on the Network Address Translation terminology. Understanding these terms is paramount to understanding the NAT configuration as a whole.

▶ When studying, focus on the static NAT configurations first, because these are the simplest. After you master this configuration, move on to NAT overload, followed by dynamic NAT.

Introduction

Welcome to NAT, Part 2. It's now time to move from the soft and squishy GUI way of working through NAT into the "real man's way" of configuring NAT—from the command line. Performing the NAT configuration using the command-line interface puts hair on your chest (my apologies to the women using this style of configuration) and also gives you plenty more flexibility than using the SDM GUI. This chapter builds on the foundational concepts and terminology from Chapter 20, "Enabling Internet Connectivity with NAT," applying the concepts directly in command-line configuration. However, because the terminology of NAT is so unique and potentially confusing, I would like to review the terms with you before we begin into the configuration to keep you from having to flip back and forth between chapters. We'll then walk through the command-line configuration of static NAT, dynamic NAT, and NAT overload.

Reviewing NAT Concepts

Objective:

▶ Explain the basic operation of NAT

Let's start by reviewing the three forms of NAT:

▶ **Static NAT:** This form of NAT provides a one-to-one translation between IP addresses (typically public and private). These types of mappings are usually used to allow Internet clients to access internal servers. It can be either a full IP address translation or translations of individual TCP or UDP ports.

▶ **Dynamic NAT:** This form of NAT translates one pool of IP addresses to another. This is typically used as a temporary solution when companies or departments merge that have duplicate address schemes. Of the three NAT forms, this is used the least often.

▶ **NAT overload/PAT:** This form of NAT allows multiple internal clients (typically using private IP address) to share one or more public IP addresses. This is accomplished by using unique source port numbers for each request coming from the public IP address. This is the most common form of NAT.

In addition to reviewing the forms of NAT, I'd like to reiterate the terminology used when referencing logical locations on the network. Understanding the NAT terminology is more important now than in the SDM, because the SDM accomplishes most everything for you without requiring a deep understanding.

▶ **Inside/outside:** These NAT descriptors refer to where a device is physically located. If a device is "inside," it is under your control; it is in your network. If a device is "outside," it is not under your control; it is outside your network.

▶ **Local/global:** These NAT descriptors refer to where an IP address is located *from the perspective of a NAT device*. The NAT device is a network device that has its address translated through a NAT router. It could be a PC, a server, an Xbox, or any other type of host that has a private address that is translated to a real address on the Internet. If the IP address is considered "local," it is seen as a device on the local subnet from the perspective of a NAT device (this may or may not be true). If the IP address is considered "global," it is seen as not on the local subnet from the perspective of a NAT device.

Figure 21.1 shows these types of addresses on the network.

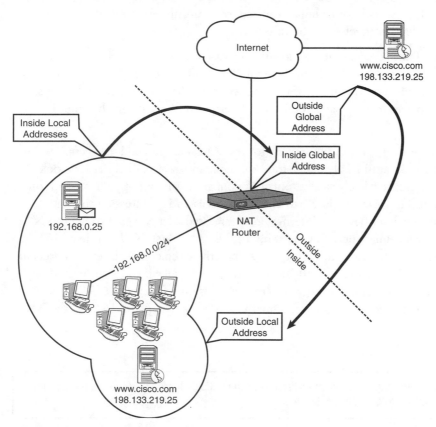

FIGURE 21.1 NAT terminology.

▶ **Inside local addresses:** These addresses are the easiest to understand because they refer to everything inside your network. An address "inside" is physically located inside your network. From the perspective of the NAT device, it is "local," meaning that it is seen on the internal network. If an inside local address were to communicate with another inside local address, that communication would be described as standard LAN connectivity. No routers would be needed.

▶ **Inside global addresses:** Now the terms begin to mix a little bit. Let's break this down into the individual pieces: First, the address is "inside," which means that it is physically located on your network; it is under your control. "Global" means that it is seen as an IP address, not on the local subnet from the perspective of one of your NAT devices. Put all this together and you are left with the Internet valid IP address assigned to your router that is directly connected to the Internet. This is where a fundamental understanding of inside and outside can really help. If the address were an "outside global," it would not be under your control, meaning that it could be any of the millions of devices attached to the Internet.

▶ **Outside global addresses:** Outside global addresses refer to devices that are physically "outside" your network—outside your control. These addresses are "global," meaning that the NAT devices on the inside of your network see these as nonlocal addresses. Put these two pieces together and you have a description of a standard Internet IP address.

▶ **Outside local addresses:** I saved the best for last. Outside local addresses confused me for quite some time until I fully understood the capabilities of NAT. First let's look at the pieces. This address is physically "outside" your network, out of your control, out on the Internet. However, it appears to NAT devices as an IP address on the "local" subnet. What this describes is an Internet host translated as it comes through the NAT router *into* your local network. You can think of this as "reverse NAT," or just NAT in the other direction. As shown in Figure 21.1, when the cisco.com web server speaks to the internal hosts on the 192.168.0.0/24 network, they believe it to be co-located on the local subnet with them. They come to this conclusion because the NAT router translates the outside global address to something local (perhaps 192.168.0.1, the NAT gateway's address).

TIP

Understanding the four NAT address descriptors listed is useful not only for the CCNA exam, but also for understanding any real-world NAT documentation.

NAT Configurations

Objective:

▶ Configure NAT for given network requirements

Configuring NAT is not all that bad as long as you focus on your objective. I mention this because the syntax can be quite daunting when you see all the options available to you. Advanced NAT configurations can get quite complex.

> **TIP**
>
> For the CCNA and ICND2 exams, you should be able to perform these three NAT-related tasks:
>
> ▶ Configure static NAT, translating an inside global address (or port number) to an inside local address, such as a web, DNS, or email server.
>
> ▶ Configure dynamic NAT, translating a pool of inside local addresses to a pool of outside global addresses.
>
> ▶ Configure NAT overload, translating many inside local addresses to a single inside global address.
>
> Of these three, I would especially focus on the first and third configurations, because they are more common in the real world.

With that said, it's time to walk through these configurations one at a time.

Static NAT

As discussed earlier, static NAT performs a one-to-one mapping from an inside local address to an inside global address (in English: from a private to a public address). This could mean that all traffic is translated between these addresses, or it could mean that you just choose certain ports through which to translate. As I go through the syntax, I will expand a little more on this. Figure 21.2 adds a network diagram to this syntax.

Before we get into the syntax, I want to make sure you've got the terms down. The internal network consists of the 192.168.1.0/24 addresses. In NAT terms, these are all inside local addresses. The router has a single Internet IP address of 5.1.1.10. This is considered the inside global address. The rest of the hosts on the Internet that will be accessing your internal servers all have outside global addresses.

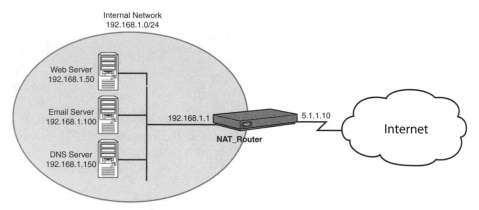

FIGURE 21.2 Static NAT configuration.

Scenario 1

Configure a static NAT translation so that if any request on any port is received on the inside global address of the NAT_Router, it forwards that request to the internal web server.

Here we go! First, get familiar with the current interfaces:

```
NAT_Router#show ip interface brief
Interface               IP-Address      OK? Method Status        Protocol
FastEthernet0           192.168.1.1     YES manual up            up
Serial0                 5.1.1.10        YES manual up            up
```

Everything is as shown in Figure 21.2. The first step in configuring NAT is to identify your inside and outside interfaces to the router. This is done on a per-interface basis:

```
NAT_Router#configure terminal
Enter configuration commands, one per line.  End with CNTL/Z.
NAT_Router(config)#interface fastethernet0
NAT_Router(config-if)#ip nat inside  !identifies internal interface
NAT_Router(config-if)#exit
NAT_Router(config)#interface serial0
NAT_Router(config-if)#ip nat outside !identifies external interface
NAT_Router(config-if)#exit
NAT_Router(config)#
```

With these interfaces identified to the router, it now knows which interface(s) are considered outside and inside. Setting up the static NAT translation is a little more difficult.

Static NAT configurations are set up in global configuration mode with the ip nat syntax:

```
NAT_Router(config)#ip nat ?
  inside     Inside address translation
  log        NAT Logging
  outside    Outside address translation
```

```
pool          Define pool of addresses
service       Special translation for application using non-standard port
translation   NAT translation entry configuration
```

The primary keywords to consider are inside and outside. These two commands perform exactly the same function from different perspectives. If you choose the inside keyword, the syntax that follows translates an inside address to an outside address. If you choose the outside keyword, the syntax that follows translates an outside address to an inside address. Because NAT translations are always two-way, the keyword you choose influences the order you use for the addresses in the upcoming syntax. To avoid confusion, I recommend picking one method (inside or outside) and using it exclusively.

Many moons ago, I chose to use inside, so that's what I'll do here:

```
NAT_Router(config)#ip nat inside ?
  destination  Destination address translation
  source       Source address translation
```

The choice now is whether to translate the inside *source* IP address or inside *destination* IP address.

If you are looking from the perspective of the *inside* device (what was chosen when the inside keyword was used rather than outside), you need to translate the internal device's source IP address rather than its various destination IP addresses. (See how this can get confusing if you alternate between the inside and outside keywords?)

```
NAT_Router(config)#ip nat inside source ?
  list       Specify access list describing local addresses
  route-map  Specify route-map
  static     Specify static local->global mapping
```

At this point, the router wants to know what type of translation you want to perform. The list keyword is used to perform dynamic NAT translations. Using route maps for NAT is far beyond the scope of the CCNA (and perhaps even the CCNP). In this case, you need to define a static translation:

```
NAT_Router(config)#ip nat inside source static ?
  A.B.C.D  Inside local IP address
  esp      IPSec-ESP (Tunnel mode) support
  network  Subnet translation
  tcp      Transmission Control Protocol
  udp      User Datagram Protocol
```

The router would now like to have either the inside local address or the protocol information. This scenario requests a full translation from the router's inside global address to the web server's inside local address. If you were choosing to use NAT to translate individual ports, you would use either TCP or UDP protocols. For this scenario, you can enter the web server's inside local address:

```
NAT_Router(config)#ip nat inside source static 192.168.1.50 ?
  A.B.C.D  Inside global IP address
```

The router now needs to know what inside global address to use. In this example, the router's inside global address is 5.1.1.10, which is the same IP address assigned to its Serial0 interface. In the real world, you have the option of purchasing blocks of IP addresses from your ISP. You can then translate each of these public addresses to an inside local address *without the address even being assigned to an interface*! All you need to do is create static NAT mappings for each of the addresses that you have been assigned by the ISP, and your router automatically responds to them on the interface(s) you have designated as `ip nat outside` interfaces. This example has only a single IP address, so that's plugged in here:

```
NAT_Router(config)#ip nat inside source static 192.168.1.50 5.1.1.10 ?
  extendable  Extend this translation when used
  no-alias    Do not create an alias for the global address
  <cr>
```

The `extendable` keyword enables you to have multiple inside global addresses mapped to the same inside local address (all the mappings must be marked with the `extendable` keyword). The `no-alias` command enables you to set up a one-way NAT mapping from the inside to outside. (The outside interface does not pass requests through to the inside host, but the inside host is translated to the outside.) In this case, you're not adding either of these special functions, so you can just press the Enter key. Awesome!

You can verify this configuration by using either the `show running-config` command or the much more concise `show ip nat translations`:

```
NAT_Router#show ip nat translations
Pro Inside global      Inside local      Outside local      Outside global
--- 5.1.1.10           192.168.1.50      ---                ---
```

Because this is a manually defined static entry, only the inside global and inside local fields are populated. If a host tried to connect to this entry (to access the internal web server), you would see the outside local and outside global columns populate as well. Let me generate some traffic from the outside to show you what this will look like:

```
NAT_Router#show ip nat translations
Pro Inside global  Inside local      Outside local      Outside global
--- 5.1.1.10       192.168.1.50      ---                ---
tcp 5.1.1.10:80    192.168.1.50:80   52.1.9.3:3367      52.1.9.3:3367
```

In this case, an outside host accesses the 5.1.1.10 address with a web browser (TCP port 80). You can see that it keeps the original static entry and adds a line below it, showing the outside local and outside global addresses of the external client. In this case, they are the same because the outside host appears as an outside host to the web server (the outside local address). Port 3367 is the dynamically generated source port number of the outside host, and port 80 is the destination port number sent to the web server. Scenario 1 accomplished!

Scenario 2

Configure two additional static NAT translations. If the NAT_Router receives a request to its inside global address that uses SMTP, it should be sent to the internal email server. If the NAT router receives a DNS request on the inside global address, it should forward it to the internal DNS server. All other traffic should keep forwarding to the internal web server.

Wow! What a scenario! To tackle this, you must remember the universal rule of routing: The more specific matches *always win*. So, if you were to add specific static NAT entries that forward just a single port number, it would always overrule the forward all entry configured for the web server in Scenario 1. Let's walk through these using context-sensitive help one more time, with a little less commentary:

```
NAT_Router(config)#ip nat ?
  inside       Inside address translation
  log          NAT Logging
  outside      Outside address translation
  pool         Define pool of addresses
  service      Special translation for application using non-standard port
  translation  NAT translation entry configuration

NAT_Router(config)#ip nat inside ?
  destination  Destination address translation
  source       Source address translation

NAT_Router(config)#ip nat inside source ?
  list       Specify access list describing local addresses
  route-map  Specify route-map
  static     Specify static local->global mapping

NAT_Router(config)#ip nat inside source static ?
  A.B.C.D  Inside local IP address
  esp      IPSec-ESP (Tunnel mode) support
  network  Subnet translation
  tcp      Transmission Control Protocol
  udp      User Datagram Protocol
```

So far, the static NAT mapping has been configured in exactly the same fashion as the previous one. Now we'll add a little twist: Because we are just forwarding specific ports to the internal server, we need to choose the protocol those ports are using. The scenario calls for us to forward SMTP traffic to the internal E-Mail server and DNS traffic to the internal DNS server. SMTP uses TCP port 25, and DNS traffic uses UDP port 53 (remember this from Chapter 19, "Using Cisco Access Lists"?), so here's how the syntax continues. First, we'll focus on creating the map for the E-Mail server:

```
NAT_Router(config)#ip nat inside source static tcp ?
  A.B.C.D  Inside local IP address
```

```
NAT_Router(config)#ip nat inside source static tcp 192.168.1.100 ?
  <1-65535>  Local UDP/TCP port

NAT_Router(config)#ip nat inside source static tcp 192.168.1.100 25 ?
  A.B.C.D    Inside global IP address
  interface  Specify interface for global address
```

All righty, then. A specific static NAT mapping has been configured that uses the TCP proto-col and that points to the inside local address of 192.168.1.100 with inside local port 25. Isn't that interesting? Now it's time to specify an inside local port as well! This opens a bunch of possibilities. But before I expand on those, let's finish the command:

```
NAT_Router(config)#ip nat inside source static tcp 192.168.1.100 25
5.1.1.10 ?
  <1-65535>  Global UDP/TCP port

NAT_Router(config)#ip nat inside source static tcp 192.168.1.100 25
5.1.1.10 25 ?
  extendable  Extend this translation when used
  no-alias    Do not create an alias for the global address
  <cr>
NAT_Router(config)#ip nat inside source static tcp 192.168.1.100 25
5.1.1.10 25
NAT_Router(config)#^Z
NAT_Router#show ip nat translations
Pro Inside global     Inside local      Outside local      Outside global
--- 5.1.1.10          192.168.1.50      - - -              - - -
tcp 5.1.1.10:25       192.168.1.100:25  - - -              - - -
```

Did you see that? Not only was the command finished and the static NAT mapping added to the table, but now you can see the possibility for the *global TCP/UDP port!* This enables you to perform the fantastic configuration of *port redirection.* Here's the idea: Perhaps for security reasons, you didn't want to have the internal email server answering SMTP requests on port 25, so the internal port on the server is changed to 5525. Now none of the internal clients can access that email server via port 25; however, the NAT router can redirect incoming Internet requests on port 25 to the inside local port 5525! All this is seamless to the Internet clients. Are you as excited about this as I am?

Finally, let's add the last NAT translation for the DNS server:

```
NAT_Router(config)#ip nat inside source static udp ?
  A.B.C.D  Inside local IP address

NAT_Router(config)#ip nat inside source static udp 192.168.1.150 ?
  <1-65535>  Local UDP/TCP port

NAT_Router(config)#ip nat inside source static udp 192.168.1.150 53 ?
  A.B.C.D    Inside global IP address
  interface  Specify interface for global address
```

```
NAT_Router(config)#ip nat inside source static udp 192.168.1.150 53
5.1.1.10 ?
  <1-65535>  Global UDP/TCP port

NAT_Router(config)#ip nat inside source static udp 192.168.1.150 53
5.1.1.10 53
NAT_Router(config)#^Z
NAT_Router#show ip nat translations
Pro Inside global      Inside local       Outside local      Outside global
--- 5.1.1.10           192.168.1.50       ---                ---
tcp 5.1.1.10:25        192.168.1.100:25   ---                ---
udp 5.1.1.10:53        192.168.1.150:53   ---                ---
```

Perfect! Three static NAT entries have now been added. Before we move on, let me call your attention to the context-sensitive help after the local port information has been entered:

```
NAT_Router(config)#ip nat inside source static udp 192.168.1.150 53 ?
  A.B.C.D    Inside global IP address
  interface  Specify interface for global address
```

So far, you have been entering the inside global address that you would like to translate. However, there may be an occasion when you do not know what your global address may be (primarily when using DHCP for your Internet address). In this case, you can use the `interface` keyword rather than an inside global address to translate requests received on the outside interface to internal hosts. This can be especially useful when using a Cisco router to perform NAT on a cable or DSL connection at a home.

```
NAT_Router(config)#ip nat inside source static udp 192.168.1.150 53 interface serial 0
53
```

Dynamic Pool Translations

The next step is to move from the manual, static NAT entries to allowing the router to do the work for you. Dynamic NAT enables you to define a pool of addresses to translate *from* and a pool of addresses to translate *to*. The primary application of dynamic translations is to temporarily overcome overlapping IP addresses. For example, a company might use subnets of the 10.0.0.0/8 address range for its internal addressing. This company might merge with another company that uses the same internal address space (this happens all the time). The IT staff could implement an intermediary design that uses NAT to translate between the two networks. When performing this type of translation, hosts must refer to each other by hostname rather than IP address, thus requiring a DNS server be in place. When the NAT router sees a reply from a remote DNS server, it changes the remote IP address to something other than an overlapping IP address.

Although the CCNA-level NAT does not get deep into design for overlapping IP addresses, you need to know the basic configurations of dynamic NAT. These configurations also act as springboards into the NAT overload configuration. First, examine Figure 21.3, a dynamic NAT network diagram.

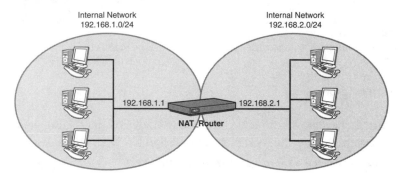

FIGURE 21.3 Dynamic NAT translations.

Scenario 3

Configure the NAT_Router so that hosts from the 192.168.1.0/24 network are seen as IP addresses 192.168.2.200 to 225 when accessing the hosts in the 192.168.2.0/24 network. Likewise, the hosts from the 192.168.1.0/24 network should be seen as IP addresses 192.168.1.200 to 225 when accessing the hosts in the 192.168.1.0/24 network.

This configuration is known as a two-way dynamic NAT configuration. The truth is, the NAT_Router in the middle of the diagram is not doing any routing. It's just translating between the subnets. If you ever aspire to move on and tackle the CCIE lab, these sorts of tricks are key to have in your tool belt. Here's the configuration walkthrough:

1. As before, configure the interfaces as NAT outside and inside interfaces. In this case, it does not really matter which one is set up as inside or outside, because just a private network is being translated.

```
NAT_Router#show ip interface brief
Interface               IP-Address      OK? Method Status      Protocol
FastEthernet0           192.168.1.1     YES manual up          up
Serial0                 192.168.2.1     YES manual up          up
NAT_Router#conf t
Enter configuration commands, one per line.  End with CNTL/Z.
NAT_Router(config)#interface fastethernet0
NAT_Router(config-if)#ip nat inside
NAT_Router(config-if)#exit
NAT_Router(config)#interface serial0
NAT_Router(config-if)#ip nat outside
NAT_Router(config-if)#exit
NAT_Router(config)#
```

2. Now you are introduced to a new concept: the NAT pool. This pool defines what addresses you will translate. Based on the scenarios, you need to create two NAT pools: one for the 192.168.2.200 to 225 range and one for the 192.168.1.200 to 225 range:

```
NAT_Router(config)#ip nat ?
  inside        Inside address translation
  log           NAT Logging
  outside       Outside address translation
  pool          Define pool of addresses
  service       Special translation for application using non-standard port
  translation   NAT translation entry configuration

NAT_Router(config)#ip nat pool ?
  WORD   Pool name

NAT_Router(config)#ip nat pool NETWORK1 ?
  A.B.C.D         Start IP address
  netmask         Specify the network mask
  prefix-length   Specify the prefix length

NAT_Router(config)#ip nat pool NETWORK1 192.168.1.200 ?
  A.B.C.D   End IP address

NAT_Router(config)#ip nat pool NETWORK1 192.168.1.200 192.168.1.225 ?
  netmask         Specify the network mask
  prefix-length   Specify the prefix length

NAT_Router(config)#ip nat pool NETWORK1 192.168.1.200 192.168.1.225
prefix-length ?
  <1-32>   Prefix length

NAT_Router(config)#ip nat pool NETWORK1 192.168.1.200 192.168.1.225
prefix-length 24
NAT_ROUTER(config)#
```

This command creates a NAT pool called Network1 that defines the correct address range necessary. Notice that this is one of the first commands you have seen that enables you to use CIDR notation (also known as "bit notation") for your subnet mask. You now need to create a second NAT pool for the other network range:

```
NAT_Router(config)#ip nat pool NETWORK2 192.168.2.200 192.168.2.225
prefix-length 24
```

3. You must now create a couple of standard access lists that will define the addresses that *will be translated*. This is one of the nonsecurity uses of an access list.

```
NAT_Router(config)#access-list 50 permit 192.168.1.0 0.0.0.255
NAT_Router(config)#access-list 51 permit 192.168.2.0 0.0.0.255
```

4. Now you can put all the pieces together and turn on the NAT translation between the networks. The first thing is to define a translation going from the 192.168.1.0/24 subnet to the 192.168.2.0/24 network:

```
NAT_Router(config)#ip nat ?
  inside       Inside address translation
  log          NAT Logging
  outside      Outside address translation
  pool         Define pool of addresses
  service      Special translation for application using non-standard port
  translation  NAT translation entry configuration

NAT_Router(config)#ip nat inside ?
  destination  Destination address translation
  source       Source address translation

NAT_Router(config)#ip nat inside source ?
  list       Specify access list describing local addresses
  route-map  Specify route-map
  static     Specify static local->global mapping

NAT_Router(config)#ip nat inside source list ?
  <1-2699>  Access list number for local addresses
  WORD      Access list name for local addresses

NAT_Router(config)#ip nat inside source list 50 ?
  interface  Specify interface for global address
  pool       Name pool of global addresses

NAT_Router(config)#ip nat inside source list 50 pool ?
  WORD  Pool name for global addresses

NAT_Router(config)#ip nat inside source list 50 pool NETWORK2 ?
  overload  Overload an address translation
  <cr>

NAT_Router(config)#ip nat inside source list 50 pool NETWORK2
NAT_Router(config)#
```

If you were to read the preceding line of syntax in English, it would sound something like this: "Translate the internal addresses defined in access list 50 into the pool of addresses defined in the NAT pool NETWORK2." Keep a mental note of that over-load keyword you see in the final-context sensitive help; you'll make use of that soon. For now, let's define the translation going back the other way:

```
NAT_Router(config)#ip nat outside source list 51 pool NETWORK1
NAT_Router(config)#
```

Notice that this time an outside-to-inside translation is configured because the interface is marked as connected to the 192.168.2.0/24 subnet as the outside interface.

At this point, the networks are translating quite well. Remember that the pool of 25 addresses defined earlier allows only 25 consecutive sessions between the subnets. Any consecutive sessions above that number will fail.

NAT Overload

Finally it's time to explore the feature that made NAT famous around the network world: NAT overload. NAT overload is the official name of the feature that allows multiple hosts to share a single IP address. When Microsoft began allowing its servers to perform routing with the Routing and Remote Access administrative tools, it decided to call the feature Port Address Translation (PAT), which caught on in many circles. I prefer to use the term NAT overload because NAT can statically translate TCP or UDP ports to different inside local address—the true "port address translation."

The configuration of NAT overload is a piece of cake, especially now that you've seen the prior dynamic NAT configuration.

Scenario 4

Configure the network pictured in Figure 21.4 for NAT overload, allowing all internal clients to access the Internet. In addition, configure a static entry that sends any incoming request on TCP port 80 or 443 to the internal web server.

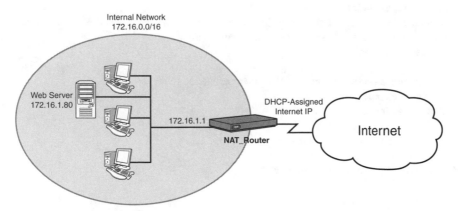

FIGURE 21.4 NAT overload configuration.

Let's walk through this new scenario step by step. In Figure 21.4, a typical network is connected to the Internet through the NAT_Router. The router needs to be configured to perform NAT overload to allow all the internal clients to access the Internet through a single IP address. Notice as well that the Internet IP address is assigned via DHCP, so there's no way to be sure what the inside global address is at any point in time. Here goes!

This first thing is to become familiar with NAT_Router:

```
NAT_Router#show ip interface brief
Interface               IP-Address      OK? Method Status      Protocol
FastEthernet0           172.16.1.1      YES manual up          up
Serial0                 68.3.160.5      YES DHCP   up          up
```

Now it's time to identify the interfaces to the NAT process:

```
NAT_Router#configure terminal
Enter configuration commands, one per line.  End with CNTL/Z.
NAT_Router(config)#interface fastEthernet 0
NAT_Router(config-if)#ip nat inside
NAT_Router(config-if)#exit
NAT_Router(config)#interface serial 0
NAT_Router(config-if)#ip nat outside
```

Now, just as with the dynamic NAT, you need to create an access list that identifies the addresses to be translated by NAT. Use a named access list this time:

```
NAT_Router(config)#ip access-list ?
  extended     Extended Access List
  log-update   Control access list log updates
  logging      Control access list logging
  standard     Standard Access List

NAT_Router(config)#ip access-list standard ?
  <1-99>       Standard IP access-list number
  <1300-1999>  Standard IP access-list number (expanded range)
  WORD         Access-list name

NAT_Router(config)#ip access-list standard INTERNAL_ADDRESSES
NAT_Router(config-std-nacl)#permit ?
  Hostname or A.B.C.D  Address to match
  any                  Any source host
  host                 A single host address

NAT_Router(config-std-nacl)#permit 172.16.0.0 ?
  A.B.C.D  Wildcard bits
  log      Log matches against this entry
  <cr>

NAT_Router(config-std-nacl)#permit 172.16.0.0 0.0.255.255
```

Perfect! Now on to the final command that will enable NAT overload for the addresses that have been defined. Again, the ip nat syntax from global configuration mode is used to set this up:

```
NAT_Router(config)#ip nat ?
  inside       Inside address translation
```

```
  log          NAT Logging
  outside      Outside address translation
  pool         Define pool of addresses
  service      Special translation for application using non-standard port
  translation  NAT translation entry configuration

NAT_Router(config)#ip nat inside ?
  destination  Destination address translation
  source       Source address translation

NAT_Router(config)#ip nat inside source ?
  list       Specify access list describing local addresses
  route-map  Specify route-map
  static     Specify static local->global mapping
```

This is where the router asks you to specify the internal addresses to be translated. Previously, the static keyword was used to perform 1:1 IP address or port translations; now the list keyword designates a list of internal addresses to be translated. The access list just created specifies which internal addresses will translate.

```
NAT_Router(config)#ip nat inside source list ?
  <1-2699>  Access list number for local addresses
  WORD      Access list name for local addresses

NAT_Router(config)#ip nat inside source list INTERNAL_ADDRESSES ?
  interface  Specify interface for global address
  pool       Name pool of global addresses
```

Now the router needs to know what inside global address the inside local addresses should use. You can designate this either by using a NAT pool (as shown with the dynamic NAT configuration) or by specifying an outgoing interface to use. Because you do not know what inside global address you will have (because of the DHCP configuration), you need to specify the outgoing interface.

```
NAT_Router(config)#ip nat inside source list INTERNAL_ADDRESSES interface ?
  Async             Async interface
  BVI               Bridge-Group Virtual Interface
  CTunnel           CTunnel interface
  Dialer            Dialer interface
  FastEthernet      FastEthernet IEEE 802.3
  Lex               Lex interface
  Loopback          Loopback interface
  Multilink         Multilink-group interface
  Null              Null interface
  Serial            Serial
  Tunnel            Tunnel interface
  Vif               PGM Multicast Host interface
  Virtual-Template  Virtual Template interface
  Virtual-TokenRing Virtual TokenRing
```

```
NAT_Router(config)#ip nat inside source list INTERNAL_ADDRESSES interface
serial 0 ?
  overload  Overload an address translation
  <cr>

NAT_Router(config)#ip nat inside source list INTERNAL_ADDRESSES interface
serial 0 overload
```

There it is—the magic overload keyword. That's all it takes to turn on NAT overload for the interface connected to the Internet. The router now translates thousands of internal hosts through a single IP address. One more thing needs to be done to complete the scenario: Add the static NAT translation for the web server. By adding this configuration, you combine NAT overload with static NAT, which is a very common configuration. Here goes:

```
NAT_Router(config)#ip nat ?
  inside       Inside address translation
  log          NAT Logging
  outside      Outside address translation
  pool         Define pool of addresses
  service      Special translation for application using non-standard port
  translation  NAT translation entry configuration

NAT_Router(config)#ip nat inside ?
  destination  Destination address translation
  source       Source address translation

NAT_Router(config)#ip nat inside source ?
  list       Specify access list describing local addresses
  route-map  Specify route-map
  static     Specify static local->global mapping

NAT_Router(config)#ip nat inside source static ?
  A.B.C.D  Inside local IP address
  esp      IPSec-ESP (Tunnel mode) support
  network  Subnet translation
  tcp      Transmission Control Protocol
  udp      User Datagram Protocol

NAT_Router(config)#ip nat inside source static tcp ?
  A.B.C.D  Inside local IP address

NAT_Router(config)#ip nat inside source static tcp 172.16.1.80 ?
  <1-65535>  Local UDP/TCP port

NAT_Router(config)#ip nat inside source static tcp 172.16.1.80 80 ?
  A.B.C.D    Inside global IP address
  interface  Specify interface for global address
```

```
NAT_Router(config)#ip nat inside source static tcp 172.16.1.80 80
interface ?
  Async               Async interface
  BVI                 Bridge-Group Virtual Interface
  CTunnel             CTunnel interface
  Dialer              Dialer interface
  FastEthernet        FastEthernet IEEE 802.3
  Lex                 Lex interface
  Loopback            Loopback interface
  Multilink           Multilink-group interface
  Null                Null interface
  Serial              Serial
  Tunnel              Tunnel interface
  Vif                 PGM Multicast Host interface
  Virtual-Template    Virtual Template interface
  Virtual-TokenRing   Virtual TokenRing

NAT_Router(config)#ip nat inside source static tcp 172.16.1.80 80
interface serial 0 ?
  <1-65535>  Global UDP/TCP port

NAT_Router(config)#ip nat inside static tcp 172.16.1.80 80
interface serial 0 80
```

Beautiful. This has added the line that will translate incoming requests to the web server *in addition to performing NAT overload for all other internal clients.* If some internal clients are accessing the Internet, you can verify that the translations are working properly:

```
NAT_Router#show ip nat translation
Pro Inside global     Inside local       Outside local        Outside global
tcp 68.3.160.5:39449 172.16.1.15:39449  66.102.7.104:80      66.102.7.104:80
tcp 68.3.160.5:39450 172.16.1.150:39450 66.102.7.147:80      66.102.7.147:80
udp 68.3.160.5:43617 172.16.1.25:43617  207.228.226.5:53     207.228.226.5:53
udp 68.3.160.5:43617 172.16.1.13:43617  64.233.161.9:53      64.233.161.9:53
udp 68.3.160.5:43617 172.16.1.14:43617  192.52.178.30:53     192.52.178.30:53
udp 68.3.160.5:347   172.16.1.13:347    202.71.97.92:123     202.71.97.92:123
tcp 68.3.160.5:39453 172.16.1.76:39453  207.228.243.100:80 207.228.243.100:80
tcp 68.3.160.5:39454 172.16.1.182:39454 207.228.243.100:80 207.228.243.100:80
tcp 68.3.160.5:39446 172.16.1.87:39446  67.138.240.17:110  67.138.240.17:110
tcp 68.3.160.5:39448 172.16.1.140:39448 67.138.240.17:110  67.138.240.17:110
udp 68.3.160.5:43617 172.16.1.140:43617 216.239.36.10:53   216.239.36.10:53
tcp 68.3.160.5:80    172.16.1.80:80      ---                --- !Web Server
udp 68.3.160.5:43617 172.16.1.67:43617  216.239.53.9:53     216.239.53.9:53
udp 68.3.160.5:43617 172.16.1.220:43617 192.5.6.30:53       192.5.6.30:53
tcp 68.3.160.5:37389 172.16.1.82:37389  68.6.19.2:110       68.6.19.2:110
tcp 68.3.160.5:39447 172.16.1.77:39447  68.6.19.2:110       68.6.19.2:110
tcp 68.3.160.5:39451 172.16.1.77:39451  64.233.167.147:80   64.233.167.147:80
tcp 68.3.160.5:39452 172.16.1.15:39452  64.233.167.147:80   64.233.167.147:80
udp 68.3.160.5:40477 172.16.1.25:40477  216.115.25.17:5061 216.115.25.17:5061
```

```
udp 68.3.160.5:40478 172.16.1.142:40478 216.115.25.17:5061 216.115.25.17:5061
udp 68.3.160.5:43617 172.16.1.150:43617 216.239.32.10:53   216.239.32.10:53
```

Holy cow! They sure are working, and it looks like the internal clients have taken advantage of that fact. If you look down the list of inside local addresses, you can see what inside hosts are accessing the Internet (along with what source port they are using to establish the request). Also, take a look at the inside global address; notice anything odd? It's the same address the whole way down, just using different port numbers. This is the perfect picture of NAT overload. Finally, take a look at the translation with the "Web Server" comment next to it. This is the static NAT entry that was added for the internal web server. There are no outside local/global addresses for this because it is not in use at this time.

TIP

NAT Overload also works with a pool of addresses. In our example, we configured everything to overload the Serial 0 interface. We could also create a pool of IP addresses (see Scenario 3 where we configure dynamic NAT) and use NAT overload to translate many addresses to the pool. The advantage of doing this is that once a single IP address in the pool is "maxed out" (all the port numbers have been used up), the router can begin using a second IP address from the pool. If we created a pool of addresses for our translation, we could use the following command to enable NAT Overload:

```
NAT_Router(config)#ip nat inside source list INTERNAL_ADDRESSES pool
NAT_POOL overload
```

You may encounter this in the ICND2 or CCNA certification exams.

Verifying NAT Operation

Objectives:

▶ Configure NAT for given network requirements

▶ Troubleshoot NAT issues

Although a `show running-config` command is always useful to show what commands you have entered into your router to get NAT running, you can use a few commands to ensure that NAT is operational. The primary command you have seen many times at this point: `show ip nat translations`. This command gives you a snapshot view of what current NAT translations are active on your router. Its sidekick command, `show ip nat statistics`, gives you a view of how many translations are currently active, how many total translations have occurred, and how much of your NAT pool is being used (if performing dynamic NAT). Sample output from this command follows:

```
NAT_Router#show ip nat statistics
Total active translations: 12 (0 static, 12 dynamic; 11 extended)
Outside interfaces:
  Serial0
Inside interfaces:
  FastEthernet0
Hits: 38415022  Misses: 567286
Expired translations: 568274
Dynamic mappings:
-- Inside Source
[Id: 1] access-list NAT_TRANSLATION interface Ethernet0 refcount 4
```

Remember that the number of "hits" and "misses" does not reflect how many NAT translations have been successful or unsuccessful. Rather, it reflects how many times a packet matches an existing translation in the table (a hit) and how many times a new translation needed to be created (a miss).

Troubleshooting NAT Operation

Objective:

▶ Troubleshoot NAT issues

NAT troubleshooting usually focuses on misconfiguration of some sort. It never fails that I'll go through the complexity of creating access lists and statically mapping private and public addresses and port numbers only to forget to label the inside and outside interfaces using the `ip nat inside` and `outside` commands. So the first step of troubleshooting should always be to verify your configuration! Remember, if you are using a router-on-a-stick configuration to route between VLANs, the `ip nat inside` command needs to be on each subinterface for NAT to translate correctly and not only on the physical interface. That rule goes for any configuration that uses subinterfaces, including Frame Relay, which we'll talk about in Chapter 23, "Using Frame Relay Connections."

If you have checked your configuration completely and found no missing links, use the verification commands we just discussed to find out if NAT translations are occurring on the router. If you see plenty of translations displayed using the `show ip nat translations` command, it may just be that the client you are using has a bad configuration or an unreachable DNS server. That brings up another point: always attempt to access a server by IP address rather than hostname. You don't want to get knee-deep in NAT troubleshooting only to find out it was a DNS issue. My favorite test is to ping the IP address 4.2.2.2 (a well-known public DNS server) from the internal client. If you attempt the ping and it is successful, try initiating a TCP connection. This brings up a big tip:

> **TIP**
>
> An extremely handy way to test TCP connections is to use a modified syntax of the `telnet` command. For example, if I wanted to test a connection to www.google.com without opening a web browser, I could enter `telnet www.google.com 80`, which initiates a TCP connection attempt on port 80. If you are successful, your command prompt will most likely blank out or return some scrambled information. This isn't the information you are looking for; you want to know if the connection was successful. The test I use most often is to Telnet to 4.2.2.2 (the now-famous DNS server address using port 53, the TCP DNS port used for server record replication) using the syntax `telnet 4.2.2.2 53`. This allows me to test connectivity without needing to resolve a DNS hostname.

If you find that your connection attempts are failing from the internal client, move your tests to the router. Attempt the same `ping` commands and port-based `telnet` commands from the router. This will test your connectivity without the NAT process in the way. If the connection attempts fail, you most likely have an ISP connection or routing issue. Check your default route and attempt to ping the next-hop IP address attached to the default route. Use the troubleshooting techniques discussed in Chapters 10 through 12 to get your router communicating on the Internet.

If you find that the connection attempts are successful from the router but are still unsuccessful from the client, it may be time to use the `debug ip nat` command to find the issue. I hesitate to recommend this command, because it has the potential to overload a production router to the point of crashing. This command dumps translations to the screen anytime a NAT translation occurs. This following is a sample of what this looks like. Keep in mind that this output resulted from my enabling the debug for about one second on a network running in my home—and I'm showing you only about a quarter of the output!

```
NAT_ROUTER#debug ip nat
*Mar  1 00:24:57.503: NAT*: s=172.30.2.27->68.110.171.98, d=69.59.234.120 [27622]
*Mar  1 00:24:57.575: NAT*: s=69.59.234.120, d=68.110.171.98->172.30.2.27 [56108]
*Mar  1 00:25:15.583: NAT*: s=172.30.2.27->68.110.171.98, d=69.59.234.120 [27624]
*Mar  1 00:25:15.651: NAT*: s=69.59.234.120, d=68.110.171.98->172.30.2.27 [10038]
*Mar  1 00:25:33.659: NAT*: s=172.30.2.27->68.110.171.98, d=69.59.234.120 [27626]
*Mar  1 00:25:33.731: NAT*: s=69.59.234.120, d=68.110.171.98->172.30.2.27 [29444]
*Mar  1 00:25:46.659: NAT*: s=172.30.2.27->68.110.171.98, d=69.59.234.120 [27628]
*Mar  1 00:25:46.731: NAT*: s=69.59.234.120, d=68.110.171.98->172.30.2.27 [43578]
*Mar  1 00:25:46.743: NAT*: s=172.30.2.27->68.110.171.98, d=69.59.234.120 [27629]
*Mar  1 00:25:46.751: NAT*: s=172.30.2.27->68.110.171.98, d=69.59.234.120 [27630]
*Mar  1 00:25:46.843: NAT*: s=69.59.234.120, d=68.110.171.98->172.30.2.27 [43694]
*Mar  1 00:25:49.407: NAT*: s=69.59.234.120, d=68.110.171.98->172.30.2.27 [46478]
*Mar  1 00:25:51.739: NAT*: s=172.30.2.27->68.110.171.98, d=69.59.234.120 [27708]
*Mar  1 00:25:51.807: NAT*: s=69.59.234.120, d=68.110.171.98->172.30.2.27 [49083]
*Mar  1 00:26:04.227: NAT*: s=172.30.2.27->68.110.171.98, d=69.59.234.120 [28129]
*Mar  1 00:26:04.295: NAT*: s=69.59.234.120, d=68.110.171.98->172.30.2.27 [62725]
*Mar  1 00:26:04.299: NAT*: s=69.59.234.120, d=68.110.171.98->172.30.2.27 [62727]
*Mar  1 00:26:04.311: NAT*: s=172.30.2.27->68.110.171.98, d=69.59.234.120 [28130]
```

```
*Mar  1 00:26:09.815: NAT*: s=172.30.2.27->68.110.171.98, d=69.59.234.120 [28131]
*Mar  1 00:26:09.887: NAT*: s=69.59.234.120, d=68.110.171.98->172.30.2.27 [3141]
*Mar  1 00:26:27.895: NAT*: s=172.30.2.27->68.110.171.98, d=69.59.234.120 [28133]
*Mar  1 00:26:27.967: NAT*: s=69.59.234.120, d=68.110.171.98->172.30.2.27 [22794]
```

Each line represents a packet passing through the NAT process. You can quickly see why this can overwhelm a router in an active business environment.

Finally, you may encounter a situation in which a bad NAT translation is kept in the table. This happens frequently when you change your internal IP address scheme in some way, especially when you change individual host addresses that were just accessing the Internet. Although waiting for some time for the translations to time out solves the problem, impatient administrators may want to use the `clear ip nat translation *` command to wipe out any dynamically created NAT entries. This is not likely to disrupt service to your internal network, because active NAT translations immediately re-create themselves as the internal host sends data to or receives data from the Internet.

Chapter Summary

Network Address Translation (NAT) has become so successful for prolonging the life of IPv4 that it has now become a prohibitor of a progressive move to TCP/IP version 6. Because of its widespread use, NAT features have grown over the years to provide a solution to almost any network situation.

A company planning to use NAT will deploy one of the three private address ranges on its internal network, which are prevented from routing to the Internet. The company will then use one of the three forms of NAT—static NAT, dynamic NAT, or NAT overload—to translate these private ranges onto the Internet. Most networks use a combination of NAT overload and static NAT to accomplish most major network objectives.

Most of the challenge with NAT is learning the terminology that describes the different addresses on a network. Inside local addresses are internal to a network. The inside global address represents the public Internet address assigned to your router. Outside global addresses represent all the hosts outside your network attached to the Internet with Internet IP addresses. Finally, outside local addresses represent hosts outside your network as they are seen by the internal NAT hosts.

Key Terms

- ▶ Network Address Translation (NAT)
- ▶ Port Address Translation (PAT)
- ▶ Static NAT
- ▶ Dynamic NAT
- ▶ NAT overload
- ▶ Private IP addresses
- ▶ Public IP addresses
- ▶ Inside local address
- ▶ Inside global address
- ▶ Outside local address
- ▶ Outside global address
- ▶ Port redirection
- ▶ NAT pool

Apply Your Knowledge

Exercise

21.1 Configuring NAT for a Home Network Environment

You want to deploy NAT on a home network. This network has five internal hosts and receives a public Internet IP address through DHCP on a DSL connection. The Cisco 1700 router should use NAT overload to enable all internal clients to access the Internet. In addition, you would like to use Windows Remote Desktop Client (TCP port 3389) to access your home PC (192.168.1.100) from anywhere in the world. Figure 21.5 shows this home network with relevant addressing details.

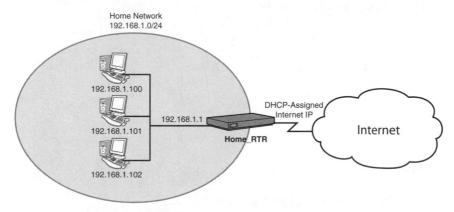

FIGURE 21.5 Home network diagram.

Estimated Time: 5 to 10 minutes

1. This is something that any CCNA student can do at home, provided you have a high-speed Internet connection. The first thing you need to do is verify your router configuration and identify your inside and outside interfaces:

```
Home_Router#show ip int brief
Interface              IP-Address       OK? Method Status      Protocol
FastEthernet0          192.168.1.1      YES manual up          up
Ethernet0              68.209.55.8      YES DHCP   up          up
Home_Router#configure terminal
Enter configuration commands, one per line.  End with CNTL/Z.
Home_Router(config)#int fastethernet0
Home_Router(config-if)#ip nat inside
Home_Router(config-if)#exit
Home_Router(config)#int ethernet0
Home_Router(config-if)#ip nat outside
```

2. Now you need to configure an access list that matches the internal IP addresses to be translated:

```
Home_Router(config)#ip access-list ?
  extended    Extended Access List
  log-update  Control access list log updates
  logging     Control access list logging
  standard    Standard Access List

Home_Router(config)#ip access-list standard ?
  <1-99>      Standard IP access-list number
  <1300-1999> Standard IP access-list number (expanded range)
  WORD        Access-list name

Home_Router(config)#ip access-list standard INSIDE_IP
Home_Router(config-std-nacl)#permit ?
  Hostname or A.B.C.D  Address to match
  any                  Any source host
  host                 A single host address

Home_Router(config-std-nacl)#permit 192.168.1.0 ?
  A.B.C.D  Wildcard bits
  log      Log matches against this entry
  <cr>

Home_Router(config-std-nacl)#permit 192.168.1.0 0.0.0.255
Home_Router(config-std-nacl)#exit
Home_Router(config)#
```

3. Now that the access list is defined, you can put NAT overload into action:

```
Home_Router(config)#ip nat ?
  inside       Inside address translation
  log          NAT Logging
  outside      Outside address translation
  pool         Define pool of addresses
  service      Special translation for application using non-standard port
  translation  NAT translation entry configuration

Home_Router(config)#ip nat inside ?
  destination  Destination address translation
  source       Source address translation

Home_Router(config)#ip nat inside source ?
  list       Specify access list describing local addresses
  route-map  Specify route-map
  static     Specify static local->global mapping

Home_Router(config)#ip nat inside source list ?
  <1-2699>  Access list number for local addresses
  WORD      Access list name for local addresses
```

```
Home_Router(config)#ip nat inside source list INSIDE_IP ?
  interface  Specify interface for global address
  pool       Name pool of global addresses

Home_Router(config)#ip nat inside source list INSIDE_IP interface
ethernet 0 ?
  overload  Overload an address translation
  <cr>

Home_Router(config)#ip nat inside source list INSIDE_IP interface
ethernet 0 overload
Home_Router(config)#
```

4. The NAT overload configuration is in place; clients now can access the Internet with the single DHCP-assigned address from the DSL provider. Now you need to configure your static NAT entry to allow remote desktop access to your internal PC:

```
Home_Router(config)#ip nat ?
  inside       Inside address translation
  log          NAT Logging
  outside      Outside address translation
  pool         Define pool of addresses
  service      Special translation for application using non-standard port
  translation  NAT translation entry configuration

Home_Router(config)#ip nat inside source ?
  list       Specify access list describing local addresses
  route-map  Specify route-map
  static     Specify static local->global mapping

Home_Router(config)#ip nat inside source static ?
  A.B.C.D  Inside local IP address
  esp      IPSec-ESP (Tunnel mode) support
  network  Subnet translation
  tcp      Transmission Control Protocol
  udp      User Datagram Protocol

Home_Router(config)#ip nat inside source static tcp ?
  A.B.C.D  Inside local IP address

Home_Router(config)#ip nat inside source static tcp 192.168.1.100 ?
  <1-65535>  Local UDP/TCP port

Home_Router(config)#ip nat inside source static tcp 192.168.1.100 3389 ?
  A.B.C.D    Inside global IP address
  interface  Specify interface for global address
```

```
Home_Router(config)#$ inside source static tcp 192.168.1.100 3389
interface ethernet 0 ?
  <1-65535>  Global UDP/TCP port

Home_Router(config)#$ inside source static tcp 192.168.1.100 3389
interface ethernet 0 3389
```

5. The configuration is now complete.

Exam Questions

1. You are working through NAT issues for your organization, and you notice that some NAT translations are "stuck" in the table. What command allows you to clear existing mappings from the
   table?

   ○ **A.** `delete ip nat translation *`

   ○ **B.** `clear ip nat translation *`

   ○ **C.** `erase ip nat translation *`

   ○ **D.** `no ip nat translation *`

2. Which of the following forms of NAT incorporates the source IP address (inside local) along with
   the source port number to make every translation unique?

   ○ **A.** Static NAT

   ○ **B.** Dynamic NAT

   ○ **C.** NAT overload

   ○ **D.** NAT port mapping

3. Which of the following commands enables an FTP server with the inside local address 10.5.9.100
   to be accessed from a Serial0 interface (that is directly connected to the Internet)?

   ○ **A.** `ip nat inside source static tcp interface serial 0 21`
         `10.5.9.100 21`

   ○ **B.** `ip nat inside source static tcp 10.5.9.100 21 interface`
         `serial 0 21`

   ○ **C.** `ip nat inside destination static tcp interface serial 0 21`
         `10.5.9.100 21`

   ○ **D.** `ip nat inside destination static tcp 10.5.9.100 21 interface`
         `serial 0 21`

4. You are configuring NAT on your company router to provide Internet access to the internal subnets. The router has a single interface connecting to the Internet and two interfaces connecting to
different subnets of your corporate network. What is the proper configuration of the `ip nat`
`inside` and `ip nat outside` commands?

- ○ **A.** The ISP interface should be configured with `ip nat inside`, and only a single
  interface connecting to the corporate network should have the `ip nat outside`
  designation.

- ○ **B.** All three interfaces should be configured with the `ip nat inside` commands,
  because they are all under your authority.

- ○ **C.** Only one of the interfaces connecting to the corporate network can be configured with
  the `ip nat inside` command, and the ISP interface should be configured with `ip`
  `nat outside`.

- ○ **D.** The two interfaces connecting to the corporate network should be configured with the
  `ip nat inside` command, and the ISP interface should be configured with `ip`
  `nat outside`.

5. While viewing the output of the `show ip nat statistics` command, you notice that a large
number of packets are labeled as a "miss." What causes this issue?

- ○ **A.** You have not labeled an accurate outside interface for NAT.

- ○ **B.** The command used for NAT overload is missing the `overload` keyword at the end of
  the syntax.

- ○ **C.** Your network has many new sessions that do not have an existing NAT translation.

- ○ **D.** The interface configured with the `ip nat outside` command is probably down.

6. Which of the following represent a private IP address? (Choose two)

- ○ **A.** 192.168.5.205

- ○ **B.** 172.32.65.31

- ○ **C.** 10.168.5.205

- ○ **D.** 224.16.23.1

7. The configuration of dynamic NAT requires the use of an _____, which is a list of the inside
global addresses that the Cisco router uses when translating the inside local addresses.

- ○ **A.** Inside interface

- ○ **B.** Access list

- ○ **C.** Outside interface

- ○ **D.** IP NAT pool

8. What command is necessary to designate the inside interface in a NAT configuration?

- ○ **A.** `nat interface inside`
- ○ **B.** `nat inside interface`
- ○ **C.** `ip nat inside`
- ○ **D.** `ip inside interface`

9. You would like to see the active NAT translations that are happening on your router. Your primary interest is in the inside local IPs that are being translated. What command shows you this information?

- ○ **A.** `show ip nat statistics`
- ○ **B.** `show ip nat translations`
- ○ **C.** `show ip interface`
- ○ **D.** `show running-config`

10. You verify that NAT is functioning by using the `show ip nat translations` command. You notice the following output displayed to the terminal window:

```
NAT_Router#show ip nat translations
Pro Inside global     Inside local      Outside local      Outside global
--- 5.1.1.10          192.168.1.50      ---                ---
```

What does this entry represent?

- ○ **A.** A static NAT translation between 5.1.1.10 and 192.168.1.50
- ○ **B.** A dynamic NAT translation between 5.1.1.10 and 192.168.1.50
- ○ **C.** A malfunctioning NAT translation. Each translation should have all four columns filled in with IP address information.
- ○ **D.** A static NAT translation between 5.1.1.10 and 192.168.1.50 that is currently not in use

Answers to Exam Questions

1. B. By issuing the `clear ip nat translation *` command, you erase the router's entire NAT translation table. Although this sounds devastating, it typically does not cause any connection issues, because the table is dynamically rebuilt. The other answers are invalid syntax.

2. C. NAT overload uses the source port number to send many unique requests out a single public IP address. Answer A is incorrect because static NAT performs 1:1 translations from public to private IP addresses. Answer B is incorrect because dynamic NAT performs many 1:1 translations without requiring manual entries. Answer D is incorrect because NAT port mapping is not a valid form of NAT.

3. **B.** This syntax correctly lists the source address (inside local) and port number first and the inside global address and port second. The `ip nat inside destination` syntax enables you to specify only a list of inside global addresses and does not work for this situation. Answers A, C, and D are invalid syntax.

4. **D.** The `ip nat inside` and `ip nat outside` commands specify to the router the interfaces connecting to the corporate network and to the ISP, respectively. You can label as many interfaces as you want with either the `ip nat inside` or `outside` syntax.

5. **C.** When you view the output of the `show ip nat statistics` command, the number of hits and misses represents how many packets had an existing NAT translation already in the table (a hit) or required a new NAT translation to be created (a miss). It is not uncommon to have many misses in a busy network.

6. **A, C.** The private address ranges are 10.x.x.x, 172.16.x.x to 172.31.x.x, and 192.168.x.x. Answers B and D fall outside these ranges.

7. **D.** Dynamic NAT requires the use of an IP NAT pool that lists the inside global addresses (typically Internet-valid) that will be used for the translation. Answer B is incorrect because access lists are used to define the inside local addresses that will be translated. Answers A and C are incorrect because the inside and outside interfaces must be defined but do not define what addresses are to be translated.

8. **C.** The `ip nat inside` command designates the inside interface to the NAT router. The other commands are considered invalid syntax.

9. **B.** The `show ip nat translations` command shows you all active translations currently in place on your router. It includes the inside local and global and the outside local and global addresses for each translation. Answer A is incorrect because the `show ip nat statistics` command tells you only how many translations are currently happening. Answer C is incorrect because the `show ip interface` command does not give you any NAT statistics. Answer D is incorrect because the `show running-config` command tells you only the NAT configurations you have set up.

10. **D.** This is a trick question that claims the "choose the *best* answer" mantra. Answer A is correct; it does represent a static NAT mapping. But answer D is *more* correct because it is a static NAT mapping not in use. If the static NAT mapping were in use, the outside local and global columns would have the IP address information of the outside host currently using the translation.

Suggested Readings and Resources

1. Cisco TAC NAT Configuration Syntax, http://www.cisco.com/univercd/cc/td/doc/product/software/ios122/122cgcr/fipr_c/ipcprt1/1cfipadr.htm#wp1042290

2. Chris Ward and Jeremy Cioara. *Exam Cram 2 CCNA Practice Questions*. Que Publishing, 2004.

3. How Network Address Translation Works, http://computer.howstuffworks.com/nat1.htm

CHAPTER TWENTY-TWO

Wide Area Network Connections

Objectives

This chapter covers the following Cisco-specific objectives for the "Implement and verify WAN links" section of the 640-802 CCNA exam:

▶ **Describe different methods for connecting to a WAN**

▶ **Configure and verify a basic WAN serial connection**

▶ **Configure and verify a PPP connection between Cisco routers**

▶ **Troubleshoot WAN implementation issues**

Outline

Study Strategies

▶ Read the information presented in the chapter, paying special attention to tables, Notes, and Exam Alerts.

▶ Although Wide Area Network configuration is important, many of the advanced configuration options discussed are reserved for the CCNP BCRAN exam. At the CCNA level, be sure to focus on understanding the concepts thoroughly.

▶ Because it is in widespread use, focus your energy on learning the ideas behind the PPP protocol. Be sure to pay special attention to the authentication concepts.

Introduction

In nearly all traditional Cisco texts, Wide Area Networks (WANs) are typically moved to the end of the book. This is amusing to me because WAN connectivity is usually listed in the top three functions of a router. WAN connections do just that: connect networks that have a wide area separating them. This type of connection requires you to work with one or more service providers that supply the logical connections between your locations.

The good news about WAN connections is this: These technologies only encompass the Physical and Data Link layers of the OSI Model. Just like the concepts of ethernet and token ring, WAN links are just another method of transporting data between devices. So with only two layers worth of technology, WAN links should be fairly simple to learn, right? Well, that's the bad news: Because of the ever-increasing demands of the IT machine, WAN links have become increasingly complex to the point where they can be a specialization in themselves. Thankfully, the CCNA exam focuses primarily on two specific types of WAN connections:

▶ Leased Lines

▶ Frame Relay

> **EXAM ALERT**
>
> To prepare for the CCNA exam, you need to be very familiar with these WAN connections. Those preparing for ICND1 exam should focus their studies primarily on Leased Line concepts and configurations.

Although there are many more WAN connection types, these are currently the most popular. By studying these WAN connections you will learn the foundation concepts behind WAN connections in general, making it easier to learn any new WAN technologies as they emerge.

WAN Connection Types

Objective:

▶ Describe different methods for connecting to a WAN

The following three categories of WAN connections comprise most of the connections used by businesses around the world. As the name implies, each of the WAN connection categories contains multiple connection types. If you ever called a service provider and asked for a packet-switched connection, the next question would inevitably be, "What type?"

Leased Lines

This connection category is what most people are familiar with when they hear the term, "WAN connection." A leased line connection provides a dedicated, point-to-point link between two locations. The beauty of this connection type is that you have a virtual private road between your sites. You have complete control over the traffic on that road; nobody else can share the road with you. If you have a T1-speed connection (1.544Mbps) between your locations, that bandwidth is always dedicated to you, regardless of whether you use it or not. Therefore, leased lines are typically the most expensive connection types.

In the Field

The two factors that directly affect the cost of a leased line are

▶ How far apart, geographically, the sites are located

▶ The amount of bandwidth required

Leased lines are the most appropriate when you need a fixed amount of bandwidth and complete control over all your traffic. Companies that are implementing Voice over IP (VoIP), which runs their telephone system over the data network, will usually vie for leased line connections. Because the telecommunications carrier (service provider) is dedicating the leased line bandwidth to you, they can provide a guaranteed level of service. This not only includes the uptime (reliability) of the line, but also delay requirements. The delay of the line is how long it takes a packet to get from the entry point to the end of the connection. Long delays can cause the quality of a VoIP call to degrade to the point of sounding like a bad cellular phone call. Because the service provider typically has end-to-end control over a leased line connection, they can guarantee a specific level of delay.

Circuit-Switched Networks

Anytime you hear the hum of a dial tone followed by the rhythmic beeping of digits, you are more than likely connected to a circuit-switched network. This type of connection establishes a dedicated channel (or circuit) for the duration of the transmission, and then tears down the channel when the transmission is complete. This is known as a *dial-on-demand connection*. The largest circuit-switched network in the world is the telephone system, which links together many different network segments to create an end-to-end circuit for each telephone call.

Circuit-switched networks can be called a "connection-oriented" network type. They are most useful when you have small amounts of data to reliably send at a time. Some circuit-switched networks charge on a per-use or per-minute basis (primarily ISDN), so the amount you pay for the connection is directly related to how much you use it. This type of connection would be ideal for a small office that uses local area network (LAN) connectivity during the day and then replicates all the updated data back to the main site in the evening. For example, you might have a sales office that creates a log of transactions that it sends back to the corporate headquarters at night.

Packet-Switched Networks

Packet-switched networks enable the service provider to create a large pool of bandwidth for their clients, rather than dedicate specific amounts of bandwidth to each client (as in leased lines). The client can then dictate what circuits they would like established through the service provider network between their sites (these are called *permanent virtual circuits*), providing an end-to-end connection. By using packet-switched networks to provide WAN connectivity, you can gain lower-cost WAN connections that can potentially provide more bandwidth to your locations.

When you sign up for a packet-switched network, the service provider gives you a guaranteed level of bandwidth. The higher your service guarantee, the more you pay for the connection on a monthly basis. The great aspect of a packet switched network is that you usually get more than you are guaranteed; depending on the type of contract you negotiate with the service provider, you could get much more bandwidth than you are guaranteed. However, you must realize that this bandwidth is just that: non-guaranteed. If you send extra traffic during a busy time of day, the service provider can drop the traffic and be well within the service contract. This also applies for delay guarantees. Because traffic sent through a packet-switched network may take different paths (depending on the service provider's infrastructure) to reach the destination, most service providers offer a very loose delay guarantee (if they decide to offer one at all).

Broadband

Broadband technology, in its base definition, is a system that enables you to send multiple signals over a wire at one time. The alternative technology, baseband, enables you to send only a single signal over the wire at a time. Broadband connections primarily encompass small office/home office (SOHO) WAN links that use cable modem or DSL technology to connect to the Internet. A cable service provider sends multiple signals over a cable coaxial line, enabling a home user to run many services, such as cable television, high-speed Internet, and telephone service, over a single line. Telephone providers are offering the same services through the copper phone line connections.

Medium and large businesses are just now beginning to consider cable and DSL connections as backup Internet connections for their main offices. Broadband technology is one of the newest WAN connection offerings to market, and has yet to prove its reliability on a long-term basis.

Virtual Private Networks (VPNs)

VPNs are not a specific type of WAN connection, but are often used to accomplish the same purpose as a WAN connection. Connections to the Internet have become widely available at an extremely low cost (when compared against the other types of WAN connectivity). Rather than purchasing dedicated circuits between locations, you can just purchase a standard Internet connection at each site. The quality of your Internet connection determines the quality of your WAN connectivity. After all sites have a connection to the Internet, you can then create tunnels through the Internet to each location, enabling the sites to connect through a full-mesh relationship (every site is directly connected, through the Internet, to every other site). These tunnels isolate the interoffice connectivity from the rest of the Internet traffic and secure the traffic through heavy encryption algorithms.

The VPN tunnels are created with the application of a heavy amount of encryption to the traffic sent between the locations. Because sending your company's private data across a public network, such as the Internet, could be perilous, you should scramble (encrypt) your data before sending it. Because the process of encrypting and de-encrypting data is extremely hard on a router processor, you may choose to offload this work to a router VPN card (a hardware add-on), a PIX firewall (Cisco's firewall platform), or a VPN concentrator (a specific device manages and maintains many VPN connections). Within this concept lie the advantages and disadvantages of using VPNs for your WAN connections. The major advantage is the cost: You can establish full connectivity between all your locations for a small fraction of what it would cost to purchase dedicated WAN links. You can also allow home users to connect into the office through a VPN connection to allow for telecommuting employees. The disadvantage is the delay incurred in applying the VPN encryption algorithms and the unreliable nature of the Internet. Although the Internet is the most redundant network in the world, because of the massive amount of traffic that crosses the Internet daily, the delay can be inconsistent.

Metropolitan Ethernet (Metro Ethernet)

Metro ethernet technology began to emerge early in the new millennium as a viable alternative to traditional WAN connections when connecting offices within a metropolitan area (primarily major cities). At the end of the century, .com-based businesses were booming. Many of these companies began laying complex fiber optic–based networks throughout many of the major metropolitan areas of the nation. When the world economy plummeted at the turn of the century, many of these .com companies went out of business, leaving huge amounts of unmanaged fiber cable under the city streets. This fiber was quickly acquired by local service providers and is slowly being leased to their customers.

Using this fiber to connect offices in the same general region allows for WAN links at speeds of 1000Mbps or greater, at a fraction of the cost of a standard T1 line. The WAN link can even terminate onto a standard Category 5E/6 UTP copper cable and plug directly into a switch using a fiber to copper converter at the customer premise. This enables the WAN connections to be managed completely through VLANs with no dedicated router hardware in place. The connections, which are already fast enough, become even faster.

Metro ethernet is beginning to stretch even between cities, as service providers are planting fiber optic cable runs between major metropolitan areas. It shouldn't be too long before intra-nation WAN links are rated in terms of Gbps as a standard. Metro ethernet is becoming quite popular in government organizations that have many locations in the same general geographic region.

> **EXAM ALERT**
>
> For the ICND1 exam, you should be familiar with the following network types:
> ▶ Leased Lines
>
> For the ICND2 and CCNA exams, you should be familiar with the following network types:
> ▶ Leased Lines
> ▶ Packet Switched

The WAN Physical Layer

The physical connections for WANs are very diverse, primarily because of the diverse form factors that were created by CSU/DSU manufacturers. The Channel Service Unit/Data Service Unit (CSU/DSU) device is the box that connects and converts your WAN cabling to the service provider's WAN cabling. Although CSU/DSUs often have many lights, buttons, and LCD displays, they are typically nothing more than a glorified terminal adapter, converting between the service provider's cable and your local router connection. Figure 22.1 shows a typical physical layout for a WAN connection.

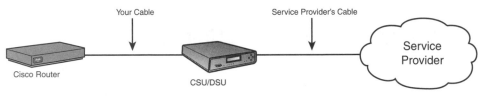

FIGURE 22.1 WAN physical connection points.

If a CSU/DSU is involved, you will be responsible for purchasing the cable that connects your router to the CSU/DSU unit.

Cisco routers primarily use serial interfaces when connecting to a WAN. The Cisco interfaces come in two types: DB-60 serial interfaces and Smart Serial interfaces. Typically, older routers use the DB-60 style interfaces, whereas newer routers use the Smart Serial interfaces. The DB-60 interface received its name because of the 60 pins in the interface. Smart Serial interfaces are much more space efficient, and can squeeze two interfaces into the same WAN Interface Card (WIC) that the DB-60 interface used.

These WIC interfaces can be installed into any of Cisco's mainline routers (1700 series, 2600/2800 series, 3600/3800 series).

After you have installed the interface, you must then purchase the cable that connects your router to the CSU/DSU. This cable converts from one of Cisco's two proprietary interface types (DB-60 or Smart Serial) to a standards-based CSU/DSU connector. Five primary standard connectors have been created for the CSU/DSU units: V.35, X.21, EIA/TIA-232, EIA/TIA-449, and EIA/TIA-530. The most common connector in North America is V.35.

Notice how these cables convert from the Cisco proprietary Smart Serial or V.35 connector to the industry standard V.35 connector, which would connect to the CSU/DSU device.

T1 interfaces use an RJ-48 connector. These interface types usually come with a built-in CSU/DSU, which eliminates the need to purchase an outside box and thereby eliminates another point of potential failure in your network. Upon initial inspection, the RJ-48 connector looks exactly like the RJ-45 connector used for ethernet technology, but don't be fooled! The RJ-48 connector is very different. First off, it is fastened to Shielded Twisted Pair cabling (STP) instead of the standard Unshielded Twisted Pair (UTP) of ethernet. This reduces line noise on these connections. This is important because WAN connectivity is much more susceptible to interference than LAN cabling. In addition, the voltage sent across these wires, the pin-out arrangement, and the line capacitance is different on the RJ-48 connection than RJ-45.

WAN Data Link Encapsulations

After you have the Physical layer plugged in, you must move up to the Data Link WAN encapsulation. Just as with the Physical layer, a variety of standards are available for the data link connections. However, the choice of the Data Link protocol is usually much simpler. As long as your WAN connection supports the Data Link encapsulation you use and you are using the same type of encapsulation on both ends of the connection, the WAN link will work. Sometimes, the type of WAN connection you are using forces you to choose one, specific Data Link encapsulation. For example, if you sign up with a service provider for a Frame Relay connection, you must use Frame Relay Data Link encapsulation. Likewise, if you sign up for an ATM connection, you must use ATM encapsulation. Other times, there may be some flexibility on the choice of protocol you can use. For example, if you sign up for a point-to-point T1 connection, you can use Cisco HDLC, SLIP, or PPP for your data link encapsulation. Here is a brief description of each of the encapsulation types.

Serial Line Internet Protocol (SLIP)

SLIP is a standards-based protocol for point-to-point serial connections that use only TCP/IP. This was primarily used for dial-up connections to the Internet back in the earlier days of the Internet. It has been widely replaced by PPP.

Point-to-Point Protocol (PPP)

This protocol has largely replaced SLIP connections for point-to-point WAN connections and dial-up networking. PPP was released as an improvement to SLIP and added support for non-TCP/IP protocols and encrypted authentication (among many other features). PPP is the most popular protocol for connecting point-to-point WAN connections.

Cisco High-Level Data Link Control (HDLC)

HDLC was originally designed as an open standard protocol, meaning all routers could support it. However, the open standard version of HDLC was pretty horrible. It did not support multiple network-layer protocols, which meant that you could support only one protocol (such as TCP/IP, IPX/SPX, or AppleTalk) over your WAN connection. In view of this shortcoming, Cisco modified the standard HDLC to support this missing feature. However, anytime a standard is modified, the protocol becomes proprietary. In this case, you can use HDLC only on Cisco routers to connect to other Cisco routers. HDLC is the default encapsulation on all serial interfaces on Cisco routers. Although HDLC does not have as many features as PPP, it does offer very low overhead, which makes your WAN connections very efficient.

X.25 Link Access Procedure, Balanced (LAPB)

This encapsulation is used on X.25-based networks, which is the predecessor to Frame Relay. Although X.25 is used rarely in well-developed countries, it has widespread use in countries not as technologically advanced.

Frame Relay

This encapsulation relates directly to the Frame Relay WAN connection, which is the faster successor to X.25. Frame Relay increased its speed capabilities by removing much of the error correction that is no longer needed on the more reliable circuits of today. Frame Relay has widespread use in nearly all well-developed areas.

Asynchronous Transfer Mode (ATM)

This technology is very similar to frame relay, but chops packets into very small pieces (53 bytes each) called *cells*. Because all the frames are exactly the same size, routers are able to process them much quicker. ATM also has the capability to run at very fast speeds because it adapts to run over fiber optic cabling.

PPP over Ethernet (PPPoE) and PPP over ATM (PPPoA)

These technologies have been implemented to allow service providers to harness the features of PPP on an ethernet or ATM connection. This technology is primarily used in DSL high-speed Internet deployments.

> **EXAM ALERT**
>
> The ICND1 exam requires you to be familiar with the configuration of HDLC and PPP. The CCNA exam requires you to be familiar with the configuration of HDLC, PPP, and Frame Relay encapsulation types.

Cisco HDLC

As mentioned previously, HDLC in its truest form is an industry standard created by the International Organization for Standardization (ISO). These are the same folks who created the OSI Model (bless their hearts). Because the ISO version of HDLC lacked the support for multiple protocol use, Cisco modified it and caused HDLC on Cisco routers to become a proprietary protocol.

The beauty of HDLC is that it is very simple and works out of the box. Typically, if you are deploying a WAN connection with a Cisco router on each side of the link, it eliminates plenty of troubleshooting involved in trying to enable the connection with HDLC, even if you plan on using PPP in the long run. Because HDLC is so simple, there are no options to negotiate and you can rule it out of any troubleshooting you may encounter. If the link is not coming up, it is usually something on the service provider side of the business.

Because HDLC is enabled by default, you don't need to perform any additional configuration for the data link configuration of your serial interfaces. However, if the data link encapsulation was changed to something other than HDLC, you can re-enable HDLC by moving into interface configuration mode for the serial interface you want to use and type the command `encapsulation hdlc`.

PPP

Objectives:

▶ Configure and verify a PPP connection between Cisco routers

▶ Configure and verify a basic WAN serial connection

The PPP protocol has become the industry standard for connecting multi-vendor environments over WANs. Whenever people think about using an "industry standard" for anything, they usually think of the bland, saltine-cracker type of protocol. Surprisingly, PPP defies the norm and is one of the most feature-packed WAN protocols in existence. Although it functions at the Data Link layer of network connectivity, it comprises multiple sub-protocols that serve multiple functions. This provides you with a feature-rich connection, even when bringing up a WAN link between non-Cisco devices.

PPP can function over nearly any type of WAN connection that does not implement its own, specific mechanism for transporting data (such as frame relay and ATM). This means you can use PPP to connect if you are using an asynchronous (modem-like) connection or a synchronous (high-speed) point-to-point serial connection.

Although PPP fills a single layer on the OSI Model (the Data Link layer), it has multiple "sub-layers" that give it all its functionality. Each sub-layer adds specific functionality to the PPP protocol suite. Figure 22.2 depicts the three PPP sub-layers as they relate to the OSI model. Notice that all three of these sub-layers fit into the single Data Link layer.

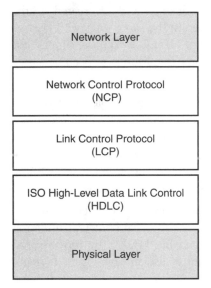

FIGURE 22.2 PPP sub-layers.

It is easy to get confused when expanding the already confusing OSI model into sub-layers for a specific protocol. This is just a logical view of the PPP protocol describing how it is able to include all the functions it advertises. The following sections look at each of these sub-layers, one at a time.

EXAM ALERT

You need to know the sub-layers of PPP and their functions for the CCNA exam because these directly relate to the features PPP provides.

Sub-Layer 1: ISO HDLC

Initially, seeing this layer in PPP seems quite odd. Wasn't HDLC a competing protocol to PPP? This sub-layer of PPP comprises the industry standard ISO HDLC. This sub-layer is responsible for allowing PPP to be supported by multiple devices. It gives the devices that run PPP common ground to stand on when they communicate with each other. As you will see in just a moment, the LCP layer above is responsible for negotiating all the features of HDLC. Because all devices that run HDLC may not support every single feature, the HDLC sub-layer enables the base PPP communication to continue, even if the platforms support different features.

Sub-Layer 2: Link Control Protocol (LCP)

You can think of the LCP sub-layer as the feature negotiation layer. All the features that PPP supports are negotiated by LCP. These features are

- ▶ Authentication
- ▶ Callback
- ▶ Compression
- ▶ Multilink

> **EXAM ALERT**
> Be able to pick the features negotiated by LCP out of a line-up.

Authentication

The authentication features of PPP enable you to require a username and password for the connecting device to bring up the WAN connection. This is not a very important feature on leased line, point-to-point connections because the only way a hacker would be able to get a device connected to the WAN would be to render one of the on-site administrators unconscious and replace the on-site router with one of the hacker's own. The PPP authentication features are most useful for dial-up connections that could be reached by users connected to the Public Switched Telephone Network (PSTN).

For example, you may choose to connect a modem to your router through the AUX port to allow dial-up access, should all the LAN and WAN connectivity to the router fail. This modem would be assigned a phone number, accessible from any computer modem in the world. PPP authentication would require a username and password to be entered before the modem connection would bridge a successful connection.

There are two types of authentication supported by PPP: the Password Authentication Protocol (PAP) and the Challenge Handshake Authentication Protocol (CHAP).

PAP

This authentication protocol is one of the earliest authentication types to be released for WAN connectivity. If PAP is enabled for the connection, the call flow progresses as follows:

1. Client dials up to a router running PPP.

2. After the link (connection) is established, *the client* sends its username and password at the LCP (feature) layer.

3. The PPP router checks the username and password against its user database and allows or denies the client.

Although this list of three steps is a logical authentication process, it has a few flaws. First off, the client dictates the timing of sending the username and password; the server (router running PPP) receives the username and password whenever the client decides to send it. This causes the PAP mechanism to be susceptible to playback attacks. This is a type of attack where a hacker captures (sniff) packets from a conversation and then plays the packets back in an attempt to mirror the connection. Because the client is in complete control of the authentication attempt, the server accepts the played-back packets whenever the client decides to send them.

The authentication of PAP is also done in clear text, which makes it even more vulnerable to packet-sniffing intruders. Anyone who does have a way of monitoring the connection can capture the packets, break them open, and find the username and password used for authentication in clear text. Can you say, "network devastation"?

With all this being said, the only reason you would choose to use the PAP method for authentication is if you were using very old equipment that did not support the newer method of authentication, CHAP.

CHAP

CHAP is a much more secure procedure for connecting to a PPP-based system. The authentication process for CHAP goes like this:

1. Client dials up to a router running PPP.

2. The *router* sends a challenge message to the client.

3. The client responds with the *hash* of the password it is configured to use.

4. The router looks up the password hash against its database. If the hash matches, the client is allowed into the network.

5. After the client is authenticated, the router sends re-authentication messages at random intervals, requiring the client to send the password hash whenever prompted.

Doesn't that list already make you feel better than PAP? The first thing to notice is that the router (server) is in control of the authentication process. Rather than accepting the username and password whenever the client decides to send it, the router demands the username and password on its timeframe. If the client isn't ready to ante up with the credentials, the server immediately terminates the connection. This makes performing a playback attack much more difficult to accomplish.

Even if a hacker were to successfully execute a playback attack with CHAP, the random authentication interval ensures the hacker will not be connected for long. Executing the initial playback attack would require intricate timing for the hacker to be successful. The random authentication requests would be nearly impossible to keep up.

The clear text issues have also been solved by using a system known as *password hashing*. Without getting too deep into cryptography and security mechanisms, you must understand that this is not the same thing as encrypting a password and sending it across the network. Given the time, nearly any encryption algorithm can be broken if the data is captured. Using a hashed version of the password means that the client never actually sends the real password across the line. To accomplish this, the router (PPP server) and the PPP client must be configured to have the identical password. Before the client sends the password, it runs an irreversible mathematical algorithm on the password. The result of that algorithm is called the hash, which is sent to the server. The server runs the same algorithm on its password and compares the two hashes. If the answer is the same, the client successfully authenticates.

Now, you may be thinking the same thing I did when I first heard about this process, "Well, can't you just get the mathematical formula and reverse it to figure out what the password is from the hash? For example, if the formula is *(the password)∞2 = the hash*, could you just take *the (hash÷2) = the password*?" Fair question, but just wait until you see the formula. The hashing method (formula) used is known as the MD5 hash. This formula has been *engineered* with the sole purpose of being irreversible. With that in mind, someone might capture the password hash and find out that it is 5,381,120,123,590. Now the trick is to reverse-engineer an irreversible formula to figure out how the algorithm came up with that answer. It would be much easier for hackers to render the IT staff unconscious at whatever site they were looking to compromise and steal the servers containing the data they needed.

Callback

Just as the name implies, the PPP callback functionality enables a dial-up server (or router) running PPP to use a predefined number to call the person back who initially dialed into the location. One of the major advantages of this function is the increased security: It requires the dial-up user to authenticate and then be present at the predefined phone number to be able to receive the return call. The other advantage is the toll consolidation. If you have long distance users dialing into the network, you leave your company at the mercy of the long distance carriers of your users. By using PPP callback, you can ensure that the company long distance charges are applied, which are typically much lower than normal carrier charges.

A PPP callback process goes through the following steps:

1. A user dials into a router using PPP and authenticates.

2. Upon a successful authentication, the router terminates the connection (typically without any notification) and dials the user back at the predefined number configured by the administrator.

3. Upon reconnect, the user authenticates a second time.

4. Upon a successful authentication, the user is granted network access.

Compression

When I first heard about compression on a WAN link, my mind flashed back to the days of the Stacker compression program of Microsoft DOS. This program slowed your computer down to a crawl to gain a few megabytes of storage space on a hard disk. Surprisingly, one of the two compression algorithms used on PPP WAN connections is named "Stacker"; however, the effects are much less devastating than they were with the old DOS program.

Using compression to make your WAN connection more efficient is not a new concept. These technologies have been around since the days of DOS. However, these technologies have become much more viable on today's networks because of the increase in CPU and memory resources on network equipment. The tradeoff when choosing to use compression is that you gain more WAN bandwidth by sacrificing your router's processor and memory resources. How much you sacrifice depends on the type of compression algorithm you use.

Stacker

The compression type analyzes the data that is being sent and replaces continuous streams of characters with codes. These codes are stored in a dictionary and looked up on the other end of the connection to rebuild the original data. The Stacker algorithm (which is actually called Lempel-Ziv) uses a "flat dictionary-style compression." This means that for every packet of data, it goes through the same process: Look up the character streams in the dictionary, replace the characters with codes, begin again. Therefore, it is very good for network connections that have constantly varying data types (such as SQL, HTTP, FTP, and so on) crossing them. It doesn't matter what the previous traffic was; the same compression algorithm is applied. The Stacker algorithm is notoriously heavy on CPU resources and has less effect on the router's memory resources.

Predictor

This compression algorithm received its name because it literally attempts to predict the next character stream that will be sent or received. It uses a similar dictionary lookup process as Stacker; however, it takes the most common characters looked up and builds a cached index file. Anytime some traffic needs to be sent or received, the index file is checked first. If the character stream (or codes) is not found in the index file, it then consults the full dictionary to find the necessary compression or decompression algorithm. Therefore, the Predictor algorithm works best on network connections that have fairly similar traffic patterns (that can be cached in the index file). For example, perhaps you have a WAN link back to a central office that houses an intranet server that users access to update the corporate e-commerce website. In this case, the traffic patterns would be very similar (HTTP/HTTPS) for most times of the day. The Predictor algorithm usually uses more memory resources and has less effect on the router's CPU than the Stacker algorithm (as long as the traffic patterns do not vary largely).

Microsoft Point-to-Point Compression

Microsoft has its own compression algorithm for PPP, aptly named the Microsoft Point-to-Point Compression (MPPC). This protocol offers slightly improved processor and bandwidth utilization for Microsoft Windows–based clients. Because other devices, such as Cisco routers, would need to support this compression algorithm for Microsoft Windows to use it, Microsoft released the algorithm as an RFC standard (RFC 2118). Under the licensing in this RFC, Microsoft permits other vendors to implement MPPC solely for the purpose of connecting to other MPCC clients. MPPC therefore is used only to allow Windows dial-up users to use compression.

Multilink

PPP multilink enables you to bundle multiple WAN connections into a single, logical connection. This could be as small as bundling two 33.6Kbps modems together to make a 67.2Kbps connection, or bundling four T1 lines together to give yourself a 6.176Mbps connection. The separate interfaces that are bundled together are no longer seen as individual interfaces, but rather join a larger "logical" multilink interface. You can assign this single interface its own IP address, configure authentication, or optimize the logical line with compression. It acts and feels like a real interface, even though it could potentially comprise many physical links.

There are two major benefits to using Multilink PPP (MLPPP). First off, the logical link becomes a single point of management. Rather than figuring out what the traffic utilization is on all the individual physical lines, you can focus your monitoring software (if you have some) on just a single interface. The second benefit to MLPPP is the fact that all physical links bundled in the logical group get *exact* load balancing. When I say "exact," I mean the down-to-the-exact-bit-level kind of exact. MLPPP chops all your packets (referred to as *fragmentation*) into exactly equal sizes before it sends them across the line. This leads to the one drawback of using MLPPP: slightly increased processor and memory utilization on your router.

Sub-Layer 3: Network Control Protocol

The final sub-layer of PPP is what gives it the functionality to allow multiple Network layer protocols to run across a single WAN link at any given time. I think of this layer as the PPP DUPLO® LEGO® block connector. Have you ever seen the DUPLO® blocks for small children? They all have that standard connector with which any other DUPLO® can connect so the child can put any two pieces together (which provides positive affirmation, I'm sure). In that same sense, the Network Control Protocol (NCP) sub-layer of PPP has open-source, network-layer connectors that anyone can plug into. For example, the TCP/IP protocol has a connector called IPCP (the CP stands for "control protocol") that enables TCP/IP to run across a PPP WAN link. IPX/SPX has a connector called IPXCP. With the open-source nature of this protocol, I could create a "Jeremy protocol" and then write a JeremyCP to allow it to run across a PPP WAN link. Cisco has written its own extension called CDPCP that enables the Cisco Discovery Protocol to run across a PPP WAN link, which enables the routers on each end of the connection to use CDP to see each other.

Configuring PPP

Objectives:

▶ Configure and verify a basic WAN serial connection

▶ Configure and verify a PPP connection between Cisco routers

The configuration of PPP without any options does not even deserve its own section. All you need to do is access the interface you would like to enable to run PPP and type the command encapsulation ppp. After you do that on both sides of the connection, you're finished. For example, if I wanted to configure PPP on the Serial 0 interface of a router, here is the process:

```
AccessServer#configure terminal
Enter configuration commands, one per line.  End with CNTL/Z.
AccessServer(config)#interface serial 0
AccessServer(config-if)#encapsulation ppp
```

After you begin turning on the options, the configuration can get a little more complex. This chapter discusses turning on PPP authentication and compression technology.

Authentication

The CCNA exam focuses on configuring PPP authentication between two Cisco routers rather than using authentication for dial-up users (this is covered in the Building Cisco Remote Access Networks CCNP course). Typically, when Cisco routers are performing authentication on a WAN link, the routers will be configured as two-way authentication. Two-way authentication means that both routers authenticate each other. Typically, when a dial-up user connects to a router, one-way authentication is performed (the user must authenticate to the Cisco router, not vice-versa).

To set up CHAP PPP authentication, you must do the following:

1. Turn on PPP encapsulation.

2. Configure the necessary hostname for the authenticating routers.

3. Create user accounts on each side of the connection.

4. Turn on CHAP PPP authentication.

At first, these steps may seem somewhat cryptic, but let me walk you through a configuration example and explain how all these pieces fit together. Refer to Figure 22.3 for a visual of this example configuration.

FIGURE 22.3 PPP authentication example.

This sample configuration enables two-way, CHAP PPP authentication between the Robin and Pigeon routers. For the sake of brevity, assume the router hostnames are already configured and PPP encapsulation has been enabled under the serial interfaces.

Before you begin, you need to understand the significance of the router hostname. By default, when a Cisco router attempts to authenticate with another router, it uses the router hostname as its PPP username to authenticate with the other side. In this example, the router with the hostname "Robin" crosses the PPP link and attempts to authenticate with the Pigeon router, using the username "Robin." The Pigeon router attempts to authenticate with the Robin router, using the username "Pigeon." You therefore need to create user accounts on each router that match the usernames the routers will use when authenticating. The following syntax accomplishes this:

```
Pigeon#configure terminal
Enter configuration commands, one per line.  End with CNTL/Z.
Pigeon(config)#username Robin password cisco

Robin#configure terminal
Enter configuration commands, one per line.  End with CNTL/Z.
Robin(config)#username Pigeon password cisco
```

Now, when the Robin router comes over to the Pigeon router and says "My username is Robin," the Pigeon router has a user database that identifies that username. Likewise, the Pigeon router can now authenticate the Robin router. If you have any experience with Windows administration, this is an identical concept to creating user accounts for people to log on to their PCs.

CAUTION

The CHAP username and passwords are both case sensitive. If the hostname of your router begins with a capital letter, ensure you create the user account the same way.

When using CHAP authentication, you must use the same password for both user accounts. In this case, both the Pigeon and Robin router share the password "cisco." It must remain the same on both sides because CHAP never actually sends the password across the wire; it sends only the MD5 hash version of it. When the receiving side gets the hash, it runs the MD5 algorithm on its own password and compares the two hashes. If they match, authentication succeeds. The following is the complete configuration of both the Pigeon and Robin routers to enable CHAP PPP authentication:

```
Pigeon#configure terminal
Enter configuration commands, one per line.  End with CNTL/Z.
Pigeon(config)#username Robin password cisco
Pigeon(config)#interface serial 0
Pigeon(config-if)#encapsulation ppp
Pigeon(config-if)#ppp authentication chap

Robin#configure terminal
Enter configuration commands, one per line.  End with CNTL/Z.
Robin(config)#username Pigeon password cisco
Robin(config)#interface serial 0
Robin(config-if)#encapsulation ppp
Robin(config-if)#ppp authentication chap
```

EXAM ALERT

Be prepared to configure a PPP encapsulated, CHAP authenticated leased line connection in an exam environment. Be absolutely sure you understand that the passwords must be the same on both routers when configuring CHAP authentication.

Compression

Enabling PPP compression is a piece of cake. You just have to make sure that both sides of the connection enable it; if only one side of the connection enables it, the link fails. Using the Pigeon and Robin scenario again, the following shows the steps you can take to enable compression:

```
Pigeon#configure terminal
Enter configuration commands, one per line.  End with CNTL/Z.
Pigeon(config)#interface serial 0
Pigeon(config-if)#compress  ?
  mppc       MPPC compression type
  predictor  predictor compression type
  stac       stac compression algorithm
  <cr>
```

That's it! Just use the compress command and type the mode of compression you would like to use, and let the bandwidth savings begin.

Verifying PPP

Objectives:

▶ Configure and verify a basic WAN serial connection

▶ Configure and verify a PPP connection between Cisco routers

To ensure your PPP connection came up successfully, you can always use the ol' faithful show ip interface brief command.

```
Pigeon#show ip interface brief
Interface          IP-Address      OK? Method Status      Protocol
FastEthernet0      10.1.1.2        YES NVRAM  up          up
Serial0            10.2.2.2        YES manual up          up
```

In this case, all is well with the Serial 0 PPP connection between the routers because the Protocol is stated as up. Remember, the Status column generally dictates the Physical layer connectivity, whereas the Protocol column focuses on the Data Link connectivity.

If you want to get a little more in depth with the PPP negotiation on the interface, issue the show interface <*interface*> command as follows:

```
Pigeon#show interface serial 0
Serial0 is up, line protocol is up
  Hardware is PowerQUICC Serial
  Internet address is 10.2.2.2/24
  MTU 1500 bytes, BW 1544 Kbit, DLY 20000 usec,
     reliability 255/255, txload 1/255, rxload 1/255
  Encapsulation PPP, loopback not set
  Keepalive set (10 sec)
  LCP Open
  Open: IPCP, CCP, CDPCP
  Last input 00:00:51, output 00:00:01, output hang never
  Last clearing of "show interface" counters 05:07:30
  Input queue: 0/75/0/0 (size/max/drops/flushes); Total output drops: 0
  Queueing strategy: weighted fair
  Output queue: 0/1000/64/0 (size/max total/threshold/drops)
     Conversations  0/1/256 (active/max active/max total)
     Reserved Conversations 0/0 (allocated/max allocated)
     Available Bandwidth 1158 kilobits/sec
  5 minute input rate 0 bits/sec, 0 packets/sec
  5 minute output rate 0 bits/sec, 0 packets/sec
     4127 packets input, 168000 bytes, 0 no buffer
     Received 0 broadcasts, 0 runts, 0 giants, 0 throttles
     84 input errors, 0 CRC, 84 frame, 0 overrun, 0 ignored, 0 abort
     8196 packets output, 404090 bytes, 0 underruns
     0 output errors, 0 collisions, 163 interface resets
     0 output buffer failures, 0 output buffers swapped out
     326 carrier transitions
     DCD=up  DSR=up  DTR=up  RTS=up  CTS=up
```

As you can see from the output above, the router has negotiated Link Control Protocol (LCP) options, which is indicated by the `LCP Open` state. If the LCP negotiations had failed (most likely because of an authentication problem), the LCP state would rotate between `Listen`, `ACKSent`, or `TERMSent`. This is the Cisco router trying to go through the negotiation of the LCP options. In the line below `LCP Open`, you can verify all the Network layer communication occurring across the PPP link. In this case, you can see IPCP (indicates the TCP/IP protocol), CCP (Indicates compression is in effect—compressed control protocol [CCP]), and CDPCP (indicates the Cisco Discovery Protocol [CDP]). Technically, CDP is a Data Link protocol; however, Cisco adopted it to connect into the PPP options as a Layer 3 protocol.

EXAM ALERT

Be able to interpret the `show interface` command output as it relates to the PPP options.

Finally, if you would like to see how your PPP compression is working out, you can type the command `show compress`. This gives you the compression statistics for the line:

```
Pigeon#show compress
 Serial0
        Software compression enabled
        uncompressed bytes xmt/rcv 4215/4956
        compressed    bytes xmt/rcv 0/0
        1  min avg ratio xmt/rcv 0.223/4.621
        5  min avg ratio xmt/rcv 0.284/4.621
        10 min avg ratio xmt/rcv 0.270/1.372
        no bufs xmt 0 no bufs rcv 0
        resyncs 0
```

In this case, you have no compressed bytes because all the traffic sent over the PPP link was generated by the routers themselves (this traffic is exempt from compression).

Troubleshooting PPP

Objectives:

▶ Configure and verify a basic WAN serial connection

▶ Configure and verify a PPP connection between Cisco routers

▶ Troubleshoot WAN implementation issues

Whenever you reach the troubleshooting section for any topic, you can be guaranteed some `debug` output. In this case, the `debug` commands for PPP are pretty darn useful: Most of the output is easy to understand. The most useful command that I have found to troubleshoot a PPP link is the `debug ppp negotiation` command. Check out this output:

```
Pigeon#debug ppp negotiation
1d02h: Se0 PPP: Using default call direction
1d02h: Se0 PPP: Treating connection as a dedicated line
1d02h: Se0 PPP: Phase is ESTABLISHING, Active Open [0 sess, 1 load]
1d02h: Se0 LCP: O CONFREQ [Closed] id 157 len 15
1d02h: Se0 LCP:    AuthProto CHAP (0x0305C22305)
1d02h: Se0 LCP:    MagicNumber 0x0709760C (0x05060709760C)
1d02h: Se0 LCP: I CONFREQ [REQsent] id 208 len 15
1d02h: Se0 LCP:    AuthProto CHAP (0x0305C22305)
1d02h: Se0 LCP:    MagicNumber 0x22D5B7B3 (0x050622D5B7B3)
1d02h: Se0 LCP: O CONFACK [REQsent] id 208 len 15
1d02h: Se0 LCP:    AuthProto CHAP (0x0305C22305)
1d02h: Se0 LCP:    MagicNumber 0x22D5B7B3 (0x050622D5B7B3)
1d02h: Se0 LCP: TIMEout: State ACKsent
1d02h: Se0 LCP: O CONFREQ [ACKsent] id 158 len 15
1d02h: Se0 LCP:    AuthProto CHAP (0x0305C22305)
1d02h: Se0 LCP:    MagicNumber 0x0709760C (0x05060709760C)
1d02h: Se0 LCP: I CONFACK [ACKsent] id 158 len 15
1d02h: Se0 LCP:    AuthProto CHAP (0x0305C22305)
1d02h: Se0 LCP:    MagicNumber 0x0709760C (0x05060709760C)
1d02h: Se0 LCP: State is Open
1d02h: Se0 PPP: Phase is AUTHENTICATING, by both [0 sess, 1 load]
1d02h: Se0 CHAP: O CHALLENGE id 156 len 27 from "Pigeon"
1d02h: Se0 CHAP: I CHALLENGE id 2 len 26 from "Robin"
1d02h: Se0 CHAP: O RESPONSE id 2 len 27 from "Pigeon"
1d02h: Se0 CHAP: I RESPONSE id 156 len 26 from "Robin"
1d02h: Se0 CHAP: O SUCCESS id 156 len 4
1d02h: Se0 CHAP: I SUCCESS id 2 len 4
1d02h: Se0 PPP: Phase is UP [0 sess, 1 load]
1d02h: Se0 IPCP: O CONFREQ [Closed] id 4 len 10
1d02h: Se0 IPCP:    Address 10.2.2.2 (0x03060A020202)
1d02h: Se0 CCP: O CONFREQ [Closed] id 4 len 6
1d02h: Se0 CCP:    Predictor1 (0x0102)
1d02h: Se0 CDPCP: O CONFREQ [Closed] id 4 len 4
1d02h: Se0 IPCP: I CONFREQ [REQsent] id 5 len 10
1d02h: Se0 IPCP:    Address 10.2.2.1 (0x03060A020201)
1d02h: Se0 IPCP: O CONFACK [REQsent] id 5 len 10
1d02h: Se0 IPCP:    Address 10.2.2.1 (0x03060A020201)
1d02h: Se0 CCP: I CONFREQ [REQsent] id 2 len 6
1d02h: Se0 CCP:    Predictor1 (0x0102)
1d02h: Se0 CCP: O CONFACK [REQsent] id 2 len 6
1d02h: Se0 CCP:    Predictor1 (0x0102)
1d02h: Se0 CDPCP: I CONFREQ [REQsent] id 5 len 4
1d02h: Se0 CDPCP: O CONFACK [REQsent] id 5 len 4
1d02h: Se0 IPCP: I CONFACK [ACKsent] id 4 len 10
1d02h: Se0 IPCP:    Address 10.2.2.2 (0x03060A020202)
1d02h: Se0 IPCP: State is Open
1d02h: Se0 CCP: I CONFACK [ACKsent] id 4 len 6
1d02h: Se0 CCP:    Predictor1 (0x0102)
```

```
1d02h: Se0 CCP: State is Open
1d02h: Se0 CDPCP: I CONFACK [ACKsent] id 4 len 4
1d02h: Se0 CDPCP: State is Open
1d02h: Se0 IPCP: Install route to 10.2.2.1
1d02h: %LINEPROTO-5-UPDOWN: Line protocol on Interface Serial0,
3changed state to up
```

Isn't that some great stuff?!? Okay, it does take a little bit of screening through all the output, but if you look about halfway through, you can see the exchange of the Robin and Pigeon host-names. This shows the challenge/response action of the CHAP protocol. Thankfully, you can see a SUCCESS message to finish it off, showing the Pigeon and Robin routers have successful-ly authenticated each other. Near the bottom of the output, you see the CCP (compression negotiation) negotiate the Predictor algorithm between the two routers. Finally, at the end of the output, you see the link come up.

If your PPP connection is failing, this debug command will definitely show you the cause (as long as the failure is related to PPP). Another popular command is debug ppp authentica-tion, which gives the same output, but slims it down to just the authentication information (because this is where many failures occur).

Chapter Summary

Managing WAN connections is one of the primary functions of a router. WAN connections tie distant locations together into a common network infrastructure. Choosing a WAN connection has become more difficult in recent years because there are now many more WAN connection technologies at our disposal. However, the most popular WAN connection technologies boil down to three main categories: Leased Lines, Circuit Switched, and Packet Switched.

After you have chosen the Physical connection type you would like to use, you can then move up to the Data Link connectivity. For leased line connections, the two major protocols in use today are HDLC and PPP. On a Cisco router, HDLC has been modified to support multiple upper-layer protocols and has thus become proprietary. HDLC's major feature is the low amount of network overhead it causes on the WAN connection. Other than that, it is feature-less. PPP is the more popular data link protocol because it supports multi-vendor interoperability and a plethora of features.

Key Terms

- leased lines
- packet-switched networks
- circuit-switched networks
- broadband
- Virtual Private Networks (VPNs)
- Integrated Services Digital Network (ISDN)
- metro ethernet
- X.25
- Frame Relay
- Asychronous Transfer Mode (ATM)
- High-level Data Link Control (HDLC)
- Point-to-Point Protocol (PPP)

- PPP over Ethernet (PPPoE)
- PPP over ATM (PPPoA)
- V.35
- X.21
- EIA/TIA-232, -449, and -530
- Link Control Protocol (LCP)
- Network Control Protocol (NCP)
- Password Authentication Protocol (PAP)
- Challenge Handshake Authentication Protocol (CHAP)
- stacker compression
- predictor compression
- Microsoft Point-to-Point Compression (MPPC)

Apply Your Knowledge

Exercises

22.1 Troubleshooting PPP Connections

One of the most common problems encountered when troubleshooting a PPP connection is authentication failures, which are due to the many parameters that must match for the link to successfully authenticate. In this exercise, you will incorrectly configure PPP authentication and walk through the steps necessary to troubleshoot the connection. Refer to Figure 22.4 for a visual of the connection.

FIGURE 22.4   PPP troubleshooting network diagram.

Estimated Time: 5-10 minutes

What you will do is configure the two routers for CHAP authentication across the PPP connection. However, you will configure the username/password combination on one side of the connection as all lowercase and watch the story unfold. First, get the PPP connection running:

```
Daniel#show ip interface brief
Interface          IP-Address      OK? Method Status        Protocol
FastEthernet0      10.1.1.2        YES NVRAM  up            up
Serial0            192.168.40.2    YES manual up            down
Daniel#configure terminal
Enter configuration commands, one per line.  End with CNTL/Z.
Daniel(config)#interface serial 0
Daniel(config-if)#encapsulation ppp
```

You now have the Daniel rotuer configured for PPP; now configure the Ezekiel router on the other side.

```
Ezekiel#show ip interface brief
Interface    IP-Address     OK? Method Status              Protocol
Ethernet0    192.168.1.40   YES NVRAM  up                  up
Serial0      192.168.40.1   YES manual up                  down
Serial1      unassigned     YES NVRAM  administratively down down
Ezekiel#configure terminal
Enter configuration commands, one per line.  End with CNTL/Z.
Ezekiel(config)#interface serial 0
Ezekiel(config-if)#encapsulation ppp
00:07:36: %LINEPROTO-5-UPDOWN: Line protocol on Interface Serial0,
3 changed state to up
1d14h: %LINEPROTO-5-UPDOWN: Line protocol on Interface Serial0,
3 changed state to up
Ezekiel(config-if)#^Z
```

```
1d14h: %SYS-5-CONFIG_I: Configured from console by console
Ezekiel#ping 192.168.40.2
Type escape sequence to abort.
Sending 5, 100-byte ICMP Echos to 192.168.40.2, timeout is 2 seconds:
!!!!!
Success rate is 100 percent (5/5), round-trip min/avg/max = 56/59/72 ms
```

It looks like the PPP link has been brought up successfully and you are now able to ping between the two routers. Now add the authentication piece to the picture:

```
Ezekiel#configure terminal
Enter configuration commands, one per line.  End with CNTL/Z.
Ezekiel(config)#username Daniel password examprep
Ezekiel(config)#interface serial 0
Ezekiel(config-if)#ppp authentication chap
00:11:11: %LINEPROTO-5-UPDOWN: Line protocol on Interface Serial0,
3 changed state to down
```

Notice that as soon as you turned on CHAP authentication for one side of the connection, the link went down. This is because one side of the connection is configured to require authentication while the other is not configured to support it. You can solve that problem and, at the same time, introduce the authentication configuration error.

```
Daniel#configure terminal
Enter configuration commands, one per line.  End with CNTL/Z.
Daniel(config-if)#exit
Daniel(config)#username Ezekiel password examcram
Daniel(config)#interface serial 0
Daniel(config-if)#ppp authentication chap
Daniel(config-if)#exit
Daniel(config)#exit
1d14h: %SYS-5-CONFIG_I: Configured from console by console
Daniel#show ip interface brief
Interface          IP-Address      OK? Method Status      Protocol
FastEthernet0      10.1.1.2        YES NVRAM  up          up
Serial0            192.168.40.2    YES manual up          down
```

Notice that the password examcram was used for the Ezekiel account rather than examprep. Because CHAP requires both passwords to be the same on both sides of the connection, the Serial0 link remains down. Now, if we did not know about this configuration error, the troubleshooting process would go something like this:

```
Daniel#show interface serial 0
Serial0 is up, line protocol is down
  Hardware is PowerQUICC Serial
  Internet address is 192.168.40.2/24
  MTU 1500 bytes, BW 1544 Kbit, DLY 20000 usec,
     reliability 255/255, txload 1/255, rxload 1/255
  Encapsulation PPP, loopback not set
  Keepalive set (10 sec)
```

```
        LCP Listen
        Closed: IPCP, CCP, CDPCP
        Last input 00:00:01, output 00:00:01, output hang never
        Last clearing of "show interface" counters 16:52:28
        Input queue: 0/75/0/0 (size/max/drops/flushes); Total output drops: 0
        Queueing strategy: weighted fair
    <…output removed for brevity...>
```

Notice first that the line protocol is down, which indicates a Data Link failure. When you look down at the PPP negotiation (LCP), you can see that it is in the Listen state and the NCP protocol communication is Closed. This means the LCP layer of PPP has not successfully negotiated, and points you in the correct direction for troubleshooting. Now is a good time to perform a debug and see whether you can weed out what is going on.

```
    Daniel#debug ppp negotiation
    PPP protocol negotiation debugging is on
    Daniel#
    1d14h: Se0 LCP: TIMEout: State Listen
    1d14h: Se0 LCP: O CONFREQ [Listen] id 51 len 15
    1d14h: Se0 LCP:    AuthProto CHAP (0x0305C22305)
    1d14h: Se0 LCP:    MagicNumber 0x098EF573 (0x0506098EF573)
    1d14h: Se0 LCP: I CONFACK [REQsent] id 51 len 15
    1d14h: Se0 LCP:    AuthProto CHAP (0x0305C22305)
    1d14h: Se0 LCP:    MagicNumber 0x098EF573 (0x0506098EF573)
    1d14h: Se0 LCP: I CONFREQ [ACKrcvd] id 131 len 15
    1d14h: Se0 LCP:    AuthProto CHAP (0x0305C22305)
    1d14h: Se0 LCP:    MagicNumber 0x002934B3 (0x0506002934B3)
    1d14h: Se0 LCP: O CONFACK [ACKrcvd] id 131 len 15
    1d14h: Se0 LCP:    AuthProto CHAP (0x0305C22305)
    1d14h: Se0 LCP:    MagicNumber 0x002934B3 (0x0506002934B3)
    Daniel#
    1d14h: Se0 LCP: State is Open
    1d14h: Se0 PPP: Phase is AUTHENTICATING, by both [0 sess, 1 load]
    1d14h: Se0 CHAP: O CHALLENGE id 144 len 27 from "Daniel"
    1d14h: Se0 CHAP: I CHALLENGE id 45 len 28 from "Ezekiel"
    1d14h: Se0 CHAP: O RESPONSE id 45 len 27 from "Daniel"
    1d14h: Se0 CHAP: I RESPONSE id 144 len 28 from "Ezekiel"
    1d14h: Se0 CHAP: O FAILURE id 144 len 25 msg is "MD/DES compare failed"
    1d14h: Se0 PPP: Phase is TERMINATING [0 sess, 1 load]
    1d14h: Se0 LCP: O TERMREQ [Open] id 52 len 4
    1d14h: Se0 CHAP: LCP not open, discarding packet
    1d14h: Se0 LCP: I TERMREQ [TERMsent] id 132 len 4
    1d14h: Se0 LCP: O TERMACK [TERMsent] id 132 len 4
    Daniel#
    1d14h: Se0 LCP: TIMEout: State TERMsent
    1d14h: Se0 LCP: O TERMREQ [TERMsent] id 53 len 4
    1d14h: Se0 LCP: I TERMACK [TERMsent] id 53 len 4
    1d14h: Se0 LCP: State is Closed
    1d14h: Se0 PPP: Phase is DOWN [0 sess, 1 load]
    1d14h: Se0 PPP: Phase is ESTABLISHING, Passive Open [0 sess, 1 load]
```

You can watch in amazement as PPP goes from the Listen state into the REQ/ACK state (where it begins to negotiate the connection and authentication protocol). After the LCP state is Open, the full authentication phase begins. About halfway through the CHALLENGE/RESPONSE messages, you see the glaring FAILURE message that shows that the MD/DES compare failed. This means the password hashes are not the same for these routers. If you kept this debug turned on, it would continue to loop through the process again and again until you fixed the mismatched password. Turn off the debug and fix the password, and see what happens.

```
Daniel#u all
All possible debugging has been turned off
Daniel#configure terminal
Enter configuration commands, one per line.  End with CNTL/Z.
Daniel(config)#no username Ezekiel password examcram
Daniel(config)#username Ezekiel password examprep
Daniel(config)#
00:40:34: %LINEPROTO-5-UPDOWN: Line protocol on Interface Serial0,
3 changed state to up
1d14h: %LINEPROTO-5-UPDOWN: Line protocol on Interface Serial0,
3 changed state to up
```

Wow! Just like that, the link has come online. The configuration is now successful.

Review Questions

1. List the three categories of WAN connections.

2. You are installing a new serial WAN connection into your offices in Tucson, Arizona. The service has already terminated their end of the connection at the premises and provided you with a CSU/DSU device. What physical connections should you use on your Cisco router?

3. What four features are negotiated by PPP's LCP?

4. What is the function of PPP's Network Control Protocol?

5. PPP has the capability to use two different compression algorithms. What are they? What is the effect of these algorithms on your router? Why would you choose to use one algorithm over the other?

Exam Questions

1. Which of the following network types would encompass Frame Relay and X.25?

   ○ **A.** Leased lines

   ○ **B.** Circuit-switched networks

   ○ **C.** Packet-switched networks

   ○ **D.** Broadband

2. What type of serial transition cable should you use to connect your Cisco router to a CSU/DSU device that has a V.35 female connector?

○ **A.** V.35 male on the Cisco side to V.35 male on the CSU/DSU

○ **B.** DB-60 male on the Cisco side to V.35 male on the CSU/DSU

○ **C.** DB-60 male on the Cisco side to V.35 female on the CSU/DSU

○ **D.** V.35 male on the Cisco side to V.35 female on the CSU/DSU

3. What type of packet is used during the initial PPP link establishment process?

○ **A.** Authentication

○ **B.** LCP

○ **C.** NCP

○ **D.** HDLC

4. Which of the following describes the Password Authentication Protocol (PAP) used by PPP during the LCP process? (Choose 2.)

○ **A.** PAP exchanges passwords in clear text.

○ **B.** PAP uses a MD5 hashing function to send password information.

○ **C.** PAP enables the server to be in control of the authentication attempt.

○ **D.** PAP enables the client to be in control of the authentication attempt.

5. When is CHAP authentication performed?

○ **A.** On a certain time interval

○ **B.** When the user decides to send the username/password

○ **C.** When the link connection is established

○ **D.** When the link connection is established and on a periodic interval

6. What Cisco IOS configuration mode should you be in to enable PPP authentication?

○ **A.** Global configuration mode

○ **B.** Router configuration mode

○ **C.** Interface configuration mode

○ **D.** PPP LCP configuration mode

7. What type of WAN connection enables the company to purchase a simple Internet connection and tunnel their information through the network between their sites?

   ○ **A.** Leased lines

   ○ **B.** Circuit-switched

   ○ **C.** Packet-switched

   ○ **D.** Virtual private network

8. What verification command can show you the current state of the PPP Link Control Protocol?

   ○ **A.** `show interface`

   ○ **B.** `show ip interface`

   ○ **C.** `show ppp interface`

   ○ **D.** `show wan interface`

9. Which of the following PPP sub-layers is responsible for Network layer protocol negotiation?

   ○ **A.** HDLC

   ○ **B.** CDP

   ○ **C.** LCP

   ○ **D.** NCP

10. Which of the following WAN connection categories would include dial-up modems?

   ○ **A.** Leased lines

   ○ **B.** Circuit-switched

   ○ **C.** Packet-switched

   ○ **D.** Metro ethernet

Answers to Review Questions

1. The three WAN connection categories are leased line, circuit switched, and packet switched.

2. When configuring the physical connectivity for a serial WAN connection, you need to purchase either a DB-60 or Smart Serial WIC card for your router. From there, you need to purchase a cable that converts from the DB-60 or Smart Serial card of your Cisco router to the industry standard adapter found on the CSU/DSU device that connects to the service provider.

3. The four features negotiated by the PPP Link Control Protocol (LCP) are compression, callback, multilink, and authentication.

4. The Network Control Protocol (NCP) enables the router to encapsulate multiple upper-layer protocols (such as IP, IPX, and Appletalk) over a PPP WAN connection.

5. The two PPP compression algorithms are Stacker and Predictor. The Stacker algorithm requires more processor resources and fewer memory resources. The Predictor algorithm uses more memory resources and fewer processor resources. Stacker is the best algorithm to use when there are varying traffic types crossing the PPP WAN connection. Predictor works best when you have similar traffic types using the PPP WAN connection.

Answers to Exam Questions

1. **C**. Frame Relay and X.25 fall under the packet-switched networks category. These networks establish connections through a service provider cloud using virtual circuits. Answer B is incorrect because circuit-switched networks include technologies such as modems and ISDN. Answer A is incorrect because leased lines use dedicated bandwidth between locations. Answer D is incorrect because broadband encompasses DSL and cable modem technology.

2. **B.** The Cisco side of the connection always uses either a DB-60 or Smart Serial connector (these are always male because the router has female ports). Because the CSU/DSU has a V.35 female connector, you should be using a V.35 male transition cable. All other answers are incorrect because they use either the wrong connector type or gender on the Cisco side.

3. **B.** The Link Control Protocol (LCP) is used to negotiate all options related to PPP during the link establishment phase. The Network Control Protocol (NCP) negotiates the upper-layer protocols only after the initial PPP link has been established. The HDLC layer of PPP is what allows for multivendor interoperability with the protocol. Answer A is incorrect because an authentication packet falls under the LCP negotiations. Answer C is incorrect because NCP negotiates the upper-layer protocols. Answer D is incorrect because HDLC is used to give PPP an industry standard foundation when connecting to non-Cisco equipment.

4. **A, D.** PAP is the older of the two PPP authentication protocols. It has major security flaws, including the sending of passwords in clear text and allowing the client to choose when it sends the password. Answers B and C are incorrect because the MD5 hashing and server control is a function of the CHAP.

5. **D.** CHAP requires authentication both when the link is initially established and on a periodic basis thereafter. This is awesome because it combats playback attacks and packet sniffing (passwords are not sent). PAP requires authentication only when the link is initially established and when the client chooses to send the credentials, which is why answers B and C are incorrect. Answer A is incorrect because CHAP also sends authentication credentials when the link is initially established.

6. **C.** You enable PPP authentication from the interface configuration mode by typing the command `ppp authentication <chap/pap>`. All other answers are either irrelevant or non-existent (there is no PPP LCP configuration mode in the Cisco IOS).

7. **D.** VPNs enable companies to purchase simple Internet connections and tunnel their information through the networks between their sites. This information is heavily encrypted to ensure it is not compromised crossing the public network. This is far cheaper than any other type of WAN connection, but can suffer from the heavy encryption slowdown. Answers A, B, and C are incorrect because leased lines and circuit-switched and packet-switched networks require no tunneling or encryption capabilities.

8. **A.** The `show interface` command is used to verify the current state of the PPP LCP negotiations. This shows `Open`, `Listen`, `ACKSent`, or `TERMSent`, depending on the state of LCP at the time (you want LCP to show `Open`). The other `show` commands are either irrelevant or would produce invalid syntax.

9. **D.** NCP is used to negotiate the Network layer protocols. These negotiations are typically shown as in the syntax `<negotiated protocol>CP` in `show interface` output, such as IPCP (for the IP protocol), CDPCP (for the CDP protocol), or IPXCP (for the IPX protocol). Answer A is incorrect because HDLC is used at a lower layer of PPP to provide multi-vendor interoperability, and answer C is incorrect because LCP is used to negotiate PPP features. Answer B is incorrect because CDP has nothing to do with WAN links.

10. **B.** Circuit-switched connections encompass anything that has to dial a number to make a connection. These connections typically use the telephone company as a backbone. Answer C is incorrect as packet-switched networks include technologies such as X.25 and Frame Relay. Answer A is incorrect because leased lines do not dial because they are permanently established connections. Answer D is incorrect because metro ethernet is extremely high-speed connections running through a metropolitan area.

Suggested Reading and Resources

1. Cisco Introduction to WAN Technologies, http://www.cisco.com/ univercd/cc/td/doc/cisintwk/ito_doc/introwan.htm.

2. Ward, Chris and Cioara, Jeremy. *Exam Cram 2 CCNA Practice Questions*. Que Publishing, 2004.

3. Quinn, Eric and Glauser, Fred. *BCRAN Exam Cram 2 (Exam 642-821)*. Que Publishing, 2003.

CHAPTER TWENTY-THREE

Frame Relay

Objectives

This chapter covers the following Cisco-specified objectives for the "Implement and verify WAN links" section of the 640-802 CCNA exam:

▶ **Describe different methods for connecting to a WAN**

▶ **Configure and verify Frame Relay on Cisco routers**

▶ **Troubleshoot WAN implementation issues**

Outline

Study Strategies

▶ Read the information presented in the chapter, paying special attention to tables, Notes, and Exam Alerts.

▶ Spend as much time as you find necessary on the terms and concepts of Frame Relay. After you fully understand the operation, the configuration is not very difficult.

▶ Although configuration questions may exist, the CCNA exam typically focuses on the concepts behind Frame Relay, with many of the configurations reserved for the CCNP BCRAN exam.

Introduction

Up until now, most of the WAN connection types discussed so far have provided dedicated bandwidth. For example, if you purchase a point-to-point leased-line connection at a T1 speed, you have 1.544Mbps at your disposal, 24 hours a day. This bandwidth is there regardless of whether you use it or not. Likewise, if you are using an ISDN BRI connection and dial the line up, you have 128Kbps of bandwidth at your disposal. Your network might not choose to send a single packet across the line; regardless, the 128Kbps of bandwidth sits there waiting. But with Frame Relay (and packet-switched networking, in general), the service providers had a novel idea: If you're not using your bandwidth, should it just sit there? I think not.

Welcome to the world of Frame Relay, the first connection type where lightning-bolt WAN links terminate into some sort of fluffy cloud rather than going directly to another router. This is a place where your destination address is not actually at the destination, but rather, terminates at the source. With Frame Relay, the bandwidth you pay for might just be the beginning of the bandwidth you get. Yes, my friends, you have entered the WAN Link Twilight Zone.

Frame Relay Overview

Objective:

▶ Describe different methods for connecting to a WAN

Frame Relay is by far the most conceptually complex topic in the CCNA-level material. Much as with subnetting, though, after you get it, you'll think it's the greatest thing since sliced bread. However, until you get to that point, you'll probably think people that use Frame Relay are insane. Unfortunately (or fortunately, depending on your perspective), Frame Relay is one of the more popular WAN connection types in use in production networks. It offers the high speed demanded by the networks of today at cut-rate prices that managers love.

Frame Relay connections work quite differently than the typical WAN connections discussed thus far. Rather than have a single connection from a location to another location (also known as point-to-point), you might have a connection going from one location to five other locations out a single, physical serial interface. You start to get the feel that this is an ethernet-style connection where any device connected to a hub can reach any other device plugged into the same hub. Depending on your Frame Relay configuration, this may not be far from the truth. Rather than connect sites together through individual physical interfaces, Frame Relay connects sites together with virtual circuits.

Virtual Circuits

Objective:

▶ Describe different methods for connecting to a WAN

Virtual circuits are logical links through service provider networks that give routers the impression that they are linked directly together. Take a look at Figure 23.1. You have a router on each side of the service provider cloud, connected through a virtual circuit, signified by a dotted line through the cloud. These routers believe they are connected directly together (as if the cloud weren't there). You could even do a `traceroute` command between these routers and it would show only a single hop. However, if you peeled back that cloud, you would find that these routers are nowhere near directly connected. They would be going through many service provider routers, through many different networks. Truth be told, the technology underneath that Frame Relay cloud probably isn't even Frame Relay. When a frame gets sent through that cloud, its headers are most likely stripped and replaced many times; it's shaken, stirred, and spun around. But by the time it reaches the other end of the virtual circuit, the original Frame Relay headers are placed back on and a dazed and confused packet walks out of the cloud reporting that it traveled only a single hop between the source and the destination. For now, it's best to say that what happens in the cloud, stays in the cloud. Unless you're a service provider, this is how most network administrators prefer to leave it.

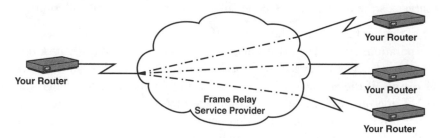

FIGURE 23.1 Typical Frame Relay network diagram.

Although you aren't concerned with what happens within the cloud, you do need to understand the circuits that ride over the cloud. These virtual circuits define the devices you are able to reach. The more virtual circuits you purchase to connect your various locations, the more redundant the connections will be; at the same time, the monthly cost will rise significantly. Therefore, there are three major design strategies to provisioning Frame Relay virtual circuits.

Hub and Spoke Design

Every network looks for cost efficiency. Redundancy is often sacrificed on the altar of monthly cost. Thus, the hub and spoke Frame Relay network design is one of the more common. In this configuration, you pick a centralized location (most likely, your largest, most connected office) as the "hub" of the network. All other locations are considered "spokes" and have a single virtual circuit connection back to the hub. Figure 23.2 gives a visual of what this looks like.

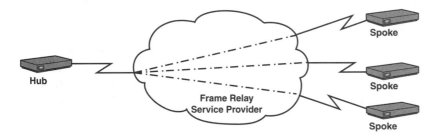

FIGURE 23.2   Hub and spoke Frame Relay design.

Initially, it appears as though the spoke offices will be unable to reach each other. However, you can configure them to traverse through the hub location if they ever need to communicate. Typically, in this network design, the spoke offices rarely communicate with each other. Rather, they access servers, store information, send email, and so on through the hub office.

The major advantage of this configuration is the cost. It offers the cheapest monthly price tag, which cost-cutting corporations enjoy. The disadvantages are beginning to mount against this design, however. The redundancy is sorely lacking. If a single router (the central router) loses connectivity for any reason (if the router crashes, if a trenching company cuts through the line), your entire WAN goes down. The other disadvantage of this design is beginning to eclipse even redundancy. It is the disadvantage of tandem switching. Any time the spoke offices need to reach each other, they must go through the hub office. This is considered a *tandem switch*. Tandem switching takes time and adds delay for the end-to-end connection. Up until modern times, this was no big deal; file transfers between spoke offices would just move a little slower. One technology has pushed tandem switching from a priority level of "No big deal" to "Heaven help us, the sky is falling." That technology is Voice over IP (VoIP).

VoIP technology involves moving the telephone system from running on its own network to using the data network as a backbone for communication. VoIP has very strict delay requirements that can be easily exceeded anytime sources of delay (such as a tandem switch) are introduced. Now, anytime employees working in the spoke offices call each other (which happens quite a bit more frequently than file transfer), the call quality may sound like a bad cell phone call. Therefore, most companies that are looking to move into a VoIP environment typically redesign their Frame Relay network to minimize the number of tandem switches that occur.

Partial Mesh Design

You can think of the partial mesh Frame Relay design as the compromise between network administrators and cost-saving managers. In this configuration, key sites have redundant virtual circuit connections through the cloud, as shown in Figure 23.3.

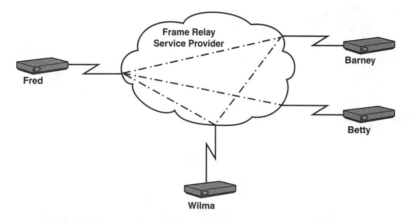

FIGURE 23.3 Partial mesh Frame Relay design.

This gives them a level of redundancy and minimizes the number of tandem switches required for them to communicate. Less critical locations have fewer virtual circuit connections, which keeps the cost lower.

Full Mesh Design

If the partial mesh design is a compromise between the network administrators and managers, then the full mesh design implies that the network administrators won. This design is every Cisco network administrator's picture of perfection over a Frame Relay cloud. It gives every site a direct virtual circuit to every other site, as shown in Figure 23.4. This design gives maximum redundancy and minimum packet latency (latency describes how long it takes a packet to reach each location). Of course, this type of service comes at a cost, the highest cost of all Frame Relay network designs.

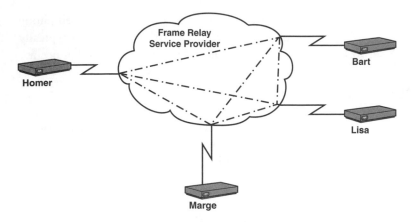

FIGURE 23.4   Full mesh Frame Relay design.

Frame Relay Terminology

Objective:

▶ Describe different methods for connecting to a WAN

As with most Cisco concepts, you'll find that the configuration piece of Frame Relay is fairly simple; the difficulty appears when you try to understand the concepts behind the configuration. Frame Relay introduces a plethora of new terms that describe the end-to-end communication. The first term you have already seen: a virtual circuit. You'll now find out that there are two types of virtual circuits.

Permanent Virtual Circuit

A permanent virtual circuit (PVC) is a permanently established circuit through the Frame Relay service provider network. It enables the routers at each end to communicate with each other without any setup process. A PVC closely emulates a leased-line connection between your devices.

Switched Virtual Circuit

A switched virtual circuit (SVC) gives you an "on-demand" connection through the Frame Relay cloud. The connection from end-to-end is built as the routers require it and may be billed on a usage basis (very much like ISDN connections). SVC connections have largely decreased in use in recent years (almost to the point of non-existence) because service providers no longer have true end-to-end Frame Relay connections, but rather, convert from Frame Relay to some other network type after you transmit data into the cloud. If this seems odd, remember: What happens in the cloud, stays in the cloud.

Local Management Interface

The local management interface (LMI) signaling is the "language of love" between your router and the service provider. Using LMI, the service provider can transmit status information about the state of your virtual circuits to your router. In recent versions of the IOS, your router can auto-detect what LMI language the service provider uses. In older IOS versions, this must be manually configured under the interface.

Data Link Connection Identifier

It is a little known fact that router serial interfaces do not have MAC addresses. MAC addresses are related only to LAN connections. WAN connections therefore all have different Layer 2 addresses that they use to identify the other side of the connection. In the case of Frame Relay, this is known as a *Data Link Connection Identifier* (DLCI). Communicating through DLCIs is unlike most other network communication that you've seen thus far. Rather than access a destination DLCI number to reach the remote router, you *leave on a local* DLCI number to reach a remote router. This is very similar to the way airline travel works. When you want to fly to a remote destination, say North Dakota, you might leave on flight #4513. When you want to return from North Dakota to your original location, you might leave on flight #4839. This means that the DLCI numbers you use are *locally significant*; the DLCIs you have in Arizona matter only to the router in Arizona. The DLCIs you have in North Dakota matter only to the router in North Dakota. Look at Figure 23.5 for a network diagram.

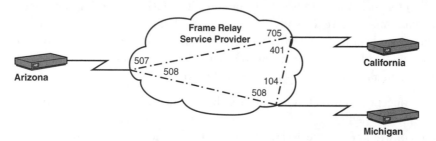

FIGURE 23.5 Frame Relay DLCIs.

Figure 23.5 shows a full mesh design with three locations: Arizona, California, and Michigan. At each location, the routers have two virtual circuits that enable them to reach the other locations. Now remember, the way DLCIs work is you leave on a local DLCI number rather than access a remote DLCI, so if Arizona wants to reach California, it uses DLCI number 507 to get there. If California wants to get back to Arizona, it uses DLCI 705. Likewise, California uses DLCI 401 to reach the router in Michigan.

Because DLCIs are locally significant, service providers can do whatever they want with them. Take a look at the DLCI connection between Arizona and Michigan. It's not a mistype! Arizona is assigned to use DLCI 508 to reach Michigan. Michigan also uses DLCI 508 to reach Arizona. This seems to make no sense until you realize that the DLCI number 508 means something totally different if it is received in Arizona than if it is received in Michigan. Remember: *locally* significant. The service provider probably has DLCI 508 in use in many locations for many different customers. As long as the set of DLCIs is unique at each location, everything is fine with the Frame Relay standards.

Local Access Rate

The Local Access Rate (commonly called the *line speed*) is the maximum physical speed that your Frame Relay connection can attain. Today's Frame Relay connections can usually reach up to T3 speeds (just over 44Mbps). This maximum can vary depending on the area in which you are and the service provider you are using. This does not define how fast your virtual circuits can travel. That's the job of the Committed Information Rate (which is covered next). However, the accumulation of all the bandwidth on all your virtual circuits can never exceed the router's Local Access Rate.

Committed Information Rate

With a Frame Relay connection, really just two things heavily affect the price of the connection: first, the number of virtual circuits you purchase, and second, the Committed Information Rate (CIR) for each one of those virtual circuits. The CIR is the minimum speed the service provider commits to give you for the circuit at all times. It's your guarantee. Typically, you get more bandwidth than what your CIR dictates, but if the service provider starts running thin on bandwidth allocations, it can contractually cut your location's virtual circuits down to the minimum amount of bandwidth defined by your CIR.

Now here's the major concept: Each PVC you purchase has its own CIR. This can be mind-boggling because you just learned about the Local Access Rate, which defines the maximum physical speed of the connection. Frame Relay enables you to divide up your connections, assigning a CIR for each PVC destination. Take a look at Figure 23.6.

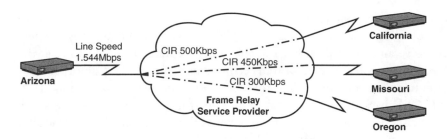

FIGURE 23.6 Frame Relay CIR.

You now have a hub and spoke Frame Relay design where Arizona is connected to California, Missouri, and Oregon. Focus for the moment on Arizona: The Local Access Rate is shown as T1 speed—1.544Mbps. Each PVC has its own CIR: The PVC to California is rated at a CIR of 500Kbps, the PVC to Missouri uses a CIR of 450Kbps, and the connection to Oregon uses a 300Kbps CIR. Notice that the total bandwidth of all the PVCs does not exceed the Local Access Rate of the line. Remember, the CIR is the minimum amount of bandwidth the service provider gives you. If you oversubscribe your Local Access Rate with the sum of all the CIRs, you may be physically limiting how much bandwidth the service provider would be willing to give you (and paying too much for your connection).

Many service providers offer extremely low-cost Frame Relay connections that are rated at a zero CIR. This means that you'll probably get bandwidth, but the service provider does not guarantee anything. When signing up for one of these connections, be sure to use a reputable service provider because some of the smaller service providers may be oversubscribing their network with these connections and not have enough bandwidth to give you a reliable connection.

Backwards Explicit Congestion Notification

Because service providers allow you to burst above your CIR (using more bandwidth than you're paying for), you have the potential of taking advantage of the service provider. If not configured differently, your router will attempt to send across all PVCs at the maximum speed the physical interface can handle (your Local Access Rate). If there is a large mismatch between your CIR and the Local Access Rate, your PVC will soon begin to become congested. The service provider will send messages to the router sending the large amount of traffic attempting to tell it to slow down. This is known as a Backwards Explicit Congestion Notification (BECN) message. The method the service provider uses to send this notification is important to understand.

Because of the way PVCs are engineered, the service provider cannot communicate directly to the router sending the data. Instead, it modifies the headers of return traffic to notify the person sending the excessive amount of data. For example, imagine that you were sitting at the Arizona location (from the prior Figure 23.6) transferring a large file to the California location via FTP. The entire time you are sending this file, the California site is sending TCP Acknowledgments (ACKs) back to confirm the data receipt. If the Arizona site is excessively exceeding the CIR, the service provider flips a bit (known as the BECN bit) in the header of the ACK messages to notify the sender that it needs to slow down.

By default, your Cisco router ignores the BECN message (what audacity!). It does so because BECN response falls under a major configuration called Frame Relay Traffic Shaping, which you'll learn plenty about if you decide to continue on into the CCNP courses. It is to your advantage to drop your speed when you receive a BECN message because the service provider will soon thereafter liquidate the vast majority of your traffic in the Frame Relay cloud, causing drastic performance reductions.

Forward Explicit Congestion Notification

This one is one of the most misunderstood of all Frame Relay terms. After you understand the concept of a BECN, it seems logical to assume a Forward Explicit Congestion Notification (FECN) tells the receiving side of the connection to slow down. This is not true at all. Why would a Frame Relay service provider tell the *receiver* to slow down? It is not sending any traffic, just receiving it. Instead, a FECN message is used to tell the receiver to generate traffic that the service provider can tag with a BECN to tell the sender to slow down. I'm sure you're thinking, "What?!?" Here's an example.

Again, you have a device in Arizona sending traffic to the California location. This time, they are sending an enormous video stream (which uses UDP communication). UDP requires no acknowledgments, so the service provider has no return traffic to mark as a BECN to tell the sender to slow down. Instead, it tags some of the traffic heading to the receiver. This is known as a FECN (it uses the same bit in the header as the BECN, but is interpreted as a FECN because it is sent the other way). If the receiving router is configured to support FECNs, it generates some "junk" (called a Q.922 test frame), puts it in a frame, and sends it back to the sender. The junk in the packet is really junk. The sending router in Arizona drops it after it is received. All it's there for is to give the service provider something to tag to tell Arizona to slow down. So, a FECN message is just a method to generate some traffic so the service provider can send a BECN.

Discard Eligible

This term describes any traffic that you send above the CIR you have purchased. Because you are using bandwidth that you did not pay for, the service provider automatically tags your packets as Discard Eligible (written as D_e—that's D subscript e). Just because a packet is marked D_e doesn't mean it will be discarded. Most of the time it makes it across the Frame

Relay network just fine. What the D_e marking means is if the service provider experiences congestion, guess which packets are the first to go—yep, the packets tagged as D_e.

When you get deeper into Frame Relay traffic shaping (later in your Cisco career), you'll discover that there's a way to mark your own traffic D_e. This enables you to be selective with what traffic is marked D_e rather than use the random selection of the service provider. This can keep your high-priority traffic from being sent above the CIR.

The Nature of NBMA Networks

Objective:

▶ Describe different methods for connecting to a WAN

Frame Relay networks fall under the umbrella of Non-Broadcast Multi-Access (NBMA) networks. As the name implies, these networks allow multiple devices to access the network, but do not allow broadcast between them. Although this is their default behavior, you can configure your Cisco router to treat the network however you'd like. Because NBMA networks allow traffic between only the sites for which you purchase PVCs, this leads to some very odd configurations. The hub and spoke topology can be very confusing to manage until you understand the problems associated with these network types.

One of the major problems that can be encountered is that of running distance vector routing protocols over a Frame Relay network. These routing protocols (which include RIP, IGRP, and even EIGRP) have a built-in loop prevention mechanism called *split-horizon*. This mechanism prevents a router from sending an update out the same interface as that on which it received an update. Figure 23.7 shows where the problems begin with the default Frame Relay configuration.

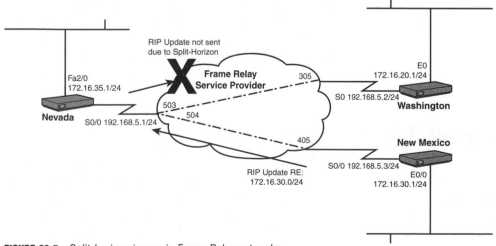

FIGURE 23.7   Split-horizon issues in Frame Relay networks.

This figure shows a typical hub and spoke configuration between Nevada, Washington, and New Mexico. Because this network is so simple, this company has decided to use the RIP routing protocol. Here's how the problem starts: New Mexico sends an RIP routing update to Nevada regarding its 172.16.30.0/24 network. Nevada receives the update coming in its S0 interface. Now the spilt-horizon rule steps in and tells the Nevada router not to send that routing update back out the interface on which it was received. Washington never hears about the 172.16.30.0 network through the RIP protocol and is unable to access any devices at that location. The same thing goes for the Washington network. The advertisement reaches the Nevada router, but is never sent to New Mexico because of the split-horizon rule.

Two methods are used to solve this problem. First, you can disable the split-horizon mechanism altogether. This is a risky move because you are then relying on the other loop prevention mechanisms to keep a loop from happening in the network. The second method is to use subinterfaces.

> **EXAM ALERT**
>
> Know the terminology behind Frame Relay. Especially ensure you understand the CIR and DLCI concepts.

Subinterfaces

Objective:

▶ Describe different methods for connecting to a WAN

Using subinterfaces to solve your split-horizon problem is the best way to go. Subinterfaces enable you to break your single, physical interface into multiple, logical interfaces. You still have only a single physical connection to the Frame Relay service provider, however, your router sees it as multiple connections. There are two categories of Frame Relay subinterfaces: point-to-point and multipoint. Only the point-to-point interface type is designed to fix the split-horizon issue by creating a subinterface for each PVC connection. However, because we're talking about subinterfaces, it would be a good idea to talk about multipoint as well.

Multipoint Subinterfaces

Forgive me for allowing my opinion to get in the way of a neutral CCNA book, but multipoint interfaces are about as useful as a squirt gun for a scuba diver. This subinterface type enables you to have multiple PVCs terminating under a single, logical subinterface. This type of subinterface is how a physical interface behaves if no subinterfaces are created. It still encounters the same split-horizon issues, forcing you to disable split-horizon. You might wonder, "How is this type of subinterface helpful then?" Like I said…squirt gun for a scuba diver. Multipoint subinterfaces can be useful in other, non–Frame Relay deployments, but in Frame Relay they cause more trouble than anything.

Point-to-Point Subinterfaces

This subinterface type enables you to logically design your Frame Relay network as a series of point-to-point connections, no matter how complex your PVC configuration may be. Each PVC circuit is assigned to a single, point-to-point subinterface. This solves the split-horizon issue without much intervention from you because the Cisco router now sees each PVC as its own interface. For example, if a routing update is received on Serial 0, split-horizon blocks that update from being sent back out Serial 0. After you configure point-to-point subinterfaces correctly, the router sees an update come in on one of the subinterfaces, such as Serial 0.10. It has no problem sending that update out another subinterface, such as Serial 0.20, because it sees these interfaces as two, distinct ports.

Address Mapping in Frame Relay

Objective:

▶ Configure and verify Frame Relay on Cisco routers

Frame Relay functions at the Data Link layer of the OSI model. It provides services for the WAN just as ethernet provides services for the LAN. Because everything we do today typically relies on IP addresses, Frame Relay needs to have a way of mapping its Data Link layer address (a DLCI) to a Network layer address (typically an IP address). For example, your router may know that it can reach some location through DLCI 505, but DLCI 505 doesn't really mean anything to your router. Your router works with IP addresses, not DLCI numbers. So to allow DLCI 505 to mean something, your router needs to somehow map this to the IP address that DLCI 505 can reach. There are two methods you can use to accomplish this: Inverse ARP and static mappings.

Inverse ARP

Inverse ARP is the router's automated method to map DLCIs to IP addresses. It works as follows:

1. You connect your router to the Frame Relay service provider through a serial interface.

2. The service provider uses LMI to identify your router and send your router a list of DLCIs it can use to reach your remote sites.

3. Your router sends Inverse ARP messages to each one of these DLCI numbers. This Inverse ARP message carries the simple message, "Hello DLCI! Please send your IP address."

4. The remote router receives the message and responds with its IP address.

5. Your router maps the DLCI number to the IP address it received.

The router sends these Inverse ARP messages to each DLCI number it has received until it has a complete mapping table of DLCI numbers to IP addresses. All along, you as the administrator have done…nothing! This is a completely automated process that makes the Frame Relay setup seamless for small environments. The only drawback to this method is it does not work for subinterfaces. For Inverse ARP to function properly, you must leave all assigned DLCIs under the physical interface, which causes this interface to become a multipoint interface (if you have multiple DLCI numbers). As you have already seen, multipoint interfaces have problems with split-horizon.

Static Mappings

The alternative to allowing Inverse ARP to automatically configure your environment is to use static maps. This method is also specific to multipoint-style interfaces. Using this method, you can manually enter the DLCI to IP address mapping for each PVC. This gives you complete control over the mapping process and enables you to have more than one interface (unlike Inverse ARP). The specifics of this configuration, along with the considerations for point-to-point interfaces, are covered later in this chapter.

> **EXAM ALERT**
>
> Know what the differences are between Inverse ARP Frame Relay configuration and static mappings.

Configuring Frame Relay

Objective:

▶ Configure and verify Frame Relay on Cisco routers

Configuring Frame Relay can be very simple or slightly complex, depending on your network requirements and design. I'd like to walk you through three configuration scenarios, explaining step-by-step how each piece is configured. By the time you're finished here, you'll be a Frame Relay expert. The three configuration scenarios are as follows:

▶ Configuring Frame Relay for a single neighbor

▶ Configuring Frame Relay that uses a multipoint interface

▶ Configuring Frame Relay that uses a point-to-point interface

Configuring Frame Relay for a Single Neighbor

This configuration is the simplest one to set up for Frame Relay. Because the router does most of the work for you in this configuration, many people call this a *Frame Relay auto-configuration*. It is helpful to walk through this configuration step-by-step, first looking at Figure 23.8.

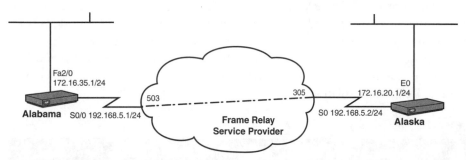

FIGURE 23.8 Simple Frame Relay configuration.

There are two locations in this scenario: Alabama and Alaska. This configuration is really a point-to-point style connection, we're just going through a Frame Relay cloud to accomplish it. Alabama uses DLCI 503 to reach Alaska, and Alaska uses DLCI 305 to reach Alabama. You've already configured the necessary IP addresses for the network requirements; all that's left to do is configure the Frame Relay connection. Let's have at it!

Step 1: Turn on Frame Relay Encapsulation

Start on the Alabama router to get familiar with your surroundings:

```
Alabama#show ip interface brief
Interface       IP-Address      OK? Method Status                Protocol
Serial0/0       192.168.5.1     YES manual administratively down down
Serial0/1       unassigned      YES unset  administratively down down
Serial0/2       unassigned      YES unset  administratively down down
Serial0/3       unassigned      YES unset  administratively down down
FastEthernet2/0 172.16.35.1     YES manual up                    up
```

It looks as though the Fast Ethernet interface is up and running, and the Serial 0/0 interface has an IP address, but needs a little work beyond. First turn on the Frame Relay encapsulation:

```
Alabama#configure terminal
Enter configuration commands, one per line.  End with CNTL/Z.
Alabama(config)#interface serial 0/0
Alabama(config-if)#encapsulation frame-relay ?
  ietf  Use RFC1490/RFC2427 encapsulation
  <cr>

Alabama(config-if)#encapsulation frame-relay
Alabama(config-if)#
```

Take a look at this. When you access the Serial interface and type **encapsulation frame-relay ?**, you are given the option of either hitting the Enter key or adding the `ietf` keyword after the command. If you just press the Enter key, the router uses Cisco proprietary Frame Relay encapsulation. The Cisco proprietary version of encapsulation came out before the industry standard (`ietf`) Frame Relay encapsulation and uses a slightly different method for identifying the Layer 3 protocol (IP, IPX, and so on) that is being encapsulated. This makes it incompatible with the industry standard Frame Relay encapsulation. What it boils down to is this: If you are connecting two Cisco routers over a Frame Relay network, use the command `encapsulation frame-relay` to configure each side. If you are connecting your Cisco router to a non-Cisco device, use the command `encapsulation frame-relay ietf` to use the industry standard Frame Relay encapsulation.

> **EXAM ALERT**
>
> Be sure to know how to configure Frame Relay encapsulation between Cisco and non-Cisco routers.

The example wants to connect two Cisco routers, so you can use the Cisco proprietary encapsulation. Watch what happens when the Serial 0/0 interface on the Alabama router is brought up:

```
Alabama(config-if)#no shutdown
Alabama(config-if)#
*Mar  1 00:23:40.571: %LINK-3-UPDOWN: Interface Serial0/0,
3changed state to up
Alabama(config-if)#
*Mar  1 00:23:51.571: %LINEPROTO-5-UPDOWN: Line protocol on Interface
3Serial0/0, changed state to up
```

It looks like the interface has come up, so now it's time get out to privileged mode and verify that everything is working as expected. The first command you can use to check the connection is `show frame-relay lmi`. Remember, LMI (the Local Management Interface) is the language of love between you and your service provider. The service provider uses this language to send status messages, DLCI information, and line statistics to your local router. This is the lowest level of Frame Relay communication. If it is not working, nothing will be working.

```
Alabama#show frame-relay lmi

LMI Statistics for interface Serial0/0 (Frame Relay DTE) LMI TYPE = CISCO
  Invalid Unnumbered info 0         Invalid Prot Disc 0
  Invalid dummy Call Ref 0          Invalid Msg Type 0
  Invalid Status Message 0          Invalid Lock Shift 0
  Invalid Information ID 0          Invalid Report IE Len 0
  Invalid Report Request 0          Invalid Keep IE Len 0
  Num Status Enq. Sent 36           Num Status msgs Rcvd 35
  Num Update Status Rcvd 0           Num Status Timeouts 1
```

Focus on the key information here, which has been conveniently bolded for you. You can see that you have sent 36 status messages and received 35 messages. This is good. These numbers should be relatively equal and increasing on a steady basis. If the connection is failing, you will see the `Num Status Timeouts` field increment steadily. You can think of these messages as keepalives for your Frame Relay connection. Your router is saying "Hello" to the service provider (`Num Status Enq. Sent`) and the service provider is saying "Hello back" (`Num Status msgs Rcvd`). Now let's move up to the next level.

```
Alabama#show frame-relay pvc

PVC Statistics for interface Serial0/0 (Frame Relay DTE)

                Active      Inactive      Deleted        Static
  Local           0            0             0              0
  Switched        0            0             0              0
  Unused          0            1             0              0

DLCI = 503, DLCI USAGE = UNUSED, PVC STATUS = INACTIVE, INTERFACE =
ÂSerial0/0

  input pkts 0           output pkts 0          in bytes 0
  out bytes 0            dropped pkts 0         in pkts dropped 0
  out pkts dropped 0             out bytes dropped 0
  in FECN pkts 0         in BECN pkts 0         out FECN pkts 0
  out BECN pkts 0        in DE pkts 0           out DE pkts 0
  out bcast pkts 0       out bcast bytes 0
  5 minute input rate 0 bits/sec, 0 packets/sec
  5 minute output rate 0 bits/sec, 0 packets/sec
  switched pkts 0
  Detailed packet drop counters:
  no out intf 0          out intf down 0        no out PVC 0
  in PVC down 0          out PVC down 0         pkt too big 0
  shaping Q full 0       pkt above DE 0         policing drop 0
  pvc create time 00:09:59, last time pvc status changed 00:09:34
```

By using the `show frame-relay pvc` command, you can see all your virtual circuit connections over the Frame Relay cloud. Notice that none of this has been configured. The service provider actually sent the usable DLCI information to you with the LMI signaling! Your router (Alabama) received DLCI 503 from the service provider. Referring back to the network diagram in Figure 23.8, you can see that this is exactly the DLCI information you want to receive. But there seems to be a problem: The DLCI is marked as `INACTIVE`. This is where understanding the four PVC states can come in very handy:

▶ **Active**—A PVC marked as ACTIVE is successfully connected through between the two endpoints (routers). This is the normal state if everything is working properly.

▶ **Inactive**—A PVC marked as INACTIVE is working properly on your end of the connection (the local side); however, the other side of the connection is either not configured or offline.

▶ **Deleted**—A PVC marked as DELETED is having problems at your side (local side) of the connection. Most likely, you are attempting to use a DLCI number that the service provider has not configured.

▶ **Static**—A PVC marked as STATIC has been manually entered by you (the administrator) rather than dynamically discovered from the service provider.

> **EXAM ALERT**
>
> Understanding the states of a PVC can be quite useful in both the real world and the testing environment.

Whew! Quite a bit of information there applies directly to what you are seeing right now. Because the PVC is marked as INACTIVE, it means that your side (Alabama) is working just fine; it's the remote side (Alaska) that is having the problem. This is where you suddenly realize that you are not just the administrator in Alabama, but also the administrator for Alaska as well. You need to jump on a plane (or use a telnet connection) to reach the Alaska router and configure that side of the connection.

```
Alaska#show ip interface brief
Interface       IP-Address      OK? Method Status                 Protocol
Ethernet0       172.16.20.1     YES NVRAM  up                     up
Ethernet1       unassigned      YES unset  administratively down  down
Serial0         192.168.5.2     YES NVRAM  administratively down  down
Serial1         unassigned      YES unset  administratively down  down
```

It looks as if Alaska is in the same state as Alabama was when you first got involved in the configuration. Turn on Frame Relay encapsulation and power on the interface:

```
Alaska#configure terminal
Enter configuration commands, one per line.  End with CNTL/Z.
Alaska(config)#interface serial 0
Alaska(config-if)#encapsulation frame-relay
Alaska(config-if)#no shutdown
Alaska(config-if)#
00:26:42: %LINK-3-UPDOWN: Interface Serial0, changed state to up
00:26:53: %LINEPROTO-5-UPDOWN: Line protocol on Interface Serial0,
3changed state to up
00:28:42: %FR-5-DLCICHANGE: Interface Serial0 - DLCI 305 state
3changed to ACTIVE
```

Take a look at that—the Line Protocol (data link connectivity) on the Serial interface came up and the DLCI 305 went ACTIVE. Now do the same verification commands you did on Alabama to see what things look like:

```
Alaska(config-if)#^Z
Alaska#show frame lmi

LMI Statistics for interface Serial0 (Frame Relay DTE) LMI TYPE = CISCO
    Invalid Unnumbered info 0          Invalid Prot Disc 0
    Invalid dummy Call Ref 0           Invalid Msg Type 0
    Invalid Status Message 0           Invalid Lock Shift 0
    Invalid Information ID 0           Invalid Report IE Len 0
    Invalid Report Request 0           Invalid Keep IE Len 0
    Num Status Enq. Sent 53            Num Status msgs Rcvd 54
    Num Update Status Rcvd 0           Num Status Timeouts 0
Alaska#show frame pvc

PVC Statistics for interface Serial0 (Frame Relay DTE)

DLCI = 305, DLCI USAGE = LOCAL, PVC STATUS = ACTIVE, INTERFACE = Serial0

    input pkts 1          output pkts 1          in bytes 30
    out bytes 30          dropped pkts 0         in FECN pkts 0
    in BECN pkts 0        out FECN pkts 0        out BECN pkts 0
    in DE pkts 0          out DE pkts 0
    out bcast pkts 1      out bcast bytes 30
    pvc create time 00:00:59, last time pvc status changed 00:01:00
```

Right on! The PVC status is now viewed as ACTIVE from the perspective of Alaska, which implicitly implies that Alabama is working as well (because ACTIVE indicates both sides of the connection are working as they should). So, hold your breath—now it's time to do the final test: to ping from Alaska to Alabama, which acts as an end-to-end test of Network layer (Layer 3) connectivity:

```
Alaska#ping 192.168.5.1
Type escape sequence to abort.
Sending 5, 100-byte ICMP Echos to 192.168.5.1, timeout is 2 seconds:
!!!!!
Success rate is 100 percent (5/5), round-trip min/avg/max = 60/60/60 ms
```

YES!!! That's exactly what you want to see. Five exclamation points indicating five successful, round-trip ping messages over the Frame Relay network. Isn't this exciting?

So let me summarize what it took to get a point-to-point Frame Relay connection running:

1. Turn on Frame Relay encapsulation.

That's it! Of course, there are some prerequisite steps, such as assigning IP addresses and turning on the interface. It may have seemed like a bigger process because of the verification commands that were performed. However, if you have just a single connection over the Frame Relay cloud, the service provider sends both sides of the connection their DLCI information through LMI signaling. The router then uses Inverse ARP messages to discover the IP address on the remote end of the connection. After the remote IP address is discovered, the router makes the connection between the local DLCI and remote IP address. Look at one more show command:

```
Alaska#show frame-relay map
Serial0 (up): ip 192.168.5.1 dlci 305(0x131,0x4C10), dynamic,
              broadcast,, status defined, active
```

From the Alaska router's perspective, you can see from using the show frame-relay map command that the router has mapped the Alabama router's IP address (192.168.5.1) to the local DLCI the Alaska router uses to reach that IP address (305). You can also see that this map was dynamically defined, which means that the Cisco router made this link between IP and DLCI numbers with Inverse ARP.

So the key to allowing Cisco routers to configure the Frame Relay connection themselves is to ensure the LMI is working correctly between your router and the service provider, which brings us to the closing point of this section.

If you are using an extremely old version of the IOS (any version earlier than 11.2), the router is unable to auto-detect what LMI language the service provider is using. This means you must manually configure it with the following syntax:

```
Router(config-if)#frame-relay lmi-type ?
  cisco
  ansi
  q933a
```

To determine which LMI signaling you should use, you need to contact your service provider.

EXAM ALERT

Be sure to know the LMI types and be able to pick them out of a line-up. It is also key to remember that "ietf" is a Frame Relay encapsulation type. IETF is not an LMI type.

Configuring Frame Relay That Uses a Multipoint Interface

Now, the scenario has expanded with the addition of another office to the mix. This change is reflected in Figure 23.9.

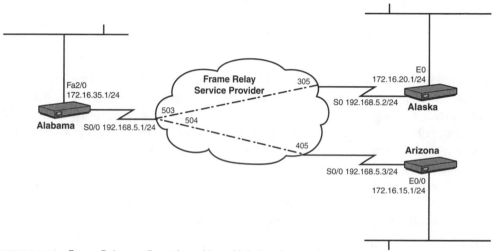

FIGURE 23.9 Frame Relay configuration with multiple locations.

The Arizona office has entered the picture and moved this story to a hub and spoke design. Alabama is the hub of the network, having PVC connections to both Alaska and Arizona. To save on cost, Alaska and Arizona are not directly connected and must use their PVC to Alabama anytime they would like to reach each other. Notice the IP addressing in this figure as well: All routers are configured on the same subnet (192.168.5.0/24) for their WAN connections. This IP addressing tells you that you are using a point-to-multipoint design. The routers think the WAN operates just like an ethernet network where all points connected to the network are able to reach all other points in the network. If you were using a point-to-point design (a much better design, in my humble opinion), each PVC would be on its own subnet, just as if you had point-to-point WAN links through the Frame Relay cloud. The point-to-point design is discussed a little bit later; for now, it's time to focus on making the point-to-multipoint design work successfully.

Configuring a multipoint interface can be done in two ways: You can either place the configuration under the physical interface itself or use a subinterface. Let me demonstrate. You've already done plenty of configuration on the physical interface, just by placing commands directly under the Serial interface. If you want to configure a subinterface, this is how the process looks:

```
Alaska#configure terminal
Enter configuration commands, one per line.  End with CNTL/Z.
Alaska(config)#interface serial 0.?
  <0-4294967295>  Serial interface number

Alaska(config)#interface serial 0.10 ?
  multipoint      Treat as a multipoint link
  point-to-point  Treat as a point-to-point link

Alaska(config)#interface serial 0.10 multipoint
Alaska(config-subif)#
```

In this case, the multipoint subinterface Serial 0.10 has been created. The subinterface number you choose is completely up to you. As you can see, you can use numbers from zero up to slightly more than 4 billion (Cisco is all about flexibility). In this case, I chose 10. If you were using this for your Frame Relay configuration, you could remove all commands from the physical interface (Serial 0) except for the encapsulation frame-relay command and place them under the subinterface. At this point, there's no real advantage to configuring Frame Relay with subinterfaces because you are using a multipoint configuration. After you get to point-to-point, you'll see the many advantages of this configuration. For now, you can save a little complexity and just configure everything under the physical interface.

If you had a full mesh Frame Relay design where every location had a PVC to every other location, this setup would take care of itself just like the previous configuration you saw. Each location would send an Inverse ARP message out on its PVCs and figure out how to connect to everyone else. However, if you look at the figure, you can see that there is no full mesh of virtual circuits. Alabama will work just fine in this design because it has PVCs to each location. Alaska and Arizona are going to have some problems if you just leave everything in its default configuration. The Inverse ARP message will be able to discover Alabama because it is directly at the end of the PVC; however, the Inverse ARP message does not "bounce through." Alaska does not discover Arizona and vice versa. This is where Frame Relay maps come in handy. You can manually configure each site by defining static maps dictating which DLCIs connect to each remote IP address. Even though it is not necessary to manually configure Alabama, it is a good practice not to mix dynamic and static configurations. If you want to use dynamic, it should be in use everywhere. Likewise, if you want to use static, use it everywhere. So the first thing to do is to configure the hub of the network, Alabama:

```
Alabama#configure terminal
Enter configuration commands, one per line.  End with CNTL/Z.
Alabama(config)#interface serial 0/0
Alabama(config-if)#frame-relay map ?
  bridge  Bridging
  ip      IP
  llc2    llc2

Alabama(config-if)#frame-relay map ip ?
```

```
    A.B.C.D  Protocol specific address

Alabama(config-if)#frame-relay map ip 192.168.5.2 ?
  <16-1007>  DLCI

Alabama(config-if)#frame-relay map ip 192.168.5.2 503 ?
  broadcast            Broadcasts should be forwarded to this address
  cisco                Use CISCO Encapsulation
  compress             Enable TCP/IP and RTP/IP header compression
  ietf                 Use RFC1490/RFC2427 Encapsulation
  nocompress           Do not compress TCP/IP headers
  payload-compression  Use payload compression
  rtp                  RTP header compression parameters
  tcp                  TCP header compression parameters
  <cr>

Alabama(config-if)#frame-relay map ip 192.168.5.2 503 broadcast
Alabama(config-if)#frame-relay map ip 192.168.5.3 504 broadcast
```

You've now statically mapped the DLCI numbers to the remote IP addresses. Remember, after you do this, you've overruled the Inverse ARP process; you are now taking the role of Inverse ARP under your belt. Look at the first static map: It tells the router, "If you would like to reach the *remote* IP address 192.168.5.2, use the *local* DLCI number 503." Likewise, the second line says, "To reach the *remote* IP address 192.168.5.3, use the *local* DLCI number 504."

It's also important to talk about the last option added to the syntax, broadcast. By default, your router treats the Frame Relay cloud just like the type of network it is: NBMA. Therefore, your routing protocols (which use multicast and broadcast traffic) will not work over a Frame Relay network. If you would like the router to forward broadcasts over the Frame Relay cloud, attach the broadcast keyword onto the end of the Frame Relay map.

You can also see from the context-sensitive help that you have many other options in addition to the broadcast keyword that you can add to the end of the Frame Relay map. Most of these options deal with the various flavors of compression that you can enable over the Frame Relay network if you wish. However, the other two highlighted options are of key importance. The keywords cisco and ietf define whether the remote router is a Cisco router or some other brand that uses the IETF industry-standard Frame Relay encapsulation. You might have noticed that neither command was entered under the map statement. The Cisco router uses the Cisco Frame Relay encapsulation by default. If you are connecting to non-Cisco routers, be sure to add the ietf keyword to the each map.

Now you can move on to the Alaska and Arizona routers:

```
Alaska#configure terminal
Enter configuration commands, one per line.  End with CNTL/Z.
Alaska(config)#interface serial 0
Alaska(config-if)#frame map ip 192.168.5.1 305 broadcast
```

```
Alaska(config-if)#frame map ip 192.168.5.3 305 broadcast

Arizona#configure terminal
Enter configuration commands, one per line.  End with CNTL/Z.
Arizona(config)#interface serial 0/0
Arizona(config-if)#frame map ip 192.168.5.1 405 broadcast
Arizona(config-if)#frame map ip 192.168.5.2 405 broadcast
```

Take a look at this: On the Arizona and Alaska routers, both remote IP addresses have been mapped to the same DLCI number. This is why you could not use Inverse ARP to solve this whole scenario: It would have detected only the directly connected neighbor—Alabama, in this case. Because I'm still sitting on the Arizona router, I perform the verification from there:

Arizona#**show frame-relay lmi**

```
LMI Statistics for interface Serial0/0 (Frame Relay DTE) LMI TYPE = CISCO
  Invalid Unnumbered info 0        Invalid Prot Disc 0
  Invalid dummy Call Ref 0         Invalid Msg Type 0
  Invalid Status Message 0         Invalid Lock Shift 0
  Invalid Information ID 0         Invalid Report IE Len 0
  Invalid Report Request 0         Invalid Keep IE Len 0
  Num Status Enq. Sent 1336        Num Status msgs Rcvd 1337
  Num Update Status Rcvd 0         Num Status Timeouts 2
  Last Full Status Req 00:00:23    Last Full Status Rcvd 00:00:23
```

It looks like the LMI information is being received successfully. Now examine the PVC status and mappings:

Arizona#**show frame-relay pvc**

```
PVC Statistics for interface Serial0/0 (Frame Relay DTE)
```

	Active	Inactive	Deleted	Static
Local	1	0	0	0
Switched	0	0	0	0
Unused	0	0	0	0

DLCI = 405, DLCI USAGE = **LOCAL, PVC STATUS = ACTIVE**, INTERFACE = Serial0/0

```
  input pkts 0           output pkts 0        in bytes 0
  out bytes 0            dropped pkts 0       in pkts dropped 0
  out pkts dropped 0              out bytes dropped 0
  in FECN pkts 0         in BECN pkts 0       out FECN pkts 0
  out BECN pkts 0        in DE pkts 0         out DE pkts 0
  out bcast pkts 0       out bcast bytes 0
  5 minute input rate 0 bits/sec, 0 packets/sec
  5 minute output rate 0 bits/sec, 0 packets/sec
  pvc create time 00:15:57, last time pvc status changed 00:00:20
```

```
Arizona#show frame-relay map
Serial0/0 (up): ip 192.168.5.1 dlci 405(0x195,0x6450), static,
              broadcast,
              CISCO, status defined, active
Serial0/0 (up): ip 192.168.5.2 dlci 405(0x195,0x6450), static,
              broadcast,
              CISCO, status defined, active
```

Based on the output from the show frame-relay pvc and show frame-relay map commands, it looks like DLCI 405 is ACTIVE and statically mapped to both the remote IP addresses it is able to reach. Because it tests round-trip connectivity, the final ping test verifies that the rest of the locations are configured correctly as well:

```
Arizona#ping 192.168.5.1

Type escape sequence to abort.
Sending 5, 100-byte ICMP Echos to 192.168.5.1, timeout is 2 seconds:
!!!!!
Success rate is 100 percent (5/5), round-trip min/avg/max = 56/58/60 ms

Arizona#ping 192.168.5.2

Type escape sequence to abort.
Sending 5, 100-byte ICMP Echos to 192.168.5.2, timeout is 2 seconds:
!!!!!
Success rate is 100 percent (5/5), round-trip min/avg/max = 116/117/124 ms
```

Take a look at that—successful pings everywhere! However, things are not as peachy as they may seem initially. Compare those round trip times for the two destinations. When the first ping was performed from Arizona to Alabama, the average round-trip response time was 58ms. The second ping went from Arizona to Alaska, and the round-trip response time effectively *doubled*, moving up to 117ms! Although the hub and spoke topologies are very cost effective, they can have devastating effects on delay-sensitive traffic, such as Citrix, Voice over IP, or Video over IP.

Now that the Frame Relay network is working correctly, it may be tempting to walk away cheering and feeling quite fantastic about the general state of your life. However, one more thing needs to be checked. Take a look again at Figure 23.8. Each location has a LAN connection, representing the offices in those locations. Although the Frame Relay network may be humming along, you still need to check the routing tables to ensure each one of these locations is able to reach the other. Behind the scenes, I've configured EIGRP for Autonomous System 100 on each router, sending and receiving advertisements on all interfaces. Look at the routing table on Alabama first:

```
Alabama#show ip route
Codes: C - connected, S - static, R - RIP, M - mobile, B - BGP
       D - EIGRP, EX - EIGRP external, O - OSPF, IA - OSPF inter area
       N1 - OSPF NSSA external type 1, N2 - OSPF NSSA external type 2
```

```
        E1 - OSPF external type 1, E2 - OSPF external type 2
        i - IS-IS, L1 - IS-IS level-1, L2 - IS-IS level-2, ia - IS-IS
        * - candidate default, U - per-user static route, o - ODR
        P - periodic downloaded static route
Gateway of last resort is not set
     172.16.0.0/24 is subnetted, 3 subnets
C       172.16.35.0 is directly connected, FastEthernet2/0
D       172.16.20.0 [90/20537600] via 192.168.5.2, 00:00:35, Serial0/0
D       172.16.15.0 [90/20537600] via 192.168.5.3, 00:00:03, Serial0/0
C    192.168.5.0/24 is directly connected, Serial0/0
```

Whew! Everything looks good. As you can see, the highlighted output shows the Alabama router has learned about the networks in Alaska and Arizona just fine. Just to be certain of things, jump over to Arizona and verify the routing table over there.

```
Arizona#show ip route
Codes: C - connected, S - static, R - RIP, M - mobile, B - BGP
        D - EIGRP, EX - EIGRP external, O - OSPF, IA - OSPF inter area
        N1 - OSPF NSSA external type 1, N2 - OSPF NSSA external type 2
        E1 - OSPF external type 1, E2 - OSPF external type 2
        i - IS-IS, su - IS-IS summary, L1 - IS-IS level-1, L2 - IS-IS level-2
        ia - IS-IS inter area, * - candidate default, U - per-user static
        o - ODR, P - periodic downloaded static route
Gateway of last resort is not set
     172.16.0.0/24 is subnetted, 2 subnets
D       172.16.35.0 [90/2172416] via 192.168.5.1, 00:02:12, Serial0/0
C       172.16.15.0 is directly connected, Ethernet0/0
C    192.168.5.0/24 is directly connected, Serial0/0
```

Uh-oh. That warm, fuzzy feeling is slipping away. It appears that Arizona has learned about only the Alabama network, and is not showing Alaska in the routing table. It's a good idea to verify the Alaska routing table as well.

```
Alaska#show ip route
Codes: C - connected, S - static, I - IGRP, R - RIP, M - mobile, B - BGP
        D - EIGRP, EX - EIGRP external, O - OSPF, IA - OSPF inter area
        N1 - OSPF NSSA external type 1, N2 - OSPF NSSA external type 2
        E1 - OSPF external type 1, E2 - OSPF external type 2, E - EGP
        i - IS-IS, L1 - IS-IS level-1, L2 - IS-IS level-2, * - default
        U - per-user static route, o - ODR
Gateway of last resort is not set
     172.16.0.0/24 is subnetted, 2 subnets
D       172.16.35.0 [90/2172416] via 192.168.5.1, 00:03:22, Serial0
C       172.16.20.0 is directly connected, Ethernet0
C    192.168.5.0/24 is directly connected, Serial0
```

Sure enough, Alaska is not learning about the Arizona network either. You have just experienced the split-horizon routing rule taking effect. The Alabama router is acting as the hub of the network. As it receives incoming routing updates on its Serial 0 interface from the Alaska and Arizona routers, the split-horizon rule jumps in and restricts the Alabama router's capability to send those updates back out of the interface on which it was received. There are two ways to solve this problem. First, you could move from a multipoint configuration to a point-to-point configuration (the safer, more preferred method), or disable the split-horizon routing rule completely (opening yourself up to the potential of routing loops). Remember, these routing rules have been put in place for a reason. Disabling them is like skydiving without a back-up parachute. Most of the time, you should be fine, but just wait until that unusual situation. There may be very little chance of a safe landing.

Because this is a multipoint configuration, you can go ahead and disable the split-horizon features for now. The point-to-point solution is explained in just a moment. You need to be careful to disable split-horizon only at the key points of a network. If you disable it everywhere, you will most certainly end up with routing loops. In this case, you need to disable it at the network hub: Alabama. If you turn it off on this router, the routing updates will be received on the Serial 0 interface and sent right back out the same interface, allowing Arizona and Alaska to hear about each other. Here's how it's done:

```
Alabama#configure terminal
Enter configuration commands, one per line.  End with CNTL/Z.
Alabama(config)#interface serial 0/0
Alabama(config-if)#no ip split-horizon ?
  eigrp  Enhanced Interior Gateway Routing Protocol (EIGRP)
  <cr>
Alabama(config-if)#no ip split-horizon eigrp ?
  <1-65535>  Autonomous system number
Alabama(config-if)#no ip split-horizon eigrp 100
*Mar  1 00:45:29.507: %DUAL-5-NBRCHANGE: IP-EIGRP(0) 100: Neighbor
Â192.168.5.3 (Serial0/0) is down: split horizon changed
*Mar  1 00:45:29.507: destroy peer: 192.168.5.3
*Mar  1 00:45:29.507: %DUAL-5-NBRCHANGE: IP-EIGRP(0) 100: Neighbor
Â192.168.5.2 (Serial0/0) is down: split horizon changed
*Mar  1 00:45:29.507: destroy peer: 192.168.5.2
Alabama(config-if)#
*Mar  1 00:46:19.647: %DUAL-5-NBRCHANGE: IP-EIGRP(0) 100: Neighbor
Â192.168.5.2 (Serial0/0) is up: new adjacency
*Mar  1 00:46:38.111: %DUAL-5-NBRCHANGE: IP-EIGRP(0) 100: Neighbor
Â192.168.5.3 (Serial0/0) is up: new adjacency
```

You can see that turning off split-horizon for the EIGRP routing system caused the neighbors to reset themselves because of the configuration change. Now that they've come back up, you can verify the Alaska and Arizona routing tables:

```
Alaska#show ip route
Codes: C - connected, S - static, I - IGRP, R - RIP, M - mobile, B - BGP
       D - EIGRP, EX - EIGRP external, O - OSPF, IA - OSPF inter area
       N1 - OSPF NSSA external type 1, N2 - OSPF NSSA external type 2
```

```
              E1 - OSPF external type 1, E2 - OSPF external type 2, E - EGP
              i - IS-IS, L1 - IS-IS level-1, L2 - IS-IS level-2, * - default
              U - per-user static route, o - ODR
Gateway of last resort is not set
      172.16.0.0/24 is subnetted, 3 subnets
D        172.16.35.0 [90/2172416] via 192.168.5.1, 00:02:12, Serial0
C        172.16.20.0 is directly connected, Ethernet0
D        172.16.15.0 [90/21049600] via 192.168.5.1, 00:02:12, Serial0
C     192.168.5.0/24 is directly connected, Serial0

Arizona#show ip route
Codes: C - connected, S - static, R - RIP, M - mobile, B - BGP
       D - EIGRP, EX - EIGRP external, O - OSPF, IA - OSPF inter area
       N1 - OSPF NSSA external type 1, N2 - OSPF NSSA external type 2
       E1 - OSPF external type 1, E2 - OSPF external type 2
       i - IS-IS, su - IS-IS summary, L1 - IS-IS level-1, L2 - IS-IS level-2
       ia - IS-IS inter area, * - candidate default, U - per-user static
       o - ODR, P - periodic downloaded static route
Gateway of last resort is not set
      172.16.0.0/24 is subnetted, 3 subnets
D        172.16.35.0 [90/2172416] via 192.168.5.1, 00:02:57, Serial0/0
D        172.16.20.0 [90/21049600] via 192.168.5.1, 00:02:33, Serial0/0
C        172.16.15.0 is directly connected, Ethernet0/0
C     192.168.5.0/24 is directly connected, Serial0/0
```

Excellent! The remote sites are now seeing each other's LAN connections in the routing table. The multipoint Frame Relay configuration is complete.

Configuring Frame Relay That Uses Point-to-Point Interfaces

I'm so excited! All this configuration has led up to this point: my highly suggested and preferred Frame Relay configuration, point-to-point subinterfaces. As you just saw, configuring Frame Relay using multipoint connections can be confusing because you have multiple, non–directly connected sites tied together through a single physical interface. In addition, it can cause some technical problems, primarily with routing protocols. Now, enter point-to-point subinterfaces into the configuration and these problems slowly melt away.

The configuration of point-to-point subinterfaces does require a little more work than multipoint because it requires you to create a logical subinterface for each PVC coming out of your locations. To explain this, let me introduce the next scenario to be configured. It involves setting up a network very similar to the previous, multipoint configuration. This time, a router known as Salmon will be the hub. BlueGill and Trout will act as the spokes. Take a look at the logical diagram in Figure 23.10.

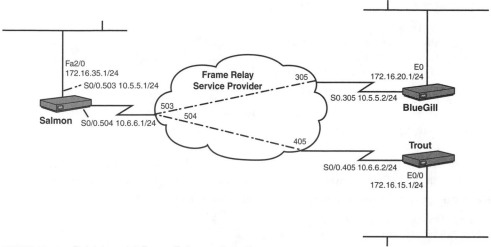

FIGURE 23.10 Point-to-point Frame Relay configuration.

Can you see the difference between the point-to-point and multipoint configurations at the hub router? Instead of having a single IP address and interface connected to the Frame Relay cloud, you now have two *logical subinterfaces* connected to the Frame Relay cloud: Serial0/0.503 and Serial0/0.504. Each one of these subinterfaces is on its own subnet. Now, the split-horizon problems from before are automatically solved through the creation of these subinterfaces. When the router receives a routing update on Serial0/0.503, it has no problem sending it out Serial0/0.504, and vice versa. Now you may argue that it is still sending it out the same physical interface, which is true. However, the router doesn't see it this way. After you create the two subinterfaces, the router sees them as two completely independent connections. The only disadvantage of a point-to-point configuration is that you must configure a separate subnet for each PVC, whereas the multipoint allowed all routers to share a common subnet.

With that foundation in place, let's jump straight into the configuration and fill in the gaps as you go. I'm going to begin with the hub of the network: the great Salmon router. First, familiarize yourself with the surroundings:

```
Salmon#show ip interface brief
Interface          IP-Address      OK? Method Status                Protocol
Serial0/0          unassigned      YES manual up                    up
Serial0/1          unassigned      YES NVRAM  administratively down down
Serial0/2          unassigned      YES NVRAM  administratively down down
Serial0/3          unassigned      YES NVRAM  administratively down down
Ethernet1/0        unassigned      YES NVRAM  administratively down down
FastEthernet2/0    172.16.35.1     YES NVRAM  up                    up
```

Good—the Serial0/0 interface has no IP configuration. Let's begin:

```
Salmon#configure terminal
Enter configuration commands, one per line.  End with CNTL/Z.
Salmon(config)#interface serial 0/0
Salmon(config-if)#encapsulation frame-relay
Salmon(config-if)#exit
Salmon(config)#
*Mar  1 02:06:37.787: %LINEPROTO-5-UPDOWN: Line protocol on
3Interface Serial0/0, changed state to up
```

The first move is to enable Frame Relay encapsulation on the physical interface. Notice that the line protocol immediately comes online. At this point, you are finished with the physical interface configuration. Now you can move to the subinterfaces.

```
Salmon(config)#interface serial 0/0.?
  <0-4294967295>  Serial interface number

Salmon(config)#interface serial 0/0.503 ?
  multipoint      Treat as a multipoint link
  point-to-point  Treat as a point-to-point link

Salmon(config)#interface serial 0/0.503 point-to-point
Salmon(config-subif)#
```

We've just created the subinterface Serial0/0.503 in a point-to-point configuration, as shown in Figure 23.10. The fact that the subinterface number matches the local DLCI used for the connection holds no functional significance whatsoever. It is just a common practice to have your subinterface number match the DLCI number for administrative identification purposes. Now that you are in the subinterface configuration mode, you can set up the logical parameters. This will take just two settings:

```
Salmon(config-subif)#ip address 10.5.5.1 255.255.255.0
Salmon(config-subif)#frame-relay interface-dlci 503
Salmon(config-fr-dlci)#exit
Salmon(config-subif)#exit
Salmon(config)#
```

The two commands necessary assigned the IP address and the local DLCI number to the subinterface. No complex mappings. No broadcast keywords. Just an IP address and DLCI number. Simple is good. Now add the second subinterface to the configuration and verify how everything looks:

```
Salmon(config)#interface serial 0/0.504 point-to-point
Salmon(config-subif)#ip address 10.6.6.1 255.255.255.0
Salmon(config-subif)#frame-relay interface-dlci 504
Salmon(config-fr-dlci)#end
Salmon#
```

```
*Mar  1 02:14:31.287: %SYS-5-CONFIG_I: Configured from console by console
Salmon#show ip interface brief
Interface        IP-Address      OK? Method Status              Protocol
Serial0/0        unassigned      YES manual up                  up
Serial0/0.503    10.5.5.1        YES manual up                  up
Serial0/0.504    10.6.6.1        YES manual up                  up
Serial0/1        unassigned      YES NVRAM  administratively down down
Serial0/2        unassigned      YES NVRAM  administratively down down
Serial0/3        unassigned      YES NVRAM  administratively down down
Ethernet1/0      unassigned      YES NVRAM  administratively down down
FastEthernet2/0  172.16.35.1     YES NVRAM  up                  up
```

Have you ever had a fresh chocolate chip cookie, pulled right out of the oven, cooked to a golden crisp that literally melts in your mouth? That's the only thing that might be better than a configuration like this. Look at that!!! You have two logical subinterfaces configured perfectly on their own subnets. The router also knows what DLCI number it is able to use to reach the other side of the connection. One quick note: Have you been noticing how the router moves you into a DLCI configuration mode after you enter the `frame-relay interface-dlci` command? When you get into the advanced Frame Relay configurations, you will be able to assign certain traffic shaping parameters to each one of those connections that tell the router how fast it should send to each site, among many other things. That's for the CCNP certification. For now, go ahead and bring up the two spoke routers:

```
BlueGill#show ip interface brief
Interface       IP-Address      OK? Method Status              Protocol
Ethernet0       172.16.20.1     YES NVRAM  up                  up
Ethernet1       unassigned      YES unset  administratively down down
Serial0         unassigned      YES NVRAM  up                  down
Serial1         unassigned      YES unset  administratively down down
BlueGill#configure terminal
Enter configuration commands, one per line.  End with CNTL/Z.
BlueGill(config)#interface serial 0
BlueGill(config-if)#encapsulation frame-relay
*Mar  1 02:19:32.011: %LINEPROTO-5-UPDOWN: Line protocol on
ÂInterface Serial0, changed state to up
BlueGill(config-if)#exit
BlueGill(config)#interface serial 0.305 point-to-point
BlueGill(config-subif)#ip address 10.5.5.2 255.255.255.0
BlueGill(config-subif)#frame-relay interface-dlci 305
02:20:18: %FR-5-DLCICHANGE: Interface Serial0 - DLCI 305 state
Âchanged to ACTIVE
BlueGill(config-fr-dlci)#^Z
BlueGill#

Trout#show ip interface brief
Interface        IP-Address      OK? Method Status              Protocol
Ethernet0/0      172.16.15.1     YES NVRAM  up                  up
```

```
Serial0/0              unassigned      YES NVRAM  up          down
Trout#configure terminal
Enter configuration commands, one per line.  End with CNTL/Z.
Trout(config)#interface serial 0/0
Trout(config-if)#encapsulation frame-relay
*Mar  1 02:29:36.081: %LINEPROTO-5-UPDOWN: Line protocol on Interface
ÂSerial0/0, changed state to up
Trout(config-if)#exit
Trout(config)#interface serial 0/0.405 point-to-point
Trout(config-subif)#ip address 10.6.6.2 255.255.255.0
Trout(config-subif)#frame-relay interface-dlci 405
02:33:18: %FR-5-DLCICHANGE: Interface Serial0/0 - DLCI 405 state
Âchanged to ACTIVE
Trout(config-fr-dlci)#^Z
Trout#
```

Did you see those DLCIs go ACTIVE? That's a really good sign that things are working just fine. Behind the scenes, I also configured the EIGRP process on all three routers to include all attached interfaces. Because I'm currently connected to the Trout router, I'll verify everything is working okay from here:

```
Trout#ping 10.6.6.1
Type escape sequence to abort.
Sending 5, 100-byte ICMP Echos to 10.6.6.1, timeout is 2 seconds:
!!!!!
Success rate is 100 percent (5/5), round-trip min/avg/max = 56/58/60 ms

Trout#ping 10.5.5.2
Type escape sequence to abort.
Sending 5, 100-byte ICMP Echos to 10.5.5.2, timeout is 2 seconds:
!!!!!
Success rate is 100 percent (5/5), round-trip min/avg/max = 116/116/117 ms
Trout#show ip route
Codes: C - connected, S - static, R - RIP, M - mobile, B - BGP
       D - EIGRP, EX - EIGRP external, O - OSPF, IA - OSPF inter area
       N1 - OSPF NSSA external type 1, N2 - OSPF NSSA external type 2
       E1 - OSPF external type 1, E2 - OSPF external type 2
       i - IS-IS, su - IS-IS summary, L1 - IS-IS level-1, L2 - IS-IS level-2
       ia - IS-IS inter area, * - candidate default, U - per-user static
       o - ODR, P - periodic downloaded static route
Gateway of last resort is not set
     172.16.0.0/24 is subnetted, 3 subnets
D       172.16.35.0 [90/2172416] via 10.6.6.1, 00:05:21, Serial0/0.405
D       172.16.20.0 [90/21049600] via 10.6.6.1, 00:05:21, Serial0/0.405
C       172.16.15.0 is directly connected, Ethernet0/0
     10.0.0.0/24 is subnetted, 2 subnets
C       10.6.6.0 is directly connected, Serial0/0.405
D       10.5.5.0 [90/21024000] via 10.6.6.1, 00:05:21, Serial0/0.405
```

Sweet! The first ping tested connectivity from the Trout router to the Salmon router. The second ping tested connectivity from the Trout router to the BlueGill router. Finally, by examining the routing table, you can see that the Trout router has already learned about the LANs behind Trout and BlueGill, and has even learned about the PVC between Salmon and BlueGill (this is the last bolded entry in the routing table). This is a key feature of the point-to-point configuration. Because every PVC is seen as its own subnet, routing protocols enable your routers to learn about those connections without requiring the messy maps of multipoint configurations. Just like that, you have a point-to-point Frame Relay configuration.

Verifying Frame Relay

Objective:

▶ Configure and verify Frame Relay on Cisco routers

As you have gone through the three different configurations of Frame Relay, you have really seen the Frame Relay verification commands in action. However, it's time for a formal introduction of the three major commands you use when ensuring all is well with your Frame Relay configuration.

show frame-relay lmi

This command enables you to verify your communication with the Frame Relay service provider.

```
Salmon#show frame-relay lmi
LMI Statistics for interface Serial0/0 (Frame Relay DTE) LMI TYPE = CISCO
  Invalid Unnumbered info 0          Invalid Prot Disc 0
  Invalid dummy Call Ref 0           Invalid Msg Type 0
  Invalid Status Message 0           Invalid Lock Shift 0
  Invalid Information ID 0           Invalid Report IE Len 0
  Invalid Report Request 0           Invalid Keep IE Len 0
  Num Status Enq. Sent 258           Num Status msgs Rcvd 259
  Num Update Status Rcvd 0           Num Status Timeouts 0
  Last Full Status Req 00:00:07      Last Full Status Rcvd 00:00:07
```

Notice that the Num Status Enq. Sent and Num Status msgs Rcvd fields are relatively the same. This indicates that your communication with the service provider is excellent.

show frame-relay pvc

This command enables you to see, in detail, all the PVC connections your router has established through the cloud.

```
Trout#show frame-relay pvc
PVC Statistics for interface Serial0/0 (Frame Relay DTE)
              Active      Inactive      Deleted      Static
  Local         1            0             0            0
  Switched      0            0             0            0
  Unused        0            0             0            0
DLCI = 405, DLCI USAGE = LOCAL, PVC STATUS = ACTIVE, INTERFACE =
ÂSerial0/0.405
  input pkts 643          output pkts 638           in bytes 54196
  out bytes 51074         dropped pkts 0            in pkts dropped 0
  out pkts dropped 0          out bytes dropped 0
  in FECN pkts 0          in BECN pkts 0            out FECN pkts 0
  out BECN pkts 0         in DE pkts 0              out DE pkts 0
  out bcast pkts 624      out bcast bytes 49746
  5 minute input rate 0 bits/sec, 0 packets/sec
  5 minute output rate 0 bits/sec, 0 packets/sec
  pvc create time 00:45:12, last time pvc status changed 00:45:12
```

The main information you'll grab from this output is the status of the circuit (shown here as ACTIVE) and the DLCI number (shown here as 405). It's sometimes nice to see the packet statistics for the PVCs as well to ensure traffic is passing between your locations.

show frame-relay map

This command is my favorite command to verify my Frame Relay circuits.

```
Stitch#show frame-relay map
Serial0/0.405 (up): point-to-point dlci, dlci 405(0x195,0x6450), broadcast
          status defined, active
```

This is the most concise way of finding out your DLCI number and the state of the circuit, without being overwhelmed with all the statistics for the line.

Troubleshooting Frame Relay

Objective:

▶ Troubleshoot WAN implementation issues

Alas, when all is not well with your Frame Relay connections, the debug commands come to the rescue. Thankfully, for most troubleshooting scenarios, there is just one debug command that can expose the problem. Before you get into the debug, though, you'll quickly see that the standard show commands from the verification section can give quite a bit of useful information. Take a look:

```
Stitch#show frame-relay map
Serial0/0.407 (down): point-to-point dlci, dlci 407(0x197,0x6470), broadcast
        status deleted
Serial0/0.405 (up): point-to-point dlci, dlci 405(0x195,0x6450), broadcast
        status defined, active
Serial0/0.406 (down): point-to-point dlci, dlci 406(0x196,0x6460), broadcast
        status defined, inactive
```

Just a simple show frame-relay map command can point you in the initial direction for troubleshooting the circuit. As you can see from the output, there are three different DLCI numbers in three different activity states. First up is DLCI 407, which is in a status of DELETED. This means that the router is attempting to communicate with the service provider through DLCI 407, but the service provider has no idea what the router is talking about. They have no DLCI 407 defined. In this case, the configuration problem is most likely on your own router. Typing the DLCI number incorrectly is one likely cause. Otherwise, the service provider dropped the ball and did not accurately set up the connections. The second DLCI in the list is DLCI 405, which is in a status of ACTIVE. This is a good circuit, going through to the other end of the connection. The final DLCI in the list is DLCI 406, which is in a status of INACTIVE. This means that the end of the connection is configured, and the service provider recognizes the DLCI you are attempting to use. The other end of the connection is where the problem lies. They have either configured an incorrect DLCI or have not configured the interface at all.

Just from this initial output, you can figure out a direction or a location to begin your troubleshooting efforts. Now comes the lower-level debug troubleshooting.

```
Salmon#debug frame-relay lmi
Frame Relay LMI debugging is on
Displaying all Frame Relay LMI data
*Mar  1 00:05:07.215: Serial0/0(out): StEnq, myseq 1, yourseen 0, DTE down
*Mar  1 00:05:07.215: datagramstart = 0x1DA2F74, datagramsize = 14
*Mar  1 00:05:07.215: FR encap = 0x00010308
*Mar  1 00:05:07.215: 00 75 95 01 01 01 03 02 01 00
*Mar  1 00:05:17.215: Serial0/0(out): StEnq, myseq 2, yourseen 0, DTE down
*Mar  1 00:05:17.215: datagramstart = 0x1C01254, datagramsize = 14
*Mar  1 00:05:17.215: FR encap = 0x00010308
*Mar  1 00:05:17.215: 00 75 95 01 01 00 03 02 02 00
*Mar  1 00:05:27.215: Serial0/0(out): StEnq, myseq 3, yourseen 0, DTE down
*Mar  1 00:05:27.215: datagramstart = 0x1DA21B4, datagramsize = 14
*Mar  1 00:05:27.215: FR encap = 0x00010308
*Mar  1 00:05:27.215: 00 75 95 01 01 00 03 02 03 00
*Mar  1 00:05:37.215: Serial0/0(out): StEnq, myseq 4, yourseen 0, DTE down
*Mar  1 00:05:37.215: datagramstart = 0x1C00494, datagramsize = 14
*Mar  1 00:05:37.215: FR encap = 0x00010308
*Mar  1 00:05:37.215: 00 75 95 01 01 00 03 02 04 00
```

The most useful debug is typically the debug frame-relay lmi because this focuses on your direct communication with the service provider. At first, this output looks quite cryptic, but take a look at the highlighted information. You can see the sequence numbers increasing on your end (that's the myseq field), but the service provider doesn't see this. This most likely indicates that the Frame Relay LMI language is mismatched between you and the service provider. Here's how to fix the problem:

```
Salmon#show frame-relay lmi

LMI Statistics for interface Serial0/0 (Frame Relay DTE) LMI TYPE = ANSI
  Invalid Unnumbered info 0          Invalid Prot Disc 0
  Invalid dummy Call Ref 0           Invalid Msg Type 0
  Invalid Status Message 0           Invalid Lock Shift 0
  Invalid Information ID 0           Invalid Report IE Len 0
  Invalid Report Request 0           Invalid Keep IE Len 0
  Num Status Enq. Sent 49            Num Status msgs Rcvd 14
  Num Update Status Rcvd 0           Num Status Timeouts 34
Salmon#configure terminal
Enter configuration commands, one per line.  End with CNTL/Z.
Salmon(config)#interface serial 0/0
Salmon(config-if)#
*Mar  1 00:08:47.215: Serial0/0(out): StEnq, myseq 23, yourseen 0, DTE down
*Mar  1 00:08:47.215: datagramstart = 0x1C019D4, datagramsize = 14
*Mar  1 00:08:47.215: FR encap = 0x00010308
*Mar  1 00:08:47.215: 00 75 95 01 01 00 03 02 17 00
*Mar  1 00:08:47.215:
Salmon(config-if)#frame lmi-type cisco
*Mar  1 00:08:57.215: Serial0/0(out): StEnq, myseq 1, yourseen 0, DTE down
*Mar  1 00:08:57.215: datagramstart = 0x1DA2BB4, datagramsize = 13
*Mar  1 00:08:57.215: FR encap = 0xFCF10309
*Mar  1 00:08:57.215: 00 75 01 01 00 03 02 01 00
*Mar  1 00:08:57.227: Serial0/0(in): Status, myseq 1
*Mar  1 00:08:57.227: RT IE 1, length 1, type 0
*Mar  1 00:08:57.227: KA IE 3, length 2, yourseq 1 , myseq 1
*Mar  1 00:08:57.227: PVC IE 0x7 , length 0x6 , dlci 503, status 0x0 , bw 0
*Mar  1 00:08:57.227: PVC IE 0x7 , length 0x6 , dlci 504, status 0x0 , bw 0
*Mar  1 00:09:07.215: Serial0/0(out): StEnq, myseq 2, yourseen 1, DTE down
*Mar  1 00:09:07.215: datagramstart = 0x1DA22F4, datagramsize = 13
*Mar  1 00:09:07.215: FR encap = 0xFCF10309
*Mar  1 00:09:07.215: 00 75 01 01 01 03 02 02 01
*Mar  1 00:09:07.235: Serial0/0(in): Status, myseq 2
*Mar  1 00:09:07.235: RT IE 1, length 1, type 0
*Mar  1 00:09:07.235: KA IE 3, length 2, yourseq 2 , myseq 2
*Mar  1 00:09:07.235: PVC IE 0x7 , length 0x6 , dlci 503, status 0x0 , bw 0
*Mar  1 00:09:07.235: PVC IE 0x7 , length 0x6 , dlci 504, status 0x0 , bw 0
```

Sure enough, you saw that the LMI type was hard-coded as ANSI. After it was changed over to Cisco, the debug showed the sequence numbers matching up between your router and the service provider. Right after the sequence number synchronization, the service provider's router delivers the DLCI information to your router. This is where it pays to know the status codes. These are not covered on the CCNA exam, but are tested on when you get into the CCNP level exams:

Status 0x0 = INACTIVE

Status 0x2 = ACTIVE

Status 0x4 = DELETED

In this case, you can see that both DLCI 503 and 504 are marked as INACTIVE.

Most of the Frame Relay troubleshooting comes from a misconfiguration of the Frame Relay DLCI. It's very easy to map the wrong DLCI to the wrong IP address because Frame Relay uses a very different addressing perspective than most other networking technologies. Understanding the Frame Relay circuit states can really help in isolating the problem quickly.

Chapter Summary

This chapter has taken you from the basics of Frame Relay into a fairly complex configuration using subinterfaces. The steepest part of the learning curve in the Frame Relay world is in trying to understand the terminology. Frame Relay uses a new set of Layer 2 addresses known as DLCIs. These are your logical addresses, which enable you to communicate with remote devices over the Frame Relay cloud. Unlike typical addressing, DLCIs work through a localized system—that is, you leave on a local DLCI to reach a remote destination over a PVC. This PVC is established for you by a service provider (after you have paid an excessive amount of money) and is one of the primary criteria that determine your monthly cost for the line. The other cost-affecting criterion is the CIR you purchase for each circuit. This is the speed that the service provider commits to give you for each PVC you purchase. Many times, you will be able to burst above this speed if extra bandwidth is available.

After you understand the terminology of Frame Relay, you have three different configuration options. For simple network designs, you can let the Inverse ARP system take care of the Frame Relay setup for you. If you just enable Frame Relay encapsulation on your Serial interface, the router can configure itself. It does this by using LMI signaling to receive all its DLCI information from the service provider. The router can then use Inverse ARP to discover the remote devices. As your network becomes more advanced and uses multiple virtual circuits, you can rely on a multipoint or point-to-point configuration. The advantage of multipoint is that all the routers connected to the Frame Relay cloud can share a common subnet. The major problem with this configuration comes from the routing loop prevention mechanism split-horizon. This prevents a router from sending a routing update out the same interface as that over which it was received. Coming to the rescue are point-to-point subinterfaces. These enable you to statically assign a DLCI number to a dedicated subinterface. Because each PVC has its own subinterface, there are no problems with split-horizon.

Key Terms

- ▶ virtual circuit

- ▶ permanent virtual circuit (PVC)

- ▶ switched virtual circuit (SVC)

- ▶ hub and spoke design

- ▶ partial mesh design

- ▶ full mesh design

- ▶ Local Management Interface (LMI)

- ▶ Data Link Connection Identifier (DLCI)

- ▶ local access rate/line speed

- ▶ Committed Information Rate (CIR)

- ▶ Backwards Explicit Congestion Notification (BECN)

- ▶ Forward Explicit Congestion Notification (FECN)

- ▶ Discard Eligible (D_e)

- ▶ Non-Broadcast Multi-Access (NBMA)

- ▶ split-horizon

- ▶ point-to-point subinterfaces

- ▶ point-to-multipoint/multipoint subinterfaces

- ▶ Frame Relay map

- ▶ inverse ARP

- ▶ static mappings

- ▶ Cisco Frame Relay encapsulation

- ▶ IETF Frame Relay encapsulation

- ▶ ACTIVE, INACTIVE, and DELETED PVC status

- ▶ Cisco, ANSI, and Q933A LMI signaling

Apply Your Knowledge

Exercises

23.1 Configuring Frame Relay in a Partial Mesh Environment

Trees Unlimited Inc., a well-to-do lumber company, has offered you an exorbitant amount of money to convert their point-to-point T1 infrastructure into a partial mesh Frame Relay environment. They have four locations with a variety of connectivity requirements. The circuits have been installed and provisioned at each of their four locations, shown in Figure 23.11.

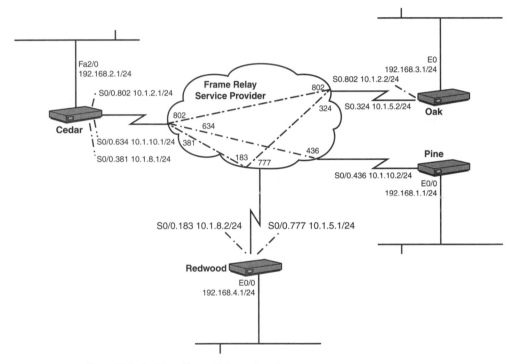

FIGURE 23.11 Trees Unlimited Inc. Frame Relay network.

Your goal is to configure the Frame Relay network as shown in the network diagram. You also need to enable EIGRP routing for autonomous system 50 for all networks to ensure routes are accurately advertised around the network.

Estimated Time: 15–20 minutes

Wow! What a scenario! It looks overwhelming at first. Take this one router at a time, starting with the hub of the network: Cedar. As shown in this diagram, it's clear that the network designer decided to go with a point-to-point setup because every PVC is assigned its own subnet. Also, take a look at the PVC between the Cedar and Oak routers. That's not a misprint! It is a common practice for Frame Relay service providers to use the same DLCI number on both sides of the connection. Because DLCIs are locally significant, accessing DLCI 802 at the Cedar location means something completely different than accessing DLCI 802 at the Oak location. With those prerequisites in place, you can jump right into the configuration:

```
Cedar#show ip interface brief
Interface       IP-Address    OK? Method Status                 Protocol
Serial0/0       unassigned    YES NVRAM  up                     down
Serial0/1       unassigned    YES NVRAM  administratively down  down
Serial0/2       unassigned    YES NVRAM  administratively down  down
Serial0/3       unassigned    YES NVRAM  administratively down  down
Ethernet1/0     unassigned    YES NVRAM  administratively down  down
FastEthernet2/0 192.168.2.1   YES manual up                     up
Cedar#configure terminal
Enter configuration commands, one per line.  End with CNTL/Z.
Cedar(config)#interface serial 0/0
Cedar(config-if)#encapsulation frame-relay
Cedar(config-if)#exit
*Mar  1 00:03:40.059: %LINEPROTO-5-UPDOWN: Line protocol on Interface
3Serial0/0, changed state to up
Cedar(config)#interface serial 0/0.802 point-to-point
Cedar(config-subif)#ip address 10.1.2.1 255.255.255.0
Cedar(config-subif)#frame-relay interface-dlci 802
Cedar(config-fr-dlci)#exit
Cedar(config-subif)#exit
Cedar(config)#interface serial 0/0.634 point-to-point
Cedar(config-subif)#ip address 10.1.10.1 255.255.255.0
Cedar(config-subif)#frame-relay interface-dlci 634
Cedar(config-fr-dlci)#exit
Cedar(config-subif)#exit
Cedar(config)#interface serial 0/0.381 point-to-point
Cedar(config-subif)#ip address 10.1.8.1 255.255.255.0
Cedar(config-subif)#frame-relay interface-dlci 381
Cedar(config-fr-dlci)#exit
Cedar(config-subif)#exit
Cedar(config)#router eigrp 50
Cedar(config-router)#network 10.0.0.0
Cedar(config-router)#network 192.168.2.0
Cedar(config-router)#no auto-summary
Cedar(config-router)#exit
Cedar(config)#exit
*Mar  1 00:05:17.535: %SYS-5-CONFIG_I: Configured from console by
3console
Cedar#show ip interface brief
```

```
Interface          IP-Address     OK? Method Status               Protocol
Serial0/0          unassigned     YES NVRAM  up                   up
Serial0/0.381      10.1.8.1       YES manual down                 down
Serial0/0.634      10.1.10.1      YES manual up                   up
Serial0/0.802      10.1.2.1       YES manual down                 down
Serial0/1          unassigned     YES NVRAM  administratively down down
Serial0/2          unassigned     YES NVRAM  administratively down down
Serial0/3          unassigned     YES NVRAM  administratively down down
Ethernet1/0        unassigned     YES NVRAM  administratively down down
FastEthernet2/0    192.168.2.1    YES manual up                   up
```

Initially, it may look like there is a problem here. Only one of the subinterfaces has come up, but when you look back at the network diagram (in Figure 23.11), you can see that subinterface Serial0/0.634 on the Cedar router connects down to the Pine router. Pine happens to be the only router that does not have multiple PVC connections. In this case, Inverse ARP took care of the mapping on that side of the connection, which brings the interface up. The rest of them require the remote router be configured before the operational status goes active. Before you leave the Cedar router, you need to do one more verification command:

```
Cedar#show frame-relay pvc

PVC Statistics for interface Serial0/0 (Frame Relay DTE)

              Active      Inactive      Deleted       Static
  Local         0            3             0             0
  Switched      0            0             0             0
  Unused        0            0             0             0

DLCI = 381, DLCI USAGE = LOCAL, PVC STATUS = INACTIVE, INTERFACE =
ÂSerial0/0.381

    input pkts 0           output pkts 0          in bytes 0
    out bytes 0            dropped pkts 0         in pkts dropped 0
    out pkts dropped 0          out bytes dropped 0
    in FECN pkts 0         in BECN pkts 0         out FECN pkts 0
    out BECN pkts 0        in DE pkts 0           out DE pkts 0
    out bcast pkts 0       out bcast bytes 0
    5 minute input rate 0 bits/sec, 0 packets/sec
    5 minute output rate 0 bits/sec, 0 packets/sec
    pvc create time 00:06:56, last time pvc status changed 00:06:56

DLCI = 634, DLCI USAGE = LOCAL, PVC STATUS = INACTIVE, INTERFACE =
ÂSerial0/0.634

    input pkts 0           output pkts 86         in bytes 0
    out bytes 14864        dropped pkts 0         in pkts dropped 0
    out pkts dropped 0          out bytes dropped 0
    in FECN pkts 0         in BECN pkts 0         out FECN pkts 0
    out BECN pkts 0        in DE pkts 0           out DE pkts 0
    out bcast pkts 86      out bcast bytes 14864
```

```
5 minute input rate 0 bits/sec, 0 packets/sec
5 minute output rate 0 bits/sec, 0 packets/sec
pvc create time 00:06:58, last time pvc status changed 00:00:08

DLCI = 802, DLCI USAGE = LOCAL, PVC STATUS = INACTIVE, INTERFACE =
➥Serial0/0.802

  input pkts 0            output pkts 0          in bytes 0
  out bytes 0            dropped pkts 0          in pkts dropped 0
  out pkts dropped 0          out bytes dropped 0
  in FECN pkts 0         in BECN pkts 0          out FECN pkts 0
  out BECN pkts 0        in DE pkts 0            out DE pkts 0
  out bcast pkts 0          out bcast bytes 0
  5 minute input rate 0 bits/sec, 0 packets/sec
  5 minute output rate 0 bits/sec, 0 packets/sec
  pvc create time 00:06:59, last time pvc status changed 00:06:59
```

Just as expected: Every DLCI is marked as INACTIVE. This is actually good news: It says that the remote side is not configured correctly; however, your side is configured just fine (otherwise the PVC status would be set to DELETED). Now move on to the Oak location.

```
Oak#show ip interface brief
Interface      IP-Address    OK? Method Status               Protocol
Ethernet0      192.168.3.1   YES manual up                   up
Ethernet1      unassigned    YES unset  administratively down down
Serial0        unassigned    YES unset  up                   down
Serial1        unassigned    YES unset  administratively down down
Oak#configure terminal
Enter configuration commands, one per line.  End with CNTL/Z.
Oak(config)#interface serial 0
Oak(config-if)#encapsulation frame-relay
Oak(config-if)#exit
00:20:01: %LINEPROTO-5-UPDOWN: Line protocol on Interface Serial0,
3changed state to up
00:20:02: %LINK-3-UPDOWN: Interface Serial0, changed state to up
00:20:02: %FR-5-DLCICHANGE: Interface Serial0 - DLCI 802 state
3changed to ACTIVE
Oak(config)#interface serial 0.802 point-to-point
Oak(config-subif)#ip address 10.1.2.2 255.255.255.0
Oak(config-subif)#frame-relay interface-dlci 802
Oak(config-fr-dlci)#exit
Oak(config-subif)#exit
Oak(config)#interface serial 0.324 point-to-point
Oak(config-subif)#ip address 10.1.5.2 255.255.255.0
Oak(config-subif)#frame-relay interface-dlci 324
00:20:57: %LINEPROTO-5-UPDOWN: Line protocol on Interface Serial0.324,
3changed state to down
Oak(config-fr-dlci)#exit
Oak(config-subif)#exit
```

```
Oak(config)#router eigrp 50
Oak(config-router)#network 10.0.0.0
Oak(config-router)#network 192.168.3.0
Oak(config-router)#no auto-summary
Oak(config-router)#exit
Oak(config)#exit
00:21:19: %SYS-5-CONFIG_I: Configured from console by console
Oak#show ip interface brief
Interface    IP-Address   OK? Method Status               Protocol
Ethernet0    192.168.3.1  YES manual up                   up
Ethernet1    unassigned   YES unset  administratively down down
Serial0      unassigned   YES unset  up                   up
Serial0.324  10.1.5.2     YES manual down                 down
Serial0.802  10.1.2.2     YES manual up                   up
Serial1      unassigned   YES unset  administratively down down
Oak#ping 10.1.2.1

Type escape sequence to abort.
Sending 5, 100-byte ICMP Echos to 10.1.2.1, timeout is 2 seconds:
!!!!!
Success rate is 100 percent (5/5), round-trip min/avg/max = 60/60/60 ms
```

Nice. Now you can ping successfully between the Oak and Cedar locations because you have configured both sides of the connection. Did you notice that DLCI 802 went ACTIVE as soon as you turned on Frame Relay encapsulation? The Oak router used Inverse ARP to detect that the Cedar router had been configured on the other end of the connection. Now you can continue around the network diagram in a clockwise fashion and set up the Pine router.

```
Pine#show ip interface brief
Interface    IP-Address   OK? Method Status               Protocol
Ethernet0/0  192.168.1.1  YES manual up                   up
Serial0/0    unassigned   YES NVRAM  up                   down
Pine#configure terminal
Enter configuration commands, one per line.  End with CNTL/Z.
Pine(config)#interface serial 0/0
Pine(config-if)#encapsulation frame-relay
Pine(config-if)#exit
*Mar  1 00:22:51.147: %LINEPROTO-5-UPDOWN: Line protocol on Interface
3Serial0/0, changed state to up
Pine(config)#interface serial 0/0.436 point-to-point
Pine(config-subif)#ip address 10.1.10.2 255.255.255.0
Pine(config-subif)#frame-relay interface-dlci 436
Pine(config-fr-dlci)#exit
Pine(config-subif)#exit
Pine(config)#router eigrp 50
Pine(config-router)#network 10.0.0.0
Pine(config-router)#network 192.168.1.0
```

```
Pine(config-router)#no auto-summary
Pine(config-router)#exit
Pine(config)#
Pine(config)#exit
*Mar  1 00:23:45.504: %SYS-5-CONFIG_I: Configured from console by
3console
Pine#show ip interface brief
Interface        IP-Address      OK? Method Status        Protocol
Ethernet0/0      192.168.1.1     YES manual up            up
Serial0/0        unassigned      YES NVRAM  up            up
Serial0/0.436    10.1.10.2       YES manual up            up
Pine#ping 10.1.10.1

Type escape sequence to abort.
Sending 5, 100-byte ICMP Echos to 10.1.10.1, timeout is 2 seconds:
!!!!!
Success rate is 100 percent (5/5), round-trip min/avg/max = 56/57/60 ms
```

Excellent. You can ping to the Cedar router. You now have three routers configured in this story; take a moment to check the routing table and see whether EIGRP is doing its job:

```
Pine#show ip route
Codes: C - connected, S - static, R - RIP, M - mobile, B - BGP
       D - EIGRP, EX - EIGRP external, O - OSPF, IA - OSPF inter area
       N1 - OSPF NSSA external type 1, N2 - OSPF NSSA external type 2
       E1 - OSPF external type 1, E2 - OSPF external type 2
       i - IS-IS, su - IS-IS summary, L1 - IS-IS level-1, L2 - IS-IS
       ia - IS-IS inter area, * - candidate default, U - per-user static
       o - ODR, P - periodic downloaded static route

Gateway of last resort is not set

     10.0.0.0/24 is subnetted, 2 subnets
C       10.1.10.0 is directly connected, Serial0/0.436
D       10.1.2.0 [90/21024000] via 10.1.10.1, 00:02:02, Serial0/0.436
C    192.168.1.0/24 is directly connected, Ethernet0/0
D    192.168.2.0/24 [90/2172416] via 10.1.10.1, 00:02:02, Serial0/0.436
D    192.168.3.0/24 [90/21049600] via 10.1.10.1, 00:02:02, Serial0/0.436
Pine#ping 192.168.3.1

Type escape sequence to abort.
Sending 5, 100-byte ICMP Echos to 192.168.3.1, timeout is 2 seconds:
!!!!!
Success rate is 100 percent (5/5), round-trip min/avg/max = 116/116/117 ms
```

Everything looks good here! Just for fun, I sent a ping from the Pine router over to the LAN interface of Oak and it looks as sweet as...well, a chocolate chip cookie. Now take on the final router configuration:

```
Redwood#show ip interface brief
Interface        IP-Address      OK? Method Status        Protocol
Ethernet0/0      192.168.4.1     YES manual up            up
Serial0/0        unassigned      YES unset  up            down
Redwood#configure terminal
Enter configuration commands, one per line.  End with CNTL/Z.
Redwood(config)#interface serial 0/0
Redwood(config-if)#encapsulation frame-relay
Redwood(config-if)#exit
*Mar  1 00:35:28.484: %LINEPROTO-5-UPDOWN: Line protocol on Interface
3Serial0/0, changed state to up
Redwood(config)#interface serial 0/0.183 point-to-point
Redwood(config-subif)#ip address 10.1.8.2 255.255.255.0
Redwood(config-subif)#frame-relay interface-dlci 183
Redwood(config-fr-dlci)#exit
Redwood(config-subif)#exit
Redwood(config)#interface serial 0/0.777 point-to-point
Redwood(config-subif)#ip address 10.1.5.1 255.255.255.0
Redwood(config-subif)#frame-relay interface-dlci 777
Redwood(config-fr-dlci)#exit
Redwood(config-subif)#exit
Redwood(config)#router eigrp 50
Redwood(config-router)#network 10.0.0.0
*Mar  1 00:37:12.411: %DUAL-5-NBRCHANGE: IP-EIGRP(0) 50: Neighbor 10.1.8.1
(Serial0/0.183) is up: new adjacency
*Mar  1 00:37:14.714: %DUAL-5-NBRCHANGE: IP-EIGRP(0) 50: Neighbor 10.1.5.2
(Serial0/0.777) is up: new adjacency
Redwood(config-router)#network 192.168.4.0
Redwood(config-router)#no auto-summary
Redwood(config-router)#^Z
Redwood#
*Mar  1 00:37:30.316: %SYS-5-CONFIG_I: Configured from console by console
Redwood#show ip interface brief
Interface        IP-Address      OK? Method Status        Protocol
Ethernet0/0      192.168.4.1     YES manual up            up
Serial0/0        unassigned      YES unset  up            up
Serial0/0.183    10.1.8.2        YES manual up            up
Serial0/0.777    10.1.5.1        YES manual up            up
Redwood#show ip route
Codes: C - connected, S - static, R - RIP, M - mobile, B - BGP
       D - EIGRP, EX - EIGRP external, O - OSPF, IA - OSPF inter area
       N1 - OSPF NSSA external type 1, N2 - OSPF NSSA external type 2
       E1 - OSPF external type 1, E2 - OSPF external type 2
       i - IS-IS, su - IS-IS summary, L1 - IS-IS level-1, L2 - IS-IS
       ia - IS-IS inter area, * - candidate default, U - per-user static
       o - ODR, P - periodic downloaded static route

Gateway of last resort is not set
```

```
C    192.168.4.0/24 is directly connected, Ethernet0/0
     10.0.0.0/24 is subnetted, 4 subnets
D       10.1.10.0 [90/21024000] via 10.1.8.1, 00:00:12, Serial0/0.183
C       10.1.8.0 is directly connected, Serial0/0.183
D       10.1.2.0 [90/2681856] via 10.1.5.2, 00:00:12, Serial0/0.777
C       10.1.5.0 is directly connected, Serial0/0.777
D    192.168.1.0/24 [90/21049600] via 10.1.8.1, 00:00:12, Serial0/0.183
D    192.168.2.0/24 [90/2172416] via 10.1.8.1, 00:00:12, Serial0/0.183
D    192.168.3.0/24 [90/2195456] via 10.1.5.2, 00:00:13, Serial0/0.777
```

Well, it looks like your work here is done. All that's left to do is to collect that exorbitant check from the wealthy tree company!

Review Questions

1. There are three virtual circuit design strategies for a Frame Relay cloud. Explain what these are and the advantages and disadvantages associated with each.

2. Write a brief definition for the following terms:

    ▶ Local Management Interface

    ▶ Data Link Connection Identifier

    ▶ Local Access Rate

    ▶ Committed Information Rate

3. When you connect a router to a Frame Relay network, the service provider transmits DLCI information to your router via LMI. How does the router then find the Layer 3 address to associate with the circuit?

4. When connecting a router to a Frame Relay network with multiple destinations, split-horizon issues can occur. Explain why this is and the two methods you could use to fix these issues.

5. You are troubleshooting a Frame Relay network. It appears that your router is not receiving any DLCI information. What command(s) would you use to begin troubleshooting this problem and why?

Exam Questions

1. Into what categories of network does Frame Relay fit? (Choose 2.)

    ○ **A.** Circuit-switched

    ○ **B.** Packet-switched

    ○ **C.** Broadcast multi-access

    ○ **D.** NBMA

2. Which of the following connections describe an on-demand circuit through the Frame Relay cloud that is created when needed and then destroyed after data has been transmitted?

   ○ **A.** PVC

   ○ **B.** SVC

   ○ **C.** DID

   ○ **D.** DOD

3. Which of the following are valid LMI signaling types? (Choose 3.)

   ○ **A.** Cisco

   ○ **B.** IETF

   ○ **C.** ANSI

   ○ **D.** Q.933a

4. According to Figure 23.12, what DLCI would be used if a client in Minnesota wanted to send information to a server in California?

   ○ **A.** 501

   ○ **B.** 502

   ○ **C.** 601

   ○ **D.** 602

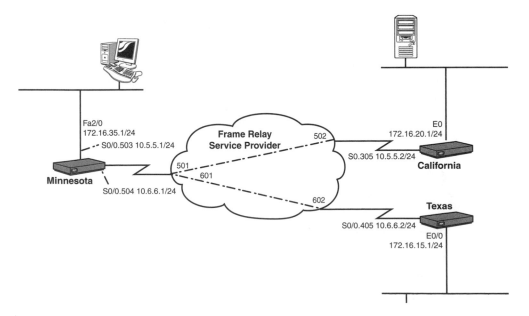

5. A router connected to a Frame Relay service provider can occasionally send faster than the subscribed _____, but never faster than the _____.

- ○ **A.** Local Access Rate, CIR
- ○ **B.** Virtual Circuit Speed, CIR
- ○ **C.** CIR, Virtual Circuit Speed
- ○ **D.** CIR, Local Access Rate

6. If your router is sending too much information into the Frame Relay cloud, the service provider tags any return traffic with a _____ to notify your router to reduce its transmission rate.

- ○ **A.** D_e
- ○ **B.** BECN
- ○ **C.** FECN
- ○ **D.** Burst

7. By default, Cisco routers receive LMI messages from the service provider that provide all usable DLCI numbers for the local circuit. How does your router find out the remote devices it is able to reach?

- ○ **A.** The router sends Hello messages down each virtual circuit.
- ○ **B.** The router uses CDP to discover its directly connected neighbors.
- ○ **C.** The router uses Inverse ARP messages.
- ○ **D.** The router does not need to do anything; LMI signaling from the service provider auto-configures the router.

8. You have two routers connected over a Frame Relay network. The router in Arizona has the IP address 10.1.1.1/24 and uses a local DLCI of 512. The router in Michigan has the IP address 10.1.1.2/24 and uses a local DLCI of 598. Which syntax among the following choices correctly creates a static map that enables Arizona to reach Michigan and allows routing protocol functionality?

- ○ **A.** frame-relay map ip 10.1.1.2 512 broadcast
- ○ **B.** frame-relay map ip 10.1.1.1 512 broadcast
- ○ **C.** frame-relay map ip 10.1.1.2 598 broadcast
- ○ **D.** frame-relay map ip 10.1.1.1 598 broadcast

9. You are configuring your router's Serial 0 interface to communicate across the Frame Relay cloud with a non-Cisco router. You would like to use the Inverse ARP feature of the router to avoid configuring static maps; what command would you use to enable this feature?

   ○ **A.** encapsulation frame-relay

   ○ **B.** inverse-arp frame-relay

   ○ **C.** ietf inverse-arp

   ○ **D.** encapsulation frame-relay ietf

10. You are troubleshooting your Frame Relay connections. After typing in the show frame-relay pvc command, one of your PVCs shows up as DELETED. What causes this?

   ○ **A.** Your router is incorrectly configured. You need to add the right DLCI information and the circuit should come up.

   ○ **B.** The remote router is incorrectly configured.

   ○ **C.** You are physically disconnected from the service provider.

   ○ **D.** You need to switch from a multipoint configuration to a point-to-point configuration and create a subinterface for each PVC you plan on using.

Answers to Review Questions

1. The three Frame Relay virtual circuit design strategies are hub and spoke, partial mesh, and full mesh. Hub and spoke is the cheapest design; however, it also offers the least amount of redundancy. If the hub location fails, the entire WAN mesh goes down. In addition, the hub and spoke design increases the amount of delay for packets traveling between the spoke locations. This can be devastating for VoIP traffic. Partial mesh designs connect key sites with multiple virtual circuits. This offers redundancy for those key locations, but can become a more costly design. Full mesh offers the ultimate level of redundancy and delay guarantees, but requires a huge monthly cost to support the large number of circuits.

2. Local Management Interface (LMI): This is the language spoken between your Frame Relay router and the service provider that is used to provide DLCI status and traffic statistics.

   Data Link Connection Identifier (DLCI): This is the Data Link address used to identify virtual circuits in the Frame Relay cloud.

   Local Access Rate: This is the maximum physical speed your interface connected to the Frame Relay cloud can use.

   Committed Information Rate: This is the level of bandwidth the service provider commits to give you on a regular basis.

3. After your router receives DLCI information, it sends Inverse ARP messages to each DLCI number requesting the Layer 3 address of the remote router.

4. Split-horizon is a loop-prevention mechanism that prevents a router from advertising a route out the same interface that received the original route advertisement. It can cause problems with Frame Relay because a hub router could have multiple destinations connected to a single physical interface. When those destinations send advertisements to the hub router, split horizon prevents the router from propagating the advertisements to other remote offices. The two methods you can use to resolve this issue are disabling the split-horizon mechanism or using point-to-point subinterfaces.

5. The command you would be most likely to use to troubleshoot the failed DLCI communication is the `show frame-relay lmi` command. It enables you to focus on the communication with the Frame Relay service provider. If necessary, you may also use the `debug frame-relay lmi` command to probe deeper into the messages exchanged between your router and the service provider.

Answers to Exam Questions

1. **B, D**. Frame Relay is considered a packet-switched network and operates in much the same way as X.25 and ATM. Rather than have users connected directly together over leased lines, virtual circuits are established through the service provider network. Frame Relay also falls under the NBMA category. This means that, by default, multiple devices can access the network, but broadcast messages are not forwarded. Answer A is incorrect because circuit-switched networks encompass connections that use the telephone company as a backbone. Answer C is incorrect because it describes ethernet connectivity, not Frame Relay.

2. **B, A.** SVC is an on-demand circuit through the Frame Relay cloud that is created when needed and then destroyed after data has been transmitted. This circuit type is not commonly used and has been widely replaced by PVCs, which is Answer A. Answers C and D are incorrect because these acronyms have nothing to do with Frame Relay.

3. **A, C, D.** The valid LMI signaling methods are Cisco, ANSI, and Q.933a. Answer B is incorrect because IETF represents the industry standard Frame Relay encapsulation that allows non-Cisco devices to interoperate with Cisco devices over a Frame Relay cloud.

4. **A.** DLCI addressing works exactly opposite of how most folks think it should work. Rather than send to a destination DLCI number, you leave on a local DLCI number. In this case, the Minnesota router would leave on DLCI 501 to reach the California office. Answer B is incorrect because California would leave on DLCI 502 to get to Arizona. Answers C and D are incorrect because they reference the connection between Minnesota and Texas.

5. **D.** A router connected to a Frame Relay service provider can often send faster than the Committed Information Rate (CIR), but never faster than the Local Access Rate. The CIR describes the minimum amount of bandwidth that the service provider contractually guarantees the client. The Local Access Rate references the fastest physical speed the line can handle. Answers B and C are incorrect because there is no such thing as a Virtual Circuit Speed. Answer A is incorrect because the terms are reversed.

6. **B.** The service provider tags any return traffic with a Backwards Explicit Congestion Notification (BECN) marking. By default, your router ignores these notifications. Answer A is incorrect because Discard Eligible (D_e) describes markings placed on any traffic sent above the CIR. Answer C is incorrect because Forward Explicit Congestion Notification (FECN) markings are placed on packets if there is no return traffic that can be marked with BECNs to tell the sender to slow down. Answer D is what happens to a balloon if you poke it with a needle.

7. **C.** After the routers receive the DLCI information through LMI signaling, they send Inverse ARP messages through to the other side of the connection. This enables them to discover the remote IP addresses they are able to reach. Answer A is incorrect because Hello messages are specific to routing protocols such as OSPF and EIGRP. Answer B is incorrect because Cisco Discovery Protocol enables you to see information just about directly connected Cisco devices. Answer D is incorrect because LMI can only give your routers the DLCI numbers it can use to reach remote devices, but cannot tell the router how the remote devices are configured.

8. **A.** The correct syntax of the Frame Relay map command is `frame-relay map ip <remote_ip_address> <local_dlci> broadcast`. The `broadcast` keyword enables routing protocol updates to function. In this case, Arizona is trying to reach the remote IP address in Michigan of 10.1.1.2, and uses the local DLCI of 512 to get there. All other answers use either the wrong DLCI or IP address.

9. **D.** To use the industry standard Frame Relay encapsulation, you need to type in `encapsulation frame-relay ietf`. This enables Inverse ARP to map your Frame Relay circuits for you. Answer A is incorrect because this uses the Cisco proprietary Frame Relay encapsulation that does not work with any non-Cisco gear. The other two answers use invalid syntax and commands.

10. **A.** Three primary PVC states indicate the status of the line. ACTIVE means there are no problems. INACTIVE means that there is a problem with the remote router, which rules out Answer B. DELETED means that there is a problem with your local router. Typically, this is caused by using the incorrect DLCI information. Answer D is eliminated because multipoint and point-to-point designs use DLCI information in the same way. If the DLCI shows up as DELETED under a multipoint configuration, it shows up as DELETED under a point-to-point configuration. Finally, if you were physically disconnected from the service provider, you would not see DLCI information (because LMI is used to send the DLCI status to your router), making answer C incorrect.

Suggested Reading and Resources

1. Cisco TAC Configuring Frame Relay, http://www.cisco.com/univercd/cc/td/doc/product/software/ios121/121cgcr/wan_c/wcdfrely.htm.

2. Ward, Chris and Cioara, Jeremy. *Exam Cram 2 CCNA Practice Questions*. Que Publishing, 2004.

3. Chin, Jonathan. *Cisco Frame Relay Solutions Guide*. Cisco Press, 2004.

CHAPTER TWENTY-FOUR

Understanding VPN Connectivity

Objectives

This chapter covers the following Cisco-specified objectives for the "Implement and verify WAN links" section of the 640-802 CCNA exam:

► **Describe different methods for connecting to a WAN**

► **Describe VPN technology (including: importance, benefits, role, impact, components)**

Outline

Study Strategies

▶ Read the information presented in the chapter, paying special attention to Notes.

▶ VPN connections are becoming increasingly prevalent in the industry. Although VPNs were not a major topic on the ICND1, ICND2, or CCNA exams at their initial release (and at the time of this writing), you can expect more VPN topics to be added as time passes.

▶ Because of the complexity, VPN configurations are not part of the ICND1, ICND2, or CCNA exams. Focus your study on the benefits of VPN connections and why an organization would choose VPN connectivity.

Introduction

Internet connectivity is everywhere. My wife and I (Jeremy) recently took a trip to Honduras to assist some of the struggling areas. After flying through a rainforest, our plane touched down in the main city. We were quickly escorted to a van where we drove with many others for a couple hours to a remote region of the country. I'll never forget the irony of the scene when I arrived. A woman was washing clothes in a bucket on the corner. Directly across from her was a small building with a flashing sign that said "Internet Cafe." Amazing!

Therein lies the concept: If the Internet is everywhere, and just about every major organization has an Internet connection, why not use the Internet as a style of "WAN link" to connect offices? This is the idea of virtual private networks (VPNs). This network connection style is considered virtually private because we are really sending our corporate internal data over a public network—the Internet, to be exact. So as you can imagine, you have plenty of security considerations to think through before you launch your company's internal records into the great Internet abyss.

Understanding VPN Connectivity

Objective:

▶ Describe different methods for connecting to a WAN

Anyone who has ever set up a private point-to-point WAN link between two offices can probably attest to some of the challenges: long wait times (it can take months to get a private line installed), high monthly costs, and technical issues between your equipment and the carrier. On the other hand, Internet connections are relatively inexpensive and typically faster to install. These are just a few of the reasons why VPN connectivity has become so popular. As I just mentioned, VPN connectivity allows any location that has Internet connectivity to bring up a virtual private line between locations, allowing true any-to-any connectivity, as shown in Figure 24.1.

The focus of most of this chapter is the "private" piece of the VPN acronym. For the VPN to be considered a secure means of transferring data, that data must be heavily encrypted.

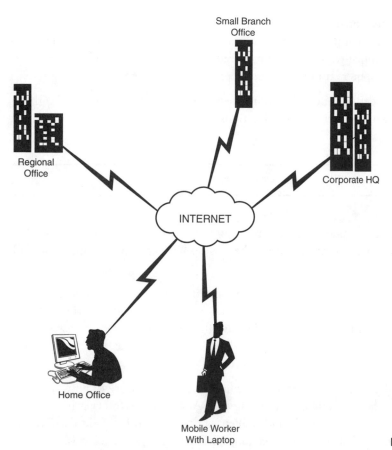

FIGURE 24.1 VPN topology.

VPN Benefits and Considerations

We have already discussed some of the benefits of VPN connectivity. Here is a list of all the benefits of using VPN connections over private lines:

▶ **Cost savings:** Internet connectivity is considerably cheaper than private-line connections. Likewise, a corporation could use a single Internet connection to communicate with many branch offices using VPN technology. In the private-line arena, each of the branch office connections would be a recurring monthly cost.

▶ **Remote-access connections:** If a corporation used only private-line connections, mobile workers and telecommuters would be limited to dialup technology to obtain remote access to the company. Dialup is considered extremely slow by today's standards. Many newer computers no longer feature preinstalled modems.

▶ **Scalability:** VPN connections allow the company to grow to add new locations without adding significant infrastructure considerations.

> **TIP**
>
> Be sure to understand the benefits of VPN connectivity over leased-line connections.

Looking at this list of benefits, it may seem like a no-brainer to choose VPN connections over other styles of WAN connectivity. Unfortunately, there is no perfect WAN connection, and VPN has its share of drawbacks:

▶ **Higher overhead:** Because of the significant amount of encryption that must be performed on all data sent over the VPN, VPN technology does cause more overhead than a traditional WAN link. This can manifest itself in many ways: the processor and memory utilization of your router or firewall will increase, more delay in sending and receiving packets, and more overhead in the header of each packet sent.

▶ **Varying service levels:** Because the Internet is considered the "network of networks," there is no guarantee when sending and receiving data. Although the Internet has been proven time and time again to be stable and resilient, a downstream ISP failure can cause your data to reroute through a slower connection, causing varying service levels. This makes deploying real-time applications such as voice and video over IP a challenge.

▶ **Security considerations:** Although varying levels of encryption and authentication can be applied to your VPN connection(s), the data is still being sent over a public network. Some high-security organizations may find this risk unacceptable.

Types of VPNs

VPN connections come in two major genres: site-to-site and remote-access VPNs. Let's talk about each of these individually.

Site-to-Site VPNs

Site-to-site VPNs are the direct replacement for private-line WAN connections. They allow offices to maintain permanent or semipermanent connections between each other through the Internet, as shown in Figure 24.2.

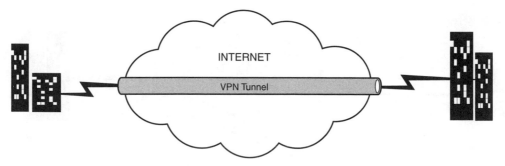

FIGURE 24.2   Site-to-site VPN technology.

One of the first things you'll notice when you look at Figure 24.2 is that VPN connections are commonly represented by a tunnel. That picture has even moved into common IT lingo. You'll hear things like "The VPN tunnel is down" and "Our VPN tunnel uses AES encryption." This terminology comes from the concepts behind the VPN; these connection types create a logical tunnel through the Internet. From the perspective of the internal user, she is unable to see any of the devices that the data passes through on the Internet. Likewise, the Internet cannot see any of the data contained on the inside of the tunnel; it is all encrypted. This effectively simulates a private-line feel between the two (or more) offices.

I mentioned that the VPN connection can be permanent or semipermanent. This is really up to the network administrator. The benefit of using a permanent VPN connection is the "always there" feeling. When you transmit data between the two locations, it immediately passes through without delay. The drawback of this connection is that router or firewall resources are always being consumed to maintain the VPN connection. Semipermanent connections are an "on-demand" style of VPN. When the VPN is needed, the router or firewall establishes the VPN connection. When the VPN is no longer required (data is no longer attempting to pass between offices), the router or firewall tears down the tunnel. Because the router or firewall does not need to maintain idle VPN connections, a semipermanent connection allows you to maximize your resources. On the flip side, VPN connections take a moment to establish when data needs to be transmitted. This may result in the initial connection attempt between offices experiencing delay or failure while the VPN tunnel is formed.

Remote-Access VPNs

Remote-access VPNs typically are used to allow telecommuting or mobile workers to connect to the corporate network from home or hotel-like locations, as shown in Figure 24.3.

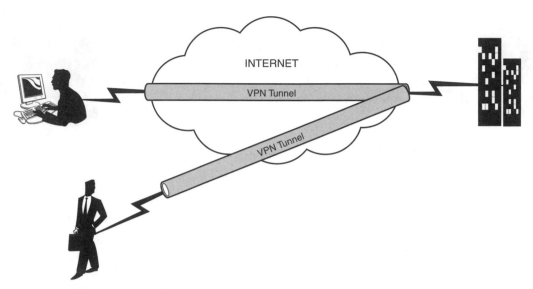

FIGURE 24.3   Remote-access VPN technology.

Remote-access VPNs are always on-demand in nature rather than being a permanent connection. When a user wants to connect, he typically opens VPN software installed on his laptop by an administrator. After selecting the VPN connection he wants to use and clicking a connect button, he is be prompted for his user credentials. This can range from a simple username and password to a token-based system requiring a credit card-style device that generates a password that is valid for only 60 seconds. (This can get into some very cool security stuff, but we won't go there yet.)

Remote-access VPNs (and even some site-to-site VPNs) are configured through a system Cisco calls Cisco Easy VPN. If you look at the command-line configuration of an Easy VPN device (which is well beyond the CCNA), you quickly realize that it's anything but easy to set up. Cisco calls this configuration Easy VPN because the VPN client (called the Easy VPN Remote device) requires very little configuration. Just about all of the setup is done on the Easy VPN Server. When the Easy VPN Remote client connects, the Easy VPN Server chooses the type of encryption, authentication, and other settings that the VPN tunnel will use and transmits those settings to the Easy VPN Remote device. Easy, right? At least from the client perspective. The Easy VPN Server requires quite a bit of configuration for this to work correctly.

Within the last few years, a new style of remote-access VPN connection has emerged, called an SSL (Secure Socket Layer) VPN. Many people call this a WebVPN or clientless VPN connection. Here's the concept: We have long used security for websites. Any site you connect to using the https://*sitename* string uses the SSL protocol to create a secure, encrypted session. When using an SSL VPN connection, the remote-access client accesses a secure web page, managed by your Cisco router or firewall and is prompted for a username and password. As soon as the client successfully authenticates, the web page turns into a type of portal that allows a VPN-style connection as long as the web page remains open. This phenomenal new type of connection allows you to have remote-access VPN clients without the need to install client software or have extensive training teaching remote users how to use the VPN connection.

The SSL VPN comes in two forms:

▶ **Clientless:** The purely clientless SSL VPN connection allows you to create a web page listing the resources that the user can access after he or she has successfully authenticated to the VPN. For example, the user would connect, enter his or her username and password, and be redirected to a web page with links to all the common resources the user could access. The clientless VPN does not allow users to use applications on their own PC over the VPN.

▶ **Thin client:** The thin-client form of the SSL VPN asks to install an ActiveX- or Java-based plug-in after the user has successfully authenticated to the VPN. This plug-in allows other applications (only TCP-based applications at this time) to run from the user's PC across the VPN. An example of this connection type in action goes something like this: The user opens the SSL VPN web page in her browser and is prompted for a username and password. After she enters the correct authentication credentials, the web page asks the user if she wants to install the thin client. If she accepts this request, a small program downloads and runs. Depending on how you (as the network administrator) structure the SSL VPN, the web page can then redirect to a "quick link" page with access to many of the common resources inside the network. You could also just have the web page redirect to a "Connection Successful" message. The user can now open TCP-based applications (such as email or web browsing, to name a couple) and access servers located at the corporate office through the VPN.

Let me mention off the CCNA record that I believe this new SSL VPN connection will be the "wave of the future" in regards to remote-access VPNs. Cisco has already released a new implementation called the Cisco Secure Desktop. Check this out: When the thin client downloads to the user's PC, it also installs a "secure desktop" system that takes over the user's Windows desktop environment. The thin client tracks any files that the user downloads from the corporate office. When the user disconnects from the VPN, all the secure corporate files are removed from her PC (they literally disappear)! When the user reconnects to the VPN, the SSL VPN thin client automatically replaces all the files that the user previously had on her PC, in the respective locations. Isn't that amazing? The secure desktop system ensures that if the end user's PC is stolen or compromised (such as by a worm or virus), the corporate data will be inaccessible. Nice.

> **NOTE**
>
> Be sure to understand the difference between site-to-site and remote-access VPN connectivity.

The Pieces That Make a VPN Tick

Objective:

▶ Describe VPN technology (including: importance, benefits, role, impact, components)

To run a VPN connection, you must have a router or firewall that supports VPN connectivity (such as the Cisco ISR or ASA Firewall) and a VPN client (only if you are deploying a remote-access VPN).

Most of the modern business-class routers manufactured by Cisco are considered Integrated Services Routers (ISRs). These routers are designed to fill multiple roles in a network, one of which is managing site-to-site and remote-access VPN connectivity. However, to support VPNs, you may need to upgrade the IOS version that the router is running to a version that supports security features. Cisco also supports the ASA Firewall (previously known as the PIX Firewall). The ASA firewall is designed to handle many security aspects of the network and supports both site-to-site and remote-access VPN connections. Depending on the size and needs of your business, you can choose one or both product lines. ISRs are designed to handle routing as their primary function (which they do quite well) and handle VPNs as a secondary function (which they do fairly well). The ASA is designed to handle VPNs and other firewall processes as its primary function (which it does quite well) and routing as a secondary function (which it does fairly well).

If you are managing a site-to-site connection, two routers or two ASA firewalls are all that will be required. If you are managing remote-access VPN connections, you will also need to consider a VPN client. These clients can come in many forms:

▶ **Cisco VPN client:** If you purchase a Cisco SmartNET agreement (Cisco's fancy name for an extended support and warranty agreement) with your ISR router or ASA firewall, you can download the latest versions of the Cisco VPN client. This provides the most compatibility (supports many features) when used with the Cisco VPN solution. For example, you can enable a VPN-triggered firewall that begins working as soon as the user connects to the VPN. This firewall can protect the client from being compromised by Internet-based attacks while connected to the VPN. When the user disconnects from the VPN, the firewall disables itself to allow unfiltered Internet and local network access. The rules of this firewall can be controlled by the Cisco administrator (that's you!).

▶ **Certicom client:** The Certicom client is a widely supported VPN client that can be installed on portable devices such as a PDA. This allows the user to connect to the corporate VPN from the PDA device and perform tasks such as checking corporate email.

▶ **Cisco VPN 3002 hardware client:** You can install this lower-cost device in a small office/home office (SOHO) environment. It establishes on-demand VPN connections when data that needs to cross the VPN is sent. This can be done without installing any software on the client PCs or requiring extra training on the use of VPN software. Although this product is considered end of life (EOL—no longer manufactured by Cisco), other products like this are manufactured by third-party companies that are compatible with the Cisco VPN solution.

▶ **Third-party IPsec VPN software:** The industry-standard IPsec protocol is supported in many other VPN clients. So, if you or your company has purchased some other non-Cisco, IPsec-compatible VPN software, chances are you can make it work with the Cisco VPN solution. It may just take a little more work!

Understanding IPsec

Objective:

▶ Describe VPN technology (including: importance, benefits, role, impact, components)

I've mentioned the IPsec protocol a few times, so let's now take a moment to discuss the role it plays. First, the name IPsec is short for IP Security, which is a suite of subprotocols (much in the same way that TCP/IP is a suite of subprotocols) that is used to protect data crossing a network. Because IPsec operates at the network layer of the OSI model, it can protect data from the transport layer and above. This means that IPsec can protect any type of TCP- or UDP-based communication. This gives IPsec a large advantage over other encryption protocols, such as SSH and SSL. These encryption protocols work at the transport layer and are restricted to specific ports. For example, SSH encrypts only TCP port 22 by default, and SSL encrypts only TCP port 443 by default.

You might be wondering, "Why is IPsec a suite of protocols? Isn't it just supposed to encrypt the data?" Excellent question. There are a couple ways to answer this. First, the makers of IPsec realized that there was far more to protecting data than just performing encryption. Encrypted packets can still be captured and used maliciously. For example, say you send some data encrypted using IPsec that transfers $1,000 to a bank account. An attacker could capture the data and resend it many times to cause multiple transfers to go through, even though the attacker cannot see the actual data in the packet.

The second answer to the question is a little more complex. IPsec is considered a suite of protocols, but it is unable to provide any direct security features in and of itself. Now, if that doesn't blow your mind, nothing will! Here's the idea: IPsec is better described as a framework of protocols, as shown in Figure 24.4.

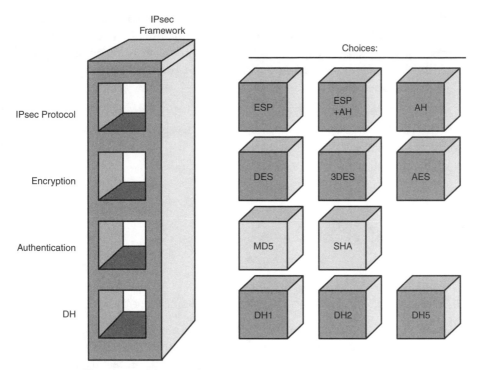

FIGURE 24.4 IPsec protocol framework.

Each of the categories shown in Figure 24.4 (IPsec Protocol, Encryption, Authentication, and DH) is an open hole to be filled with a standard. Think of these holes as being like an audio CD player. The CD player doesn't choose what type of music to play; that's the job of the CD. When you put in a jazz CD, the CD player reads the data and outputs jazz sounds to the speakers. In the same way, the IPsec protocol acts as a "player" for whatever type of security you want to add. This is extremely powerful, because it allows the IPsec protocol to continue to be used regardless of advances in cryptography. For example, 20 years from now, many of the encryption methods we use today will probably be obsolete or considered extremely weak. With the IPsec protocol framework, we can remove those older encryption standards and plug in new ones. The IPsec protocol itself does not change!

Now that we've discussed the IPsec protocol framework, let's get a basic understanding of the function of each of those holes.

Encryption

Encryption is officially called data confidentiality. Its function is to make any data that you send unreadable to unauthorized devices and yet understandable to authorized devices. To fully understand how this is possible, you would need to read a book on data cryptography.

(Warning: These books typically weigh more than a small car and are guaranteed to put most people to sleep within minutes.) Rather than get into advanced cryptography, let me give you the basic premise. Each device that wants to encrypt or decrypt data needs the appropriate key. A key is an extremely advanced mathematical formula that is designed to scramble data when it is sent between devices. Figure 24.5 illustrates this process.

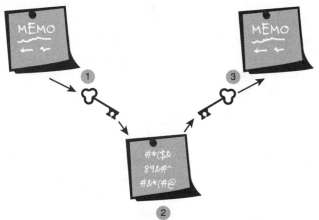

FIGURE 24.5 Encryption/decryption process.

Based on the figure, the encryption steps are as follows:

1. Clear-text (unencrypted) data is sent to the encryption algorithm (key). The key runs the data through a sophisticated mathematical formula that renders the data unreadable.

2. The encrypted data is transmitted across the potentially unsecured network and is received by the destination device.

3. The destination device uses the same key to decrypt the scrambled data, returning it to its original, clear-text form.

This process is technically called symmetric encryption. In this type of encryption, the same key is used to encrypt and decrypt data. It is a faster, more efficient style of encryption. Asymmetric encryption uses two keys: one to encrypt and another to decrypt. We'll talk about asymmetric encryption in a moment.

Although many symmetric encryption algorithms are available, three types of symmetric encryption commonly are used to secure data. Each one offers varying levels of encryption strength:

▶ **Data Encryption Standard (DES) algorithm:** DES was one of the first encryption algorithms to be used. It was originally developed by IBM to support a 56-bit key (the longer the key, the more secure the algorithm). By today's standards, DES is considered a relatively weak encryption method.

▶ **Triple DES (3DES) algorithm:** To address the weaknesses of DES, the 3DES algorithm was produced. This algorithm did not reinvent the wheel of encryption. Instead, it ran the DES algorithm three times with different encryption keys (thus the name 3DES). This significantly improved the strength of the original DES algorithm.

▶ **Advanced Encryption Standard (AES):** AES is one of the newer encryption algorithms. It was created by Rijndael (a group of two Belgian cryptographers) in response to a competition created by the National Institute of Standards and Technology (NIST)—a division of the U.S. government. It was designed to increase encryption strength beyond the DES and 3DES standards and yet be more efficient on the device's processor. As it stands today, AES offers 128-, 192-, and 256-bit encryption.

Diffie-Hellman

The Diffie-Hellman (DH) key exchange algorithm addresses a gigantic missing piece of the symmetric encryption systems we just talked about. Again, the symmetric encryption algorithms (including DES, 3DES, and AES) use a "shared key" approach in which the same key can encrypt and decrypt data. This is very efficient on processing cycles, but it raises a question. If the same key encrypts and decrypts data, how do both of the devices get the key? Simple! The devices just send the key to each other over the network. So, next question: If they just send the key to each other over the network, couldn't someone intercept the key and use it to decode all the transmissions? Ah, now *that* is the problem, and this is where the DH key exchange algorithm comes in.

The goal of the DH algorithm is to give devices a way to securely exchange the shared key over a public network. To accomplish this, it uses an advanced process in which both endpoints exchange results to a mathematical formula over a clear network. Using these results, each VPN endpoint can determine a shared secret value that is used to generate symmetrical encryption keys (which are much easier for the devices to process) to use for the VPN session.

> **NOTE**
>
> As you might be able to tell, I am avoiding a detailed explanation of the mathematics behind the Diffie-Hellman algorithm. If you would like a deeper understanding of this process, visit http://en.wikipedia.org/wiki/Diffie-Hellman.

The DH key exchange algorithm uses monstrously huge numbers (some more than 300 digits long) to accomplish its mathematical cryptographic process. Although DH is much more secure than symmetric encryption, it is much harder on the device's processor. This is why DH cryptography is used only briefly at the start of the session to generate symmetric encryption keys.

Secure Socket Layer (SSL)

Although the Diffie-Hellman algorithm has long been used to secure symmetric encryption key exchange over a public network, SSL is a cryptographic protocol that provides secure communications over the Internet for things such as web browsing, instant messaging, and email. It is discussed here because SSL VPNs are continuing to increase in popularity.

As with Diffie-Hellman, the goal of SSL is to provide secure communications over a public network. To accomplish this, SSL uses a dual-key approach. Each device uses a public and private key system. These keys are reverse mathematical formulas to each other. In other words, anything that the public key encrypts, the private key can decrypt. Anything that the private key encrypts, the public key can decrypt. The public and private keys use mathematical algorithms that are so complex that it is impossible for someone who has one key to generate the opposite. For example, if you have a public key, it is feasibly impossible to figure out what the private key is, and vice versa. With this in mind, look at Figure 24.6, which illustrates the key exchange process.

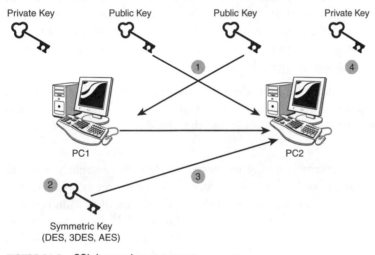

FIGURE 24.6 SSL key exchange process.

The SSL key exchange goes through the following steps:

1. PC1 and PC2 send each other their respective public key encryption formula.

2. One of the devices (PC1 in this example) generates a shared-secret key (symmetric encryption) that will be used to encrypt and decrypt data for the session.

3. PC1 encrypts the shared-secret key using the public key of PC2 and transmits the key to PC2.

4. PC2 decrypts the shared-secret key using its private key. Now that both PC1 and PC2 have the same shared-secret key, it can and will be used to encrypt and decrypt all communication for the secured session.

SSL uses asymmetric encryption (public and private keys) at the start of the conversation to provide a secure exchange of a shared secret key. As soon as the devices have the shared secret key, the SSL session converts to using symmetric encryption because it is much more efficient on the device's processors.

> **NOTE**
>
> Keep in mind that this is just a discussion of the encryption component of SSL. SSL also provides a number of other security measures.

Authentication/Data Integrity

When many IT people think of authentication, they equate it to entering a username and password to log on to a PC. This form of authentication is designed to verify that the person using the computer is who he says he is. Authentication as it applies to IPsec performs a similar, but not identical, job. When sending data over an unsecured network, you must ensure that the data received is exactly the same as the data sent and that the data is received from a trusted source. If the data changed somewhere between the sending and receiving devices, the security protocol should detect the change and reject the data.

Authentication is often used synonymously with the terms data integrity and hashing in the IPsec world. Technically speaking, authentication verifies that the device sending the data is the "true" device (not a fake). Data integrity ensures that the data does not change from one end to the other.

The process to accomplish data integrity is similar to encryption, but with a slightly different angle. As with encryption, hashing passes all the data contained in the packet (above Layer 3) through a mathematical algorithm. However, the job of this mathematical algorithm is not to scramble the data, but rather to come up with a result, which is known as the hash. As an example, the mathematical algorithm might say something like "Add up all the vowels in this data packet," and the result might be 96. This result (known as the hash) is then appended to the end of the data and is sent to the receiver, as shown in Figure 24.7.

The step-by-step hashing process goes like this:

1. The sending device passes the data to be transferred through a hashing algorithm and comes up with a result (the hash).

2. The hash is appended to the data and is sent to the receiving device.

3. The receiving device receives the data and runs it through the same hashing algorithm to generate a result. The result is then compared to the result that was originally appended to the data. If the hashed values are the same, the receiving device is assured that the data did not change during transmission. If the values are different, the data did change, and the receiving device discards it.

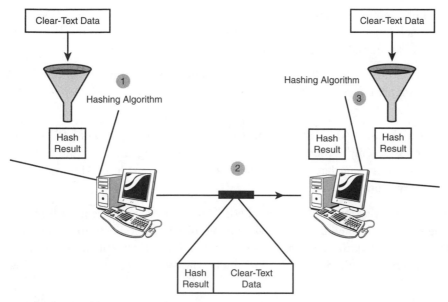

FIGURE 24.7 Hashing/data integrity process.

The hashing algorithm is obviously much more complex than simply adding up all the vowels in the data. Currently, two widely supported hashing algorithms are used:

▶ **Message Digest 5 (MD5)** was created in 1991 by Ronald Rivest, an MIT professor. Uses a 128-bit hashing algorithm.

▶ **Secure Hash Algorithm 1 (SHA-1)** was published in 1995 by the NIST to increase the strength of the original MD5 algorithm. Generally uses a 160-bit hashing algorithm.

As with encryption, the more bits that are used in the hashing algorithm, the stronger it becomes. You should use the strongest hashing algorithm that your VPN platform supports.

IPsec Protocols

The final "piece" of the IPsec framework is the IPsec protocol itself. As I mentioned, the individuals who created IPsec wanted it to be a protocol that would last through the ages. To make this happen, they even granted the flexibility to change the entire protocol engine! Today we use blocks such as Diffie-Hellman, encryption, and authentication, but maybe in 10 years some new security method will be added to the bundle. Perhaps biometric VPN security will be an option. Users would be required to complete a retinal scan to authenticate to the VPN (I can feel my sci-fi movie self emerging). We might need to add a "retinal block" to the IPsec protocol framework that is required for VPN establishment.

Okay, my example is a little out there, but the concept is sound. The IPsec protocol framework can be extended to support future security methods. Currently, you can use two "engines" for IPsec:

▶ **Authentication Header (AH):** The AH protocol was the first IPsec engine to be released. It supported only authentication (verifying the sending and receiving devices) and data integrity (ensuring that data does not change in transmission). AH does not support any encryption.

▶ **Encapsulating Security Payload (ESP):** The ESP protocol was the second IPsec engine to be released. It filled in the massive missing piece of AH: encryption. The ESP protocol supports all three pieces of the IPsec framework: authentication, data integrity, and encryption. Because of this, it is by far the more popular of the two IPsec engines.

Chapter Summary

The popularity of VPN technology can only increase as time goes on. The availability and low cost of Internet connection has made this method of communicating very convenient for corporations to use. Keep in mind that although VPNs are scalable, flexible, and low-cost, they also suffer the same drawbacks of normal Internet connectivity. There is no guarantee of consistent low-delay, high-speed service 24 hours a day. Likewise, the overhead that VPN connections add to your devices is a large consideration when choosing which WAN technology your organization will use.

Modern VPNs are powered by the IP Security (IPsec) protocol, which is a framework of subprotocols in which each plays a role in keeping the connection secure. When designing a VPN, you must choose the appropriate levels of encryption, authentication, and Diffie-Hellman (DH) to balance performance and security. Keep in mind that there is far more to IPsec and cryptography in general than what is presented in this chapter. This chapter was designed to give you enough understanding that you can recognize terms and functions of the VPN components both in the real world and on the CCNA exam.

Key Terms

- Virtual private network (VPN)
- Site-to-site VPN
- Remote-access VPN
- SSL or web VPN
- Cisco Easy VPN Server
- Cisco Easy VPN Remote
- IP Security (IPsec) protocol
- Authentication
- Encryption
- Hashing

- Data integrity
- Diffie-Hellman (DH)
- Data Encryption Standard (DES)
- Triple DES (3DES)
- Advanced Encryption Standard (AES)
- Message Digest 5 (MD5)
- Secure Hash Algorithm 1 (SHA-1)
- Authentication Header (AH)
- Encapsulating Security Payload (ESP)

Apply Your Knowledge

Review Questions

1. What are the three benefits of using VPN connectivity over private lines?

2. Describe the two types of VPN implementations. What would be an ideal use of each?

3. The three primary security techniques used over VPN connections are encryption, authentication, and data integrity. Briefly describe the purpose of each.

4. What are the differences between asymmetric and symmetric encryption?

5. Briefly describe how SSL can securely send an encryption/decryption key over a public network.

Exam Questions

1. Your organization has just opened a new office in Detroit. You have existing offices in Phoenix, San Diego, and Albuquerque that are tied together using VPN technology. What physical or logical changes should you add to support the VPN connection to the new office?

   ○ **A.** No new interfaces are needed. The VPN configuration needs only to be applied to the router.

   ○ **B.** No new interfaces are needed. You need to communicate with the ISP to provision a new DLCI.

   ○ **C.** A new serial interface needs to be added to the router to support the new connection. The encapsulation should be set to match the service provider's requirements.

   ○ **D.** A new Fast Ethernet interface needs to be added to the router to support the new connection. You must communicate with the service provider to provision the new circuit.

2. Which of the following is *not* a valid benefit of using VPN technology?

   ○ **A.** Lower costs

   ○ **B.** More flexibility when configuring site-to-site connections

   ○ **C.** The ability to support telecommuters

   ○ **D.** Lower network overhead

3. What is needed to support an SSL VPN connection?

○ **A.** The router should be configured to support SSL VPN connections. The client can connect using a standard web browser.

○ **B.** The router should be configured to support SSL VPN connections. The client must use the Cisco VPN client when connecting.

○ **C.** The router should be configured to support SSL VPN connections. The client must use a third-party thin client to connect.

○ **D.** The router does not need to be configured to support SSL VPN connections. The client platform delivers all configuration when it connects.

4. What platforms can support site-to-site and remote-access VPNs? (Choose two)

○ **A.** Cisco IOS

○ **B.** Cisco IPS Appliance

○ **C.** Cisco Catalyst 3550

○ **D.** Cisco ASA 5500

5. Which of the following is *not* a component of the IPsec framework?

○ **A.** ESP

○ **B.** SHA-1

○ **C.** TCP

○ **D.** MD5

○ **E.** AES

6. Which of the following represent data integrity algorithms? (Choose two)

○ **A.** AES

○ **B.** MD5

○ **C.** DES

○ **D.** 3DES

○ **E.** SHA-1

7. Which of the following are symmetric encryption algorithms? (Choose two)

   ○ **A.** DH

   ○ **B.** SHA-1

   ○ **C.** DES

   ○ **D.** AES

8. You have just finished proposing a new VPN solution to your organization's upper management. They have approved the solution, provided that you use the strongest level of encryption possible. What algorithm will you choose?

   ○ **A.** 3DES

   ○ **B.** AES

   ○ **C.** SHA-1

   ○ **D.** MD5

9. You would like to implement IPsec over your LAN network. You are not as interested in encryption features, because they can cause tremendous overhead, but you would like to implement authentication and data integrity features. What IPsec protocol will you use?

   ○ **A.** AH

   ○ **B.** DH

   ○ **C.** ESP

   ○ **D.** SHA-1

10. What process passes data through a mathematical algorithm to generate a 128- or 160-bit result?

   ○ **A.** Encryption

   ○ **B.** Diffie-Hellman

   ○ **C.** Hashing

   ○ **D.** ESP

Answers to Review Questions

1. VPN connectivity is more cost-effective and scalable than leased-line connections. In addition, it provides the capability for remote-access connections (such as telecommuters or mobile workers).

2. VPN connections can be either site-to-site or remote-access. Site-to-site is the direct replacement for a leased line and acts as a permanent connection between offices. Remote-access connections allow users to connect to the corporate network from a remote location, such as a home or motel.

3. Encryption is designed to scramble data before it is sent and descramble it at the remote end. This keeps people from intercepting and interpreting data that is communicated over a network. Authentication ensures that the devices sending and receiving data are really who they say they are. Data integrity ensures that data does not change when it is sent across the network.

4. Asymmetric encryption uses a public and private key system. Each key is the reverse of the other (the public key can decrypt what the private key encrypts, and vice versa). This encryption type is very processor-intensive. Symmetric encryption uses the same key to encrypt and decrypt data. It is much more processor-efficient than asymmetric encryption.

5. SSL can secure communication over a public network between two devices. The devices first exchange public keys and use the opposite device's public key to encrypt a session key. The encrypted session key is then exchanged between the devices and is decrypted using the private key. After this, the session key is used to encrypt and decrypt all communication between the two devices.

Answers to Exam Questions

1. **A.** A big advantage of VPN connections is their flexibility and scalability. If you need to add a new office, all you need to do is apply the necessary configuration to the router, allowing it to connect through the Internet to the new office. No new interfaces are necessary to accomplish this.

2. **D.** VPN solutions offer many benefits, but lower network overhead is not one of them. Because the VPN forms a tunnel through the public network, new IP headers must be generated and applied to the packet. This increases the network overhead for this type of connection.

3. **A.** SSL VPN connections allow you to deploy a VPN solution without installing a client on the end-user PC. To connect to the VPN, the user opens a web page hosted by the router or ASA device and authenticates. The web page then becomes a VPN portal. This is why SSL VPNs are often called WebVPNs.

4. **A, D.** Specific feature sets of the Cisco IOS (used on routers) can support site-to-site and remote-access VPNs. Cisco also manufactures the ASA 5500 series security appliance, which is specifically designed to support VPN solutions.

5. **C.** The TCP protocol fits into the TCP/IP protocol suite rather than the IPsec protocol suite. All other protocols listed are either encryption, authentication, or IPsec core protocols.

6. **B, E.** The two data integrity algorithms are MD5 (128-bit hash) and SHA-1 (160-bit hash).

7. **C, D.** The two encryption algorithms are DES (offering 56-bit encryption) and AES (offering 128-, 192-, and 256-bit encryption).

8. **B.** AES currently offers the strongest levels of encryption possible for symmetric encryption. It can reach up to 256-bit encryption.

9. **A.** The Authentication Header (AH) is the older of the two IPsec core protocols. It supports only authentication and data integrity features. The Encapsulating Security Payload (ESP) adds encryption.

10. **C.** Hashing features pass data through a mathematical algorithm to generate a hash used for data integrity. Passing data through an algorithm to scramble it is called encryption.

Suggested Readings and Resources

1. Wikipedia cryptography explanation, http://en.wikipedia.org/wiki/Cryptography

2. Richard Deal. *The Complete Cisco VPN Configuration Guide*. Cisco Press, 2005.

3. Bruce Schneier. *Applied Cryptography: Protocols, Algorithms, and Source Code in C*, Second Edition. Wiley, 1996.

4. Chris Ward and Jeremy Cioara. *Exam Cram 2 CCNA Practice Questions*. Que Publishing, 2004.

Fast Facts

OSI Model in Review

Table FF.1 lists the seven layers of the OSI model and significant aspects of each layer.

TABLE FF.1   The OSI Model

OSI Layer	Important Functions
Application	Provides an interface between a host's communication software and any necessary external applications. Evaluates what resources are necessary and available resources for communication between two devices. Synchronizes client/server applications. Provides error control and data integrity between applications. Provides system-independent processes to a host.
Presentation	Presents data to the application layer. Acts as a data format translator. Handles the structuring of data and negotiating data transfer syntax to Layer 7. Processes involved include data encryption, decryption, compression, and decompression.
Session	Handles dialog control among devices. Determines the beginning, middle, and end of a session or conversation that occurs between applications (intermediary).
Transport	Manages end-to-end connections and data delivery between two hosts. Segments and reassembles data. Provides transparent data transfer by hiding details of the transmission from the upper layers.
Network	Determines best path for packet delivery across the network. Determines logical addressing, which can identify the destination of a packet or datagram. Uses data packets (IP, IPX) and route update packets (RIP, EIGRP, and so on). Uses routed protocols IP, IPX, and AppleTalk DDP. Devices include routers and Layer 3 switches.
Data Link	Ensures reliable data transfer from the Network layer to the Physical layer. Oversees physical or hardware addressing. Formats packets into a frame. Provides error notification. Devices include bridges and Layer 2 switches.
Physical	Moves bits between nodes. Assists with the activation, maintenance, and deactivation of physical connectivity between devices. Devices include hubs and repeaters.

Application Protocols Supported by the Application Layer

TABLE FF.2 Application Layer Protocols

Application Protocols	Function
Telnet	A TCP/IP protocol that provides terminal emulation to a remote host by creating a virtual terminal. TeraTerm is one program that can be installed on a user computer to create Telnet sessions. This protocol requires authentication via a username and password.
Hypertext Transfer Protocol (HTTP)	Enables web browsing with the transmission of Hypertext Markup Language (HTML) documents on the Internet.
Secure Hypertext Transfer Protocol (HTTPS)	Enables secure web browsing. A secure connection is indicated when the URL begins with https:// or when a lock symbol is in the lower-right corner of the web page that is being viewed.
File Transfer Protocol (FTP)	Allows a user to transfer files. Provides access to files and directories.
Trivial File Transfer Protocol (TFTP)	A bare-bones version of FTP that does not provide access to directories. With TFTP you can simply send and receive files. Unlike FTP, TFTP is not secure and sends smaller blocks of data.
Domain Name System (DNS)	Resolves hostnames such as cisco.com into IP addresses.
Simple Mail Transfer Protocol (SMTP)	Sends email across the network.
Post Office Protocol 3 (POP3)	Receives email by accessing a network server.
Network File System (NFS)	Allows users with different operating systems (that is, NT and Unix workstations) to share files through a network. Remote files appear as though they reside on a local machine even though the local machine might be "diskless."
Network News Transfer Protocol (NNTP)	Offers access to Usenet newsgroup postings.
Simple Network Management Protocol (SNMP)	Monitors the network and manages configurations. Collects statistics to analyze network performance and ensure network security.
Network Time Protocol (NTP)	Synchronizes clocks on the Internet to provide accurate local time on the user system.
Dynamic Host Configuration Protocol (DHCP)	Works dynamically to provide an IP address, subnet mask, domain name, and a default gateway for routers. Works with DNS and WINS (used for NetBIOS addressing).

TABLE FF.3 Control Information for Each Layer

OSI Layer	Control Information Name
Application	Data
Presentation	
Session	
Transport	Segment
Network	Packet
Data Link	Frame
Physical	Bit

TABLE FF.4 OSI Layers and Related TCP/IP Layers

OSI Layer	TCP/IP Layer
Application	Application
Presentation	
Session	
Transport	Transport
Network	Internet
Data Link	
Physical	Network Access

TCP uses Positive Acknowledgment and Retransmission (PAR):

1. The source device begins a timer when a segment is sent and retransmits if the timer runs out before an acknowledgment is received.

2. The source device keeps track of segments that are sent and requires an acknowledgment for each segment.

3. The destination device acknowledges when a segment is received by sending a packet to the source that iterates the next sequence number it is looking for from the source.

TABLE FF.5 The TCP Segment Header Format

Source Port	Destination Port
Sequence Number	
Acknowledgment Number	
Miscellaneous Flags	Window (Flow Control)
Checksum	Urgent
Options	

CCNA Exam Prep (Exam 640-802), Second Edition

TABLE FF.6 Applications Using TCP and Related Ports

Application	Port Number(s)
FTP	20, 21
Telnet	23
SMTP	25
DNS (zone transfers)	53
HTTP	80
POP3	110
NNTP	119
HTTPS	443

TABLE FF.7 The UDP Header

Source Port	Destination Port
Length	Checksum

TABLE FF.8 Applications Using UDP and Related Ports

Application	Port Number(s)
DHCP	67, 68
DNS (name resolution)	53
TFTP	69
NTP	123
SNMP	161

Network Domains

Two domains determine data transport reliability:

- **Broadcast domain:** A group of nodes that can receive each other's broadcast messages and are segmented by routers.

- **Collision domain:** A group of nodes that share the same media and are segmented by switches. A collision occurs if two nodes attempt a simultaneous transmission. *Carrier Sense Multiple Access Collision Detection (CSMA/CD)* sends a jam signal to notify the devices that there has been a collision. The devices then halt transmission for a random backoff time.

Cabling, Lines, and Services

▶ **Bandwidth:** The total amount of information that can traverse a communications medium measured in millions of bits per second. Bandwidth is helpful for network performance analysis. Also, availability is increasing but limited.

▶ **Crosstalk:** An electrical or magnetic field that is a result of one communications signal that can affect the signal in a nearby circuit.

> **Near-end Crosstalk (NEXT):** Crosstalk measured at the transmitting end of a cable.

> **Far-end Crosstalk (FEXT):** Crosstalk measured at the far end of the cable from where the transmission was sent.

Unshielded twisted-pair (UTP) cables are vulnerable to Electromagnetic Interference (EMI) and use an RJ-45 connector. Fiber-optic cables are not susceptible to EMI.

Use a straight-through cable to connect the following devices:

▶ Terminated directly into a dedicated hub or switch port

▶ From a PC to a switch or a hub

▶ From a router to a switch or a hub

Use a cross-over cable to connect the following devices:

▶ From switch to switch

▶ From router to router

▶ From PC to PC

▶ From a PC to a router

▶ From a hub to a hub

▶ From a hub to a switch

Spread Spectrum Wireless LANs allow for high-speed transmissions over short distances.

Wireless Fidelity (Wi-Fi) is defined by IEEE 802.11.

TABLE FF.9   Summary of Ethernet 802.3 Characteristics

Standard	Speed	Media Type	Connector Used
10BASE-2	10Mbps	RG-58 coaxial	BNC
10BASE-5	10Mbps	RG-58 coaxial	BNC
10BASE-T	10Mbps	Category 3, 4, or 5 UTP or STP	RJ-45
10BASE-FL	10Mbps	Fiber-optic	SC or ST

TABLE FF.10   Comparison of Fast Ethernet 802.3u Characteristics

Standard	Speed	Media Type	Connector Used
100BASE-T4	100Mbps	Category 3, 4, or 5 UTP or STP	RJ-45
100BASE-TX	100Mbps	Category 5 UTP or STP	RJ-45
100BASE-FX	100Mbps	Fiber-optic	SC or ST

TABLE FF.11   Summary of Gigabit Ethernet 802.3ab Characteristics

Standard	Speed	Media Type	Connector Used
1000BASE-T or 1000BASE-TX	1000Mbps or 1Gbps	Category 5 UTP or higher	RJ-45

TABLE FF.12   Comparison of Gigabit Ethernet 802.3z Characteristics

Standard	Speed	Media Type	Connector Used
1000BASE-CX	1000Mbps or 1Gbps	Shielded copper wire	Nine-pin shielded connector
1000BASE-SX	1000Mbps or 1Gbps	MM fiber-optic	SC or ST
1000BASE-LX	1000Mbps or 1Gbps	MM or SM fiber-optic	SC or ST

MAC Addressing

A MAC address is hard-coded (burned in) on the network interface controller (NIC) of the Physical layer device attached to the network. Each MAC address must be unique and use the following format:

- Consist of 48 bits (or 6 bytes).

- Displayed by 12 hexadecimal digits (0 through 9, A through F).

- First six hexadecimal digits in the address are a vendor code or organizationally unique identifier (OUI) assigned to that NIC manufacturer.

- Last six hexadecimal digits are assigned by the NIC manufacturer and must be different from any other number assigned by that manufacturer.

Example of a MAC address: 00:00:07:A9:B2:EB

The OUI in this example is 00:00:07.

The broadcast address value is FFFF.FFFF.FFFF.

Framing and Duplex Types

802.3 frame information and parameters are as follows:

- The data-link header portion of the frame contains the Destination MAC address (6 bytes), Source MAC address (6 bytes), and Length (2 bytes).

- The Logical Link Control portion of the frame contains Destination Service Access Point (DSAP), Source Service Access Point (SSAP), and Control information. All three are 1 byte long. The Service Access Point (SAP) identifies an upper-layer protocol such as IP (06) or IPX (E0).

- The Data and cyclical redundancy check (CRC) portion of the frame is also called the data-link trailer. The Data field can be anywhere from 43 to 1497 bytes long. The frame check sequence (FCS) field is 4 bytes long. FCS or CRC provides error detection.

Bridges and switches examine the source MAC address of each inbound frame to learn MAC addresses.

Switches are multiport bridges that use ASIC hardware chips for frame forwarding. Dedicated bandwidth enables the switch port to guarantee the speed assigned to that port. For example, 100Mbps port connections get 100Mbps transmission rates.

Hubs use half-duplex technology. Switches can be set up for full duplex.

WAN Interfaces

WAN interfaces are used to provide a point of interconnection between Cisco routers and other network devices. Types of WAN interfaces include

- Basic Rate Interface (BRI)
- Synchronous Serial
- Asynchronous Serial
- High-Speed Serial Interface (HSSI)
- T1 Controller Card

BRI is an Integrated Services Digital Network (ISDN) line that consists of two 64Kbps bearer (B) channels and one 16Kbps data (D) channel.

DCE equipment might consist of a

▶ Modem

▶ Channel Service Unit/Data Service Unit (CSU/DSU)

▶ BRI NT-1

DTE equipment might consist of a

▶ Router

▶ PC

▶ Server

Memory Types

Four memory components are used by Cisco devices. Those components include ROM, flash, RAM, and NVRAM.

RAM contains the running IOS, with the exception of run from flash (RFF) routers. RAM also contains the running configuration or the active configuration that is used after a machine is booted.

IOS File Naming Conventions

Given the example filename c2600-ipbase-1.122-1.T.bin, from left to right, each portion of the filename represents the following:

▶ **c2600:** Hardware platform (Cisco 2600 router)

▶ **ipbase:** Feature set

▶ **1:** File format (compressed relocatable)

▶ **122:** IOS version number

▶ **l:** Maintenance release number

▶ **T:** Train identifier

Utilities Using ICMP

Internet Control Messaging Protocol (ICMP) is used by ping and traceroute utilities. Packet Internet Groper (ping) allows you to validate that an IP address exists and can accept requests.

► Ping is an echo and the response is an echo response.

► Routers send Destination Unreachable messages when they can't reach the destination network and they are forced to drop the packet. The router that drops the packet sends the ICMP DU message.

A traceroute traces the route or path taken from a client to a remote host. Traceroute also reports the IP addresses of the routers at each next hop on the way to the destination. This is especially useful when you suspect that a router on the route to an unreachable network is responsible for dropping the packet.

Network Security

Three classes of attack are commonly found in today's network environment:

► Access attacks

► Reconnaissance attacks

► Denial of service (DoS) attacks

Access Attacks

An access attack is just what it sounds like: an attempt to access another user account or network device through improper means. The four main types of access attacks are

► Password attacks

► Trust exploitation

► Port redirection

► Man-in-the-middle

Reconnaissance Attacks

The four main subcategories or methods for gathering network data for a reconnaissance attack are

- ► Packet sniffers
- ► Port scans
- ► Ping sweeps
- ► Information queries

Denial of Service (DoS) Attacks

DoS attacks are often implemented by a hacker as a means of denying a service that is normally available to a user or organization. The three main types of DoS attacks are

- ► Distributed DoS
- ► TCP SYN
- ► Smurf

Mitigating Network Threats

The following actions can be taken to lessen the impact of an attack on a network:

- ► Authentication, Authorization, and Accounting (AAA)
- ► Cisco access control lists (ACLs)
- ► Cisco IOS Secure Management features: SSH, SNMP, Syslog, and NTP
- ► Encryption protocols: SSH, IPsec, and SSL
- ► Security appliances and applications: Firewall, IPS, and IDS

IP Addressing

IPv4 addresses

- ► Consist of 32 bits.
- ► Are broken into four octets (8 bits each).

- Use dotted-decimal format; an example is 172.16.122.204.

- Minimum value (per octet) is 0, and the maximum value is 255.

- 0.0.0.0 is a network ID.

- 255.255.255.255 is a broadcast IP.

TABLE FF.13   IPv4 Address Classes

	First Octet	Second Octet	Third Octet	Fourth Octet
Class A	Network	Host	Host	Host
Class B	Network	Network	Host	Host
Class C	Network	Network	Network	Host

TCP/IP defines two additional address classes:

- **Class D:** Used for multicast addresses.

- **Class E:** Used for research purposes.

TABLE FF.14   Address Class Ranges

Class	First Octet Decimal Range
A	1 to 126
B	128 to 191
C	192 to 223
D	224 to 239
E	240 to 255

The 127.x.x.x address range is reserved for loopback addresses.

Default subnet masks:

- **Class A:** 255.0.0.0

- **Class B:** 255.255.0.0

- **Class C:** 255.255.255.0

Classless Addressing

Classless Interdomain Routing (CIDR) notation might also be used to identify the subnet mask. The CIDR notation for each network class can be determined by counting the 1s in binary or the number of bits that make up the network portion of the address.

The mask is written in slash notation as follows:

▶ **Class A:** /8

▶ **Class B:** /16

▶ **Class C:** /24

Private Ranges

IANA private address space allocations:

▶ **Class A:** 10.0.0.0 to 10.255.255.255

▶ **Class B:** 172.16.0.0 to 172.31.255.255

▶ **Class C:** 192.168.0.0 to 192.168.255.255

Subnetting

TABLE FF.15   Decimal to Binary Conversions

Class	First Octet Decimal Range
0	00000000
128	10000000
192	11000000
224	11100000
240	11110000
248	11111000
252	11111100
254	11111110
255	11111111

To calculate the hosts in a subnet, we can use the formula $2^H - 2$. The exponent H represents the number of host bits in a network.

To calculate the networks in a subnet, we can use the formula $2^N - 2$. The exponent N represents the number of subnet bits in a network.

The range of valid IP addresses in a subnet is the first IP address after the Network ID and the last IP address before the broadcast IP address.

The following represents IP subnetting:

IP address = 100.15.209.0

Subnet mask = 255.255.254.0

Network ID = 100.15.208.0

Broadcast IP = 100.15.209.255

Valid IP range = 100.15.208.1 to 100.15.209.254

IPv6

IPv6 is a workable IP version that was created in the event that the IP space from IPv4 is exhausted.

IPv6 address format summary:

▶ Defined by RFC 2373 and RFC 237.

▶ Consists of 128 bits, with a 64-bit network prefix and a 64-bit local identifier.

▶ Represented by 32 hexadecimal digits broken into eight smaller groups of four.

▶ Utilizes CIDR notation (slash notation) to discern a subnet range, so you might see the same IP address subnetted and written out as
2001:0BD2:0200:08F1:0000:0000:0000:16AB/16.

The same IPv6 IP address can be written out in all of the following ways:

2001:**0**BD2:**0**200:**0**8F1:0000:0000:0000:16AB

2001:BD2:200:8F1:0:0:0:16AB

2001:BD2:200:8F1::16AB

Types of IPv6 Addresses

▶ **Link-local addresses:** Addresses that have the shortest reach of the IP address types. They can only go as far as the Layer 2 domain. These addresses are autogenerated with or without the use of a DHCP server. So, when an IPv6 node goes online, this address is assigned automatically.

▶ **Unique/site-local addresses:** Addresses that have a broader scope than link-local addresses. They can expand to the size of an organization and are used to describe the boundary of the organizational network. These are the private addresses for IPv6.

▶ **Global addresses:** Addresses that have the broadest scope of all. As the name indicates, these addresses are for global use—that is, for Internet communications.

▶ **Multicast:** Addresses that are extremely important because of their use in group communications and broadcast messaging.

Integrating IPv4 and IPv6

There are several ways to integrate IPv4 and IPv6 addressing. You can implement dual-stack, tunneling, or translation techniques to help IPv4 and IPv6 addresses exist together on the network simultaneously.

Layer 3 Functions

Routers and Layer 3 switches perform the following functions:

▶ Do not forward broadcasts or multicasts by default.

▶ Make best path decisions.

▶ Filter packets with access lists.

▶ Remove and add Layer 2 frames.

▶ Use quality of service (QoS) rules for traffic types.

Routers decide which interface to forward a packet through by examining the network portion of each IP address.

IOS Terminal Access Methodologies

To gain access to an EXEC session to an IOS for configuration and administration, you can use the following methods:

- ▶ **Console:** Out-of-band CLI access via a rollover cable connected to the COM port of your terminal PC.

- ▶ **Auxiliary:** Out-of-band CLI access via rollover cable connected to external modem for remote access.

- ▶ **Telnet:** In-band CLI access to an active IP address on the device's vty lines using the Telnet protocol. Requires configuration.

- ▶ **SSH:** Secure encrypted in-band CLI access to an active IP address using the SSH protocol. Requires configuration.

- ▶ **HTTP/HTTPS:** In-band GUI access to an active IP address using the HTTP or HTTPS protocol. Requires configuration.

IOS Boot Processes

To solidify the startup process, the following is a recap of the stages of the bootup, any fallback procedures, and the memory locations involved:

1. POST located in ROM tests hardware.

2. Bootstrap located in ROM looks at boot field in configuration register to locate IOS. 0x2100 boots to ROMmon located in ROM.

3. 0x2101 to 0x210F prompt bootstrap to parse startup-config in NVRAM for any `boot system` commands. If there are any commands, do what they say.

4. If no `boot system` commands, load first file in flash. If no file in flash, TFTP boot. If no IOS file found from TFTP, go to ROMmon mode.

5. After IOS is loaded, check configuration register. If 0x2142, ignore startup-config in NVRAM. If 0x2102, load startup-config in NVRAM. If no startup-config, TFTP autoinstall. If no TFTP autoinstall configuration found, enter Setup Mode.

IOS Navigation

TABLE FF.16   IOS Navigation Modes

Mode	Prompt	Description
User EXEC	`Router>`	Basic troubleshooting and verification
Privileged EXEC	`Router#`	All available commands, including `delete`, `clear`, `erase`, `configure`, `copy`, and `reload`
Global configuration	`Router(config)#`	Configurations that apply to the entire device
Line configuration	`Router(config-line)#`	Configurations that apply to the terminal lines into a device
Interface configuration	`Router(config-if)#`	Configurations that apply to interfaces
Subinterface configuration	`Router(config-subif)#`	Configurations that apply to logical extensions of the physical interface
Router configuration	`Router(config-router)#`	Configurations that apply to routing protocols
VLAN configuration	`Switch(vlan)#`	VLAN-specific configurations in switches

Context-Sensitive Help

The question mark shows all the available commands at that particular prompt. To see all the available commands that start with a letter or letter(s), type the letter(s) immediately followed by a question mark. To see the list of commands that follows a keyword, type the keyword, a space, and a question mark. Commands can be abbreviated as long as there are enough characters to recognize what command you are entering.

Terminal Editing Keys

TABLE FF.17   Cisco IOS Terminal Editing Keystrokes

Keystroke	Function
Ctrl+A	Moves the cursor to the beginning of the command line.
Ctrl+E	Moves the cursor to the end of the command line.
Ctrl+B	Moves the cursor back one character.
Ctrl+F	Moves the cursor forward one character.
Esc+B	Moves the cursor back one word.
Esc+F	Moves the cursor forward one word.

Syntax Errors

▶ **Ambiguous command:** This error is displayed when you have not typed enough characters for the IOS to distinguish which command you want to use. In other words, several commands start with those same characters, so you must type more letters of the command for the IOS to recognize your particular command.

▶ **Incomplete command:** The IOS has recognized your keyword syntax with this error message; however, you need to add more keywords to tell the IOS what you want to do with this command.

▶ **Invalid input:** Also known as the "fat finger" error, this console error message is displayed when you mistype a command. The IOS displays a caret (^) up to the point where the IOS could understand your command.

Global Configuration Commands

TABLE FF.18   Global Configuration Commands

Command	Description
config-register *register*	Alters the configuration register.
boot system *location*	Specifies location to load IOS.
hostname *hostname*	Changes the name of the Cisco router or switch.
banner motd *char banner char*	Creates a message of the day login banner.
ip host *name ipaddress*	Configures a static mapping of a hostname to an IP address.
ip name-server *ip*	Specifies a DNS server IP address for dynamic name resolution.
ip domain-lookup	Enables automatic name resolution.
ip domain-name	Assigns a domain name to a Cisco device.

Securing the IOS

First and foremost, ensure that you physically secure access to your Cisco devices so that there are no intentional or unintentional disruptions or access to the device itself.

To secure user EXEC access to your console port:

```
Router(config)#line console 0
Router(config-line)#login
Router(config-line)#password password
```

To secure user EXEC access to your aux port:

```
Router(config)#line aux 0
Router(config-line)#login
Router(config-line)#password password
```

To secure user EXEC access to all five Telnet lines:

```
Router(config)#line vty 0 4
Router(config-line)#login
Router(config-line)#password password
```

To secure access to privileged EXEC mode:

```
Router(config)#enable secret password
Router(config)#enable password password
```

The `enable secret` global configuration command encrypts the password using a MD5 hash. If the `enable secret` and `enable password` commands are used at the same time, the `enable secret` password is used.

To encrypt the `enable password` and the line passwords, use the `service password-encryption` command.

SSH

To secure terminal access to the Cisco device, use SSH over Telnet. The steps to configure SSH are as follows:

1. Configure a hostname on the device other than the default hostname.

2. Configure a domain name for the Cisco device.

3. Generate an RSA key (recommended to be at least 1024 bits) with the `crypto key generate` command.

4. Create a username/password combination with the `username username password password` command.

5. (Optional) Limit the vty lines to allow SSH with only the `transport input SSH` command.

Interface Configuration Commands

TABLE FF.19   Interface Configuration Commands

Command	Description
ip address ip *subnetmask*	Assigns an IP address to an interface.
no shutdown	Administratively enables an interface.
full-duplex	Changes the duplex setting to full duplex.
clock rate *speed*	Sets the timing speed of the network on a DCE interface in bps.
bandwidth *speed*	Sets the logical bandwidth setting for routing protocols in Kbps.
ip address dhcp	Dynamically assigns an IP address to an interface from a DHCP server.

Switch Commands

TABLE FF.20   Switch Configuration Commands

Command	Description
interface range *media range*	Configures several interfaces with the same parameters.
ip address *ipaddress*	Assigns an IP address to a VLAN interface.
ip default-gateway *ip*	Sets the gateway of last resort for a Layer 2 switch.
speed *speed*	Changes the speed of an autosensing link in Mbps.
duplex *duplex*	Sets the duplex of a switchport.

The copy Command

The copy command is used to copy files from one location to another. For example, to save the current configuration, we copy the running-config in RAM to the startup-config in NVRAM using the copy running-config startup-config command.

The copy command is used to copy files between our device and a TFTP server. For instance, copy flash tftp backs up the IOS in flash to a TFTP server. copy flash tftp can be used to upgrade, downgrade, or restore an IOS back onto our device. Before copying to a TFTP server, follow these steps:

1. The TFTP server must have the TFTP service running.

2. Our device must be cabled correctly. If a switch, plug the TFTP server into the switch with a straight-through Ethernet cable. If going directly between a router and the TFTP server, use a cross-over cable.

3. You must have IP connectivity to the server.

4. There must be enough room on the TFTP server and your device's memory to store these files.

The show Command

TABLE FF.21 General show Commands

Command	Mode	Output
show running-config	Privileged	Current active configuration in RAM.
show startup-config	Privileged	Configuration stored in NVRAM that is loaded on reboot.
show interfaces	User and privileged	Status of the interfaces as well as physical and logical address, encapsulation, bandwidth, reliability, load, MTU, duplex, broadcasts, collisions, and frame errors.
show ip interface brief	User and privileged	Status of the interfaces and their logical addresses.
show controller	User and privileged	Microcode of the interface including DCE/DTE cable connection.
show flash	User and privileged	Filenames and sizes of IOS files stored in flash memory.
show version	User and privileged	IOS version, system uptime, amount of RAM, NVRAM, flash memory, and configuration register.

Interface Status

TABLE FF.22 Interface Status Values

Layer 1	Layer 2 (Line Protocol)	Possible Symptoms
Up	Up	None. Interface is functional.
Up	Down	Encapsulation mismatch, lack of clocking on serial interfaces.
Down	Down	Cable is disconnected or attached to a shutdown interface on the far-end device.
Administratively down	Down	Local interface was not enabled with the no shutdown command.

Cisco Discovery Protocol

- ▶ Proprietary Cisco Layer 2 protocol that uses multicast to gather hardware and protocol information about directly connected devices.

- ▶ Network layer protocol and media independent.

- ▶ Enabled by default on all Cisco devices, but can be disabled globally:

  ```
  Router(config)#no cdp run
  ```

  or can be disabled on interface-by-interface basis:

  ```
  Router(config-if)#no cdp enable
  ```

- ▶ To learn the remote device's Layer 3 address and IOS version

  ```
  Router>show cdp neighbor detail
  ```

  or

  ```
  Router>show cdp entry *
  ```

Telnet

Telnet enables a virtual terminal connection to a remote device's IP address using the Application layer protocol called Telnet (TCP port 23 at the Transport layer).

To Telnet from IOS, enter the keyword `telnet` followed by the IP address or hostname. If you enter only an IP address or hostname in user or privileged EXEC, IOS automatically assumes that you are Telnetting. To Telnet to a Cisco device, the vty passwords must be set, or you receive the "Password required, but none set" error. To access Privileged EXEC in a Telnet session, you must have enable password set, or you receive the "% No password set" error.

- ▶ To suspend the Telnet session, press Ctrl+Shift+6, x.

- ▶ To see a list of the active sessions in the originating router, use the `show sessions` command.

- ▶ To resume a suspended session, press the Enter key from user EXEC or privileged EXEC mode, or enter `resume` followed by the session number.

- ▶ To close a Telnet session from the device you are Telnetted into, enter `exit` or `logout` from user EXEC or privileged EXEC mode.

- ▶ To close a Telnet session from the originating device, enter `disconnect` followed by the session number.

- ▶ To see log messages in your Telnet session, use the privileged EXEC mode command `terminal monitor` in the device that you are Telnetted into.

DHCP

Your Cisco device can act as a DHCP server and respond to DHCP requests on a segment. To configure the Cisco device as a DHCP server, you must first enable the interface that will receive the DHCP requests and assign an IP address to it. After the interface is enabled, you define the DHCP address pool with the `ip dhcp pool` *poolname* global configuration command. In `dhcp-config` mode, you can define the DHCP address scope with the `network` command followed by the IP subnet to be assigned. You can also define additional parameters such as the default gateway, DNS server, domain name, and length of the IP lease. To exclude IP addresses from being assigned (such as if you have statically assigned them to specific devices), use the `ip dhcp excluded-address` *ip-address* command to remove the IP(s) from the scope.

To verify the devices that have been assigned IP addresses from the DHCP address scope, use the `show dhcp bindings` command.

Switches

Switches have the following functions:

▶ Segment LANs into multiple collision domains.

▶ Learn MAC addresses by examining the source MAC address of each frame received and store them in a CAM table.

▶ Base their forwarding decisions based on the destination MAC address of an Ethernet frame.

▶ Flood broadcast, multicast, and unknown unicast frames out all ports except the one it was received.

A switch has three methods of forwarding frames:

▶ **Store-and-forward:** Latency varying transmission method that buffers the entire frame and calculates the CRC before forwarding the frame.

▶ **Cut-through:** Only looks at the destination MAC address in an Ethernet frame and forwards it.

▶ **Fragment-free:** Checks the first 64 bytes for frame fragments (due to collisions) before forwarding the fame.

Duplex Connections

▶ Half-duplex interfaces have one-way communication with suboptimal throughput because they operate in a collision domain in which CSMA/CD must be enabled. When connected to a hub, they must run half duplex.

▶ Full-duplex interfaces simultaneously send and receive, allowing higher throughput because CSMA/CD is disabled. Connections to other switches or devices can be full duplex.

Spanning Tree Protocol IEEE 802.1d

STP is a Layer 2 protocol that is used to prevent switching loops in networks with redundant switched paths.

TABLE FF.23   STP Port States

State	Function	Transition Time
Disabled	The interface is administratively shut down or disabled from port violation.	NA
Blocking	Does not forward any user data. All ports start out in this state. Does not send, but still can receive BPDUs to react to topology changes.	0 to 20 seconds
Listening	Begins to transition to a forwarding state by listening and sending BPDUs. No user data sent.	15 seconds
Learning	Begins to build MAC addresses learned on the interface. No user data sent.	15 seconds
Forwarding	User data forwarded.	

STP elects root bridge/switch by determining which switch has the lowest Bridge ID in the topology learned from sending and receiving BPDUs. Bridge ID is a combination of Priority and MAC address.

All nonroot switches determine root port based on the fastest (lowest cumulative cost) path back to root switch. If a tie occurs, the Bridge ID followed by port priority and port number are the tie breakers.

On each segment, the switch advertising the fastest way back to the root switch is the designated port for that segment.

If port is not a root or a designated port, it is blocking.

TABLE FF.24 Port Cost Values

Interface	Cost
10Gbps	2
1Gbps	4
100Mbps	19
10Mbps	100

STP Configuration

STP is enabled by default for all VLANs in a switch. To change the priority to a lower value for root switch elections, use one of the following commands:

```
Switch(config)#spanning-tree vlan 1 priority 4096
```

or

```
Switch(config)#spanning-tree vlan 1 root
```

STP Topology Changes and Enhancements

In the event of a topology change, formerly blocked ports might transition to a forwarding state. It might take up to 50 seconds to transition from a blocking state to a forwarding state.

An exception to these 50 seconds is if the following Cisco enhancements are in place to speed up convergence:

▸ **PortFast** skips the listening and learning states on end-devices such as servers, PCs, and printers. PortFast can cause switching loops if a hub or switch is connected. BPDU Guard adds protection by disabling a port if the interface receives a BPDU.

▸ **UplinkFast** skips the listening and learning transitions when a direct failure occurs on its root port on a switch with redundant uplinks to a distribution switch.

▸ **BackboneFast** speeds up convergence by skipping the max age time when switches learn of a failure indirectly.

EtherChannel

EtherChannel is a Cisco method of bundling redundant links between switches to act as a single aggregated link. This allows utilization of all the link's bandwidth, because STP treats the link as a single interface (no blocking/discarding ports). In the case of a link failure, EtherChannel automatically distributes the traffic load over the remaining links in milliseconds.

To add an interface to an EtherChannel bundle (up to eight), use the `channel-group chan-nel#` `mode on` command in the interface configuration.

Rapid Spanning Tree Protocol

RSTP IEEE 802.1w incorporates several of Cisco's STP enhancements and ensures a safe and quick transition to a forwarding state and topology convergence by removing the overdependence on STP timers.

TABLE FF.25 RSTP Port States

State	Function	802.1d STP Equivalent
Disabled	The interface is administratively shut down or disabled from port violation.	Disabled
Discarding	Does not forward any user data. All ports start out in this state. Does not send, but still can receive BPDUs to react to topology changes.	Blocking and listening
Learning	Begins to build MAC addresses learned on the interface. No user data is sent.	Learning
Forwarding	User data is forwarded.	Forwarding

TABLE FF.26 RSTP Port Roles

State	Function	802.1d STP Equivalent
Root	The forwarding interface with the fastest (lowest cumulative path cost) to the root switch.	Root
Designated	On each segment, this forwarding interface is responsible for forwarding frames from one segment to the next.	Designated
Discarding	If the interface is not a root or designated port, it is discarding. Discarding ports are nonforwarding interfaces that do not forward traffic to avoid switching loops.	Blocking
Alternate	An interface in a discarding state that becomes the root port for a segment if the existing root port fails. Occurs when there are redundant links to the root switch in a switched network.	NA
Backup	An interface in a discarding state that becomes the designated port for a segment if the existing designated port fails. Occurs when there are redundant links to the same segment.	NA

TABLE FF.27 RSTP Link Types

State	Function
Link type point-to-point	Full-duplex links between switches
Link type shared	Half-duplex links between switches or hubs
Edge type	Connections to end devices such as PCs, printers, and servers

RSTP Convergence

Edge ports immediately transition to a forwarding state when connected to RSTP ports. For point-to-point link types, transitioning to a forwarding state involves a synchronization process:

1. After switches are connected to a point-to-point link, they exchange BPDUs.

2. If a switch determines its port will become a designated port, it sends a proposal to start forwarding to its neighbor.

3. The neighboring switch receives the proposal. If its port is a root port, it synchronizes the change by putting all nonedge ports into a discarding state and sending an agreement back to the original switch. If its port is a discarding port, it does not respond to the proposal.

4. The original switch immediately transitions to a forwarding state if it receives an agreement or eventually transitions to a forwarding state after a forward delay occurs.

RSTP uses BPDUs as keepalives to detect if a neighboring switch goes down. When the topology change is detected, RSTP immediately starts aging out the affected MAC address and tells its neighbors to do the same.

Virtual LANs (VLANs)

VLANs logically divide a switch into multiple broadcast domains at Layer 2.

Each VLAN can represent a logical grouping of users by function or department. As users in these VLANs move, we simply need to change the VLAN assigned to their switch port. VLANs also enhance security because users in one VLAN cannot communicate to users in another VLAN without the use of a Layer 3 device providing inter-VLAN routing.

VLAN Configuration

VLANs can be statically assigned to switch access ports or dynamically assigned by using a VMPS. By default, all interfaces are assigned to the management VLAN, VLAN 1.

To configure a VLAN:

1. Create the VLAN in global configuration:

```
Switch(config)#vlan 2
Switch(config-vlan)#
```

2. The VLAN must be named:

```
Switch(config-vlan)#vlan 2 name ExamPrep
```

3. The desired ports must be added to the new VLAN:

```
Switch(config)#interface FastEthernet 0/1
Switch(config-if)#switchport access vlan 2
```

Voice VLANs

Voice VLANs are used to separate VoIP traffic from data on an access port for QoS, manageability, and traffic confinement.

```
Switch(config-if)#switchport voice vlan 30
```

Trunks

VLANS can span multiple switches using trunks. Trunks multiplex traffic from all VLANs over a single connection. The VLAN identifier is tagged over the trunk using one of the following tagging methods:

▶ **ISL:** A Cisco-proprietary trunk that encapsulates the original Ethernet frame with a 26-byte header and a 4-byte CRC.

▶ **IEEE 802.1q:** Standards-based VLAN tagging that inserts a 4-byte tag in the original Ethernet frame. Traffic originating from the native VLAN (VLAN 1 by default) is not tagged over the trunk. If native VLAN configuration does not match on both sides, this could cause VLAN leakage.

Trunk Configuration

```
Switch(config)#interface FastEthernet 0/24
Switch(config-if)#switchport trunk encapsulation [isl|dot1q]
Switch(config-if)#switchport mode trunk
```

Trunks can be secured by allowing only specific VLANs to traverse to switches that specifically require access to those VLANs. The command to specify the VLANs to be included in the "allowed list of VLANs" is switchport trunk allowed vlan {add ¦ remove ¦ except} *vlan_list*.

VLAN Trunking Protocol

Cisco created VTP to minimize the amount of VLAN administration in switches by enabling a VTP server to multicast VTP advertisements to other switches in the same VTP domain. Switches receiving these advertisements synchronize their VLAN database with the VLAN information advertised from the server, assuming that the revision number is higher.

TABLE FF.28 VTP Modes

Mode	Function
Server	Default VTP mode that enables you to create, modify, and delete VLANS. These VLANs are advertised to other switches and saved in the VLAN database.
Client	Cannot create, modify, or delete VLANs. Forwards advertisements received from the server, but does not save the VLAN configuration in the VLAN database.
Transparent	Creates, modifies, and deletes VLANs only on the local switch. Does not participate in VTP but forwards VTP advertisements received from servers. Also saves the VLAN configuration in the VLAN database.

VTP Configuration

Changing the VTP domain name from NULL to ExamPrep:

```
Switch(config)#vtp domain ExamPrep
```

Setting the device VLAN database password to examcram:

```
Switch(config)#vtp password examcram
```

Setting the device to VTP TRANSPARENT mode:

```
Switch(config)#vtp transparent
```

InterVLAN Routing

InterVLAN routing requires a Layer 3 device such as router or a Layer 3 switch:

▶ **Router-on-a-stick:** The connection between router and switch must be at least Fast Ethernet speeds and must be a trunk. The router interface consists of subinterfaces to assign an IP gateway for each VLAN. The VLAN is associated with a subinterface using the encapsulation command:

```
Router(config)#interface FastEthernet 0/1.2
Router(config-subif)#ip address 192.168.2.1 255.255.255.0
Router(config-subif)#encapsulation dot1q 2
Router(config)#interface FastEthernet 0/1.3
Router(config-subif)#ip address 192.168.3.1 255.255.255.0
Router(config-subif)#encapsulation dot1q 3
```

▶ **Switched virtual interfaces:** VLAN interfaces configured in a Layer 3 switch that enables inter-VLAN routing using ASIC technology:

```
Router(config)#interface Vlan 2
Router(config-if)#ip address 192.168.2.1 255.255.255.0
Router(config)#interface Vlan 3
Router(config-if)#ip address 192.168.3.1 255.255.255.0
```

Port Security

Here's the configuration that limits the number of MAC addresses that can be dynamically learned on a switch port:

```
Switch(config-if)#switchport mode access
Switch(config-if)#switchport port-security
Switch(config-if)#switchport port-security maximum 1
Switch(config-if)#switchport port-security violation {protect ¦ restrict ¦ shutdown}
```

If a violation occurs, the default response of a Catalyst switch is to shut down the port. To have the port increase a violation counter and alert an administrator using SNMP, use the `restrict` keyword. The `protect` keyword allows only traffic from the secure port and drops packets from other MAC addresses until the number of MAC addresses drops below the maximum.

To secure an interface by statically assigning the permitted MAC address(es) attached to the port, use the `switchport port-security mac-address` *MAC_address* command on the interface. Alternatively, you can have the switch learn these addresses up to the maximum by using sticky-learned addresses with the command `switchport port-security mac-address sticky`.

Routing Characteristics

Packets originating from a nonrouting device destined for another network are sent to their default gateway (Layer 3 device on segment). The router consults its routing table to determine if the destination network can be reached. If not, the ICMP Destination Unreachable message is sent to the source. If so, packet is forwarded out interface associated with the destination network in routing table.

Routing Sources

▶ **Connected interfaces:** As soon as we assign an IP address to a working (up/line protocol up) interface, the router associates the entire subnet of the interface's IP address in the routing table.

▶ **Static routes:** Manual entries that an administrator enters into the configuration that describe the destination network and the next hop (router along the destination path).

▶ **Routing protocols:** Protocols exchanged between routing devices to dynamically advertise networks.

When multiple routing sources are advertising the same IP subnet, the router uses the source with the lowest administrative distance.

TABLE FF.29   Default Administrative Distances

Routed Source	Default Distance
Connected	0
Static route	1
EIGRP (internal)	90
OSPF	110
RIPv1 and v2	120
EIGRP (external)	170

Static and Default Routes

Static routes are useful in stub networks in which we want to control the routing behavior by manually configuring destination networks into the routing table:

```
Router(config)#ip route 10.0.0.0 255.0.0.0 192.168.2.5
```

A floating static route can be configured when redundant connections exist and you want to use the redundant link if the primary fails. This is configured by adding a higher administrative distance at the end of a static route:

```
Router(config)#ip route 10.0.0.0 255.0.0.0 192.168.2.9 2
```

A default route is a gateway of last resort for a router when there isn't a specific match for an IP destination network in the routing table (such as packets destined for the Internet):

```
Router(config)#ip route 0.0.0.0 0.0.0.0 serial 0/0
```

With routing protocols, you can specify a default network, which is a network in the routing table that routing devices consider to be the gateway of last resort. Using their routing protocols, they determine the best path to the default network:

```
Router(config)#ip default-network 192.168.1.0
```

Dynamic Routing Protocols

In complex networks with multiple pathways to destinations, dynamic routing protocols enable routers to advertise their networks to each other and dynamically react to topology changes.

Routing protocols determine the best path based on the lowest metric.

Routing Metrics

Because one of the core responsibilities of routing protocols is to build routing tables to determine optimal routing paths, we need to have some means of measuring which routes are preferred when there are multiple pathways to a destination. Routing protocols use some measure of metrics to identify which routes are optimal to reach a destination network. The lowest cumulative metric to a destination is the preferred path and the one that ultimately enters the routing table. Different routing protocols use one or several of the following metrics to calculate the best path.

TABLE FF.30   Routing Metrics

Metric	Description
Hop count	The number of routing devices that the packet must travel to reach a destination network
Bandwidth	The cumulative bandwidth of the links to the destination in kilobits per second
Delay	The length of time (measured in microseconds) a packet takes from source to destination
Reliability	The consistency of the links and paths toward the destination based on error rates of the interfaces
Load	The cumulative amount of congestion or saturation of the links toward the destination
MTU	The maximum frame size that is allowed to traverse the links to the destination
Cost	An arbitrary number typically based on the link's bandwidth

Interior and Exterior Gateway Routing Protocols

▶ **Interior gateway routing protocols:** IG routing protocols advertise networks and metrics within an autonomous system.

▶ **Exterior gateway routing protocols:** EG routing protocols advertise networks in between autonomous systems.

Classful and Classless Routing Updates

▶ **Classful routing:** The routing updates only contain the classful networks without any subnet mask. Summarization is automatically done when a router advertises a network out an interface that is not within the same major subnet. Classful routing protocols must have a FLSM design and do not operate correctly with discontiguous networks.

▶ **Classless routing:** The routing updates can contain subnetted networks because the subnet mask is advertised in the updates. Route summarization can be manually configured at any bit boundary. Classless routing protocols support VLSM designs and discontiguous networks.

Routing Protocol Classes

▶ **Distance vector:** The entire routing table is periodically sent to directly connected neighbors regardless of a topology change. These routing protocols manipulate the routing table updates before sending that information to their neighbors and are slow to converge when a topology change occurs.

▶ **Link state:** All possible link states are stored in an independent topology table in which the best routes are calculated and put into the routing table. The topology table is initially synchronized with discovered neighbors followed by frequent hello messages. These routing protocols are faster to converge than distance vector routing protocols.

▶ **Hybrid:** By using the best characteristics from link-state and routing protocols, these advanced routing protocols efficiently and quickly build their routing information and converge when topology changes occur.

Redistribution

Redistribution is the method of configuring routing protocols to advertise networks from other routing protocols:

▶ **One-way redistribution:** Networks from an edge protocol are injected into a more robust core routing protocol, but not the other way around. This method is the safest way to perform redistribution.

▶ **Two-way redistribution:** Networks from each routing protocol are injected into the other. This is the least preferred method because it is possible that suboptimal routing or routing loops might occur because of the network design or the difference in convergence times when a topology change occurs.

Distance Vector Routing Loop Mitigation

Distance vector routing protocols contain several measures to prevent routing loops:

▶ **Maximum hop counts:** To ensure that routing metrics do not increment until infinity in a routing loop, distance vector routing protocols have a maximum hop count.

TABLE FF.31   Maximum Hop Counts

Protocol	Distance Vector/Link State/Hybrid	Maximum Hop Count
RIPv1	Distance vector	15
RIPv2	Distance vector	15
EIGRP	Hybrid	224
OSPF	Link state	Infinite

- ▶ **Split horizon:** Subnets learned from neighbor routers should not be sent back out the same interface from which the original update came.

- ▶ **Route poisoning with poison reverse:** When a route to a subnet fails, the subnet is advertised with an infinite metric. Routers receiving the poisoned route override the split horizon rule and send a poison reverse back to the source.

- ▶ **Hold-down timers:** The amount of time a router ignores any information about an alternative route with a higher metric to a poisoned subnet.

- ▶ **Flash updates/triggered updates:** When a route fails, the router immediately shoots out an update as opposed to waiting for a normal update interval.

RIP and RIPv2

TABLE FF.32   RIP and RIPv2 Comparison

	RIPv1	RIPv2
Classful/classless	Classful	Both
Algorithm	Bellman-Ford	Bellman-Ford
Metric	Hops	Hops
Maximum hop count	15	15
Infinite metric	16	16
Hello/dead time	30/180	30/180
Updates	Broadcast	Multicast (224.0.0.9)
Update authentication	No	Yes
Load balancing	Equal paths	Equal Paths

RIP Configuration

The configuration for RIP is seamless as long as you remember these two simple rules:

1. Advertise only your directly connected networks.

2. Advertise only the classful network.

```
Router(config)#router rip
Router(config-router)#network 192.168.7.0
Router(config-router)#network 172.17.0.0
```

RIPv2 Configuration

```
Router(config)#router rip
Router(config-router)#network 192.168.7.0
Router(config-router)#network 172.17.0.0
Router(config-router)#version 2
Router(config-router)#no auto-summary
```

Verifying and Troubleshooting RIP

TABLE FF.33   Verifying and Troubleshooting RIP Commands

Command	Output
show ip route	The routing table with RIP entries represented as "R"
show ip protocols	RIP timers, advertised networks
debug ip rip	Real-time display of RIP routing updates being sent and received

Before using any debug commands, verify the processor utilization using the show process-es command.

OSPF Characteristics

TABLE FF.34   OSPF Characteristics

	OSPF
Classful/classless	Classless
Algorithm	Dijkstra SPF
Metric	Cost (10^8/bandwidth bps)
Maximum hop count	None
Areas or autonomous system configuration	Areas

TABLE FF.34 *Continued*

	OSPF
Hello/dead time	10/40, 30/120
Cisco or IETF	IETF
Updates	Multicast (224.0.0.5, 224.0.0.6)
Load balancing	Equal paths
Routed protocols	IP

OSPF is a link-state routing protocol that automatically discovers its neighbors by sending hello messages to 224.0.0.5. After the neighbors are discovered, they form an adjacency by synchronizing their databases. This database lists all possible routes that the neighbor is aware of in the topology. Each subnet learned has a cost associated with it, which is calculated by taking 10^8/bandwidth. The paths with the lowest cost to a destination are put in the routing table.

TABLE FF.35 Cost Values Based on Bandwidth

Bandwidth	OSPF Cost
56Kbps	1785
64Kbps	1562
T1 (1.544 Mbps)	64
E1 (2048 Mbps)	48
Ethernet (10 Mbps)	10
Fast Ethernet (100 Mbps)	1
Gigabit Ethernet (1000 Mbps)	1

OSPF uses areas to limit the size of the topology table for devices inside that area, which allows for smaller updates and faster convergence. ABRs that sit on the border of these areas have a hierarchically function over other routers because they manually summarize networks to the rest of the OSPF autonomous system. The result of this summarization is a smaller topology and routing table because the individual subnets are not being advertised. In addition, topology changes are confined inside the area where the change occurred because other areas are not aware of the individual subnets.

Areas can be numbered from 0 to 65535. Area 0 is known as the backbone area in which all other areas must connect. An area can be configured as a stub area in which ABRs advertise default routes instead of summarized networks into an area to minimize the topology and route tables.

In broadcast and nonbroadcast multiaccess topologies, OSPF decreases the amount of update overhead by electing a DR and BDR. The DR and BDR are determined by the router that has the highest priority. In the case of a tie, the highest Router ID is a tiebreaker.

The Router ID is determined by the highest active loopback IP address that is configured when the OSPF process starts. The loopback interface is a virtual interface that does not go down unless the router is turned off. In the absence of any loopback interfaces, the highest active physical IP address is used. It is common to use a host mask (255.255.255.255) on a loopback interface.

When a topology change occurs, the update is sent to the DR and BDR to the 224.0.0.6 multicast address. The DR is responsible for sending that update to the rest of the OSPF routers by multicasting the update to 224.00.5. When a device receives an update, it immediately floods it to its neighbors before calculating the topology change.

OSPF Configuration

The first step should be to configure the loopback interface to establish the Router ID:

```
Router(config)#interface loopback 0
Router(config-if)#ip address 10.1.42.1 255.255.255.255
```

You must specify an OSPF process ID between 1 and 65535. The OSPF process ID identifies a unique instance of an OSPF process and is locally significant (does not have to match in all routers in the OSPF autonomous system):

```
Router(config)#router ospf 1
```

To associate the networks to OSPF areas, you must specify the network followed by the wild-card mask and the area:

```
Router(config-router)#network 192.168.1.0 0.0.0.255 area 0
```

The area can be designated as a stub area as long as there is only one pathway in and out of the area:

```
Router(config-router)#area 1 stub
```

To change the cost of a link on an interface, you must navigate to the interface and use the following command:

```
Router(config-if)#ip ospf cost 30
```

On broadcast and nonbroadcast multiaccess topologies, you should force the election by changing the default OSPF priority on the interface:

```
Router(config-if)#ip ospf priority 5
```

Verifying and Troubleshooting OSPF

TABLE FF.36 Verifying and Troubleshooting OSPF Commands

Command	Output
show ip route	The routing table with OSPF entries represented as "O." Routes learned from other areas also have an interarea indicator ("IA").
show ip protocols	OSPF process ID and advertised networks.
show ip ospf interface	Local router's router ID, interface topology type, link cost and priority, router ID for the DR and BDR on the segment, hello/dead intervals, and a count of how many neighbors and adjacencies.
show ip ospf neighbor	Neighbor table to verify neighbor IDs and if neighbor is DR or BDR.
show ip ospf database	OSPF subnets and advertising routers in the topology table.
debug ip ospf events	Real-time display of LSAs and LSUs being sent and received.

EIGRP Characteristics

TABLE FF.37 EIGRP Characteristics

	EIGRP
Classful/classless	Both
Algorithm	DUAL
Metric	32-bit composite (bandwidth plus delay)
Maximum hop count	224
Areas or autonomous system configuration	Autonomous systems
Hello/dead time	5/15, 60/180
Cisco or IETF	Cisco
Load balancing	Unequal paths
Routed protocols	IP, IPX, AppleTalk
Redistribution	Automatic with matching IGRP autonomous system number
Administrative distance	90 for internally learned networks 170 for externally learned networks
Updates	Multicast (224.0.0.10)

In the EIGRP topology table, EIGRP maintains the advertised distance and the feasible distance to every subnet. The subnet(s) with the lowest feasible distance is the route that is placed in the routing table known as the successor route. If the advertised distance of an alternative route is lower than the feasible distance of the successor route, it is a feasible successor, which is used if the successor route fails. This is why EIGRP's DUAL algorithm makes it the fastest-converging routing protocol.

In cases in which there isn't a feasible successor, the route goes from a passive state to an active state. The state is active because the router is actively querying its neighbor for alternative paths to the destination. If a reply indicates an alternative path, that link is used.

EIGRP Configuration

Similar to IGRP, EIGRP uses the concept of autonomous system numbers in the configuration. These autonomous system numbers must match in all configured Cisco routing devices:

```
Router(config)#router eigrp 100
Router(config-router)#network 192.168.7.0
Router(config-router)#network 172.17.0.0
```

EIGRP can also load-balance over unequal paths using the `variance` command:

```
Router(config-router)#variance 10
```

Similar to RIPv2, EIGRP can be configured as classless supporting VLSM, discontiguous networks, and manual route summarization:

```
Router(config-router)#no auto-summary
```

Verifying and Troubleshooting EIGRP

TABLE FF.38 Verifying and Troubleshooting EIGRP Commands

Command	Output
`show ip route`	The routing table with OSPF entries represented as "D." External route entries learned from redistribution also have an "EX" indicator.
`show ip protocols`	EIGRP autonomous system and advertised networks.
`show ip eigrp neighbors`	Neighbor table to verify neighbors in neighbor table.
`show ip eigrp topology`	EIGRP-learned subnets and the calculated successors for each subnet based on the lowest composite metric.
`debug ip eigrp`	Real-time display of hellos and updates being sent and received.

Passive Interfaces

When interfaces are not connected to other routing devices, or you want to designate certain devices that should not receive routing updates, you can configure those interfaces as passive interfaces. When an interface is designated as a passive interface, routing updates are not sent out that interface. However, incoming updates can still be received and processed. To configure the passive interfaces, use the `passive-interface` command in the routing process:

```
Router(config-router)#passive-interface fastethernet 0/0
```

Wireless Networking

Wireless networks have impacted our existing network environments profoundly over the last few years. Because this is the newest topic on the CCENT and CCNA exams, much of what you need to know is the foundations of wireless:

▶ Wireless networks exist by using FCC unmanaged/unregulated radio frequency (RF) signals. This allows corporations to implement wireless technology without FCC approval.

▶ The primary technologies that exist today are 802.11b, 802.11g, and 802.11a. 802.11b/g uses the 2.4GHz frequency range. 802.11a uses the 5GHz frequency range. The 2.4GHz band is much more saturated with consumer electronics (such as cordless phones and microwaves) than the 5GHz band. 802.11n is still in draft status at the time of this writing.

▶ Higher radio frequencies can handle more bandwidth, but they have less range than the lower radio frequencies.

▶ When wireless technology is implemented in a larger building, adjacent wireless access points should use different channels to avoid interfering with each other.

▶ The primary channels used in the U.S. for 802.11b/g are channels 1, 6, and 11. These three channels do not have any overlapping frequencies with each other.

▶ The Wi-Fi Alliance was an organization whose aim was to create a cross-vendor certification of wireless equipment. Purchasing equipment certified by the Wi-Fi Alliance ensures that all the wireless networking gear you use will be compatible with each other.

Wireless Security and Implementation

Because wireless networking has become so prevalent in businesses, it is imperative that every network technician know the foundations of wireless security. Table FF.39 breaks down the wireless encryption standards currently available.

TABLE FF.39 Wireless Encryption Standards

Security Standard	Encryption Strength	Key Distribution	Encryption Cipher
WEP	40-bit	Preshared keys	RC4
WEP2	104-bit	Preshared keys	RC4
WPA	128-bit	Preshared keys or 802.1x; TKIP allows dynamic key rotation	RC4
WPA2 (802.11i)	Varied strength; currently up to 256-bit	Preshared keys or 802.1x	AES

Wireless authentication adds an entirely new layer of security to your wireless network. Rather than simply requiring a preshared key (PSK) to gain access to the WLAN, users must authenticate using one of many EAP methods. Encryption keys are dynamically generated after a successful authentication.

Network authentication for LAN environments is called 802.1x (also known as EAP over LAN [EAPOL]).

When implementing wireless access points, you can choose to use a Basic Service Set (BSS), which is a single access point. Or you can choose to use an Extended Service Set (ESS), which is two or more BSSs that tie users to the same LAN. These typically have overlapping coverage areas.

The farther you move from a wireless access point, the more your speed decreases. 802.11a/b/g have the following steps:

802.11a and 802.11g:

- ▶ Step 1: 54Mbps
- ▶ Step 2: 48Mbps
- ▶ Step 3: 36Mbps
- ▶ Step 4: 24Mbps
- ▶ Step 5: 18Mbps
- ▶ Step 6: 12Mbps
- ▶ Step 7: 9Mbps
- ▶ Step 8: 6Mbps

802.11b:

- ▶ Step 1: 11Mbps
- ▶ Step 2: 5.5Mbps

▶ Step 3: 2Mbps

▶ Step 4: 1Mbps

Implementing a wireless network typically should be done in four steps:

1. Ensure hardwired operation.

2. Install the wireless access point in your tested switchport.

3. Configure a basic wireless network, and test it.

4. Add wireless security, and test it.

Cisco Access Lists

Access lists are a Cisco configuration paramount to enabling your router to do any major task. The following facts are relevant to access lists:

▶ A Cisco access list is nothing more than an ordered list of permit and deny statements.

▶ They are read by the router in a top-down format. As soon as a match condition is reached, the access list stops processing.

▶ If you reach the end of an access list and have not been explicitly permitted, you are implicitly denied.

▶ Numbered and named access lists do not allow you to reorder statements; however, named access lists allow you to delete individual access list lines.

Access lists have a number of functions on the Cisco router. The primary access lists uses are

▶ Packet filtering

▶ Quality of Service (QoS)

▶ Network Address Translation (NAT)

▶ Route filtering

There are two types of IP-based access lists:

▶ Standard access lists are capable of filtering traffic based only on the source IP address.

▶ Extended access lists are capable of filtering traffic based on protocol, source address, source port number, destination address, and destination port number.

IP Standard access lists use numbers 1 to 99, and IP Extended access lists use numbers 100 to 199.

The configuration of a standard access list uses the following syntax:

```
Router(config)#access-list <1-99> <permit/deny> <source_IP_address> <wildcard_mask>
```

The following configuration creates access list 25, which permits a single host (10.1.1.5) and the 192.168.1.0/24 subnet:

```
Router(config)#access-list 25 permit 10.1.1.5 0.0.0.0
Router(config)#access-list 25 permit 192.168.1.0 0.0.0.255
```

As a shortcut, you can use the host keyword instead of a wildcard mask of 0.0.0.0 and the any keyword instead of a wildcard mask of 255.255.255.255. The following example shows these keywords in action:

```
Router(config)#access-list 25 permit host 10.1.1.5
Router(config)#access-list 25 deny any
```

When looking to apply an access list to an interface, remember the following mantra:

One access list

- ▶ Per protocol
- ▶ Per interface
- ▶ Per direction

When trying to find what direction to apply an access list, picture yourself as a router. Hold out an arm to represent an interface. If the traffic is moving away from your body, it should be applied out (outbound) on the interface. If the traffic is coming into your body, it should be applied in (inbound) on the interface. Standard access lists are always applied closest to the destination. Extended access lists are always applied closest to the source.

The following is the generic syntax used to apply access lists to an interface:

```
Router(config-if)#ip access-group <access-list_number> <in/out>
```

The following configuration applies access list 25 in the inbound direction:

```
Router(config-if)#ip access-group 25 in
```

Access lists can also be applied to vty ports to restrict Telnet access to your router. The following configuration applies access list 25 to a router's vty ports:

```
Router(config)#line vty 0 4
Router(config-line)#access-class 25 in
```

Extended access list configuration gets slightly more complex than a standard access list. The following is the generic syntax used to create an extended access list:

```
Router(config)#access-list <100-199> <permit/deny> <protocol> <source_IP_address>
<wildcard_mask> <source_port_number> <destination_IP_address> <wildcard_mask>
<destination_port_number>
```

There are many IP-based protocols that extended access lists can permit or deny. The following is a list of the protocols you should be familiar with:

▶ **IP** permits or denies source/destination addresses using the entire TCP/IP protocol suite. Using this keyword permits or denies *all* access from a source to a destination.

▶ **TCP** permits or denies source/destination addresses using TCP-based applications. The most common applications include FTP, Telnet, SMTP, and HTTP.

▶ **UDP** permits or denies source/destination addresses using UDP-based applications. The most common applications include DNS and TFTP.

▶ **ICMP** permits or denies source/destination addresses using ICMP-based applications. The most common applications include Echo, Echo-Reply, and Unreachables.

When configuring extended access lists, you rarely, if ever, know a network device's source port number information. This number is randomly generated by the host's operating system. You should leave it blank for any CCNA-level configuration you perform.

You need to know these commonly used port numbers for the CCNA exam:

TCP Ports

▶ Port 21: FTP

▶ Port 22: SSH

▶ Port 23: Telnet

▶ Port 25: SMTP

▶ Port 80: HTTP

▶ Port 443: HTTPS

UDP Ports

▶ Port 53: DNS

▶ Port 69: TFTP

The following access list permits a single host (10.1.1.5) to access any destination using port 80 (HTTP):

```
Router(config)#access-list 150 permit tcp host 10.1.1.5 any eq 80
```

The following access list denies a network subnet (172.16.70.0/24) from accessing a single host (172.16.50.100) using port 21 (FTP):

```
Router(config)#access-list 125 deny tcp 172.16.70.0 0.0.0.255 host 172.16.50.100 eq 21
```

Often, you need to end an access list with a "permit all" statement. The following examples show how to accomplish this:

Standard access list example:

```
Router(config)#access-list 12 permit any
```

Extended access list example:

```
Router(config)#access-list 125 permit ip any any
```

Often, a router connected to the Internet denies all incoming traffic to secure the internal network. However, this prevents internal users from receiving responses to their common web browsing requests. The following extended access list entry permits any return traffic that is a response to a request originated from the internal network:

```
Router(config)#access-list 150 permit tcp any any established
```

You can verify access lists using a few show commands:

▶ show running-config shows the full access list configuration and the interfaces where you have applied them.

▶ show ip interface shows the inbound and outbound access lists applied to each interface.

▶ show access-lists shows all access lists created on the router and the number of times each entry has been matched.

▶ show ip access-lists shows just the IP-based access lists on the router and the number of times each entry has been matched.

Network Address Translation (NAT)

NAT is in use on virtually every Internet-connected router in the world today. This technology acts as a security boundary and Internet address sharing system. The following facts are relevant to NAT.

NAT typically operates by translating private IP addresses to public Internet addresses. The following are the private address ranges as defined by RFC 1918:

- **Class A:** 10.X.X.X
- **Class B:** 172.16.X.X to 172.31.X.X
- **Class C:** 192.168.X.X

The three primary forms of NAT are as follows:

- **Static NAT** allows you to manually map one IP address to another in a one-to-one relationship.
- **Dynamic NAT** allows you to define a pool of addresses to be translated along with a pool of addresses they will be translated to.
- **NAT Overload/PAT** allows a single Internet IP address to support many internal clients.

The standards bodies have developed many terms to describe the location of an IP address in the world of NAT:

- **Inside local addresses:** Refers to everything inside your network.
- **Inside global addresses:** The Internet valid IP address assigned to your router that is directly connected to the Internet.
- **Outside global addresses:** A standard Internet IP address accessible from any host connected to the Internet.
- **Outside local addresses:** How an Internet host is seen by the internal network as it is translated through the NAT router into your local network.

The following shows a Static NAT configuration fully translating 192.168.1.50 (on the internal network) to 5.1.1.10 (on the Internet). It then shows a single Static NAT port translation mapping 192.168.1.150 port 53 (DNS) on the internal network to 5.1.1.11 port 53 on the Internet:

```
NAT_Router(config)#interface fastethernet0
NAT_Router(config-if)#ip nat inside
NAT_Router(config)#interface serial0
NAT_Router(config-if)#ip nat outside
NAT_Router(config)#ip nat inside source static 192.168.1.50 5.1.1.10
NAT_Router(config)#ip nat inside source static udp 192.168.1.150 53 5.1.1.11 53
```

The following shows a NAT Overload/PAT configuration translating the entire internal network (192.168.1.0/24) to a single Internet address assigned to the Serial0 interface:

```
NAT_Router(config)#interface fastethernet0
NAT_Router(config-if)#ip nat inside
NAT_Router(config)#interface serial0
NAT_Router(config-if)#ip nat outside
NAT_Router(config)#access-list 50 permit 192.168.1.0 0.0.0.255
NAT_Router(config)#ip nat inside source list 50 interface serial0 overload
```

Wide-Area Networks

Wide area network (WAN) connections tie together geographically distant locations, enabling them to communicate as if directly connected. The following facts are relevant to WANs.

WAN technologies only encompass the Physical and Data Link layers of the OSI model. The three major categories of WAN technology used to connect networks today are as follows:

▶ **Leased lines** provide a dedicated, point-to-point link between two locations.

▶ **Circuit-switched networks** establish a dedicated channel (or circuit) for the duration of the transmission and then tear down the channel when the transmission is complete.

▶ **Packet-switched networks** enable the service provider to create a large pool of bandwidth for its clients, who establish connections through the shared bandwidth using virtual circuits.

Cisco routers connect to most WAN connections through their serial ports. The Cisco side of the connection uses either a DB-60 or Smart Serial port. The CSU/DSU that the Cisco router connects to has one of five standard connectors: V.35, X.21, EIA/TIA-232, EIA/TIA-449, or EIA/TIA-530.

At the Data Link layer, Cisco routers primarily use one of two WAN encapsulations for leased-line and circuit-switched networks:

▶ **Point-to-Point Protocol (PPP):** The most popular, industry-standard, feature-packed protocol for connecting routers

▶ **Cisco High-level Data Link Control (HDLC):** A Cisco-proprietary, low-overhead protocol that makes your WAN connections very efficient between Cisco devices

HDLC is the default encapsulation on all Cisco serial interfaces. However, PPP is used to gain more features and industry standard capabilities when connecting over the WAN. It is made up of three sublayers:

▶ **ISO HDLC** is responsible for enabling PPP to be supported by multiple devices.

▶ **Link Control Protocol (LCP)** is the feature negotiation layer that performs the following functions:

- ▶ **Authentication** requires a username and password for the connecting device.

  - ▶ **Callback** enables a dialup server (or router) running PPP to call back the person who initially dialed into the location using a predefined number.

  - ▶ **Compression** makes WAN connections more efficient by minimizing the amount of data sent.

  - ▶ **Multilink** bundles multiple WAN connections (or WAN channels in the case of ISDN) into a single, logical connection.

- ▶ **Network Control Protocol (NCP)** gives PPP the functionality to enable multiple Network layer protocols to run across a single WAN link at any given time.

When configuring PPP authentication, you can choose between two authentication protocols:

- ▶ **Password Authentication Protocol (PAP)** sends username and password once in clear-text format when authenticating.

- ▶ **Challenge Handshake Authentication Protocol (CHAP)** sends a username and hashed password when demanded by the CHAP server.

When configuring PPP compression, you can choose between three compression types:

- ▶ **Stacker:** A flat compression algorithm that is notoriously heavy on CPU resources and has less effect on the router's memory resources. Useful for WAN links with many traffic patterns.

- ▶ **Predictor:** A dictionary-based compression algorithm that is notoriously heavy on memory resources and has less effect on the router's CPU resources. Useful for WAN links with similar traffic patterns.

- ▶ **Microsoft Point-to-Point Compression (MPPC):** Used for Microsoft Windows dialup clients wanting to use compression.

To activate PPP encapsulation on an interface, use the following syntax:

```
Router(config)#interface serial 0
Router(config-if)#encapsulation ppp
```

When adding CHAP authentication to your configuration, you need to ensure that you create a user account that matches the hostname of the other side of the connection. In addition, the passwords must be the same on both sides. Here is a PPP CHAP authentication configuration between the Kirk and Spock routers:

```
Kirk(config)#username Spock password cisco
Kirk(config)#interface serial 0
Kirk(config-if)#encapsulation ppp
```

```
Kirk(config-if)#ppp authentication chap

Spock(config)#username Kirk password cisco
Spock(config)#interface serial 0
Spock(config-if)#encapsulation ppp
Spock(config-if)#ppp authentication chap
```

To enable PPP compression on an interface, you can use the following syntax:

```
Router(config-if)#compress ?
  mppc       MPPC compression type
  predictor  predictor compression type
  stac       stac compression algorithm
```

The show interface command is one of the most useful when verifying the PPP configuration. The connection is active when the LCP Open tag is seen, as shown here:

```
Router#show interface serial 0
Serial0 is up, line protocol is up
  Hardware is PowerQUICC Serial
  Internet address is 10.2.2.2/24
  MTU 1500 bytes, BW 1544 Kbit, DLY 20000 usec,
    reliability 255/255, txload 1/255, rxload 1/255
  Encapsulation PPP, loopback not set
  Keepalive set (10 sec)
  LCP Open
  Open: IPCP, CCP, CDPCP
```

When troubleshooting PPP authentication issues, use the debug ppp authentication command to observe the authentication process as it occurs.

Frame Relay

Frame Relay is the only packet-switched network tested on the CCNA exam. It is one of the more popular connections in businesses today. The following facts are relevant to Frame Relay.

Frame Relay offers the high speeds demanded by the networks of today at cut-rate prices. Rather than connecting sites through individual physical interfaces, Frame Relay connects sites using virtual circuits. Virtual circuits are logical links through service provider networks that give routers the impression that they are directly linked. The more virtual circuits purchased to connect network locations, the more redundant the network connections will be; at the same time, the monthly cost will rise significantly. Because of this, there are three design strategies for provisioning virtual circuits:

- **Hub and spoke:** A centralized location (most likely, your largest, most connected office) acts as the network's "hub." All other locations are considered "spokes" and have a single virtual circuit connection back to the hub.

▶ **Partial mesh:** Key network sites have redundant virtual circuit connections through the Frame Relay cloud. Other noncritical sites might only have a single virtual circuit.

▶ **Full mesh:** Every site has a direct virtual circuit to every other site in the network.

Frame Relay also introduces another set of terminology that CCNA candidates should be familiar with:

▶ **Permanent Virtual Circuit (PVC):** A permanently "nailed-up" circuit through the Frame Relay service provider network.

▶ **Switched Virtual Circuit (SVC):** An "on-demand" connection through the Frame Relay cloud.

▶ **Local Management Interface (LMI):** Signaling between your router and the Frame Relay service provider.

▶ **Data Link Connection Identifier (DLCI):** The Data Link layer addressing used by Frame Relay to identify endpoints connected to the Frame Relay service provider.

▶ **Local access rate:** The maximum physical speed that a Frame Relay connection can attain.

▶ **Committed Information Rate (CIR):** The minimum speed the service provider commits to give you for a virtual circuit at all times.

▶ **Backward Explicit Congestion Notification (BECN):** A message sent by the service provider notifying a router sending at an excessive data rate to reduce its speed.

▶ **Forward Explicit Congestion Notification (FECN):** A message sent by the service provider notifying a receiving router to send information that can be tagged as a BECN to tell a router sending at an excessive data rate to reduce its speed.

▶ **Discard Eligible (DE):** Describes any traffic that you send above the CIR you have purchased.

To provide more logical configurations, Cisco routers can create multiple subinterfaces that can connect to any number of virtual circuits. Two types of subinterfaces can be created:

▶ **Point-to-point subinterfaces** are assigned to a single virtual circuit. Only one DLCI number assigned per point-to-point subinterface.

▶ **Multipoint subinterfaces** are assigned to one or more virtual circuits. Numerous DLCI numbers can be mapped under a multipoint subinterface.

Using multipoint interfaces or the physical Serial interface for multiple virtual circuits causes known problems with the distance vector routing protocol loop-prevention mechanism, split horizon.

Cisco routers initially receive a list of DLCIs they can reach from the Frame Relay service provider. There are two ways they can map the DLCI number to the remote IP address it can reach at the other end of the connection:

▶ **Inverse ARP** enables the router to send messages down each one of the DLCI numbers to discover the router's IP address on the remote end.

▶ **Static mappings** allow the Cisco administrator to manually map each DLCI number to the router's IP address on the remote end.

Understanding the states of a Frame Relay PVC can be quite useful in both the real world and the testing environment:

▶ **Active:** The PVC is successfully connected through between the two endpoints (routers). This is the normal state if everything is working properly.

▶ **Inactive:** The PVC is working properly on your end of the connection (the local side); however, the other side of the connection is either not configured or offline.

▶ **Deleted:** The PVC is having problems on your end (the local side) of the connection. Most likely, you are attempting to use a DLCI number that the service provider has not configured.

▶ **Static:** The PVC has been manually entered by you (the administrator) rather than being dynamically discovered from the service provider.

Configuring a Frame Relay interface for a single virtual circuit requires the following minimal configuration:

```
Router(config)#interface serial 0
Router(config-if)#encapsulation frame-relay
```

If you are connecting to a non-Cisco router through the Frame Relay cloud, use the command `encapsulation frame-relay ietf` to enable your interface with the industry standard Frame Relay encapsulation.

If you are using an extremely old version of the IOS (any version earlier than 11.2), the router is unable to autodetect what LMI language the service provider is using. This means that you must manually configure it using the following syntax:

```
Router(config-if)#frame-relay lmi-type ?
  cisco
  ansi
  q933a
```

The following is a sample configuration of a multipoint interface using static Frame Relay maps. In this case, 192.168.5.1 is the remote end IP address and DLCI 405 is used to get there. Likewise, 192.168.5.2 is another remote-end router that can be reached through DLCI 406:

```
Router(config)#interface serial 0/0.10 multipoint
Router(config-if)#frame map ip 192.168.5.1 405 broadcast
Router(config-if)#frame map ip 192.168.5.2 406 broadcast
```

The following is a sample configuration using the same setup as the preceding example, but using point-to-point interfaces:

```
Router(config)#interface serial 0/0.405 point-to-point
Router(config-if)#frame-relay interface-dlci 405
Router(config)#interface serial 0/0.406 point-to-point
Router(config-if)#frame-relay interface-dlci 406
```

When troubleshooting Frame Relay connections, start with the `show frame-relay lmi` command to check connectivity to the service provider. From there, use `show frame-relay pvc` to check the status of the virtual circuits.

VPN Connectivity

VPN technology allows businesses to use their existing Internet connections to connect to other offices (site-to-site VPNs) or allow telecommuting or mobile users to connect into the office network from their PCs (remote-access VPN).

VPNs provide a variety of benefits over private-line connections:

▶ Cost savings over private-line connections

▶ Remote-access connections for telecommuting or mobile users

▶ Scalability

At the same time, VPNs have some major drawbacks:

▶ Higher overhead

▶ Varying service levels

▶ Additional security considerations

VPN connections come in two major genres: site-to-site and remote-access VPNs.

Site-to-site VPNs are the direct replacement for private-line WAN connections. They allow offices to maintain permanent or semipermanent connections between each other through the Internet.

Remote-access VPNs typically are used to allow telecommuting or mobile workers to connect to the corporate network from home or hotel-like locations. These remote-access VPNs come in a couple of styles: client-based (requires the installation of a VPN client) and clientless (also known as SSL or WebVPN; users connect through a secure web page).

The key protocol that drives VPN connections is IPsec. This is actually a suite of protocols that provide standards for encryption, authentication, and data integrity.

Three primary encryption standards are used with IPsec:

▶ **Data Encryption Standard (DES) algorithm** was originally developed by IBM to support a 56-bit key.

▶ **Triple DES (3DES) algorithm** uses three different DES keys to encrypt data, thus tripling the strength of DES.

▶ **Advanced Encryption Standard (AES)** currently offers 128-, 192-, and 256-bit encryption.

Currently, two data-integrity standards are used with IPsec:

▶ **Message Digest 5 (MD5)** uses a 128-bit hashing algorithm.

▶ **Secure Hash Algorithm 1 (SHA**-1) uses a 160-bit hashing algorithm.

Practice Exam

1. As you are trying to enter a command in the IOS, you receive the console message "Invalid input detected at ^." What should you do to correct this?

   ○ **A.** Enter more characters for the IOS to understand the command.

   ○ **B.** Enter more keywords so that the IOS understands what you want to do with the command.

   ○ **C.** Check your typing syntax.

   ○ **D.** Check your console connection.

2. According to the following access list, what would happen to a packet coming from the source address 192.168.5.67?

```
access-list 50 permit 192.168.5.16 0.0.0.15
access-list 50 permit 192.168.5.32 0.0.0.15
access-list 50 permit 192.168.5.48 0.0.0.7
access-list 50 permit 192.168.5.0 0.0.0.0
```

   ○ **A.** The packet would be denied because of the implicit deny statement.

   ○ **B.** The packet would be permitted because of the `permit 192.168.5.32 0.0.0.15` statement.

   ○ **C.** The packet would be permitted because of the `permit 192.168.5.48 0.0.0.7` statement.

   ○ **D.** The packet would be permitted because of the `permit 192.168.5.0 0.0.0.0` statement.

3. Which of the following are Application layer protocols? (Choose the three best answers)

   ○ **A.** Telnet

   ○ **B.** JPEG

   ○ **C.** HTTP

   ○ **D.** FTP

4. Which of the following commands will enable you to specify the datagram size in a ping to 10.1.1.1?

   ○ **A.** Router>**ping -l**

   ○ **B.** Router#**ping**

   ○ **C.** Router#**ping 10.1.1.1**

   ○ **D.** Router>**ping 10.1.1.1**

5. Your company has an internal web server that must be accessed from the Internet. This internal web server has the IP address 172.16.55.10. The router accesses the Internet through the FastEthernet0/1 interface. What NAT syntax is necessary to forward HTTP requests to the internal web server?

   ○ **A.** ip nat outside destination tcp 80 fastEthernet0/1
       172.16.55.10 80

   ○ **B.** ip nat inside source static tcp 172.16.55.10 80 interface
       fastEthernet 0/1 80

   ○ **C.** ip nat outsidsource tcp 80 172.16.55.10 80 interface
       fastEthe ernet0/1 80

   ○ **D.** ip nat inside destination static tcp 172.16.55.10 80
       interface fastEthernet 0/1 80

6. Which Application layer protocol resolves hostnames or fully qualified domain names (FQDNs) such as www.cisco.com into IP addresses?

   ○ **A.** SMTP

   ○ **B.** NFS

   ○ **C.** NNTP

   ○ **D.** DNS

7. Which of the following configuration registers causes the IOS to boot from flash if no boot system commands are present?

   ○ **A.** 0x2100

   ○ **B.** 0x2106

   ○ **C.** 0x2140

   ○ **D.** 0x210P

8. When connecting a serial cable from the CSU/DSU to your Cisco router, what two standards are supported on the Cisco end of the connection? (Choose two)

◯   **A.**   EIA/TIA-449

◯   **B.**   Smart Serial

◯   **C.**   DB-60

◯   **D.**   RJ-45

9. Which layer of the OSI model handles dialog control among devices?

◯   **A.**   Application

◯   **B.**   Presentation

◯   **C.**   Session

◯   **D.**   Transport

10. Which of the following STP 802.11d port states actively learns MAC addresses? (Choose all that apply)

◯   **A.**   Blocking

◯   **B.**   Learning

◯   **C.**   Listening

◯   **D.**   Forwarding

11. Which of the following IP addresses represent public addresses? (Choose two)

◯   **A.**   192.186.6.32

◯   **B.**   172.31.20.55

◯   **C.**   172.200.166.99

◯   **D.**   10.255.255.5

◯   **E.**   172.17.50.2

12. SNMP uses which port number?

◯   **A.**   67

◯   **B.**   68

◯   **C.**   69

◯   **D.**   161

13. At the end of the Setup Mode dialog, you are asked whether you want to keep the configuration you created. This configuration will be present even if you reboot the device. Where is this configuration stored?

   ○ **A.** NVRAM

   ○ **B.** RAM

   ○ **C.** ROM

   ○ **D.** Flash

14. Which of the following is a form of DoS attack? (Choose three)

   ○ **A.** TCP SYN

   ○ **B.** Smurf

   ○ **C.** DDoS

   ○ **D.** Trust exploitation

15. Which of the following are valid LMI signaling types? (Choose three)

   ○ **A.** Cisco

   ○ **B.** ANSI

   ○ **C.** ITU-T

   ○ **D.** Q.933a

   ○ **E.** IETF

16. _____ is an electrical or magnetic field that is a result of one communications signal that can affect the signal in a nearby circuit.

   ○ **A.** EMI

   ○ **B.** Attenuation

   ○ **C.** Crosstalk

   ○ **D.** Bandwidth

17. Which of the following is *not* an advantage of areas in OSPF?

   ○ **A.** ABRs perform automatic summarization.

   ○ **B.** Smaller topology tables

   ○ **C.** Confinement of topology changes

   ○ **D.** Speed up convergence

18. You would like to keep Network 1 (shown in the following figure) from accessing the Internet. Where would be the most efficient location to apply the access list ?

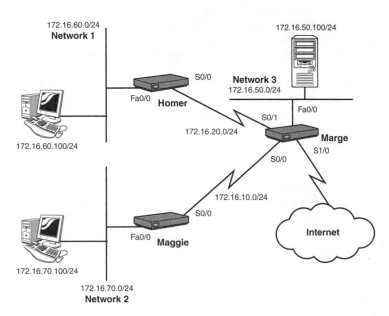

```
access-list 75 deny 172.16.60.0 0.0.0.255
access-list 75 permit any
```

- ○ **A.** On the Homer router, Fa0/0 inbound
- ○ **B.** On the Homer router, Fa0/0 outbound
- ○ **C.** On the Homer router, S0/0 inbound
- ○ **D.** On the Homer router, S0/0 outbound
- ○ **E.** On the Marge router, S0/1 inbound
- ○ **F.** On the Marge router, S0/1 outbound
- ○ **G.** On the Marge router, S1/0 inbound
- ○ **H.** On the Marge router, S1/0 outbound

19. What type of UTP cable would you use to connect a switch to a PC?

- ○ **A.** Coaxial cable
- ○ **B.** Straight-through cable
- ○ **C.** Cross-over cable
- ○ **D.** Thin coaxial

20. Given the following output, which of the following statements is false?

```
Routing Protocol is "rip"
  Sending updates every 30 seconds, next due in 2 seconds
  Invalid after 180 seconds, hold down 180, flushed after 240
  Outgoing update filter list for all interfaces is not set
  Incoming update filter list for all interfaces is not set
  Redistributing: rip
  Default version control: send version 2, receive version 2
    Interface        Send  Recv   Key-chain
    Ethernet0         2     2     examprep
    Serial0           2     2
  Routing for Networks:
    172.19.0.0
    10.2.0.0
  Routing Information Sources:
    Gateway          Distance      Last Update
  Distance:           80
```

- ○ **A.** The administrative distance has been changed.

- ○ **B.** This is version 2 of RIP.

- ○ **C.** Update authentication is configured.

- ○ **D.** The router configuration looks like the following:

    ```
    Router(config)#router rip
    Router(config-router)#version 2
    Router(config-router)#network 10.2.0.0
    Router(config-router)#network 172.19.0.0
    ```

21. Which of the following forms of NAT allows you to translate one group of IP addresses to another in a 1:1 relationship with minimal configuration?

- ○ **A.** Port Address Translation

- ○ **B.** Static NAT

- ○ **C.** NAT Overload

- ○ **D.** Dynamic NAT

22. The Ethernet IEEE 802.3 specification defines which of the following LAN standards? (Choose the three best answers)

- ○ **A.** 10BASE-2

- ○ **B.** 10BASE-5

- ○ **C.** 10BASE-T

- ○ **D.** Wi-Fi

23. Which of the following networks are contained in the summarized CIDR route of 192.168.64.0 /19? (Choose all that apply)

   ○ **A.** 192.168.96.0 /24

   ○ **B.** 192.168.60.0 /24

   ○ **C.** 192.168.80.0 /24

   ○ **D.** 192.168.101.0 /24

24. Which of the following encapsulation types can be used on leased-line connections? (Choose two)

   ○ **A.** HDLC

   ○ **B.** Frame Relay

   ○ **C.** ISDN

   ○ **D.** PPP

25. Which devices are implemented at the Physical layer of the OSI model? (Choose the two best answers)

   ○ **A.** Switch

   ○ **B.** Bridge

   ○ **C.** Hub

   ○ **D.** Repeater

26. Which of the following are 802.3 MAC sublayer Ethernet addresses? (Choose the three best answers)

   ○ **A.** IP address

   ○ **B.** Unicast address

   ○ **C.** Multicast address

   ○ **D.** Broadcast address

27. You add a switch to your VTP domain, and all your VLANs in the domain vanish. What is a likely cause of this behavior?

   ○ **A.** The new switch has a higher revision number in client mode.

   ○ **B.** The new switch has a higher revision number in server mode.

   ○ **C.** The existing switches have a higher revision number than the new switch.

   ○ **D.** Someone went to each switch and deleted the VLANs without your knowing.

28. Which of the following match the correct encryption algorithm with the wireless security standard? (Choose two)

   ◯ **A.** WPA / TKIP

   ◯ **B.** WPA 2 / TKIP

   ◯ **C.** WPA / AES

   ◯ **D.** WPA2 / AES

29. Which Ethernet MAC 802.3 sublayer address type always starts with the hexadecimal characters 0100.5E?

   ◯ **A.** Unicast address

   ◯ **B.** Multicast address

   ◯ **C.** Broadcast address

   ◯ **D.** IP address

30. You no longer have IP connectivity to a remote router at a customer's site. From your location, what terminal option can you use to gain access to an EXEC session on the remote router?

   ◯ **A.** Console port

   ◯ **B.** Telnet

   ◯ **C.** SSH

   ◯ **D.** Auxiliary port

31. Your manager wants you to convert the company's leased-line connections to a Frame Relay topology. He wants to use the lowest-cost solution available. What topology should you design?

   ◯ **A.** Full mesh

   ◯ **B.** Partial mesh

   ◯ **C.** Hub and spoke

   ◯ **D.** NBMA

32. _____ occurs when a switch creates a dedicated path for sending and receiving transmissions with each connected host.

   ◯ **A.** Microsegmentation

   ◯ **B.** Half duplex

   ◯ **C.** Full duplex

   ◯ **D.** CSMA/CD

33. You want to speed up convergence on switch ports connected to hosts, but you are afraid of someone plugging in a switch or hub and causing a loop. Which features address both requirements? (Choose two)

    ○ **A.** BackboneFast

    ○ **B.** PortFast

    ○ **C.** UplinkFast

    ○ **D.** BPDU Guard

34. How many wireless channels are available in the U.S. for the 2.4GHz band without overlapping frequencies for close-proximity wireless access points?

    ○ **A.** 1

    ○ **B.** 3

    ○ **C.** 11

    ○ **D.** 23

35. Which devices are implemented at the Data Link layer of the OSI model? (Choose the two best answers)

    ○ **A.** Hub

    ○ **B.** Repeater

    ○ **C.** Switch

    ○ **D.** Bridge

36. What range represents the first octet value of a Class A address?

    ○ **A.** 0 to 126

    ○ **B.** 1 to 126

    ○ **C.** 128 to 191

    ○ **D.** 192 to 223

37. The EIGRP routing protocol is advertising the 172.16.0.0 network. In the same autonomous system, RIP is advertising the 10.0.0.0 network. What will the contents of the routing table look like in a router running both routing protocols?

    ○ **A.** 10.0.0.0 and 172.16.0.0 will be learned through EIGRP because it has a lower administrative distance.

    ○ **B.** 10.0.0.0 and 172.16.0.0 will be learned through RIP because it has a higher administrative distance.

    ○ **C.** 10.0.0.0 will be learned through EIGRP, and 172.16.0.0 will be learned through RIP.

    ○ **D.** 10.0.0.0 will be learned through RIP, and 172.16.0.0 will be learned through EIGRP.

38. You are configuring the Internet connection for the network pictured in the following figure. The initial NAT Overload configuration has been set up; you must now publish the internal FTP and web server to the Internet. What commands will accomplish this? (Choose two)

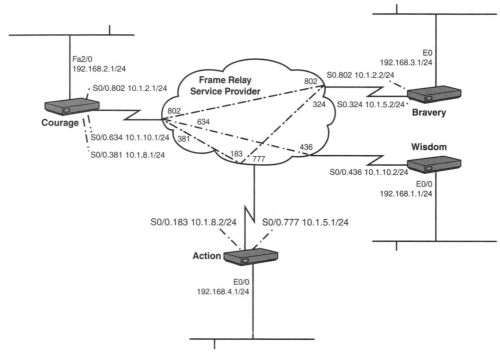

○ **A.** `ip nat inside source static tcp 80 192.168.254.100 80 24.15.240.9`

○ **B.** `ip nat inside source static tcp 192.168.254.50 20 24.15.240.9 20`

○ **C.** `ip nat inside source static tcp 192.168.254.50 21 24.15.240.9 21`

○ **D.** `ip nat inside source static tcp 192.168.254.100 80 24.15.240.9 80`

○ **E.** `ip nat inside source static tcp 21 192.168.254.50 21 24.15.240.9`

39. What can be installed in a router's T1 slot to communicate with and control the 24 DS0 channels?

○ **A.** GBIC

○ **B.** T1 controller card

○ **C.** BRI, NT1

○ **D.** HSSI

40. What is the end result of the 192.168.2.0 network based on the following output?

```
RouterA#debug ip rip
RIP protocol debugging is on
RouterA#
00:26:27: RIP: received v1 update from 192.168.1.6 on Serial0/0
00:26:27:      192.168.2.0 in 12 hops
00:26:37: RIP: received v1 update from 192.168.1.12 on Serial0/1
00:26:37:      192.168.2.0 in 12 hops
```

   ○ **A.** The router forwards packets to 192.168.1.6 because it received that update first.

   ○ **B.** The router forwards packets to 192.168.1.12 because it received that update last.

   ○ **C.** The router ignores the updates because the maximum hop count is reached.

   ○ **D.** Both entries are put in the router, and it load-balances over both links.

41. You need to block a host from Internet access by using an access list. When creating the access list, you use the syntax `access-list 99` to start the command. What type of access list is this?

   ○ **A.** An IP standard access list

   ○ **B.** An IP extended access list

   ○ **C.** An IP standard expanded range access list

   ○ **D.** An IP extended expanded range access list

42. What is 00111000 10110011 01010111 11011010 converted into decimal format?

   ○ **A.** 56.179.87.217

   ○ **B.** 56.179.87.218

   ○ **C.** 56.179.87.219

   ○ **D.** 56.179.87.220

43. Which of the following is *not* a difference between RIPv2 and EIGRP?

   ○ **A.** EIGRP can be configured as classless.

   ○ **B.** EIGRP requires all routers to be Cisco.

   ○ **C.** EIGRP supports IP, IPX, and AppleTalk.

   ○ **D.** EIGRP can distinguish between internal and external networks.

44. You are configuring your Cisco 2600XM series router to connect across the WAN to a Cisco 3800 series router. You would like to use the default WAN encapsulation. Will this work?

   ○ **A.** Yes. All Cisco routers support the same WAN encapsulation standards.

   ○ **B.** Yes. Newer Cisco routers support different WAN encapsulation standards, but they are backward-compatible with older WAN encapsulation types.

   ○ **C.** No. Newer Cisco routers use PPP as their WAN encapsulation types, and older Cisco routers use HDLC.

   ○ **D.** No. Newer Cisco routers use the industry-standard HDLC, and older Cisco routers use a proprietary version.

45. What is the broadcast IP of 212.84.5.66/26?

   ○ **A.** 212.84.5.125

   ○ **B.** 212.84.5.126

   ○ **C.** 212.84.5.127

   ○ **D.** 212.84.5.128

46. Which of the following statements is true about the 10.1.100.0 network based on the following output?

```
CstmrARtr#show ip route
...output omitted...

Gateway of last resort is 192.168.1.9 to network 0.0.0.0

D    10.1.100.0 /24 [90/16] via 192.168.1.9, 00:00:11, Serial0
C    172.17.0.0/16 is directly connected, Ethernet0
D    172.16.0.0/16 [90/2340] via 172.17.0.2, 00:00:02, Ethernet0
     192.168.1.0/30 is subnetted, 1 subnets
C       192.168.1.8 is directly connected, Serial0
```

   ○ **A.** The 10.1.100.0 network is 16 hops away.

   ○ **B.** EIGRP is configured to be classless.

   ○ **C.** Serial 0 has an IP address of 192.168.1.9.

   ○ **D.** The maximum hop count has been reached.

47. Which of the following commands would you enter to see the output shown here?

```
PVC Statistics for interface Serial0 (Frame Relay DCE)
       Active    Inactive   Deleted    Static
       Local     1          0          0         0
       Switched  0          0          0         0
       Unused    0          0          0         0

DLCI = 101, DLCI USAGE = LOCAL, PVC STATUS = ACTIVE, INTERFACE = Serial0

 input pkts 207      output pkts 239      in bytes 15223
 out bytes 14062     dropped pkts 0       in FECN pkts 0
 in BECN pkts 0      out FECN pkts 0      out BECN pkts 0
 in DE pkts 0        out DE pkts 0
 out bcast pkts 17   out bcast bytes 3264
 PVC create time 00:11:32, last time PVC status changed 00:11:32
Router1#
```

- ○ **A.** show frame relay lmi
- ○ **B.** show frame relay pvc
- ○ **C.** show frame relay virtual circuit
- ○ **D.** show frame relay all

48. What is the network ID of 212.84.5.66/26?

- ○ **A.** 212.84.5.0
- ○ **B.** 212.84.5.64
- ○ **C.** 212.84.5.128
- ○ **D.** 212.84.5.192

49. You change the VLAN configuration of the Layer 2 switch port connected to your management terminal from VLAN 1 to VLAN 3. As you complete the configuration, your Telnet connection is suddenly disconnected. What is the most probable reason?

- ○ **A.** An IP access list was created in the switch.
- ○ **B.** Someone changed the IP address in VLAN 3.
- ○ **C.** The switch's IP address is in the management VLAN.
- ○ **D.** Someone changed the password on the switch's vty lines.

50. Which of the following are valid interface connections for serial WAN connections? (Choose three)

   ○ **A.** EIA/TIA-449

   ○ **B.** V.35

   ○ **C.** RJ-48

   ○ **D.** RJ-44

   ○ **E.** X.21

51. What does the c2600 portion of the Cisco IOS filename c2600-ipbase-1.122-1.T.bin represent?

   ○ **A.** Hardware platform

   ○ **B.** Feature set

   ○ **C.** Train identifier

   ○ **D.** IOS version

52. After Telnetting from Router A into Router B, you realize that your `debug` outputs are not showing on the terminal screen in Router B. How can you remedy this?

   ○ **A.** RouterA#**terminal monitor**

   ○ **B.** RouterA(config-line)#**terminal monitor**

   ○ **C.** RouterB(config-line)#**terminal monitor**

   ○ **D.** RouterB#**terminal monitor**

53. You have created an access list and applied it inbound for your router's Internet connection. You want the router to send a message out the console port whenever inbound access is denied because of this access list. What command can you add to the end of your access list statements to enable this feature?

   ○ **A.** report

   ○ **B.** logging

   ○ **C.** log

   ○ **D.** record

   ○ **E.** match

54. Which of the following statements is false regarding the successor and feasible successor?

○ **A.** The lowest feasible distance is the successor route.

○ **B.** Both are located in the topology database.

○ **C.** The feasible successor is determined if the feasible distance is less than the advertised distance of the successor route.

○ **D.** The successor route is placed in the routing table.

55. What allows an end device to receive power over a copper Ethernet cable?

○ **A.** Long-Reach Ethernet

○ **B.** Gigabit Ethernet

○ **C.** Fast Ethernet

○ **D.** Power over Ethernet

56. What command configures a default route in a Layer 2 switch?

○ **A.** `ip route 0.0.0.0 0.0.0.0 FastEthernet 0/0`

○ **B.** `ip default-gateway 172.16.1.1`

○ **C.** `ip default-network 192.168.1.0`

○ **D.** `default-route 172.16.1.1`

57. You are using a Cisco 7921 Wireless VoIP device. While speaking to your coworker on the phone, you are walking through multiple wireless cells. What type of network topology is this?

○ **A.** Multiservice

○ **B.** Roaming

○ **C.** Basic Service Set

○ **D.** Extended Service Set

58. You walk away from your terminal for five minutes to get some coffee. When you return, you notice that someone has made configuration changes to your router. Which three commands will keep this from happening in the future?

○ **A.** `Router(config-line)#line-timeout 1`

○ **B.** `Router(config-line)#login`

○ **C.** `Router(config)#password password`

○ **D.** `Router(config)#exec-timeout 1`

○ **E.** `Router(config-line)#password password`

○ **F.** `Router(config-line)#exec-timeout 1`

59. Your new junior technician can't figure out why traffic from VLAN 1 isn't being tagged with a VLAN identifier over the 802.1q trunk port. What should you tell him?

○ **A.** They are baby giant frames, so there is no room in the frame.

○ **B.** They are from the native VLAN.

○ **C.** VLAN 1 should not be forwarded over a trunk.

○ **D.** Only one VLAN is allowed over a trunk.

60. You are configuring an office to use a Cisco router to connect to the Internet. The onsite network administrator wants to publish an internal email server, two internal web servers, and an internal FTP server to the Internet so that outside users can access them. What is necessary for this configuration?

○ **A.** You need a public Internet IP address for each internal server. These addresses can be mapped using Static NAT features.

○ **B.** You need a single public Internet IP address for this configuration, and you use NAT Overload to share it between all four internal servers.

○ **C.** You need a single public Internet IP address for this configuration, and you use Static NAT to map specific ports to all four internal servers.

○ **D.** You need two public Internet IP addresses to accommodate the internal web servers. The FTP and email server can be mapped to individual ports on either of the addresses.

61. Which of the following conditions could cause the port to transition to a disabled state? (Choose all that apply)

○ **A.** A BPDU is detected on a BPDU Guard-enabled port.

○ **B.** The port is not a root or designated port.

○ **C.** The switch connected to your port has a faster way back to the root.

○ **D.** A port security violation has occurred.

62. Which of the following is *not* true of a loopback interface with OSPF?

○ **A.** It is a virtual interface.

○ **B.** It commonly has a 255.255.255.255 netmask.

○ **C.** It ensures that an interface is always active for OSPF processes.

○ **D.** The higher physical interface number becomes the Router ID.

63. Which of the following topologies is shown in the figure?

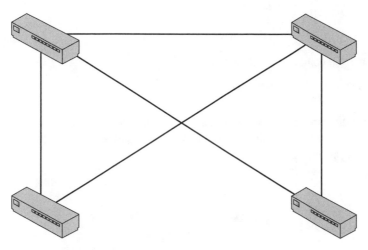

○ **A.** Partial mesh

○ **B.** Full mesh

○ **C.** Ring mesh

○ **D.** Hub and spoke

64. Given the following output, how can we close Telnet session 2? (Choose two)

```
CCNA2620#show sessions
Conn    Host              Address           Idle      Conn Name
  1     131.108.100.152   131.108.100.152   0      131.108.100.152
 *2      126.102.57.63     126.102.57.63    0       126.102.57.63
```

○ **A.** Press the Enter key and enter `exit`.

○ **B.** Enter `disconnect 2`.

○ **C.** Press the Enter key and enter `disconnect 2`.

○ **D.** Enter `close 2`.

65. Which of the following is *not* a characteristic of link-state routing protocols?

○ **A.** VLSM support

○ **B.** Route summarization at any bit level

○ **C.** Full routing updates at regular intervals

○ **D.** Discontiguous network support

66. Which of the following is *not* part of the VLAN configuration process?

    ◯ **A.** Name the VLAN.

    ◯ **B.** Create the VLAN.

    ◯ **C.** Set the VTP domain to client mode.

    ◯ **D.** Assign the VLAN to a switch port.

67. You have just finished proposing a new VPN solution to your organization's upper management. They have approved the solution, provided that you use the strongest level of encryption possible. What algorithm will you choose?

    ◯ **A.** SHA-1

    ◯ **B.** AES

    ◯ **C.** 3DES

    ◯ **D.** MD5

68. You connected your switch into a device at half duplex. What is a possible reason for not using full duplex?

    ◯ **A.** It is a 10Mbps port.

    ◯ **B.** You are connecting it to another switch.

    ◯ **C.** You are using a straight-through cable.

    ◯ **D.** You are connected to a hub.

69. Which of the following is *not* an additional feature of RIPv2 over RIPv1?

    ◯ **A.** Full update followed by hellos

    ◯ **B.** Update authentication

    ◯ **C.** Multicast updates

    ◯ **D.** Classless support

70. How many bits are there in an IPv6 address?

    ◯ **A.** 32 bits

    ◯ **B.** 64 bits

    ◯ **C.** 96 bits

    ◯ **D.** 128 bits

71. Which of the following are encryption protocols? (Choose three)

    ◯ **A.** IPsec

    ◯ **B.** SSL

    ◯ **C.** NTP

    ◯ **D.** SSH

72. Private addressing for IPv6 is represented by what kind of address?

    ◯ **A.** Link-local

    ◯ **B.** Global

    ◯ **C.** Unique/site-local

    ◯ **D.** Multicast

Answers to Practice Exam

Answers at a Glance

1. C	25. C, D	49. C
2. A	26. B, C, D	50. A, B, E
3. A, C, D	27. B	51. A
4. B	28. A, D	52. D
5. B	29. B	53. C
6. D	30. D	54. C
7. B	31. C	55. D
8. B, C	32. A	56. B
9. C	33. B, D	57. D
10. B, D	34. B	58. B, E, F
11. A, C	35. C, D	59. B
12. D	36. B	60. D
13. A	37. D	61. A, D
14. A, B, C	38. C, D	62. D
15. A, B, D	39. B	63. A
16. C	40. D	64. A, B
17. A	41. A	65. C
18. F	42. B	66. C
19. B	43. A	67. B
20. D	44. A	68. D
21. D	45. C	69. A
22. A, B, C	46. B	70. D
23. C	47. B	71. A, B, D
24. A, D	48. B	72. C

Answers with Explanations

1. **C.** The "Invalid input detected at ^" terminal message indicates that the IOS understood the configuration command up to the ^. This type of message is typical when the command contains a typo. Answer A is the correction for an "Ambiguous Command" message. Answer B is the correction for an "Incomplete Command" message. Answer D is incorrect because the terminal session is still connected.

2. **A.** The packet would be denied because of the implicit deny statement at the end of the access list. Answer B is incorrect because the first `permit` statement matches only the range of addresses from 192.168.5.16 to 31. Answer C is incorrect because the third `permit` statement matches only the range of addresses from 192.168.5.48 to 63. Answer D is incorrect because the last `permit` statement matches only the 192.168.5.0 network address.

3. **A, C, D.** Telnet, HTTP, and FTP are all protocols supported by Layer 7, or the Application layer, of the OSI model. Answer B is incorrect because JPEG is a Layer 6, or Presentation layer, supported protocol.

4. **B.** You must use an extended ping to specify the datagram size when pinging an IP address. To do an extended ping in the Cisco IOS, you must be in privileged EXEC mode, and the command is `ping` without specifying an IP address. Answer A is incorrect because it is a DOS command, not an IOS command. Answer C is incorrect because you do not specify the IP address after the `ping` keyword. Answer D is incorrect because you must be in privileged EXEC mode.

5. **B.** The `ip nat` syntax can be quite cryptic, because the Cisco router gives you plenty of flexibility with the form and directions of NAT translation. In this case, we are looking to create a Static NAT translation to allow TCP port 80 (HTTP) to pass through the Cisco router to the internal web server. There are two ways to accomplish this. We can create a Static NAT translation from the inside perspective or from the outside perspective. In this question, the only correct answer is the translation performed from the inside: `ip nat inside source static tcp 172.16.55.10 80 interface fastEthernet 0/1 80`. If we were to perform the Static NAT translation from the outside perspective, we would not be given the option to choose to translate from an interface (fastEthernet 0/1 in this case). Answers A, C, and D would result in an invalid syntax message.

6. **D.** DNS resolves hostnames into IP addresses. Answer A is incorrect because SMTP sends email across the network. Answer B is incorrect because NFS allows users with different operating systems (that is, NT and UNIX workstations) to share files. Answer C is incorrect because NNTP offers access to Usenet newsgroup postings.

7. **B.** If the boot field in the configuration register is 2-F, the router or switch will load the IOS from flash when no `boot system` commands are present. Answers A and C will load into ROMmon because the boot field is 0. Answer D has a P in the boot field, which is not a valid hexadecimal character.

8. **B, C.** Cisco routers typically support DB-60, which is a 60-pin connection. Only one DB-60 interface is supported per WIC card. Because of this, Cisco developed the Smart Serial connector, which is much smaller and supports more condensed interfaces. Answer A is incorrect because EIA/TIA-449 connects to the CSU/DSU side of the connection. Answer D is incorrect because this is a LAN interface standard.

9. **C.** The Session layer of the OSI model handles dialog control among devices and determines the beginning, middle, and end of a session or conversation that occurs between applications (intermediary). The Application layer (Answer A) provides an interface between a host's communication software and any necessary external applications. The Presentation layer (Answer B) presents data to the Application layer. The Transport layer (Answer D) manages end-to-end connections and data delivery between two hosts.

10. **B, D.** During the learning and forwarding STP port states, the switch actively learns MAC addresses it receives on that interface. Answers A and C are incorrect because MAC addresses are not learned during the blocking and listening port states.

11. **A, C.** The only private addresses are from the ranges 10.0.0.0 to 10.255.255.255, 172.16.0.0 to 172.31.255.255, and 192.168.0.0 to 192.168.255.255. Because Answers A and C fall outside those ranges, they are considered public IP addresses.

12. **D.** SNMP uses port number 161. Answers A and B are incorrect because DHCP uses port numbers 67 and 68. Answer C is incorrect because TFTP uses port number 69.

13. **A.** When a configuration is saved, it is stored in NVRAM as the startup-config. Answer B is incorrect because the running-config is stored in RAM. Answer C is incorrect because POST, ROMmon, and RxBoot are located in ROM. Answer D is incorrect because the compressed IOS file is stored in flash.

14. **A, B, C.** TCP SYN, smurf, and DDoS are all types of DoS attacks. Answer D is incorrect because trust exploitation is a type of access attack.

15. **A, B, D.** Answers A, B, and D are all valid signaling types for Local Management Interface (LMI). Answer C is incorrect because the ITU-T is a standards organization that actually created the Q.933a standard. Answer E is incorrect because this is the industry-standard type of Frame Relay encapsulation, not an LMI signaling type.

16. **C.** Crosstalk is an electrical or magnetic field that is a result of one communications signal that can affect the signal in a nearby circuit. Answer A is incorrect because EMI is the interference caused by electromagnetic signals. Answer B is incorrect because attenuation occurs over long distances as a signal loses strength. Answer D is incorrect because bandwidth is the total amount of information that can traverse a communications medium measured in millions of bits per second.

17. **A.** OSPF ABRs do not perform automatic summarization. Route summarization entries must be manually configured with the `area area# range summaryaddress` command. Answers B, C, and D are all valid advantages of OSPF.

18. **F.** When applying standard access lists, it's always best to apply them closest to the destination. Because they can only permit or deny based on the source address, placing them too close to the source might allow or deny too much access. For example, if the access list were placed on the Fa0/0 port of the Homer router, Network 1 would not be able to access any resources on the network. All other answers are incorrect because they are not the closest to the Internet destination.

19. **B.** When connecting a switch to a PC, you must use a straight-through UTP cable. Answer A is incorrect because coaxial cable is typically used for cable television. Answer C is incorrect because cross-over cables are used to connect like devices, such as switches to other switches or PCs to other PCs. Answer D is incorrect because thin coaxial (also known as thinnet) is used in older network topologies.

20. **D.** Answer D is the false answer because you must configure directly connected classful networks. Thus, 10.2.0.0 is incorrect because the classful network should be 10.0.0.0. Answer B is incorrect because, based on the output, the routing protocol configured is RIPv2 with update authentication. Answer A is incorrect because the administrative distance for RIPv2 is 120; however, the output shows the AD as 80. Answer C is incorrect because the output does show that update authentication is indeed configured.

21. **D.** Dynamic NAT allows you to configure multiple pools of IP addresses and translate between them. The router dynamically matches each IP address to one another as a request is made. Answer A is incorrect because Port Address Translation (PAT) is just another name for NAT Overload. Answer B is incorrect because although Static NAT could perform this task, it would take quite a bit of configuration to manually map IP addresses in large pools. Answer C is incorrect because NAT Overload takes a group of IP addresses and translates them to a single (overloaded) IP address.

22. **A, B, C.** 10BASE-2, 10BASE-5, and 10BASE-T are all 10Mbps IEEE 802.3 Ethernet standards. Answer D is incorrect because Wi-Fi is a wireless technology that is defined by IEEE 802.11.

23. **C.** The summary route for 192.168.64.0 /19 summarized the networks from 192.168.64.0 /24 to 192.168.95.0 /24. Because 5 bits were stolen (2^5 = 32), 32 networks are being summarized. Answers A, B, and D are incorrect because these do not fall in the summary range.

24. **A, D.** HDLC and PPP are the only encapsulation types supported by Cisco on leased-line connections. Answer B is incorrect because Frame Relay is an encapsulation used on a Frame Relay packet-switched network. Answer C is incorrect because ISDN is a type of circuit-switched technology.

25. **C, D.** Hubs and repeaters are hardware devices used at the Physical layer of the OSI model to extend a network. Answers A and B are incorrect because switches and bridges are hardware devices used at the Data Link layer to segment a network.

26. **B, C, D.** Unicast, multicast, and broadcast addresses are Ethernet address types used at the 802.3 MAC sublayer. Answer A is incorrect because IP addresses are logical addresses used at the Network layer of the OSI model.

27. **B.** If you add another switch to a VTP domain that is in server mode and has a higher revision number, other switches in the VTP domain use the VLANs in the new server's database. If there are no VLANs in the database, the other switches remove all the VLANs in their databases as well. Answer A is incorrect because a switch in client mode does not advertise its own VLANs. Answer C is incorrect because devices with a higher revision number ignore the VTP advertisements of the new server. Answer D is possible, but Answer B is more likely than someone deleting your VLANs without you knowing.

28. **A, D.** The WPA algorithm uses the TKIP algorithm to generate dynamic keys during a wireless session. This helped handle many of the security concerns of WEP. WPA2 (also known as 802.11i) uses the AES encryption algorithm, which is considered one of the best encryption standards available.

29. **B.** All multicast addresses start with 0100.5E. Answer A is incorrect because unicast addresses start with the OUI of the manufacturer NIC. Answer C is incorrect because broadcast addresses begin with FFFF.FF. Answer D is incorrect because IP addresses are not Ethernet MAC sublayer addresses, and they use dotted-decimal format rather than hexadecimal format.

30. **D.** Modems typically are connected to the auxiliary port and are used as a "last-resort" method of accessing the remote router. Answers B and C are incorrect: Because you no longer have IP connectivity to the router, you cannot use SSH and Telnet. Answer A is incorrect: You cannot console into the router because it is in a remote location. The only viable solution left is to call into a modem that is connected through the Auxiliary port.

31. **C.** For a low-cost connection, you could use a hub-and-spoke topology. With this design, you would need only a connection from the hub office to each of the spokes. Answer A is incorrect because each router would need a separate connection for every other router in the topology. This would be quite expensive in a large topology. Answer B is incorrect because you would still have more connections than a hub and spoke. Answer D is incorrect because nonbroadcast multiaccess (NBMA) does not affect the cost of Frame Relay.

32. **A.** Microsegmentation occurs when a switch creates a dedicated path for sending and receiving transmissions with each connected host. Answer B is incorrect because half duplex allows only one-way data transmission. Answer C is incorrect because full duplex allows two-way data transmission. Answer D is incorrect because CSMA/CD is an algorithm used for arbitration on an Ethernet network.

33. **B, D.** To speed up convergence for end devices such as computers, servers, and printers, you can enable PortFast, which bypasses the listening and learning port states. To keep that port from having a hub or switch connect to it and causing loops, you can enable BPDU Guard, which disables the interface if it receives a BPDU. Answers A and C will not speed up convergence for end devices.

34. **B.** In the U.S., only three nonoverlapping channels are available for the 2.4GHz band. Europe has four nonoverlapping channels, because access to other unlicensed RF bands is available. The moral of the story? If you're having trouble finding a free wireless channel in your area, move to Europe.

35. **C, D.** Switches and bridges are hardware devices used at the Data Link layer to segment a network. Answers A and B are incorrect because hubs and repeaters are hardware devices used at the Physical layer of the OSI model to extend a network.

36. **B.** Class A addresses have a first octet value of 1 to 126. Class B addresses have a first octet value of 128 to 191. Class C addresses have a first octet value of 192 to 223. Answers A, C, and D are incorrect because they do not correctly identify this range.

37. **D.** Routing protocols do not advertise each others' networks unless redistribution has occurred. Answers A and B are incorrect: Because the routing protocols are not advertising the same network, administrative distance does not play into this. Answer C is incorrect because it reverses the networks the routing protocols are advertising.

38. **C, D.** The generic Static NAT syntax for TCP translations is `ip nat inside source static tcp` *inside_ip inside_port outside_ip*/*outside_interface outside_port*. In this case, only Answers C and D match this syntax. Answers A and E flip the IP address and port numbers in the wrong location, which produces a syntax error. Answer B uses port 20, which is used by FTP; however, only port 21 is used to initiate an FTP session. After a client initiates the incoming FTP session on port 21, the FTP server establishes an outgoing FTP data connection using port 20. Because of this, no incoming NAT translation is necessary for TCP port 20.

39. **B.** A T1 controller card can be installed in a router's T1 slot to communicate with and control the 24 DS0 channels. Answer A is incorrect because a GBIC interface module can be inserted into the Gigabit Ethernet slot to allow for different media connections to that port. Answer C is incorrect because if it is not built in on a Cisco router via a BRI-U interface, the service provider requires separate BRI NT-1 hardware as a termination point for the communications line, which then connects to the Cisco router. Answer D is incorrect because HSSI is a high-speed interface that offers up to 52Mbps transmission rates to the WAN from a Cisco router.

40. **D.** Because the update is coming from two different sources with the same metric, RIP load-balances over both equal paths. Answers A and B are incorrect because the order in which the updates were received is negligible. Answer C is incorrect because the maximum hop count for RIP is 15.

41. **A.** Standard IP access lists are numbered from 1 to 99. Answer B is incorrect because extended IP access lists are numbered from 100 to 199. Answer C is incorrect because the expanded range standard access list is 1300 to 1999. Answer D is incorrect because the expanded range extended access list is 2000 to 2699.

42. **B.** The first octet is 32+16+8=56. The second octet is 128+32+16+2+1=179. The third octet is 64+16+4+2+1=87. The last octet is 128+64+16+8+2=218. So the address in dotted-decimal format is 56.179.87.218. The last bit in the last octet is 0, which means that any address ending with an odd-numbered octet can be eliminated. All other answers have the wrong decimal conversion.

43. **A.** EIGRP and RIPv2 can both be configured as classless routing protocols using the `no auto-summary` command. All other answers are unique differences between RIPv2 and EIGRP.

44. **A.** Cisco routers (new and old) all use a Cisco-proprietary version of HDLC on their serial connections. Although there is an industry-standard HDLC, very few vendors support it. Answer B is incorrect because there are no "backward-compatible" WAN standards. Answers C and D are incorrect because newer Cisco routers still use the Cisco-proprietary HDLC as the default encapsulation.

45. **C.** The broadcast IP of 212.84.5.66/26 is 212.84.5.127. The next network ID after 212.84.5.64 is 212.84.5.128. To determine the broadcast IP, you subtract 1 from the next network ID, which in this case is 212.84.5.127. All other answers are incorrect because they are not the broadcast IP.

46. **B.** 10.1.100.0 shows a subnet mask of /24, which means that it was not automatically summarized to its classful boundary of 10.0.0.0/8. Because this network is learned from EIGRP, the administrator had to make this classless by using the no auto-summary command. Answers A and D are incorrect because hop count is not a factor in this case; EIGRP does not use hop count as its metric. Answer C is incorrect because Serial 0 has the IP address of 192.168.1.8 displayed as the connected interface entry.

47. **B.** The show frame relay pvc command provides you with statistics for each configured connection, as well as traffic statistics. Answer A is incorrect because the output is not for LMI statistics. Answers C and D are incorrect because there are no such commands.

48. **B.** The network ID of 212.84.5.66/26 is 212.84.5.64. The CIDR notation represents subnet mask 255.255.255.192. The binary equivalent of the subnet mask host field is 11000000. The binary equivalent of the 212.84.5.66 host field is 01000010. Using Boolean AND, the network ID is 212.84.5.64. Therefore, Answers A, C, and D are incorrect.

49. **C.** VLAN 1, the management VLAN, contains the IP address for the switch and CDP and VTP advertisements. If your terminal computer is not connected to the management VLAN, you cannot Telnet to that switch. Answer A is incorrect because an IP access list cannot be configured in Layer 2 switches. Answer B is incorrect because the management VLAN is VLAN 1. Answer D will not disconnect the active Telnet session.

50. **A, B, E.** The five primary standards that are used for serial interface connections (to the CSU/DSU) are V.35, X.21, EIA/TIA-232, EIA/TIA-449, and EIA/TIA-530. Answers C and D are incorrect because RJ-48 is the standard for a T1 connection, and RJ-44 is not a defined standard.

51. **A.** The c2600 portion of the IOS filename represents the hardware platform. In this case, it is a Cisco 2600 series router. Answer B is incorrect because the term ipbase refers to the IP Base feature set. Answer C is incorrect because the train identifier is T for Technical. Answer D is incorrect because the IOS version is represented by 122, or version 12.2.

52. **D.** The terminal monitor command copies and consoles messages to the Telnet sessions of an IOS router or switch. This command is done in privileged EXEC mode in the device you are Telnetted into. Answers A, B, and C are incorrect because they are either on the wrong router or in the wrong mode.

53. **C.** If you add the log keyword to the end of an access list entry, the router reports any matches on that line to the console port. This logging can also be redirected to a reporting server. Answers A, B, D, and E are invalid syntax.

54. **C.** The feasible successor is determined if the route's advertised distance is less than the feasible distance of the successor route in the routing table. The feasible successor and the successor router are both maintained in the topology table. Answers A, B, and D are true regarding the successor and feasible successor.

55. **D.** Power over Ethernet is a technology that allows an end device to receive power over a copper Ethernet cable. Answer A is incorrect because Long-Reach Ethernet (LRE) is an Ethernet specification developed by Cisco to provide broadband service over existing telephone-grade or Category 1, 2, or 3 wiring. Answers B and C are incorrect because Gigabit Ethernet and Fast Ethernet standards do not include the ability to supply power to an end device.

56. B. Because this is a Layer 2 switch, the gateway of last resort is configured by setting the default gateway. Answers A and C are incorrect because you cannot configure a default route or a default network in a Layer 2 switch. Answer D is not a valid command.

57. D. An Extended Service Set (ESS) wireless topology is the combination of two or more Basic Service Set (BSS) networks. This allows client roaming (between wireless cells) without service interruption.

58. B, E, F. To secure your console connection when you walk away from the IOS terminal, you need to decrease the exec-timeout and set the login and password. These configurations must be performed in line configuration mode. All other answers are incorrect because they are performed in the wrong configuration mode.

59. B. With 802.1q trunks, traffic originating from the native VLAN is not tagged with a VLAN identifier. Answer A is incorrect because information can always be added to a frame, even if it is a baby giant. Answer C is incorrect because VLAN 1 is always forwarded over a trunk by default. Answer D is incorrect because many VLANs can be sent over a trunk.

60. D. NAT can accomplish some pretty amazing feats; however, sharing an IP address for two servers that use the same port number is not one of them. In this case, you need two public Internet addresses to allow both internal web servers to be accessed on TCP port 80. The other servers can use port 21 (FTP) and port 25 (SMTP) on either of the public Internet IP addresses. Answer A could be used to solve this problem, but it is not the best solution because it would be more costly to deploy than Answer D. Answer B is incorrect because NAT Overload would let the servers share a single IP address only when accessing the Internet, not when the requests originate from the Internet. Answer C is incorrect because you could only map TCP port 80 on the single IP address to one of the internal web servers. The other internal web server could not be accessed from the Internet.

61. A, D. The port will become disabled if a BPDU is detected on a BPDU Guard-enabled port, as well as if there is a port security violation. Answers B and C are incorrect because that would cause the port to be in a blocking state.

62. D. When using loopback interfaces with OSPF, the physical interfaces are no longer used to determine the Router ID. All other answers are true and play a significant role in the OSPF Router ID.

63. A. There are redundant links between the routers. However, there are not redundant links between all the routers. Answer B is incorrect because there are not redundant links between all the routers. Answer C is incorrect because even though the connections form a ring as shown here, if it were in the cloud, it would not look like this. Answer D is incorrect because it is not a star or hub-and-spoke topology—there is no central point.

64. A, B. To disconnect the Telnet session, you can enter `disconnect` followed by the session number in the originating router. Or you can press the Enter key to resume the Telnet session and enter `exit` in the device you are Telnetted into to close the Telnet session. Answer C is incorrect because pressing Enter first resumes your session with the remote router and causes the `disconnect` command to fail. Answer D is incorrect because it is invalid syntax.

65. C. Link-state routing protocols (OSPF and IS-IS) do not send full routing updates at regular intervals. Answers A, B, and D are characteristic of link-state routing protocols; however, this question is looking for the false answer.

66. C. Setting the VTP domain to client mode does not allow you to configure any VLANs on the switch. Answers A, B, and D typically are performed during a VLAN configuration process.

67. B. AES currently offers the strongest levels of encryption possible for symmetric encryption. It can reach up to 256-bit encryption.

68. D. When connecting to a hub, you must have the port running in half duplex, because CSMA/CD must be enabled. Answer A is incorrect because the speed is irrelevant. Answer B is incorrect because you can run full duplex when connecting to switches. Answer C is incorrect because it does not matter what cable is used.

69. A. RIPv2 has update authentication and multicasts updates to 224.0.0.9 and can support classless routing. Answer A is not a feature because RIPv2 is a distance vector routing protocol that sends continuous updates every 30 seconds instead of Hello messages, such as RIPv1.

70. D. IPv6 addresses consist of 128 bits. Answer A is the correct bit count of an IPv4 address. Answers B and C are incorrect because they are not valid IP address bit counts.

71. A, B, D. IPsec, SSL, and SSH are all encryption protocols. Answer C is incorrect because NTP (Network Time Protocol) synchronizes clocks on a network.

72. C. Unique/site-local addresses are the private address space for IPv6. Answer A is incorrect because link-local addresses represent the address automatically assigned to a device at Layer 2. Answer B is incorrect because a global address is a public IP address. Answer D is incorrect because a multicast address in IPv6 is the same as a broadcast IP address.

What's on the CD-ROM

The CD-ROM features an innovative practice test engine powered by MeasureUp™, giving you yet another effective tool to assess your readiness for the exam.

Multiple Test Modes

MeasureUp practice tests can be used in Study, Certification, or Custom Mode.

Study Mode

Tests administered in Study Mode allow you to request the correct answer(s) to and an explanation for each question during the test. These tests are not timed.

You can also specify the objectives or missed questions you want to include in your test, the timer length, and other test properties.

In Study Mode, you receive automatic feedback on all correct and incorrect answers. The detailed answer explanations are a superb learning tool in their own right.

Certification Mode

Tests administered in Certification Mode closely simulate the actual testing environment you will encounter when taking a licensure exam and are timed. These tests do not allow you to request the answer(s) and/or explanation to each question until after the exam.

Custom Mode

Custom Mode allows you to specify your preferred testing environment. Use this mode to specify the categories you want to include in your test, timer length, number of questions, and other test properties. You can modify the testing environment during the test by clicking the Options button.

Attention to Exam Objectives

MeasureUp practice tests are designed to appropriately balance the questions over each technical area covered by a specific exam. All concepts from the actual exam are covered thoroughly to ensure that you're prepared for the exam.

Installing the CD

The system requirements are as follows:

- Windows 95, 98, Me, NT 4, 2000, XP, or Vista
- 14MB of disk space for the testing engine
- An average of 2MB of disk space for each individual test
- Control Panel Regional Settings must be set to English (United States)
- PC only

To install the CD-ROM, follow these instructions:

1. Close all applications before beginning this installation.
2. Insert the CD into your CD-ROM drive. If the setup starts automatically, go to step 6. If the setup does not start automatically, continue with step 3.
3. Select **Start**, **Run**.
4. Click **Browse** to locate the MeasureUp CD. In the Browse dialog box, from the Look In drop-down list, select the CD-ROM drive.
5. In the Browse dialog box, double-click **Setup.exe**. In the Run dialog box, click **OK** to begin the installation.
6. On the Welcome screen, click **MeasureUp Practice Questions** to begin the installation.
7. Follow the Certification Prep Wizard by clicking **Next**.
8. To agree to the Software License Agreement, click **Yes**.
9. On the Choose Destination Location screen, click **Next** to install the software to C:\Program Files\Certification Preparation. If you cannot locate MeasureUp Practice Tests on the Start menu, see the next section.
10. On the Setup Type screen, select **Typical Setup**. Click **Next** to continue.
11. In the Select Program Folder screen, you can name the program folder where your tests will be located. To select the default, simply click **Next**, and the installation continues.

12. After the installation is complete, verify that **Yes, I Want to Restart My Computer Now** is selected. If you select **No, I Will Restart My Computer Later**, you cannot use the program until you restart your computer.

13. Click **Finish**.

14. After restarting your computer, choose **Start**, **Programs**, **Certification Preparation**, **Certification Preparation**, **MeasureUp Practice Tests**.

15. On the MeasureUp Welcome Screen, click **Create User Profile**.

16. In the User Profile dialog box, complete the mandatory fields, and click **Create Profile**.

17. Select the practice test you want to access, and click **Start Test**.

Creating a Shortcut to the MeasureUp Practice Tests

To create a shortcut to the MeasureUp practice tests, follow these steps:

1. Right-click your desktop.

2. From the shortcut menu, select **New**, **Shortcut**.

3. Browse to C:\Program Files\MeasureUp Practice Tests, and select the **MeasureUpCertification.exe** or **Localware.exe** file.

4. Click **OK**.

5. Click **Next**.

6. Rename the shortcut MeasureUp.

7. Click **Finish**.

After you complete step 7, use the MeasureUp shortcut on your desktop to access the MeasureUp products you ordered.

Technical Support

If you encounter problems with the MeasureUp test engine on the CD-ROM, please contact MeasureUp at 800-649-1687, or email support@measureup.com. Support hours of operation are 7:30 a.m. to 4:30 p.m. EST. In addition, you can find Frequently Asked Questions (FAQs) in the Support area at www.measureup.com. If you would like to purchase additional MeasureUp products, call (678) 356-5050 or 800-649-1687, or visit www.measureup.com.

Glossary

10BASE-T An IEEE 802.3 Ethernet standard that has a maximum segment length of 100m and has a 10Mbps data transmission speed. 10BASE-T can use Category 3, 4, or 5 unshielded twisted-pair (UTP) or shielded twisted-pair (STP) cables for connectivity.

802.11a An IEEE wireless networking standard released in 1999 that uses the 5GHz frequency range. 802.11a clients can theoretically transmit at a maximum speed of 54Mbps.

802.11b An IEEE wireless networking standard released in 1999 that uses the 2.4GHz frequency range. 802.11b clients can theoretically transmit at a maximum speed of 11Mbps.

802.11g An IEEE wireless networking standard released in 2003 that uses the 2.4GHz frequency range. 802.11g clients can theoretically transmit at a maximum speed of 54Mbps. This standard is backward-compatible with 802.11b clients.

802.11n A predraft standard for wireless networking that uses Multiple Input, Multiple Output (MIMO) signals to achieve higher throughput. Current predraft equipment uses the 2.4GHz frequency range.

802.1q An IEEE frame-tagging method over trunk ports that insert the 4-byte VLAN identifier inside the original Ethernet frame.

802.1x An authentication protocol geared toward LAN environments. 802.1x requires that users authenticate to the network before they are granted wired or wireless access.

A

AAA (Authentication, Authorization, and Accounting)   A group of three services that are used in conjunction with an authentication server and a software service such as Terminal Access Controller Access Control System (TACACS) or Remote Authentication Dial-in User Service (RADIUS) to provide a secure network connection with a record of user activities.

ABR (Area Border Router)   A router that sits between multiple areas in a hierarchical OSPF network. These routers are responsible for summarizing subnets to the rest of the OSPF autonomous system. Because they must maintain topology information from several areas, these routers are typically robust in resources.

access attack   A class of attack in which a hacker attempts to access another user account or network device through improper means.

access-class   The command used to apply an access list to vty ports.

access port   A switch port that has a single VLAN assigned to it. These are typically used for connectivity between end devices.

ACTIVE, INACTIVE, and DELETED PVC status   The three states of a Frame Relay PVC. Active means that the connection is good on both ends. Inactive means that the remote router is misconfigured. Deleted means that the local router is misconfigured.

adjacency   A term that describes the state after two OSPF neighbors have synchronized their topology databases.

administrative distance   An arbitrary value between 1 and 255 that is assigned to determine the trustworthiness of the routing sources.

advertised distance   The composite metric to a destination that is being advertised from our EIGRP neighbors.

AES (Advanced Encryption Standard)   The newest encryption algorithm. It is managed by the National Institute of Standards and Technology (NIST), a division of the U.S. government. It was designed to increase encryption strength beyond the DES and 3DES standards and yet be more efficient on the device's processor. As it stands today, AES offers 128-, 192-, and 256-bit encryption.

AH (Authentication Header)   One of the components that powers the IPsec security suite of protocols. AH defines capabilities for authentication and data-integrity algorithms but does not provide the capability for encryption.

Application layer   Layer 7 of the OSI model. Provides an interface between a host's communication software and any necessary external applications (that is, email, file transfers, and terminal emulation). This layer can also evaluate what resources are necessary to communicate between two devices and determine their availability.

area   A subdivision of an autonomous system composed of groups of contiguous networks and attached hosts. Used in link-state routing protocols to minimize routing update overhead and confine network instability.

ARP (Address Resolution Protocol) A protocol that maps a known IP address to a MAC address by sending a broadcast ARP. When the destination IP address is on another subnet, the sender broadcasts ARP for the router's Ethernet port or default gateway, so the MAC address sent back is that of the router's Ethernet port.

ASP (AppleTalk Session Protocol) A session layer protocol that manages client/server based communications, but is specific to AppleTalk client and server devices.

asynchronous A serial interface that does not synchronize the clocks for the bit stream of the sending and receiving end of a serial link.

ATM (Asynchronous Transfer Mode) A packet-switched connection type that reaches high speeds by dividing all packets into equal-sized cells of 53 bytes each.

attenuation A term used to describe how a signal loses strength over long distances.

authentication The process of requiring or prompting for credentials before a device can access the network.

autonomous system A collection of routing devices under the same administrative control.

autonomous system number An indicator in an IGRP and EIGRP configuration that identifies the autonomous system to which the routers are actively sending routing updates.

auxiliary port An out-of-band management connection used to connect to an external modem with a rollover cable.

B

backbone area Also known as the transit area, Area 0 is an area to which all other areas must connect.

BackboneFast Cisco STP enhancement that skips the max-age timer when switches learn of a failure indirectly.

backbone router Any router that is connected to Area 0.

Backward Explicit Congestion Notification (BECN) A signaling method used by a Frame Relay service provider that attempts to drop the speed of a router sending excessive data.

balanced hybrid routing protocol A class of routing protocol that uses the best characteristics from link-state and routing protocols. These advanced routing protocols efficiently and quickly build their routing information and converge when topology changes occur.

bandwidth The total amount of information that can traverse a communications medium measured in millions of bits per second. Bandwidth is helpful for network performance analysis. Also, availability is increasing but limited.

bandwidth *speed* An interface configuration command that assigns a logical speed to the interface for accurate routing metrics.

banner motd *delimiting_char banner delimiting_char* A global configuration command to create a message-of-the-day login banner.

BDR (Backup Designated Router) A router that is elected in OSPF as a redundant device in case the Designated Router fails.

bearer channel (B channel) Used as a building block for ISDN connections. Provides 64Kbps of bandwidth per channel.

Bellman-Ford Algorithm A routing algorithm used by RIP and IGRP, which entails routing updates being received and updated before propagating the message to other routing devices.

binary A computer language that is represented by a bit value of 0 or 1.

blocking Ports that are not the root or the designated port in a STP election that are left in a blocking state. Data is not transmitted on these ports, but BPDUs can still be received.

Bluetooth A wireless technology that uses a short-range wireless radio connection to allow various devices to interconnect. Such devices include cell phones, PCs, and personal digital assistants (PDAs). The only requirement to establish connectivity is a 10 meter range (approximately 33 feet) between communicating devices. When in range, Bluetooth uses an RF link in the 2.4GHz range that has a 720Kbps per channel capacity to transfer voice or data.

BOD (Bandwidth on Demand) A Cisco extension to the PPP Multilink concept that allows more DDR connections to be brought up as bandwidth is needed and disconnected as bandwidth is not needed.

Boolean AND A mathematical operation that can be used to identify the network ID and broadcast IP given an IP address and subnet mask.

boot field The last hexadecimal character in a configuration register that specifies where to find an IOS.

bootstrap Instructions loaded from ROM to activate the IOS loading code.

boot system *location filename* A global configuration command that specifies locations and filenames to load the IOS.

BPDU (Bridge Protocol Data Unit) A Layer 2 message sent in an STP environment to advertise bridge IDs, root bridge MAC addresses, and root path costs.

BPDU Guard A Cisco enhancement to PortFast that prevents loops by moving an access port to a disabled state if a BPDU is received.

BRI (Basic Rate Interface) An Integrated Services Digital Network (ISDN) line that consists of two 64Kbps bearer (B) channels and one 16Kbps data (D) channel. Voice, video, and data traffic can be carried over the B channels. Signals between telephone company switches use the D channel.

bridge A hardware device at the Data Link layer that connects two segments in a single network or connects two networks. They simply forward data between those segments/networks without analyzing or redirecting the data.

bridge ID A Spanning Tree Protocol switch identifier composed of a combination of bridge priority and MAC address.

broadband A term used to describe high-speed Internet connections such as DSL or cable modems.

broadcast An Ethernet LAN address in which a frame is sent to all devices in the same LAN. Broadcast addresses are always the same value—FFFF.FFFF.FFFF.

broadcast domain A group of nodes that can receive each other's broadcast messages and are segmented by routers.

broadcast IP The last IP address in a network. Every host bit for the broadcast IP address is turned on (or all 1s).

broadcast multiaccess (BMA) topology Consists of multiple devices that access the same medium and can hear each others' broadcasts and multicast messages such as Ethernet networks.

broadcast subnet The last subnet in a network, which has all 1s in the subnet field.

BSS (Basic Service Set) Describes a network topology with an independent wireless access point managing a group of clients.

bus topology A network topology that is set up so that the network nodes are connected via a single cable (also referred to as a trunk or a backbone). Electrical signals are sent from one end of the cable to the other.

C

CAM (Content-Addressable Memory) table A table in RAM that stores MAC addresses in a switch.

CAS (Channel Associated Signaling) A type of connection that incorporates signaling information with the data being sent. Also called Robbed Bit Signaling (RBS).

CCS (Common Channel Signaling) A type of connection that separates signaling information from the data transmission. ISDN is a CCS-style technology.

CDP (Cisco Discovery Protocol) A Layer 2 Cisco-proprietary protocol that advertises information to directly connected Cisco neighbors.

cdp enable An interface configuration command to enable CDP on an interface (on by default).

cdp run A global configuration command to enable CDP on a device (on by default).

CHAP (Challenge Handshake Authentication Protocol) A strong authentication type used with PPP encapsulation. Passwords are hashed and sent multiple times over the course of a WAN connection.

CIR (Committed Information Rate) The minimum speed guaranteed to a customer by a Frame Relay service provider.

Circuit Switched Network A WAN connection type that encompasses dial-on-demand technologies such as modems and ISDN.

Cisco, ANSI, and Q933A LMI signaling The three forms of Frame Relay LMI signaling. Cisco IOS 11.2 and later automatically detect the Frame Relay signaling type. Earlier versions of the IOS must be coded manually.

Cisco Frame Relay Encapsulation A Cisco-proprietary Frame Relay encapsulation that can be used only when communicating through a Frame Relay service provider to other Cisco routers.

classful routing protocol Routing updates contain only the classful networks, without any subnet mask. Summarization is automatically done when a router advertises a network out an interface that is not within the same major subnet. Classful routing protocols must have a FLSM design and do not operate correctly with discontiguous networks.

Classless Interdomain Routing (CIDR) A way to allocate and specify Internet addresses used in routing. Offers more flexibility than the original system of IP address classes.

classless routing protocol Routing updates can contain subnetted networks because the subnet mask is advertised in the updates. Route summarization can be manually configured at any bit boundary. Classless routing protocols support VLSM designs and discontiguous networks.

CLI (command-line interface) An interface that defines the method used to communicate with an operating system. In the case of Cisco, this is IOS.

client mode A VTP mode in which you cannot create, modify, or delete VLANs. Forwards advertisements received from the server but does not save VLAN configuration to the VLAN database.

clock rate speed An interface configuration command that specifies the clocking speed in bps.

collision domain A group of nodes that share the same media and are segmented by switches. A collision occurs if two nodes attempt a simultaneous transmission.

composite metric A metric used by IGRP and EIGRP composed of bandwidth plus delay by default. Can also support Reliability, Load, and MTU as well.

config-register register A global configuration command to alter the configuration register.

configuration register A 16-bit (four hexadecimal characters) value in NVRAM that specifies how the router or switch should operate during initialization.

connected interface As soon as we assign an IP address to a working (up/line protocol up) interface, the router associates the entire subnet of the interface's IP address in the routing table.

console port An out-of-band management connection used to connect to a PC with a rollover cable.

copy from to A privileged EXEC command that copies files from one location to another.

cost An arbitrary number typically based on the link's bandwidth.

count to infinity When routers are continuously passing updates to unreachable networks between each other in a routing loop, the metric continues to increase forever.

CPE (Customer Premises Equipment) Refers to equipment located on the customer premises, such as the router and typically the CSU/DSU.

crosstalk An electrical or magnetic field that is a result of one communications signal that can affect the signal in a nearby circuit.

CSMA/CD A process that sends a jam signal to notify the devices that there has been a collision. The devices then halt transmission for a random back-off time.

CSU/DSU (Channel Service Unit/Data Service Unit) A device that serves as an intermediary between the service provider and the WAN router. In most cases, the CSU/DSU provides clocking for the router.

Ctrl+Shift+6, x   A keystroke to suspend Telnet sessions and cancel lookups and pings.

cut-through   A frame transmission method that looks only at the destination MAC address in an Ethernet frame and forwards it.

D

data integrity   Using measures to ensure that data does not change in transmission. This typically is described as hashing data.

Data Link layer   Layer 2 of the OSI model. Ensures reliable data transfer from the Network layer to the Physical layer for transmission across the network.

data packet   A packet that transports data across the internetwork and is supported by IP and IPX protocols.

DCE (Data Circuit-Terminating Equipment)   Also called Data Communications Equipment. The term used to identify a device that connects the Data Terminal Equipment (DTE) to a service provider's communications line. Types of DCE are modems, CSU/DSUs, and BRI NT-1s.

DDR (Dial-on-Demand Routing)   A technology used to bring up network connections when needed and disconnect them after the need is satisfied. Typically used for ISDN connections.

DE (Discard Eligible)   Any traffic exceeding the CIR in a Frame Relay network is automatically marked by the service provider as Discard Eligible, which means that it could be dropped in case of network congestion.

default gateway   A gateway of last resort in switches and PCs. This default gateway is the IP address that hosts and switches send their traffic to when the destination is on another segment.

default route   A gateway of last resort for a router when there isn't a specific match for an IP destination network in the routing table (such as packets destined for the Internet).

demarc (demarcation)   The point at which the telco terminates its line to the customer.

DES (Data Encryption Standard)   One of the first electronic encryption algorithms to be used. It was originally developed by IBM to support a 56-bit key. By today's standards, DES is considered a relatively weak encryption.

designated port   On each STP segment, the switch with the lowest cumulative cost to the root has the designated port.

dialer interface   A logical interface that contains a configuration that can be applied to a physical interface when needed.

dialer list/dialer group   The syntax used to create a list of interesting traffic (dialer list) and apply that list to an interface (dialer group).

dialer map   Used to manually map a remote IP address to the phone number a router should dial to reach it.

dialer pool   A pool of physical interfaces that a logical, dialer interface can draw from when attempting to make a connection.

dialer profile   A newer form of DDR connection that allows you to define different configurations to be applied to an ISDN interface when certain destinations are dialed.

Diffie-Hellman Algorithm   An asymmetric (public and private key) algorithm that allows for secure exchange of encryption keys over a public network.

Digital Signal Level 1 (DS1)   Also called a T1, this line offers a 1.544Mbps data transmission speed. A single T1 consists of 24 digital signal level 0 (DS0) channels that are 64Kbps each and an additional 8Kbps that are reserved for management overhead.

Dijkstra SPF Algorithm   A routing algorithm used by OSPF and IS-IS that builds and calculates the shortest path to all known destinations.

discarding state   A Rapid Spanning Tree nonforwarding port state that entails a port that does not participate in the switched topology because BPDU updates are not actively being sent and MAC addresses are not being learned. Similar to 802.1d Spanning Tree Protocol's blocking state.

disconnect *conn#*   A user or privileged EXEC command to disconnect a suspended Telnet session.

discontiguous network   A major network separated by another major network that is automatically summarized, causing routing confusion.

distance vector routing protocol   A class of routing protocol in which the entire routing table is periodically sent to directly connected neighbors regardless of a topology change. These routing protocols manipulate the routing table updates before sending that information to their neighbors and are slow to converge when a topology change occurs.

distributed DoS attack   A type of DoS attack in which multiple systems are compromised to send a DoS attack to a specific target.

DLCI (Data Link Connection Identifier)   A data link address used by Frame Relay.

DNA SCP (Digital Network Architecture Session Control Protocol)   A proprietary Digital Equipment Corporation Networking (DECnet) Session layer protocol. Also referred to as a DECnet session.

DNS (Domain Name System)   An Application layer protocol that resolves hostnames and fully qualified domain names, such as www.cisco.com, into IP addresses.

DoS (denial of service) attack   A class of attack that is implemented to deny a service that is normally available to a user or organization.

DR (Designated Router)   Elected in OSPF to minimize routing update overhead that can occur in broadcast and nonbroadcast multiaccess topologies.

DTE (Data Terminal Equipment)   A device at the user end of a network that is connected to the service provider via the DCE device. Types of DTE are PCs, routers, and servers.

DTP (Dynamic Trunking Protocol)   A protocol used by Cisco to negotiate trunking.

DUAL (Diffusing Update Algorithm)   The algorithm used by EIGRP to determine the best loop-free path to a destination, as well as alternative paths in certain conditions.

dual-ring topology   A network topology that uses two rings for redundancy purposes. If a failure occurs on one ring, the other provides operability.

duplex   A device's communication mode. Can be either half duplex or full duplex, depending on the connection type.

Dynamic Host Configuration Protocol (DHCP) An Application layer protocol that works dynamically to provide an IP address, subnet mask, domain name, and default gateway to network clients.

dynamic NAT   Automatically performs NAT translations between two or more pools of addresses.

E

EGP (Exterior Gateway Protocol)   A routing protocol that advertises networks between autonomous systems.

EIA/TIA-232, -449, and -530   Physical serial interface standards on CSU/DSU devices.

EIGRP (Enhanced Interior Gateway Routing Protocol)   A Cisco-proprietary enhancement of IGRP to support classless routing, multiple routed protocols, a 32-bit composite metric, and the DUAL algorithm for fast convergence and loop-free routing.

EMI (electromagnetic interference)   The interference caused by electromagnetic signals, which can decrease data integrity.

enable password *password*   A global configuration command that sets a clear-text password for entering privileged EXEC mode.

enable secret *password*   A global configuration command that sets an MD5 encrypted password for entering privileged EXEC mode.

Encapsulating Security Payload (ESP)   One of the engines that can power the IPsec security suite of protocols. ESP defines capabilities for authentication, data integrity, and encryption algorithms.

encapsulation   The process of adding a header or trailer to the Protocol Data Unit at each layer of the OSI model.

encryption   The process of scrambling data, thus making it unreadable, before transmitting it over the network.

erase startup-config   A privileged EXEC command that deletes the startup-config in NVRAM to return the router or switch to the original "out-of-box" configuration after reboot.

Error-Disabled   A port security state in which a violation has occurred and the interface has been disabled.

ESS (Extended Service Set)   A wireless topology that includes two or more wireless access points, providing extended wireless coverage across the network.

EtherChannel   A Cisco link aggregation method that bundles multiple links between two switches into a single logical link.

Ethernet   A LAN specification introduced in the 1970s when Xerox needed a networking system to connect PCs.

exec-timeout *minutes seconds*   A line configuration command that specifies the length of terminal inactivity before closing the EXEC session.

extended access list A list of permit and deny statements capable of matching network traffic based on the protocol used, source IP address, source port number, destination IP address, and destination port number.

F

feasible distance The composite metric composed of the advertised distance to a destination plus the composite metric to reach that advertising router from the local router.

feasible successor route A backup route in the EIGRP topology table that is enabled if the successor route fails. Determined if the advertised distance of the candidate feasible successor is less than the feasible distance of the successor route.

FECN (Forward Explicit Congestion Notification) A signaling method used by a Frame Relay service provider. It attempts to drop the speed of a router sending excessive data by having a receiving router send traffic back to the sender tagged as a BECN message.

FEXT (Far-End Crosstalk) The crosstalk measured at the far end of the cable from where the transmission was sent.

fiber A cable that uses light rather than electrical signals to send data transmissions. These optical light signals travel a fiberglass core, and you might hear this technology referred to as fiber optics or optical cabling. Fiber is not susceptible to electromagnetic interference.

filter A program or device that uses a defined set of criteria to break up data and signals.

flapping A term used to describe a failing interface that is constantly going up and down.

flash A type of system memory that is installed on either an electrically erasable, programmable, read-only memory (EEP-ROM), or Personal Computer Memory Card International Association (PCMCIA) card. Flash memory contains the Cisco Internetworking Operating System (IOS) image. The router uses flash by default to locate the IOS when it is booted. Configuration files might also be stored on a flash card. Flash is also nonvolatile memory.

floating route A route with a higher administrative distance that enters the routing table when the primary route fails.

flow control A process that provides buffer controls that prevent packet flooding to the destination host. Buffers store bursts of data for processing when the transmission is complete.

FLSM (Fixed-Length Subnet Mask) A design that assumes that subnet routes from different parts of their classful network all use the same subnet mask that they use. Any subnetted networks must contain the same subnet mask throughout the topology.

forward-delay timer The time to transition from listening to learning and learning to forwarding. Each forward delay is 15 seconds.

forwarding An STP port state in which the interface transmits and receives data.

fragment-free A frame transmission method that checks the first 64 bytes for frame fragments (due to collisions) before forwarding the frame.

frame   A packet that is formatted by the Data Link layer of the OSI model for transmission to the Physical layer.

Frame Relay   One of the more popular packet-switched connection types that establishes site-to-site connections through a service provider network. Can attain speeds up to T3 and uses DLCI numbers as its Layer 2 addressing.

FTP (File Transfer Protocol)   An Application layer protocol that allows a user to transfer files and provides access to files and directories.

full duplex   Bidirectional transmissions enabling higher throughput because CSMA/CD is disabled. Connections to other switches or devices can be full duplex.

full-mesh design   A costly, but fully redundant, packet-switched network design in which all routers are directly connected to all other routers through virtual circuits.

full-mesh topology   A network topology that is set up so that each device is directly connected to every other device on the network. This connection method has built-in redundancy. If one link goes down, the device transmits via another link.

G

GBIC (Gigabit Interface Converter)   An interface module that can be inserted into the Gigabit Ethernet slot on a switch to allow for different media connections to that port. The physical media can range from copper to single-mode fiber. A GBIC is also hot-swappable, so it can be installed without interrupting service to that switch.

global address   A type of IPv6 address with the broadest scope. These addresses are for global use—that is, for Internet communications.

H

half duplex   One-way communication transmission with suboptimal throughput because it operates in a collision domain in which CSMA/CD must be enabled. When connected to a hub, half duplex must be run.

hashing   The process of running data through an algorithm that generates a result based on the actual data. This result is known as the hash. In most cases, this result is then sent with the data to the receiving device. The receiving device can then rerun the hash algorithm and compare the results to ensure that the data did not change in transmission.

HDLC (High-level Data Link Control)   A WAN encapsulation that can be used over leased lines and circuit-switched connections. Does not have many features, but uses minimal network overhead when communicating. Cisco's version of HDLC is proprietary.

hold-down timer   A routing loop mitigation process in which a router ignores any information about an alternative route with a higher metric to a poisoned subnet for an amount of time.

hop   A metric determined by the number of routers along the destination path.

host mask   255.255.255.255 or /32 subnet mask used on loopback interfaces to represent a single host.

hostname *hostname*   A global configuration command to name the router.

HSSI (High-Speed Serial Interface)   A high-speed interface that offers up to 52Mbps transmission rates to the WAN from a Cisco router. The higher speed capacity is relevant if the corporate backbone requires high-speed Internet access and VPN connectivity.

HTTP (Hypertext Transfer Protocol)   An Application layer protocol that enables web browsing with the transmission of Hypertext Markup Language (HTML) documents on the Internet.

HTTPS (Secure Hypertext Transfer Protocol)   An Application layer protocol that enables secure web browsing using SSL. A secure connection is indicated when the URL begins with https:// or when there is a lock symbol in the lower-right corner of the web page that is being viewed.

hub   A multiple port repeater. A smaller hub consists of four or five ports and might be called a workgroup hub. When data is received, the hub then retransmits that data on all the other ports.

hub-and-spoke design   One of the lowest-cost designs in a packet-switched network. All offices connect to a central office (the hub) through a single virtual circuit connection. If the hub router goes down, all connectivity through the packet-switched network is lost.

I–J–K

ICMP (Internet Control Messaging Protocol)   A Network layer protocol that provides ping and traceroute utilities.

idle timer/fast idle timer   Configuration parameters used with DDR connections to set the amount of time the connection should stay online without seeing interesting traffic.

IDS (Intrusion Detection System)   A passive device that listens to traffic passing through a network to generate alerts and issue TCP resets if necessary.

IETF Frame Relay Encapsulation   An industry-standard Frame Relay encapsulation that can be used when communicating with non-Cisco routers through a Frame Relay service provider.

IGP (Interior Gateway Protocol)   A routing protocol that advertises networks and metrics within an autonomous system.

IGRP (Interior Gateway Routing Protocol)   A Cisco-proprietary distance vector routing protocol that uses a composite metric to determine the optimal path.

in-band   Management signals traversing over the same networking paths and interfaces as the data stream.

information query   A type of query that is sent via the Internet to resolve hostnames from IP addresses or vice versa.

infrared   A wireless technology that uses infrared beams to pass data across the network. A television remote uses infrared technology to send requests to the television set. Speeds can reach a maximum of 16Mpbs, and signals are used for short distance communications.

inside global address   NAT terminology that describes the public address assigned to the NAT gateway.

inside local address NAT terminology that describes the private addresses behind the NAT gateway.

Integrated Services Digital Network (ISDN) A circuit-switched network that combines multiple B channels that can handle 64Kbps each with a single signaling (D) channel to form a WAN connection between two locations.

interesting traffic Used when configuring DDR to tell the router what traffic is valuable enough to initiate a call using the DDR connection.

interface configuration A configuration mode that sets parameters specific to the interface.

interface range *media port_range* A switch global configuration command that navigates several switch ports that will ultimately share similar configuration parameters.

internetwork The connection of more than one network. These networks are linked by hardware devices to function as a larger single network. An internetwork can also be called an internet.

inter-VLAN routing Traffic routed from one VLAN to another by using an external router or a Layer 3 switch.

inverse ARP A method that allows a Frame Relay router to automatically discover the remote routers by sending Inverse ARP messages to each local DLCI number it receives from the service provider.

inverse mask/wildcard mask A complete reversal of the subnet mask that is used primarily when configuring OSPF and access list.

IOS The software developed and maintained by Cisco to support a full array of system functions, applications (including Internet applications), and network hardware in a single software package.

IP (Internet Protocol) A Network layer protocol that uses logical or virtual addressing to get a packet from a source to its destination. IP addresses are used by routers to make forwarding decisions.

ip access-group A command used to apply an access list to an interface.

ip address *address subnet_mask* An interface configuration command that assigns an IP address to an interface.

ip address dhcp An interface configuration command that dynamically obtains an IP address for the interface.

ip default-gateway *gateway_IP* A switch global configuration command that sets a default route/gateway of last resort for a Layer 2 switch.

ip dhcp pool A global configuration command that defines a DHCP address pool.

ip domain-lookup A global configuration command that enables dynamic name resolution lookups.

ip host *hostname IP* A global configuration command to create a static map of an IP address to a hostname.

ip name-server *dns_server_IP* A global configuration command that specifies up to six DNS servers for dynamic resolution.

IPS (Intrusion Prevention System) An active device that is inline with the traffic path on a network. An IPS listens promiscuously to all incoming traffic to identify attacks, which the system can then block.

IP Security (IPsec)   A protocol framework that provides many types of security for network communication. IPsec is commonly used in VPN connections.

IPv4 (IP version 4)   A version of IP addressing that uses 32-bit addresses grouped into four octets. Each octet has a minimum value of 0 and a maximum value of 255. IPv4 addresses are presented in dotted decimal format.

IPv6 (IP version 6)   An IP address format that was created in the event that the IPv4 address space is exhausted. IPv6 addresses are 128 bits long and are represented by 32 hexadecimal digits broken into eight smaller groups of 4 bits, which are separated by colons.

ISL (interswitch link)   A Cisco frame-tagging method over trunk ports that encapsulates the original frame with a 26-byte header and a 4-byte CRC.

L

LACP (Link Aggregation Control Protocol)   An IEEE standardized dynamic bundling protocol for negotiating EtherChannel bundles.

LAN (local-area network)   An internetwork that is limited to a local or small geographic area. An example of a LAN would be the individual computers or workstations that are connected on one floor of a building.

LCP (Link Control Protocol)   A sublayer protocol of PPP responsible for negotiating authentication, multilink, compression, and callback.

learning   An STP port state in which the interface begins to build MAC addresses learned on the interface.

leased line   Typically the most expensive WAN connection that constructs a dedicated, point-to-point connection between locations.

line configuration   A configuration mode that sets parameters specific to the terminal line.

link-local address   An IPv6 address type that can only go as far as the Layer 2 domain. These addresses are autogenerated when an IPv6 node goes online and are assigned automatically.

link-state routing protocol   A class of routing protocols in which all possible link states are stored in an independent topology table in which the best routes are calculated and put into the routing table. The topology table is initially synchronized with discovered neighbors followed by frequent hello messages. These routing protocols are faster to converge than distance vector routing protocols.

listening   An STP port state in which the interface begins to transition to a forwarding state by listening and sending BPDUs. No user data sent.

LLC (Logical Link Control)   A Data Link sublayer defined by IEEE 802.2.

LMI (Local Management Interface)   The signaling method used between a Frame Relay service provider and the customer premises equipment.

local access rate/line speed The maximum physical speed a WAN connection is capable of reaching.

`login` A line configuration command that enables prompting of a password on the terminal lines.

longest-match rule In routing logic, dictates that when there are several subnetted entries for a destination network, the smallest and most specific subnet is chosen over others.

loopback interface A virtual interface that does not go down unless the router is turned off. Used by OSPF to determine the Router ID.

LRE (Long-Reach Ethernet) An Ethernet specification developed by Cisco to provide broadband service over existing telephone-grade or Category 1, 2, or 3 wiring. Speeds vary between 5 to 15Mbps and can reach a maximum segment length of up to 5000m.

LSA (Link State Advertisement) Used by OSPF to send hello messages and update information on attached interfaces, metrics used, and other variables.

LSU (Link State Update) A specific type of LSA that entails new information being sent to neighbor routers after an adjacency has been formed with that neighbor.

M

MAC (Media Access Control) A Data Link sublayer defined by IEEE 802.3.

MAC address A hard-coded (burned-in) address on the network interface controller (NIC) of the Physical layer node attached to the network.

MAN (Metropolitan Area Network) An internetwork that is larger than a LAN but smaller than or equal in size to a WAN.

management VLAN VLAN 1 by default. The management VLAN contains the switch's management IP address and CDP and VTP advertisements.

man-in-the-middle attack A type of access attack that occurs when a hacker eavesdrops or listens for network traffic and intercepts a data transmission. As soon as the transmission is intercepted, the untrustworthy host can position itself between the two communicating hosts, interpret the data, and steal information from the packets sent.

max-age timer The maximum length of time a bridge port saves its configuration BPDU information. The value is 20 seconds by default.

MD5 (Message Digest 5) A hashing algorithm created in 1991 by Ronald Rivest, an MIT professor. Uses a 128-bit hash.

Metro Ethernet A new type of technology allowing for low-cost, high-speed fiber connections between offices within metropolitan areas.

microsegmentation The process in which a switch creates a dedicated path for sending and receiving transmissions with each connected host. Each host then has a separate collision domain and a dedicated bandwidth.

MIMO (Multiple Input, Multiple Output) An implementation of 802.11 wireless technology that uses multiple antennas at both the transmitter and receiver to improve the performance of the wireless connection.

MPPC (Microsoft Point-to-Point Compression) A PPP compression algorithm developed by Microsoft for Windows dial-up clients.

modem A device that converts a digital signal into an analog signal for transmission over a telephone line. The signal is converted back into a digital format when it reaches the device on the other end of that telephone line.

multicast An Ethernet LAN address in which a frame can be sent to a group of devices in the same LAN. IEEE Ethernet multicast addresses always begin with 0100.5E in hexadecimal format. The last three bytes can be any combination.

multimode A type of fiber cable that is generally used for shorter distances and is ideal for a campus-sized network.

multiplexing Combining multiple messages over a single channel.

N

named access list An access list identified by a name rather than a number. Can be standard or extended, and allows the deletion of individual access list lines.

NAT (Network Address Translation) A technique that translates a private IP address to a public IP address for outbound transmission to the Internet. NAT also translates a public IP address to a private IP address for inbound transmission on the internal network.

native VLAN VLAN 1 by default. Traffic originating from the native VLAN is not tagged over the trunk link.

NAT overload Allows multiple internal clients to share a single Internet IP address using port numbers to distinguish requests.

NAT pool NAT terminology that describes a pool of addresses that a router can use for NAT translations.

NBMA (nonbroadcast multiaccess) A WAN network design that allows multiple clients to attach, but not send broadcast messages to each other. Frame Relay is an example of an NBMA network.

NCP (Network Control Protocol) A sublayer protocol of PPP responsible for enabling multiple Network layer protocols to work over a PPP-encapsulated WAN connection.

neighbor table A table used by link-state and balanced hybrid routing protocols that maintains all neighbors discovered by receiving hello messages from other routers using the same routing protocol.

network ID Also called a network number or subnet ID, this address is the first IP address in a network. Every host bit for the network ID address is turned off (or all 0s).

network interface A network component that provides connectivity from an end-user PC or laptop to the public network. Depending on the interface, you might see up to three light-emitting diodes (LEDs) that help to determine status of the connection.

Network layer Layer 3 of the OSI model. Determines the best path for packet delivery across the network. Routed protocols such as IP are used to determine logical addressing that can identify the destination of a packet or datagram. The most common network device found at the Network layer is a router; however, Layer 3 switches might also be implemented.

NEXT (Near-End Crosstalk) The crosstalk measured at the transmitting end of a cable.

NFS (Network File System) (pertaining to a session layer) A Session layer protocol that accesses remote resources transparently and represents files and directories as if local to the user system.

NFS (Network File System) (pertaining to an application layer) An Application layer protocol that allows users with different operating systems (that is, NT and Unix workstations) to share files.

NNTP (Network News Transfer Protocol) An Application layer protocol that offers access to Usenet newsgroup postings.

nonbroadcast multiaccess topology Consists of multiple devices that access the same medium and cannot hear each other's broadcasts and multicast messages such as Frame Relay networks.

no shutdown An interface configuration command that administratively enables an interface.

NTP (Network Time Protocol) An Application layer protocol that synchronizes clocks on the Internet to provide accurate local time on the user system.

NVRAM (Nonvolatile Random-Access Memory) A type of system memory that stores the startup configuration. This configuration is loaded when the router is booted.

O

ODR (On-Demand Routing) An enhancement to CDP that enables a stub router to advertise the connected IP prefix.

OSI model A layered architecture model created by the International Organization for Standardization (ISO) to internetwork various vendor specific networks.

OSPF (Open Shortest Path First) An open-standard classless routing protocol that uses cost as a metric and uses areas to minimize routing overhead.

OSPF priority An arbitrary number configured on an OSPF interface to influence a DR and BDR election. Default is 1.

Out-of-band Management signals traversing a dedicated channel separate from the data stream.

outside global address NAT terminology that describes an Internet valid address accessible from any device connected to the Internet.

outside local address NAT terminology that describes an Internet valid address as it is seen from the internal network.

P

packet A unit of data that contains control information and might also be referred to as a datagram. Packets are used by the Network layer of the OSI model.

packet sniffer A software program or piece of hardware that captures, decodes, and analyzes traffic sent over a network.

packet-switched network A type of WAN connection that establishes connections using virtual circuits. ATM, Frame Relay, and X.25 fall under this category of connection.

PAgP (Port Aggregation Protocol) A proprietary dynamic bundling protocol for negotiating EtherChannel bundles.

PAP (Password Authentication Protocol) A weak authentication type used with PPP encapsulation. Usernames and passwords are transmitted a single time in clear-text format.

partial-mesh design A packet-switched network design that compromises between cost and redundancy by providing key locations with multiple virtual circuit connections.

partial-mesh topology A network topology that has direct connectivity between some of the network devices, but not all of them, such as the full mesh topology.

passive interface A routing process command that defines an interface that stops sending routing updates. The interface still can accept routing updates.

password attack A type of access attack in which a hacker attempts to obtain a password for a device.

password *password* A line configuration command that specifies the password to be prompted on a terminal line.

PAT (Port Address Translation) A technique that translates a Transport protocol connection (TCP or UDP) from an outside network host/port to an internal network host/port.

PDU (Protocol Data Unit) A unit that includes the message and the protocol/control information from the forwarding layer of the OSI model.

Physical layer Layer 1 of the OSI model. Moves bits between nodes. Electrical, mechanical, procedural, and functional requirements are defined at the Physical layer to assist with the activation, maintenance, and deactivation of physical connectivity between devices.

ping (Packet Internet Groper) An echo request sent by a device that uses ICMP at the Network layer to validate that an IP address exists and can accept requests. The response is called an echo response.

ping sweep A tool that sends an echo request to numerous host IP addresses at the same time to see which host(s) respond(s) with an echo reply.

POE (Power over Ethernet) A technology that allows an end device to receive power over a copper Ethernet cable. End devices that might use PoE include IP telephones, wireless access points, video cameras, and card scanners.

point-to-multipoint/multipoint subinterface A subinterface that allows multiple DLCI numbers to be mapped to remote IP addresses under the same logical interface.

point-to-point subinterface A subinterface typically used for Frame Relay that assigns a single DLCI number to a single subinterface and creates a point-to-point style connection through a packet-switched cloud.

point-to-point topology A network topology in which two routing devices are separated by a segment.

poison reverse   A routing loop mitigation process in which a router receives a poisoned route and overrides the split horizon rule to send the subnet as "possibly down" back to the source.

POP3 (Post Office Protocol 3)   An Application layer protocol that receives email by accessing an Internet server.

PortFast   A Cisco STP enhancement that skips the listening and learning port states for end-devices.

port redirection   NAT terminology that describes statically translating from one port to another.

port scan   A software program that surveys a host network for open ports.

port security   A method to limit the number of MAC addresses that are dynamically learned on a switch port.

POST (power-on self test)   A test performed by a ROM chip to initially test the hardware on bootup.

PPP (Point-to-Point Protocol)   A WAN encapsulation type that provides many features and is supported by nearly all router vendors.

PPP multilink   An industry-standard feature that allows multiple connections to be bundled into a single, logical connection between two network locations.

PPPoA (PPP over ATM)   An encapsulation typically used by DSL service providers to gain the features of PPP over an ATM connection.

PPPoE (PPP over Ethernet)   An encapsulation typically used by DSL service providers to gain the features of PPP over an Ethernet connection.

predictor compression   A dictionary-based compression type that attempts to predict the traffic patterns that will be sent over a WAN connection. Is good for links that have very few types of traffic. Uses more memory resources than the sister compression type, Stacker.

Presentation layer   Layer 6 of the OSI model. Presents data to the Application layer and acts as a data format translator.

PRI (Primary Rate Interface)   A type of ISDN connection that uses 23 B channels and a single D channel. Provides bandwidth equivalent to a T1 line.

private IP address   An address that is not routable over the Internet. These include the 10.0.0.0/8 network, the 172.16.0.0 to 172.31.255.255/16 networks, and the 192.168.0.0 to 192.168.255.255/24 networks.

privileged EXEC   The highest privileged command mode, which allows full access to all commands.

process ID   A number between 1 and 65535 that represents a unique instance of an OSPF process. The process ID is locally significant (it does not have to match in all routers in the OSPF autonomous system).

protect   A port security violation action in which frames from unsecure MAC addresses are dropped until the number of MAC addresses drops below the maximum.

proxy ARP (Proxy Address Resolution Protocol)   A protocol that allows a router to respond to an ARP request that has been sent to a remote host. Some UNIX machines (especially Solaris) rely on Proxy ARP versus default gateways.

public IP address   An address that is routable over the Internet.

PVC (Permanent Virtual Circuit)   A permanently established virtual circuit through a service provider network.

PVST (Per-VLAN Spanning Tree)   An instance of Spanning Tree Protocol runs for each active VLAN in a switched network.

Q

Q.921   The ISDN D channel protocol used at the Data Link layer.

Q.931   The ISDN D channel protocol used at the Network layer.

QoS (quality of service)   The method of prioritizing certain types of traffic when congestion affects performance.

R

RAM (Random-Access Memory)   A type of memory that is used for short-term storage of a machine's running IOS and running configuration. This is the only type of system memory that is not permanent.

RARP (Reverse Address Resolution Protocol) A protocol that maps a known MAC address to an IP address.

reconnaissance attack   A class of passive attack in which a hacker surveys a network and collects data for a future attack.

redistribution   A method of configuring routing protocols to advertise networks from other routing protocols.

reload   A privileged EXEC command to perform a reboot of the router or switch.

remote-access VPN   A VPN connection type that allows telecommuting or mobile workers to connect to the corporate network from their PCs.

repeater   A device consisting of a transmitter and a receiver. When the repeater receives a signal, it amplifies the signal and then retransmits. This effectively enables the signal to travel over a greater distance.

restrict   A port security violation action in which a violation increases the violation counter and an SNMP alert is generated.

resume _conn#_   A user or privileged EXEC command resumes a suspended Telnet session.

RF (radio frequency)   A method of broadcasting that uses alternating current to produce radio waves. RF typically is used in 802.11 wireless networking.

ring topology   A network topology that is set up so that one device is directly connected to two other devices on the same network. When a device emits a data signal transmission, it is sent in a single direction to the next connected device. The transmission continues to pass along each device successively until it arrives back at the original transmitting device. This method creates a ring or a loop.

RIP (Routing Information Protocol) A standard distance vector routing protocol that uses hop count as its only metric.

RIPv2 (RIP version 2) An enhancement to RIP to support classless updates, router authentication, and multicast updates.

ROM (Read-Only Memory) A type of system memory that contains the basic code for booting a device and maintaining power-on self test (POST), ROM Monitor (ROMmon), bootstrap, and RxBoot.

ROMmon (ROM Monitor) A small codeset in ROM that allows you to perform elementary functions to manually get the router or switch back to a functioning state.

root bridge The base of the STP topology calculations elected based on the lowest Bridge ID.

root port A nonroot bridge port that has the lowest cumulative cost to a root bridge.

routed protocol A protocol such as IP that can be routed using a router.

route poison A routing loop mitigation process in which a router sets a failed subnet to an infinite metric and advertises it to its neighbor.

router ID The IP address by which a device is known to an OSPF autonomous system. Determined by the highest active loopback IP address that is configured when the OSPF process starts. If your router does not have a loopback interface, it uses the highest physical interface IP address.

router-on-a-stick An inter-VLAN routing method by trunking to an external router with subinterfaces.

route summarization The process of advertising multiple network IDs into a single route.

route update packet A packet that sends updates to neighbor routers about all networks connected to that internetwork and is supported by routing protocols such as RIP, EIGRP, and OSPF.

routing protocol A protocol that exchanges network routes between routing devices to dynamically advertise networks. RIP, OSPF, and EIGRP are examples of routing protocols.

routing table The routing logic stored in RAM, where packet forwarding decisions are made.

RPC (Remote Procedure Call) A Session layer protocol that is the basis for client/server communications. Calls are created on the client and then carried out on the server.

RSTP (Rapid Spanning Tree Protocol) IEEE 802.1w RSTP incorporates similar technologies as Cisco's PortFast, UplinkFast, and BackboneFast.

running-config The active configuration running in RAM.

RxBoot Also known as a mini-IOS, RxBoot is a limited IOS in ROM with enough functionality to load an IOS from a TFTP server.

S

SAN (Storage-Area Network) A subnetwork or special-purpose network. Allows users on a larger network to connect various data storage devices with clusters of data servers.

SDM (Security Device Manager) A web-based tool that was developed by Cisco for its IOS software-based routers. SDM gives users the option to configure and monitor a router without relying heavily on the CLI.

server mode The default VTP mode that enables you to create, modify, and delete VLANS. These VLANs are advertised to other switches and saved in the VLAN database.

service password-encryption A global configuration command that encrypts all passwords that are clear text in the configuration.

Session layer Layer 5 of the OSI model. Handles dialog control among devices.

setup mode An interactive dialog session to establish an initial configuration. Setup mode is automatically loaded when there is a missing startup-config in NVRAM.

SHA-1 (Secure Hash Algorithm 1) A hashing algorithm published in 1995 by the NIST to increase the strength of the hash algorithm from the original MD5 standard. Uses a 160-bit hash.

show cdp neighbors A user or privileged EXEC command to display the device ID, local interface, holdtime, capability, platform, and port ID learned from CDP advertisements of directly connected neighbors.

show cdp neighbors detail A user or privileged EXEC command to display the output of the show cdp neighbors command in addition to the Cisco IOS version and the Layer 3 address of directly connected neighbors.

show controller A user or privileged EXEC command to display the interface microcode including whether a DTE or DCE cable is connected to the interface.

show dhcp lease A user or privileged EXEC command to display the IP address assigned to the interface(s) configured by the ip address dhcp command.

show flash A user or privileged EXEC command to display the filenames and sizes of IOS files stored in flash memory.

show interfaces A user or privileged EXEC command to display the status of the interfaces as well as physical and logical address, encapsulation, bandwidth, reliability, load, MTU, duplex, broadcasts, collisions, and frame errors.

show ip dhcp bindings A user or privileged EXEC command to display the IP addresses dynamically assigned to devices from the DHCP-enabled router.

show ip interface brief A user or privileged EXEC command to display a summary of the interface statuses and logical addressing.

show sessions A user or privileged EXEC command to verify active Telnet sessions initiated from local device.

show version A user or privileged EXEC command to display the IOS version, system uptime, amount of RAM, NVRAM, flash memory, and configuration register.

SIA (Stuck In Active) timer   Enabled when an EIGRP router goes into an active state in the event of a topology change. The SIA timer is the amount of time a neighbor EIGRP router has to respond to a query. The default is 180 seconds.

single-mode   A type of fiber cable that is used to span longer distances than multi-mode fiber. Single-mode fiber also allows for a higher data rate and faster data transmission speeds.

site-to-site VPN   A VPN configuration that directly replaces a private line connection by establishing a permanent or semipermanent connection between sites.

SMTP (Simple Mail Transfer Protocol)   An Application layer protocol that sends email across the network.

smurf attack   A type of DoS attack in which multiple broadcast ping requests are sent to a single target from a spoofed IP address.

SNMP (Simple Network Management Protocol)   An Application layer protocol that monitors the network and manages configurations.

SPID (Service Provider Identifier)   Sometimes required on ISDN lines upon dial-in for billing purposes.

split-horizon   A distance vector routing protocol loop-prevention mechanism that prevents data from being sent back in the direction from which it was received.

SQL (Structured Query Language)   A Session layer protocol that functions as a query language that requests, updates, and manages databases.

SSH (Secure Shell)   A protocol that enables terminal encrypted connections to remote devices with an IP address.

SSL (Secure Socket Layer)   A protocol that provides a secure channel between two devices at the Application layer (Layer 7) of the OSI model.

SSL VPN   Also known as WebVPN. Allows users to connect to a VPN without requiring a client installation. Users access the VPN using a secure web page.

stacker compression   A flat compression type that uses the same compression algorithm for all traffic types. Is a good compression for links that have many types of traffic. Uses more processor resources than the sister compression type, Predictor.

standard access list   A list of permit and deny statements that can match network traffic based on the source IP address only.

star topology   A network topology that is the most commonly implemented network design. With this topology, there is a central device with separate connections to each end node. Each connection uses a separate cable. You might also hear this called a hub-and-spoke topology.

startup-config   A saved configuration stored in NVRAM that is loaded when the router or switch boots.

static Frame Relay map   A manual method of mapping a local DLCI number to the remote IP address it is capable of reaching over a Frame Relay cloud.

static NAT   Manually maps a NAT-translated address, typically between a public Internet address and a private internal address.

static route A manual entry that an administrator enters into the configuration that describes the destination network and the next hop.

sticky secure MAC address A MAC address dynamically learned using port security that the switch automatically configures to be secure MAC addresses.

store-and-forward A latency-varying transmission method that buffers the entire frame and calculates the CRC before forwarding the frame.

STP (Spanning Tree Protocol) A Layer 2 protocol that eliminates loops caused by redundant connections on a switched network.

STP (Shielded Twisted-pair) cable A branch of twisted-pair cabling that uses an additional shield that provides an additional reduction of interference and attenuation.

stub network A network with a single entry and exit point.

stub routing An EIGRP routing feature that minimizes convergence in hub-and-spoke networks.

subinterface A logical extension of a physical interface that is treated by the IOS as an actual interface.

subnet (subnetwork) A smaller network created from a Class A, B, or C network.

subnet mask A 32-bit address used by a network device to identify which part of an IP address is the subnet portion.

subnetting The process of breaking a large network of IP addresses into smaller, more manageable address ranges.

successor route The route in a topology table with the lowest feasible distance to a subnet. This route is also placed in the routing table.

supernet A summarized route.

SVI (Switched Virtual Interface) Created in a Layer 3 switch to perform inter-VLAN routing.

switch A multiport bridge that uses an Application-Specific Integrated Circuit (ASIC) to forward frames at the Data Link layer. Each port of the switch has dedicated bandwidth.

Switched Virtual Circuit (SVC) An on-demand virtual circuit through a service provider network.

switchport trunk allowed vlan An interface configuration command that specifies which VLANs or VLAN ranges are permitted over a trunk link.

synchronization A Rapid Spanning Tree Protocol process of blocking all nonedge point-to-point links before sending a proposal to ensure that a change in a switched topology gets accurately synchronized with all other local ports.

synchronous A serial interface that synchronizes clocks for the bit stream of both the sending and receiving end of a serial link.

SYSLOG A management feature that collects log messages from a Cisco device and sends them to a syslog server to keep a record of any network occurrences.

T

TCP (Transmission Control Protocol)   A reliable connection-oriented Transport layer protocol. TCP uses acknowledgments, sequencing, and flow control to ensure reliability.

TCP Established   A type of extended access list entry that can be added to allow return traffic, satisfying a client request.

TCP/IP (Transmission Control Protocol/Internet Protocol)   A suite of protocols developed by the Department of Defense to help develop internetworks.

TCP SYN attack   A type of DoS attack in which a SYN request is sent to a device with a spoofed IP address. The attacking system does not acknowledge the resulting SYN-ACK, which causes the session connection queues to fill up and stop taking new connection requests.

Telnet   A TCP/IP protocol that provides terminal emulation to a remote host by creating a virtual terminal.

telnet *IP_address*   A user or privileged EXEC command to initiate a virtual terminal session to a remote device.

terminal editing key   A shortcut key to navigate the cursor in lieu of the arrow keys.

TFTP (Trivial File Transfer Protocol)   An Application layer protocol that is a barebones version of FTP that does not provide access to directories. With TFTP, you can simply send and receive files.

token passing   A process in which a 3-byte token (or special bit pattern) is inserted in a frame and passed in a single direction from one node to another until it forms a complete loop. The node that has possession of the token is the only one that can send data at any given time on that LAN. Because only one node can send data at a time, collisions are avoided.

Token Ring   A LAN protocol that uses a token-passing media access technology in a physical ring or physical star topology, which creates a logical ring topology. Token Ring is defined by the IEEE 802.5 standard.

topology table   A table used by link-state and balanced hybrid routing protocols that maintains every possible route to any given subnet along with its associated metric.

traceroute   A Network layer tool that traces the route or path taken from a client to a remote host. Traceroute also reports the IP addresses of the routers at each next hop on the way to the destination.

transparent bridge   A bridge that goes unnoticed by the other devices on a network.

transparent mode   A VTP mode in which you can create, modify, and delete VLANs only on the local switch. Transparent switches do not participate in VTP but forward VTP advertisements received from servers. Also saves VLAN configuration in a VLAN database.

Transport layer   Layer 4 of the OSI model. Responsible for end-to-end connections and data delivery between two hosts. The capability to segment and reassemble data is a key function of this layer.

triggered update   A routing loop mitigation process in which a router immediately shoots out an update as opposed to waiting for the normal update interval.

Triple DES (3DES) algorithm Produced to address the weaknesses of DES. This algorithm did not reinvent the wheel of encryption, so to speak. Instead, it ran the DES algorithm three times with different keys (thus the term 3DES). This significantly improved the strength of the original DES algorithm.

trunk An interconnection between switches that multiplexes traffic from all VLANs to other switches.

trust exploitation A type of access attack that occurs when a device or group of devices on a shared segment erroneously trust information that has been provided by an untrustworthy source.

U

UDP (User Datagram Protocol) An unreliable connectionless Transport layer protocol. UDP headers contain only the source and destination ports, a length field, and a checksum.

unicast An Ethernet LAN address that identifies the MAC address of an individual LAN or NIC card.

unique/site-local address An IPv6 address type that can expand to the size of an organization and that is used to describe the boundary of the organizational network. This is the private addressing for IPv6.

UplinkFast A Cisco STP enhancement that skips the listening and learning port states on redundant trunk links to distribution layer switch.

user EXEC An initial command mode with limited commands to test connectivity and verify statistics.

UTP (Unshielded Twisted-Pair) cable A branch of twisted-pair cabling that uses four pairs of colored wire. UTP is vulnerable to EMI and uses an RJ-45 connector. There are five categories of UTP cable, labeled Category 1 to Category 5.

V

V.35 A physical serial interface standard on CSU/DSU devices.

variance A multiplier used in IGRP and EIGRP that enables these routing protocols to load balance over unequal paths.

virtual circuit A logical connection through a service provider network that makes the attached routers believe they are directly connected.

VLAN A Layer 2 method of segmenting broadcast domains. Each VLAN created in a switch represents a logical grouping of devices into their own broadcast domain.

VLSM (Variable-Length Subnet Mask) A design that allows you to allocate an IP subnet according to the needed number of hosts for that subnet. Requires classless routing.

VMPS (VLAN Membership Policy Server) A dynamic method of associating MAC addresses with VLANs.

voice VLAN Sometimes called auxiliary VLANs, voice VLANs create a separate broadcast domain on an access port to logically segment and administer VoIP traffic.

VPN (Virtual Private Network)   A type of network connection that allows secure transmission of network data over the Internet between two or more locations.

VTP (VLAN Trunking Protocol)   A Layer 2 Cisco-proprietary protocol that minimizes the administrative overhead involved in replicating VLAN configurations by having a VTP server advertise the VLAN configurations.

VTP domain   A collection of switches participating in VTP advertisements.

VTP pruning   Reduces unnecessary flooded traffic, such as broadcast, multicast, unknown, and flooded unicast packets to other switches by repressing flooded traffic to switches from inactive VLANs.

W

WAN (wide-area network)   An internetwork that covers more than one geographical area.

WebVPN   Also known as an SSL VPN. Allows users to connect to a VPN without requiring a client installation. Users access the VPN using a secure web page.

Wi-Fi Alliance   A group of large companies that own and control the Wi-Fi Certified logo and ensure that 802.11 wireless equipment is cross-compatible.

wildcard mask   Sometimes referred to as an inverse mask. Used to identify to the IOS how much of an IP address should be applied to a criterion in a configuration statement. A 0 means that the corresponding bit must match. A 1 means to ignore the corresponding bit value.

windowing   A process used by TCP in which windows are determined by the receiving system to limit the amount of data segments (bytes) that can be sent by the source device without an acknowledgment from the recipient. Window sizes vary and can change throughout the duration of a connection.

wireless cell   Defines a region of coverage by a wireless access point.

wireless channel   Defines distinct ranges of radio frequencies that are used for 802.11 transmission. Your goal in designing wireless networks is to ensure that wireless coverage from adjacent access points uses different channels so as not to interfere with each other.

wireless fidelity (Wi-Fi)   A wireless networking standard defined by IEEE 802.11. The 802.11 standard allows for transmission speeds of up to 1 to 2Mbps and uses a radio frequency of 2.4GHz.

wireless roaming   The ability of a wireless client to move between different wireless access points without losing network connectivity.

WPA (Wi-Fi Protected Access)   Offers a stronger encryption scheme than the original WEP standard without changing wireless hardware requirements. Implements Temporal Key Integrity Protocol (TKIP) and the Message Integrity Code (MIC).

WPA2 (Wi-Fi Protected Access 2)   Also known as 802.11i. Implements a stronger security system for wireless networks using the Advanced Encryption Standard (AES) encryption cipher.

X–Y–Z

X.21 A physical serial interface standard on CSU/DSU devices.

X.25 The predecessor packet-switched technology to Frame Relay. X.25 used excessive error checking, which slowed down the connection.

X Window A Session layer protocol that communicates with remote UNIX machines and allows the user to operate the device as if it is attached locally.

zero subnet rule The first subnet in a network that has all binary 0s in the subnet field.

Index

NUMBERS

E

F

M

Q - R

W